> FOR SOME MYSTERIOUS REASON MY *POWER RING* HAS NO EFFECT ON THAT FLYING BOMB! WHICHEVER WAY I TURN—IT SWERVES RIGHT AFTER ME!

SHOWCASE PRESENTS
GREEN LANTERN
VOLUME ONE

Julius Schwartz Editor-Original Series

Bob Harras Group Editor-Collected Editions

Robert Greenberger Editor

Robbin Brosterman Design Director-Books

DC COMICS

Diane Nelson President

Dan DiDio and **Jim Lee** Co-Publishers

Geoff Johns Chief Creative Officer

Patrick Caldon EVP-Finance and Administration

John Rood EVP-Sales, Marketing and Business Development

Amy Genkins SVP-Business and Legal Affairs

Steve Rotterdam SVP-Sales and Marketing

John Cunningham VP-Marketing

Terri Cunningham VP-Managing Editor

Alison Gill VP-Manufacturing

David Hyde VP-Publicity

Sue Pohja VP-Book Trade Sales

Alysse Soll VP-Advertising and Custom Publishing

Bob Wayne VP-Sales

Mark Chiarello Art Director

Cover illustration by Gill Kane and Joe Giella
Cover color by Alex Sinclair

SHOWCASE PRESENTS GREEN LANTERN VOL. ONE
Published by DC Comics. Cover and compilation
Copyright © 2010 DC Comics. All Rights Reserved.
Originally published in single magazine form in GREEN LANTERN 1-17,
SHOWCASE 22-24 © 1959-1963 DC Comics. All Rights Reserved.
All characters, their distinctive likenesses and related elements featured in
this publication are trademarks of DC Comics. The stories, characters and
incidents featured in this publication are entirely fictional.

DC Comics, 1700 Broadway, New York, NY 10019
A Warner Bros. Entertainment Company
Printed by Transcontinental Gagne, Louiseville, QC, Canada (10/20/10)
First Printing.
ISBN: 978-1-4012-2946-7

TABLE OF CONTENTS

STORIES BY **JOHN BROOME**   ART BY **GIL KANE** AND **JOE GIELLA**   EXCEPT WHERE NOTED

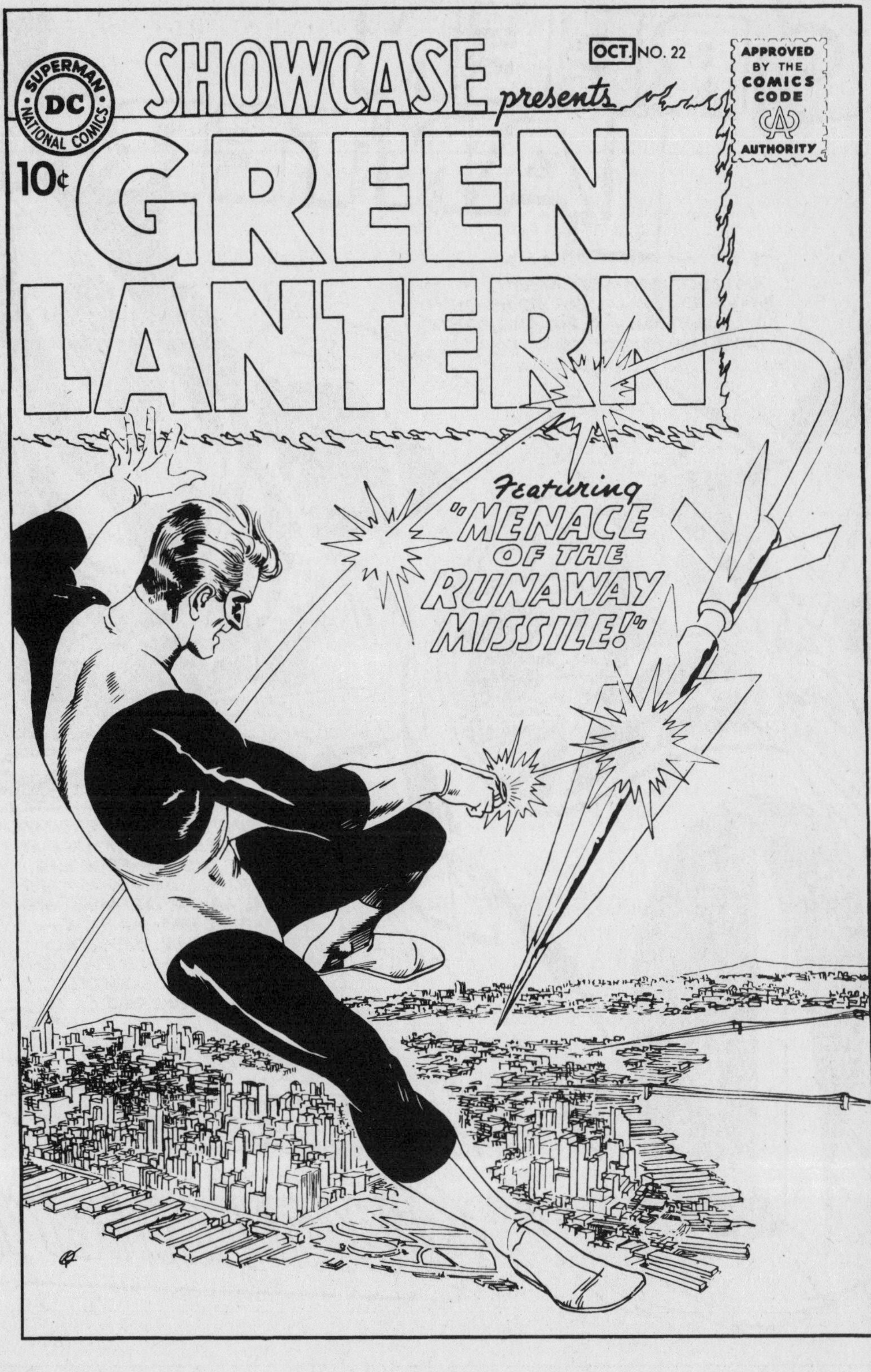
SHOWCASE presents
OCT. NO. 22
APPROVED BY THE COMICS CODE AUTHORITY
SUPERMAN DC NATIONAL COMICS
10¢
GREEN LANTERN
Featuring "MENACE OF THE RUNAWAY MISSILE!"

GREEN LANTERN
THIS PILOT TRAINER WASN'T MEANT TO FLY--IT HAS NO WINGS! BUT SOMETHING--SOME INCREDIBLE FORCE--IS FLYING ME IN IT!
HAL JORDAN HAD A FINE REPUTATION AS AN ACE TEST PILOT WHOSE REMARKABLE LACK OF FEAR WAS KNOWN TO ALL HIS ASSOCIATES! BUT HAL NEVER DREAMED HIS REPUTATION WAS SO WIDESPREAD THAT AN UNEARTHLY BEING WOULD SINGLE HIM OUT TO RECEIVE THE GREATEST GIFT IN THE UNIVERSE!
SOS
Green Lantern
N-624

IN A DESOLATE SPOT IN THE SOUTHWEST *U.S.A.*, WHERE A STRANGE CRAFT HAS CRASH-LANDED...

...AND INSIDE, AN ALIEN BEING IS GIVING OFF HIS LAST THOUGHTS...

NO USE...FOOLING YOURSELF, *ABIN SUR*...YOU ARE DYING! YOU HAVE ONLY A SHORT TIME LEFT TO LIVE...

AND YOU KNOW WHAT YOUR DUTY IS...TO PASS ON THE *BATTERY OF POWER* TO...A DESERVING ONE! IT IS...WHAT YOU WOULD HAVE BEEN OBLIGED TO DO HAD YOU MET...DISASTER ON YOUR *OWN* WORLD..

...AND YOU MUST DO IT HERE...ON EARTH! YOU MUST TRY TO FIND A *DESERVING* EARTHMAN... AND PASS ON THE *BATTERY OF POWER* TO *HIM*...! BUT YOU MUST *HURRY*...

AS THE STRICKEN SPACEMAN PRESSES HIS FINGER RING TO THE OBJECT BESIDE HIM...

BATTERY OF POWER -- SEEK IN THIS STRANGE WORLD...IF THERE BE A DESERVING ONE HERE! SEEK AND FIND...AND BRING HIM TO ME!

FROM THE GREEN RING A BOLT OF PURE ENERGY RISES...

HE MUST BE ONE WITH-OUT FEAR! ENTIRELY WITH-OUT FEAR! HURRY!! THE TIME IS SHORT!

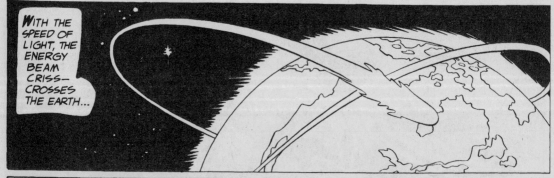

WITH THE SPEED OF LIGHT, THE ENERGY BEAM CRISS-CROSSES THE EARTH...

MEANWHILE, AT THE **FERRIS AIRCRAFT COMPANY**, HAL JORDAN, TEST PILOT, SITS IN A TRAINER OF HIS OWN DESIGN...

THIS FLIGHTLESS TRAINER WILL HELP TURN OUT SPACE PILOTS OF THE FUTURE--!

SUDDENLY, A GREEN GLOW SURROUNDS THE FLYER...

eh? WHAT'S THAT STRANGE LIGHT SURROUNDING ME!? I--I SEEM TO BE **MOVING**!

BEFORE HAL CAN TAKE A BREATH...

I'M SCOOTING THROUGH THE AIR AT FANTASTIC SPEED! B--BUT HOW CAN SUCH AN INCREDIBLE THING HAPPEN?

WHEN THE FLIGHT ABRUPTLY CEASES...

I KNOW I DIDN'T LEAVE EARTH--BUT THAT SURE LOOKS LIKE A WRECKED SPACESHIP LYING THERE--!

AND AS THE PILOT APPROACHES THE VESSEL...

COME IN, HAL JORDAN!

GOOD GOSH! A SPACEMAN-- COMMUNICATING WITH ME BY **TELEPATHY**!

3

STARTLED, THE CRACK TEST PILOT ENTERS THE WRECKED SHIP...

I AM *ABIN SUR*... I AM NOT OF EARTH--BUT OF A FAR DISTANT PLANET--AND I AM... DYING...

HOW CAN I HELP--

NO... IT IS TOO LATE TO HELP ME... BESIDES, I MUST SPEAK TO YOU... OF A MORE IMPORTANT MATTER...

MORE IMPORTANT... THAN YOUR *LIFE?*

YES... LOOK AT THIS *BATTERY,* HAL JORDAN...

WHY... IT LOOKS LIKE A *GREEN LANTERN*...

YES... IN YOUR WORDS... A *GREEN LANTERN*... BUT ACTUALLY IT IS A *BATTERY OF POWER*... GIVEN ONLY TO SELECTED SPACE-PATROLMEN IN THE SUPER-GALACTIC SYSTEM... TO BE USED AS A WEAPON AGAINST FORCES OF EVIL AND INJUSTICE...

IT IS OUR DUTY... WHEN DISASTER STRIKES... TO PASS ON THE *BATTERY OF POWER*... TO ANOTHER WHO IS *FEARLESS*... AND *HONEST!* COME CLOSER TO ME...

YES... BY THE GREEN BEAM OF MY RING... I SEE THAT YOU ARE HONEST! AND THE *BATTERY* HAS ALREADY SELECTED YOU AS ONE BORN WITHOUT FEAR! SO YOU PASS BOTH TESTS, HAL JORDAN...

4

"*THERE IS STILL MUCH TO TELL YOU... AND ONLY MOMENTS LEFT! MY SHIP WAS BATTERED... IN THE DEADLY RADIATION BANDS SURROUNDING YOUR PLANET...*"

"*A TERRIBLE BLAST OF YELLOW LIGHT-- SIMILAR TO YOUR AURORA BOREALIS-- BLINDED ME AT THE CONTROLS...*"

YELLOW LIGHT-- STUNNING ME--!

"*THEN I CRASHED...*"

ONLY SECONDS LEFT TO TELL YOU... ONCE YOU HAVE THE BATTERY YOU WILL HAVE POWER OVER EVERYTHING--EXCEPT WHAT IS YELLOW!

THE UNIQUE METAL WHICH CHARGES THE BATTERY WITH ITS WONDROUS POWER HAS A YELLOW IMPURITY IN IT! STRANGELY ENOUGH, IF THE YELLOW IMPURITY IS REMOVED, THE BATTERY LOSES ITS POWER!

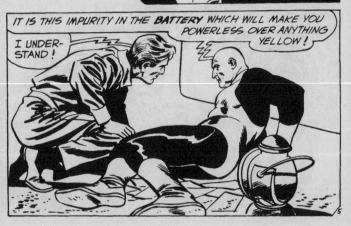

IT IS THIS IMPURITY IN THE BATTERY WHICH WILL MAKE YOU POWERLESS OVER ANYTHING YELLOW!

I UNDERSTAND!

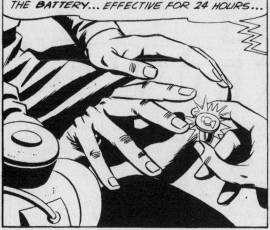

NOW TAKE MY RING... LET ME PUT IT ON YOU--! WITH THIS RING YOU WILL DRAIN POWER FROM THE *BATTERY*... EFFECTIVE FOR 24 HOURS...

NOW... I'VE TOLD YOU ALL... DO NOT FAIL ME...

GONE! HE... BREATHED HIS LAST!

AFTER HAL JORDAN HAS FOLLOWED THE SPACE-MAN'S ORDERS IN DISPOSING OF ALL REMNANTS OF HIM AND HIS ROCKET...

THE SPACEMAN TOLD ME TO TAKE HIS SPECIAL UNIFORM! AND I VOWED TO HIM THAT I WOULD CARRY OUT MY NEW RESPONSIBILITIES TO THE BEST OF MY ABILITY!

AS THE STILL-DAZED TEST PILOT TRIES OUT HIS NEW *POWER*...

LIFTING A CLIFF INTO THE AIR! I CAN DO ANYTHING I WANT WITH THIS RING... ANYTHING I *WILL* TO HAPPEN... I CAN MAKE HAPPEN!

BUT TO BE SAFE, I MUST USE IT ONLY IN THE GREATEST SECRECY! I KNOW--! I'LL ADOPT A *SECRET IDENTITY*-- I'LL CALL MYSELF *GREEN LANTERN*-- AFTER THE POWER BATTERY!

AND IN TIME, I HOPE TO MAKE *GREEN LANTERN* A NAME TO BE FEARED BY EVIL DOERS EVERY-WHERE!

The End

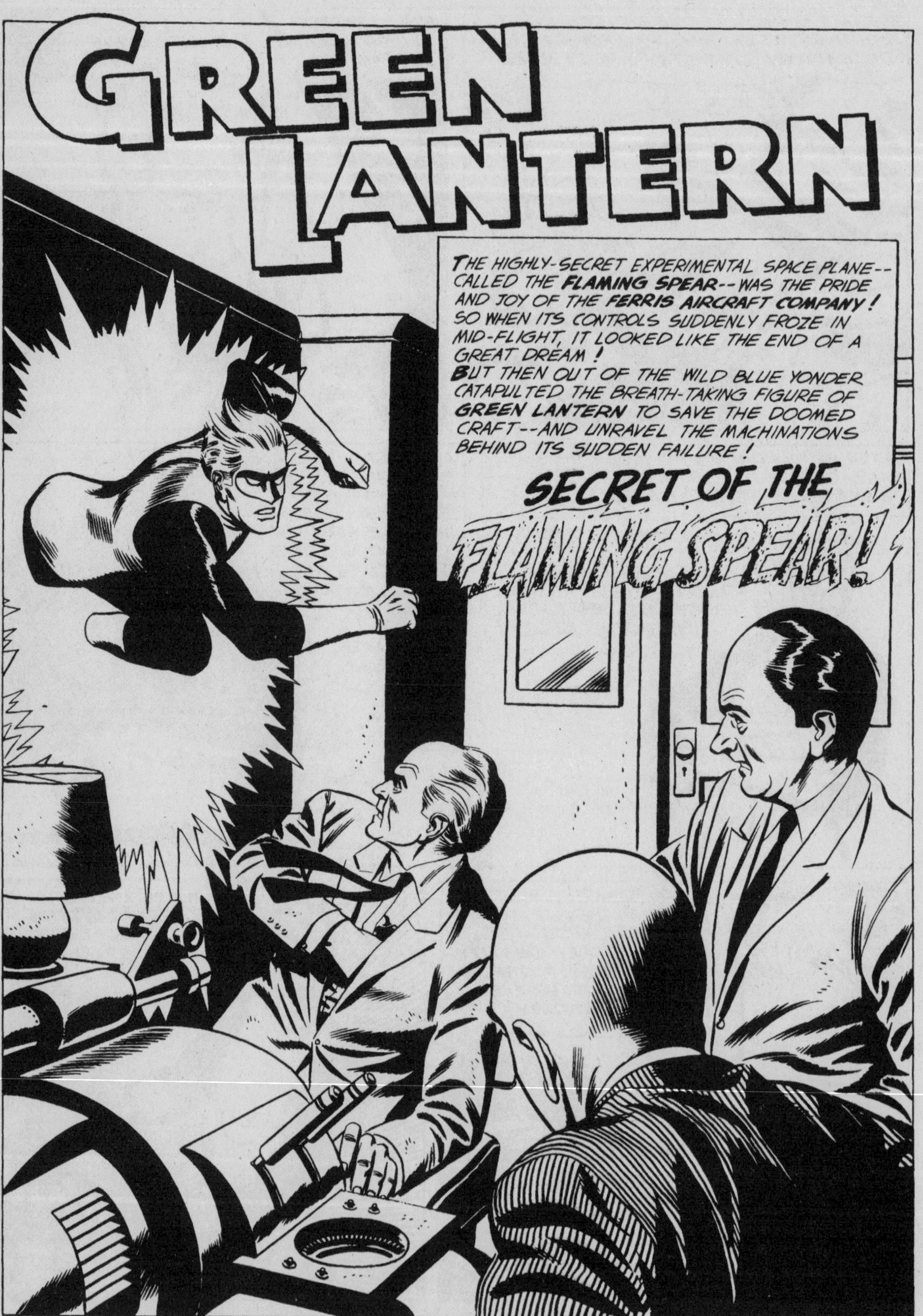
GREEN LANTERN
THE HIGHLY-SECRET EXPERIMENTAL SPACE PLANE--CALLED THE FLAMING SPEAR--WAS THE PRIDE AND JOY OF THE FERRIS AIRCRAFT COMPANY! SO WHEN ITS CONTROLS SUDDENLY FROZE IN MID-FLIGHT, IT LOOKED LIKE THE END OF A GREAT DREAM!
BUT THEN OUT OF THE WILD BLUE YONDER CATAPULTED THE BREATH-TAKING FIGURE OF GREEN LANTERN TO SAVE THE DOOMED CRAFT--AND UNRAVEL THE MACHINATIONS BEHIND ITS SUDDEN FAILURE!
SECRET OF THE FLAMING SPEAR!

IN THE MAIN OFFICE OF THE *FERRIS AIRCRAFT COMPANY.*

HAL JORDAN, WHERE HAVE YOU BEEN? WE LOOKED EVERYWHERE FOR YOU--!

ER--THERE WAS SOMETHING I HAD TO ATTEND TO, CAROL...

CAROL FERRIS, DAUGHTER OF THE BOSS, FREQUENTLY ACTS LIKE THE BOSS HERSELF...

REALLY, MR. JORDAN, IT SEEMS TO ME YOU SHOULD ATTEND TO YOUR OWN AFFAIRS ON YOUR OWN TIME!

I'M RECEIVING YOU LOUD AND CLEAR, MISS FERRIS..

...BUT HOW ABOUT DINNER AND A DANCE TONIGHT, CAROL?

AS LONG AS IT'S NOT ON COMPANY TIME--THAT WOULD BE WONDERFUL!

BUT BEFORE EMPLOYEE-RELATIONS CAN GET ANY WARMER...

CALLING TOWER! THIS IS THE *FLAMING SPEAR!* I'M IN TROUBLE!

Eh?

CONTROLS FROZEN! I'M IN A DIVE! C--CAN'T PULL OUT!

IT'S FRANK NICHOLS! DAD SENT HIM UP IN THE *FLAMING SPEAR* WHEN YOU WEREN'T AROUND, HAL!

POOR FRANK-- HE HASN'T A CHANCE!

ONE CHANCE--IN THE PERSON OF *GREEN LANTERN!*

2

THE NEXT MOMENT... WHERE'S HAL? HE--HE WAS JUST STANDING HERE BESIDE ME!

IN HAL JORDAN'S DRESSING ROOM AT THE HANGAR, A GREEN-CLAD FIGURE MURMURS A SOLEMN OATH...

IN BRIGHTEST DAY... IN BLACKEST NIGHT, NO EVIL SHALL ESCAPE MY SIGHT! LET THOSE WHO WORSHIP EVIL'S MIGHT BEWARE MY POWER--GREEN LANTERN'S LIGHT!

THEN, LIKE A JAVELIN OF LIGHT, THE EMERALD CRUSADER CLEAVES THROUGH THE AIR...

FLYING... WHAT A STRANGE SENSATION... I WONDER IF I'LL EVER GET USED TO IT... BUT THERE'S THE PLANE--!

AT THE LAST MOMENT THE POWER-PACKED GREEN BEAM SEIZES THE PLUNGING CRAFT...

GRIPPING IT! ALL I HAVE TO DO IS USE MY WILL POWER--AND THE BEAM DOES THE REST!

WHEN THE PLANE HAS BEEN SAFELY GROUNDED...

SAY--YOU SAVED MY LIFE! BUT-- WHO ARE YOU?

GREEN LANTERN IS MY NAME!

WAIT... WHAT'S THIS?

3

UNDER THE PENETRATING FORCE OF THE AMAZING BEAM A TELLTALE SIGN IS REVEALED...

THAT WAS NO *ACCIDENT* THAT CAUSED THIS PLANE TO CRASH! SOMETHING -- SOME OUTSIDE RADIATION LOCKED THE CONTROLS!

AS *GREEN LANTERN* SWINGS THE RING-BEAM AROUND..

AND THE RADIATION IS STILL COMING INTO THE PLANE...INVISIBLE-- EXCEPT IN MY GREEN BEAM!

NO TIME TO ANSWER QUESTIONS NOW! I'VE GOT... THINGS TO DO!

WAIT'LL I TELL THE FELLOWS ABOUT *THIS!*

AS THE *GREEN GLADIATOR* STREAKS THROUGH THE AIR...

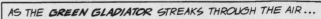

EH? THE RADIATION -- SUDDENLY STOPPED! MAYBE I CAN *STILL* FIND OUT WHERE IT CAME FROM... AND *WHO* SENT IT...

...BY CONTINUING EXACTLY IN THIS DIRECTION! ALL RADIATION TRAVELS IN A *STRAIGHT LINE* -- AND IF I HOLD MY COURSE THIS WAY I OUGHT TO COME TO ITS POINT OF ORIGIN!

IN A HOUSE NOT FAR OFF...

I CAN'T UNDERSTAND IT! OUR RADIATION-SENDER BROUGHT THE PLANE DOWN -- BUT IT DIDN'T CRASH!

14

BUT WE SAW IT DIVE--OUT OF CONTROL!

THERE'S NOTHING WRONG WITH THE RADIATION--SENDER! I'M SURE OF IT!

LET'S GO OVER TO THE FIELD AND FIND OUT WHAT'S HAP--WHAT'S THAT *GREEN LIGHT* COMING THROUGH THE WALL ?!

THE NEXT INSTANT A STARTLING APPARITION APPEARS...

JUST AS I FIGURED! *SABOTEURS!*

WH-WHAT'S THAT ? IT AIN'T A *BIRD*--

IT AIN'T A *PLANE!*

AND IT SURE AIN'T *SUPERMAN!*

WHOEVER HE IS, HE'S NOT PAYING US A FRIENDLY VISIT! *SHOOT HIM DOWN!*

BUT AS THE BULLETS WING AT THE GREEN--CLAD CHAMPION...

HE--HE'S EXPLODING OUR BULLETS IN MID-AIR--LIKE FIRECRACKERS!

CUTE TRICKS YOU CAN DO WITH THIS POWER BEAM...

POW!

POW!

5

THEIR GUNS EMPTIED IN VAIN, ONE OF THE TRIO IN DESPERATION GRABS UP A HEAVY **YELLOW** LAMP...

NOW THEY'RE STARTING TO THROW THINGS! BUT THAT WON'T HELP THEM -- ANY MORE THAN THEIR PISTOLS DID!

BUT THEN AS THE **EMERALD GLADIATOR** TURNS HIS BEAM ON THE HURTLING LAMP.

THE LAMP IS STILL COMING AT ME! I--I HAVE NO CONTROL OVER IT!

WE LAMPED HIM OUT!

WE BETTER GET OUT OF HERE!

WHEN THE **GREEN LANTERN** COMES TO HIS SENSES...

A **YELLOW** LAMP--I SHOULD HAVE KNOWN! MY BEAM HAS NO POWER OVER ANYTHING YELLOW! BUT--WHERE ARE THOSE SABOTEURS?

THERE THEY GO! BUT THEIR GETAWAY SPEED ISN'T AS FAST AS MY POWER-RAY...

HOWEVER, AS THE **GREEN BEAM** LANCES OUT...

GREAT SCOTT! I CAN'T STOP THE CAR! IT'S YELLOW TOO! IN THAT CASE--

6

MADE THE BEAM ERUPT INTO ICE-PICKS TO PUNCTURE THE BLACK TIRES!

AS THE TRIO TRIES TO FLEE ON FOOT, THE BEAM SPLITS INTO A THREE-WAY LASSO..

YOU THREE ARE COMING WITH ME TO THE NEAREST OFFICE OF THE *F.B.I.*!

LATER AT THE *FERRIS COMPANY* OFFICE...

HAL! WE JUST GOT A FLASH OVER THE RADIO-- THE SABOTEURS WHO TRIED TO CRASH OUR PLANE HAVE BEEN CAUGHT!

BY SOMEONE NAMED *GREEN LANTERN!*

WOULD YOU KNOW ANYTHING ABOUT THIS, HAL JORDAN?

WH-- HOW COULD I--

NEVER MIND-- IT'S A GOOD PIECE OF WORK-- WHOEVER THIS *GREEN LANTERN* IS! BUT I'M GLAD YOU CAME IN, HAL--

YOU CAN BE THE FIRST TO HEAR AN IMPORTANT ANNOUNCEMENT CONCERNING THE MANAGEMENT OF THE *FERRIS AIRCRAFT COMPANY!*

HAL, WHEN CAROL HERE WAS BORN I WAS DOWN-HEARTED--I WAS HOPING FOR A **SON** TO TAKE OVER THIS BUSINESS! BUT AS THINGS HAVE TURNED OUT--

CAROL HAS PROVEN HERSELF TO BE AS GOOD AS ANY SON! SHE'S GOT A REAL FINE BUSINESS HEAD ON HER SHOULDERS! SO--I'VE COME TO A DECISION...

I'VE ALWAYS WANTED TO TRAVEL AROUND THE WORLD BEFORE I GET TOO OLD TO ENJOY MYSELF! MRS. FERRIS AND I WILL BE GONE **TWO YEARS**...

...AND DURING THAT TIME CAROL WILL BE IN **SOLE CHARGE** OF THIS COMPANY!

OH, BOY! I'VE GOT A HUNCH THIS ISN'T GOING TO TURN OUT SO GOOD--FOR **ME**!

AFTER WILLARD FERRIS HAS TAKEN HIS LEAVE...

WE'RE STILL GOING DANCING TONIGHT, AREN'T WE, CAROL?

MR. JORDAN, PUH-LEASE!

FROM NOW ON THE RELATIONS BETWEEN US WILL BE **STRICTLY BUSINESS**!

BUT--!

MY HUNCH WAS RIGHT!

NO HARM IN MIXING BUSINESS WITH PLEASURE--

YOU HEARD WHAT DAD SAID! I'VE GOT TO SATISFY HIS FAITH IN ME--

AND THAT MEANS THAT DURING THE NEXT TWO YEARS I'LL HAVE ABSOLUTELY NO TIME FOR ROMANCE! I'M YOUR BOSS, MR. JORDAN-- AND THAT'S *ORDERS!*

Whew!

TWO YEARS!?

LATER, A CRESTFALLEN PILOT MOONS OVER HIS FATE...

sigh MY *POWER RING* CAN DO ANYTHING FOR ME EXCEPT GET ME THE ONE THING IN THE WORLD I WANT MOST--*CAROL!*

The End

GREEN LANTERN

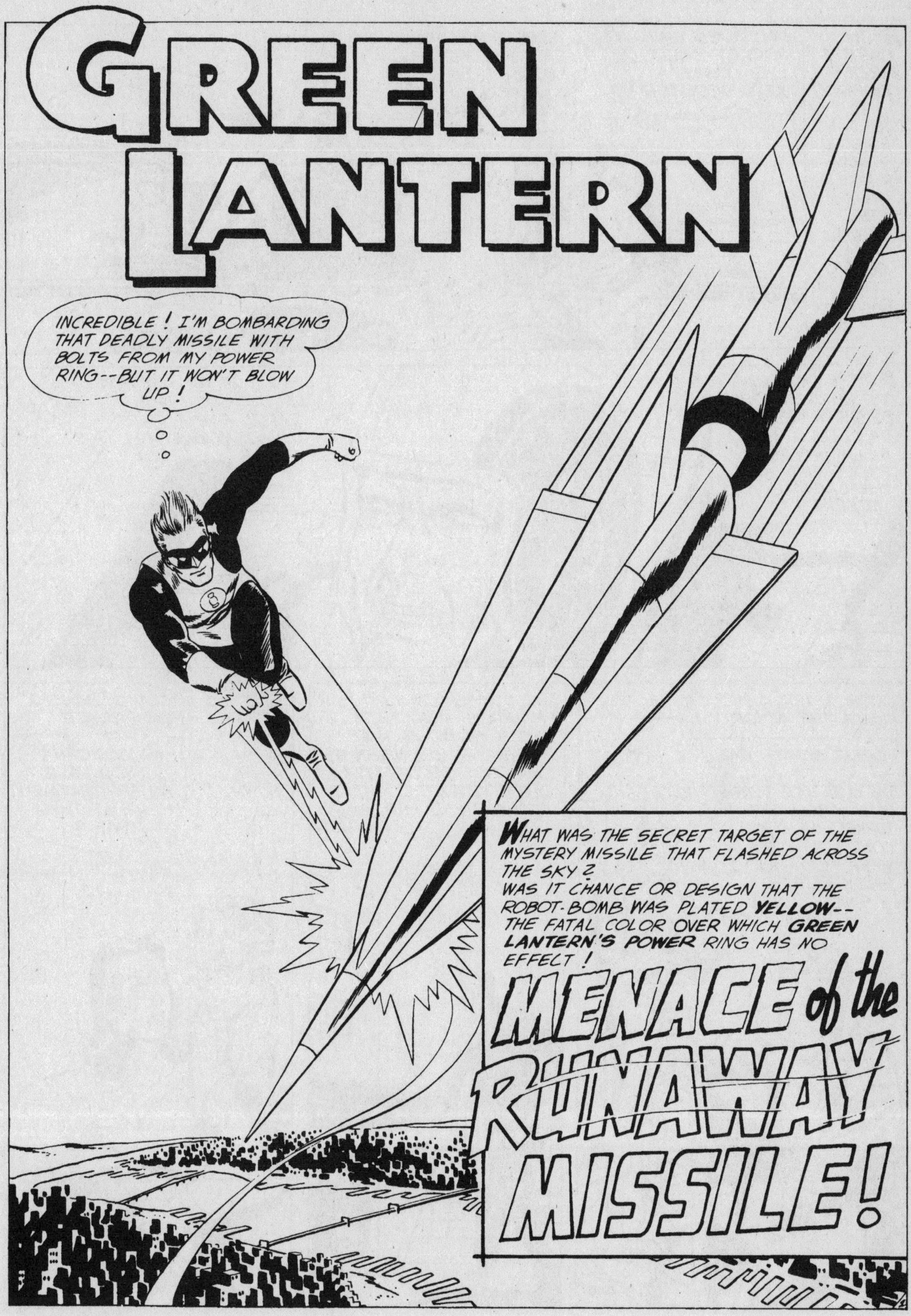
GREEN LANTERN
INCREDIBLE! I'M BOMBARDING THAT DEADLY MISSILE WITH BOLTS FROM MY POWER RING--BUT IT WON'T BLOW UP!
WHAT WAS THE SECRET TARGET OF THE MYSTERY MISSILE THAT FLASHED ACROSS THE SKY? WAS IT CHANCE OR DESIGN THAT THE ROBOT-BOMB WAS PLATED YELLOW-- THE FATAL COLOR OVER WHICH GREEN LANTERN'S POWER RING HAS NO EFFECT!
MENACE of the RUNAWAY MISSILE!

AT THE FERRIS AIRCRAFT COMPANY, HAL JORDAN TESTS OUT A NEW ROCKET-MOTOR TIED DOWN TO A SLED ON RAILS...

HAL RIDES THAT ROCKET-SLED LIKE IT WAS A KID'S SCOOTER!

THERE'S NO DANGER ON EARTH HE WON'T TACKLE--HE'S UTTERLY *FEARLESS!*

BUT THE ONLOOKING GROUND CREW WOULD BE SURPRISED IF THEY COULD READ THE DAUNTLESS PILOT'S MIND AT THIS CRITICAL MOMENT!

I'VE GOT TO SUMMON UP ENOUGH COURAGE TO ASK CAROL FOR A DATE-- *TONIGHT!*

LATER, AFTER A SUCCESSFUL TESTING OF THE MOTOR...

GREAT GOING, HAL!

THE LAST TIME I TRIED TO DATE CAROL, SHE TURNED ME DOWN COLD! THAT WAS A WEEK AGO--AND I HAVEN'T TRIED SINCE...

SHE INSISTS NOW THAT HER FATHER IS AWAY AND SHE'S MY BOSS THAT RELATIONS BETWEEN US CAN ONLY BE *OFFICIAL!* BUT I'VE GOT TO MAKE HER CHANGE HER MIND!

SLIPPING INTO THE "BOSS'S" CITADEL--HER PRIVATE OFFICE...

HI, HONEY!

MR. JORDAN! DO YOU HAVE AN APPOINTMENT HERE AT THIS TIME?

2

NO, BUT I'VE GOT A GRIEVANCE! YOU WANT TO KEEP YOUR EMPLOYEES HAPPY, DON'T YOU?

THAT DEPENDS!

THIS IS SOMETHING I CAN'T TAKE UP WITH THE GRIEVANCE COMMITTEE! I PREFER TO DISCUSS IT PERSONALLY WITH THE BOSS--AT DINNER, A RIDE IN THE COUNTRY!

IMPOSSIBLE!

FOR ONE THING, I'M GOING TO THE *CELEBRITIES BALL* TONIGHT! NATURALLY, YOU WON'T BE THERE, MR. JORDAN! YOU'RE NOT THAT FAMOUS YET...

BUT IT MIGHT INTEREST YOU TO KNOW THAT I EXPECT TO MEET THE MYSTERIOUS *GREEN LANTERN* AT THE BALL! I HEAR *HE'S* BEING INVITED!

OH?!

MOMENTS LATER...

FUNNY! RIGHT AFTER I TOLD HAL ABOUT MEETING *GREEN LANTERN* TONIGHT, HE STOPPED BOTHERING ME AND LEFT! I *WONDER WHY...!*

SO *GREEN LANTERN* IS INVITED TO THE *CELEBRITIES BALL?* WELL--IN THAT CASE *CAROL* HAS A DATE WITH *ME* TONIGHT--WHETHER SHE REALIZES IT OR NOT!

3

BEHIND CLOSED DOORS IN HAL JORDAN'S DRESSING ROOM AT THE HANGAR, A SOLEMN OATH RESOUNDS..

IN BRIGHTEST DAY... IN BLACKEST NIGHT, NO EVIL SHALL ESCAPE MY SIGHT! LET THOSE WHO WORSHIP EVIL'S MIGHT BEWARE MY POWER-- GREEN LANTERN'S LIGHT!

AT THE FAMED *CELEBRITIES BALL* THAT EVENING...

SINCE *GREEN LANTERN* AND I WERE INTRODUCED TO EACH OTHER, HE'S INSISTED WE HAVE *EVERY DANCE!* HE--HE'S FASCINATING!

I EXPECTED TO BE THRILLED MEETING *GREEN LANTERN*... BUT I DIDN'T EXPECT *THIS* TO HAPPEN! HE'S GOT MY HEART ACTING LIKE A JUMPING JACK!

ON THE TERRACE OVERLOOKING THE FRAGRANT NIGHT...

I NEVER THOUGHT I COULD GO FOR ANY MAN BUT HAL JORDAN! BUT NOW--NOW I'M NOT SO SURE! HE'S DRAWING ME CLOSER--GOING TO KISS ME...

AT THAT MOMENT A FEARSOME SHAPE PLUMMETS TOWARD *COAST CITY*...

SUDDENLY THE EVER-WATCHFUL EYE OF **GREEN LANTERN** SPIES A DREAD SIGHT...

GREAT SCOTT!

AN INSTANT LATER, CAROL IS LEFT WITH EMPTY ARMS...

OF ALL THE NERVE--! HE FLEW OUT ON ME-- RIGHT IN THE MIDDLE OF A KISS!

FLASHING THROUGH THE AIR, GREEN LANTERN BEAMS HIS **POWER RING** AT THE MISSILE...

A RUNAWAY ARMY MISSILE!? IF IT CONTAINS AN ATOMIC WARHEAD--IT COULD DESTROY THE ENTIRE CITY! I MUST STOP IT!

FORMING HUGE PINCERS WITH HIS BEAM, THE **EMERALD CRUSADER** GRABS AT THE PLUNGING ENGINE OF DE-STRUCTION...

MY--MY RING HAS NO EFFECT ON IT! I SHOULD HAVE NOTICED-- IT'S BECAUSE OF THE MISSILE'S **YELLOW** COLOR!

AS THE POPULACE BELOW WATCHES HORRIFIED...

MUST BE SOMETHING I CAN DO! CAN'T LET IT STRIKE THE CITY!

5

WITH SPLIT-SECONDS TO GO...

THE VERY TIP OF THE MISSILE-- IT'S **NOT** YELLOW! THAT GIVES ME A CHANCE!

AS THE **GREEN BEAM** INSTANTLY SPREADS A NET STRONGER THAN STEEL UNDER THE PROJECTILE...

WILL MY NET HOLD? THE POINT IS STRIKING IT NOW--!

IN THE INSTANTANEOUS DUEL THAT FOLLOWS, THE NET HOLDS...

IT BENT MY NET-- BUT CAN'T BREAK THROUGH!

ON THE STREET...

THERE! IT'LL BE SAFE HERE UNTIL THE ARMY SHOWS UP TO TAKE IT AWAY!

WHEN TECHNICIANS ARRIVE...

EH? YOU SAY IT'S NOT AN ARMY MISSILE, COLONEL?

THAT'S RIGHT, **GREEN LANTERN!** IT LOOKS LIKE ONE OF OURS-- BUT WE SENT OFF NO ARMY MISSILE TODAY!

UNDER FURTHER INVESTIGATION, FURTHER FACTS EMERGE FROM THE DISASSEMBLED MISSILE...

IT CONTAINS ORDINARY EXPLOSIVE--NOT A NUCLEAR WARHEAD!

ORDINARY EXPLOSIVE? THEN THAT MEANS--

6

--ITS FUNCTION WAS TO DESTROY ONLY THAT BUILDING IT WAS GOING AT!

YES, BUT ODDLY ENOUGH, *GREEN LANTERN*...

...ALTHOUGH FEW PEOPLE KNOW IT, THAT BUILDING CONTAINS THE CORE OF OUR SUPER-IMPORTANT RESEARCH FOR *HYDROGEN POWER!*

EVIDENTLY SOMEONE TRIED TO DESTROY THE GOVERN-MENT'S *H-POWER* PROJECT! BUT WHO--?

As THE *EMERALD GLADIATOR* QUESTIONS THE ARMY MAN...

COLONEL, IS THERE ANY WAY WE CAN FIND OUT WHERE THIS MISSILE CAME FROM--

THERE'S ONE POSSIBILITY...

WE HAVE AIRCRAFT SPOTTERS ALL THROUGH THIS AREA! ONE OF THEM MIGHT HAVE SEEN THE MISSILE RISE! A PROJECTILE LIKE THIS STARTS UP SLOWLY, YOU KNOW!

By EARLY MORNING *GREEN LANTERN* HAS RECEIVED A LIST OF THE OFFICIAL SPOTTER-STATIONS...

SEE YOU LATER, COLONEL! I'M GOING TO MAKE A RAPID-FIRE TOUR OF OUR CIVIL DEFENSE POSTS IN THIS AREA!

7

FINALLY, AFTER A NUMBER OF FRUITLESS STOPS...

YES, *GREEN LANTERN!* I DID SEE SOMETHING AWHILE AGO-- SUDDEN FLAMES SHOOTING UP IN THE WOOD OVER THAT WAY!

THAT COULD HAVE BEEN THE MISSILE BLASTING OFF!

IN A TWINKLING THE GREEN-CLAD CHAMPION IS ON HIS WAY...

IT WON'T TAKE ME LONG TO EXAMINE EVERY INCH OF THAT WOOD!

AFTER A SWIFT, RING-POWERED SEARCH...

THAT AREA--! IT'S CAMOUFLAGED FOR CONCEALMENT! BUT MY BEAM REVEALS A BUILDING UNDERNEATH!

INSIDE THE HIDDEN STRUCTURE, MOMENTS LATER...

GREEN LANTERN! I'VE BEEN HALF-EXPECTING *YOU*--!

AND THAT'S WHY I PREPARED THIS TELESCOPIC BATTERING RAM! YOUR VAUNTED *POWER RING* WON'T BE ABLE TO STOP *THIS!*

BUT TO THE EVILDOER'S AMAZEMENT...

HIS RING--TURNED THE BATTERING RAM INTO A STREAM OF WATER-- DOUSING ME WITH IT!

8

AS THE MIGHTY RING IS PUT TO ANOTHER USE, *GREEN LANTERN* HEAVES A SIGH OF RELIEF...

LUCKILY THE BATTERING RAM WASN'T *YELLOW!* I HATE TO THINK WHAT WOULD HAVE HAPPENED TO ME IF HE HAD KNOWN THE NULLIFYING EFFECT THAT COLOR HAS OVER THE *POWER RING!*

SOON, AT ARMY HEADQUARTERS...

HIS NAME IS *DR. PARRIS, GREEN LANTERN!* HE'S CONFESSED EVERYTHING! HE IS A BRILLIANT SCIENTIST-- WHO PUT EVIL AMBITION AHEAD OF LOYALTY TO HIS COUNTRY!

HE WANTED TO BE THE *FIRST* TO REACH THE GOAL OF USABLE *H-POWER!* HE FIGURED IF HE COULD GET THAT, NOTHING IN THE WORLD WOULD BE BEYOND HIS REACH...

THEN THAT'S WHY HE SHOT OFF THAT MISSILE --AND ATTEMPTED TO DESTROY THE GOVERNMENT *H-POWER* PROJECT!

YES! BUT THANKS TO YOU, HIS MISGUIDED AMBITION WILL LEAD HIM TO PRISON!

LATER THAT DAY, *GREEN LANTERN* GOES TO THE FERRIS AIRCRAFT COMPANY...

I'VE GOT TO APOLOGIZE TO CAROL FOR MY HASTY EXIT LAST NIGHT! ANYWAY, THAT'S MY EXCUSE FOR COMING HERE!

BUT TO THE *EMERALD GLADIATOR'S* SURPRISE...

I DON'T WANT TO LISTEN TO YOUR EXCUSES, *GREEN LANTERN!* YOU CAN JUST LEAVE--!

UH?!

BUT, CAROL-- MISS FERRIS-- WHAT HAVE I DONE?

WHAT HAVE YOU DONE? YOU-- YOU **HEEL**! LAST NIGHT YOU KISSED ME--

YOU'RE NOT OBJECTING TO **THAT**? THE WAY YOU KISSED ME, I COULD TELL--

IT'S THE WAY **YOU** KISSED ME THAT I'M REFERRING TO...

IF YOU HAD LOST YOURSELF IN THAT KISS...THE WAY I DID...YOUR EYES WOULD HAVE NATURALLY **CLOSED**...

BUT CAROL--BE REASONABLE! IF MY EYES HAD BEEN CLOSED, I WOULDN'T HAVE SEEN THAT MISSILE AND...

GOOD DAY, **MR. GREEN LANTERN**! I AM BUSY!

CAROL FERRIS PRIVATE

SLAM! SLAM!

WHEW! NOW I'M IN A **DOUBLE DOGHOUSE** AS FAR AS CAROL IS CONCERNED! BOTH AS **HAL JORDAN**--AND AS **GREEN LANTERN**! HOW COULD THINGS GET WORSE?

IN THE NEXT ISSUE OF SHOW- CASE, MORE THRILL- ING ADVEN- TURES WITH GREEN LANTERN!

The End

10

GREEN LANTERN

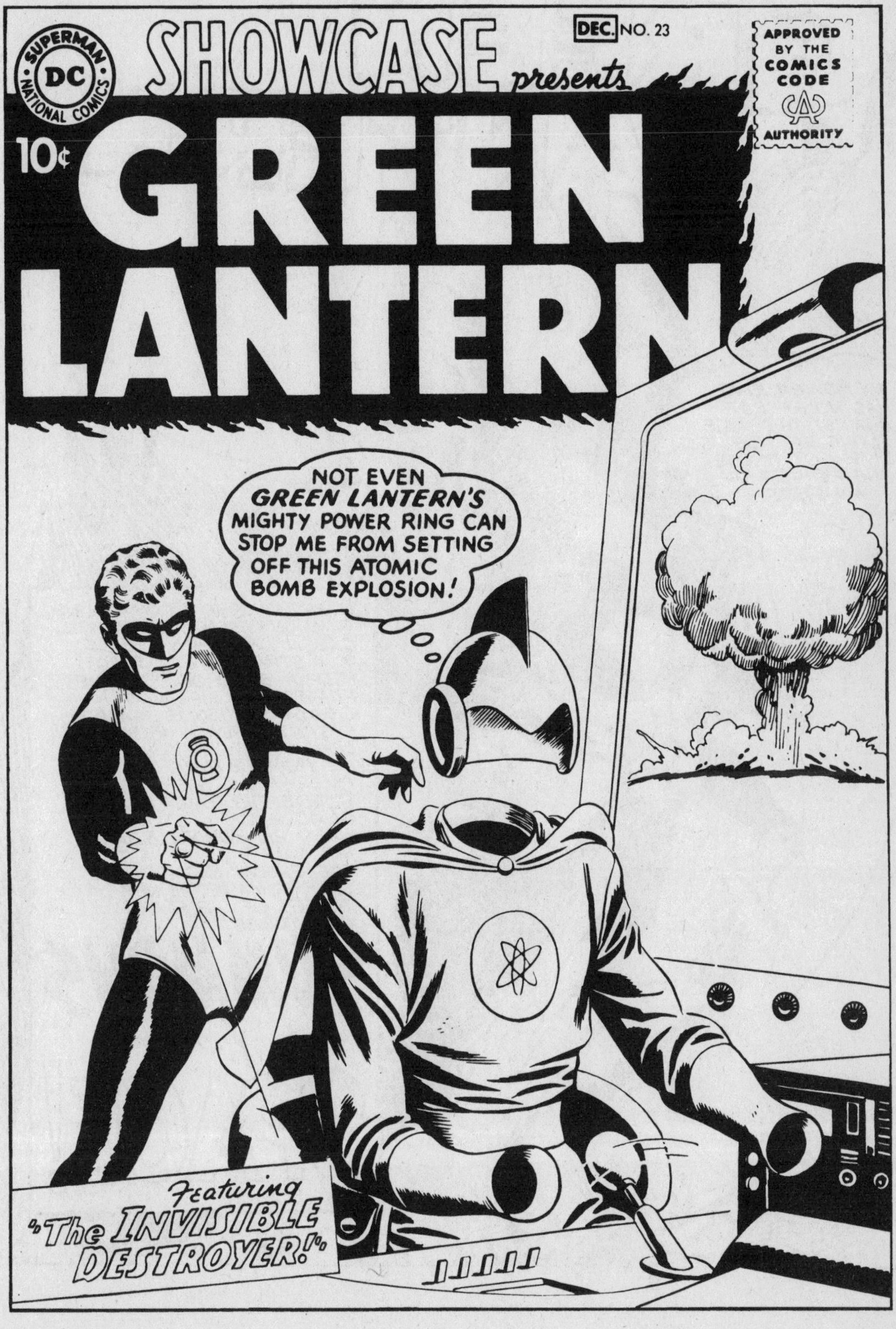
SUPERMAN
DC
NATIONAL COMICS
SHOWCASE presents
DEC. NO. 23
APPROVED BY THE COMICS CODE AUTHORITY
10¢
GREEN LANTERN
NOT EVEN GREEN LANTERN'S MIGHTY POWER RING CAN STOP ME FROM SETTING OFF THIS ATOMIC BOMB EXPLOSION!
Featuring "The INVISIBLE DESTROYER!"

GREEN LANTERN

MY *POWER RING* HAS NO EFFECT AGAINST THIS HUGE FLYING REPTILE! SO I'VE GOT TO USE THE *POWER* OF MY *FISTS!*

In RESPONSE TO A COMPELLING SUMMONS FROM OUTER SPACE, *GREEN LANTERN* SPEEDS TO A STRANGE WORLD TO HELP A BAND OF PRIMITIVE HUMANS IN A LIFE-AND-DEATH STRUGGLE AGAINST GIGANTIC FLYING REPTILES! CONFIDENTLY RELYING ON HIS *POWER RING* TO OVERWHELM THE WINGED HORDE, THE *EMERALD GLADIATOR* IS STUNNED WHEN HIS *POWER BEAM* NOT ONLY FAILS TO HALT THE ENEMY, BUT HE HIM-SELF IS MADE THE NEW TARGET OF THE FLYING CREATURES!

SUMMONS from SPACE!

LIONIZED BY SOCIETY IN *COAST CITY*, *GREEN LANTERN* --ALIAS TEST PILOT HAL JORDAN--IS INVITED TO GALA PARTIES...

US HOW YOUR *RING* WORKS, *GREEN LANTERN?*

WON'T YOU TELL

SORRY, THAT MUST REMAIN MY PERSONAL SECRET.'

BUT-- *WHO* ARE YOU SECRETLY WHEN YOU'RE *NOT* BEING *GREEN LANTERN?*

IF I TOLD YOU, IT WOULD BE *OUR* SECRET-- AND A SECRET KNOWN TO TWO, IS NO LONGER A SECRET.'

THE *EMERALD CRUSADER'S* FAME SPREADS...

GOSH, *GREEN LANTERN--* YOU'RE TAKING ME TO THE THEATER AND WE'RE USING YOUR *POWER RING* TO GET THERE!

CROSS-TOWN TRAFFIC IS SO HEAVY, WE'D MISS THE OPENING CURTAIN!

MORE AND MORE THE PAPERS CARRY STORIES AND PHOTOGRAPHS...

ZETTE

10¢

GREEN LANTERN AND DEBUTANTE LOIS FULLER AT OPERA!

...LINKING THE NAME OF *GREEN LANTERN* WITH THOSE OF THE MOST BEAUTIFUL GIRLS IN TOWN!

..."*ACTRESS BRENDA BROWN* WINS *GREEN LANTERN'S* AUTOGRAPH!'"

"...*CAREER GIRL SUSIE TAFT* SEEN AT LUNCH WITH *GREEN LANTERN...*"

2

THE NEXT DAY AT THE *FERRIS AIRCRAFT COMPANY,* HAL JORDAN AND HIS *LOVELY BOSS* CAROL FERRIS SHARE A COFFEE BREAK...

SEEN THESE SCANDALOUS NEWSPAPER ITEMS ABOUT *GREEN LANTERN?* HAL, HAVE YOU

WHAT'S SO *SCANDALOUS* ABOUT THEM, CAROL?

FORTUNATELY SHE DOESN'T DREAM THAT IN MY SECRET IDENTITY I MYSELF AM GREEN LANTERN!

I'LL TELL YOU...

IN THE LAST SEVEN DAYS HE'S BEEN REPORTED SEEN WITH SEVEN DIFFERENT BEAUTIFUL GIRLS!

WHY SHOULD THAT STRIKE YOU AS *SCANDALOUS*--UNLESS YOU WERE JEALOUS OF THE ATTENTION *GREEN LANTERN'S* GIVING THOSE--ER-- RIVALS OF YOURS?

BESIDES, CAROL, WHAT DID YOU EXPECT AFTER THE WAY YOU TREATED *GREEN LANTERN*--REFUSING EVEN TO SPEAK TO HIM ON THE PHONE!

HOW DID *YOU* KNOW THAT!?

ER--WE'VE BECOME FRIENDLY AND HE'S CONFIDED IN ME!

SO--YOU AND *GREEN LANTERN* KNOW EACH OTHER? HOW INTERESTING!

STRANGE! THE TWO MEN I FIND MOST ATTRACTIVE IN THE WORLD HAVE NOW BECOME FRIENDS! BUT...MAYBE I WAS A BIT HASTY TOWARD *GREEN LANTERN!* I WONDER!

3

HAL, DO YOU STILL WANT TO TAKE ME TO DINNER SOME EVENING?

DO I! HOW ABOUT *TONIGHT!*

NOW WAIT! YOU KNOW WHEN MY FATHER WENT OFF ON HIS ROUND-THE-WORLD TRIP AND LEFT ME IN SOLE CHARGE HERE--I PROMISED HIM TO STICK STRICTLY TO BUSINESS--

THAT'S WHY YOU AND I HAVE HAD TO STOP SEEING EACH OTHER--EXCEPT AT BUSINESS HOURS, HAL! I CAN'T AFFORD TO RISK FALLING MORE DEEPLY IN LOVE...!

OH!

BUT--MAYBE IT WOULDN'T BE SUCH A RISK IF *THREE OF US* HAD DINNER TOGETHER-- YOU, I-- AND *GREEN LANTERN!*

SINCE HE'S SUCH A FRIEND OF YOURS, HAL, I SUPPOSE YOU CAN PERSUADE HIM TO COME!

WHAT A SPOT CAROL'S PUTTING ME IN!

I'VE GOT A FEELING THAT SHE IS TRYING TO *USE ME*--IN ORDER TO GET NEXT TO *GREEN LANTERN!* I--I'M MY OWN RIVAL!

④

AFTER THE VETERAN TEST PILOT HAS PARTED FROM HIS SHAPELY EMPLOYER...

I HAD TO PROMISE CAROL TO BRING *GREEN LANTERN* TO DINNER! SHE WOULDN'T TAKE NO FOR AN ANSWER! NO *GREEN LANTERN*, SHE SAID -- NO DINNER DATE!

BUT HOW CAN I BRING *GREEN LANTERN* WHEN -- I MYSELF *AM GREEN LANTERN*? *WHOOEE!* THIS DOUBLE IDENTITY BUSINESS CAN MAKE A MAN JET-HAPPY!

IN THE PRIVACY OF HAL JORDAN'S DRESSING ROOM AT THE HANGAR...

MAYBE IF I SIT HERE ALONE AWHILE I'LL FIGURE OUT WHAT TO DO! THERE MUST BE SOME WAY OUT OF THIS DILEMMA --

EH? MY GREEN LAMP --

IT'S SIGNALING ME -- SENDING A THOUGHT OUT TO ME --!* TO THE POSSESSOR OF THE *POWER LAMP* IN SECTOR 2814...

*EDITOR'S NOTE:

GREEN LANTERN'S SECRET LAMP IS NOT OF EARTHLY ORIGIN, BUT WAS BESTOWED ON HIM BY A DYING SPACE-MAN AS DESCRIBED IN THE PREVIOUS ISSUE OF THIS MAGAZINE!

...AN EMERGENCY HAS ARISEN ON THE WORLD CALLED *VENUS* IN THE SOLAR SYSTEM IN WHICH YOU LIVE! YOU ARE THE ONLY LAMP POSSESSOR WHO CAN REACH THERE IN TIME! YOU MUST *HURRY!*

OKAY, I'M CHANGING INTO MY UNIFORM NOW!

SOON... A FAMOUS FIGURE IS TAKING THE OATH WHICH EVERY TWENTY-FOUR HOURS RENEWS THE POWER IN HIS FABULOUS RING!

IN BRIGHTEST DAY... IN BLACKEST NIGHT, NO EVIL SHALL ESCAPE MY SIGHT! LET THOSE WHO WORSHIP EVIL'S MIGHT BEWARE MY POWER -- *GREEN LANTERN'S LIGHT!*

5

PROPELLED BY HIS INVINCIBLE *POWER RING,* THE *GREEN GLADIATOR* ZOOMS OFF THE EARTH...

SOME DAY I HOPE TO FIND OUT WHO SENDS OUT THE *MYSTERIOUS THOUGHTS* THAT REACH ME THROUGH THE *POWER LAMP!* BUT UNTIL THEN...

...ALL I KNOW IS THAT THE SPACEMAN WHO PASSED THE LAMP ON TO ME MADE ME PROMISE ALWAYS TO OBEY THE COMMANDS THAT REACHED ME THROUGH IT! AND THAT MEANS I MUST ANSWER THIS SUMMONS TO *VENUS* AT ONCE!

*L*IKE A NUCLEAR-POWERED JET, *GL* CLEAVES THROUGH AIRLESS SPACE TOWARD HIS GOAL...

I WILLED MY RING TO FORM AN *AIR POCKET* AROUND ME SO THAT I CAN BREATHE! IT WILL LAST 24 HOURS--TIME ENOUGH FOR ME TO COMPLETE MY MISSION ON *VENUS*...I HOPE!

ACCORDING TO THE THOUGHTS RELAYED BY THE *LAMP,* A RACE OF HUMANS--LIKE US--IS IN SOME DREADFUL DANGER... AND I MUST HELP THEM!

*B*RIEF MOMENTS LATER, A DENSE CLOUD IS PIERCED AND...

SO THIS IS *VENUS!* THE LAMP THOUGHTS DIDN'T SAY JUST WHAT KIND OF DANGER THE HUMANS HERE WERE IN--SO I'D BETTER BE ON MY GUARD--UHH?

CONTINUED ON FOLLOWING PAGE.

6

AS THE GREEN CRUSADER WHIRLS... A HUGE *FLYING CREATURE--* OF THE *PTERODACTYL* TYPE WE HAD ON EARTH MILLIONS OF YEARS AGO-- *SWOOPING DOWN ON ME!*

INSTINCTIVELY THE LONE TRAVELER TRIES TO DEFEND HIMSELF...

MY POWER RING HAS *NO EFFECT* ON THAT *YELLOW* CREATURE!*

EDITOR'S NOTE: DUE TO AN IMPURITY IN ITS VERY NATURE, GREEN LANTERN'S POWER BEAM HAS NO EFFECT ON ANYTHING YELLOW!

THEN...

LIFTING ME IN ITS *CLAW--!*

INDOMITABLY, WITH HIS RING USELESS, THE GREEN-CLAD EARTHMAN RESORTS TO HIS POWER-PACKED FISTS!

STARTLED, THE FLYING CREATURE LETS GO OF ITS PREY--

FALLING--! BUT ITS GRIP EXHAUSTED ME--WEAKENED MY WILL POWER! CAN'T BRING MY RING INTO PLAY--!

7

DOWN, DOWN GOES THE DAZED *GL*...INTO A CREVICE IN THE GROUND...

THE ONLY THING THAT SAVED ME-- THE CREATURE IS TOO BIG TO GET INTO THIS CREVICE I FELL INTO!

LATER, AFTER THE DOWNED GLADIATOR HAS RECOVERED HIS STRENGTH...

GONE! IT FINALLY GOT TIRED OF TRYING TO GET AT ME! NOW TO HAVE A LOOK AROUND--!

ACCORDING TO THE *LAMP-THOUGHTS* THERE SHOULD BE SOME SIGN OF HUMAN HABITATION HERE! EH? WHAT'S THAT?

WHEW! BLUE-SKINNED HUMANS--LIVING IN CAVES! THEY'RE PRIMITIVE--AS OUR CAVEMEN ON EARTH WERE-- MILLIONS OF YEARS AGO!

EKA--!!

QUICKLY, THE EARTHMAN IS SURROUNDED...

GLA MIKKO A-PO!

THEY- THEY'RE TRYING TO TELL ME SOMETHING! THEY ALL SEEM EXCITED TO SEE ME!

8

PERO AB DUKA?

THIS IS AWFUL! OBVIOUSLY, THEY'RE TRYING TO TELL ME SOMETHING IMPORTANT-- BUT I CAN'T UNDERSTAND THEM! WAIT-- I WONDER--

AS THE *GREEN CHAMPION* GETS AN IDEA...

MY RING RESPONDS TO MY *WILL POWER!* WHAT IF I POINT IT AT ONE OF THESE *VENUSIANS*-- AND *WILL* IT TO UNDERSTAND WHAT HE'S TELLING ME?

--AB NULA--!

WE SEE YOU ARE A HUMAN LIKE OURSELVES! YOU MUST HELP US!

IT'S WORKING-- LIKE A CHARM!

OUR RACE IS MENACED BY WINGED RAIDERS!

THEY'RE HUGE... AND NEVER STOP HUNTING US--!

GREAT SCOTT! THE RAIDERS HE'S DESCRIBING-- SOUND LIKE THAT YELLOW CREATURE THAT ATTACKED ME!

THEY'RE TRYING TO WIPE US OUT--SO THAT THEY CAN BE THE RULING RACE ON THIS WORLD--

UHH! HERE COMES A HORDE OF THEM NOW!

9

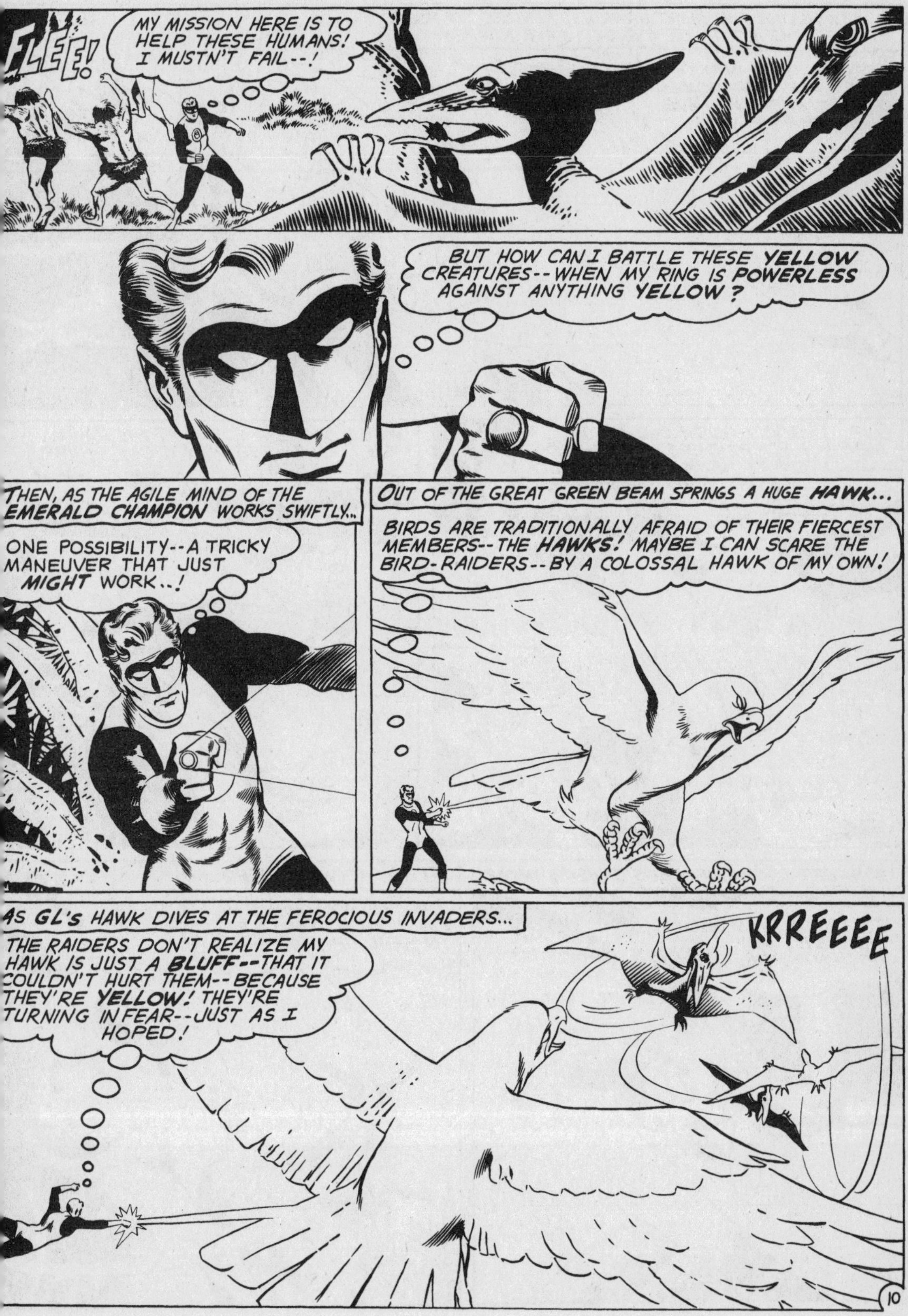
FLEEE!
MY MISSION HERE IS TO HELP THESE HUMANS! I MUSTN'T FAIL--!
BUT HOW CAN I BATTLE THESE YELLOW CREATURES--WHEN MY RING IS POWERLESS AGAINST ANYTHING YELLOW?
THEN, AS THE AGILE MIND OF THE EMERALD CHAMPION WORKS SWIFTLY..
ONE POSSIBILITY--A TRICKY MANEUVER THAT JUST MIGHT WORK..!
OUT OF THE GREAT GREEN BEAM SPRINGS A HUGE HAWK...
BIRDS ARE TRADITIONALLY AFRAID OF THEIR FIERCEST MEMBERS--THE HAWKS! MAYBE I CAN SCARE THE BIRD-RAIDERS--BY A COLOSSAL HAWK OF MY OWN!
AS GL's HAWK DIVES AT THE FEROCIOUS INVADERS...
THE RAIDERS DON'T REALIZE MY HAWK IS JUST A BLUFF--THAT IT COULDN'T HURT THEM--BECAUSE THEY'RE YELLOW! THEY'RE TURNING IN FEAR--JUST AS I HOPED!
KRREEEEE
10

IN A TWINKLING THE GIANT HAWK HAS HERDED ITS FOES TOWARD THE MOUTH OF A GREAT CAVE NEARBY...

FORCING THEM INTO THIS CAVE! ANOTHER MOMENT OR TWO AND I'LL HAVE THEM TRAPPED--!

KREEEEE

BUT THEN... GOOD GOSH! ONE OF THE BIRD-RAIDERS HAS TURNED ON MY HAWK--AND SLASHED A CLAW RIGHT THROUGH IT!

MORE OF THEM GOING AT THE HAWK! THEY--THEY SEE NOW IT CAN'T HURT THEM!

WITH JET-LIKE SWIFTNESS, GREEN LANTERN WHIRLS...

I'VE GOT THEM ALL IN THE CAVE! NOW... TO RETURN TO THE OUTSIDE--

SPLIT-SECONDS LATER...

THEY'RE FOLLOWING ME-- ONLY AN INSTANT LEFT TO SEAL UP THAT CAVE!

AS THE GREAT GREEN BEAM CAUSES A HUGE LANDSLIDE BLOCKING THE CAVE MOUTH UP FOREVER...

YOU HAVE TRAPPED OUR ENEMIES THE BIRD-RAIDERS!

THANKS TO OUR FELLOW-HUMAN, WE ARE SAVED!

LATER... THE VENUSIAN HUMANS ARE PREPARING A GREAT VICTORY FEAST-- TO WHICH I'M INVITED! THEY'RE JUST ABOUT AT THE CAVEMAN LEVEL NOW...

MAKING THEIR FIRES OUT IN THE OPEN... AND KEEPING THE FIRES LIT AND GUARDING THEM EVERY DAY! BUT THEY WON'T ALWAYS BE LIKE THIS-- ONE DAY THERE'LL BE A GREAT CIVILIZATION HERE!

AFTERWARD, AS THE EMERALD GLADIATOR STARTS HOMEWARD...

I SEE NOW WHY I WAS SENT HERE... TO PREVENT THIS BAND OF HUMANS FROM BEING WIPED OUT! HUMANS EVERYWHERE ARE IMPORTANT FOR ALL OTHER HUMANS!

HMM! BUT TO COME DOWN TO PERSONAL MATTERS--I'D BETTER HURRY! I HAVEN'T FORGOTTEN THAT I HAVE A VERY IMPORTANT DATE TONIGHT BACK HOME!

12

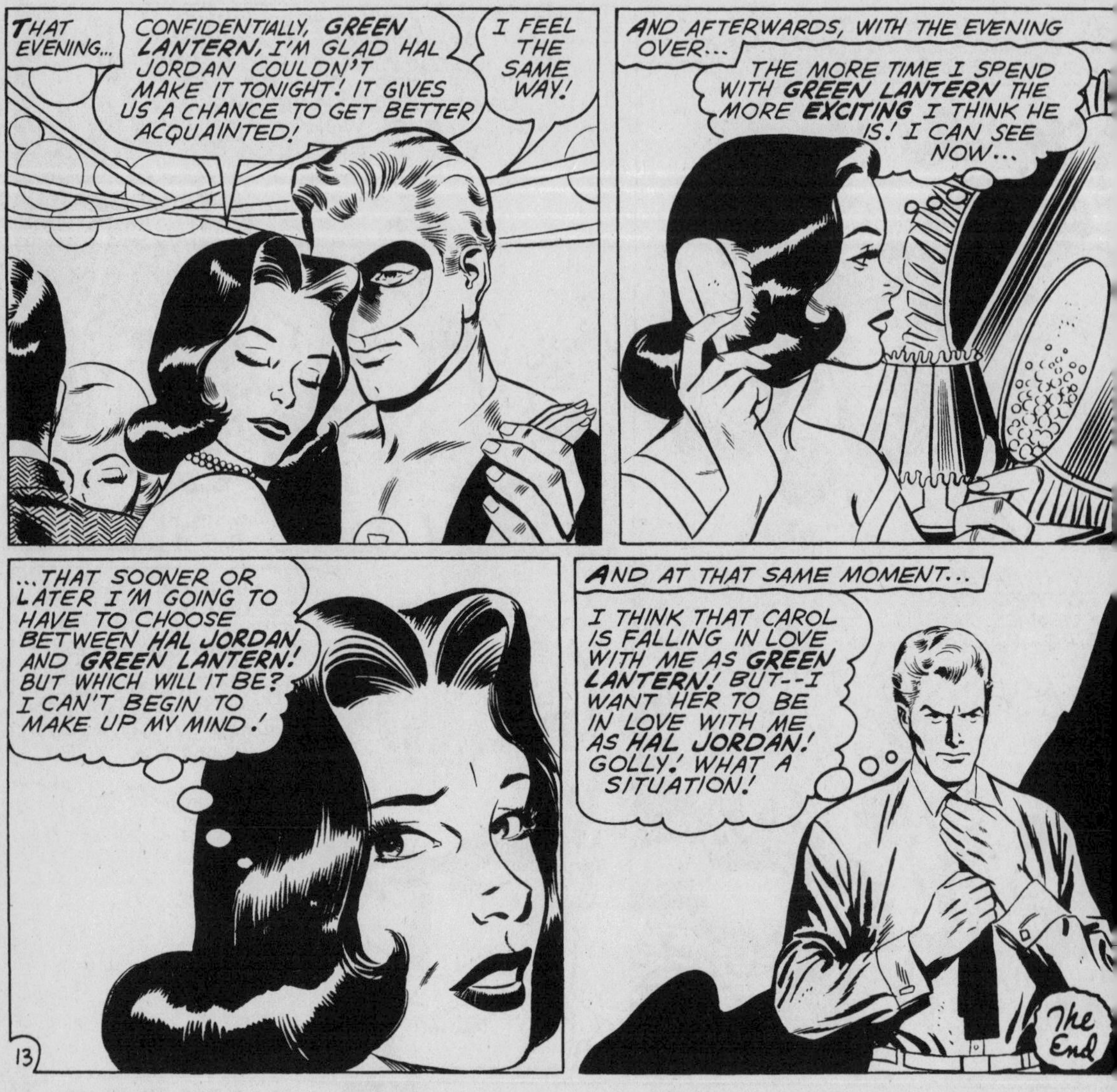
THAT EVENING...
CONFIDENTIALLY, GREEN LANTERN, I'M GLAD HAL JORDAN COULDN'T MAKE IT TONIGHT! IT GIVES US A CHANCE TO GET BETTER ACQUAINTED!
I FEEL THE SAME WAY!
AND AFTERWARDS, WITH THE EVENING OVER...
THE MORE TIME I SPEND WITH GREEN LANTERN THE MORE EXCITING I THINK HE IS! I CAN SEE NOW...
...THAT SOONER OR LATER I'M GOING TO HAVE TO CHOOSE BETWEEN HAL JORDAN AND GREEN LANTERN! BUT WHICH WILL IT BE? I CAN'T BEGIN TO MAKE UP MY MIND!
13
AND AT THAT SAME MOMENT...
I THINK THAT CAROL IS FALLING IN LOVE WITH ME AS GREEN LANTERN! BUT--I WANT HER TO BE IN LOVE WITH ME AS HAL JORDAN! GOLLY! WHAT A SITUATION!
The End

GREEN LANTERN

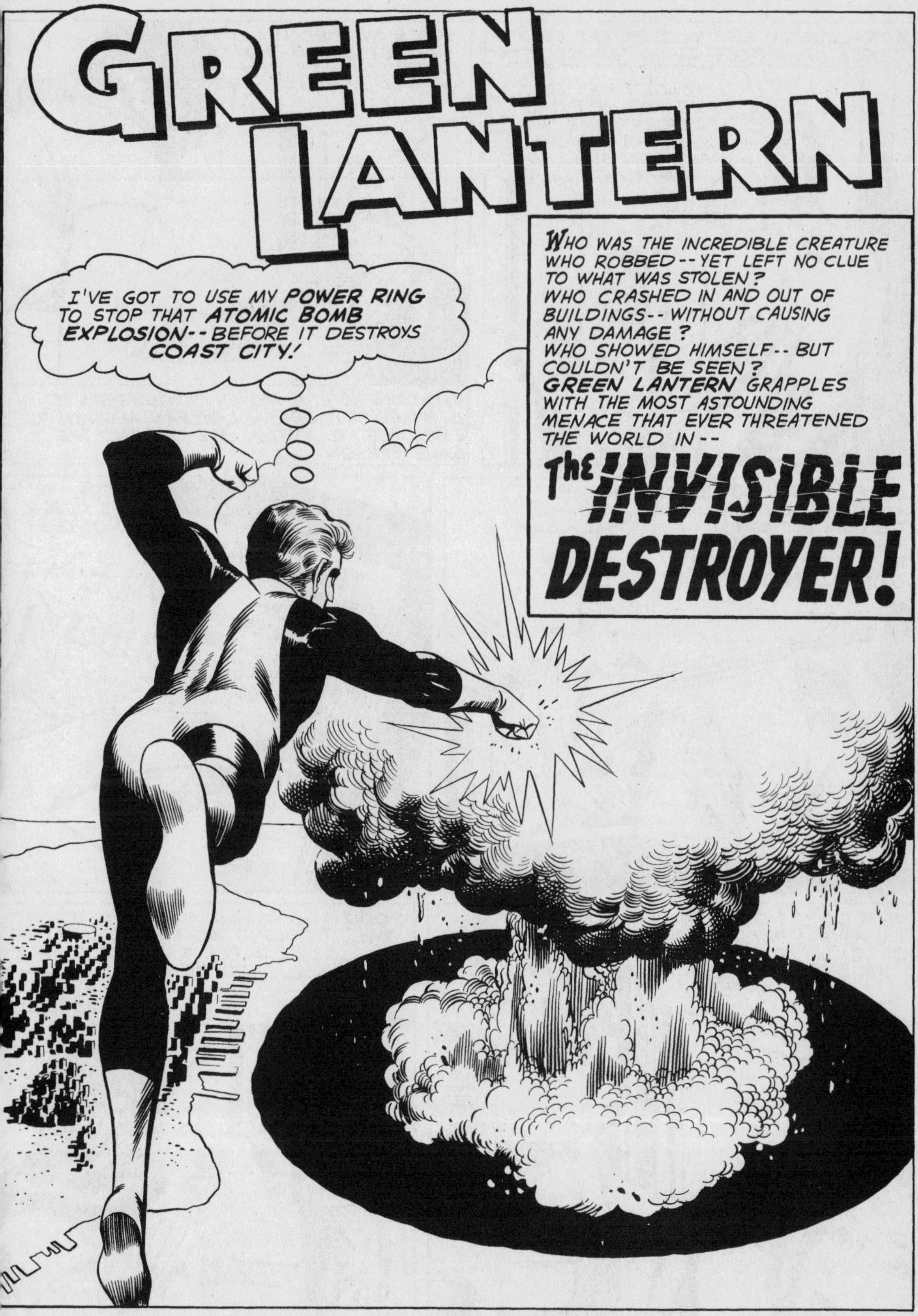
GREEN LANTERN
WHO WAS THE INCREDIBLE CREATURE WHO ROBBED--YET LEFT NO CLUE TO WHAT WAS STOLEN? WHO CRASHED IN AND OUT OF BUILDINGS--WITHOUT CAUSING ANY DAMAGE? WHO SHOWED HIMSELF--BUT COULDN'T BE SEEN? GREEN LANTERN GRAPPLES WITH THE MOST ASTOUNDING MENACE THAT EVER THREATENED THE WORLD IN--
The INVISIBLE DESTROYER!
I'VE GOT TO USE MY POWER RING TO STOP THAT ATOMIC BOMB EXPLOSION--BEFORE IT DESTROYS COAST CITY!

AS HAL JORDAN, TEST PILOT, ENTERS THE OFFICE OF HIS BOSS, CAROL FERRIS...

I WONDER WHY CAROL SENT FOR ME? IT'S THE FIRST TIME THIS WEEK SHE'S SHOWN ANY SIGN SHE KNOWS I'M ALIVE!

SINCE SHE BECAME INTERESTED IN *GREEN LANTERN* SHE'S HAD NO TIME FOR *ME* AT ALL!

*EDITOR'S NOTE! ALTHOUGH CAROL FERRIS IS UNAWARE OF IT, *GREEN LANTERN* AND HER ACE EMPLOYEE HAL JORDAN ARE ONE AND THE SAME PERSON!

OH, SO THERE YOU ARE, HAL! HAVE YOU SEEN THE ITEM IN TODAY'S NEWSPAPERS ADDRESSED TO OUR MUTUAL FRIEND *GREEN LANTERN?*

NO! WHAT ITEM--?

HERE-- IN THE *PUBLIC NOTICES!*

THE HERALD POS

ATTENTION-- GREEN LANTERN! URGENT YOU COME TO 854 WILSON AVENUE. DO NOT DELAY!

SALE ON SHOES

WHAT DO YOU MAKE OF IT, HAL?

I DON'T KNOW... BUT I'M GOING TO FIND OUT-- AS *GREEN LANTERN!*

IF *THAT'S* ALL YOU WANTED TO SEE ME ABOUT, CAROL--

GOOD-BYE!

GOING ALREADY!? WELL, IF THAT DOESN'T BEAT ALL! USUALLY HE BEGS FOR A CHANCE TO TALK TO ME--!

IN THE PRIVACY OF HAL JORDAN'S DRESSING ROOM, MOMENTS LATER...

IN BRIGHTEST DAY...IN BLACKEST NIGHT, NO EVIL SHALL ESCAPE MY SIGHT! LET THOSE WHO WORSHIP EVIL'S MIGHT BEWARE MY POWER--*GREEN LANTERN'S LIGHT!*

AND SOON... A GLITTERING EMERALD-CLAD FIGURE CLEAVES THE AIR OVER COAST CITY...

WHOEVER PUT THAT *PUBLIC NOTICE* IN THE PAPER SOUNDED LIKE HE WAS IN *TROUBLE!* LET'S SEE...*WILSON AVENUE* IS ON THE OTHER SIDE OF THE CITY... *EH?!*

PASSING OVER THE ROOFTOPS, THE KEEN EYE OF THE GREEN GLADIATOR SPIES A STRANGE SIGHT...

GREAT SCOTT! THERE'S THAT *PHANTOM THIEF*--THE ONE THE NEWSPAPERS HAVE LABELLED THE *INVISIBLE DESTROYER*-- ON THE ROOF OF THAT BUILDING!

WITHOUT HESITATION, GREEN LANTERN POWER-DIVES DOWN...

I'VE BEEN TRYING FOR DAYS TO GET A CRACK AT THIS CROOK WITH THE INCREDIBLE COSTUME THAT MAKES HIM SEEM INVISIBLE!

GREEN LANTERN! THIS IS MY LUCKY DAY!

I WAS HOPING WE'D MEET, *GREEN LANTERN*-- SO I COULD PROVE WHO WAS MORE POWERFUL -- *YOU OR I!*

INCREDIBLE--

3

MY POWER RING HAS NO EFFECT ON HIM-- HE'S WALKING RIGHT THROUGH ITS BEAM!

AS THE *EMERALD CRUSADER* IS GRIPPED IN ARMS OF TITANIC FORCE...

SEIZING ME! ≷GASP!≷ CAN HARDLY BREATHE!

HA! HA!

BUT THEN SUDDENLY, WITH *GL* ON THE VERGE OF COLLAPSE...

≷PANT!≷ HE--HE *DISAPPEARED* LIKE A PUFF OF SMOKE!

POP!

LATER, AFTER A SEARCH FOR THE *INVISIBLE DESTROYER* HAS PROVED VAIN...

NO SIGN OF HIM! WE DON'T KNOW WHAT HE WAS DOING IN THIS BUILDING, *GREEN LANTERN!* WE HAVE A *CYCLOTRON* HERE...

AND HE DIDN'T STEAL ANYTHING?

NO! HE CRASHED IN--RIGHT THROUGH A WALL WITHOUT CRACKING IT--AND LEFT WITHOUT STEALING ANYTHING THAT WE CAN SEE!

I'D BETTER BE ON MY WAY! I CAN'T DO ANY MORE HERE...

EVERY TIME THE *DESTROYER* HAS BEEN SEEN, HE'S DISAPPEARED THE SAME WAY-- SUDDENLY AND INCREDIBLY! WHO IS HE--WHERE DOES HE COME FROM?

SOON... HERE IT IS... 854 WILSON... BUT WAIT--! I'VE BEEN TO THIS HOUSE--AS HAL JORDAN! DR. PHILLIPS, THE FAMOUS AND BRILLIANT SCIENTIST, LIVES HERE!

854 WILSON

AS GREEN LANTERN ENTERS THE IMPOSING RESIDENCE...

HE WON'T RECOGNIZE ME AS HAL JORDAN, OF COURSE...

GREEN LANTERN! I'M HAPPY YOU COULD COME!

WITHOUT DELAY THE EMINENT SCIENTIST UNBURDENS HIMSELF TO THE GREEN-CLAD CHAMPION...

WHAT I HAVE TO TELL YOU WILL SOUND FANTASTIC-- UNBELIEVABLE! YOU'VE HEARD OF THE *INVISIBLE DESTROYER?*

NOT ONLY HEARD OF HIM-- BUT HAD AN ALMOST DISASTROUS ENCOUNTER WITH HIM! ON THE WAY HERE, I SAW--

NERVOUSLY THE PHYSICIST INTERRUPTS...

LISTEN! I HAVE A HABIT OF DOODLING WHILE I WORK-- YOU KNOW, MAKING DRAWINGS ON A PIECE OF PAPER-- HARDLY REALIZING WHAT I'M DOING! LOOK AT THESE, PLEASE--

IT'S THE *INVISIBLE DESTROYER!* YOU MUST HAVE SEEN HIS PICTURE IN THE PAPERS--! SOMEONE SNAPPED HIM--

I MADE THESE DRAWINGS OVER A PERIOD OF THREE DAYS, GREEN LANTERN...

...*BEFORE* I SAW HIS PICTURE IN THE PAPERS!

I TOLD YOU WHAT I HAD TO SAY WOULD SOUND FANTASTIC, *GREEN LANTERN!* BUT, WAIT-- HERE'S THE REAL *SHOCKER!*

5

AS DR. PHILLIPS REVEALS A TRULY STARTLING THEORY...

I--I FEEL THAT *I'M RESPONSIBLE* FOR THE *INVISIBLE DESTROYER!* THAT SOMEHOW HE'S BOUND UP WITH MY *IMAGINATION--!*

I DON'T FOLLOW YOU--

LOOK! HOW ELSE CAN YOU EXPLAIN THESE SKETCHES? MY IDEA IS THAT SOMEHOW A PART OF MY BRAIN -- WHILE THE REST OF IT IS OCCUPIED --HAS ACTUALLY BROUGHT THIS TERRIBLE CREATURE TO LIFE!

IT COULD HAVE BEEN DONE BY THE ACTION OF *MIND-OVER-MATTER*--BY A PART OF MY MIND THAT I'M HARDLY EVEN AWARE OF!

BUT-- THIS CREATURE IS *EVIL!* IT DESTROYS--

YOU ARE FAMILIAR WITH THE STORY OF DR. JEKYLL AND MR. HYDE? EVIL THOUGHTS MAY LURK IN OUR SUBCONSCIOUS MINDS! USUALLY WE CONTROL THEM--

THERE COULD BE A WAY TO TEST YOUR THEORY...

I CAN USE MY RING--TO PUT YOU INTO A STATE OF DEEP CONCENTRATION-- TO GIVE THE *DESTROYER* A *CHANCE* TO APPEAR--

GOOD! I MUST KNOW MY RESPONSIBILITY IN THIS MATTER!

AS THE GREAT GREEN BEAM OF THE EMERALD CHAMPION GOES TO WORK...

MY RING WILL MAKE DR. PHILLIPS CONCENTRATE COMPLETELY ON THAT FORMULA HE'S WRITING! NOW LET'S SEE WHAT HAPPENS...

6

THEN, INCREDIBLY A FEW MOMENTS LATER...

GREAT JUPITER! THE DESTROYER!

-- HE MATERIALIZED RIGHT OUT OF DR. PHILLIPS -- SPRANG INTO EXISTENCE FROM HIS BRAIN! AND DR. PHILLIPS ISN'T EVEN AWARE --!!

INSTANTLY GREEN LANTERN LUNGES AT HIS FOE...

SOMEHOW I'VE GOT TO DESTROY THIS THING -- THIS EVIL THING! I'LL RAISE MY BEAM TO ITS GREATEST STRENGTH --

BUT AS THE GREEN-CLAD HERO CATAPULTS FORWARD, HE STRIKES A WASTE BASKET...

WHAT'S THAT?

CLANG!

AND SIMULTANEOUSLY AS THE NOISE DISTRACTS THE PHYSICIST...

WH-WHAT HAPPENED?

AS DR. PHILLIPS SNAPPED BACK INTO AWARENESS OF HIS SURROUNDINGS -- THE DESTROYER DISAPPEARED! THAT PROVES HE'S RIGHT -- IT IS FROM HIS MIND!

7

As GL and the scientist confer over the dreadful development...

SO THE **DESTROYER** IS PART OF ME! I'M RESPONSIBLE FOR HIM--!

NO--NOT CONSCIOUSLY! THE GOOD PART OF YOUR MIND REFUSES TO ACKNOWLEDGE THE **DESTROYER'S** EXISTENCE! THAT'S WHY IT BLANKS OUT THE **DESTROYER'S** FACE-- SO IT APPEARS *INVISIBLE!*

OUR PROBLEM IS TO DESTROY THE **DESTROYER**-- WITHOUT HARMING YOU! WAIT--! SUPPOSE I USE MY RING TO PROBE INTO YOUR BRAIN! MAYBE I CAN **FORCE** THE CREATURE TO REVEAL ITS PLANS--WHAT IT'S UP TO!

Desperate, Dr. Phillips agrees to the proposal...

THIS IS A HUNDRED TIMES MORE DELICATE THAN BRAIN SURGERY! BUT CAN I MANAGE IT? I'VE GOT TO--FOR DR. PHILLIPS' SAKE-- AS WELL AS THE WORLD'S!

Then, after numerous vain efforts, suddenly...

GOT IT! WHEN MY RING TOUCHED A CERTAIN *TINY SPOT* IT SPRANG INTO VIEW!

SO...YOU WANT TO KNOW MY PLANS, **GREEN LANTERN?** WELL, I DON'T MIND TELLING YOU, BECAUSE YOU WON'T BE ABLE TO STOP THEM!

SO FAR I'VE ONLY BROKEN INTO PLACES WHERE *ATOMIC RADIATION* EXISTS-- LIKE THAT *CYCLOTRON!* AND THE REASON IS SIMPLE...

I *FEED* ON RADIATION! EACH DOSE THAT I ABSORB MAKES ME MORE POWERFUL! SOON I WILL BE THE *MOST POWERFUL BEING ON EARTH!*

THEN, ABRUPTLY...

HE'S BROKEN LOOSE FROM DR. PHILLIPS!

I'VE DECIDED TO STOP BOTHERING WITH SMALL AMOUNTS OF RADIATION...

I'M GOING TO SET OFF A GREAT *ATOMIC EXPLOSION!* IN ONE STROKE I'LL ABSORB ALL THE RADIATION I NEED!

NOT IF I CAN HELP IT!

BUT BEFORE THE GRIM RING-BEARER CAN REACH HIS FOE...

OHHH!

DR. PHILLIPS!?

9

A MOMENT LATER... THE STRAIN WAS TOO GREAT ON DR. PHILLIPS-- HE PASSED OUT! HE'LL BE ALL RIGHT-- HE'S COMING TO NOW--

-- BUT MEANWHILE THE *DESTROYER* GOT AWAY! I'VE GOT TO FIND HIM! THE-- THE FATE OF THE WORLD MAY BE AT STAKE!

SHORTLY, AFTER A FRANTIC SEARCH...

... AND A GREAT AMOUNT OF *NUCLEAR MATERIAL* HAS BEEN STOLEN FROM THE LOS VANEMOS BASE NEAR COAST CITY!

THAT'S MY CLUE!

A MOMENT LATER, A GREEN BOLT STREAKS FOR THE LOS VANEMOS PROVING GROUNDS...

SIGNS OF ACTIVITY AROUND THIS ABANDONED SHACK HERE ON THE GROUNDS! COULD THE *DESTROYER* BE IN THERE?

INSIDE THE SHACK... YOU'RE TOO LATE, *GREEN LANTERN!* BUT YOU CAN WATCH THE *EXPLOSION* ON THIS TELEVISION SCREEN THAT I SET UP TO VIEW MY HANDIWORK!

BUT THE INDOMITABLE SPIRIT OF THE *EMERALD GLADIATOR* REFUSES TO LET HIM GIVE UP...

THERE'S THE *ATOM BLAST!* IT WILL ONLY TAKE SPLIT-SECONDS TO SPREAD-- BUT MY RING CAN OPERATE FASTER! IT MUST OPERATE FASTER!

10

REACHING THE BLAST SITE IN A SPLIT-INSTANT, THE GREAT GREEN-CLAD CHAMPION PERFORMS AN INCREDIBLE FEAT!

THERE! MY RING HAS THROTTLED THE EXPLOSION-- SHRUNK IT TO THE SIZE OF A FIRECRACKER POP!

POOF!

AS *GREEN LANTERN* HEADS BACK FOR THE SHACK...

YOU ROBBED ME OF MY TRIUMPH, *GREEN LANTERN!* BUT IT'S A DEFEAT I SHALL TURN INTO A GREATER VICTORY-- BY DESTROYING *YOU!*

COMING AT ME! AND--MY GREEN BEAM CAN'T STOP HIM! BUT WAIT--IT MUST BE BECAUSE AS A PRODUCT OF DR. PHILLIPS' MIND HE'S *PURE ENERGY!* THAT GIVES ME AN IDEA!

YOU'LL NEVER INTERFERE WITH ME AGAIN--!

SHOOTING ENERGY BOLTS AT ME! I'VE GOT ONLY A MOMENT TO CARRY OUT MY PLAN!

POWERED BY *GL's* INDOMITABLE WILL, HIS GREAT BEAM SENDS OUT A BOLT OF *ANTI-ENERGY--!*

SCIENTISTS HAVE THEORIZED THERE IS AN *ANTI-MATTER* UNIVERSE TO COUNTERBALANCE OUR *POSITIVE MATTER* UNIVERSE! IF THE TWO SHOULD MEET, BOTH WOULD BE DESTROYED! I HOPE THE SAME HAPPENS WHEN *ANTI-ENERGY* MEETS *PURE ENERGY..!*

11

THEN... FANTASTICALLY, BEFORE *GREEN LANTERN'S* VERY EYES...

IT WORKED! THE INSTANT HE AND MY BOLT OF *ANTI ENERGY* CAME TOGETHER-- IT BLASTED HIM TO BITS! THAT-- THAT'S THE END OF THE *INVISIBLE DESTROYER!*

AND LATER, IN DR. PHILLIPS' LABORATORY...

GREEN LANTERN, YOU'VE SAVED MY LIFE-- AND MY SANITY! BUT HOW CAN I EVER THANK YOU?

DON'T TRY, DR. PHILLIPS! THE MAIN THING IS...

...WITH THE *DESTROYER* GONE, THAT TINY SPOT IN YOUR MIND THAT PRODUCED HIM IS GONE TOO! IT WILL NEVER BOTHER YOU AGAIN! SO LONG--

GOOD-BYE, *GREEN LANTERN!*

12

BUT WITH HIS *GREEN LANTERN* UNIFORM HUNG UP, SHORTLY AFTER, HAL JORDAN *STILL* HAS A PROBLEM...

HOW CAN I GET A DATE WITH MY BOSS, CAROL FERRIS? GOSH! IF I COULD ONLY SOLVE MY PROBLEM AS EASILY AS I SOLVE OTHER PERSON'S PROBLEMS!

The End.

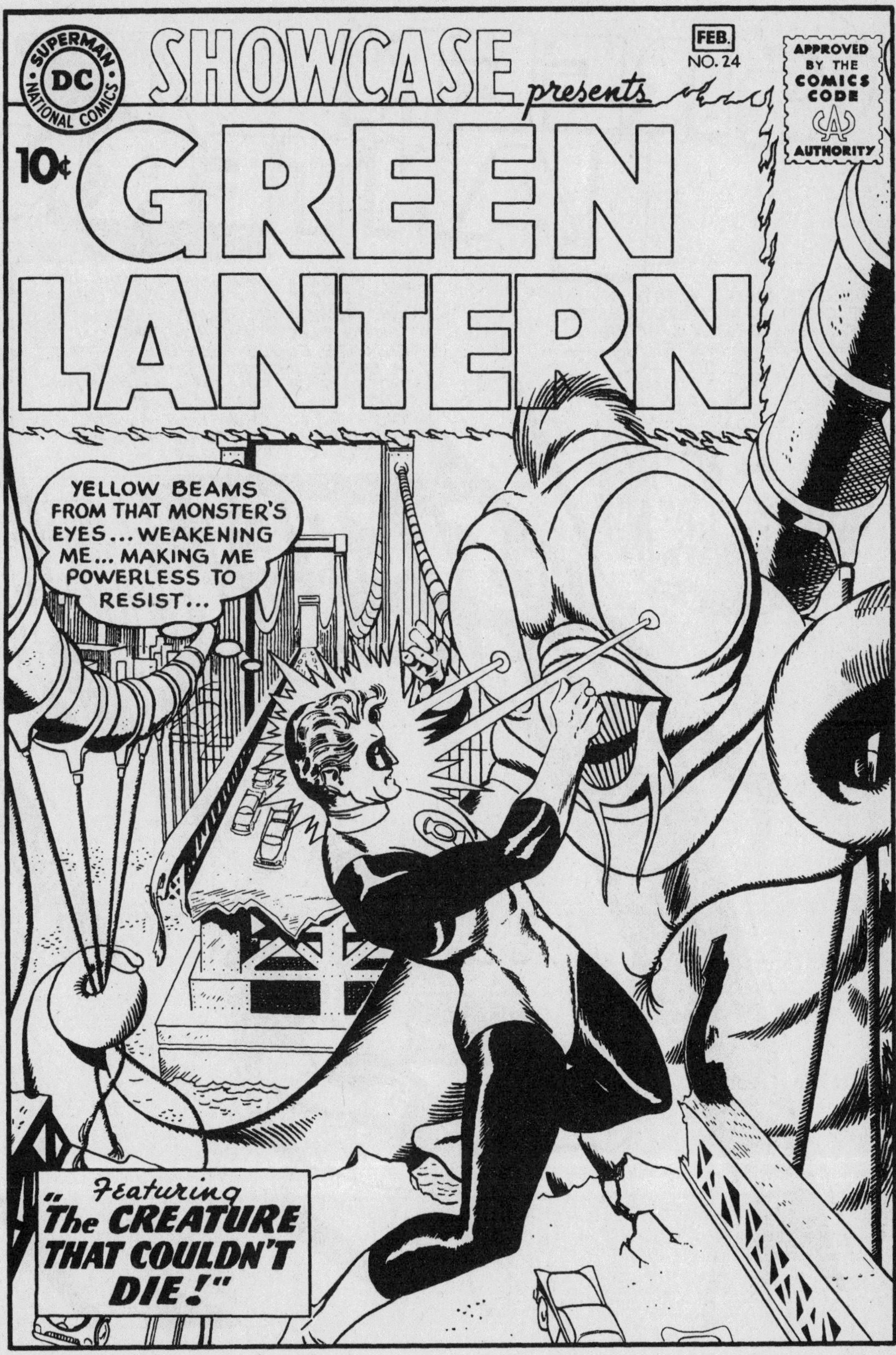
SUPERMAN DC NATIONAL COMICS
SHOWCASE presents
FEB. NO. 24
APPROVED BY THE COMICS CODE AUTHORITY
10¢
GREEN LANTERN
YELLOW BEAMS FROM THAT MONSTER'S EYES... WEAKENING ME... MAKING ME POWERLESS TO RESIST...
"Featuring "The CREATURE THAT COULDN'T DIE!"

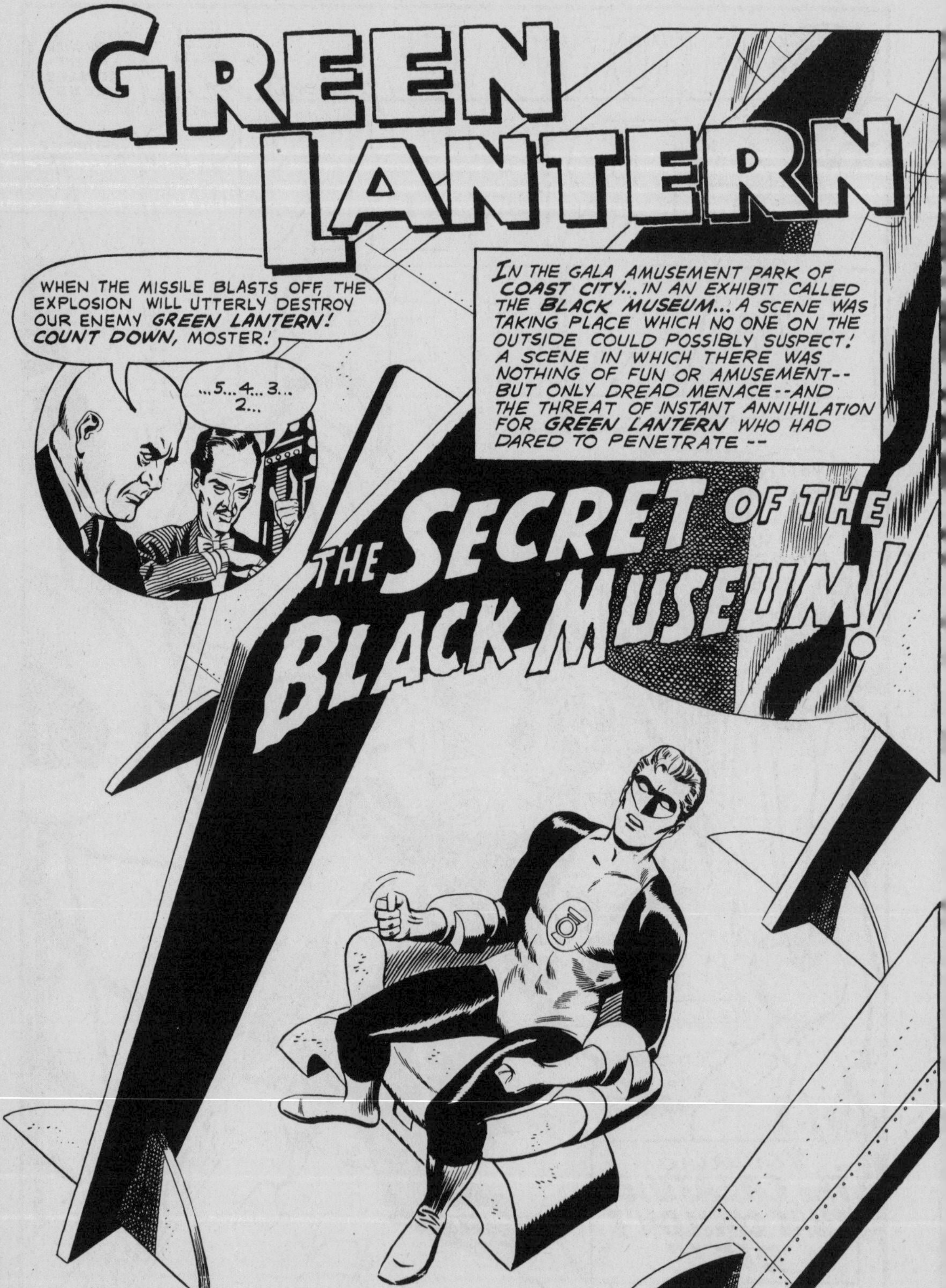
GREEN LANTERN
IN THE GALA AMUSEMENT PARK OF COAST CITY... IN AN EXHIBIT CALLED THE BLACK MUSEUM... A SCENE WAS TAKING PLACE WHICH NO ONE ON THE OUTSIDE COULD POSSIBLY SUSPECT! A SCENE IN WHICH THERE WAS NOTHING OF FUN OR AMUSEMENT--BUT ONLY DREAD MENACE--AND THE THREAT OF INSTANT ANNIHILATION FOR GREEN LANTERN WHO HAD DARED TO PENETRATE --
WHEN THE MISSILE BLASTS OFF, THE EXPLOSION WILL UTTERLY DESTROY OUR ENEMY GREEN LANTERN! COUNT DOWN, MOSTER!
...5...4...3... 2...
THE SECRET OF THE BLACK MUSEUM!

AS CAROL FERRIS CROSSES THE YARD OF THE FERRIS AIRCRAFT COMPANY WHERE SHE IS IN SOLE CONTROL...

IT'S AWFUL! I SHOULD BE KEEPING MY MIND ON BUSINESS-- AT LEAST WHILE I'M HERE AT WORK! BUT ALL I CAN THINK OF-- DAY OR NIGHT-- IS GREEN LANTERN!

I'VE EVEN CONTACTED DAD* AND PERSUADED HIM TO AGREE TO LET ME MARRY GREEN LANTERN--

*EDITOR'S NOTE: TAKING OFF ON A TWO-YEAR TRIP AROUND THE WORLD, WILLARD FERRIS LEFT HIS PRETTY DAUGHTER IN COMPLETE CHARGE OF HIS COMPANY-- ON HER PROMISE TO AVOID ANY ROMANTIC ENTANGLEMENTS!

--IF IT EVER COMES TO THAT! :SIGH!: GETTING DAD'S PERMISSION WAS A BREEZE-- BUT GETTING GREEN LANTERN TO PROPOSE IS LIKE BUCKING A TORNADO!

"FOR INSTANCE, THE OTHER NIGHT WE WERE SITTING IN THE PARK..."

CAROL, YOU'RE WONDERFUL! THERE'S NO ONE IN THE WORLD I'D RATHER BE WITH!

GO ON! TELL ME MORE...

"IT SEEMED TO ME HE WAS JUST ON THE VERGE OF 'POPPING THE QUESTION' WHEN..."

I'VE BEEN THINKING, CAROL... WHAT'S THAT--!?

HELP!

WELL, OF ALL THE UNFORTUNATE TIMES FOR SOMEONE TO CALL FOR HELP!

2

"*I MUST CONFESS IT WAS BREATHTAKING... THE MARVELOUS SPEED WITH WHKH GL AND HIS POWER RING RESCUED THE MAN FROM DROWNING...*"

YOU'LL BE ALL RIGHT! JUST RELAX!

I FELL IN THE LAKE... CAN'T SWIM...

"*I WATCHED HIM SET THE MAN SAFELY ON THE SHORE...*"

THANKS, *GREEN LANTERN!* IT WAS LIKE -- MAGIC -- THE WAY YOU RESCUED ME!

NOW HE'LL COME BACK TO ME! GOSH -- I WISH HE'D HURRY!

"*BUT WHEN THE EMERALD GLADIATOR DID RETURN, IT WAS TOO LATE! THE MOMENT HAD PASSED...*"

WHEW, IT'S LATE! AND I'VE GOT A FULL SCHEDULE TOMORROW! I GUESS I'D BETTER TAKE YOU HOME, CAROL...

OH!

AND NOW ALL I CAN DO IS WAIT... UNTIL *GREEN LANTERN* AND I ARE ALONE AGAIN! BUT WHEN -- OH, WHEN WILL THAT BE?

HI, CAROL!

As CAROL, UNAWARE THAT SHE IS GETTING HER WISH, SPEAKS TO TEST PILOT HAL JORDAN, THE SECRET *ALTER EGO* OF *GREEN LANTERN*...

YOU COME HERE TO SEE ME, SUGAR?

NOT THE WAY YOU THINK, MR. JORDAN! ARMY HEAD-QUARTERS CALLED MY OFFICE! I HAVE AN IMPORTANT MESSAGE FOR YOU...

3

THEY WANT YOU TO RETURN THE TOP-SECRET PLANS WHICH THEY ASKED YOU TO STUDY! THERE ARE SOME CHANGES THEY WANT TO MAKE IN THEM...

I SEE! ALL RIGHT, CAROL -- WILCO!

AFTER CAROL HAS GONE OFF...

I WISH CAROL WOULD LOOK AT *ME* THE WAY SHE LOOKS AT *GREEN LANTERN!* SHE SEEMS TO BE IN LOVE WITH GL -- BUT AS HAL JORDAN I DON'T RATE A TUMBLE! WHAT A SITUATION!

WHEN HAL REMOVES HIS "MONKEY SUIT" IN HIS PRIVATE DRESSING ROOM...

BUT I CAN'T WORRY ABOUT SUCH THINGS NOW! IF ARMY WANTS THOSE PLANS BACK I'D BETTER GET THEM THERE PRONTO! I'VE BEEN KEEPING THEM RIGHT ON ME HERE IN MY -- EH?

GREAT JUMPING JETS! WHERE ARE THEY? I *KNOW* I HAD THOSE PLANS IN MY POCKET!

AS THE ACE TEST PILOT FEVER-ISHLY SEARCHES FOR THE MISSING DOCUMENT...

GONE! NO TRACE OF THEM! BUT I'VE GOT TO FIND THEM! THOSE PLANS ARE FOR THE NEW *SPACEPLANE* -- THE X-500! IF THEY FELL INTO THE WRONG HANDS IT COULD BE A DISASTER!

GRIMLY BUT COOLLY, HAL CONSIDERS THE SITUATION...

I'VE GOT TO RETRACE EVERY STEP I MADE SINCE I PUT THOSE PLANS IN MY POCKET! LET ME SEE... I DEFINITELY HAD THEM AT NOONTIME WHEN I WENT TO LUNCH...

④

UHH--I REMEMBER SOMETHING! THERE WAS A CROWD JUST OUTSIDE THE COMMISSARY AT LUNCHTIME AS USUAL TODAY... AND AS I ENTERED A MAN JOSTLED ME...

"HE WAS A SMALL, DARK-FACED MAN..."

"AT THE TIME I PAID SCANT ATTENTION... BUT I REMEMBER THINKING I'D SEEN HIM SOME-WHERE BEFORE...THOUGH NOT AROUND HERE..."

I'M WILLING TO BET NOW THAT'S WHEN I LOST THE PLANS! THAT FELLOW COULD HAVE LIFTED THEM OUT OF MY POCKET WHEN HE BUMPED ME! IT'S AN OLD PICKPOCKET'S TRICK! BUT-- WHO WAS HE?

AND WHERE DID I SEE HIM BEFORE? I'VE GOT TO REMEMBER! BUT WAIT-- THERE MAY BE AN EASIER WAY THAN JUST RACKING MY BRAINS!

MY POWER RING! IT'S CAPABLE OF DOING ANY-THING I WILL IT TO DO-- SO WHY CAN'T IT PROBE MY OWN MIND FOR A MEMORY I KNOW IS BURIED THERE SOMEWHERE? GOT TO TRY IT...

AS HAL BENDS EVERY OUNCE OF HIS EXTRA-ORDINARY WILL TO THE TASK...

SOMETHING IS COMING...! BUT IT ISN'T CLEAR YET! GOT TO CONCENTRATE HARDER... HARDER!

5

THEN SUDDENLY...

GOT HIM! I REMEMBER WHERE I SAW THAT MAN *NOW*-- AT THE AMUSEMENT PARK!

IT WAS LAST WEEK-- WHEN I SPENT A FEW HOURS THERE DURING MY DAY OFF! GOLLY! THAT MAY NOT BE MUCH OF A CLUE BUT--

SPLIT-SECONDS LATER, HAL JORDAN CHANGES TO HIS *GREEN LANTERN* COSTUME...

GOT TO GET GOING--BUT I MUSTN'T FORGET TO CHARGE MY *POWER RING!* *

* EDITOR'S NOTE: GREEN LANTERN'S RING MUST BE CHARGED EVERY TWENTY-FOUR HOURS TO KEEP ITS POWER!

IN THE PRIVACY OF HAL JORDAN'S DRESSING ROOM A SOLEMN SCENE TAKES PLACE UNWITNESSED BY ANY INTRUDING EYE...

IN BRIGHTEST DAY... IN BLACKEST NIGHT, NO EVIL SHALL ESCAPE MY SIGHT! LET THOSE WHO WORSHIP EVIL'S MIGHT BEWARE MY POWER-- *GREEN LANTERN'S LIGHT!*

ACROSS THE CITY, MOMENTS AFTER, STREAKS THE AWESOME FIGURE OF THE FAMED *GREEN GLADIATOR*...

MY ONLY HOPE IS THAT THE MAN IS AN *EMPLOYEE* AT THE PARK-- OR THAT HE COMES THERE REGULARLY!

ROCKET

CONTINUED ON FOLLOWING PAGE

6

BUT THEN... AS GREEN LANTERN REACHES THE PARK, HIS KEEN EYE CATCHES A STUNNING SIGHT...

AAAAAAAAH

GREAT SCOTT! THAT "ROCKET" CAR--ON THAT ROLLER COASTER-- HAS RIPPED LOOSE FROM THE RAILS! IT'S STARTING TO PLUNGE --!

HELP!

LIKE A DAZZLING ARROW, GL WHIPS AT THE FALLING CAR...

THE CAR--IT'S YELLOW! MY RING CAN'T HANDLE IT!

EDITOR'S NOTE: DUE TO A NECESSARY IMPURITY IN THE STRANGE MATERIALS FROM WHICH IT WAS MADE, GREEN LANTERN'S RING HAS NO EFFECT ON ANYTHING YELLOW!

THE CAR IS ABOUT TO HIT THE GROUND--BUT THERE'S A MOMENT LEFT! MAYBE I CAN...

EVEN AS HE THINKS, THE EMERALD GLADIATOR ACTS, COMMANDING HIS RING TO FORM HUGE SPRINGS UNDER THE PLUMMETING CAR...

≥WHEW!≤ STOPPED IT! THE CAR LANDED ON THE SPRINGS I MADE--AND IT'S UNHARMED!

IT'S A GOOD THING THE BOTTOM OF THAT CAR WASN'T--EH? CAROL!?

GREEN LANTERN! IT LOOKS LIKE FATE JUST KEEPS THROWING US TOGETHER!

7

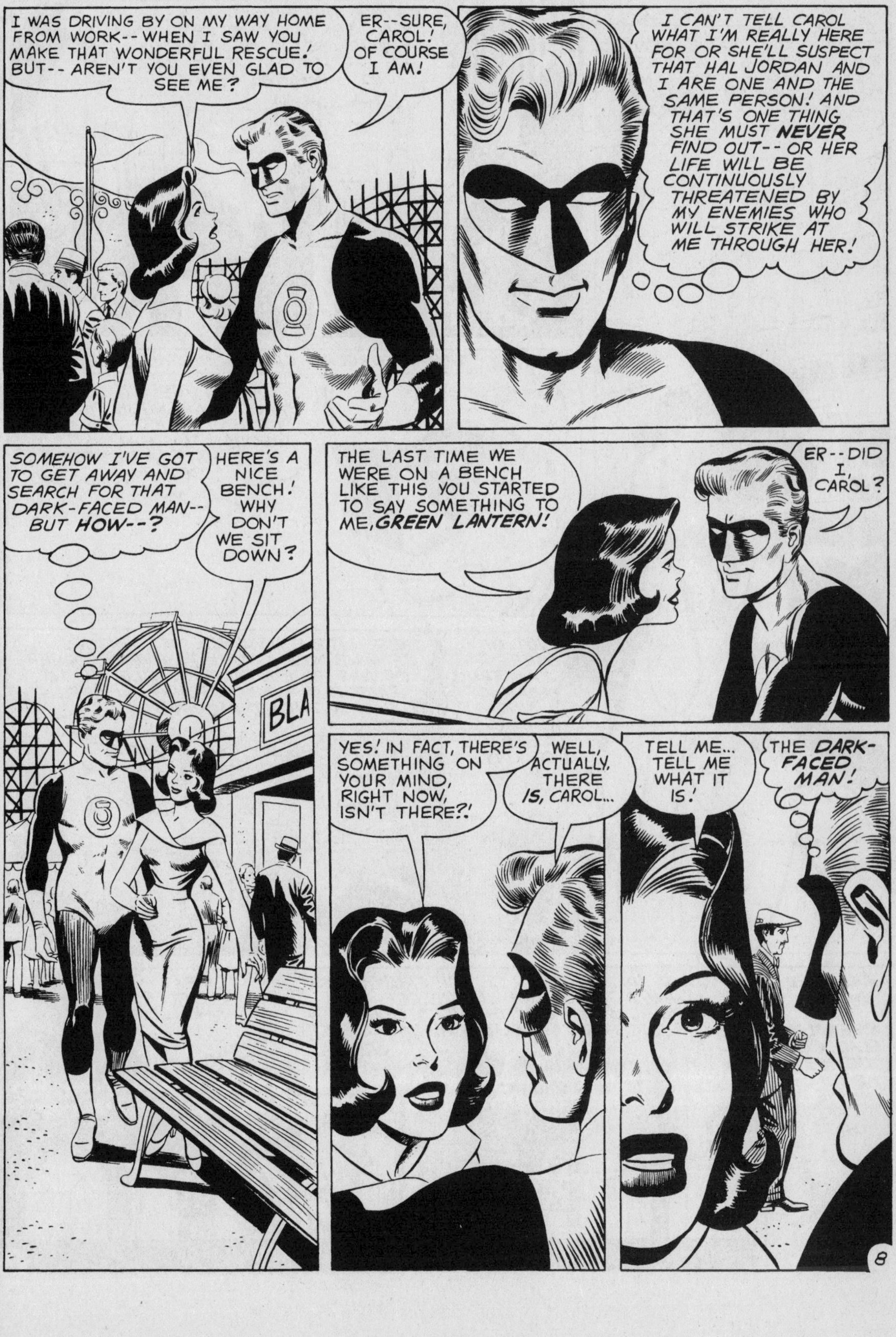
I WAS DRIVING BY ON MY WAY HOME FROM WORK-- WHEN I SAW YOU MAKE THAT WONDERFUL RESCUE! BUT-- AREN'T YOU EVEN GLAD TO SEE ME?
ER--SURE, CAROL! OF COURSE I AM!
I CAN'T TELL CAROL WHAT I'M REALLY HERE FOR OR SHE'LL SUSPECT THAT HAL JORDAN AND I ARE ONE AND THE SAME PERSON! AND THAT'S ONE THING SHE MUST NEVER FIND OUT-- OR HER LIFE WILL BE CONTINUOUSLY THREATENED BY MY ENEMIES WHO WILL STRIKE AT ME THROUGH HER!
SOMEHOW I'VE GOT TO GET AWAY AND SEARCH FOR THAT DARK-FACED MAN-- BUT HOW--?
HERE'S A NICE BENCH! WHY DON'T WE SIT DOWN?
BLA
THE LAST TIME WE WERE ON A BENCH LIKE THIS YOU STARTED TO SAY SOMETHING TO ME, GREEN LANTERN!
ER--DID I, CAROL?
YES! IN FACT, THERE'S SOMETHING ON YOUR MIND, RIGHT NOW, ISN'T THERE?!
WELL, ACTUALLY, THERE IS, CAROL...
TELL ME... TELL ME WHAT IT IS!
THE DARK-FACED MAN!
8

As CAROL TURNS, THUNDER-STRUCK...

FOR GOODNESS' SAKE--!? HE "RAN" OUT ON ME AGAIN!

HE WENT INTO THAT BUILDING-- THE *BLACK MUSEUM!*

I KNOW THIS EXHIBIT-- IT'S A SHOW OF ALL SORTS OF ROCKETS AND EXPLOSIVES! BUT-- WHAT IS THE DARK MAN DOING HERE? AND-- *WHERE IS HE?*

PUZZLED, THE GREEN-CLAD CHAMPION STARES ABOUT HIM...

I HAVE A *FEELING* SOMETHING IS WRONG IN THIS PLACE! I COULD SEARCH THROUGH THIS BUILDING, BUT I HAVE A BETTER IDEA--

OUT OF *GREEN LANTERN'S* AMAZING RING POURS A SERIES OF TINY MICRO-PHONES...

THESE LITTLE *INVISIBLE* MICROPHONES OF MINE WILL TRAVEL TO EVERY CORNER OF THIS EXHIBIT AND ENABLE ME TO FIND OUT WHAT'S GOING ON HERE *WITHOUT MOVING!*

AND SURE ENOUGH, THE *EMERALD GLADIATOR'S* DEVICE SOON PAYS OFF BIG!

...AND UNDER COVER OF OUR *FIREWORKS* EXHIBIT TONIGHT WE'LL FIRE OFF THE SPECIAL MISSILE WITH THE STOLEN PLANS FOR THE *X-500* ABOARD!

GREAT SCOTT!

9

THAT SOUNDS LIKE *SPIES!* AND THAT DARK MAN MUST BE ONE OF THEM! THE VOICE CAME FROM IN HERE--!

LOOKS LIKE QUITE A PARTY--!

GREEN LANTERN! SEIZE HIM!

THEN, UNEXPECTEDLY, A HEAVY BLOW FROM BEHIND FELLS THE EMERALD CHAMPION...

HE DIDN'T SEE ME NEAR THE DOOR AS HE CAME IN!

NICE WORK, MOSTER!

HE'S KAYOED ALL RIGHT! WHAT WILL WE DO WITH HIM?

I HAVE AN IDEA! BRING HIM THIS WAY...

SOON AFTER, OUTSIDE...

THERE GO THE *FIREWORKS* THEY HAVE EVERY NIGHT FROM THE *BLACK MUSEUM!* BUT--WHERE IS GREEN LANTERN?

BLACK M

10

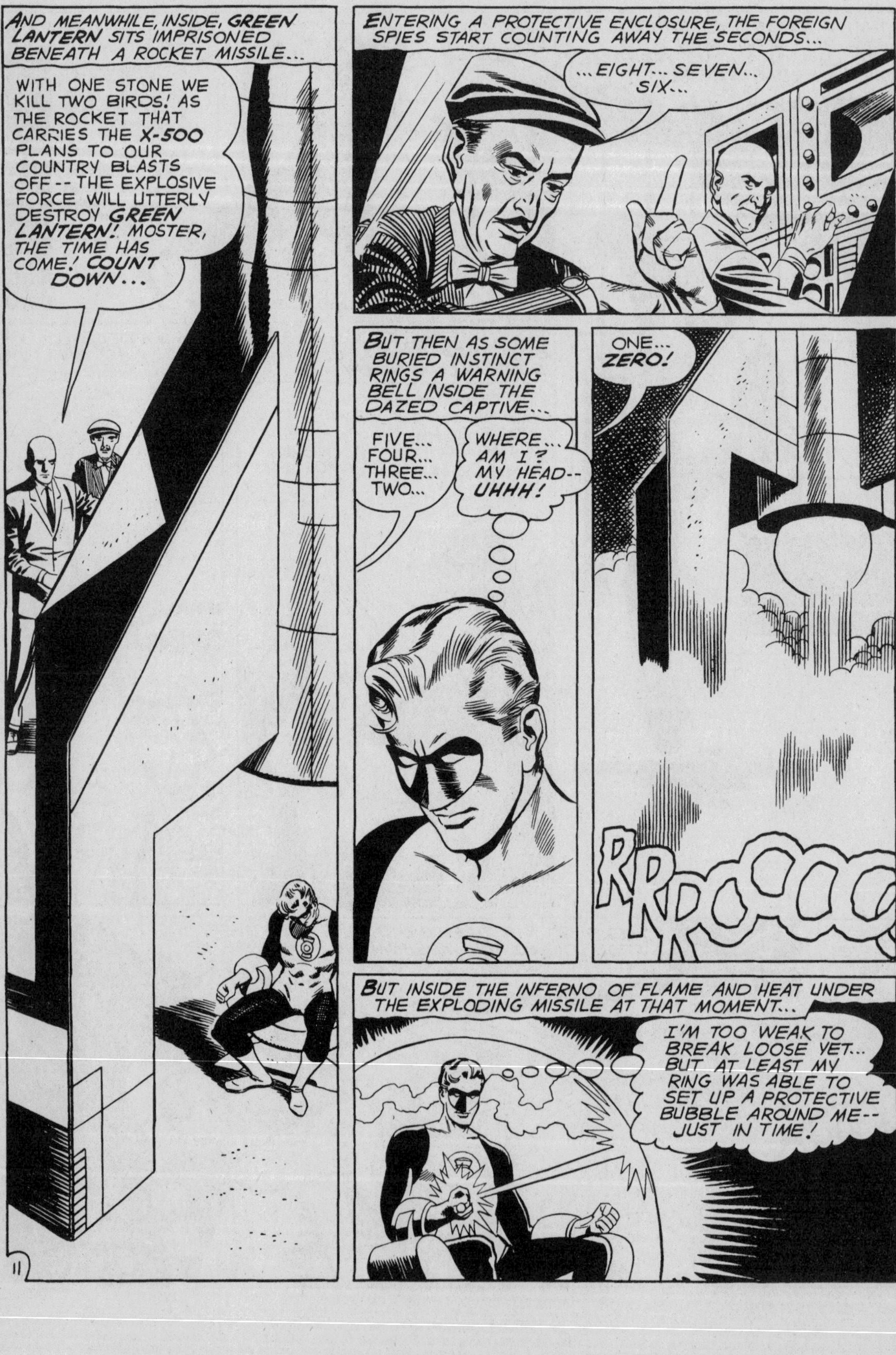
AND MEANWHILE, INSIDE, GREEN LANTERN SITS IMPRISONED BENEATH A ROCKET MISSILE...
WITH ONE STONE WE KILL TWO BIRDS! AS THE ROCKET THAT CARRIES THE X-500 PLANS TO OUR COUNTRY BLASTS OFF -- THE EXPLOSIVE FORCE WILL UTTERLY DESTROY GREEN LANTERN! MOSTER, THE TIME HAS COME! COUNT DOWN...
11
ENTERING A PROTECTIVE ENCLOSURE, THE FOREIGN SPIES START COUNTING AWAY THE SECONDS...
...EIGHT... SEVEN... SIX...
BUT THEN AS SOME BURIED INSTINCT RINGS A WARNING BELL INSIDE THE DAZED CAPTIVE...
FIVE... FOUR... THREE... TWO...
WHERE... AM I? MY HEAD-- UHHH!
ONE... ZERO!
RRROOOOO
BUT INSIDE THE INFERNO OF FLAME AND HEAT UNDER THE EXPLODING MISSILE AT THAT MOMENT...
I'M TOO WEAK TO BREAK LOOSE YET... BUT AT LEAST MY RING WAS ABLE TO SET UP A PROTECTIVE BUBBLE AROUND ME-- JUST IN TIME!

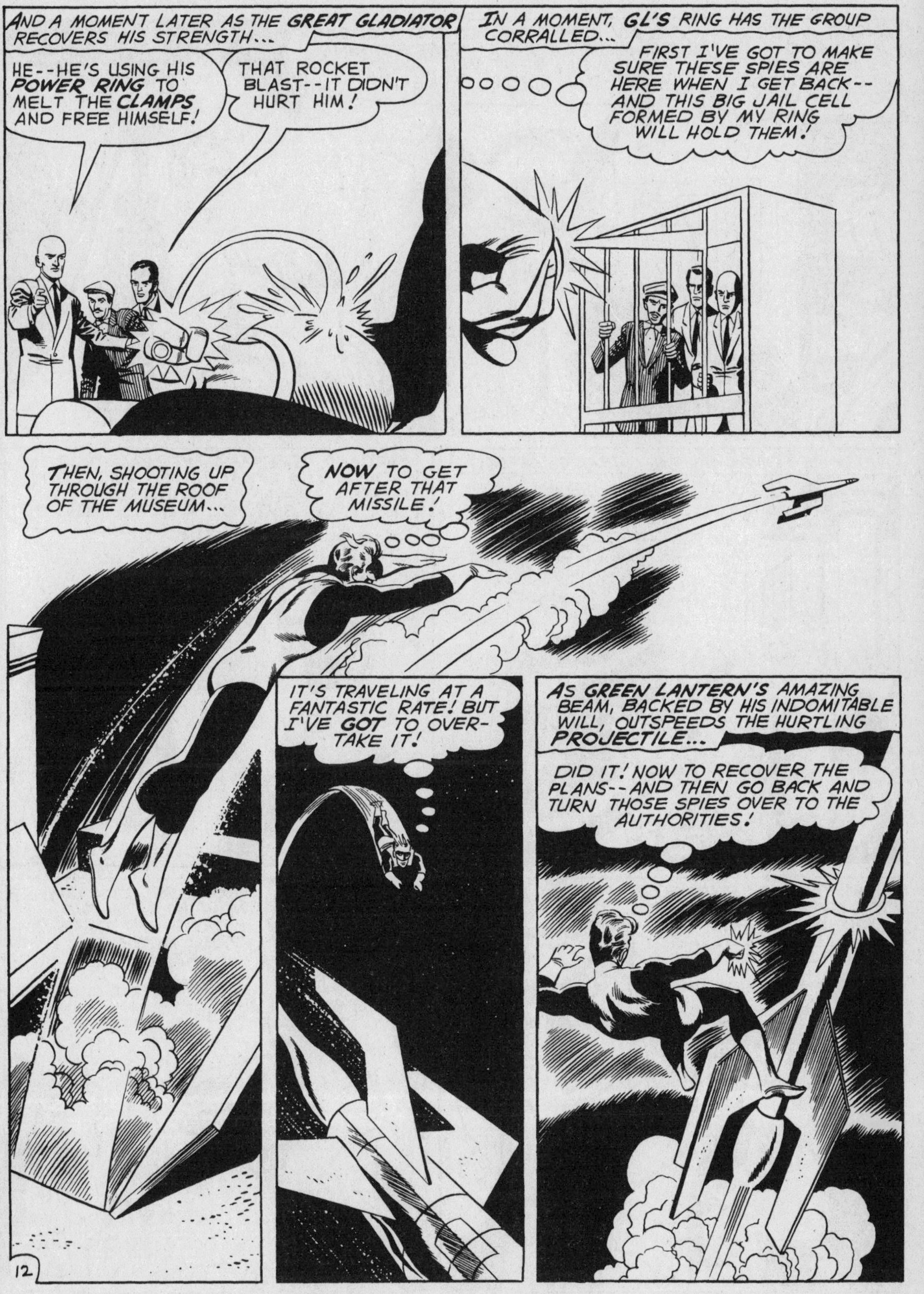
AND A MOMENT LATER AS THE GREAT GLADIATOR RECOVERS HIS STRENGTH...
HE--HE'S USING HIS POWER RING TO MELT THE CLAMPS AND FREE HIMSELF!
THAT ROCKET BLAST--IT DIDN'T HURT HIM!
IN A MOMENT, GL'S RING HAS THE GROUP CORRALLED...
FIRST I'VE GOT TO MAKE SURE THESE SPIES ARE HERE WHEN I GET BACK--AND THIS BIG JAIL CELL FORMED BY MY RING WILL HOLD THEM!
THEN, SHOOTING UP THROUGH THE ROOF OF THE MUSEUM...
NOW TO GET AFTER THAT MISSILE!
IT'S TRAVELING AT A FANTASTIC RATE! BUT I'VE GOT TO OVERTAKE IT!
AS GREEN LANTERN'S AMAZING BEAM, BACKED BY HIS INDOMITABLE WILL, OUTSPEEDS THE HURTLING PROJECTILE...
DID IT! NOW TO RECOVER THE PLANS--AND THEN GO BACK AND TURN THOSE SPIES OVER TO THE AUTHORITIES!
12

LATER, AFTER THE X-500 PLANS HAVE BEEN RETURNED TO THE ARMY...

GREEN LANTERN, YOU DID A GREAT JOB IN BREAKING UP THAT SPY RING! THE GOVERNMENT WILL AWARD YOU A SPECIAL MEDAL OF MERIT!

AFTER HE LEAVES MILITARY HEADQUARTERS...

THERE HE IS! SURROUNDED BY REPORTERS!-- BUT I'M GOING TO SPEAK TO HIM ANYWAY!

CAROL! YOU HERE TOO?

GREEN LANTERN, YOU'RE A GREAT HERO-- BUT IF YOU DON'T MIND I'D LIKE TO GIVE YOU A LITTLE ADVICE!

NEXT TIME YOU START TO PROPOSE TO A GIRL--STAY PUT UNTIL YOU'VE FINISHED!

EH?

PROPOSE TO A GIRL--? NOW WHAT IN THE WORLD PUT THAT IDEA INTO CAROL'S HEAD!?

The End.

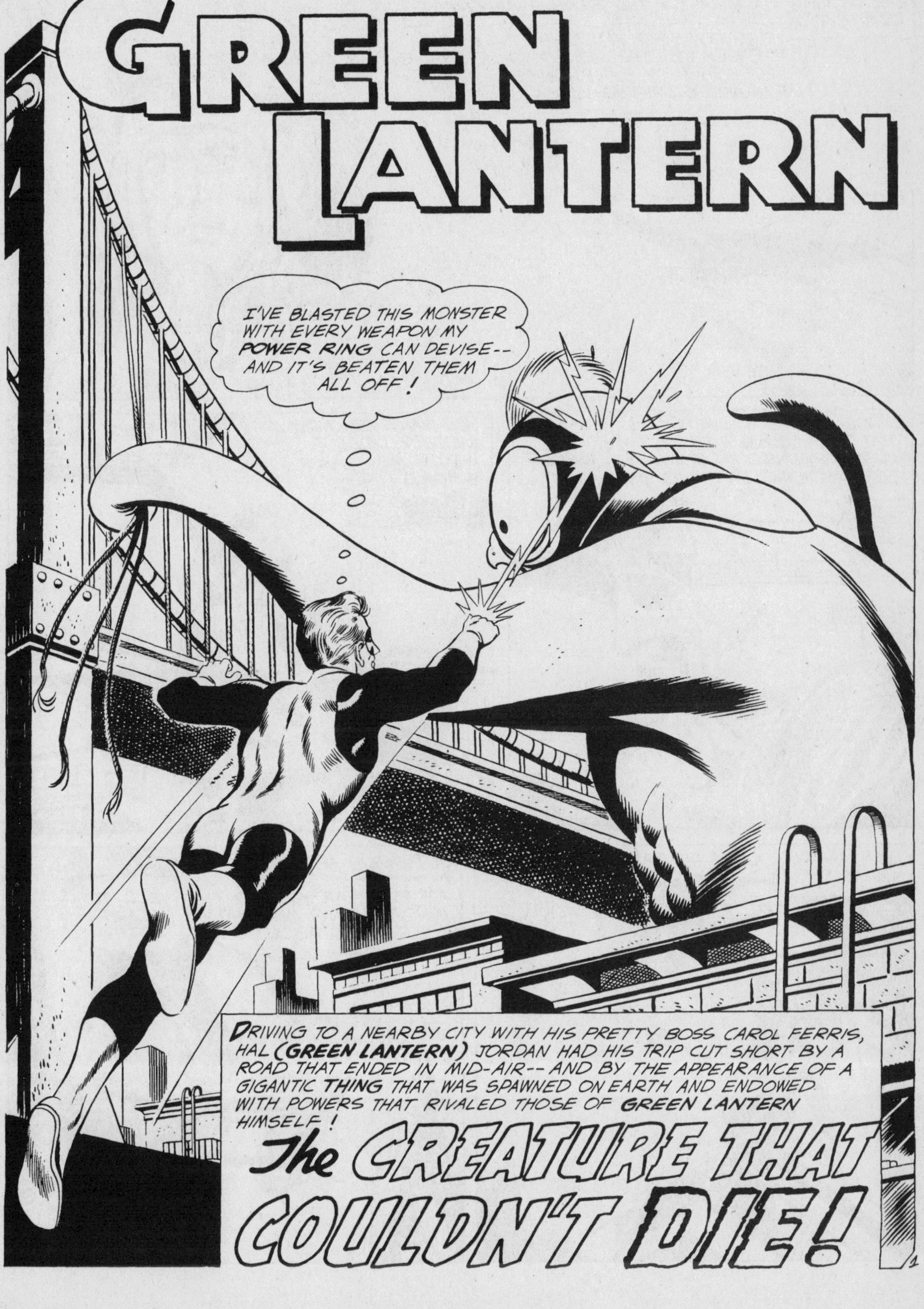
GREEN LANTERN
I'VE BLASTED THIS MONSTER WITH EVERY WEAPON MY POWER RING CAN DEVISE-- AND IT'S BEATEN THEM ALL OFF!
DRIVING TO A NEARBY CITY WITH HIS PRETTY BOSS CAROL FERRIS, HAL (GREEN LANTERN) JORDAN HAD HIS TRIP CUT SHORT BY A ROAD THAT ENDED IN MID-AIR-- AND BY THE APPEARANCE OF A GIGANTIC THING THAT WAS SPAWNED ON EARTH AND ENDOWED WITH POWERS THAT RIVALED THOSE OF GREEN LANTERN HIMSELF!
The CREATURE THAT COULDN'T DIE!
1

As TEST PILOT HAL JORDAN TRIES OUT A PLANE OVER THE PROVING GROUNDS OF THE *FERRIS AIRCRAFT COMPANY*...

THIS NEW BIRD HANDLES FINE! NOW TO CHECK OUT THE--*Eh?* A VOICE COMING THROUGH IN MY EARPHONES-- A *HEART-STOPPING VOICE!*

HAL...

HAL, THIS IS *CAROL!* I'D LIKE YOU TO DRIVE ME TO PINE CITY THIS AFTER-NOON! WHAT DO YOU SAY?

I--I'M SPEECH-LESS!

CAROL ASKING TO SPEND ALL THAT TIME ALONE WITH ME! WHAT HAPPENED?! SHE'S BEEN AVOIDING ANYTHING LIKE THIS--

WELL?

YOU WANT TO KNOW MY ANSWER, DOLL? WATCH MY *SMOKE!*

HUH?

THEN, AS THE CRACK AIRMAN SKYWRITES HIS REPLY...

THE SILLY--!

OK

BUT SOON AFTER...

IT'S YOUR PARTY, CAROL! MIND TELLING ME WHAT IT'S ALL ABOUT?

WELL, TO START WITH--

2

OUR COMPANY IS CONSIDERING A MERGER WITH A PLANT IN PINE CITY AND I HAVE TO GO THERE TO MEET THE OWNER! I FIGURED I'D ASK YOU TO DRIVE ME... ESPECIALLY SINCE I HAD SOMETHING ELSE OF IMPORTANCE TO TALK TO YOU ABOUT!

WHAT'S THAT, CAROL?

WELL, I HAD A--A *FANTASTIC DREAM* LAST NIGHT! AND I MADE UP MY MIND TO TELL YOU ABOUT IT--BUT REMEMBER, HAL, IT'S JUST A DREAM! YOU SEE...

IN IT I HAD AGREED TO *MARRY YOU*-- BUT ONLY IN ORDER TO GET *GREEN LANTERN* JEALOUS!

BOY, WHAT A DREAM! TELL ME MORE!

"THE DREAM SEEMED SO REAL! THERE WE WERE... ABOUT TO GET MARRIED..."

STILL NO SIGN OF *GREEN LANTERN!* BUT THERE'S ONLY... A FEW MINUTES LEFT! IS IT POSSIBLE... HE WON'T SHOW UP?

IN THE DREAM I WAS SURE THAT *GREEN LANTERN* WOULD APPEAR AT THE LAST MOMENT... TO SWEEP ME OFF MY FEET AND CARRY ME AWAY, YOU SEE?

UH HUH-- GO ON...

"BUT WHEN THE FATEFUL WORDS WERE UTTERED..."

I NOW PRONOUNCE YOU... MAN AND WIFE!

G-GREEN LANTERN FAILED ME!

3

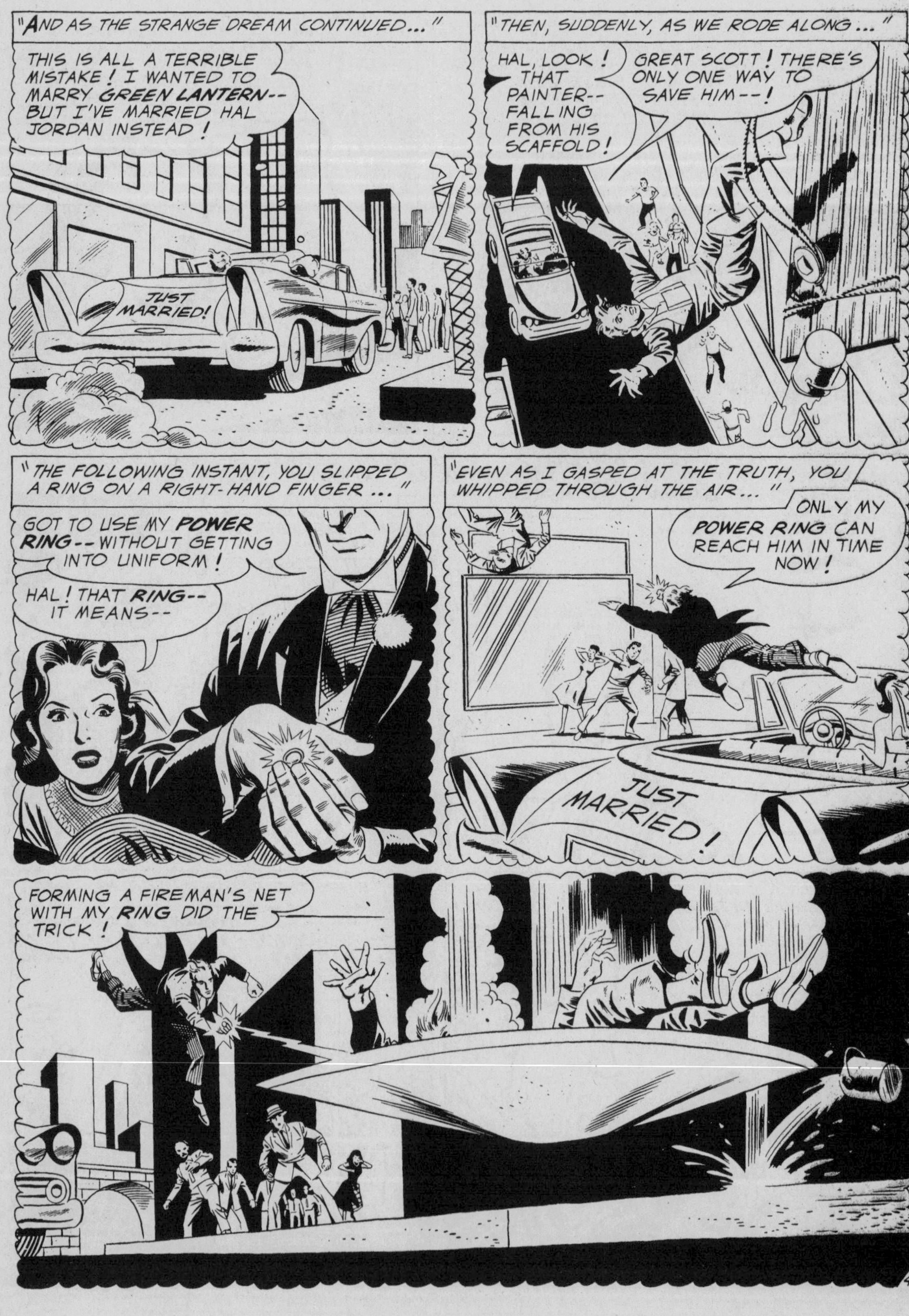
"AND AS THE STRANGE DREAM CONTINUED..."
THIS IS ALL A TERRIBLE MISTAKE! I WANTED TO MARRY GREEN LANTERN-- BUT I'VE MARRIED HAL JORDAN INSTEAD!
JUST MARRIED!
"THEN, SUDDENLY, AS WE RODE ALONG..."
HAL, LOOK! THAT PAINTER-- FALLING FROM HIS SCAFFOLD!
GREAT SCOTT! THERE'S ONLY ONE WAY TO SAVE HIM--!
"THE FOLLOWING INSTANT, YOU SLIPPED A RING ON A RIGHT-HAND FINGER..."
GOT TO USE MY POWER RING--WITHOUT GETTING INTO UNIFORM!
HAL! THAT RING-- IT MEANS--
"EVEN AS I GASPED AT THE TRUTH, YOU WHIPPED THROUGH THE AIR..."
ONLY MY POWER RING CAN REACH HIM IN TIME NOW!
JUST MARRIED!
FORMING A FIREMAN'S NET WITH MY RING DID THE TRICK!
4

SO? I MARRIED *GREEN LANTERN* AFTER ALL! HE AND HAL JORDAN ARE THE *SAME* PERSON!

"THAT'S WHERE THE DREAM ENDED!"

THIS MORNING, VIVIDLY REMEMBERING MY DREAM, IT OCCURRED TO ME THAT I HAD *NEVER* SEEN YOU AND *GREEN LANTERN* TOGETHER, HAL! I BEGAN TO THINK-- AND THAT'S WHY I ASKED YOU ON THIS RIDE...

TELL ME, HAL--ARE *YOU* REALLY *GREEN LANTERN?*

NOW, CAROL... YOU OUGHT TO KNOW BETTER THAN TO PUT FAITH IN A-- MERE *DREAM!* ACTUALLY--

BEFORE HAL CAN FINISH, THE ROAD COMES TO AN ABRUPT END--AND THE CAR PLUNGES THROUGH SPACE...

WH--WHAT'S HAPPENED TO THE ROAD--!?

AS THE CAR PLUMMETS HELPLESSLY DOWN THE SIDE OF THE MOUNTAIN...

ONLY ONE WAY TO SAVE US-- BY USING MY *POWER RING* AS HAL JORDAN! THERE ISN'T ENOUGH TIME TO SWITCH TO *GREEN LANTERN!*

Ohh!

OUT OF THE *POWER RING* FLASHES AN INTENSE *GREEN BEAM*--FORMING A PARACHUTE THAT ATTACHES ITSELF TO THE FALLING VEHICLE...

HOW STRANGELY THIS REAL-LIFE INCIDENT PARALLELS CAROL'S DREAM!

THEN, AS THE CAR MAKES A SOFT LANDING...

¡Whew! THAT WAS A CLOSE CALL! LANDED WITH JUST A COUPLE OF BOUNCES!

CAROL'S ALL RIGHT-- NOT HURT! SHE FAINTED THE MOMENT WE STARTED TO FALL! SHE NEVER DID SEE ME USE GL'S *POWER RING!*

I WONDER WHAT HAPPENED TO THAT ROAD UP THERE? WHAT COULD HAVE WIPED AWAY PART OF IT LIKE THAT?

AS HAL'S KEEN EYES SWEEP THE TERRAIN AROUND HIM...

EH? WHAT... IS... THAT!?

A CLOSER LOOK REVEALS...

A GIGANTIC FOOTPRINT-- UNLIKE ANYTHING I'VE EVER SEEN BEFORE!

CAROL WILL BE SAFE ENOUGH WHILE *GREEN LANTERN* FINDS OUT WHAT'S GOING ON HERE!

A GOOD THING I MADE SURE TO CHARGE MY RING THIS MORNING...*

Editor's Note: GREEN LANTERN'S POWER RING MUST BE RE-CHARGED EVERY 24 HOURS!

SOON, NOT FAR FROM THE ACCIDENT-SCENE...

THOSE MEN IN THAT JEEP-- WAVING FRANTICALLY AT ME!

GREEN LANTERN-- STOP! WE'VE GOT TO TALK TO YOU!

MOMENTS LATER, AS THE MEN IN THE CAR POUR OUT WILD WORDS TO THE GREEN-CLAD CHAMPION...

WE'RE SCIENTISTS--FROM THE DULONG EXPERIMENTAL STATION ON TOP OF THE MOUNTAIN--!

SOMETHING TERRIBLE HAS HAPPENED!

CALM DOWN! WE'VE **GOT** TO EXPLAIN! LISTEN, **GREEN LANTERN**--OUR WORK IN THE DULONG STATION HAS BEEN THE INVESTIGATION OF THE EFFECTS OF **COSMIC RAYS** ON VARIOUS TYPES OF MATTER...

"UP TO YESTERDAY WE HAD NO IMPORTANT RESULTS...BUT THEN THIS MORNING..."

GREAT STARS! WHAT'S HAPPENING TO THE BLOB I PLACED IN THIS TEST TUBE?

A--A SHAPE MATERIALIZING INSIDE!

"WITHIN MOMENTS, THE THING SPROUTED BEFORE MY EYES--UNTIL ..."

RUN! IT'S GROWING WILD! WE CAN'T CONTROL IT--!

I'VE **TRIED** TO SHOOT IT--!

WE COULD DO **NOTHING**, **GREEN LANTERN**! THE THING GREW TO ENORMOUS SIZE! WE'RE TRYING TO ALARM THE COUNTRY-SIDE--! IT MAY KILL-- DESTROY THOUSANDS OF PEOPLE!

YOU KEEP GOING-- SPREAD THE WARNING!

⑦

AS FOR ME, I'M GOING TO FIND THAT CREATURE-- AND *POWER-RING* BLAST IT!

BE CAREFUL, *GREEN LANTERN!* IT'S A MASS OF CONCENTRATED COSMIC RAYS-- AND CAN BE TERRIBLY DESTRUCTIVE!

NOW THAT I KNOW *WHAT* TORE A PIECE OF THAT ROAD *100* FEET UP IN THE AIR-- AND WHAT MADE THAT ENORMOUS PRINT IN THE GROUND-- I CAN DO SOMETHING ABOUT IT!

SOON, AS *GL* FOLLOWS THE TRACK OF THE HUGE FOOTPRINTS...

THERE IT IS-- NEAR THE *COAST CITY BRIDGE!* I WAS EXPECTING SOMETHING *BIG*-- BUT THIS IS MIND-STAGGERING!

RIPPING UP THAT BRIDGE-- AS IF IT WERE MADE OF PAPER! I'VE *GOT* TO STOP IT!

8

GUIDED BY GREEN LANTERN'S WILL, THE POWER RING FORMS A GIGANTIC BLAST WHICH SMASHES AT THE CREATURE...

INCREDIBLE! IT WITHSTOOD THE BLAST OF MY POWER RING!

SUDDENLY OUT OF THE EYES OF THE MONSTER FLASHES AN EERIE LIGHT...

YELLOW BEAMS FROM ITS EYES-- STUNNING ME! MY RING IS POWERLESS AGAINST ANYTHING YELLOW!

AS GL STAGGERS BACKWARD, THE COLOSSUS MOVES INTO THE CITY... STRIDES INTO A SKYSCRAPER...

LUCKY NO ONE WAS INSIDE THAT BUILD- ING! THE PEOPLE WERE WARNED AND FLED!

ALERTED BY THE GIGANTIC THREAT, MILITARY FORCES RUSH TO THE SCENE...

OUR BULLETS AND BOMBS HAVE NO EFFECT ON IT! THE MONSTER SIMPLY ABSORBS THEM!

As THE **EMERALD GLADIATOR** REGAINS HIS SENSES AND TAKES OFF AFTER THE MENACING CREATURE...

ONE OF THE SCIENTISTS WARNED ME THE MONSTER WAS A MASS OF COSMIC RAY ENERGY-- WHICH MEANS IT'S **INVULNERABLE**-- EVEN TO MY **POWER RING**!

GRIMLY, THE **GREEN CHAMPION** FOLLOWS THE MARAUDING BEAST...

I HAVE AN IDEA! MAYBE ITS VERY STRONG POINTS ARE ALSO ITS **WEAKNESS**! MAYBE IT FEEDS ON **COSMIC RAYS** TO GIVE IT ITS INCREDIBLE STRENGTH! COSMIC RAYS STRIKE EVERYWHERE...*

SCREECH!

*Editor's Note: EVERY INCH OF THE EARTH IS BOMBARDED EVERY MOMENT BY THE MYSTERIOUS **COSMIC RAYS** FROM OUTER SPACE!

...SO I **KNOW** IT'S RECEIVING THE RADIATION RIGHT NOW! IT'S JUST POSSIBLE THAT IF I CAN CUT IT OFF FROM THE **RAYS** EVEN FOR A FEW MOMENTS, IT MAY WEAKEN IT--

BENT ON TRYING OUT HIS IDEA, THE STALWART RING-WIELDER HURTLES AT HIS FANTASTIC FOE...

IT CAME OUT OF A TEST TUBE...SO MY **RING-SHIELD** AGAINST THE **COSMIC RAYS** WILL TAKE THE FORM OF A HUGE **TEST TUBE** OVER IT!

A MOMENT LATER...

I MUST BE ON THE RIGHT TRACK! IT HAS SENSED WHAT I'M DOING-- WHIRLED AT ME--BUT ALREADY THE **RING-SHIELD** IS AFFECTING IT BECAUSE THE **YELLOW BEAMS** FROM ITS EYES ARE FALLING SHORT-- CAN'T REACH ME OR THE TEST TUBE!

INSIDE THE GREAT GREEN TUBE THE COSMIC-RAY CREATURE UNDERGOES A STRANGE TRANSFORMATION...

IT'S SHRINKING IN SIZE AS FAST AS IT ORIGINALLY GREW!

THE RADIATION IN MY GREEN BEAM HAS PUT ME IN CON-TACT WITH THE MIND OF THE CREATURE! ITS THOUGHTS ARE COMING TO ME...

I'M GRATEFUL, **GREEN LANTERN**... FOR WHAT YOU'RE DOING...

CONCENTRATION OF COSMIC ENERGY... EVOLVED ME... FANTASTICALLY FAST... I MEANT NO HARM... BUT IN TRYING TO CONTROL MY ACTIONS... I CLUMSILY CAUSED DESTRUCTION...

NOW AT LAST... THANKS TO YOU... I AM NO LONGER A MENACE... TO MYSELF... OR WORLD...

DEAD... IT'S BECOME A LIFELESS BLOB!

LATER AS NEWSMEN QUIZ THE HERO IN GREEN...

SO THAT'S THE WAY YOU SUM UP THE AFFAIR, *GREEN LANTERN*?

YES! THE CREATURE WAS BORN IN A TEST TUBE--AND IT DIED IN A TEST TUBE!

AND NOW THAT THAT'S OVER... I'VE GOT ANOTHER IMPORTANT MATTER TO ATTEND TO RIGHT AWAY!

SOON AFTER, TEST PILOT HAL JORDAN MAKES HIS APPEARANCE ...

HAL! WHAT HAPPENED TO YOU?

I WENT TO--ER--GET THIS DOCTOR FOR YOU, CAROL-- BUT I SEE YOU'VE RECOVERED...

THAT EVENING, AS CAROL AND HAL READ A NEWSPAPER EXTRA...

WELL, I GUESS THIS PROVES YOU'RE NOT *GREEN LANTERN*, HAL! WHILE YOU WERE WANDERING AROUND IN SEARCH OF A DOCTOR FOR ME--*GREEN LANTERN* WAS BATTLING THAT CREATURE! OH, WELL ...

Daily Star EXTRA
GREEN LANTERN DESTROYS COSM CREATURE!

AND WHEN HAL LEAVES...

I GUESS DREAMS DON'T FORETELL THE FUTURE AFTER ALL! AND THAT MEANS I'VE STILL GOT MY PROBLEM! *HOW* AM I GOING TO GET *GREEN LANTERN* TO PROPOSE TO ME? HE'S FULL OF COURAGE--FOR *ANYTHING BUT THAT!*

The End

IF YOU HAVE BEEN THRILLED BY THE ADVENTURES OF *GREEN LANTERN* IN THE PAST THREE ISSUES OF *SHOWCASE* -- AND WOULD LIKE TO SEE HIS ADVENTURES CONTINUED IN A MAGAZINE EXCLUSIVELY HIS OWN-- PLEASE WRITE AND TELL HIM SO!

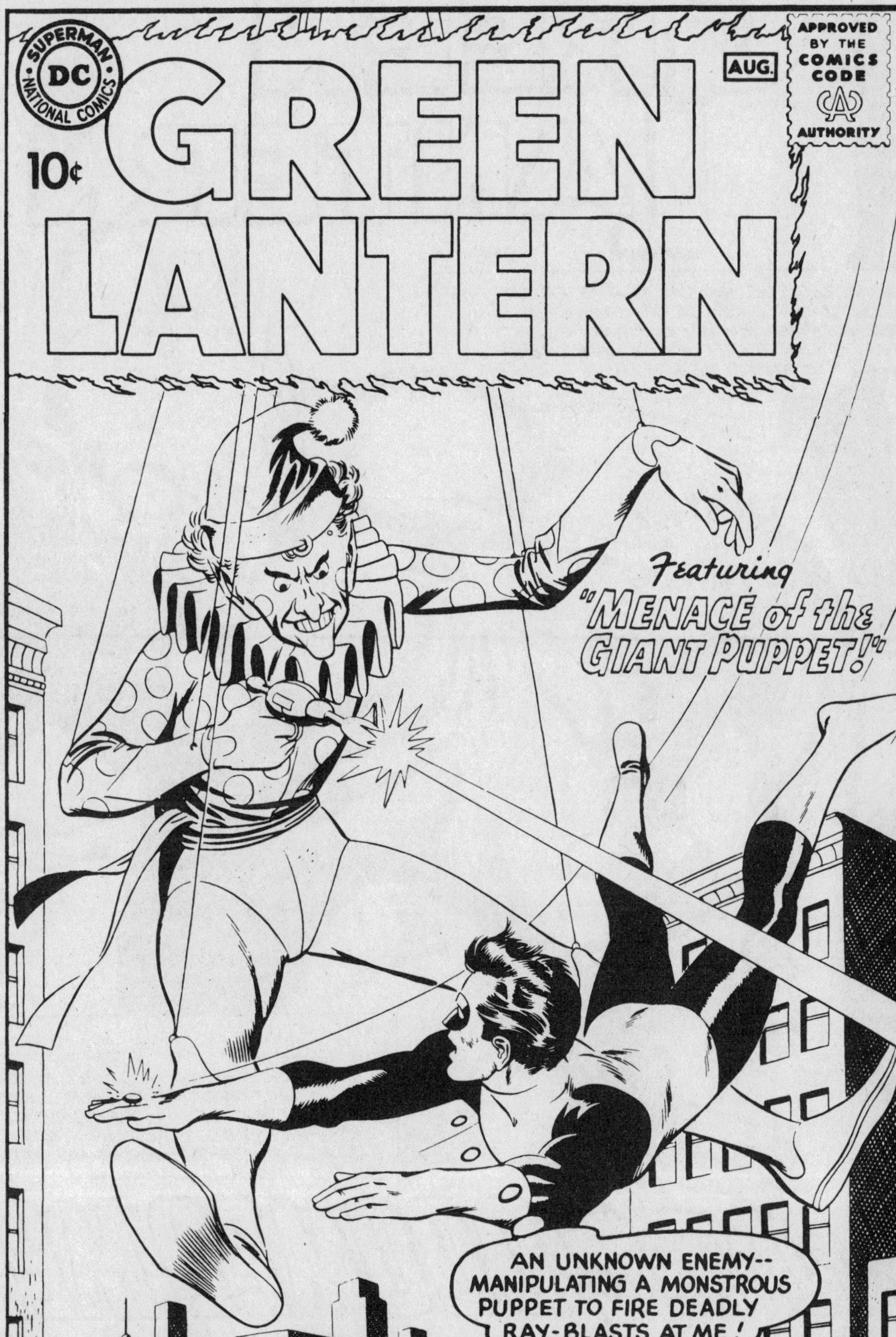
SUPERMAN
DC
NATIONAL COMICS
10¢
GREEN LANTERN
AUG.
APPROVED BY THE COMICS CODE AUTHORITY
Featuring
"MENACE of the GIANT PUPPET!"
AN UNKNOWN ENEMY-- MANIPULATING A MONSTROUS PUPPET TO FIRE DEADLY RAY-BLASTS AT ME!

GREEN LANTERN
AN INCREDIBLE MENTAL FORCE FROM THIS HUGE CREATURE... AFFECTING ME... WEAKENING MY WILL POWER... SO THAT I CAN'T GET MY POWER-RING BEAM TO REACH HIM!
ON A STRANGE AND FAR-OFF WORLD... WHERE HE HAS GONE IN RESPONSE TO A MYSTERIOUS MESSAGE RECEIVED VIA HIS BATTERY OF POWER... GREEN LANTERN BATTLES A CREATURE OF SUCH FANTASTIC STRENGTH THAT IT CAN RESIST THE POWER-RING ATTACKS OF THE EMERALD WARRIOR!
The PLANET of DOOMED MEN
1

AS ACE TEST PILOT **HAL JORDAN** PUTS A NEW EXPERIMENTAL SPACE-PLANE THROUGH ITS PACES...

HANDLES FINE...EASY AS RIDING A KIDDIE-CAR! EXCEPT THAT THIS BABY CAN **GO**...!

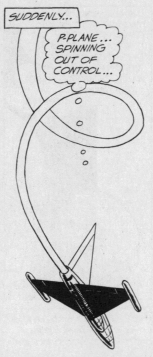

SUDDENLY...

P-PLANE... SPINNING OUT OF CONTROL...

WITH PRACTICED SKILL, AND LIGHTNING REFLEXES, THE CRACK AIRMAN BRINGS HIS CRAFT OUT OF ITS DIVE...

~WHEW!~ NOTHING WENT WRONG WITH THE PLANE-- **I** WAS AT FAULT! SUDDENLY I WENT LIMP--AS IF EVERY BIT OF ENERGY HAD BEEN DRAINED OUT OF ME --

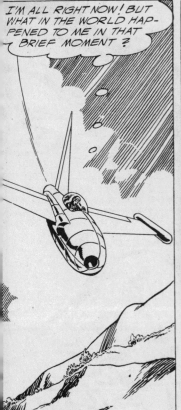

I'M ALL RIGHT NOW! BUT WHAT IN THE WORLD HAPPENED TO ME IN THAT BRIEF MOMENT?

AT THE SAME TIME ON THE FAR-DISTANT PLANET OF **OA**, IN THE CENTRAL GALAXY OF THE UNIVERSE, A GROUP SIMPLY KNOWN AS THE **GUARDIANS** IS MEETING IN SOLEMN COUNCIL...

THE **ENERGY-DUPLICATE** OF THE POSSESSOR OF A **POWER BATTERY** IN SECTOR 2814 WILL ARRIVE IN A MOMENT...

WE MUST FIND OUT IF THIS NEW POSSESSOR IS WORTHY OF HIS GREAT TRUST!

YES! AND ALSO WHETHER HE IS CAPABLE OF DEALING WITH THE TERRIBLE EMERGENCY WHICH HAS ARISEN IN HIS SECTOR...

2

THEN... AS A BLAST OF LIGHT APPEARS BEFORE THE AUGUST ASSEMBLAGE..

WH-WHERE AM I...?

WE HAVE SUMMONED YOU TO A COUNCIL OF THE **GUARDIANS**, HAL JORDAN! TO AVOID INTERFERING WITH YOUR NORMAL LIFE, WE ALLOWED YOUR CORPOREAL BODY TO REMAIN ON EARTH!

...WHILE **YOU**, THE **ENERGY-TWIN** OF THAT BODY, POSSESSING ALL OF THE KNOWLEDGE IN THE MIND OF HAL JORDAN, WILL ANSWER OUR QUESTIONS!

LET US BEGIN...

WE ALREADY KNOW MANY OF THE DETAILS INVOLVING THE TRANSFERENCE OF A **BATTERY OF POWER** TO YOU, HAL JORDAN! LET US TELL YOU FIRST WHAT **WE** KNOW! AN EARTHLY YEAR AGO...

"IN THE ARID SOUTHWEST OF YOUR COUNTRY, A CRAFT FROM OUTER SPACE CRASH-LANDED..."

"...AND INSIDE, A BEING NEVER BEFORE SEEN ON EARTH, GAVE OFF HIS LAST THOUGHTS..."

NO USE...FOOLING YOURSELF, ABIN SUR...YOU ARE DYING! YOU HAVE ONLY A SHORT TIME LEFT TO LIVE...

YOU KNOW WHAT YOUR DUTY IS... TO PASS ON THE **BATTERY OF POWER** TO...A DESERVING ONE! IT IS...WHAT YOU WOULD HAVE BEEN OBLIGED TO DO HAD YOU MET...DISASTER ON YOUR **OWN** WORLD...

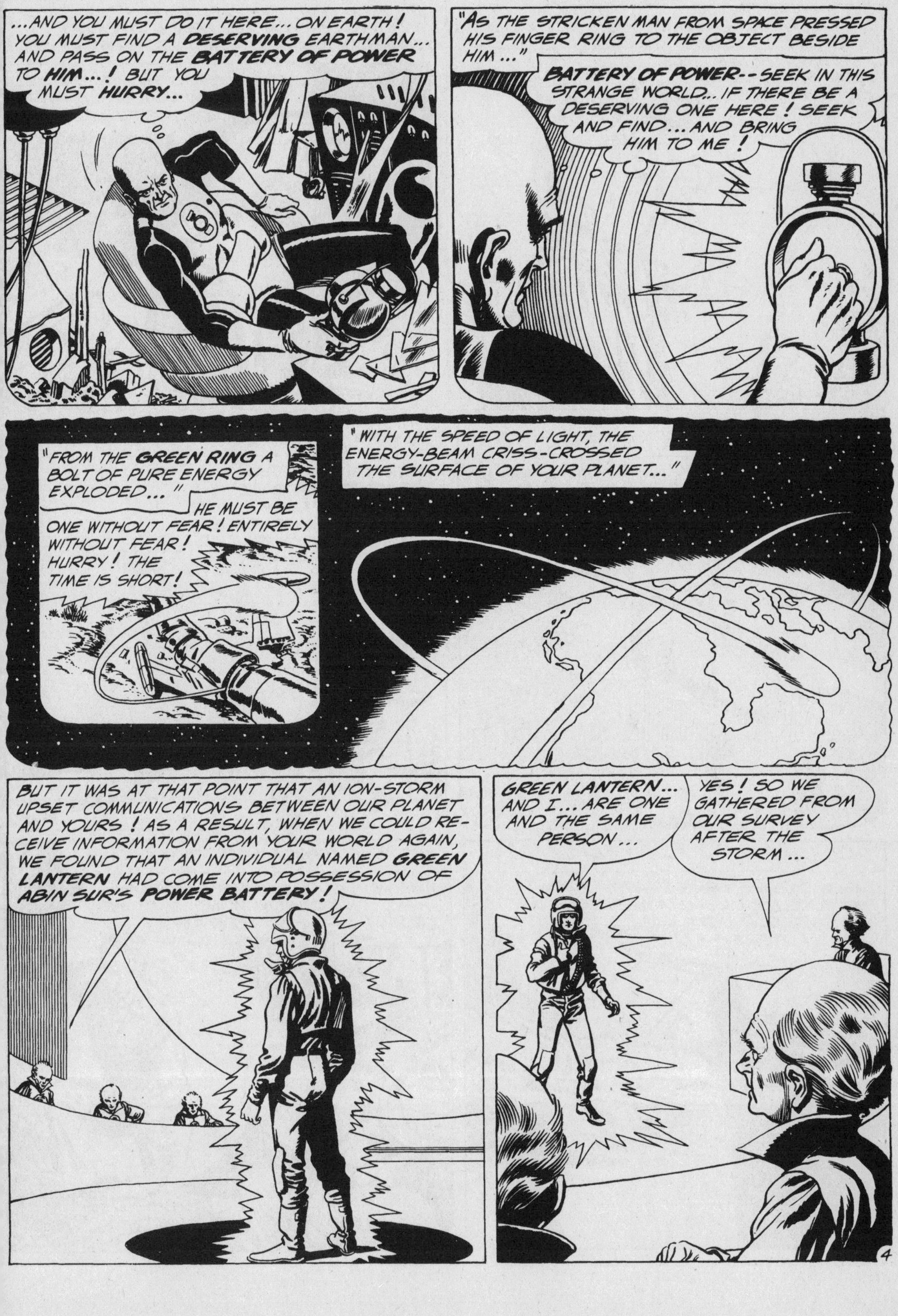
...AND YOU MUST DO IT HERE... ON EARTH! YOU MUST FIND A DESERVING EARTHMAN... AND PASS ON THE BATTERY OF POWER TO HIM...! BUT YOU MUST HURRY...
"AS THE STRICKEN MAN FROM SPACE PRESSED HIS FINGER RING TO THE OBJECT BESIDE HIM..."
BATTERY OF POWER--SEEK IN THIS STRANGE WORLD... IF THERE BE A DESERVING ONE HERE! SEEK AND FIND... AND BRING HIM TO ME!
"FROM THE GREEN RING A BOLT OF PURE ENERGY EXPLODED..."
HE MUST BE ONE WITHOUT FEAR! ENTIRELY WITHOUT FEAR! HURRY! THE TIME IS SHORT!
"WITH THE SPEED OF LIGHT, THE ENERGY-BEAM CRISS-CROSSED THE SURFACE OF YOUR PLANET..."
BUT IT WAS AT THAT POINT THAT AN ION-STORM UPSET COMMUNICATIONS BETWEEN OUR PLANET AND YOURS! AS A RESULT, WHEN WE COULD RECEIVE INFORMATION FROM YOUR WORLD AGAIN, WE FOUND THAT AN INDIVIDUAL NAMED GREEN LANTERN HAD COME INTO POSSESSION OF ABIN SUR'S POWER BATTERY!
GREEN LANTERN... AND I... ARE ONE AND THE SAME PERSON...
YES! SO WE GATHERED FROM OUR SURVEY AFTER THE STORM...
4

BUT WHAT WE WANT YOU TO DO NOW, HAL JORDAN, IS TO TELL US WHAT HAPPENED AFTER *ABIN SUR'S* GREEN BEAM WAS SENT OUT!

I REMEMBER IT ALL... SO VIVIDLY...

"*I* WAS AT THAT TIME SITTING IN A TRAINER OF MY OWN DESIGN AT THE *FERRIS AIRCRAFT COMPANY* WHERE I WORK AS A TEST PILOT..."

THIS FLIGHTLESS TRAINER WILL HELP TURN OUT SPACE PILOTS OF THE FUTURE--!

"SUDDENLY A GREEN GLOW SPRANG UP AROUND ME..."

eh? WHAT'S THAT STRANGE LIGHT SURROUNDING ME!? I--I SEEM TO BE *MOVING*!

"BEFORE I COULD EVEN TAKE A BREATH..."

I'M SCOOTING THROUGH THE AIR AT FANTASTIC SPEED! B-BUT HOW CAN SUCH AN INCREDIBLE THING HAPPEN?

"THEN, ABRUPTLY, THE FLIGHT CEASED..."

I KNOW I DIDN'T LEAVE EARTH--BUT THAT SURE LOOKS LIKE A WRECKED SPACESHIP LYING THERE--!

"AND AS I APPROACHED THE VESSEL..."

COME IN, HAL JORDAN!

GOOD GOSH! A SPACEMAN-- COMMUNICATING WITH ME BY *TELEPATHY*!

STARTLED, I ENTERED THE WRECKED SHIP..."

I AM *ABIN SUR* ... I AM NOT OF EARTH--BUT OF A FAR DISTANT PLANET--AND I AM ...DYING...

HOW CAN I HELP--

NO... IT IS TOO LATE TO HELP ME ... BESIDES, I MUST SPEAK TO YOU ...OF A MORE IMPORTANT MATTER...

MORE IMPORTANT... THAN YOUR *LIFE*?

YES... LOOK AT THE *BATTERY*, HAL JORDAN...

WHY... IT LOOKS LIKE A *GREEN LANTERN*...

YES... IN YOUR WORDS... A *GREEN LANTERN*... BUT ACTUALLY IT IS A *BATTERY OF POWER*... GIVEN ONLY TO SELECTED SPACE-PATROL MEN IN THE SUPER-GALACTIC SYSTEM ... TO BE USED AS A WEAPON AGAINST FORCES OF EVIL AND INJUSTICE...

IT IS OUR DUTY...WHEN DISASTER STRIKES...TO PASS ON THE *BATTERY OF POWER*... TO ANOTHER WHO IS FEARLESS ...AND *HONEST!* COME CLOSER TO ME ...

YES... BY THE GREEN BEAM OF MY RING...I SEE THAT YOU ARE HONEST! AND THE *BATTERY* HAS ALREADY SELECTED YOU AS ONE BORN WITHOUT FEAR! SO YOU PASS BOTH TESTS, HAL JORDAN...

6

"*THERE IS STILL MUCH TO TELL YOU... AND ONLY MOMENTS LEFT! MY SHIP WAS BATTERED... IN THE DEADLY RADIATION BANDS SURROUNDING YOUR PLANET...*"

"*A TERRIBLE BLAST OF YELLOW LIGHT-- SIMILAR TO YOUR AURORA BOREALIS-- BLINDED ME AT THE CONTROLS...*"

YELLOW LIGHT-- STUNNING ME--!

"*THEN I CRASHED...*"

ONLY SECONDS LEFT TO TELL YOU... ONCE YOU HAVE THE **BATTERY** YOU WILL HAVE POWER OVER EVERYTHING-- EXCEPT WHAT IS **YELLOW**!

THE UNIQUE **METAL** WHICH CHARGES THE **BATTERY** WITH ITS WONDROUS POWER HAS A YELLOW IMPURITY IN IT! STRANGELY ENOUGH, IF THE YELLOW IMPURITY IS REMOVED, THE **BATTERY** LOSES ITS POWER!

IT IS THIS IMPURITY IN THE **BATTERY** WHICH WILL MAKE YOU POWERLESS OVER ANYTHING YELLOW!

I UNDER-STAND!

NOW TAKE MY RING -- LET ME PUT IT ON FOR YOU --! WITH THIS RING YOU WILL DRAIN POWER FROM THE BATTERY... EFFECTIVE FOR 24 HOURS...

NOW... I'VE TOLD YOU ALL... DO NOT FAIL ME...

GONE! HE... BREATHED HIS LAST!

"AFTER I HAD FOLLOWED THE SPACEMAN'S ORDERS IN DISPOSING OF ALL REMNANTS OF HIM AND HIS ROCKET..."

THE SPACEMAN TOLD ME TO TAKE HIS SPECIAL UNIFORM! AND I VOWED TO HIM THAT I WOULD CARRY OUT MY NEW RESPONSIBILITIES TO THE BEST OF MY ABILITY!

"I WAS STILL DAZED AS I TRIED OUT MY NEW POWER..."

LIFTING A CLIFF INTO THE AIR! I CAN DO ANYTHING I WANT WITH THIS RING... ANYTHING I WILL TO HAPPEN... I CAN MAKE HAPPEN!

BUT TO BE SAFE I MUST USE IT ONLY IN THE GREATEST SECRECY! I KNOW --! I'LL ADOPT A SECRET IDENTITY -- I'LL CALL MYSELF GREEN LANTERN -- AFTER THE POWER BATTERY!

AND IN TIME I HOPE TO MAKE GREEN LANTERN A NAME TO BE FEARED BY EVIL-DOERS EVERYWHERE!

Story continued on following page.

As the **ENERGY-TWIN** of the real Hal Jordan finishes his account, the **GUARDIANS** come to a unanimous decision...

HAL JORDAN, WE DEEM YOU WORTHY OF BEING A POSSESSOR OF A **BATTERY OF POWER!**

YOU WILL NOW RETURN TO YOUR WORLD TO REJOIN THE CORPOREAL BODY OF YOUR REAL SELF!

AND THIS INTERVIEW WILL BE ERASED FROM YOUR MIND... UNTIL IT IS PROPER FOR YOU TO LEARN ABOUT US...

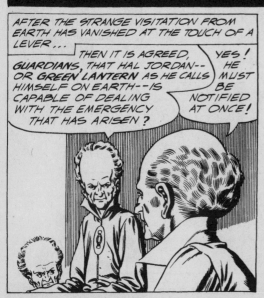

AFTER THE STRANGE VISITATION FROM EARTH HAS VANISHED AT THE TOUCH OF A LEVER...

THEN IT IS AGREED, GUARDIANS, THAT HAL JORDAN -- OR GREEN LANTERN AS HE CALLS HIMSELF ON EARTH -- IS CAPABLE OF DEALING WITH THE EMERGENCY THAT HAS ARISEN?

YES! HE MUST BE NOTIFIED AT ONCE!

BACK ON EARTH AT THIS MOMENT...

FUNNY ABOUT THAT SENSATION I HAD--BUT EVIDENTLY IT DIDN'T DO ANY HARM! I FEEL OKAY!

...BUT I'D FEEL EVEN BETTER IF I COULD GET A DATE WITH CAROL* TONIGHT!

*Editor's Note: MISS CAROL FERRIS, IN THE ABSENCE OF HER FATHER, IS IN SOLE CHARGE OF THE FERRI AIRCRAFT COMPANY WHERE HAL IS EMPLOYED AS TEST PILOT.

IN HIS PRIVATE DRESSING ROOM AT THE HANGAR, AS HAL TAKES OFF HIS FLYING TOGS...

THE TROUBLE IS, EVER SINCE CAROL MET MY ALTER EGO **GREEN LANTERN**, SHE DOESN'T SEEM TO FIND ANY TIME FOR ME! WHAT A SITUATION I'M UP AGAINST...

I'M MY OWN RIVAL FOR CAROL'S AFFECTIONS! BUT I'LL NEVER TELL HER--OR ANYONE ELSE--THAT I'M **GREEN LANTERN!** I WANT TO WIN CAROL AS MYSELF -- AS **HAL JORDAN!**

EH?

TURNING HIS EYES TO A CORNER OF THE ROOM, THE ACE TEST PILOT SEES...

A GREEN GLOW COMING THROUGH THE INVISIBILITY SHIELD PROTECTING MY POWER BATTERY!*

*Editor's Note: HAL (GREEN LANTERN) JORDAN HAS CREATED THE INVISIBILITY SHIELD TO PREVENT THE POWER BATTERY FROM BEING SEEN OR TOUCHED BY ANYONE BUT HIMSELF!

THE BATTERY IS SIGNALING ME AGAIN--PROJECTING THOUGHTS AT ME!

WIELDER OF THE GREEN BEAM OF POWER, YOU MUST TAKE CARE OF AN EMERGENCY IN YOUR SECTOR...

...ON THE WORLD OF CALOR, THE THIRD PLANET IN THE STAR-SYSTEM CLOSEST TO YOURS, A RACE OF HUMAN-TYPE BEINGS IS IN DANGER!

HE ACTS WITH COMMENDABLE SPEED... CHARGING HIS POWER RING...

...REPEATING HIS SOLEMN OATH...

IN BRIGHTEST DAY... IN BLACKEST NIGHT, NO EVIL SHALL ESCAPE MY SIGHT! LET THOSE WHO WORSHIP EVIL'S MIGHT BEWARE MY POWER-- GREEN LANTERN'S LIGHT!

AND SOON A FORMIDABLE FIGURE CLEAVES THE DARKNESS OF OUTER SPACE AROUND EARTH...

MY *RING*, OBEYING MY WILL POWER, HAS FORMED AN INVULNERABLE POCKET OF AIR AROUND ME... TO ENABLE ME TO BREATHE UNTIL I GET TO THAT STAR-SYSTEM THE *LANTERN* VOICE TOLD ABOUT!

POWERED BY HIS INVINCIBLE RING, THE *GREEN-CLAD GLADIATOR* QUICKLY REACHES HIS DESTINATION, TRILLIONS OF MILES FROM EARTH...

BUT WHO SPEAKS TO ME THROUGH THE *LANTERN*? WHOSE THOUGHTS DO I RECEIVE? WILL I EVER KNOW? WILL I EVER GET TO SEE THEM? *

EditOR's Note: GL IS UNAWARE THAT IN THE PERSON OF HIS ENERGY-DUPLICATE HE HAS ALREADY SEEN THE INCREDIBLE GUARDIANS!

ON THE PLANET...

KE-GRA-UM-NU--

WE HAVE BEEN ASKING THE SPIRIT KA-MA TO SEND US HELP--!

AS THE EMERALD CRUSADER APPROACHES...

GU-BARO! GU-NARU--

I CAN'T UNDERSTAND THEM--BUT MY *RING* WILL FIX THAT--!

UNDER GL'S AMAZING *POWER RING*, BACKED BY HIS INDOMITABLE *WILL*, THE WORDS OF THE NATIVES COME CLEAR...

WE EXPECTED YOU! WE KNEW THAT YOU WOULD COME!

WHAT?! HOW COULD THAT BE?

AFTER THE *RING-WIELDER* HAS BEEN MADE TO UNDERSTAND...

SO THAT'S IT! THEY BELIEVE THAT THIS STRANGE TREE HAS THE POWER TO GRANT THEM FAVORS--AND THEY WERE BEGGING IT FOR HELP! THEY THINK *THAT'S* HOW I CAME HERE!

BUT THEN UNDER FURTHER QUESTIONING...

DRYG-- DRYG!

DRYG!

STRANGE! I'M TRYING TO LEARN *WHAT* IT IS THAT'S THREATENING THEM! BUT THE *SAME WORD* IN THEIR LANGUAGE APPEARS IN THE GREEN BEAM--

IT MUST BE THAT THERE IS *NO* SUITABLE WORD IN ENGLISH FOR THIS *DRYG* THAT THEY'RE AFRAID OF!

THEY WANT TO SHOW ME SOME-- THING-- TAKING ME UP THIS HILL!

ON TOP OF THE CREST, *GL* VIEWS A STARTLING SPECTACLE...

GREAT SCOTT! A VALLEY FULL OF EXPLODING VOLCANOES! WHAT A STAGGERING SIGHT!

AS THE EARTHLING VIEWS THE VISTA WITH AWE...

ACCORDING TO THE *CALORIANS*, THE *DRYG*-- WHATEVER IT IS--COMES FROM THAT VALLEY! THEY SAY IT WAS *SPAWNED* IN THE TERRIBLE HEAT AND FLAME OF THE ERUPTING LAVA...

SUDDENLY...

Eh? THE NATIVES ARE RUNNING AS IF SCATTERED BY THE WIND!

DRYG! DRYG!

12

THEN...

~Whew!~ A FANTASTIC GORILLA-LIKE CREATURE-- SIXTY-FEET HIGH IF IT'S AN INCH!

MY GREEN BEAM WILL CUT HIM DOWN TO SIZE!

THAT'S ODD... MY RING DOESN'T SEEM TO BE FUNCTIONING RIGHT!

AS THE GREEN GLADIATOR ROCKETS AT HIS GARGANTUAN FOE...

AN OVERPOWERING MENTAL ENERGY FROM THAT MONSTER! IT'S PENETRATING MY BRAIN-- DRAINING MY WILL POWER! I CAN'T SUMMON ENOUGH FORCE BEHIND MY BEAM TO HIT HIM--!

AGAIN AND AGAIN, **GL'S** CHARGES COME TO NAUGHT...

STILL CAN'T REACH HIM! WITHOUT MY **WILL** BEHIND IT, THE **POWER** RING IS USELESS! AND I'M GETTING MORE FEEBLE! GOT TO TRY SOME OTHER WAY TO GRAB HIM--

MAYBE THAT'S IT! I'VE BEEN TRYING TO USE MY RING TO **GRAB** HIM-- THE WRONG TACTICS! THIS CREATURE **MUST** HAVE A **WEAKNESS**... AND IT'S JUST OCCURRED TO ME WHAT THAT MIGHT BE...!

SUDDENLY TURNING HIS *GREEN BEAM* INTO A HUGE NOZZLE, THE EARTHLING TRIES OUT HIS NEW IDEA ...

THE GORILLA CAME FROM THE INTENSE HEAT OF THAT VOLCANO VALLEY, SO MAYBE THE ONE THING IT CAN'T STAND IS *COLD*--SUCH AS THIS COATING OF *LIQUID OXYGEN**MY RING IS SPRAYING ON IT!

***Editor's Note:** LIQUID OXYGEN, AT A TEMPERATURE NEAR ABSOLUTE ZERO, IS ONE OF THE COLDEST SUBSTANCES KNOWN!

CONCENTRATING EVERY IOTA OF WILL POWER BEHIND HIS *RING*...

GOT TO KEEP PILING *MASSES OF ICE* ON HIM--IT'S THE ONLY THING THAT *WEAKENS HIM!* HE'S STRUGGLING-- TRYING TO CONCENTRATE HIS MENTAL FORCE AT ME--BUT I'M KEEPING HIM *TOO BUSY* DEFENDING HIMSELF--!

IT DIDN'T PARALYZE HIM COMPLETELY--BUT IT STUNG HIM ENOUGH TO SHIFT HIS MENTAL FORCE AWAY FROM ME! I CAN FEEL MY WILL RETURNING TO FULL POWER--!

NOW I'VE GOT HIM ENTIRELY ENCASED IN A CAKE OF ICE FORMED BY MY RING! BUT HOW TO KEEP HIM THERE--THAT'S THE QUESTION!

I'VE GOT TO KEEP THE ICE FROZEN AROUND HIM... SO THAT HE CAN'T EVER BREAK LOOSE! I KNOW A NEAT WAY OF DOING THAT--

14

THEN, AS THE GREAT *GREEN BEAM* FORMS A GIGANTIC PAIR OF ICE-TONGS...

I NOTICED A POLAR REGION AT ONE END OF THIS PLANET-- LIKE OURS ON EARTH... FULL OF *PERPETUAL ICE*...!

AND SOON... THERE! I'VE PUT THE *DRYG* "ON ICE"! COLD AS IT IS HERE, I'D SAY HE'S IN A *PERMANENT DEEP-FREEZE*!

ON THE WAY BACK TOWARD THE PRIMITIVE HUMANS OF *CALOR*...

THE CALORIANS FEARED THEY WOULD BE WIPED OUT BE-CAUSE THE *DRYG* HUNTED THEM DAY AND NIGHT, BUT THEY WON'T HAVE TO FEAR ANY MORE *NOW*...!

THEY'RE THANKING THE TREE - SPIRIT *KA-MA* FOR HAVING SENT *ME* TO RID THEM OF THE *DRYG*..!

GU-MA... KA-MA!

WELL ...NO HARM IN THEIR THINKING THAT..! I'LL JUST SLIP AWAY NOW... WITHOUT DISTURBING THEIR CEREMONY...

AS THE *GREEN GLADIATOR*, AGAIN PROTECTED BY AN AIR POCKET, ZOOMS THROUGH SPACE AFTER A MISSION WELL-ACCOMPLISHED...

I'LL JUST ABOUT HAVE TIME TO GET HOME AND *RECHARGE* MY POWER RING FOR ANOTHER 24 HOURS...

...AND MAYBE GET A DATE WITH CAROL-- IF I'M LUCKY!

The End

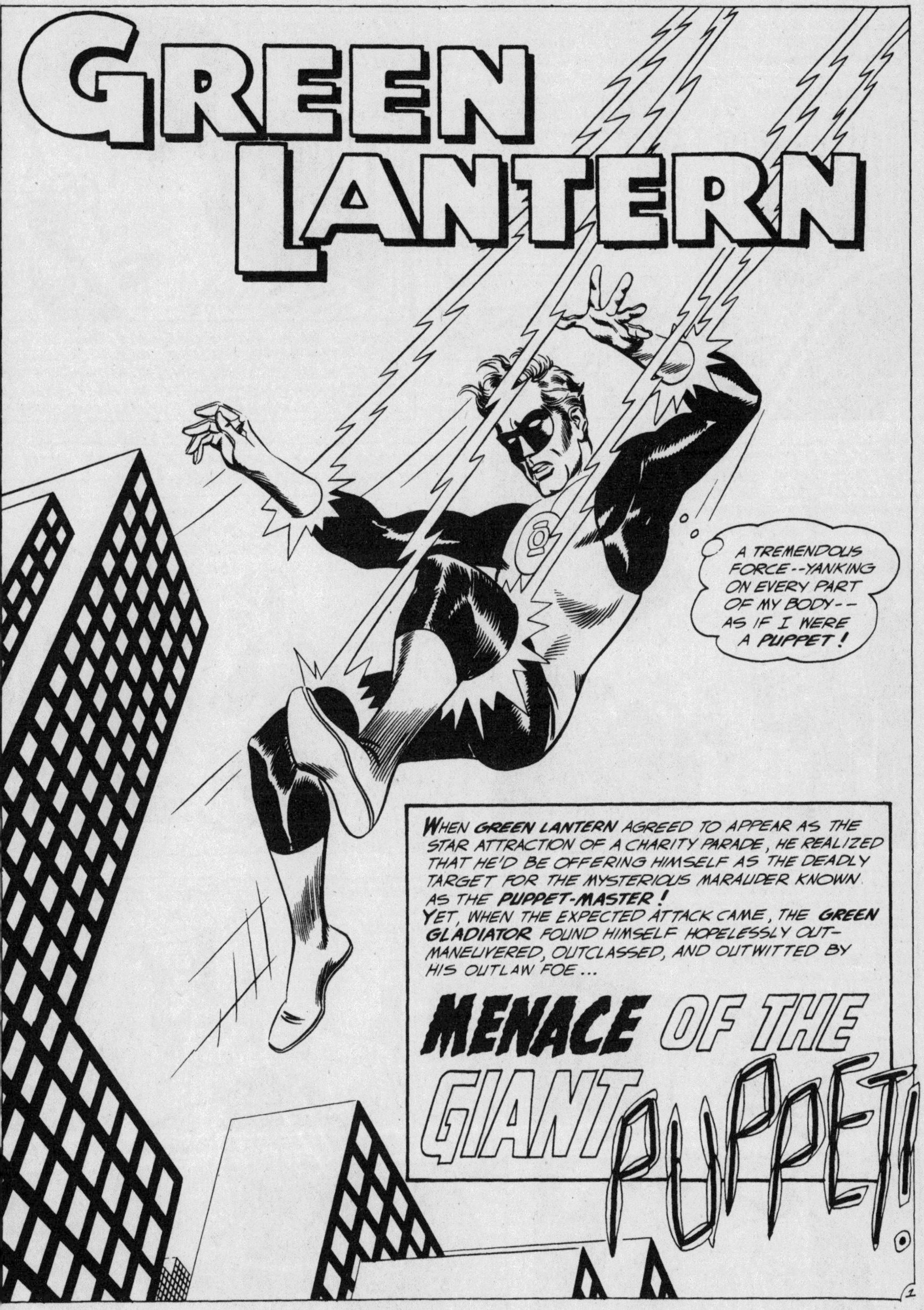
GREEN LANTERN
A TREMENDOUS FORCE--YANKING ON EVERY PART OF MY BODY--AS IF I WERE A PUPPET!
WHEN GREEN LANTERN AGREED TO APPEAR AS THE STAR ATTRACTION OF A CHARITY PARADE, HE REALIZED THAT HE'D BE OFFERING HIMSELF AS THE DEADLY TARGET FOR THE MYSTERIOUS MARAUDER KNOWN AS THE PUPPET-MASTER!
YET, WHEN THE EXPECTED ATTACK CAME, THE GREEN GLADIATOR FOUND HIMSELF HOPELESSLY OUT-MANEUVERED, OUTCLASSED, AND OUTWITTED BY HIS OUTLAW FOE...
MENACE OF THE GIANT PUPPET!
1

AS CAROL FERRIS PUTS THE FINISHING TOUCHES TO HER MAKE-UP IN THE OFFICE AT THE *FERRIS AIR-CRAFT COMPANY...*

♪♪ NIGHT AND DAY, YOU ARE THE ONE... ♪♪

YES...NIGHT AND DAY... DAY AND NIGHT... ALL I THINK ABOUT IS *GREEN LANTERN!* I WONDER IF MY DREAM WILL EVER COME TRUE.. AND THAT SOMEDAY HE AND I WILL MARRY?

I EVEN CONTACTED DAD ON HIS TRIP AND PERSUADED HIM TO AGREE TO LET ME MARRY *GREEN LANTERN*--

Editor's Note: TAKING OFF ON A TWO-YEAR, ROUND-THE-WORLD CRUISE, WILLARD FERRIS LEFT HIS PRETTY DAUGHTER IN CHARGE OF HIS COMPANY--ON CONDITION THAT SHE AVOID ANY ROMANTIC ENTANGLEMENTS!

--IF IT EVER COMES TO THAT! (SIGH!) GETTING DAD'S PERMISSION WAS A BREEZE--BUT GETTING *GREEN LANTERN* TO PROPOSE IS LIKE TRYING TO GRAB A HANDFUL OF QUICKSILVER!

"THE OTHER NIGHT, FOR EXAMPLE, WE WERE SITTING IN THE PARK, JUST THE TWO US..."

BEING WITH YOU MEANS A LOT TO ME, CAROL! YOU'RE WONDERFUL...

GO ON! TELL ME MORE...

"IT SEEMED TO ME HE WAS JUST ON THE VERGE OF 'POPPING THE QUESTION' WHEN..."

I'VE BEEN THINKING, CAROL...WHAT'S THAT--!?

HELP!

WELL, OF ALL THE UNFORTUNATE TIMES FOR SOMEONE TO *FALL INTO THE LAKE!*

YOU'LL BE ALL RIGHT! JUST RELAX!

OF COURSE, THE *EMERALD GLADIATOR* WITH HIS INCREDIBLE *POWER RING* SAVED THE MAN! BUT BY THE TIME HE GOT BACK TO ME IT WAS TOO LATE... THE MOMENT HAD PASSED AND HE NEVER DID FINISH WHAT HE STARTED TO TELL ME...

BUT MAYBE HE WILL TODAY! THE CIVIC COUNCIL IS HAVING A CHARITY PARADE AND *GREEN LANTERN* AGREED TO APPEAR IN IT! HE PROMISED TO CALL FOR ME HERE AS SOON AS IT'S OVER...

IN NEARBY *COAST CITY* MEANWHILE...

HURRAH! IT'S *GREEN LANTERN!*

THE PARADE STARTED LATE-- WHICH MEANS IT'LL BE SOME TIME BEFORE I CAN CALL FOR CAROL! I ACCEPTED AN INVITATION TO APPEAR HERE, NOT ONLY FOR CHARITY... BUT FOR ANOTHER IMPORTANT REASON...

AS THE *GREEN-CLAD CRUSADER* SWINGS ALONG, HIS *POWER RING* BLAZING, TO THE DELIGHT OF THE CROWD...

RECENTLY THERE HAS BEEN A RASH OF STRANGE BANK ROBBERIES! AND JUST THE OTHER DAY--AS HAL JORDAN, MY ALTER EGO--

"--I ENTERED THE *COAST CITY BANK* TO MAKE A DEPOSIT..."

DON'T TRY ANYTHING! HAND OVER THAT MONEY! A HOLD-UP!

"I HAD TO ACT FAST, AND I DID..."

WHILE I KEEP THIS REVOLVING DOOR TURNING AT HIGH SPEED...

I CAN CHANGE TO MY *GREEN LANTERN* COSTUME...

WITHOUT BEING SEEN!

"THEN, I SLIPPED ON THE POWER RING WHICH, AS HAL JORDAN, I ALWAYS CARRY IN MY SECRET POCKET.."

GOOD THING I CHARGED MY *RING* THIS MORNING! IT'S FULL OF POWER AND **READY TO GO!**

*GREEN LANTERN'S RING MUST BE RECHARGED EVERY 24 HOURS AT HIS MYSTIC **POWER BATTERY** IN ORDER TO BE EFFECTIVE!

"I GUESS THE CROOK DIDN'T KNOW WHAT STRUCK HIM..."

"AND THE NEXT MOMENT MY GREEN BEAM FORMED UNBREAK-ABLE MANACLES..."

THIS IS ONE PAIR OF HAND-CUFFS THAT NOT EVEN *HOUDINI* COULD GET OUT OF!

"BUT AT THE POLICE STATION SOON AFTER..."

IT'S ODD, *GREEN LANTERN!* BIFFY IS A WELL-KNOWN CROOK, BUT HE NEVER PULLED A **BANK JOB** BEFORE! I'M INCLINED TO CREDIT HIS STORY THAT HE'S BEEN UNDER SOME KIND OF A **SPELL**...

YEAH...

I KNEW WHAT I WAS DOIN', BUT I COULDN'T HELP MYSELF! IT WAS LIKE I WAS A PUPPET-- AND SOMEONE ELSE WAS MOVIN' MY HANDS AND LEGS--!

A *PUPPET!*

YAY-- GREEN LANTERN!

WE MIGHT NOT HAVE BELIEVED BIFFY--BUT HIS STORY TIED IN WITH OTHER CASES OF CRIMINALS WHO ACTED JUST LIKE HELPLESS PUPPETS WHEN I CAUGHT THEM COMMITTING THEIR CRIMES!

"AS SOON AS THE NEWSPAPERS CAUGHT WIND OF ALL THIS, THEY WASTED NO TIME IN COMING OUT WITH HEADLINES."

MORNING NEWS

MYSTERY PUPPET-MASTER RULES UNDERWORLD!

COAST CITY SENT

WILL GREEN LANTERN DEFEAT SENSATIONAL PUPPETEER OF CRIME?

CITY JOURNAL

PUPPETEER N CONTROL?

SINCE THE NEWSPAPERS HAD SET THE STAGE, I DECIDED TO GIVE MY MYSTERIOUS OPPONENT--THE **PUPPETEER**-- EVERY CHANCE TO STRIKE AT ME...IN THE HOPE IT WOULD TEMPT HIM OUT INTO THE OPEN!

AND THAT'S WHY I AGREED TO APPEAR IN THIS PARADE! BUT SO FAR--EH?

BAMM!

THEN, AS THE **GREEN-CLAD CRUSADER** WHIRLS, INSTANTLY ON THE ALERT AT THE SOUND OF **GUN-FIRE**...

BANG!

THAT HUGE PUPPET-- PART OF THE PARADE BEHIND ME--SHOOTING A GUN AT ME!

WITH TRIGGER-QUICK REFLEXES THE POWER BEAM ARCS FROM *GREEN LANTERN'S* FINGER...

TO AVOID *PANIC* IN THE CROWD, I'M USING MY RING TO TURN THE RAY-BLASTS INTO *CONFETTI* AS THEY LEAVE THE GUN! THIS WAY THE CROWD WILL THINK IT'S ALL PART OF THE PARADE--!

EEee!

AND A MOMENT LATER A HUGE GREEN LOCK-WRENCH CRUMPLES THE RAY-GUN AS IF IT WERE PAPER...

BOY, OH, BOY! WHAT A SHOW *GREEN LANTERN* IS PUTTING ON!

NOW, LET'S SEE WHERE THE PUPPET'S STRING-CONTROLS LEAD TO--AND WHO WAS WORKING IT IN SUCH DEADLY FASHION...

THE PUPPET WAS MANIPULATED FROM THIS DERRICK BACK HERE! IT WAS SUPPOSED TO BE PART OF THE PARADE--

IN THE CAB OF THE DERRICK...

THE OPERATOR OF THE DERRICK--UNCONSCIOUS! THEN--THAT MEANS THIS WAS THE WORK OF THE *PUPPET-MASTER!* BUT HE'S MANAGED TO MAKE HIS *GETAWAY!*

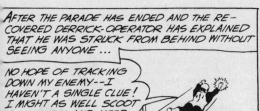

AFTER THE PARADE HAS ENDED AND THE RE-COVERED DERRICK-OPERATOR HAS EXPLAINED THAT HE WAS STRUCK FROM BEHIND WITHOUT SEEING ANYONE...

NO HOPE OF TRACKING DOWN MY ENEMY--I HAVEN'T A SINGLE CLUE! I MIGHT AS WELL SCOOT BACK NOW AND KEEP MY DATE WITH CAROL--

NOT LONG AFTER, IN A LITTLE-NOTICED LOFT BUILDING IN THE FACTORY AREA OF COAST CITY...

GREEN LANTERN ESCAPED ME! BUT I MUST GET RID OF HIM! HE'S INTERFERING WITH MY CRIMINAL OPERATIONS!

SCIENCE CAN BE USED FOR GOOD OR EVIL-- I CHOSE THE LATTER BECAUSE IT WOULD BE MORE PROFITABLE FOR ME! IT TOOK YEARS OF HARD WORK BEFORE I STARTED TO CASH IN ON MY SCIENTIFIC KNOW--HOW...

THIS IS MY PRIZE INVENTION! A MACHINE THAT PROJECTS A HYPNO-RAY WHICH FORCES ANYONE I FOCUS IT ON TO OBEY MY MENTAL COMMANDS! YET I'M NOT ALL--POWERFUL...

JUST AS A HYPNOTIZED PERSON CAN NEVER BE MADE TO DO ANYTHING HE WOULDN'T ORDINARILY DO, SO MY HYPNO-RAY CAN'T FORCE ANY-ONE TO PERFORM ACTS AGAINST HIS NATURE! THAT'S WHY I'VE ONLY FOCUSED IT SO FAR ON CRIMINALS AND USED THEM TO STEAL FOR ME!

CRIMINALS HAVE NO MENTAL BLOCKS AGAINST STEALING! THEY WILLINGLY OBEY MY ILLEGAL HYPNO-COMMANDS!

BUT NOW I'VE DECIDED TO MAKE A SUPREME EFFORT TO USE MY AMAZING MACHINE TO GET RID OF GREEN LANTERN!

I'VE ADDED A NEW Q-CIRCUIT TO MY HYPNO-RAY THAT OUGHT TO GIVE IT OVERWHELMING POWER! THERE--I'VE ZEROED IT IN ON GREEN LANTERN NOW! HE'S DANCING AT A NIGHT CLUB!

AT THAT MOMENT, IN THE POPULAR *BLUE NOTE CLUB* IN TOWN...

GREEN LANTERN, I WISH I COULD GO ON DANCING WITH YOU LIKE THIS FOR THE REST OF MY LIFE!

:SIGH:

ALL I CAN SAY TO THAT, CAROL, IS--

MY FOOT!!

WHAT--?!

SORRY, CAROL, MY...ER...FOOT SLIPPED...

STRANGE... SOMETHING SEEMED TO TUG ON MY LEG!

THEN... OOH--A NEW DANCE-STEP! SHOW ME HOW TO DO--

SOMETHING *IS* YANKING ON ME--SOME FORCE OF TREMENDOUS POWER--AS IF I WERE A *PUPPET*--! HOLY HANNAH!

IT MUST BE THE *PUPPET-MASTER!* IN SOME INCREDIBLE WAY HE'S TRYING TO GET ME IN HIS POWER! Hmmm! THAT GIVES ME AN *IDEA*...!

8

THEN SUDDENLY...

GOOD GRACIOUS! WHAT'S HAPPENING TO GL?

EEEYAH!

LIKE A HELPLESS PUPPET, THE GREEN-CLAD GLADIATOR IS PULLED ACROSS THE STREETS OF COAST CITY...

HA! HA! THIS IS WORKING OUT EASIER THAN I THOUGHT!

BUT MOMENTS LATER, INSIDE THE LOFT, GREEN LANTERN BREAKS THE INVISIBLE PUPPET-STRINGS THAT HAVE BOUND HIM...

I ONLY PRETENDED TO BE UNDER YOUR CONTROL, PUPPET-MASTER, IN ORDER TO GET YOU TO BRING ME TO YOUR SECRET HIDE-OUT!

GREAT SCOTT! IN MY ANXIETY TO GRAB HIM-- I DIDN'T NOTICE HE'S DRESSED ALL IN YELLOW!*

*Editor's Note: DUE TO AN IMPURITY ESSENTIAL TO ITS STRENGTH, GL'S RING HAS NO POWER OVER ANYTHING YELLOW!

AS THE EMERALD GLADIATOR SIZES UP THE SITUATION..

NO TIME TO DILLY-DALLY! IF MY RING WON'T HANDLE HIM, I'LL HAVE TO FIND ANOTHER WAY--!

ALL I NEED IS ONE SHOT AT GREEN LANTERN--!

SWIFTLY SEIZING A LENGTH OF HANDY CORD, GL MAKES UNEXPECTED USE OF IT...

MY **RING** CAN'T TOUCH HIM--BUT IT CAN STILL DIRECT THIS CORD TO A PERFECT LOOP AROUND HIS **WRIST!**

SECONDS AFTER, AS MORE LOOPS SNAKE AROUND THE **PUPPET MASTER**...

A LOOP AROUND HIS LEGS... ARMS... WRISTS... AND THE PUPPET-MASTER WILL BE **TAKING** COMMANDS INSTEAD OF **GIVING** THEM...

AND SOON WITH **GREEN LANTERN** "PULLING THE STRINGS"...

MARCH... PUPPET-MASTER... STRAIGHT TO POLICE HEAD-QUARTERS!

THE NEXT DAY, IN CAROL FERRIS' PRIVATE OFFICE...

I SEE BY THE PAPERS THAT **GREEN LANTERN** HAS CAPTURED THE **PUPPET-MASTER!** NOW MAYBE HE'LL GIVE ME HIS UNDIVIDED ATTENTION... OH! THAT MUST BE HIM NOW...

♪ COME IN... ♪

KNOCK! KNOCK!

News Herald-Time

GREEN LANTERN CAPTURES

OH, IT'S YOU, HAL JORDAN! I WAS EXPECTING...

--GREEN LANTERN, I BET! IT'S A SNAP TO GET CAROL TO GO FOR ME AS **GL**--BUT I'M DETERMINED TO WIN HER OVER AS MY REAL SELF-- HAL JORDAN!

MORE THRILL-PACKED ADVEN-TURES OF GREEN LANTERN IN THE NEXT ISSUE!

The End

⑩

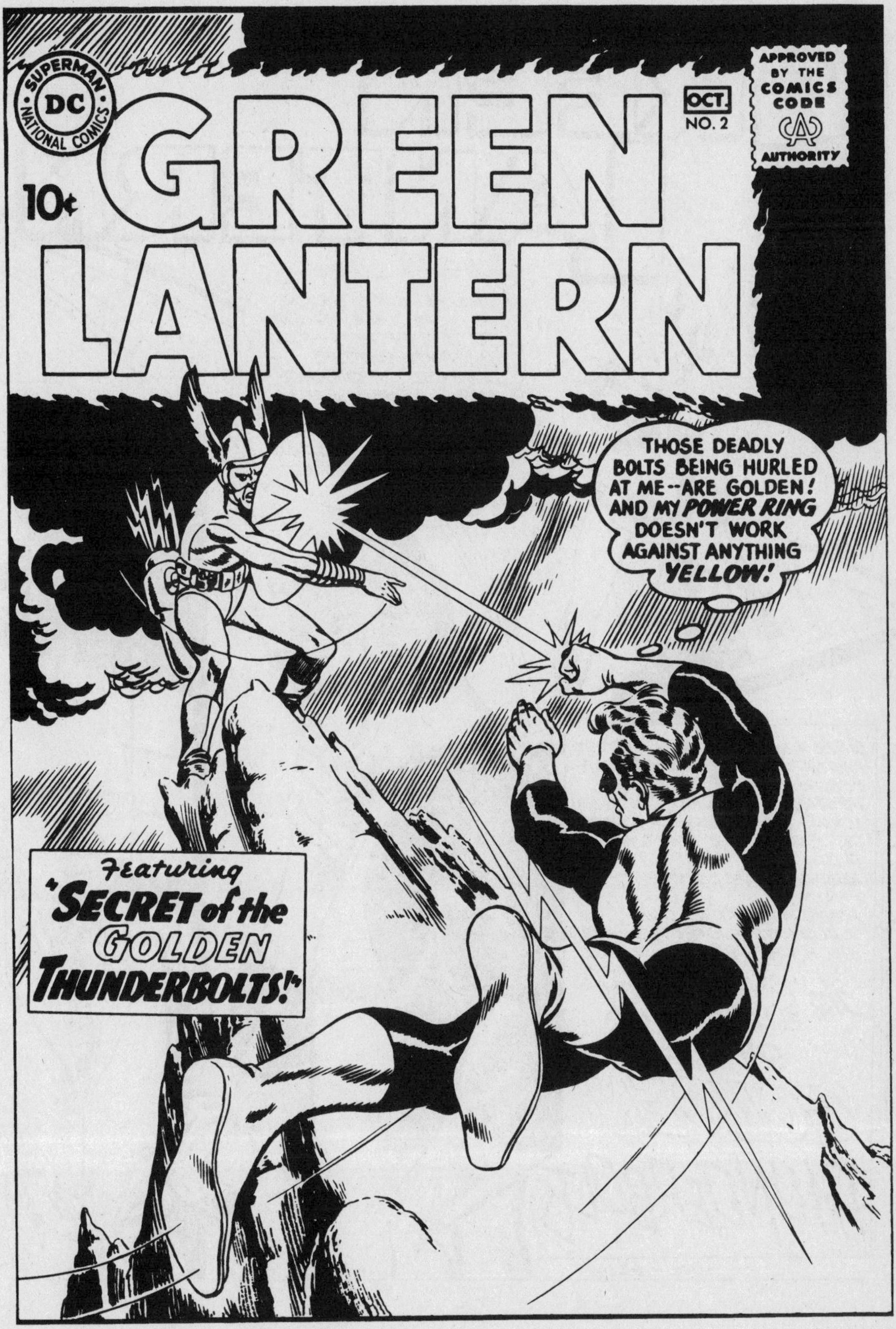
SUPERMAN DC NATIONAL COMICS
10¢
GREEN LANTERN
OCT. NO. 2
APPROVED BY THE COMICS CODE AUTHORITY
THOSE DEADLY BOLTS BEING HURLED AT ME--ARE GOLDEN! AND MY POWER RING DOESN'T WORK AGAINST ANYTHING YELLOW!
Featuring "SECRET of the GOLDEN THUNDERBOLTS!"

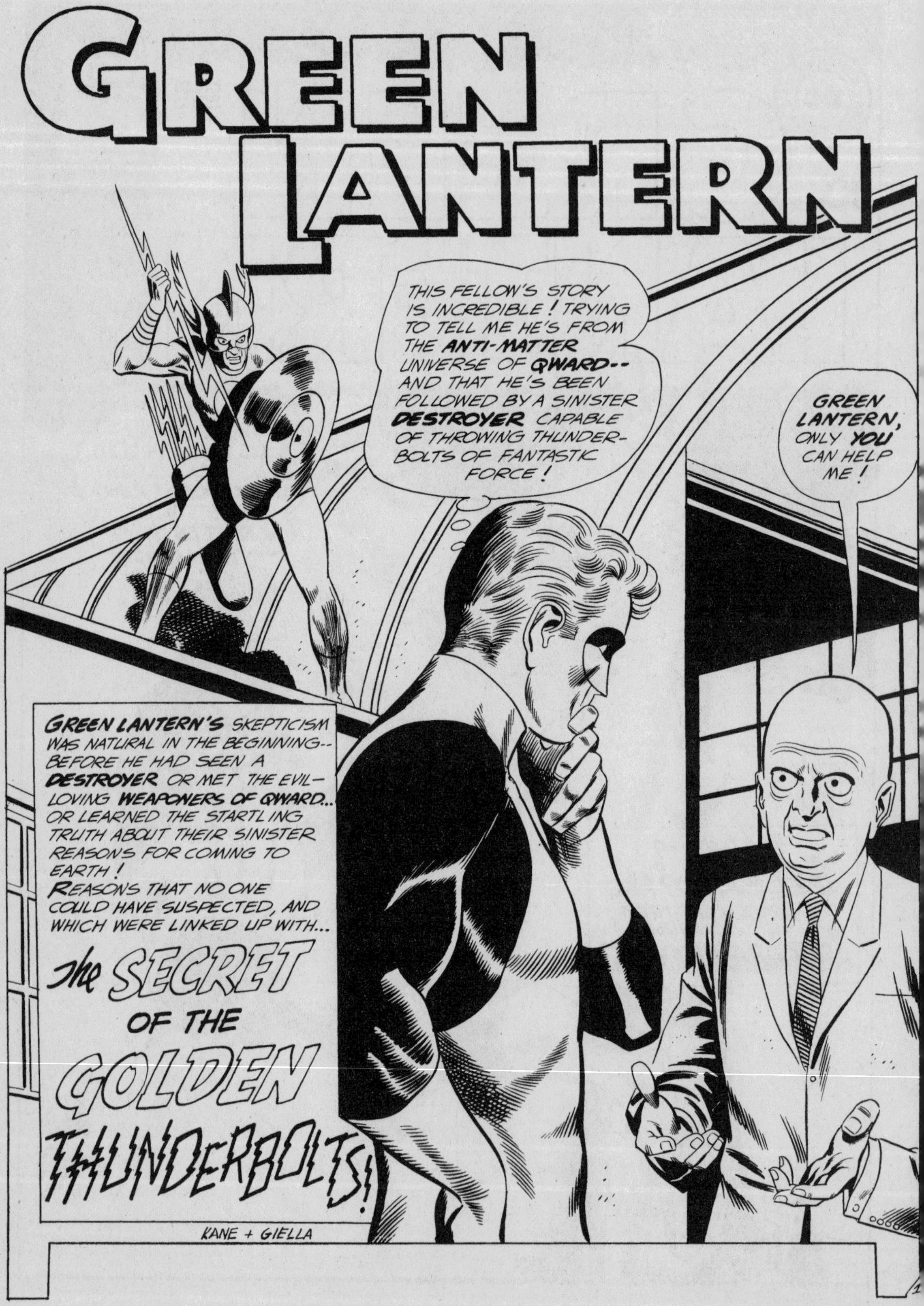
GREEN LANTERN
THIS FELLOW'S STORY IS INCREDIBLE! TRYING TO TELL ME HE'S FROM THE ANTI-MATTER UNIVERSE OF QWARD-- AND THAT HE'S BEEN FOLLOWED BY A SINISTER DESTROYER CAPABLE OF THROWING THUNDER-BOLTS OF FANTASTIC FORCE!
GREEN LANTERN, ONLY YOU CAN HELP ME!
GREEN LANTERN'S SKEPTICISM WAS NATURAL IN THE BEGINNING-- BEFORE HE HAD SEEN A DESTROYER OR MET THE EVIL-LOVING WEAPONERS OF QWARD... OR LEARNED THE STARTLING TRUTH ABOUT THEIR SINISTER REASONS FOR COMING TO EARTH! REASONS THAT NO ONE COULD HAVE SUSPECTED, AND WHICH WERE LINKED UP WITH...
The SECRET OF THE GOLDEN THUNDERBOLTS!
KANE + GIELLA

IN A CERTAIN WEST COAST CITY, ONE DAY...

GOOD GRACIOUS! WHAT IS THAT?

JEEPERS-- I WONDER HOW THAT HAPPENED?

WHO COULD HAVE CAUSED SUCH A THING?

WHAT ARE THEY SEEING...?

--A MYSTERIOUS CIRCULAR HOLE IN THE GROUND THAT STOPS ABRUPTLY AND LEADS NOWHERE AT ALL!

THE HOLE'S CUT ELECTRIC AND TELEPHONE LINES! HERE COMES AN EMERGENCY CREW TO REPAIR THEM!

AND ELSEWHERE IN THE CITY...

IT'S INCREDIBLE! IT LOOKS AS THOUGH SOMEONE BORED A HOLE RIGHT THROUGH THAT BUILDING!

LUCKILY NO ONE WAS IN IT! IT HAPPENED BEFORE ANYONE CAME TO WORK THIS MORNING!

WE'D BETTER NOTIFY THE AUTHORITIES!

MEANWHILE, UNAWARE OF THESE EVENTS, HAL JORDAN, ACE TEST PILOT, HAS OTHER THINGS ON HIS MIND THIS MOMENTOUS MORNING...

IT'S NO USE! CAROL HARDLY SEEMS TO NOTICE ME--AS HAL JORDAN! IT'S ONLY GREEN LANTERN--MY ALTER EGO-- SHE'S INTERESTED IN!

BUT I WANT TO WIN CAROL'S LOVE AS MYSELF--NOT AS *GREEN LANTERN*! I CAN'T BELIEVE THAT HER FEELING FOR *GL* IS ANYTHING BUT FASCINATION...

EH?

MR. HAL JORDAN?

YES, I'M HAL JORDAN! WHAT--?

MR. JORDAN, YOU MUST PUT ME IN TOUCH WITH *GREEN LANTERN* AT ONCE! IT IS OF THE UTMOST IMPORTANCE!

AS THE CRACK FLYER STARES IN SURPRISE AT THE ODD-LOOKING STRANGER...

I READ IN A NEWSPAPER COLUMN THAT YOU AND *GREEN LANTERN* WERE RIVALS FOR THE HAND OF MISS CAROL FERRIS! AND SINCE I DID NOT KNOW HOW TO CONTACT *GREEN LANTERN*...

YOU CAME TO ME? I SEE!

BUT *GREEN LANTERN* IS A--ER--PRETTY BUSY MAN! HE CAN'T DEAL WITH EVERY LITTLE PROBLEM THAT COMES ALONG...

"LITTLE" PROBLEMS? MR. JORDAN, PLEASE LOOK INTO MY EYES!

CURIOUS, HAL DOES AS HE IS BIDDEN...

GREAT DAY! WHAT AN EXTRAORDINARY SENSATION! I'M SEEING INCREDIBLE VISIONS--HIS *EYES* ARE TELLING ME A STORY--!

"I AM NOT OF YOUR WORLD, MR. JORDAN! I AM FROM THE UNIVERSE OF *QWARD*..."

"AN *ANTI-MATTER* UNIVERSE OCCUPYING THE SAME SPACE-CONTINUUM AS YOURS, BUT ON A DIFFERENT SPACE-TIME LEVEL!"

"YOU MAY ASK HOW I--A BEING OF ANTI-MATTER-- COULD EXIST HERE IN YOUR UNIVERSE, BUT I WILL ANSWER THAT IN DUE TIME..."

...MEAN- WHILE, MR. JORDAN, THE IMPORTANT THING I MUST BRING OUT TO YOU IS THAT OUR UNIVERSE OF *QWARD* HAS ALWAYS BEEN RULED BY EVIL-DOERS--AND LIFE THERE IS CONDUCTED ALONG LAWFUL *EVIL* LINES!

"BUT NOT ALL OF US ARE EVIL! SOME FRIENDS AND I USED TO MEET IN SECRET..."

BECAUSE WE ARE UNLAWFULLY **HONEST**, WE ARE HUNTED DOWN BY THE QWARD WEAPONERS AS **CRIMINALS**!

BECAUSE WE REFUSE TO **STEAL**, WE ARE DESPISED-- OUTCASTS!

YES! BUT MAYBE WE CAN *ESCAPE*...

ESCAPE? HOW, *TELLE-TEG? WHERE?*

I WILL EXPLAIN! AS YOU KNOW, I WORK AS A RECORD- KEEPER IN THE CITADEL OF THE *WEAPONERS!* THEY DO NOT SUSPECT THAT I AM *NOT* EVIL OR THEY WOULD HAVE IMPRISONED ME LONG AGO...

RECENTLY I LEARNED SOMETHING! THE *WEAPONERS* HAVE SUCCEEDED IN BUILD- ING A *TRANSFORMER BRIDGE* FROM OUR UNIVERSE TO THE *PLUS-MATTER* UNIVERSE IN THE SAME CONTINUUM AS OURS!

I DO NOT KNOW **WHY** THE WEAPONERS HAVE BUILT SUCH A BRIDGE--OR WHAT THEIR PLANS ARE! BUT RADIO-WAVE INFORMATION ABOUT THE OTHER UNIVERSE HAS COME TO US ACROSS THE BRIDGE! I HAVE LEARNED, FOR EXAMPLE, THAT THERE WAS ONCE A GROUP IN THE *PLUS-WORLD*...

...CALLED THE *PILGRIMS*... WHO FLED FROM OPPRESSION TO A NEW LAND! AND IT GAVE ME THIS IDEA-- WHY CAN'T **WE** WHO **HATE** EVIL FLEE TO THE OTHER UNIVERSE--WHERE IT IS *UNLAWFUL* TO BE *EVIL*--

--AND *LAWFUL* TO BE **HONEST**! OH! IF WE ONLY COULD, *TELLE-TEG!*

14

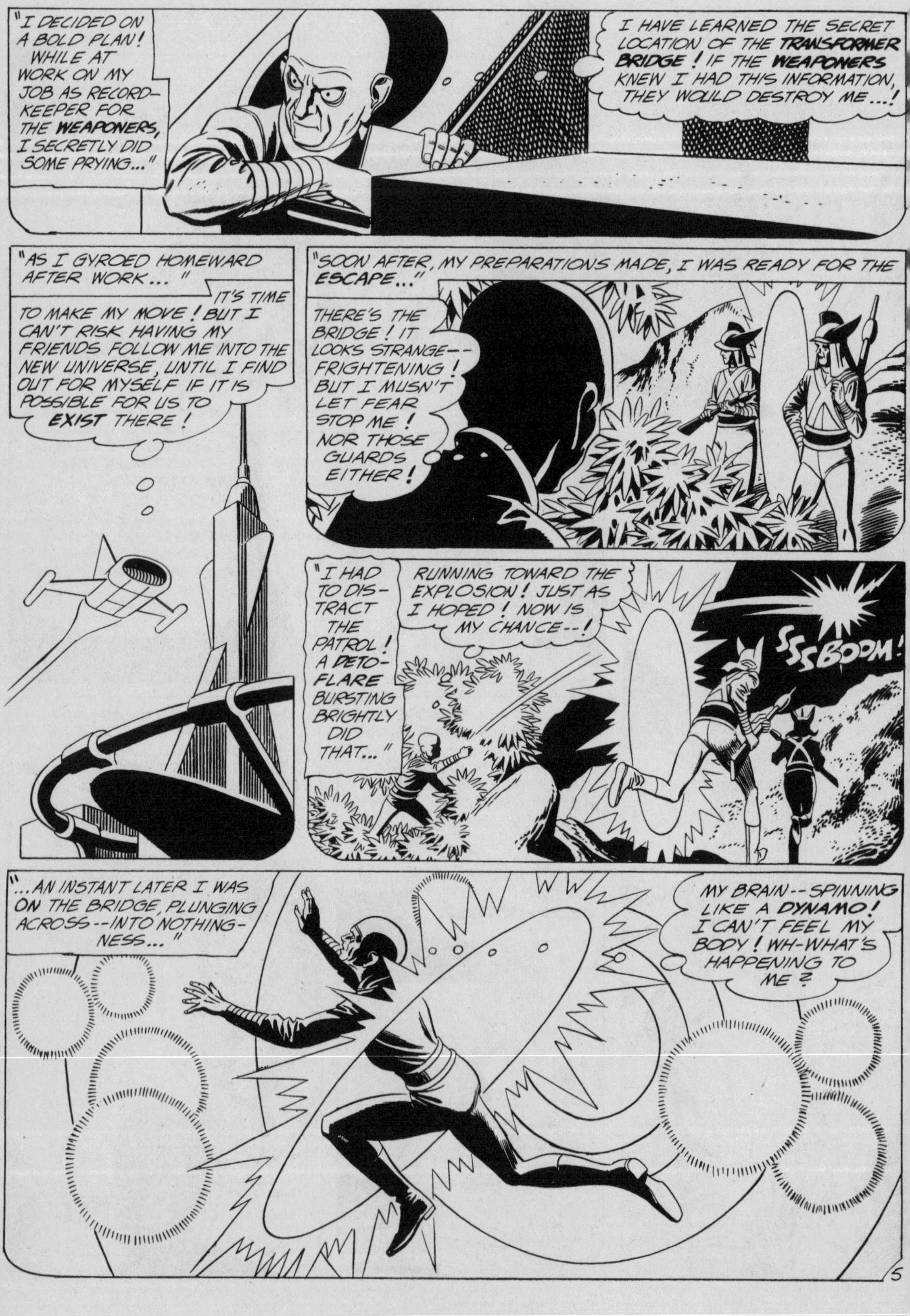
"I DECIDED ON A BOLD PLAN! WHILE AT WORK ON MY JOB AS RECORD-KEEPER FOR THE WEAPONERS, I SECRETLY DID SOME PRYING..."
I HAVE LEARNED THE SECRET LOCATION OF THE TRANSFORMER BRIDGE! IF THE WEAPONERS KNEW I HAD THIS INFORMATION, THEY WOULD DESTROY ME...!
"AS I GYROED HOMEWARD AFTER WORK..."
IT'S TIME TO MAKE MY MOVE! BUT I CAN'T RISK HAVING MY FRIENDS FOLLOW ME INTO THE NEW UNIVERSE, UNTIL I FIND OUT FOR MYSELF IF IT IS POSSIBLE FOR US TO EXIST THERE!
"SOON AFTER, MY PREPARATIONS MADE, I WAS READY FOR THE ESCAPE..."
THERE'S THE BRIDGE! IT LOOKS STRANGE-- FRIGHTENING! BUT I MUSN'T LET FEAR STOP ME! NOR THOSE GUARDS EITHER!
"I HAD TO DISTRACT THE PATROL! A DETO-FLARE BURSTING BRIGHTLY DID THAT..."
RUNNING TOWARD THE EXPLOSION! JUST AS I HOPED! NOW IS MY CHANCE--!
SSSBOOM!
"...AN INSTANT LATER I WAS ON THE BRIDGE, PLUNGING ACROSS--INTO NOTHING-NESS..."
MY BRAIN--SPINNING LIKE A DYNAMO! I CAN'T FEEL MY BODY! WH-WHAT'S HAPPENING TO ME?
5

"THEN, JUST AS SUDDENLY..."

THROUGH! AND ALIVE! SOMEHOW THE BRIDGE MUST HAVE REVERSED THE ATOMS IN MY BODY--TURNED THEM INTO PLUS-ATOMS OF THIS UNIVERSE!

-GASP- I'M

"AFTER THAT, IT DID NOT TAKE ME LONG TO LEARN YOUR LANGUAGE, TO APPEAR LIKE ONE OF YOU.."

NO ONE REALIZES THAT I AM A BEING FROM ANOTHER UNIVERSE! THE PEOPLE HERE HARDLY GIVE ME A SECOND GLANCE WHEN THEY SEE ME!

CAKE

AND I'VE LEARNED WHAT I WANT TO KNOW! THIS UNIVERSE IS THE OPPOSITE OF OURS IN EVERY WAY! IT IS RULED ALONG PRINCIPLES OF **GOOD** INSTEAD OF **EVIL**!

LAST NIGHT I WAS READY TO RETURN TO MY FRIENDS IN ORDER TO GUIDE THEM HERE! I HAD DISCOVERED THAT CHEMICALLY WE COULD EXIST IN THIS COSMOS OF YOURS! BUT THEN--**IT HAPPENED**!

WHAT WAS THAT?

"I WAS STARTING BACK! AT FIRST I SAW ONLY A SHADOW, BUT THAT WAS ENOUGH..."

A **DESTROYER OF THE WEAPONERS**! THEY HAVE FOLLOWED ME!

"BY A MIRACLE I DODGED THE **QWA-BOLT**! IT MISSED ME, BUT STRUCK A BUILDING..."

6

"I RAN! THE DESTROYER CHASED ME! SOMEHOW I ESCAPED AND HID!"

THERE IS ONLY ONE PERSON IN THIS WORLD WHO CAN HELP ME! ONLY **ONE** WHO CAN POSSIBLY DEFEAT A **DESTROYER**--AND SAVE ME AND MY FRIENDS! I MUST GET IN TOUCH WITH THE MAN CALLED **GREEN LANTERN!**

AND THAT'S WHY I HAVE COME TO YOU, MR. JORDAN!

AN INCREDIBLE TALE, AND YET IT HAS THE RING OF TRUTH! BUT THERE'S ONE WAY I CAN FIND OUT FOR CERTAIN...

WAIT HERE A MOMENT, MR. TELLE-TEG! THERE'S--ER--JUST A POSSIBILITY THAT I MIGHT BE ABLE TO CONTACT GREEN LANTERN FOR YOU...

PLEASE, MR. JORDAN-- HURRY!

BEHIND THE LOCKED DOORS OF HIS DRESSING ROOM AT THE AIRFIELD HANGAR...

I'LL TAKE TELLE-TEG BACK TO THAT BRIDGE OF HIS! IF IT REALLY EXISTS, I'LL KNOW HE ISN'T JUST SOME CRACKPOT WHO HAD A BAD DREAM!

AT HIS MYSTIC LAMP, THE **GREEN GLADIATOR** RECHARGES HIS RING FOR ANOTHER TWENTY-FOUR HOURS OF POWER...

IN BRIGHTEST DAY, IN BLACKEST NIGHT, NO EVIL SHALL ESCAPE MY SIGHT! LET THOSE WHO WORSHIP EVIL'S MIGHT BEWARE MY POWER-- GREEN LANTERN'S LIGHT!

THEN...

GREEN LANTERN! LOOK OUT!

THE **DESTROYER** HE SPOKE ABOUT!? THIS PROVES THE STORY WAS TRUE! BUT THAT TERRIBLE BOLT HE'S HURLING AT ME-- IT'S GOLDEN-- YELLOW! AND MY RING HAS NO POWER OVER ANYTHING YELLOW!*

*Editor's Note: DUE TO A NECESSARY IMPURITY IN ITS VERY NATURE, **GREEN LANTERN'S** MYSTIC RING IS POWERLESS AGAINST ANY-THING YELLOW!

AT THAT SAME MOMENT...

TELLE-TEG KNOCKED US BOTH OVER--OUT OF THE WAY OF THAT AWFUL BLAST!

AS THE EMERALD WARRIOR LEAPS TO HIS FEET AGAIN...

TELLE-TEG SAVED MY LIFE-- GAVE ME A CHANCE TO DEAL WITH THIS ASSASSIN FROM ANOTHER UNIVERSE!

BUT AS THE ALL-POWERFUL FIST FROM **GL's** RING FLASHES OUT, THE **DESTROYER** INTERRUPTS IT WITH HIS GOLDEN SHIELD AND...

MY OWN BEAM-- SHOOTING BACK AT ME!

QUICKLY, THE **GREEN-CLAD CHAMPION** DUCKS AWAY FROM HIS OWN POWER-FIST...

ABOUT TO HURL ANOTHER **QWA-BOLT** AT ME! ONLY ONE THING TO DO NOW--!

STORY CONTINUED ON FOLLOWING PAGE.

8

USING THE FULL POWERS OF HIS MAGIC BEAM, **GL** RENDERS HIMSELF **INVISIBLE**...

WHERE--

HE CAN'T SEE ME--DOESN'T KNOW WHERE TO THROW THAT BOLT! I'VE GOT TO USE THIS OPPORTUNITY TO THROW MY BEAM PAST HIS SHIELD--!

BEFORE HIS UNCANNY FOE CAN MAKE ANOTHER MOVE, **GREEN LANTERN** CASTS A **POWER-LASSO** OVER HIM...

SNARED HIM-- EH?

UHH!

AS THE CRUSADER'S EYES WHIRL MOMENTARILY TO A STRICKEN FIGURE BESIDE HIM...

TELLE-TEG! HE'S HURT--!!

GROAN!

AN INSTANT LATER, WHEN THE **RING-WIELDER** TURNS HIS ATTENTION BACK TOWARD HIS FOE...

GETTING AWAY! DURING THE DISTRACTING MOMENT THAT I TURNED ASIDE, HE MANAGED TO BREAK LOOSE FROM MY GREEN BEAM! BUT I CAN'T CHASE HIM-- MUST SEE TO **TELLE-TEG**!

BUT THEN...

DEAD... IT'S ALL OVER FOR HIM! THAT BLAST HE SAVED ME FROM--HE MUST HAVE BEEN NICKED BY THE EDGE OF IT--ENOUGH TO FINISH HIM! HE SACRIFICED HIS LIFE...TO SAVE MINE!

GRIMLY THE *EMERALD CRUSADER*, VISIBLE ONCE AGAIN, TURNS FROM A FALLEN FRIEND...

ALTHOUGH I CAN DO NOTHING FOR *TELLE-TEG* NOW--I RESOLVE TO CARRY OUT HIS MISSION--HELP HIS FRIENDS ENTER THIS UNIVERSE, AS HE WOULD HAVE DONE! BUT HOW CAN I FIND THAT BRIDGE WITHOUT--? WAIT--!

THAT *DESTROYER* MUST HAVE HEADED BACK TOWARD THE BRIDGE! BUT ALL THAT POWER HE PACKS WOULD LEAVE A RADIO-ACTIVE TRAIL-- FAINT--BUT MAYBE ENOUGH FOR MY RING TO PICK IT OUT!

I THINK I'VE GOT IT! MY RING IS ACTING LIKE A SORT OF *GEIGER-COUNTER*-- REGISTERING THE RADIATION LEFT IN THE AIR BY THE PASSAGE OF THE *DESTROYER*! I'M ON HIS TRACK!

SOON...

THERE IT IS! A HOLE INTO NOTHING-NESS ON THAT SIDE OF THE HILL--!

WITHOUT HESITATION, THE *INTREPID CRUSADER* PLUNGES INTO THE UNEARTHLY OPENING...

WHEW! IF *TELLE-TEG* HADN'T DESCRIBED THIS FANTASTIC SENSATION TO ME--I'D THINK I WAS COMING APART AT THE SEAMS! BUT I MUST KEEP GOING...

THEN, SUDDENLY...

MADE IT! THIS MUST BE THE *ANTI-MATTER UNIVERSE* OF QWARD! AND THERE ARE THE GUARDS *TELLE-TEG* SPOKE ABOUT!

10

BACKED BY **GL's** INDOMITABLE WILL POWER, THE GREEN BEAM FLASHES OUT WITH CRUSHING FORCE...

CAN'T STOP TO GET INTO A FIGHT WITH THESE PATROLS! I'VE GOT MORE IMPORTANT THINGS TO DO HERE!

AS THE EMERALD **WARRIOR** RUSHES ONWARD...

I OUGHT TO BE ABLE TO RECOGNIZE THE HIDING PLACE WHERE **TELLE-TEG'S** FRIENDS MEET IN SECRET--FROM THE DESCRIPTION IN THE ACCOUNT HE GAVE ME!

MEANWHILE IN THE CITADEL OF THE **WEAPONERS**..

WE HAVE THE BAND OF GOOD-DOERS SURROUNDED, KRAMEN! SHALL WE DESTROY THEM?

YES, IF THEY DO NOT SURRENDER AT ONCE!

AND AT THE MEETING PLACE OF THE TINY GROUP, AN AMPLIFIED TELEPATHIC VOICE PENETRATES THE INTERIOR...

SURRENDER-- OR PERISH!

WE'VE BEEN FOUND BY THE WEAPONERS!

WE CAN'T GIVE UP! IT WOULD MEAN A RAY-CELL FOR LIFE!

THEY ARE DEFYING US! FIRE AT THEM!

BUT JUST AS A DISINTEGRATIVE VOLLEY OF OVERPOWERING MIGHT HURTLES AT THE DWELLING, IT FANTASTICALLY IS COVERED BY AN IMPENETRABLE GREEN BUBBLE...

LOOKS LIKE I GOT HERE JUST IN TIME!

/11

WITH COLD FURY, THE **GREEN GLADIATOR** TURNS HIS RING ON THE MINIONS OF EVIL...

MY BEAM HAS CREATED A STINGING RAIN OF TINY STEEL PELLETS -- SHOWERING DOWN ON THEM, DRIVING THEM OFF!

A MOMENT LATER...

THEY'VE SENT IN A **THUNDERBOLT DESTROYER**! I CAN HANDLE HIM, IF I ACT **FAST** --!

FROM THE POWER BEAM EMERGES A **CHARGING FOOTBALL PLAYER** OF HUGE BULK, TO STRIKE THE **DESTROYER** FROM BEHIND BEFORE HE CAN LOOSE A BOLT!

WELL, I THINK THAT TAKES **HIM** OUT OF THE GAME!

THEN, RUSHING BACK TO TELLE-TEG'S FRIENDS...

YOU'RE ALL COMING WITH ME! HURRY! I'LL EXPLAIN AS WE GO!

SOON, ON THE **EARTH-SIDE** OF THE **TRANSFORMER-BRIDGE**...

THERE! I'VE DESTROYED THE BRIDGE-- AND SEALED UP THE OPENING! IF THE **WEAPONERS** BUILD ANOTHER BRIDGE AND TRY TO COME THROUGH, I'LL BE READY FOR THEM!

YOU'VE SAVED OUR LIVES, **GREEN LANTERN**!

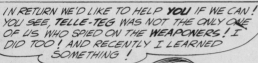

IN RETURN WE'D LIKE TO HELP **YOU** IF WE CAN! YOU SEE, **TELLE-TEG** WAS NOT THE ONLY ONE OF US WHO SPIED ON THE **WEAPONERS**! I DID TOO! AND RECENTLY I LEARNED SOMETHING!

AS THE GRATEFUL **QWARDIAN** REVEALS HIS SECRET...

WHAT?! THE **WEAPONERS** ARE OUT TO GAIN POSSESSION OF ALL THE **POWER BATTERIES** IN THIS UNIVERSE?

YES! BUT I CANNOT TELL YOU WHY THEY WANT THE BATTERIES -- OR WHAT THEIR ULTIMATE AIM IS! I KNOW NO MORE...

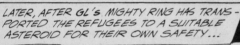

LATER, AFTER GL'S MIGHTY RING HAS TRANSPORTED THE REFUGEES TO A SUITABLE ASTEROID FOR THEIR OWN SAFETY...

FAREWELL... AND THANKS, GREEN LANTERN!

THE **WEAPONERS** WILL NEVER FIND **TELLE-TEG'S** FRIENDS WHERE I'VE LEFT THEM! ON THAT ASTEROID THEY HAVE WATER, FOOD, AND AIR -- AND THEY CAN BUILD THEIR LIVES FROM NOW ON IN FREEDOM!

AS A WEARY GLADIATOR RESTS FROM HIS LABORS...

SO THE **WEAPONERS** WANT THE MYSTIC LAMPS -- SUCH AS MINE! SOMETHING TELLS ME I HAVEN'T HEARD THE LAST OF THEM -- NOT BY A LONG QWA-SHOT!

FOR FURTHER STARTLING DEVELOPMENTS INVOLVING THE AMAZING **WEAPONERS** OF THE UNIVERSE OF **QWARD,** SEE FUTURE ISSUES OF **GREEN LANTERN** MAGAZINE!

The End

GREEN
LANTERN

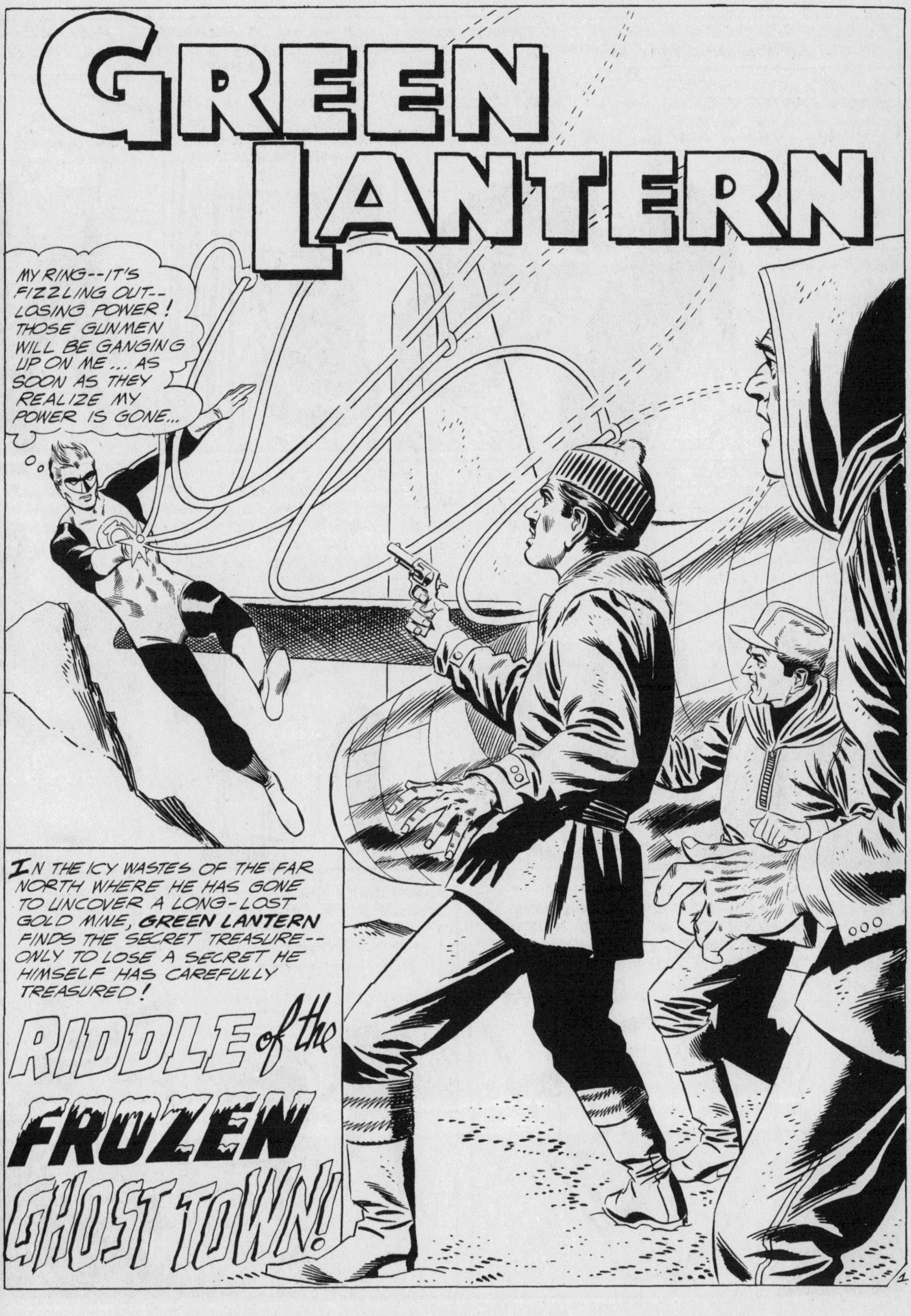
GREEN LANTERN
MY RING--IT'S FIZZLING OUT--LOSING POWER! THOSE GUNMEN WILL BE GANGING UP ON ME... AS SOON AS THEY REALIZE MY POWER IS GONE...
IN THE ICY WASTES OF THE FAR NORTH WHERE HE HAS GONE TO UNCOVER A LONG-LOST GOLD MINE, GREEN LANTERN FINDS THE SECRET TREASURE--ONLY TO LOSE A SECRET HE HIMSELF HAS CAREFULLY TREASURED!
RIDDLE of the FROZEN GHOST TOWN!
1

IN THE OFFICE OF CAROL FERRIS, TEMPORARY CHIEF OF THE **FERRIS AIRCRAFT COMPANY**...

BUT **WHY** DO YOU PREFER **GREEN LANTERN** TO ME, CAROL? IS HE BETTER LOOKING-- HAVE A MORE PLEASING PERSONALITY-- MORE STERLING CHARACTER--*

I DID NOT SUMMON YOU HERE TO QUIZ ME ON MY SOCIAL LIFE!

MR. JORDAN,

*Editor's Note:
THERE'S NO DOUBT ABOUT THE ANSWERS AS FAR AS HAL JORDAN IS CONCERNED--FOR IN HIS SECRET IDENTITY, **HE IS GREEN LANTERN!**

NOW--DOWN TO **BUSINESS**! WE'VE JUST RECEIVED NOTICE--**THOMAS KALMAKU**, YOUR MECHANIC, IS LEAVING AT THE END OF THE WEEK! WE'LL HAVE TO HIRE SOMEONE ELSE!

PIEFACE-- QUITTING?!

AS THE ACE TEST PILOT EXHIBITS EXTREME CONCERN AT THE NEWS...

LET HIM GO, CAROL! THAT ESKIMO IS A WIZARD WITH JET ENGINES AND I COULDN'T DO WITHOUT HIM! GIVE HIM A RAISE! HE'S GOT TO STAY!

WE CAN'T! HE SAID IT WASN'T MONEY! BUT IF YOU WANT TO TALK TO HIM, HAL, GO AHEAD...

SHORTLY... I WONDER WHAT'S GOT INTO **PIEFACE**? LAST TIME I SAW HIM, HE DIDN'T ACT LIKE THERE WAS ANYTHING WRONG! BUT I REALIZE NOW HOW LITTLE I KNOW ABOUT HIM-- ONLY THAT HE SERVED WITH OUR ARMED FORCES IN ALASKA...

...WHERE HE GOT TO BE AN EXPERT ON SERVICING JETS! AND THAT AFTERWARDS HE CAME DOWN HERE TO THE STATES AND GOT A JOB WITH THE **FERRIS COMPANY**--AS MY MECHANIC! HE AND I ALWAYS WORKED TOGETHER PERFECTLY--

EH?

GREAT DAY! THERE'S **PIEFACE** NOW--IN A TUSSLE WITH TWO BIG LUGS! NO TIME TO CHANGE TO MY **GREEN LANTERN** COSTUME!

AS THE CRACK AIRMAN PILES UNHESITATINGLY INTO THE FRAY...

WHAT'S GOING ON HERE?

HAL!

TWO OF YOU HEAVYWEIGHTS GANGING ON ONE LITTLE GUY? THAT'S NOT SPORTING--

SUDDENLY...

LOOKS LIKE THEY'VE DECIDED TO BREAK OFF HOSTILITIES!

AW, LET THEM GO, HAL! IT WAS JUST AN ACCIDENT--!

AN ACCIDENT?

YEAH! I WAS WALKING ALONG AND BUMPED INTO ONE OF THEM --AND THE NEXT THING I KNEW THE FIGHT STARTED! I NEVER SAW THEM BE-FORE--AN' BESIDES I'VE GOT SOME-THING MORE IMPORTANT ON MY MIND...

AS THE MECHANIC CONFIRMS HIS INTENTION OF LEAVING FERRIS...

BUT WHY? I CAN'T UNDERSTAND, PIE-FACE! HAVEN'T YOU BEEN HAPPY HERE?

SURE I HAVE! IT'S BEEN TERRIFIC-- WORKING WITH SOMEONE LIKE YOU! BUT I'VE GOT TO GO HOME!

BACK TO ALASKA?

--AND BACK TO MY PEOPLE! I NEVER TOLD YOU WHY I CAME DOWN HERE TO THE STATES, HAL! I GUESS I BETTER EXPLAIN NOW...

3

"LAST YEAR MY FATHER AND A WHITE TRAPPER NAMED JIMMY DAWES WERE TAKING A TRIP IN THE FAR NORTH, WHEN SUDDENLY..."

WHAT'S THAT? A HOLE IN THE ROCK, KALMAKU?

LET'S TAKE LOOK!

"THE 'Hole In The Rock' TURNED OUT TO BE AN OPENING IN A CAVERN LINED WITH RICH GOLD-BEARING MINERALS!"

KAL, WE'VE FOUND A FORTUNE! BUT IT WILL TAKE MONEY TO WORK THIS MINE! I'LL GO SOUTH TO RAISE THE FUNDS! MEANWHILE YOU CAN GO BACK TO YOUR VILLAGE...

GOOD! WILL WAIT FOR YOU, JIMMY...!

"THE TWO PARTNERS MADE A CAREFUL MAP OF THE AREA, THEN TORE IT EXACTLY IN HALF..."

THE ONLY WAY WE'LL FIND THIS CAVERN AGAIN, KAL, IS WHEN I RETURN AND WE PUT BOTH OF THESE MAP-HALVES TOGETHER! THIS PROTECTS BOTH OF US!

UNDERSTAND!

NOT LONG AFTER POP CAME BACK TO THE VILLAGE, HE CAME DOWN WITH A FATAL ILLNESS! BEFORE HE DIED HE PASSED ON HIS HALF OF THE MAP TO ME! I WAITED AND WAITED FOR HIS PARTNER DAWES TO COME...

...BUT HE NEVER SHOWED UP! THAT'S WHEN I DECIDED TO COME TO THE STATES--TO LOOK FOR HIM! YOU SEE, MY PEOPLE ARE VERY POOR! I WANTED TO HELP THEM WITH MY SHARE OF THE GOLD...

SO THAT'S WHAT YOU'VE BEEN DOING ON YOUR TIME OFF...

YEAH! HUNTING FOR JAMES DAWES AND THE OTHER HALF OF THIS MAP--UHH?!

GREAT FISH-HOOKS! MY MAP--THE HALF I TOLD YOU ABOUT-- IT'S GONE! I'M SURE I HAD IT ON ME A FEW MOMENTS AGO--

AS THE TRUTH DAWNS ON THE LITTLE MECHANIC...

THOSE MEN! THEY MUST HAVE BUMPED ME **ON PURPOSE**-- AND PICKED MY POCKET!

TOO LATE NOW TO TRY TO FIND THE THUGS--

HAL, THIS IS AWFUL! THAT MAP MEANT EVERYTHING TO ME--A GOLDEN OPPORTUNITY TO HELP MY PEOPLE! I... I'VE LET THEM DOWN!

MAYBE THERE'S A WAY I CAN HELP, PIE-FACE...

AS GREEN LANTERN I COULD USE MY **POWER RING** TO PROBE INTO HIS MIND--AND RE-COVER HIS PRECIOUS MAP-HALF! BUT I CAN'T LET HIM SUSPECT WHAT I'M ABOUT TO DO...

SORRY I CAN'T HELP OUT, PIEFACE! I'VE--er GOT SOME THINGS ON TAP! WE'LL TALK SOME MORE LATER, eh?

er--SURE! GOSH! HE'S NOT VERY SYMPATHETIC!

ONCE OUT OF SIGHT, HAL SPRINTS FOR HIS DRESSING ROOM WHERE MOMENTS LATER, A SOLEMN OATH IS REPEATED...

IN BRIGHTEST DAY, IN BLACKEST NIGHT, NO EVIL SHALL ESCAPE MY SIGHT! LET THOSE WHO WORSHIP EVIL'S MIGHT BEWARE MY POWER-- GREEN LANTERN'S LIGHT!

Editor's Note: CHARGING HIS RING AT HIS MYSTIC LAMP GIVES **GREEN LANTERN** TWENTY-FOUR HOURS OF POWER!

5

SOON... HI, *PIEFACE!* YOU'RE HAL JORDAN'S MECHANIC, AREN'T YOU? I JUST MET HAL--AND HE TOLD ME ALL ABOUT YOU AND YOUR PROBLEM!

H-HE *DID?*

YEP! HE EVEN SUGGESTED I MIGHT BE ABLE TO HELP YOU! WE'LL START BY FINDING THAT PRECIOUS MAP-HALF OF YOURS--

B-BUT HOW...

HOLD STILL! I'M GOING TO USE MY RING TO PROBE YOUR BRAIN--AND TRY TO FIND THE HIDDEN MEMORY-TRACES OF THAT MAP!

GREAT FISH-HOOKS!

AS THE GREAT GREEN BEAM PEERS INTO THE MIND, THE MOST MYSTERIOUS AREA IN A HUMAN.

YOU SEE, *PIEFACE,* THE MERE FACT THAT YOU *LOOKED* AT THE MAP WOULD CAUSE YOUR BRAIN TO RETAIN A MEMORY OF IT...

AH, IT'S COMING THROUGH!! HOW ABOUT IT, *PIEFACE?*

IT'S MY MAP-HALF! NO DOUBT OF IT!

LATER, AFTER A DRAWING HAS BEEN MADE OF THE ENERGY-IMAGE, *GL* SPRINGS ANOTHER SURPRISE...

PIEFACE, HOW WOULD YOU LIKE ME TO GO ALONG WITH YOU AND TRY TO FIND THE *GOLD MINE* WITH THE AID OF THIS MAP?

I--I'D LIKE NOTHING BETTER!

NOT LONG AFTERWARD, TWO FIGURES SPEED NORTHWARD ON THE WINGS OF A BLAZING GREEN BEAM...

HAL JORDAN HAS--er--DONE ME A FEW FAVORS, AND THIS WILL BE MY WAY OF RETURNING THEM!

GREEN LANTERN, YOU MAKE EVERYTHING SEEM SO EASY-- BUT I STILL DON'T UNDERSTAND--

HOW DO YOU EXPECT TO FIND THE MINE WITH ONLY **HALF** THE MAP?

THAT MAY NOT BE AS HARD AS IT SOUNDS, **PIEFACE!** OUR HALF IS THE FIRST HALF OF THE SECRET TRAIL TO THE MINE! WE'LL GO ALONG IT AS FAR AS WE CAN--AND THEN LEAVE IT TO MY **RING** TO TAKE OVER FROM THEN ON--!

AS A LABORIOUS TRAIL-TRACKING BEGINS...

THIS FROZEN BAY IS WHERE OUR MAP BEGINS! FROM HERE WE TRAVEL DUE WEST...

WITH EASE THE MYSTIC BEAM ACTS LIKE A COMPASS POINTING OUT THE WAY...

OUR NEXT LANDMARK IS A SMALL GLACIER, AND WE'VE GOT TO BE CAREFUL NOT TO GO PAST IT! THIS IS GOING TO TAKE TIME!

MANY HOURS LATER...

WHAT'S THIS OUR TRAIL HAS LED TO--?

IT'S **CAMP ARCTIC**--A FROZEN GHOST TOWN! POP TOLD ME ABOUT THIS PLACE! YEARS AGO IT USED TO BE A BUSTLING MINE CAMP, THEN IT WAS ABANDONED! BUT IT'S STILL PERFECTLY PRESERVED-- DUE TO THE GREAT COLD IN THIS VALLEY!

7

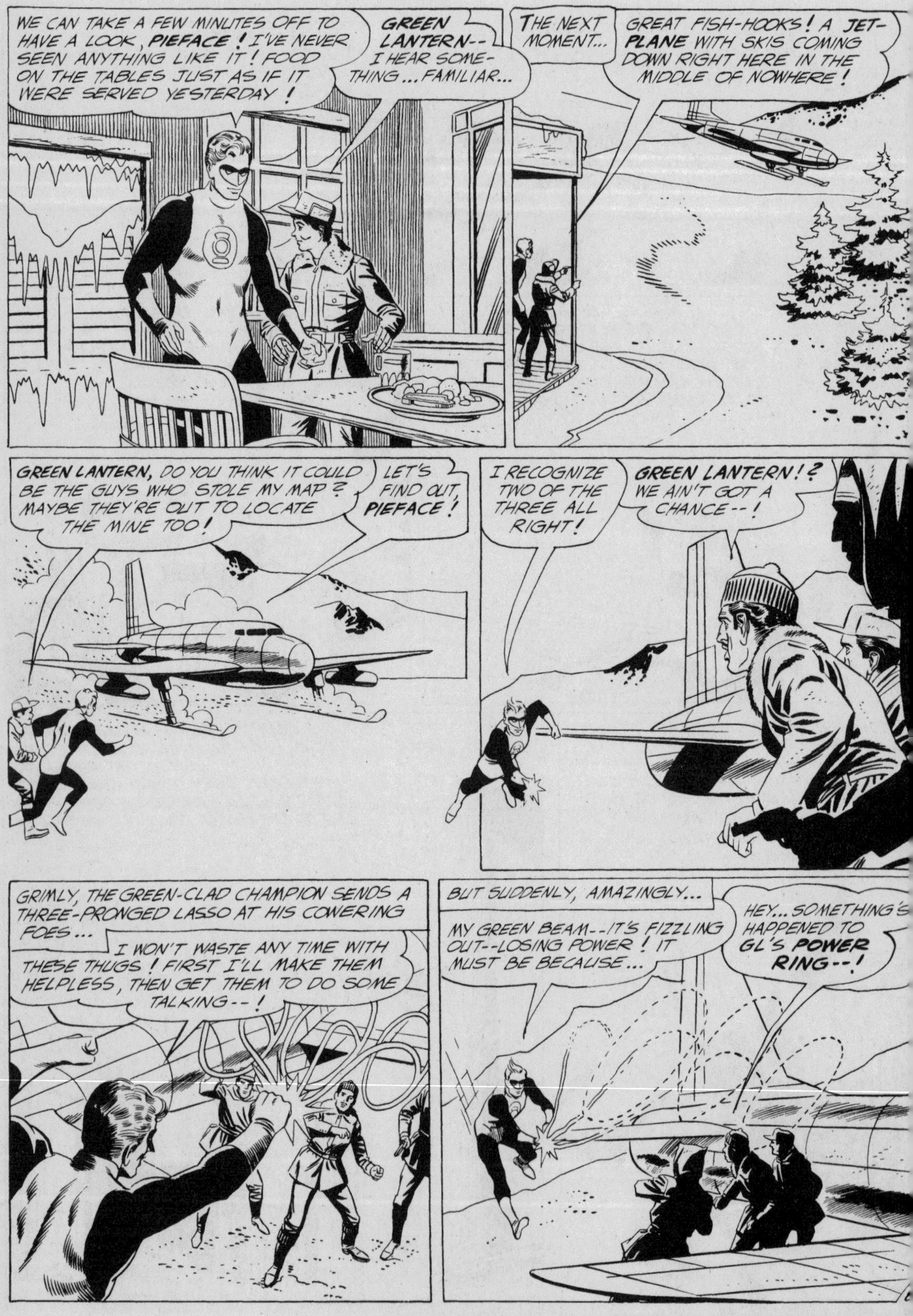
WE CAN TAKE A FEW MINUTES OFF TO HAVE A LOOK, PIEFACE! I'VE NEVER SEEN ANYTHING LIKE IT! FOOD ON THE TABLES JUST AS IF IT WERE SERVED YESTERDAY!
GREEN LANTERN-- I HEAR SOMETHING...FAMILIAR...
THE NEXT MOMENT...
GREAT FISH-HOOKS! A JET-PLANE WITH SKIS COMING DOWN RIGHT HERE IN THE MIDDLE OF NOWHERE!
GREEN LANTERN, DO YOU THINK IT COULD BE THE GUYS WHO STOLE MY MAP? MAYBE THEY'RE OUT TO LOCATE THE MINE TOO!
LET'S FIND OUT, PIEFACE!
I RECOGNIZE TWO OF THE THREE ALL RIGHT!
GREEN LANTERN!? WE AIN'T GOT A CHANCE--!
GRIMLY, THE GREEN-CLAD CHAMPION SENDS A THREE-PRONGED LASSO AT HIS COWERING FOES...
I WON'T WASTE ANY TIME WITH THESE THUGS! FIRST I'LL MAKE THEM HELPLESS, THEN GET THEM TO DO SOME TALKING--!
BUT SUDDENLY, AMAZINGLY...
MY GREEN BEAM--IT'S FIZZLING OUT--LOSING POWER! IT MUST BE BECAUSE...
HEY...SOMETHING'S HAPPENED TO GL'S POWER RING--!

AS THE TRUTH DAWNS ON THE EMERALD WARRIOR...

THE TWENTY-FOUR HOURS ARE ALMOST UP-- MY RING NEEDS *RECHARGING*--!

PILE INTO HIM-- WHILE WE STILL GOT A CHANCE!

GREAT FISH-HOOKS!

UNDER THE COMBINED ATTACK, THE *GREEN GLADIATOR* GOES DOWN, AND OUT...

HOLD IT, SHRIMP--!

YOU MUGS DON'T SCARE ME--

THAT'LL HOLD HIM!

WHAT ARE WE GONNA DO WITH *GREEN LANTERN*, DUKE? AS LONG AS HE'S ALIVE, HE COULD STYMIE OUR ACTION!

I'M WELL AWARE OF THAT, WEEPER...

...THAT'S WHY I'M GOING TO PLAY A GAME OF *FREEZE-OUT* WITH HIM! WEEPER, THERE'S A WATER SPRAY CAN IN OUR PLANE! BRING IT TO ME...

SOON, BACK AT THE DANCE PALACE IN THE FROZEN GHOST TOWN...

YOU'RE SPRAYING *GREEN LANTERN* WITH WATER, DUKE? WHAT'S THE IDEA?

THIS VALLEY *NEVER* GETS ABOVE *FREEZING*, WEEPER! WE'RE TURNING *GL* INTO A PERMANENT STATUE!

SINCE NO ONE EVER COMES HERE, *GREEN LANTERN* WILL BE A PART OF THIS FROZEN GHOST TOWN-- FOREVER!

HA! HA! WE'VE IMPROVED THIS PLACE 100 PERCENT!

AS THE TRIO DEPARTS...

UH-H-- WHERE... AM I...?

CAN'T MOVE...! ICE COVERING ME... LIKE STEEL! AND MY RING IS WITHOUT POWER...! HOW CAN I GET OUT OF THIS?

IN THE EMERGENCY, *GREEN LANTERN'S* INDOMITABLE WILL SOARS TO THE FORE...

EVEN THOUGH MY RING IS PRACTICALLY EXHAUSTED, THERE MAY BE JUST A TINY BIT OF POWER LEFT IN IT! GOT TO TRY...

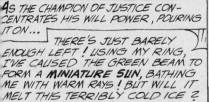

AS THE CHAMPION OF JUSTICE CONCENTRATES HIS WILL POWER, POURING IT ON...

THERE'S JUST BARELY ENOUGH LEFT! USING MY RING, I'VE CAUSED THE GREEN BEAM TO FORM A **MINIATURE SUN**, BATHING ME WITH WARM RAYS! BUT WILL IT MELT THIS TERRIBLY COLD ICE?

AGONIZING MOMENTS LATER...

IT WORKED! BUT NOW MY RING **IS** ABSOLUTELY DEAD! YET I CAN'T THINK OF GETTING HOME TO CHARGE IT--GOT TO FIND **PIEFACE** AND THOSE MEN!

MEANWHILE, IN A NEARBY BUILDING...

YOU'RE COMING WITH US, KALMAKU! WE CAN USE YOU TO DIG WHEN WE FIND THE GOLD MINE! WE'RE GOING TO TAKE A BIG LOAD OUT IN THE JET--AS MUCH AS WE CAN!

YOU CROOKS-- YOU MUST HAVE STOLEN THAT OTHER MAP-HALF TOO--FROM JIM DAWES!

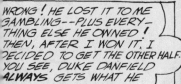

WRONG! HE LOST IT TO ME GAMBLING--PLUS EVERYTHING ELSE HE OWNED! THEN, AFTER I WON IT, I DECIDED TO GET THE OTHER HALF. YOU SEE, DUKE DANFIELD **ALWAYS** GETS WHAT HE GOES AFTER...

YOU MEAN **ALMOST** ALWAYS-- DON'T YOU, DUKE?

GREEN LANTERN AGAIN! HE'S LOOSE!

LOOK OUT FOR HIS RING!

HIS RING ISN'T WORKING!

YES--BUT PRETENDING THAT IT WAS GAVE ME JUST THE MOMENT I NEEDED TO TAKE CARE OF THESE GUNMEN!

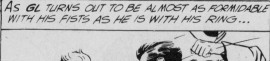

AS *GL* TURNS OUT TO BE ALMOST AS FORMIDABLE WITH HIS FISTS AS HE IS WITH HIS RING...

HUH? THE WAY *GREEN LANTERN* DID THAT-- JUST LIKE...!

AND MUCH LATER, AFTER THE BATTERED GANG HAS BEEN TURNED OVER TO THE NEAREST AUTHORITIES, AND *GREEN LANTERN* AND *PIEFACE* BETWEEN THEM HAVE FOUND THE MINE...

THAT'S RIGHT, *GREEN LANTERN!* THE MONEY FROM THIS MINE WILL TAKE CARE OF MY PEOPLE AS LONG AS THEY LIVE--AND THAT MEANS I'LL BE ABLE TO GO ON WORKING AS--er--HAL JORDAN'S MECHANIC!

THAT'S ALL I WANTED TO HEAR!

BACK IN THE STATES AGAIN, *PIEFACE* SPRINGS A SURPRISE...

WHAT'S THAT, *PIEFACE?* YOU-er--*KNOW* THAT I'M *GREEN LANTERN!?* BUT HOW--

WELL, THERE WAS THE PECULIAR WAY YOU SLUGGED THAT MAP-STEALER--LATER *GL* PULLED THE EXACT SAME STUNT! AND IT TIED IN WITH OTHER THINGS.

I GUESS YOU'D BETTER USE YOUR *POWER RING,* HUH, HAL--AND KNOCK THE KNOWLEDGE OUT OF MY HEAD! MAYBE THAT WOULD BE THE BEST THING--IT'S A TERRIBLE RESPONSIBILITY...

NO...

WE WORKED TOGETHER LONG ENOUGH, *PIEFACE!* THERE'S NO ONE I'D RATHER TRUST! *YOU'LL* KNOW THAT SECRETLY *I AM GREEN LANTERN*--BUT YOU'LL BE THE *ONLY ONE IN THE WORLD* TO KNOW IT!

GREAT FISH-HOOKS...!

SO--NOW SOMEONE ELSE SHARES *GREEN LANTERN'S* GREAT SECRET! THERE'LL BE MORE EXCITING ADVENTURES WITH *PIEFACE* IN FORTH-COMING ISSUES!

THE END

12

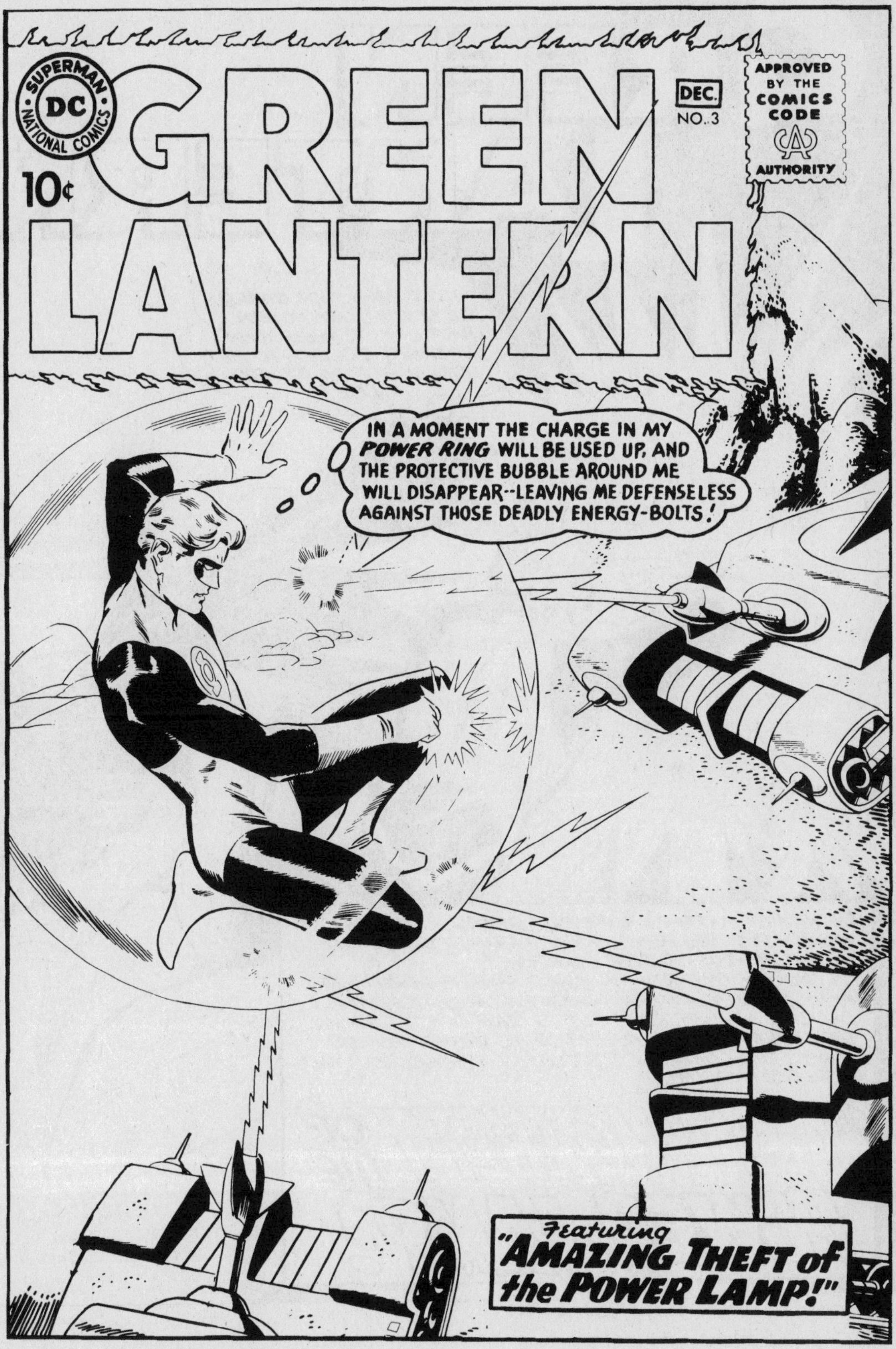
SUPERMAN DC NATIONAL COMICS
10¢
GREEN LANTERN
DEC. NO. 3
APPROVED BY THE COMICS CODE AUTHORITY
IN A MOMENT THE CHARGE IN MY POWER RING WILL BE USED UP, AND THE PROTECTIVE BUBBLE AROUND ME WILL DISAPPEAR--LEAVING ME DEFENSELESS AGAINST THOSE DEADLY ENERGY-BOLTS!
Featuring "AMAZING THEFT of the POWER LAMP!"

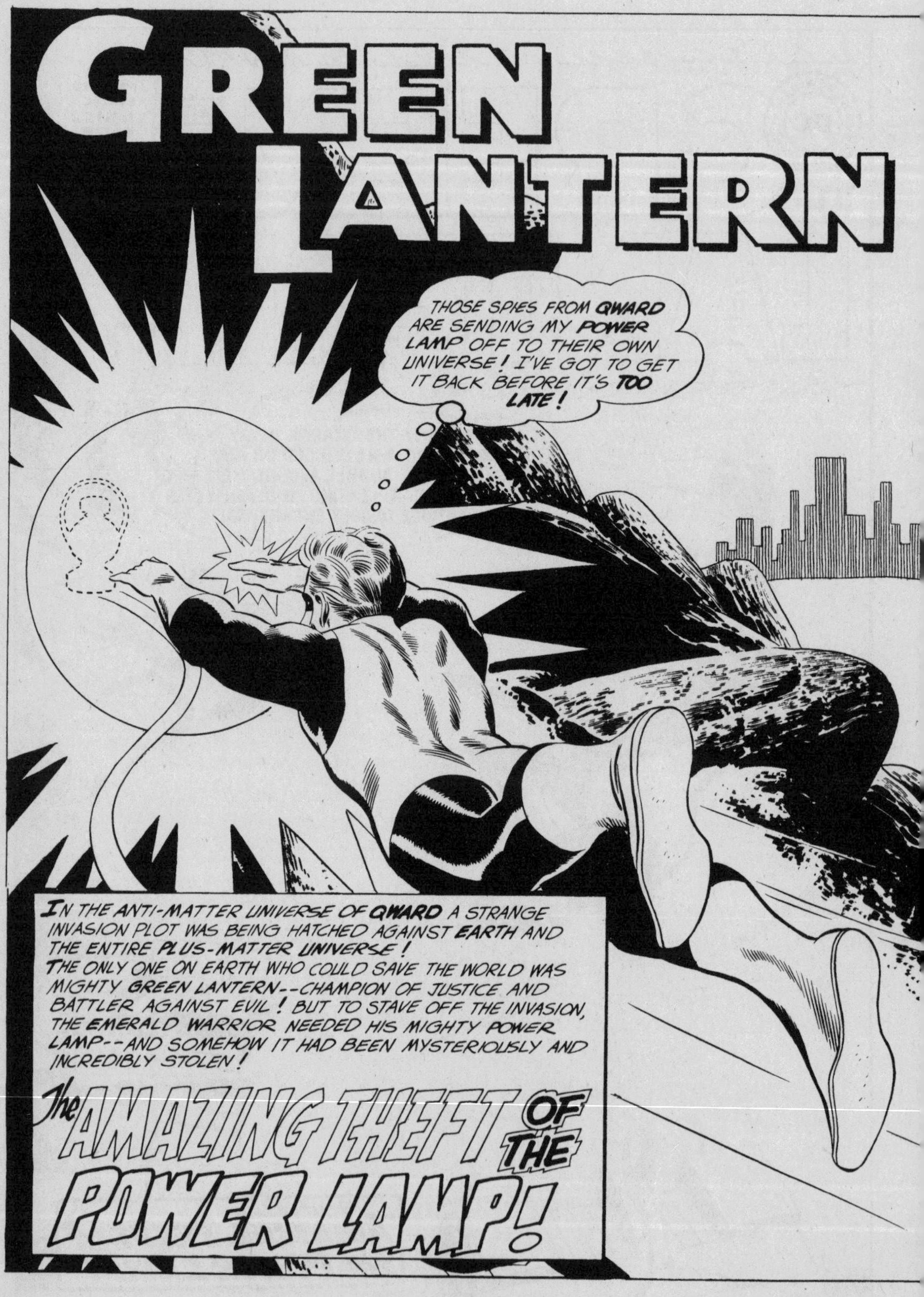
GREEN LANTERN
THOSE SPIES FROM QWARD ARE SENDING MY POWER LAMP OFF TO THEIR OWN UNIVERSE! I'VE GOT TO GET IT BACK BEFORE IT'S TOO LATE!
IN THE ANTI-MATTER UNIVERSE OF QWARD A STRANGE INVASION PLOT WAS BEING HATCHED AGAINST EARTH AND THE ENTIRE PLUS-MATTER UNIVERSE! THE ONLY ONE ON EARTH WHO COULD SAVE THE WORLD WAS MIGHTY GREEN LANTERN--CHAMPION OF JUSTICE AND BATTLER AGAINST EVIL! BUT TO STAVE OFF THE INVASION, THE EMERALD WARRIOR NEEDED HIS MIGHTY POWER LAMP--AND SOMEHOW IT HAD BEEN MYSTERIOUSLY AND INCREDIBLY STOLEN!
The AMAZING THEFT OF THE POWER LAMP!

As **GREEN LANTERN** RETURNS FROM AN EXPLOIT TOWARD HIS HOME BASE AT THE **FERRIS AIRCRAFT COMPANY**...

THAT'S ODD--I THOUGHT I HAD ANOTHER FIFTY MILES OF DESERT TO GO BEFORE I REACHED FERRIS--BUT THERE IT IS!

GUESS MY INTERNAL MILEAGE--METER NEEDS ADJUSTING--OR MAYBE I WAS DAYDREAMING! BUT ANYWAY I MIGHT AS WELL RECHARGE MY RING WHILE I'M HERE--EVEN THOUGH THERE'S STILL PLENTY OF JUICE LEFT IN IT!

ON THE WAY TO THE HANGAR, THE GREEN-CLAD CRUSADER PASSES THE MAIN BUILDING HOUSING THE EXECUTIVE OFFICES...

THERE'S CAROL... BUSY AS USUAL! BUT WAIT A SECOND...

AS THE PRETTY BOSS OF FERRIS CONTINUES WORKING WITHOUT REALIZING SHE IS BEING WATCHED...

IS THERE SOMETHING STRANGE ABOUT CAROL TODAY OR IS IT MY IMAGINATION? FUNNY...I CAN'T SEEM TO FIGURE OUT WHAT IT IS!

AND THEN...

HOLY SMOKE! NOW I KNOW I'M SEEING THINGS! I--I THOUGHT I JUST SAW HAL JORDAN!!

BUT I KNOW IT COULDN'T BE-- BECAUSE HAL JORDAN, THE TEST PILOT HERE, IS **ME!** BOTH OF US COULDN'T APPEAR ANY- WHERE AT THE **SAME TIME!**

2

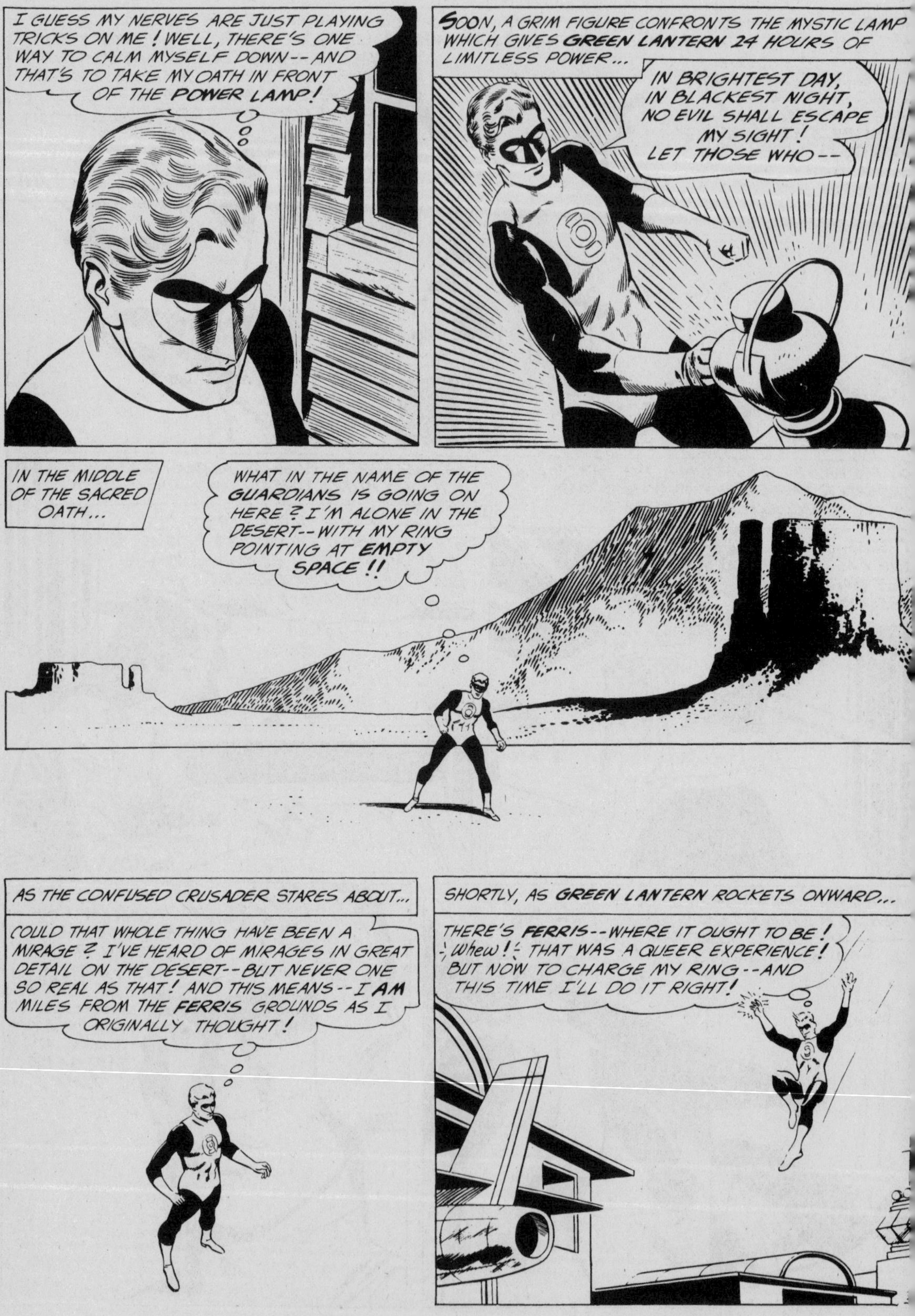
I GUESS MY NERVES ARE JUST PLAYING TRICKS ON ME! WELL, THERE'S ONE WAY TO CALM MYSELF DOWN-- AND THAT'S TO TAKE MY OATH IN FRONT OF THE POWER LAMP!
SOON, A GRIM FIGURE CONFRONTS THE MYSTIC LAMP WHICH GIVES GREEN LANTERN 24 HOURS OF LIMITLESS POWER...
IN BRIGHTEST DAY, IN BLACKEST NIGHT, NO EVIL SHALL ESCAPE MY SIGHT! LET THOSE WHO--
IN THE MIDDLE OF THE SACRED OATH...
WHAT IN THE NAME OF THE GUARDIANS IS GOING ON HERE? I'M ALONE IN THE DESERT-- WITH MY RING POINTING AT EMPTY SPACE!!
AS THE CONFUSED CRUSADER STARES ABOUT...
COULD THAT WHOLE THING HAVE BEEN A MIRAGE? I'VE HEARD OF MIRAGES IN GREAT DETAIL ON THE DESERT-- BUT NEVER ONE SO REAL AS THAT! AND THIS MEANS-- I AM MILES FROM THE FERRIS GROUNDS AS I ORIGINALLY THOUGHT!
SHORTLY, AS GREEN LANTERN ROCKETS ONWARD...
THERE'S FERRIS-- WHERE IT OUGHT TO BE! -WHEW!- THAT WAS A QUEER EXPERIENCE! BUT NOW TO CHARGE MY RING-- AND THIS TIME I'LL DO IT RIGHT!

IN THE PRIVACY OF HAL JORDAN'S DRESSING ROOM AT THE HANGAR...

I ALWAYS LEAVE MY **POWER LAMP** INVISIBLE AND WITH AN ENERGY-SHIELD AROUND IT TO PREVENT IT FROM BEING SEEN OR TOUCHED! AND THAT MEANS I'VE GOT TO USE MY RING IN ORDER TO MAKE IT VISIBLE AGAIN!

BUT AS THE GREEN BEAM FLARES INTO THE FAMILIAR CORNER...

GREAT JUPITER!! MY LAMP--IT'S **GONE**!!!

AT THAT MOMENT ON THE ROOF OF A BOARDING HOUSE IN NEARBY **COAST CITY**...

I PROMISED MRS. HENDRICKS, MY LANDLADY, THAT I'D TRY TO FIX HER **TV** AERIAL TODAY!

SUDDENLY, AS **PIEFACE**-- HAL JORDAN'S ESKIMO MECHANIC--GRIPS THE METAL PRONGS...

GREAT FISH-HOOKS! I'M GETTING SOME KIND OF RECEPTION--LIKE THOUGHTS FROM THE AERIAL!

BELOW, BEHIND CAREFULLY LOCKED DOORS...

CALLING **UNIVERSE OF QWARD***... HEADQUARTERS OF THE WEAPONERS! CALLING...

WE ARE RECEIVING YOU, DRIK! MAKE YOUR REPORT...

***Editor's Note:** AS EXPLAINED IN THE LAST ISSUE, **QWARD** IS AN **ANTI-MATTER UNIVERSE**, ON A DIFFERENT SPACE-TIME LEVEL FROM OUR **PLUS-MATTER UNIVERSE!**

WE HAVE A GREAT SUCCESS TO REPORT--BUT ALSO A PROBLEM! LET US RELATE WHAT HAS HAPPENED...

4

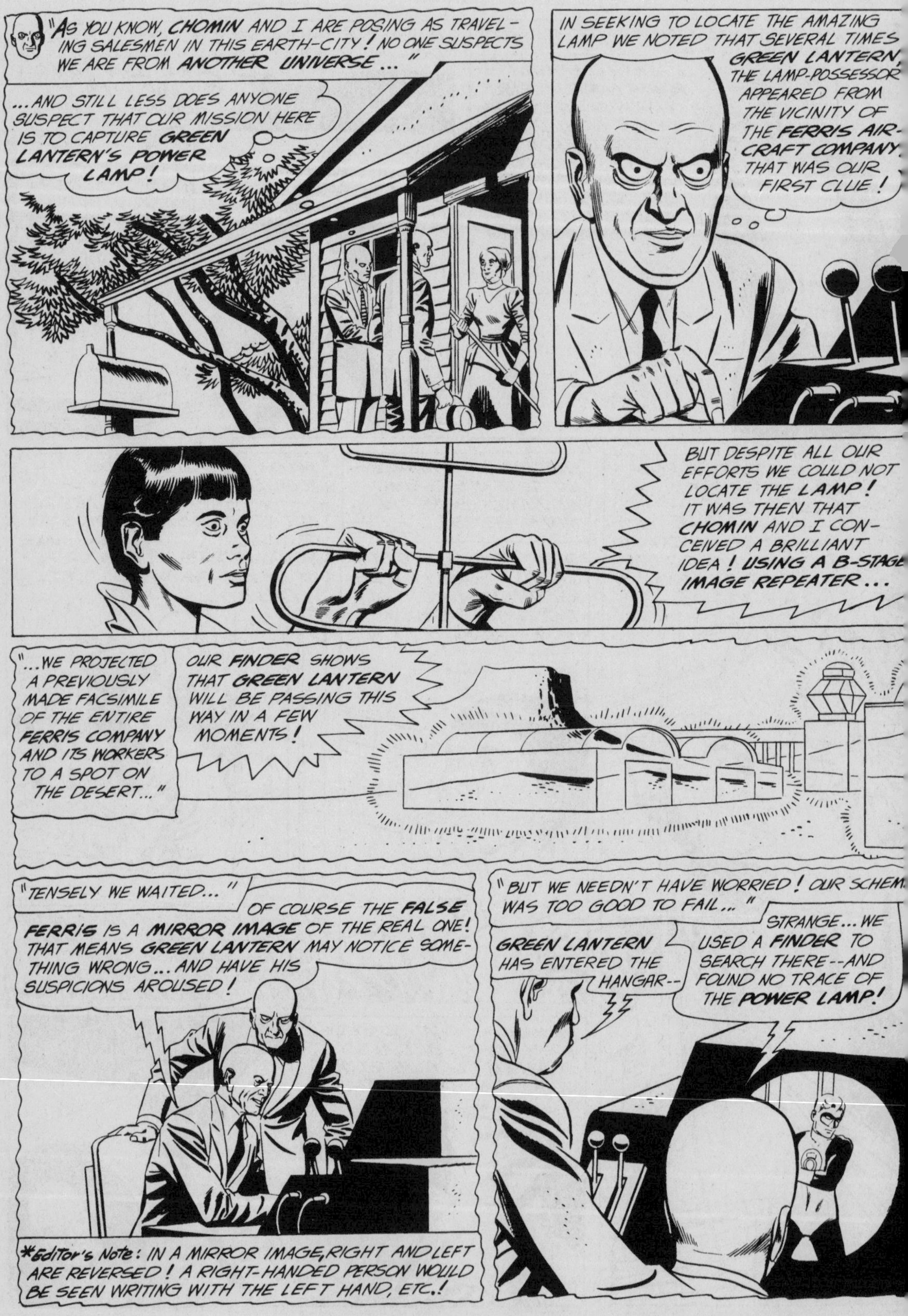
"AS YOU KNOW, CHOMIN AND I ARE POSING AS TRAVEL-ING SALESMEN IN THIS EARTH-CITY! NO ONE SUSPECTS WE ARE FROM ANOTHER UNIVERSE..."
...AND STILL LESS DOES ANYONE SUSPECT THAT OUR MISSION HERE IS TO CAPTURE GREEN LANTERN'S POWER LAMP!
IN SEEKING TO LOCATE THE AMAZING LAMP WE NOTED THAT SEVERAL TIMES GREEN LANTERN, THE LAMP-POSSESSOR APPEARED FROM THE VICINITY OF THE FERRIS AIR-CRAFT COMPANY. THAT WAS OUR FIRST CLUE!
BUT DESPITE ALL OUR EFFORTS WE COULD NOT LOCATE THE LAMP! IT WAS THEN THAT CHOMIN AND I CON-CEIVED A BRILLIANT IDEA! USING A B-STAGE IMAGE REPEATER...
"...WE PROJECTED A PREVIOUSLY MADE FACSIMILE OF THE ENTIRE FERRIS COMPANY AND ITS WORKERS TO A SPOT ON THE DESERT..."
OUR FINDER SHOWS THAT GREEN LANTERN WILL BE PASSING THIS WAY IN A FEW MOMENTS!
"TENSELY WE WAITED..."
OF COURSE THE FALSE FERRIS IS A MIRROR IMAGE OF THE REAL ONE! THAT MEANS GREEN LANTERN MAY NOTICE SOME-THING WRONG...AND HAVE HIS SUSPICIONS AROUSED!
*Editor's Note: IN A MIRROR IMAGE, RIGHT AND LEFT ARE REVERSED! A RIGHT-HANDED PERSON WOULD BE SEEN WRITING WITH THE LEFT HAND, ETC.!
"BUT WE NEEDN'T HAVE WORRIED! OUR SCHEME WAS TOO GOOD TO FAIL..."
GREEN LANTERN HAS ENTERED THE HANGAR--
STRANGE...WE USED A FINDER TO SEARCH THERE--AND FOUND NO TRACE OF THE POWER LAMP!

"THEN, THE NEXT MOMENT, THE MYSTERY WAS CLEARED UP..."

BRIGHTEST DAY...

SO THAT'S IT! HE KEEPS THE LAMP INVISIBLE SO THAT NO ONE CAN SEE IT! BUT NOW THAT WE KNOW EXACTLY WHERE IT IS IN THE *REAL HANGAR*--OUR INSTRUMENTS CAN BRING IT HERE!

"WE HAD NO MORE USE FOR THE *REFLECTED IMAGE*! WE SWITCHED IT OFF..."

BY THE TIME THE *GREEN GLADIATOR* COLLECTS HIS WITS AND REACHES THE *REAL FERRIS COMPANY*--HIS LAMP WILL BE IN OUR POSSESSION!

WE HAVE BROUGHT THE MYSTIC LAMP TO OUR ROOM!

IT IS INVISIBLE--BUT OUR Q-RAY CASTS ITS SHADOW ON THE WALL!

"BUT THEN CAME THE UN-SOLVABLE DIFFICULTY..."

ALTHOUGH OUR INSTRUMENTS BROUGHT THE LAMP HERE, WE CANNOT TOUCH IT! SOME UNSEEN FORCE PROTECTS IT! THAT IS WHY WE HAVE CONTACTED YOU--

I'VE HEARD ENOUGH!

THE TWO BOARDERS ON THE THIRD FLOOR--SPIES FROM ANOTHER UNIVERSE! I'VE GOT TO CONTACT *GREEN LANTERN* AS FAST AS POSSIBLE!

AS THE ENERGETIC YOUNG GROUND-CREWMAN SPEEDS OFF IN HIS FLASHY CAR...

I'M THE ONLY ONE IN THE WORLD WHO KNOWS THAT *GREEN LANTERN* IS REALLY HAL JORDAN--MY BOSS--AND THE TOP TEST-PILOT AT THE *FERRIS AIRCRAFT COMPANY!*

6

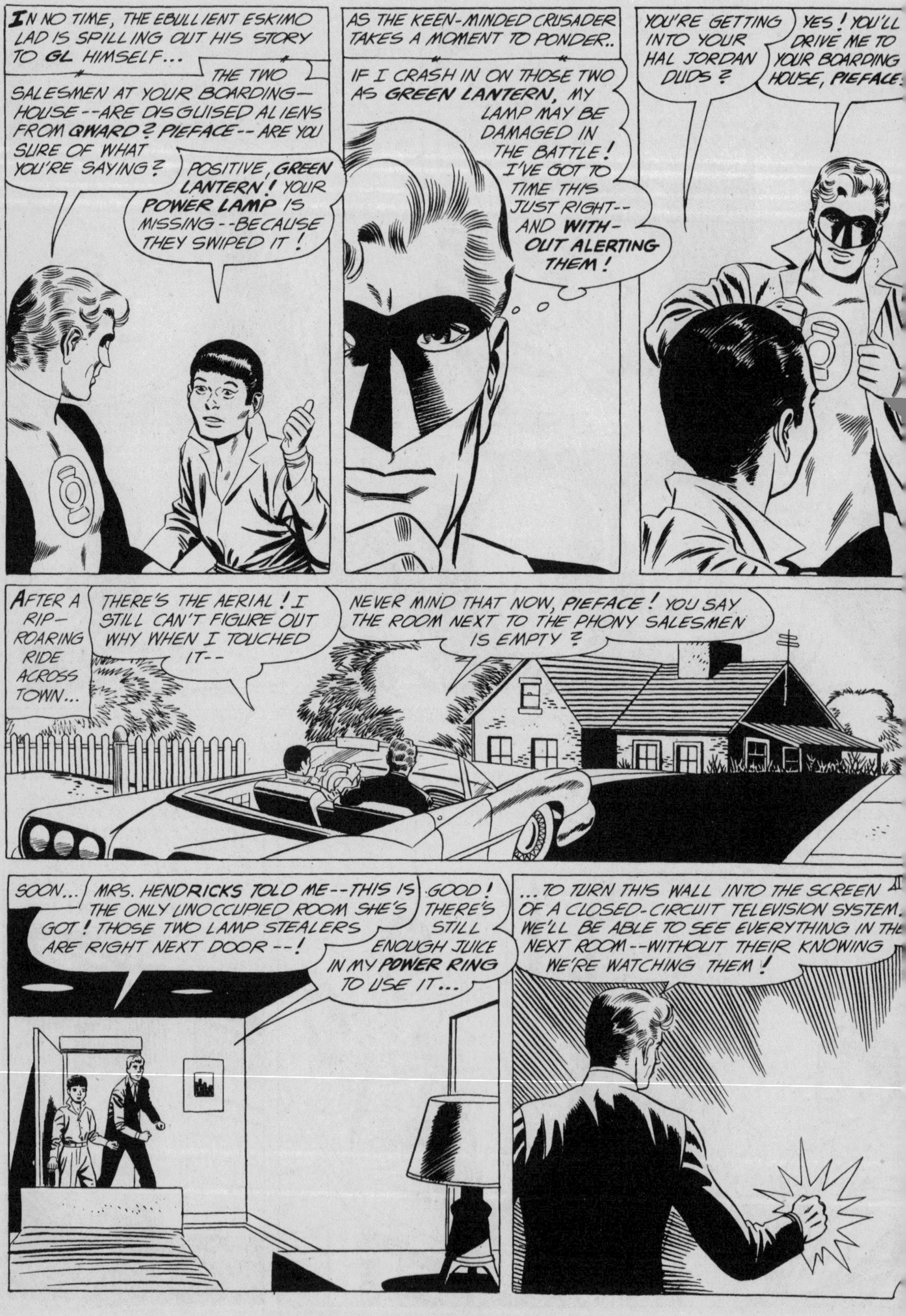
IN NO TIME, THE EBULLIENT ESKIMO LAD IS SPILLING OUT HIS STORY TO GL HIMSELF...
THE TWO SALESMEN AT YOUR BOARDING-HOUSE--ARE DISGUISED ALIENS FROM QWARD? PIEFACE--ARE YOU SURE OF WHAT YOU'RE SAYING?
POSITIVE, GREEN LANTERN! YOUR POWER LAMP IS MISSING--BECAUSE THEY SWIPED IT!
AS THE KEEN-MINDED CRUSADER TAKES A MOMENT TO PONDER..
IF I CRASH IN ON THOSE TWO AS GREEN LANTERN, MY LAMP MAY BE DAMAGED IN THE BATTLE! I'VE GOT TO TIME THIS JUST RIGHT--AND WITHOUT ALERTING THEM!
YOU'RE GETTING INTO YOUR HAL JORDAN DUDS?
YES! YOU'LL DRIVE ME TO YOUR BOARDING HOUSE, PIEFACE!
AFTER A RIP-ROARING RIDE ACROSS TOWN...
THERE'S THE AERIAL! I STILL CAN'T FIGURE OUT WHY WHEN I TOUCHED IT--
NEVER MIND THAT NOW, PIEFACE! YOU SAY THE ROOM NEXT TO THE PHONY SALESMEN IS EMPTY?
SOON...
MRS. HENDRICKS TOLD ME--THIS IS THE ONLY UNOCCUPIED ROOM SHE'S GOT! THOSE TWO LAMP STEALERS ARE RIGHT NEXT DOOR--!
GOOD! THERE'S STILL ENOUGH JUICE IN MY POWER RING TO USE IT...
...TO TURN THIS WALL INTO THE SCREEN OF A CLOSED-CIRCUIT TELEVISION SYSTEM. WE'LL BE ABLE TO SEE EVERYTHING IN THE NEXT ROOM--WITHOUT THEIR KNOWING WE'RE WATCHING THEM!

AT ONCE, THE GREAT GREEN BEAM SWINGS INTO ACTION...

GOOD GOSH! THERE'S MY *POWER LAMP*, ALL RIGHT! I CAN SEE ITS *SHADOW*! BUT--WHAT ARE THEY SAYING IN THERE--?

AS *GL's* RING CREATES A CHANNEL FOR THE *TRANSLATED THOUGHTS* OF THE ALIENS TO COME THROUGH, JUST AS THEY CAME THROUGH THE AERIAL ON THE ROOF...

THEN THAT IS THE ONLY THING TO DO! WE WILL TRANSMIT THE *POWER LAMP* TO YOU! WE CAN SEND IT EVEN THOUGH WE CAN'T TOUCH IT!

SHORTLY... ALERT! OUR *OBJECT-TRANSMITTER* IS SENDING YOU THE INVISIBLE LAMP NOW! PREPARE TO RECEIVE IT--!

AT THAT MOMENT, HAL STRIPS OFF HIS OUTER GARMENTS...

PIEFACE, I'M GOING AFTER THE LAMP--AS GREEN LANTERN! AND NO MATTER *WHERE* IT'S BEING SENT, I'M GOING TO GET IT BACK! YOU KEEP AN EYE ON THOSE PHONY SALESMEN-- DON'T LET THEM OUT OF YOUR SIGHT!

LIKE A THUNDERBOLT THE EMERALD CRUSADER DIVES AFTER HIS *POWER LAMP*...

I CAN'T OVERTAKE THE LAMP--IT'S TRAVELING AT THE SAME RATE OF SPEED AS I AM! BUT I CAN FOLLOW ITS *TRAIL* ... BY THE FAINT RADIOACTIVITY LEFT IN THE AIR...!

AND SOON AFTER, AT THE EDGE OF THE ANTI-MATTER UNIVERSE OF *QWARD* ADJOINING OURS IN THE COSMOS...

...CROSSING THE BARRIER INTO *QWARD*! I'VE BEEN THROUGH THIS BEFORE... BUT EACH TIME IT'S TERRIFYING... MYSTIFYING...

STORY CONTINUED ON FOLLOWING PAGE!

8

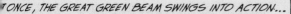
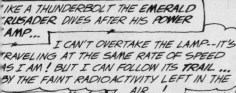

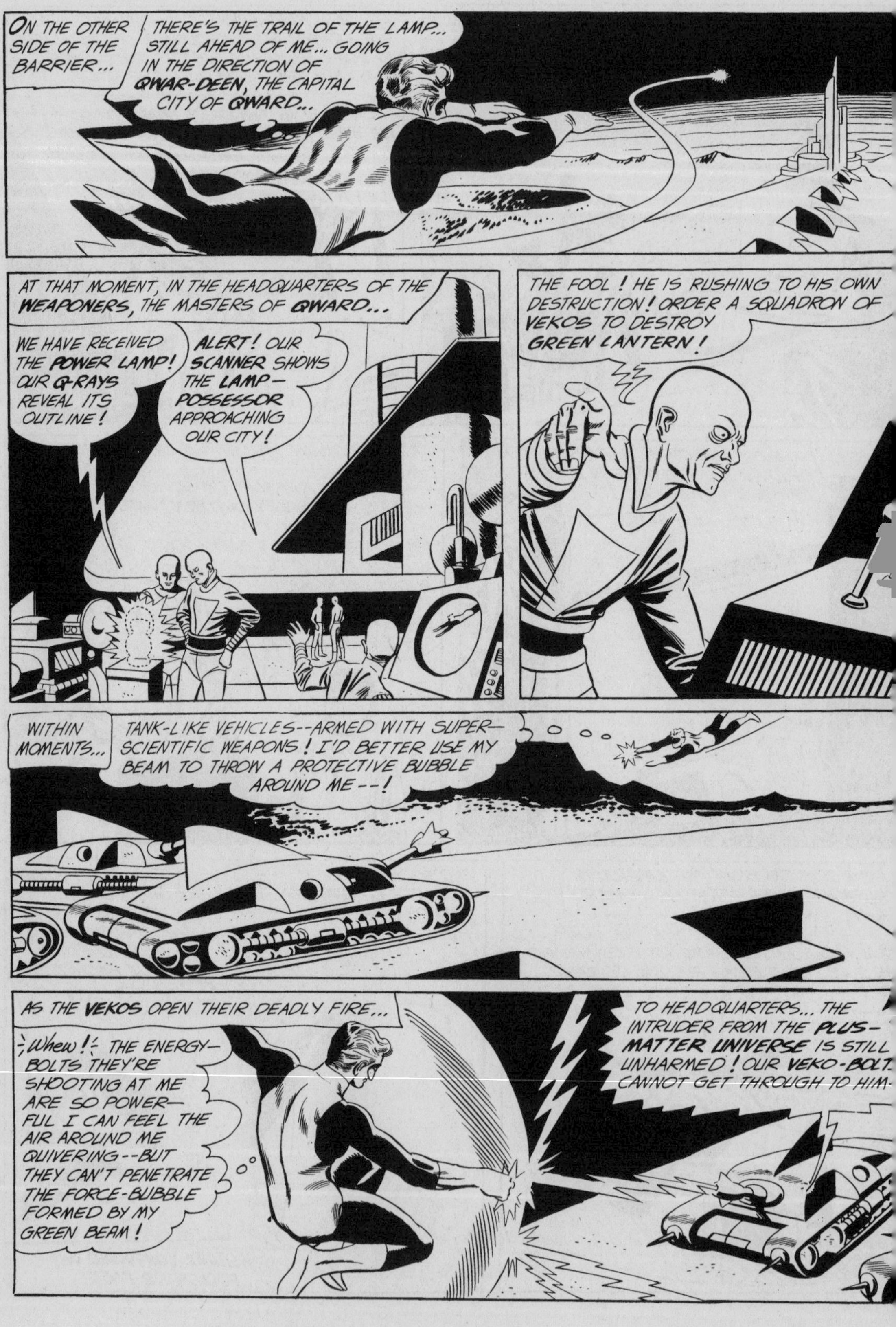

ON THE OTHER SIDE OF THE BARRIER...
THERE'S THE TRAIL OF THE LAMP... STILL AHEAD OF ME... GOING IN THE DIRECTION OF QWAR-DEEN, THE CAPITAL CITY OF QWARD...
AT THAT MOMENT, IN THE HEADQUARTERS OF THE WEAPONERS, THE MASTERS OF QWARD...
WE HAVE RECEIVED THE POWER LAMP! OUR Q-RAYS REVEAL ITS OUTLINE!
ALERT! OUR SCANNER SHOWS THE LAMP-POSSESSOR APPROACHING OUR CITY!
THE FOOL! HE IS RUSHING TO HIS OWN DESTRUCTION! ORDER A SQUADRON OF VEKOS TO DESTROY GREEN LANTERN!
WITHIN MOMENTS...
TANK-LIKE VEHICLES--ARMED WITH SUPER-SCIENTIFIC WEAPONS! I'D BETTER USE MY BEAM TO THROW A PROTECTIVE BUBBLE AROUND ME--!
AS THE VEKOS OPEN THEIR DEADLY FIRE...
Whew! THE ENERGY-BOLTS THEY'RE SHOOTING AT ME ARE SO POWERFUL I CAN FEEL THE AIR AROUND ME QUIVERING--BUT THEY CAN'T PENETRATE THE FORCE-BUBBLE FORMED BY MY GREEN BEAM!
TO HEADQUARTERS... THE INTRUDER FROM THE PLUS-MATTER UNIVERSE IS STILL UNHARMED! OUR VEKO-BOLT CANNOT GET THROUGH TO HIM-

...HERE IS ONE CERTAIN WAY WE CAN DEFEAT **GREEN LANTERN!** WE MUST **DELAY HIM** UNTIL THE POWER IN HIS RING GIVES OUT! HERE IS WHAT WE WILL DO...

As THE **WEAPONERS** ENCASE THE **POWER LAMP** IN A **YELLOW** DOME...

THIS WILL PREVENT THE EARTHMAN FROM REACHING HIS LAMP! OUR AGENTS HAVE REPORTED THAT ALL LAMP-POSSESSORS HAVE **NO POWER** OVER ANYTHING **YELLOW!** *

*Editor's Note: DUE TO A NECESSARY IMPURITY IN ITS VERY NATURE, **GREEN LANTERN'S** MYSTIC LAMP IS POWERLESS OVER ANYTHING **YELLOW!**

THUS HE WILL BE UNABLE TO PENETRATE THE DOME, AND WHEN HIS RING GIVES OUT--

ALERT! HERE HE COMES NOW! EVERYONE AWAY FROM HERE!

A MOMENT LATER, AS THE **GREEN GLADIATOR** BURSTS IN...

QUEER! I HAVE THE FEELING THIS PLACE WAS FULL OF **QWARDIANS**... UP TO A MOMENT BEFORE I ENTERED! BUT NOW...NOTHING HERE EXCEPT THAT YELLOW DOME!

AND GREAT SCOTT! THE TRAIL OF THE LAMP... IT LEADS TO THIS YELLOW DOME! I CAN'T GET AT IT--UNLESS THERE HAPPENS TO BE AN **OPENING** INTO IT--!

IN VAIN, **GREEN LANTERN** PROBES THE SURFACE OF THE STRUCTURE, SEEKING A CREVICE OR CRACK IN IT...

I'VE **GOT** TO FIND A WAY IN THERE! MY TIME--THE TWENTY-FOUR HOURS OF POWER I GET WHEN I CHARGE MY RING AT THE LAMP-- IS ALMOST UP!

10

THEN... A PIN HOLE! IT MAY BE *JUST ENOUGH* TO DO THE TRICK!

THROUGH THE DOME-HOLE DARTS A TINY BEAM, POWERED BY *GL's* WILL, TO EXPLODE THE INTERIOR...

IF THE INTERIOR ISN'T YELLOW I HAVE A CHANCE-- BY BREAKING THE WALL FROM THE INSIDE--WITH A SLEDGE-HAMMER BLOW!

DID IT! I CAN GET IN THERE NOW--!

POW!

AND THERE'S MY LAMP--THANK THE *GUARDIANS!* NOW I CAN CHARGE MY RING--AND BE PREPARED TO TAKE ON ANY FURTHER ATTACKS IN THIS UNIVERSE!

BUT AS THE *EMERALD CRUSADER* AGAIN STARTS HIS FAMILIAR OATH...

IN BRIGHTEST DAY, IN BLACKEST NIGHT, NO EVIL SHALL--eh?

SOMETHING *WRONG!* MY RING ISN'T *CHARGING!* THERE'S ONLY ONE ANSWER--

EVEN THOUGH MY BEAM ITSELF WORKS IN THIS ALIEN ANTI-MATTER UNIVERSE, I *CAN'T CHARGE* MY RING HERE! AND THAT MEANS I HAVE JUST A FEW MOMENTS OF POWER LEFT TO GET OUT OF HERE--!

At that instant, in the thought-monitoring control room where the **QWARDIAN** chieftains are concealed..

...CAN'T CHARGE MY RING...! ONLY A FEW MOMENTS OF POWER LEFT...

WE MUST PREVENT THE LAMP-POSSESSOR FROM GETTING AWAY! ALL OUR FUTURE PLANS--FOR THE INVASION OF HIS PLUS--MATTER UNIVERSE--DEPEND ON IT!

SURROUND THE DOME! ON ALL SIDES--AND BE READY TO FIRE--WITH YELLOW-FIRING RAY-GUNS!

HERE HE COMES! OPEN FIRE--! HE WILL NOT BE ABLE TO WITHSTAND US ALL--!

ZZZZZZT!

AFTER THE OPENING VOLLEY...

WE DID IT! WE HAVE SLAIN THE LAMP-POSSESSOR!!

BUT UNKNOWN TO THE **QWARDIAN** LEADERS AT THAT MOMENT...

WITH THE LAST OUNCES OF POWER LEFT IN MY RING I MADE MYSELF **INVISIBLE** AND CREATED A **FALSE IMAGE** OF MYSELF TO LEAD THE **QWARDIANS** ASTRAY! THEY BLASTED THE **IMAGE**--

LEAVING ME TO GET HOME ON JUST ABOUT **WILL POWER** ALONE!

12

SHORTLY, AS *GREEN LANTERN* PASSES THE BARRIER INTO OUR UNIVERSE, A LONG OVERDUE ACT TAKES PLACE...

IN BRIGHTEST DAY, IN BLACKEST NIGHT, NO EVIL SHALL ESCAPE MY SIGHT! LET THOSE WHO WORSHIP EVIL'S MIGHT BEWARE MY POWER--GREEN LANTERN'S LIGHT!

AND IN *COAST CITY* NOT LONG AFTERWARD, WITH THE *POWER LAMP* SECURELY HIDDEN AWAY...

WE'LL TURN THESE TWO *QWARDIANS* OVER TO THE AUTHORITIES, *PIEFACE!* THANKS FOR KEEPING AN EYE ON THEM!

A PLEASURE, GL!

AFTER THE SPIES FROM *QWARD* HAVE BEEN PLACED IN CUSTODY AND AN *INVESTIGATION* OF THEIR PRESENCE HERE HAS BEGUN...

IT'S TIME WE GOT BACK TO WORK, *PIEFACE!* HANG ON--I'LL USE MY RING TO GET US TO THE *FERRIS PLANT!*

LET'S GO!

POLICE

LATER, AS HAL JORDAN AND HIS MECHANIC LABOR OVER A JET MOTOR...

WELL! DID YOU TWO TAKE THE *MORNING OFF?* I DIDN'T SEE YOU ANY--WHERE!

ER--WE HAD THINGS TO DO, CAROL!

The End

GREEN LANTERN

GREEN LANTERN

I CREATED THAT MONSTER MYSELF-- WITH MY *POWER BEAM*! BUT NOW I'VE *GOT* TO *DESTROY* IT--BEFORE IT REACHES THAT *ATOMIC STOCK-PILE*--AND DESTROYS THE COUNTRY!

*W*HAT POSSIBLE REASON COULD *GREEN LANTERN* HAVE FOR CREATING A CREATURE THAT WOULD *THREATEN COAST CITY*?

*F*OR THE INTRIGUING ANSWER TO THIS MYSTERY IT IS NECESSARY TO DELVE INTO THE DRAMATIC--AND HIGHLY-EXPLOSIVE--SITUATION BETWEEN THE *EMERALD GLADIATOR* AND A CERTAIN LOVELY BUT DETERMINED DAMSEL NAMED *CAROL FERRIS*!

The
LEAP YEAR MENACE!

KANE + GIELLA

IN THE HEAD-QUARTERS OF THE *COAST CITY COMMUNITY CHEST*...

YES, MRS. CRANSTON! I'LL BE GLAD TO APPEAR AT THE LAUNCHING OF THE *COAST CITY COMMUNITY CHEST* DRIVE THIS AFTERNOON!

THANK YOU, *GREEN LANTERN!* YOUR PRESENCE WILL DRAW A BIG CROWD-- AND BIG DONATIONS!

COAST CITY COMM
CHEST DRIVE

AND AS THE *EMERALD GLADIATOR* EXITS FROM THE BUILDING...

THERE HE IS!

GREAT GHOSTS! IT'S THE *GREEN LANTERN FAN CLUB!* THEY'VE BEEN HOUNDING ME FOR A WEEK--BUT I'VE ALWAYS DODGED THEM UP TO NOW--!

NOW, HOWEVER, BEFORE HE CAN MOVE...

GREEN *LANTERN!* I TOUCHED HIM...I'M GOING TO FAINT...

SIGN MY AUTO-GRAPH, PLEASE!

LET GO! WE SAW HIM FIRST!

BY THE GUARDIANS! IF THIS KEEPS UP I'LL BE TORN APART! ONLY ONE WAY OUT OF THIS--

AS GL, USING HIS *POWER RING*, SOARS AWAY...

STOP HIM-- SOMEONE!

I'VE GOT TO GET AWAY! AS HAL JORDAN--MY ALTER EGO--I'VE GOT AN IMPORTANT APPOINTMENT WITH CAROL FERRIS IN JUST A FEW MINUTES!

SOON, AT THE **FERRIS AIRCRAFT COMPANY**, AFTER THE ESCAPED HERO HAS CHANGED TO HIS CIVILIAN IDENTITY...

YOU WANTED TO SEE ME, CAROL?

YES, HAL! BUT IT'S PERSONAL--AND HAS NOTHING TO DO WITH YOUR DUTIES AS A **TEST PILOT** HERE...

A GREAT LIGHT SEEMS TO BURST INSIDE THE CRACK AIRMAN...

AH! MAYBE SHE'S FINALLY REALIZED THAT IT'S **ME** SHE LOVES--AND **NOT GREEN LANTERN!**

PERSONAL, CAROL?

YES, HAL!

HAL, I REGARD YOU AS MY FRIEND-- AS JUST ABOUT THE BEST FRIEND I HAVE...

FRIEND? Hmm--THIS DOESN'T SOUND TOO PROMISING...

...AND I WANT TO GET YOUR OPINION! YOU KNOW, THIS IS **LEAP YEAR**... AND I WAS THINKING, SINCE **GREEN LANTERN** SEEMS TOO **SHY** TO PROPOSE TO ME-- WHY DON'T **I** PROPOSE TO **HIM**!?

EH?

I'M GOING TO SEE HIM AT THE **CHARITY DRIVE** THIS AFTERNOON! AND IT MAY BE A PERFECT TIME! WE'RE BOUND TO FIND OURSELVES ALONE TOGETHER...

UH...HUH...

YOU DON'T SEEM VERY ENTHUSIASTIC ABOUT MY IDEA...

I'M **NOT!** I DON'T THINK YOU OUGHT TO MARRY **GREEN LANTERN**, CAROL! HE'S--AH--TOO MUCH OF A CELEBRITY! YOU OUGHT TO MARRY SOMEBODY WHO'S LESS OF A **PUBLIC FIGURE!** SOMEBODY--

3

--SOMEBODY LIKE YOU, YOU MEAN!

WELL, THAT'S THE BEST IDEA YOU'VE OFFERED SO FAR...

I DON'T THINK IT'S ANY IDEA AT ALL, *MR. JORDAN!* FORGIVE ME FOR TAKING UP YOUR VALUABLE TIME!

SEEMS LIKE *THIS* *INTERVIEW* IS OVER...

RELUCTANTLY, HAL EXITS FROM THE LOVELY PRESENCE OF HIS BOSS...

CAROL SEEMS DETERMINED TO TAKE ADVANTAGE OF *LEAP YEAR* AND PROPOSE TO *GREEN LANTERN!* BUT IT'S AS MYSELF--*HAL JORDAN*--THAT I WANT TO WIN HER! NOT AS *GREEN LANTERN!*

AS ONE TROUBLING THOUGHT AFTER ANOTHER HARRIES THE MIND OF THE ACE TEST-PILOT...

GOLLY! WHAT WILL I DO IF SHE ACTUALLY PROPOSES? *GL* HAS TO SHOW UP AT THAT CHARITY AFFAIR THIS AFTERNOON! IT CAN'T BE AVOIDED! AND IT WILL EQUALLY BE HARD TO AVOID BEING ALONE WITH CAROL!

BUT WHAT CAN I SAY WHEN THAT MOMENT COMES? ONLY ONE WAY OUT OF THIS DILEMMA--I'VE GOT TO USE ALL MY WILES TO PREVENT CAROL FROM POPPING THE QUESTION!

LATER, BEHIND LOCKED DOORS IN THE HANGAR, A SLIGHTLY SOMBER GLADIATOR TAKES HIS OATH BEFORE THE *POWER LAMP*...

IN BRIGHTEST DAY, IN BLACKEST NIGHT, NO EVIL SHALL ESCAPE MY SIGHT! LET THOSE WHO WORSHIP EVIL'S MIGHT BEWARE MY POWER -- *GREEN LANTERN'S LIGHT!*

AND SOON AT THE TAVERN IN THE PARK, WHERE THE CHARITY AFFAIR IS ABOUT TO BEGIN...

AH! HERE COMES *GREEN LANTERN* NOW!

BUT AS A THREATENING SHOWER BIDS TO SPOIL THE FESTIVITIES...

WHAT A SHAME! WE'LL BE RAINED *OUT!*

OH, *GREEN LANTERN!* IF ONLY YOU COULD DO SOME-THING WITH YOUR *RING--!*

MY PLEASURE, MRS. CRANSTON...

THE NEXT MOMENT, AS THE DOWNPOUR STRIKES...

HOW WONDERFUL! *GREEN LANTERN* HAS RAISED A *HUGE GREEN UMBRELLA* WITH HIS *POWER RING!* IT'S POURING ALL AROUND US... BUT WE'RE DRY!

I WON'T HAVE TO KEEP THIS UMBRELLA UP FOR LONG--IT'S JUST A *SUMMER SHOWER!* MEANWHILE, I WONDER WHAT'S HAPPENED TO CAROL...

SHORTLY...

THE SUN'S OUT. AGAIN!

HERE COMES CAROL NOW-- AND FROM THAT DETERMINED LOOK IN HER EYES, I CAN SEE SHE MEANS BUSINESS!

er--WALK IN THE PARK WITH YOU? BUT, CAROL, I'M THE GUEST OF HONOR--I'VE GOT TO SPEAK HERE...

VERY WELL--THE MOMENT AFTER YOU FINISH SPEAKING THEN!

As THE TIME COMES FOR THE PRINCIPAL SPEAKER OF THE OCCASION...

THEY SAY CHARITY BEGINS AT HOME.. BUT LET US NOT FORGET, THIS CITY IS OUR HOME...

COMMUNITY CHEST

;Whew!; THOSE FAN CLUB GIRLS AGAIN! THEY'RE GETTING OUT OF HAND!

LET US THROUGH! WE WANT TO BE CLOSER TO GREEN LANTERN!

WE WANT GREEN LANTERN! WE WANT GREEN LANTERN!

--AND SO LET US CONTRIBUTE ALL WE CAN!

I BETTER TAKE CAROL FOR A WALK--IF ONLY TO GET AWAY FROM THOSE OVERENTHUSIASTIC FANS OF MINE!

COMMUNITY CHEST

AND SOON AFTER, AS POLICE HOLD BACK THE EAGER DAMSELS, GL AND CAROL SLIP OFF...

YOU--er--SAY THERE'S SOMETHING IMPORTANT ON YOUR MIND, CAROL?

I'LL FACE ANYTHING BUT THOSE GIRLS!

YES, GREEN LANTERN! SHALL WE SIT DOWN?

THERE'S NOT TOO MUCH PRIVACY HERE...BUT I GUESS IT WILL DO...

DO--FOR WHAT, CAROL? YOU'RE ACTING SO SERIOUS! YOU KNOW SOMETHING--

YOU'RE VERY PRETTY WHEN YOU'RE SERIOUS-- BUT YOU'RE EVEN MORE ATTRACTIVE WHEN YOU SMILE! NOW HOW ABOUT A LITTLE SMILE? I MEAN--

I'VE GOT TO KEEP TALKING--OR SHE'LL POP THE QUESTION!

I'VE NEVER **SEEN** YOU CARRY ON LIKE THIS, **GREEN LANTERN!** YOU'RE USUALLY SO... QUIET! ARE YOU SURE YOU'RE ALL RIGHT?

GOOD! I'VE GOT HER TO SWITCH THE CONVERSATION TO SOMETHING ELSE...

AS A MATTER OF FACT, I HAVEN'T BEEN FEELING TOO WELL... PROBABLY SOMETHING I ATE--! MAYBE I OUGHT TO--

--OUGHT TO GET **MARRIED!** **THAT'S** YOUR TROUBLE, DARLING...

LIVING BY YOUR-SELF--EATING GOODNESS KNOWS WHAT FOR MEALS! HOW CAN YOU FEEL GOOD? IT STANDS TO REASON...

EXCUSE ME, CAROL, I... CAN HARDLY HEAR YOU! THOSE NOISY MODEL AIRPLANES...

BZZZ!

I'VE GAINED A MOMENT'S TIME! BUT I'VE GOT TO DO SOMETHING DRASTIC OR SHE'LL COME OUT WITH IT AGAIN! WAIT A SECOND-- I HAVE AN IDEA...

BZZZ!

SECRETLY, THE **GREEN GLADIATOR** PREPARES HIS RING FOR ACTION...

I'VE NEVER **USED** MY RING TO **CREATE A MENACE!** BUT THAT'S WHAT I NEED NOW-- A **CHILLER-DILLER MENACE** THAT I'LL HAVE TO COMBAT-- AND GIVE ME A LEGITIMATE EXCUSE TO GET AWAY FROM HERE --AND CAROL--

BZZZZZZZ!

OUT FROM **GL'S** SIDE THE BEAM SHOOTS, UNSEEN BY HIS FAIR COMPANION...

I'LL TALK LOUDER--YELL WHAT I HAVE TO SAY, IF NECESSARY! THIS IS LEAP YEAR-- **AND IT'S A WOMAN'S PRIVILEGE TO--**

BZZZ!

CAROL! LOOK--!!

7

BUT AS CAROL TURNS, SHE DOESN'T SEE A MODEL PLANE SWOOP DOWN AND...

WHERE--? WHAT--?

THWACK!

OKAY, I SEE...IT! NOW PLEASE STOP INTERRUPTING--AND LET ME FINISH WHAT I HAVE TO SAY!

AS THIS IS LEAP YEAR--OH, NEVER MIND THE BUILDUP! I'LL GET RIGHT TO THE POINT! GREEN LANTERN, WILL YOU MARRY ME?

THERE! I'VE SAID IT! NOW HE'S GOT TO ANSWER-- ONE WAY OR ANOTHER!

AS ANXIOUS, SILENT MOMENTS PASS...

HEAVENS! I THOUGHT MY PROPOSAL MIGHT SURPRISE GREEN LANTERN! BUT I NEVER EXPECTED IT WOULD STRIKE HIM DUMB! HE HASN'T SAID A WORD--!

GREEN LANTERN, STOP PRETENDING YOU DIDN'T HEAR WHAT I SAID! YOU--OH, MY GOSH! HE'S KEELED OVER!

SOMETHING'S HAPPENED TO GREEN LANTERN! HELP!! HELP!

SOON... THANKS FOR HELPING ME, CABBIE! WE'VE GOT TO GET GREEN LANTERN TO A DOCTOR!

I KNOW WHERE THERE'S ONE NEARBY, MISS!

MEANWHILE, THE "MENACE" CREATED BY THE GREEN BEAM LIVES A LIFE OF HIS OWN...

STRANGE...I KNOW I'M A "CHILLER-DILLER" BUT WHAT THAT MEANS...OR WHAT I'M SUPPOSED TO DO...I DON'T KNOW! BUT THIS PLACE IS FULL OF ODD-LOOKING CREATURES!

AS "CHILLER-DILLER" DOES SOME SIGHTSEEING...

AS SOON AS THEY SEE ME, THEY RUN AWAY--AS IF THEY DON'T LIKE ME! WELL...IF THEY WON'T LIKE ME, I WON'T LIKE THEM!

GOOD GOSH! WHAT'S THAT?!

BUT AS THE SLIGHTLY NEAR-SIGHTED INVADER STRAIGHTENS UP...

OOOPS

GREAT SCOTT! THAT THING WILL TEAR THE CITY APART! CAN'T ANYONE DO SOMETHING?

AT NEARBY ARMY HEADQUARTERS...

...AND SEND FIFTEEN TANKS, A GUIDED MISSILE SQUADRON, THREE RECONNAISSANCE TEAMS, AND A BAZOOKA BATTALION TO SECTOR THREE--AT ONCE!

MEANWHILE... I DON'T LIKE IT HERE! THERE'S TOO MUCH *NOISE* IN THIS PLACE! I'VE GOT TO GET AWAY--*UH!*

CRASH!

THE CREATURE BACKED UP INTO THAT STATUE-- AND DEMOLISHED IT!

MUST BE SOME WAY OUT OF THIS PLACE...

HERE COMES THE ARMY! THEY'LL FINISH THAT *THING!*

MORE NOISE!? HOW DO THOSE LITTLE CREATURES STAND THIS NOISE--?

BLAM! BAM!

OUR SHELLS BOUNCE RIGHT OFF IT!

THEN, AS "*CHILLER-DILLER*" MOVES TOWARD THE RIVER-DOCKS...

ULGG! ODD... I CAN'T WALK ON THIS LIQUID MATTER!

IT'S COMING OUT!

WHAT'S IT GONNA DO NOW?

I'LL TAKE THIS "ROADWAY" OVER THE LIQUID...

AFTER THE INCREDIBLE CREATURE HURRIES ACROSS THE BRIDGE...

GENERAL! THE *THING* IS HEADING FOR OUR ATOMIC STOCKPILE! IF IT GETS INTO THAT, IT MAY BLOW UP HALF THE COUNTRY!

MR. PRESIDENT, THIS IS GENERAL WILLIS! WE NEED REINFORCEMENTS, SIR! *COAST CITY* IS ABOUT TO BE BLOWN OFF THE MAP!

AT THAT MOMENT, IN THE DOCTOR'S OFFICE WHERE *GREEN LANTERN* HAS BEEN TAKEN...

...AND THE INVULNERABLE CREATURE IS *STILL GOING!* THE NEXT FEW MINUTES WILL TELL! IT IS TOO LATE TO EVACUATE THE CITY!

HOLY SMOKE! ACCORDING TO THE DESCRIPTION OVER THE RADIO...

...IT'S THE "MENACE" I MADE WITH MY *POWER BEAM*--TO DISTRACT CAROL--THAT'S CAUSING ALL THE TROUBLE! I'VE GOT TO GET GOING--FAST!

GREEN LANTERN! ARE YOU ALL RIGHT?

HE DIDN'T ANSWER--!

HE MUST BE ALL RIGHT-- LOOK AT HIM GO!

AND IN THE VERY NICK OF TIME...

GREEN LANTERN SAVED US--HE DISSOLVED THE *MONSTER!*

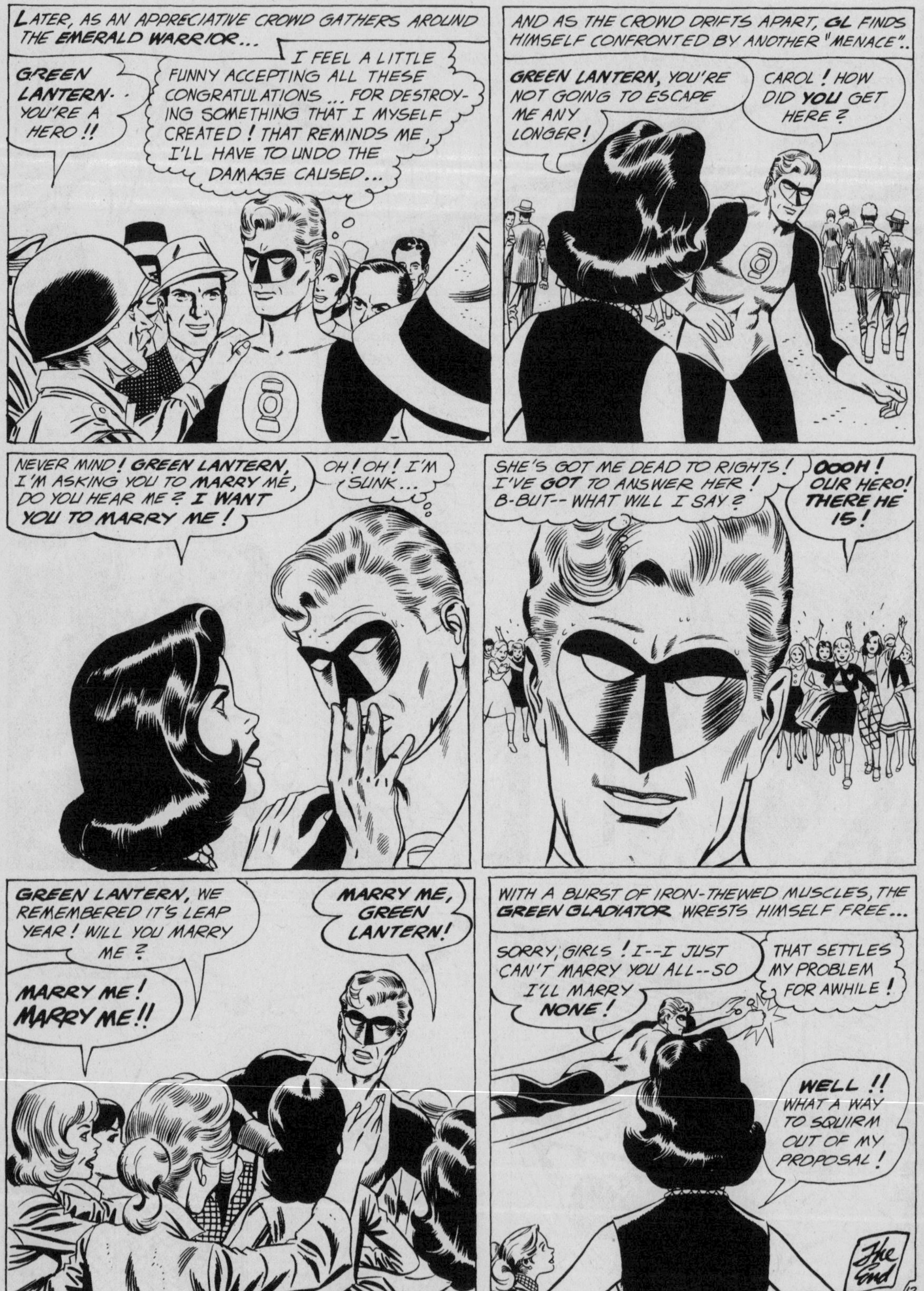
LATER, AS AN APPRECIATIVE CROWD GATHERS AROUND THE EMERALD WARRIOR...
GREEN LANTERN-- YOU'RE A HERO !!
I FEEL A LITTLE FUNNY ACCEPTING ALL THESE CONGRATULATIONS ... FOR DESTROYING SOMETHING THAT I MYSELF CREATED ! THAT REMINDS ME, I'LL HAVE TO UNDO THE DAMAGE CAUSED...
AND AS THE CROWD DRIFTS APART, GL FINDS HIMSELF CONFRONTED BY ANOTHER "MENACE"..
GREEN LANTERN, YOU'RE NOT GOING TO ESCAPE ME ANY LONGER!
CAROL ! HOW DID YOU GET HERE ?
NEVER MIND ! GREEN LANTERN, I'M ASKING YOU TO MARRY ME, DO YOU HEAR ME ? I WANT YOU TO MARRY ME !
OH ! OH ! I'M SUNK...
SHE'S GOT ME DEAD TO RIGHTS ! I'VE GOT TO ANSWER HER ! B-BUT-- WHAT WILL I SAY ?
OOOH ! OUR HERO! THERE HE IS !
GREEN LANTERN, WE REMEMBERED IT'S LEAP YEAR ! WILL YOU MARRY ME ?
MARRY ME, GREEN LANTERN!
MARRY ME ! MARRY ME !!
WITH A BURST OF IRON-THEWED MUSCLES, THE GREEN GLADIATOR WRESTS HIMSELF FREE...
SORRY, GIRLS ! I--I JUST CAN'T MARRY YOU ALL--SO I'LL MARRY NONE !
THAT SETTLES MY PROBLEM FOR AWHILE !
WELL !! WHAT A WAY TO SQUIRM OUT OF MY PROPOSAL !
The End
12

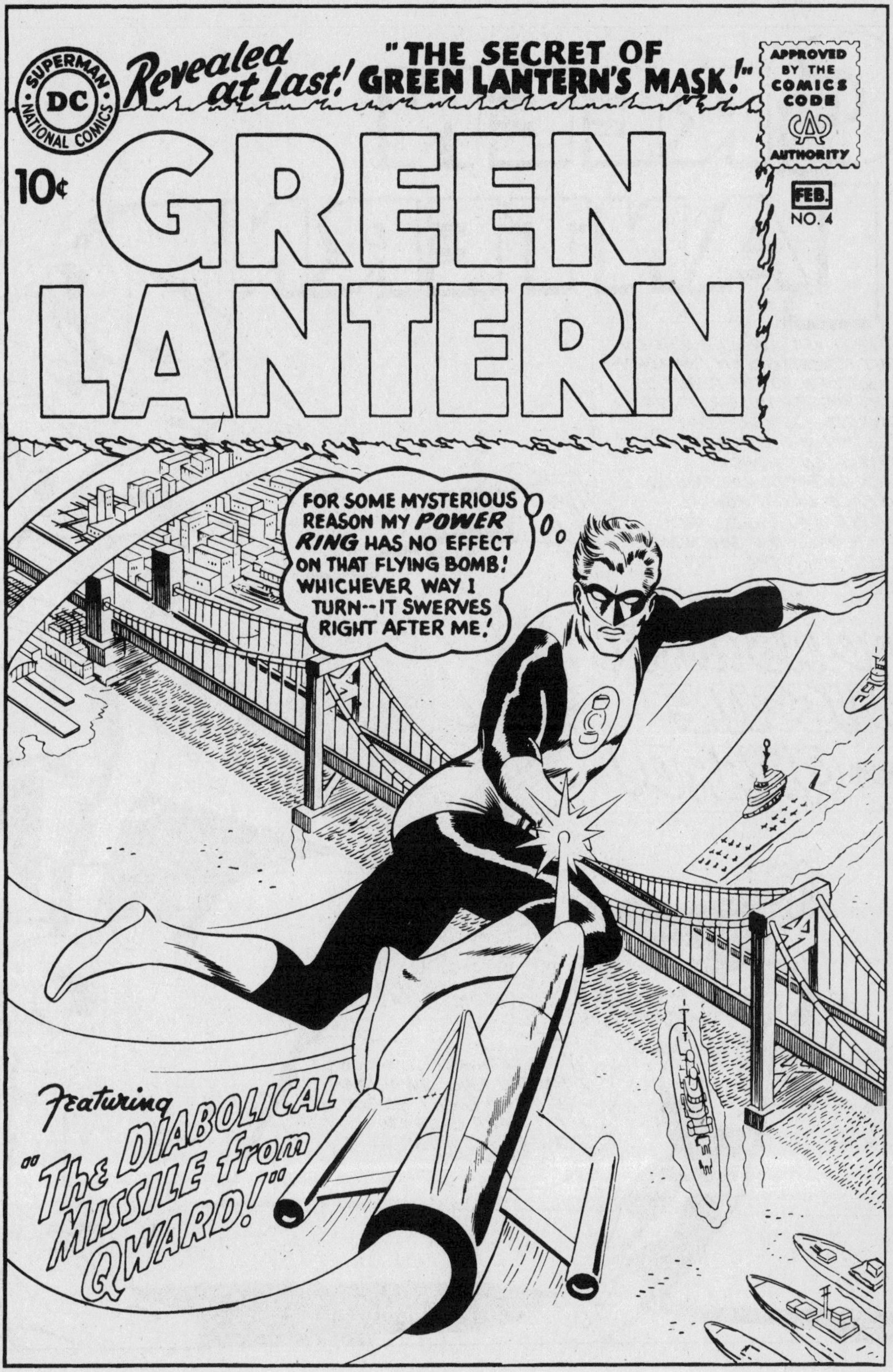
SUPERMAN DC NATIONAL COMICS
Revealed at Last! "THE SECRET OF GREEN LANTERN'S MASK!"
APPROVED BY THE COMICS CODE AUTHORITY
10¢
GREEN LANTERN
FEB. NO. 4
FOR SOME MYSTERIOUS REASON MY POWER RING HAS NO EFFECT ON THAT FLYING BOMB! WHICHEVER WAY I TURN--IT SWERVES RIGHT AFTER ME!
Featuring "The DIABOLICAL MISSILE from QWARD!"

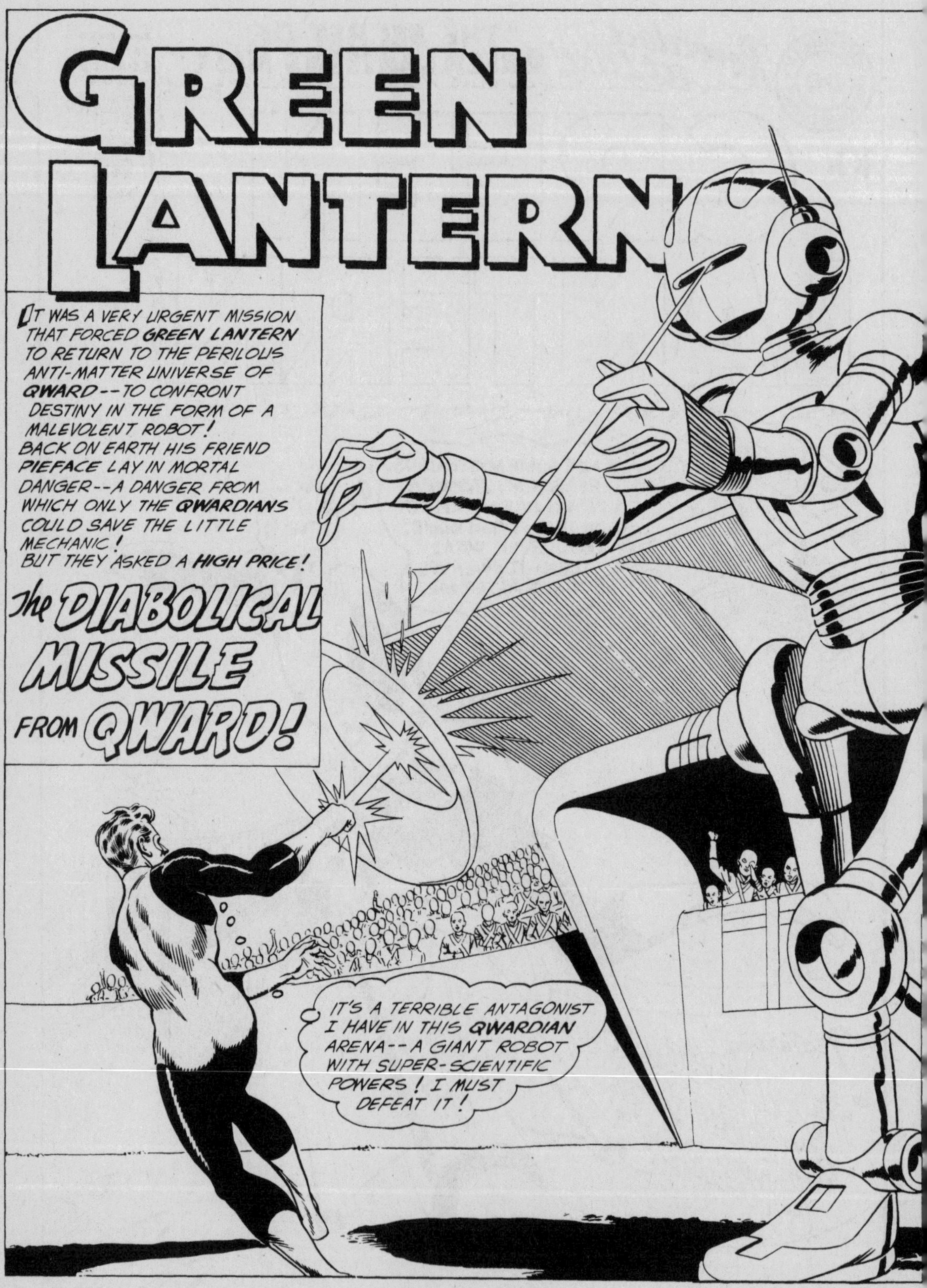
GREEN LANTERN
IT WAS A VERY URGENT MISSION THAT FORCED GREEN LANTERN TO RETURN TO THE PERILOUS ANTI-MATTER UNIVERSE OF QWARD--TO CONFRONT DESTINY IN THE FORM OF A MALEVOLENT ROBOT! BACK ON EARTH HIS FRIEND PIEFACE LAY IN MORTAL DANGER--A DANGER FROM WHICH ONLY THE QWARDIANS COULD SAVE THE LITTLE MECHANIC! BUT THEY ASKED A HIGH PRICE!
The DIABOLICAL MISSILE FROM QWARD!
IT'S A TERRIBLE ANTAGONIST I HAVE IN THIS QWARDIAN ARENA--A GIANT ROBOT WITH SUPER-SCIENTIFIC POWERS! I MUST DEFEAT IT!

ON THE ANTI-MATTER UNIVERSE OF **QWARD**, THE EXACT OPPOSITE OF OURS IN EVERY WAY, A SECRET MEETING OF THE **CHIEF WEAPONERS**, THE PLANETARY OVERLORDS...

FELLOW **WEAPONERS**, THERE IS IN THE COSMOS AN UNENDING BATTLE BETWEEN THE FORCES OF **GOOD** AND **EVIL**! AS FOR US, WE LIVE BY THE PRINCIPLES OF **EVIL**...

...JUST AS OUR NEIGHBORING UNIVERSE WITH THE PLANET **EARTH** IN IT LIVES BY THE PRINCIPLES OF **GOODNESS**--WHICH WE ABHOR! BUT IN ORDER TO DESTROY OUR MORTAL ENEMIES WE MUST FIRST DESTROY ALL THE **POWER LAMPS**...

...SUCH AS THE ONE POSSESSED BY THE EARTHMAN **GREEN LANTERN**! THEREFORE I AM PLEASED TO REPORT TO YOU TODAY THAT A GREAT STEP HAS BEEN TAKEN ON THE ROAD TO OUR EVIL DESTINY! **GREEN LANTERN IS ABOUT TO BE DESTROYED!**

RECENTLY OUR SCIENTISTS COMPLETED THIS ROBOT! IT IS PERFECT IN EVERY WAY--INCLUDING ITS DISTORTED, EVIL MIND! AND THIS ROBOT--CALLED **GNAXOS**--SOLVED OUR MOST PERPLEXING PROBLEM...

WE GAVE IT THE ASSIGNMENT OF FIGURING OUT A SURE WAY TO ELIMINATE **GREEN LANTERN**--AND IN NO TIME AT ALL ITS SUBTLE BRAIN COMPLETED THE TASK! EVEN AT THIS VERY MOMENT...

...AN **ENGINE OF DESTRUCTION** IS WINGING ITS WAY TOWARD THE **EMERALD CRUSADER** WHICH HE CAN **NEVER** HOPE TO ESCAPE!

2

AND AT THE **FERRIS AIRCRAFT COMPANY** WHERE HAL JORDAN, ACE TEST PILOT, IS EMPLOYED...

HAL, YOU SEEM A BIT WORRIED TODAY! IS ANYTHING WRONG?

I'M NOT SURE, **PIEFACE!** YOU SEE...

...MY **POWER RING**--WHICH I KEEP HERE IN THIS POCKET WHEN I'M NOT WEARING IT-- HAS BEEN EMITTING A PECULIAR TYPE OF ENERGY FOR THE PAST HOUR! IT'S AS IF...AS IF IT'S TRYING TO WARN ME OF SOME **DANGER!**

GREAT FISH-- HOOKS!

AND THAT REMINDS ME, I'D BETTER RECHARGE MY RING-- JUST IN CASE! YOU KEEP AN EYE OUT, WILL YOU, **PIEFACE?**

SURE THING, HAL! DON'T WORRY-- NO ONE WILL GET PAST **ME!**

Editor's Note :

PIEFACE--OR THOMAS KALMAKU, HAL'S CRACK ESKIMO AIRPLANE MECHANIC, TO GIVE HIM HIS REAL NAME -- IS THE ONLY PERSON ON EARTH WHO KNOWS THAT HAL JORDAN IS IN REALITY **GREEN LANTERN!** WHICH EXPLAINS THE TEST PILOT'S FREE- DOM IN DISCUSSING SUCH **TOP SECRET** MATTERS AS HIS RING AND ITS POWERS!

BEHIND CLOSED DOORS IN HAL'S DRESSING ROOM AT THE HANGAR, A SOLEMN OATH IS REPEATED...

IN BRIGHTEST DAY, IN BLACKEST NIGHT, NO EVIL SHALL ESCAPE MY SIGHT! LET THOSE WHO WORSHIP EVIL'S MIGHT BEWARE MY POWER--**GREEN LANTERN'S LIGHT!**

AND AS THE GREEN GLADIATOR EMERGES...

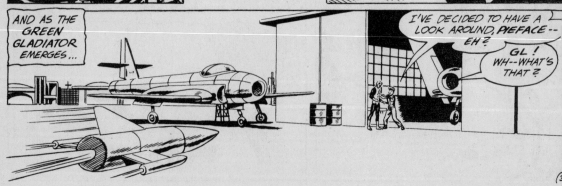

I'VE DECIDED TO HAVE A LOOK AROUND, **PIEFACE**-- EH?

GL! WH--WHAT'S THAT?

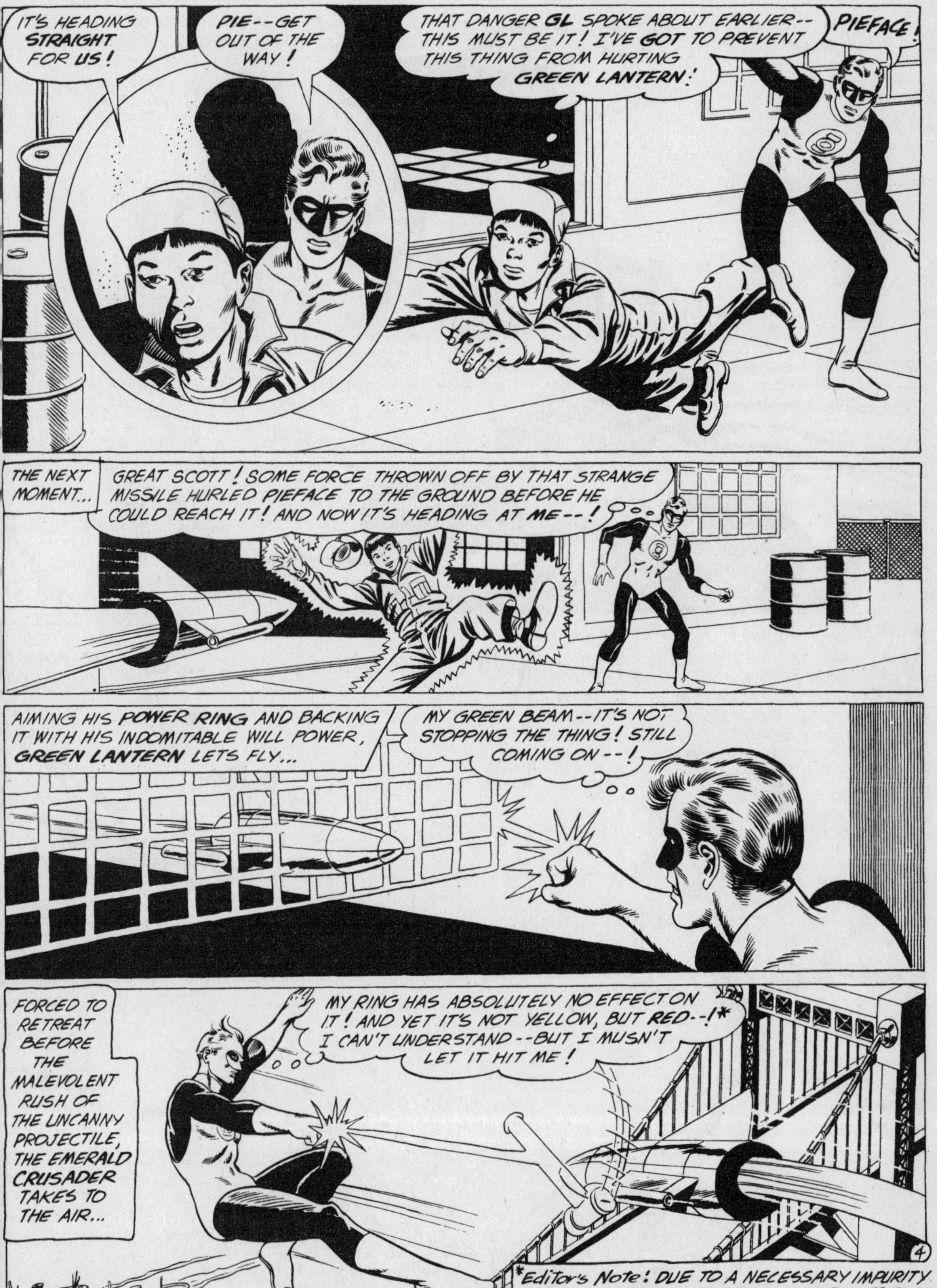
IT'S HEADING STRAIGHT FOR US!
PIE--GET OUT OF THE WAY!
THAT DANGER GL SPOKE ABOUT EARLIER-- THIS MUST BE IT! I'VE GOT TO PREVENT THIS THING FROM HURTING GREEN LANTERN!
PIEFACE!
THE NEXT MOMENT...
GREAT SCOTT! SOME FORCE THROWN OFF BY THAT STRANGE MISSILE HURLED PIEFACE TO THE GROUND BEFORE HE COULD REACH IT! AND NOW IT'S HEADING AT ME--!
AIMING HIS POWER RING AND BACKING IT WITH HIS INDOMITABLE WILL POWER, GREEN LANTERN LETS FLY...
MY GREEN BEAM--IT'S NOT STOPPING THE THING! STILL COMING ON--!
FORCED TO RETREAT BEFORE THE MALEVOLENT RUSH OF THE UNCANNY PROJECTILE, THE EMERALD CRUSADER TAKES TO THE AIR...
MY RING HAS ABSOLUTELY NO EFFECT ON IT! AND YET IT'S NOT YELLOW, BUT RED--!* I CAN'T UNDERSTAND--BUT I MUSN'T LET IT HIT ME!
4
*Editor's Note: DUE TO A NECESSARY IMPURITY IN ITS ORIGINAL MATERIALS, THE POWER RING HAS NO EFFECT ON ANYTHING YELLOW!

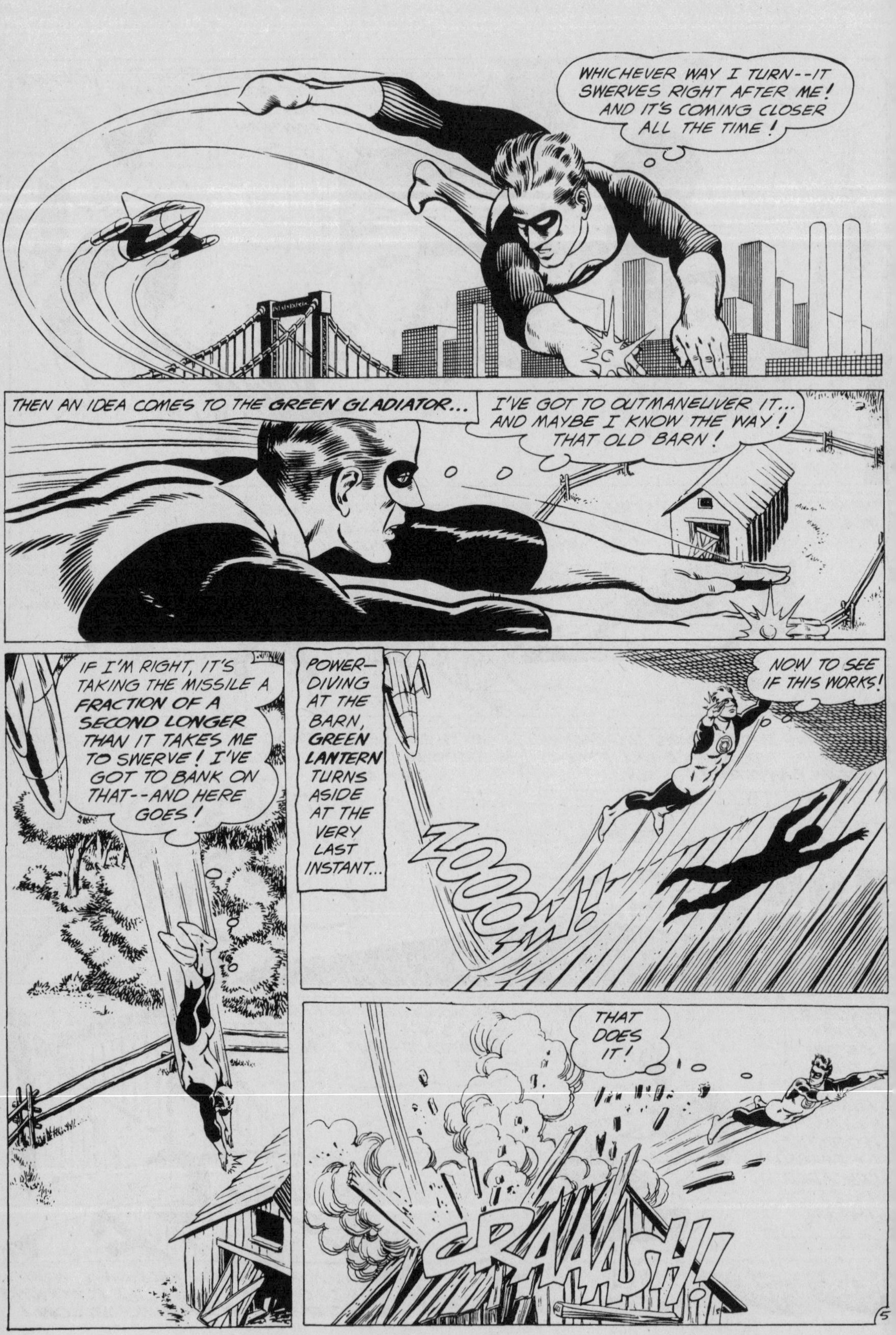
WHICHEVER WAY I TURN--IT SWERVES RIGHT AFTER ME! AND IT'S COMING CLOSER ALL THE TIME!
THEN AN IDEA COMES TO THE GREEN GLADIATOR...
I'VE GOT TO OUTMANEUVER IT... AND MAYBE I KNOW THE WAY! THAT OLD BARN!
IF I'M RIGHT, IT'S TAKING THE MISSILE A FRACTION OF A SECOND LONGER THAN IT TAKES ME TO SWERVE! I'VE GOT TO BANK ON THAT--AND HERE GOES!
POWER-DIVING AT THE BARN, GREEN LANTERN TURNS ASIDE AT THE VERY LAST INSTANT...
NOW TO SEE IF THIS WORKS!
ZOOOOM!
THAT DOES IT!
CRAAASH!
5

AS GL RUSHES BACK TO HIS MECHANIC...

WHAT'S WRONG, PAL?

HE'S IN SOME KIND OF SHOCK! THE CONTACT WITH THE MISSILE--IT'S DONE SOMETHING TO HIM! HE DOESN'T SEEM BADLY HURT, AND YET--

THAT AURA OF YELLOW RADIATION AROUND HIM-- MY RING CAN'T GET THROUGH IT TO ROUSE HIM! NO TIME TO GO FOR A DOCTOR! I'VE GOT TO FIND OUT FOR MYSELF IF HE'S ALIVE--!

ON IMPULSE THE RING-WIELDER TURNS HIS GREAT GREEN BEAM INTO A HUGE STETHOSCOPE...

THERE! I HEAR HIS HEART ALL RIGHT! HE'S STILL ALIVE! BUT WAIT A SECOND--!

THUMP!

AS A DREAD FACT DAWNS ON THE **EMERALD CRUSADER**...

GREAT SCOTT! UNLESS I'M MISTAKEN HIS HEART IS **SLOWING DOWN**! YES... LITTLE BY LITTLE IT'S BEATING **MORE** SLOWLY!

THUMP, THUMP!

IN GRIM DESPERATION AT THE PLIGHT OF HIS PLUCKY LITTLE FRIEND, THE **EMERALD CRUSADER** PLUNGES INTO ACTION...

THERE ISN'T MUCH TIME! I'VE GOT TO WORK FAST! I'M CONVINCED IT'S THAT STRANGE RADIATION AROUND HIM THAT'S ENDANGERING *PIEFACE'S* LIFE--THE RADIATION GIVEN OFF BY THAT **MISSILE**!

IF MY RING CAN'T PIERCE THAT RADIATION, NO POWER ON EARTH CAN! BUT WHOEVER MADE THIS MISSILE MAY KNOW THE ANTI- DOTE! IT'S MY ONLY HOPE! I'VE **GOT** TO FIND OUT WHERE IT CAME FROM!

AS GL'S ALL-POWERFUL RING EXAMINES THE SHATTERED PROJECTILE, A STARTLING FACT BECOMES CLEAR...

GREAT SCOTT! THE MISSILE IS REALLY *YELLOW!* BUT A BATTERY OF RED LIGHTS IN ITS INTERIOR WAS SET UP TO SHINE THROUGH ITS TRANS- PARENT METAL SKIN -- SO AS TO MAKE IT *SEEM RED !!*

SO THAT'S WHY MY RING HAD NO EFFECT ON IT! WHAT A DIABOLICAL SCHEME! SOMEONE SET IT UP THIS WAY IN ORDER TO DESTROY ME -- BY THROWING ME OFF MY GUARD! AND IT CAME WITHIN AN INCH OF SUCCEEDING! BUT WHERE --

OF COURSE! THIS MISSILE MUST HAVE COME FROM *QWARD!* I SHOULD HAVE REALIZED! ONLY MY DEADLY ENEMIES -- THE *WEAPONERS* OF *QWARD* -- HAVE THE SUPER-SCIENTIFIC KNOW-HOW NECESSARY TO CONSTRUCT SUCH A MECHANISM! AND THAT MEANS --

SNAP!

-- I'VE GOT TO GO INTO *QWARD* TO GET THE ANTIDOTE TO THE RADIATION THAT IS KILLING *PIEFACE!* NOT A MOMENT TO LOSE --!

HIS RING CLEAVING THE WAY, THE *GREEN-CLAD GLADIATOR* STREAKS THROUGH THE AIR, AS HIS THOUGHTS REVOLVE AROUND HIS STRANGE OBJECTIVE...

THE UNIVERSE OF *QWARD* -- WHAT AN INCREDIBLE PLACE! THOSE THAT TRY TO DO *GOOD* THERE ARE HOUNDED, THROWN BEHIND BARS! EVIL IS THE ACCEPTED WAY OF LIFE!

TRUTH IS SCORNED! THEY TRY TO OUT-DO EACH OTHER IN WICKEDNESS -- AND I HAVE REASON TO BELIEVE THAT LATELY *I...GREEN LANTERN...* HAVE BECOME *PUBLIC ENEMY NUMBER ONE* THERE -- WHICH IS OKAY WITH ME!

7

As **GL** nears a certain spot in the countryside near **Coast City**...

There it is--the hole in the cosmic-barrier that the **Qwardians** set up with their futuristic science to pass from their universe into ours! I've been through it before...

...but each time it's a **shock!** Feeling...of being unable...to breathe...numbness over my whole body as if I were in the grip of some...incredible force...!

But it takes only a moment to get through-- and the will power to **keep going!** Now to head for Qward City and the citadel of the **Weaponers!**

Meanwhile...

It is **Green Lantern!** He has escaped his doom!

Yes...but by coming here he has played into our hands! Fear not...!

Moments later as a vibrant green-clad figure crashes to the very heart of the **Weaponer** dynasty by means of his **power ring...**

Wait, **Green Lantern!** We know that you have come here because your friend back on Earth is in deadly danger--!

It's **Kiman--** the chief weaponer!

You know that, do you? Then you must know what I'm after!

8

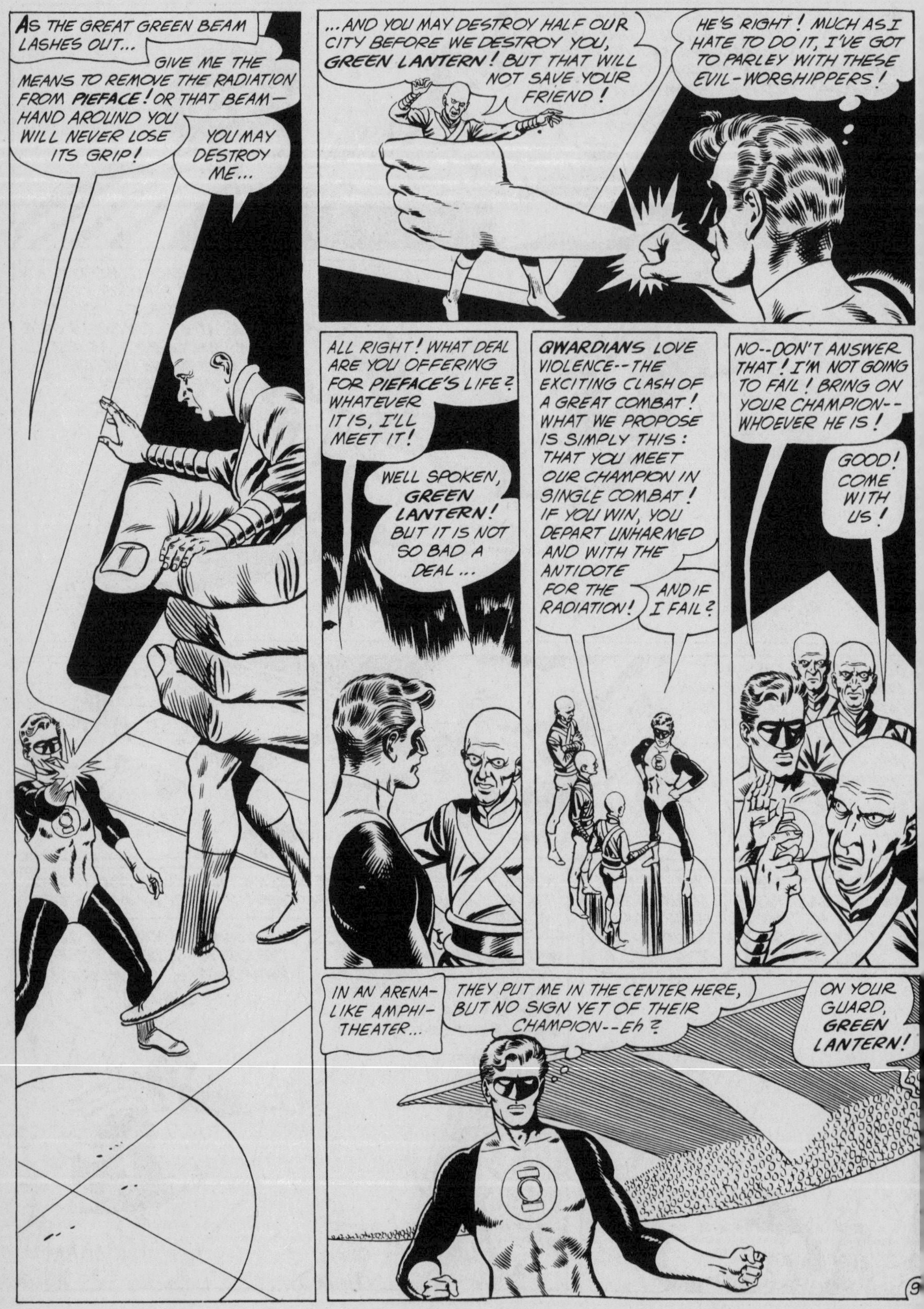
AS THE GREAT GREEN BEAM LASHES OUT...
GIVE ME THE MEANS TO REMOVE THE RADIATION FROM PIEFACE! OR THAT BEAM-HAND AROUND YOU WILL NEVER LOSE ITS GRIP!
YOU MAY DESTROY ME...
...AND YOU MAY DESTROY HALF OUR CITY BEFORE WE DESTROY YOU, GREEN LANTERN! BUT THAT WILL NOT SAVE YOUR FRIEND!
HE'S RIGHT! MUCH AS I HATE TO DO IT, I'VE GOT TO PARLEY WITH THESE EVIL-WORSHIPPERS!
ALL RIGHT! WHAT DEAL ARE YOU OFFERING FOR PIEFACE'S LIFE? WHATEVER IT IS, I'LL MEET IT!
WELL SPOKEN, GREEN LANTERN! BUT IT IS NOT SO BAD A DEAL...
QWARDIANS LOVE VIOLENCE--THE EXCITING CLASH OF A GREAT COMBAT! WHAT WE PROPOSE IS SIMPLY THIS: THAT YOU MEET OUR CHAMPION IN SINGLE COMBAT! IF YOU WIN, YOU DEPART UNHARMED AND WITH THE ANTIDOTE FOR THE RADIATION!
AND IF I FAIL?
NO--DON'T ANSWER THAT! I'M NOT GOING TO FAIL! BRING ON YOUR CHAMPION--WHOEVER HE IS!
GOOD! COME WITH US!
IN AN ARENA-LIKE AMPHITHEATER...
THEY PUT ME IN THE CENTER HERE, BUT NO SIGN YET OF THEIR CHAMPION--Eh?
ON YOUR GUARD, GREEN LANTERN!
9

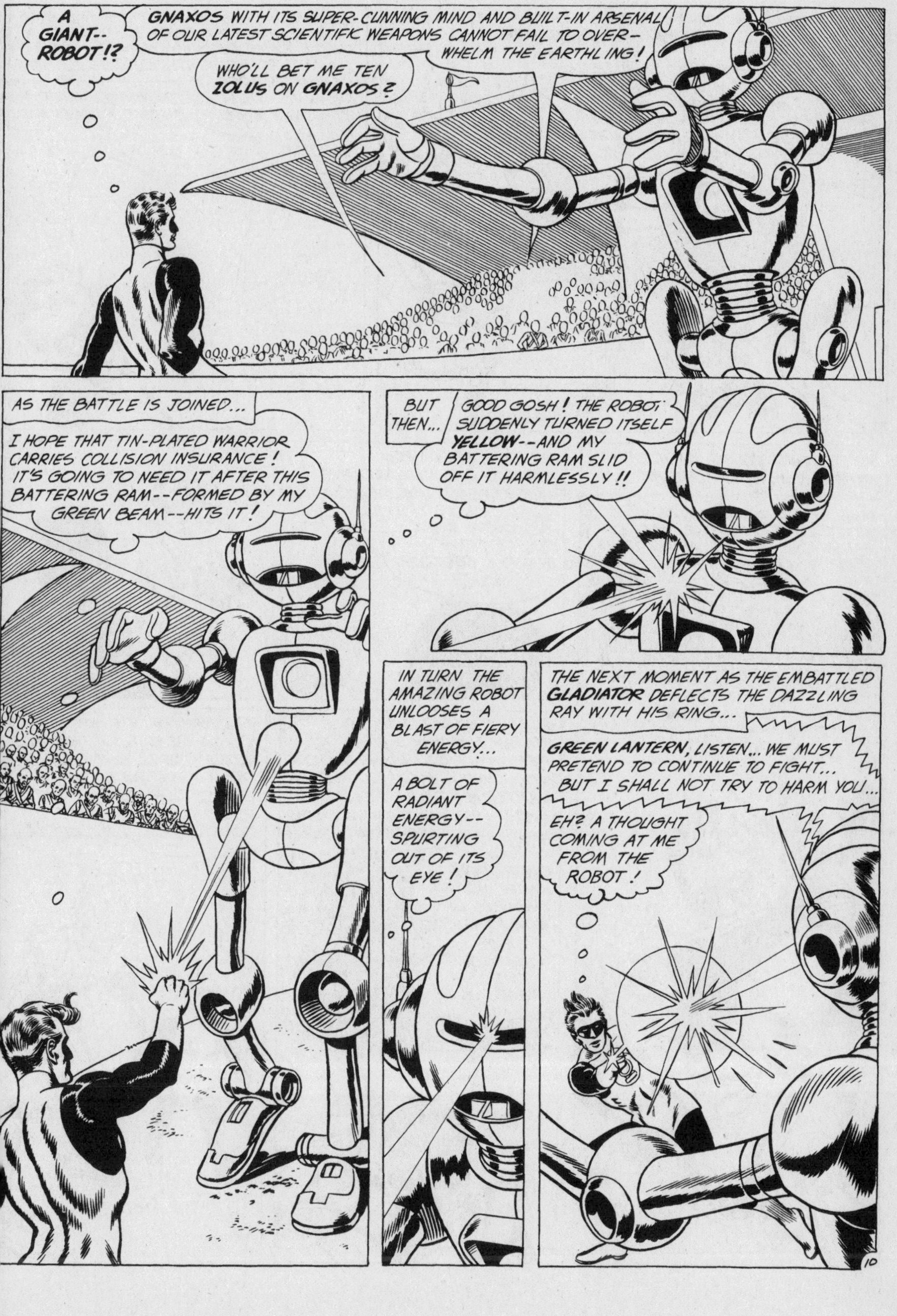
A GIANT--ROBOT!?
GNAXOS WITH ITS SUPER-CUNNING MIND AND BUILT-IN ARSENAL OF OUR LATEST SCIENTIFIC WEAPONS CANNOT FAIL TO OVERWHELM THE EARTHLING!
WHO'LL BET ME TEN ZOLUS ON GNAXOS?
AS THE BATTLE IS JOINED...
I HOPE THAT TIN-PLATED WARRIOR CARRIES COLLISION INSURANCE! IT'S GOING TO NEED IT AFTER THIS BATTERING RAM--FORMED BY MY GREEN BEAM--HITS IT!
BUT THEN...
GOOD GOSH! THE ROBOT SUDDENLY TURNED ITSELF YELLOW--AND MY BATTERING RAM SLID OFF IT HARMLESSLY!!
IN TURN THE AMAZING ROBOT UNLOOSES A BLAST OF FIERY ENERGY...
A BOLT OF RADIANT ENERGY--SPURTING OUT OF ITS EYE!
THE NEXT MOMENT AS THE EMBATTLED GLADIATOR DEFLECTS THE DAZZLING RAY WITH HIS RING...
GREEN LANTERN, LISTEN... WE MUST PRETEND TO CONTINUE TO FIGHT... BUT I SHALL NOT TRY TO HARM YOU...
EH? A THOUGHT COMING AT ME FROM THE ROBOT!
10

THEN, ANOTHER BOLT--AND ANOTHER THOUGHT MESSAGE FLASHES AT THE *EMERALD CRUSADER*...

LISTEN, *GREEN LANTERN!* EVEN THOUGH I HAVE HAD ONLY A SHORT LIFE UP TO NOW, I HAVE LEARNED THE DIFFERENCE BETWEEN *GOOD* AND *EVIL!* THOSE HUMANS WHO MADE ME--THE *QWARDIANS*--ARE EVIL!

I, GNAXOS, WAS MADE TO BE EVIL BUT SOMETHING HAPPENED TO MY BRAIN AND I HAVE BECOME *GOOD*--AND I WANT TO HELP YOU BECAUSE I HAVE LEARNED FROM PROBING YOUR MIND THAT YOU TOO ARE GOOD!

JUMPIN' JUPITER! I--I'VE FOUND AN ALLY!

AS THE TWO CLOSE WITH EACH OTHER IN MORTAL COMBAT...

TAKE THIS, *GREEN LANTERN!* IT WILL COUNTERACT THE DEADLY RADIATION THAT IS AFFECTING YOUR FRIEND! TAKE IT--AND FLEE!

BUT WHAT ABOUT YOU, GNAXOS? THE *QWARDIANS* ARE ALREADY BECOMING SUSPICIOUS! THEY'LL DISCOVER WHAT YOU'VE DONE--THEY'LL DESTROY YOU!

PERHAPS--IF THEY CAN!

BUT IF THEY DO, I SHALL PERISH THE WAY I WANT TO PERISH--FIGHTING FOR GOOD AND AGAINST EVIL! GO, *GREEN LANTERN!* I WILL HOLD THEM BACK--PREVENT THEM FROM ATTACKING YOU!

THE QWARDIANS KNOW SOMETHING IS UP NOW! THEY'RE RISING--PULLING OUT WEAPONS--!

NO, GNAXOS! I'M NOT LEAVING YOU TO DEAL WITH THIS MOB ALONE! WE'LL BOTH FIGHT THEM--AND WE'LL BOTH GET OUT OF HERE TOGETHER! COME ON--!

"WE"!?

BUT IN THE MELEE THAT FOLLOWS...

THEY'VE DOWNED THE ROBOT! I TRIED TO PROTECT IT WITH MY RING--BUT A HIGH-ENERGY SHOT SLIPPED THROUGH AND FINISHED IT!

I FEEL LIKE I'VE LOST A FRIEND! BUT I CAN'T MOURN FOR HIM ANY LONGER--I HAVE ANOTHER FRIEND TO THINK ABOUT...AND ENEMIES HERE TO SETTLE WITH!

WITH THE FURY OF VENGEANCE AND BACKED BY HIS INDOMITABLE WILL, **GL** SENDS A GREAT GREEN WAVE SURGING FROM HIS RING WITH OVERWHELMING FORCE...

MAYBE THEY DON'T HAVE **TIDAL WAVES** HERE IN THIS UNIVERSE--BUT THE **QWARDIANS** SURE KNOW WHAT ONE FEELS LIKE NOW!

SOON, OUT OF THE HALF-WRECKED CITADEL OF THE **WEAPONERS**...

WELL, IF I WASN'T **PUBLIC ENEMY NUMBER ONE** AROUND HERE BEFORE-- I SURE AM NOW! BUT FROM HERE ON IN I'VE GOT TO TRAVEL --

THROTTLING UP HIS GREEN BEAM TO ITS HIGHEST VELOCITY, THE **GREEN GLADIATOR** STREAKS BACK THE WAY HE CAME! AND SOON...

HAVE I COME IN TIME? I'LL SOON FIND OUT...!

12

HIS HEART IS STILL BEATING, BUT SO SLOW IT SEEMS ABOUT TO STOP!

THUMP

HURRIEDLY, *GL* APPLIES THE COUNTER RADIATION HE HAS BROUGHT...

WILL IT WORK? IT'S *GOT* TO!

THEN, AFTER A BREATHLESS MOMENT...

THE RADIATION IS GONE! *PIEFACE* IS GOING TO BE ALL RIGHT!

-;GROAN!;-

AND SOON...

GREEN LANTERN! WHAT HAPPENED?

THE ANTIDOTE GIVEN TO ME BY *GNAXOS* SAVED HIM!

TAKE IT EASY, FELLER-- YOU'RE OKAY NOW!

AFTER THE MECHANIC HAS LEARNED THE FULL STORY AND HAS RECOVERED COMPLETELY...

THE *QWARDIANS* AGAIN!? SOMETHING TELLS ME OUR TROUBLES WITH THEM ARE ONLY JUST BEGINNING!

IF THEY WANT TROUBLE I'M READY FOR THEM ANY TIME, *PIEFACE!*

WHAT DO YOU MEAN *YOU'RE* READY-- YOU MEAN *WE'RE* READY, DON'T YOU, *GL?!*

PIEFACE IS A GOOD FRIEND, BUT I GUESS I'LL ALWAYS KEEP IN THE BACK OF MY MIND THE MEMORY OF ONE WHO COULD HAVE BEEN MY FRIEND--IF IT HADN'T PERISHED TRYING TO SAVE ME!

The End

13

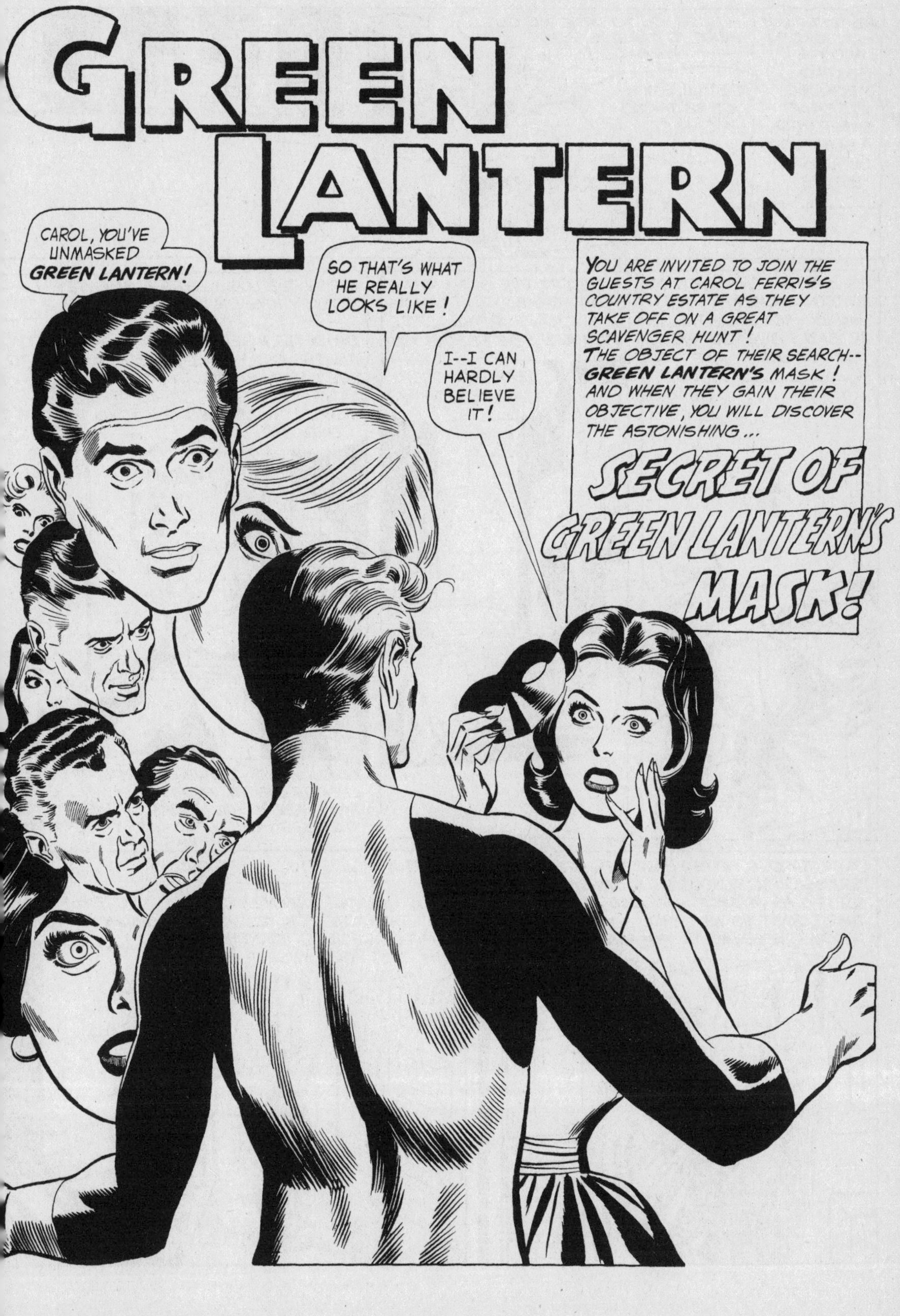
GREEN LANTERN
CAROL, YOU'VE UNMASKED GREEN LANTERN!
SO THAT'S WHAT HE REALLY LOOKS LIKE!
I--I CAN HARDLY BELIEVE IT!
YOU ARE INVITED TO JOIN THE GUESTS AT CAROL FERRIS'S COUNTRY ESTATE AS THEY TAKE OFF ON A GREAT SCAVENGER HUNT! THE OBJECT OF THEIR SEARCH-- GREEN LANTERN'S MASK! AND WHEN THEY GAIN THEIR OBJECTIVE, YOU WILL DISCOVER THE ASTONISHING...
SECRET OF GREEN LANTERN'S MASK!

As test pilot HAL JORDAN AND HIS ESKIMO MECHANIC PIEFACE SWEEP INTO A SUMPTUOUS SUBURBAN ESTATE...

NICE OF YOU TO DRIVE ME OUT HERE TO CAROL'S PLACE, PIEFACE!

I STILL SAY YOU'RE TAKING A CHANCE, HAL...

IT'S GREEN LANTERN WHO'S INVITED TO CAROL'S SOCIETY SHINDIG--NOT YOU! THEY'LL PROBABLY GIVE YOU THE BUM'S RUSH!

COULD BE--

--EXCEPT I'VE GOT A NIFTY PLAN WORKED OUT! THANKS A MILLION FOR THE LIFT, PIEFACE! BE SEEING YOU!

YEAH--SOONER THAN YOU THINK!

AFTER THE LOYAL LITTLE GREASE-MONKEY HAS DRIVEN OFF...

I'M DETERMINED TO "CRASH" THIS PARTY! IT'S THE ONLY WAY I COULD THINK OF TO SEE CAROL SOCIALLY! SINCE HER FATHER WENT OFF ON HIS ROUND-THE-WORLD TRIP,* SHE'S REFUSED TO DATE ME...

*Editor's Note: LEAVING CAROL IN SOLE CHARGE OF THE FERRIS AIRCRAFT COMPANY, WHERE HAL WORKS, ON THE PROMISE THAT SHE WOULD ENGAGE IN NO ROMANCE WHILE HE WAS GONE...

LATER, CAROL'S FATHER GAVE HER SPECIAL PERMISSION TO GO OUT WITH GREEN LANTERN! BUT IT'S AS MYSELF--AS HAL JORDAN--THAT I WANT TO WIN CAROL--NOT AS GL WHOM SHE SEEMS TO PREFER!

SHORTLY, INSIDE THE SUMPTUOUS MANSION...

er--YES, CAROL! GREEN LANTERN LEFT THIS NOTE FOR YOU AT THE PLANT! I DECIDED TO BRING IT OUT HERE MYSELF!

A NOTE--FROM GREEN LANTERN!?

As PRETTY CAROL FERRIS READS THE MISSIVE...

HE CAN'T COME! OH, HOW ANNOYING!

*Dear Carol...
Sorry to disappoint you but an emergency has come up that I must take care of!
Green Lantern*

MY GUESTS AND I WERE COUNTING ON *GREEN LANTERN* BEING HERE!

BUSINESS BEFORE PLEASURE, CAROL! IN ANY EVENT, IT GAVE ME THE IDEA OF DELIVERING THE NOTE PERSONALLY!

THANKS! AND NOW IF YOU'LL EXCUSE ME...

NOT SO FAST, CAROL! AFTER ALL, WITHOUT *GREEN LANTERN*, YOU'LL BE A MAN SHORT, AND SINCE I'M NOT DOING ANYTHING TONIGHT--

YOU WOULDN'T TURN ME AWAY, WOULD YOU, CAROL? I CAN BE VERY AMUSING! I COULD DO A FEW CARD TRICKS--

CARD TRICKS?! HOW CAN YOU POSSIBLY COMPARE *THAT* WITH WHAT *GREEN LANTERN* CAN DO?

HOWEVER, NOW THAT YOU'RE HERE, I SUPPOSE YOU MIGHT AS WELL STAY!

Whew! FOR A MINUTE I THOUGHT I WAS GOING TO NOSE-DIVE! BUT I'M IN!

MEET MY FRIEND, HAL JORDAN, EVERYBODY! HE--er--DOES CARD TRICKS!

MEANWHILE, IN A ROOM ASSIGNED TO A TRIO OF WAITERS ESPECIALLY HIRED FOR THE FESTIVE OCCASION...

I JUST HEARD THAT *GREEN LANTERN* ISN'T COMING AFTER ALL! SO WE CAN GO THROUGH WITH OUR PLAN!

GREAT! I'LL GET RIGHT INTO UNIFORM THEN!

AND SOON...

HOW DO I LOOK?

PERFECT, *WOOZY!* *GREEN LANTERN'S* OWN MOTHER WOULD BE FOOLED! NOW PUT ON YOUR MASK AND LET'S GET STARTED!

OUT IN THE DRAWING ROOM WHERE THE NEW ARRIVAL IS ENTERTAINING THE COMPANY...

HAL JORDAN TELLS THE MOST AMUSING STORIES, CAROL! HE'S REALLY FUN!

HAL *IS* OUTDOING HIMSELF TODAY! I'VE NEVER SEEN HIM LIKE THIS!

I GUESS IT'S BECAUSE HE'S TRYING TO TAKE *GREEN LANTERN'S* PLACE! BUT THAT'S IMPOSSIBLE! HE COULD NEVER IN A MILLION YEARS MATCH--eh?

LOOK-- IT'S *GREEN LANTERN!*

THIS TINY GREEN FLASHLIGHT I HAD MADE IN THE FORM OF A RING IS WORKING LIKE A CHARM!

HI, EVERY-BODY!

GREEN LANTERN, YOU'RE HERE! HOW WONDERFUL!

I FOUND I COULD MAKE IT, CAROL--SO I JUST OPENED THE THROTTLE ON MY GREEN BEAM-- AND HERE I AM! BUT DON'T LET ME INTERRUPT THINGS!

WHAT'S GOING ON HERE?

HAL JORDAN WAS GOING TO SHOW US SOME MAGIC CARD TRICKS, WEREN'T YOU, HAL?

I'VE GOT A BETTER IDEA, CAROL! WHY NOT--er--GET *GREEN LANTERN* TO DO SOME REAL MAGIC TRICKS WITH HIS *POWER RING?*

THIS JOKER IS ABOUT TO BE EXPOSED! BUT I WONDER WHO HE IS-- AND WHAT HE'S UP TO?

WELL, IF YOU ALL INSIST--!

LET'S SAY I WANT TO OPEN THAT DOOR BY REMOTE CONTROL! ALL I HAVE TO DO IS AIM MY RING AND--

AMAZING! IT'S THE FIRST TIME I'VE PERSONALLY SEEN *GREEN LANTERN* IN ACTION!

BEHIND THE DOOR...

HEH--HEH! THIS MUST LOOK LIKE *MAGIC*--FROM THE OTHER ROOM!

WONDERFUL!

DO SOMETHING ELSE!

ALL RIGHT! NOW WATCH THAT WAITER AS I FLASH MY GREEN BEAM AT HIM...

...AND CRY OUT THE MAGIC WORDS *PRESTO--CHANGEO--!*

THAT PHONEY GREEN BEAM CAN'T POSSIBLY HAVE ANY EFFECT ON THE WAITER!

THE NEXT MOMENT...

LOOK AT THAT!! HE LIFTED THE WAITER UP...!

HA! HA! I JUMPED UP HERE FROM THE FLOOR--BUT THE *POWER OF SUGGESTION* IS TERRIFIC! TO THESE SAPS IT SEEMS I WAS LIFTED UP HERE!

AS THE EMERALD-CLAD IMPOSTOR ADDRESSES HIS AUDIENCE ..

NOW, MY FRIENDS, IF YOU'LL EXCUSE ME FOR A FEW MINUTES, I JUST REMEMBERED I MUST RECHARGE *MY RING!* IT WON'T TAKE ME LONG! GO ON WITH YOUR FUN! I'LL BE RIGHT BACK!

SOON, BEHIND CLOSED DOORS...

WHAT ARE WE WAITING FOR, *WOOZY?* LET'S GET ON WITH THE BIG *JOB!*

I KNOW WHAT I'M DOING, *CHIP!* I'M GAINING THEIR *CONFIDENCE...*

IF I MOVE TOO FAST--THEY MAY GET SUSPICIOUS, SEE? LEAVE EVERYTHING TO ME-- AND DON'T WORRY!

WELL, ALL RIGHT-- BUT DON'T STALL TOO LONG!

MEANWHILE, IN ANOTHER UNUSED ROOM, HAL JORDAN SWITCHES TO HIS *GREEN LANTERN* UNIFORM ...

I THINK I HAVE AN IDEA HOW THAT IMPERSONATOR OF MINE PULLED THOSE STUNTS! AND IF I'M RIGHT, THE REAL *GREEN LANTERN* BETTER GET READY FOR *ACTION!*

BACK AT THE PARTY... A SCAVENGER HUNT? THAT'S A TERRIFIC IDEA, CAROL! BUT WHAT WILL WE GO AFTER?

THERE'S ONE OBJECT I'VE ALWAYS BEEN CURIOUS ABOUT--

HOW ABOUT THIS--THE WINNER OF OUR GAME WILL BE WHOEVER MANAGES TO BRING BACK GREEN LANTERN'S MASK!

HOW ORIGINAL!

AS BOY AND GIRL TEAMS SCATTER TO SEARCH FOR THEIR PREY, THE GREEN GLADIATOR...

MAYBE THIS WAY I'LL GET WHAT I'VE WANTED FOR A LONG TIME-- A LOOK AT GREEN LANTERN'S FACE!

HE MAY BE OUT IN THE GARDEN--!

CAROL! THERE HE IS!

LET'S GET HIM, FRED! HURRY-- BEFORE HE CAN USE HIS POWER RING TO ESCAPE US!

WHAT IN THUNDER--?

FASTER, FRED! HE'S GETTING AWAY!

SUDDENLY... HE FELL... SLIPPED ON THE FLOOR... KNOCKED HIMSELF OUT!

OH, MY!

THEN... HE'LL COME TO IN A MOMENT! HE'S NOT REALLY HURT!

...AND MEANWHILE AT LEAST I'M ABOUT TO SEE THE FACE OF MY BELOVED!

WITH A QUICK HAND CAROL FERRIS REACHES OUT...

OHHHHH... WH--WHAT HAPPENED?

HMMMM! HE'S NOT AT ALL LIKE WHAT I THOUGHT HE'D BE! IN FACT--!

I DON'T THINK I LIKE HIM ANYMORE! NOT WITH *THAT* FACE!

YOUR MASK IS THE TREASURE IN A SCAVENGER HUNT WE STARTED GREEN LANTERN. HOPE YOU DON'T MIND!

THEY GOT MY MASK! BUT THEY DIDN'T RECOGNIZE ME--SO I GUESS EVERYTHING'S STILL OKAY! LUCKILY, NO ONE EVER NOTICES A WAITER'S FACE!

AFTER THE "EMERALD CRUSADER" HAS BEEN GIVEN BACK HIS MASK...

WELL, CAROL AND FRED WON THE SCAVENGER HUNT! NOW WHAT--

LISTEN, EVERYONE! I'VE GOT ANOTHER IDEA THAT MAY AMUSE YOU...

WHAT IS IT, GREEN LANTERN?

WELL, YOU'VE SEEN THAT MY POWER RING IS CAPABLE OF INCREDIBLE STUNTS, HAVEN'T YOU? NOW I'M GOING TO SHOW YOU ONE TRICK THAT WILL REALLY STARTLE YOU...

HERE'S MY IDEA! EVERY-BODY PUT HIS JEWELS AND WATCHES ON THIS TABLE HERE! THEN, WITH MY RING I'LL SEND THEM INTO SPACE, ORBIT THEM AROUND THE MOON--AND BRING THEM BACK HERE IN LESS THAN ONE MINUTE!

SENSATIONAL!

I CAN HAVE A WATCH THAT *GREEN LANTERN* SENT AROUND THE MOON!

THAT'S FOR ME! MY PEARLS WILL BE *MORE VALU-ABLE* THAN EVER!

ME TOO!

THEY'RE FALLING FOR IT! GET READY, *CHIP!*

(I'M ALL SET!)

THEN...

NOW...AS I SPEAK THE MAGICAL WORDS--*ALIGAROO GAZAM...* AND FLASH OUT MY GREAT GREEN BEAM...

SUDDENLY IN THE MIDST OF THE "MYSTIC INCANTATION"...

HEY!! THE LIGHTS WENT OUT!

WHAT HAPPENED?

AND WHEN FINALLY LIGHT IS RESTORED...

LOOK! OUR JEWELS ARE GONE!

AND SO'S *GREEN LANTERN!*

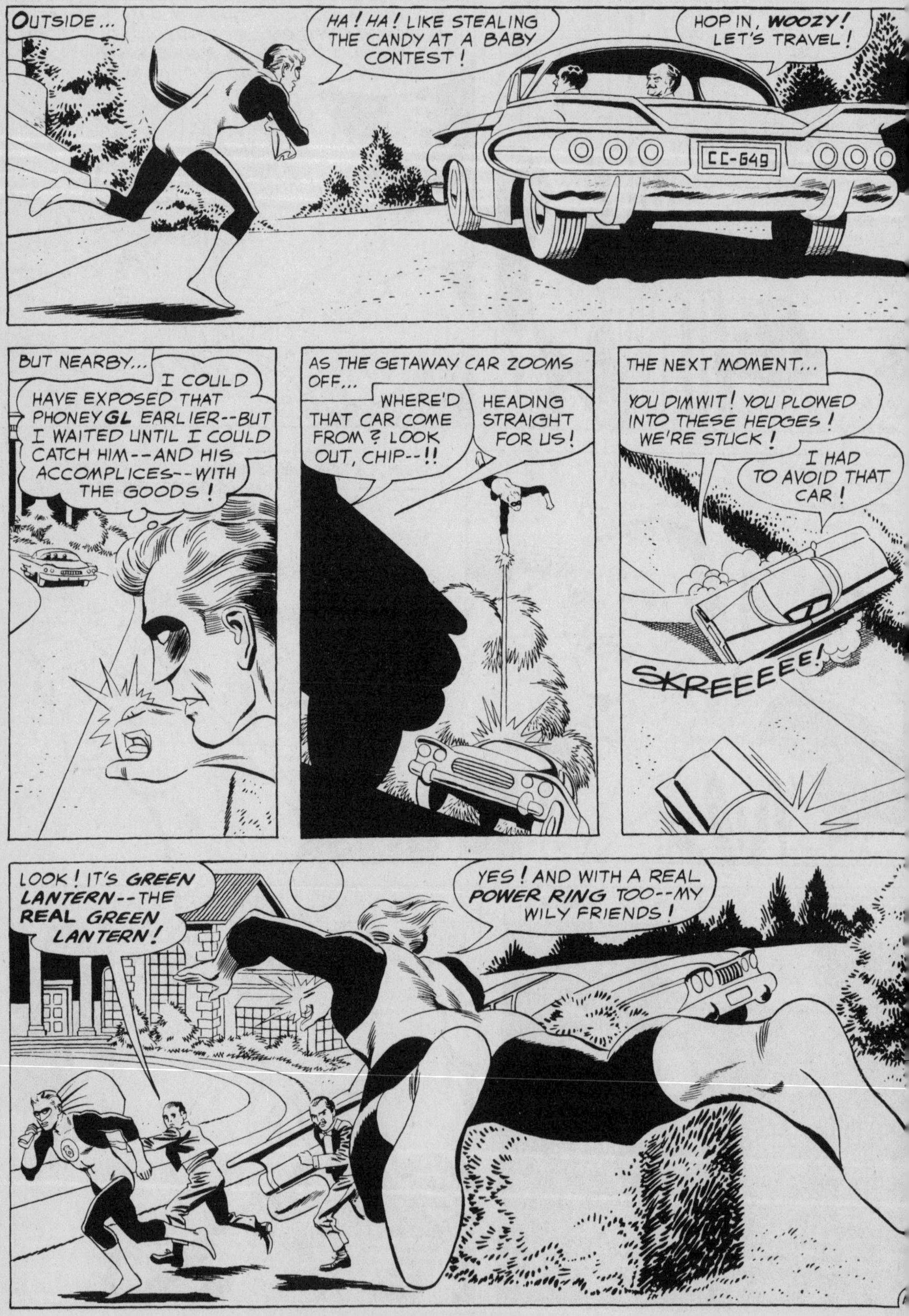
OUTSIDE...
HA! HA! LIKE STEALING THE CANDY AT A BABY CONTEST!
HOP IN, WOOZY! LET'S TRAVEL!
CC-649
BUT NEARBY...
I COULD HAVE EXPOSED THAT PHONEY GL EARLIER--BUT I WAITED UNTIL I COULD CATCH HIM--AND HIS ACCOMPLICES--WITH THE GOODS!
AS THE GETAWAY CAR ZOOMS OFF...
WHERE'D THAT CAR COME FROM? LOOK OUT, CHIP--!!
HEADING STRAIGHT FOR US!
THE NEXT MOMENT...
YOU DIMWIT! YOU PLOWED INTO THESE HEDGES! WE'RE STUCK!
I HAD TO AVOID THAT CAR!
SKREEEEEE!
LOOK! IT'S GREEN LANTERN--THE REAL GREEN LANTERN!
YES! AND WITH A REAL POWER RING TOO--MY WILY FRIENDS!

IN DESPERATION THE DESPERADOES RESOLVE TO FIGHT...

LET HIM HAVE IT, *WOOZY!*

GUNS, EH?

BACKING HIS GREEN BEAM WITH HIS FLAMING WILL POWER, THE *EMERALD CRUSADER* HANDLES THE ATTACK WITH DEXTERITY...

TURNING OUR BULLETS INTO DROPS OF WATER...

I CAN USE A LITTLE SHOWER! IT'S A HOT NIGHT!

BUT I'M GOING TO MAKE IT EVEN HOTTER FOR YOU CROOKS!

I'LL GET BACK TO CAROL'S PARTY-- AS SOON AS I TURN MY CATCH OVER TO THE POLICE! MEANWHILE, I LEFT AN EXPLANATION FOR HAL JORDAN'S DISAPPEARANCE!

AT THE PARTY...

WHAT AN EXCITING NIGHT! NOW OUR JEWELS ARE BACK--BUT WHAT'S THIS? A NOTE LYING HERE ADDRESSED TO *ME*...

I'VE BEEN A CARELESS HOSTESS-- I DIDN'T PAY ANY ATTENTION TO HAL ALL EVENING!

Dear Carol,
Since Green Lantern changed his mind and came to the party, I'm leaving! Thanks and good night.
Hal Jordan

LATER, AFTER *GREEN LANTERN* HAS RETURNED TO EXPLAIN ALL...

THE FIRST *GREEN LANTERN* WAS AN IMPOSTOR? THEN IT WASN'T YOUR *FACE* I SAW?

NO, CAROL! AND I SUPPOSE YOU'RE--er--STILL CURIOUS!

SUDDENLY, CAROL'S HAND WHIPS OUT AT *GL*'s MASK...

YES, I AM! AND THIS TIME I'M GOING TO GET THE MASK OFF THE REAL *GREEN LANTERN*-- EH?

IT WON'T COME-- IT WON'T COME OFF!

NO! MY STRINGLESS MASK IS FIXED ON BY THE FORCE OF MY *POWER RING*, CAROL! NO POWER ON EARTH CAN GET IT OFF AGAINST MY WILL!

NOW--SHALL WE JOIN THE PARTY, CAROL?

I STILL HAVEN'T SEEN THE FACE OF MY BELOVED! BUT I HAVE THE STRONGEST FEELING--THAT *SOME DAY I WILL!*

The End

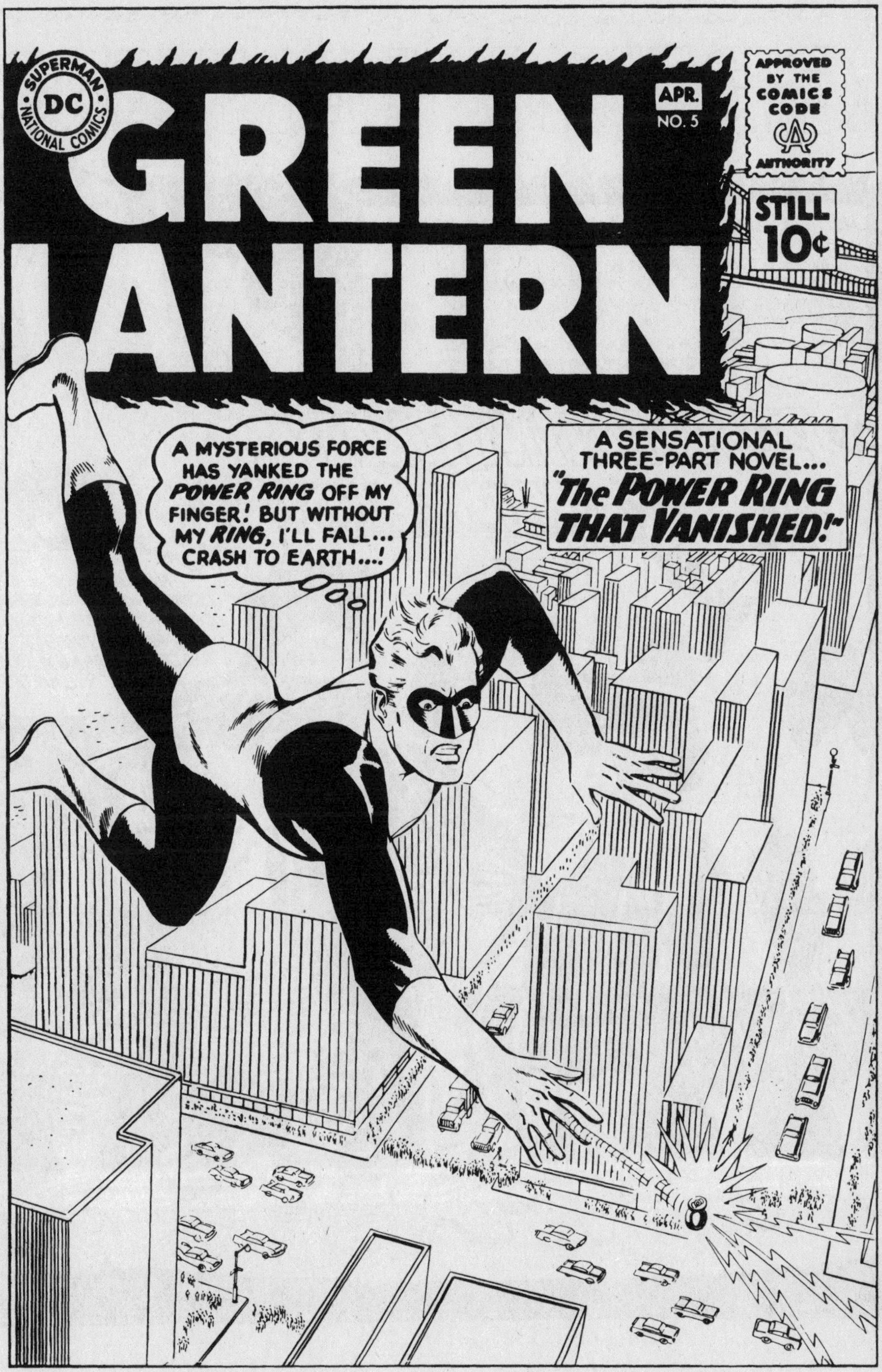
SUPERMAN DC NATIONAL COMICS
GREEN LANTERN
APR. NO. 5
APPROVED BY THE COMICS CODE AUTHORITY
STILL 10¢
A MYSTERIOUS FORCE HAS YANKED THE POWER RING OFF MY FINGER! BUT WITHOUT MY RING, I'LL FALL... CRASH TO EARTH...!
A SENSATIONAL THREE-PART NOVEL... "The POWER RING THAT VANISHED!"

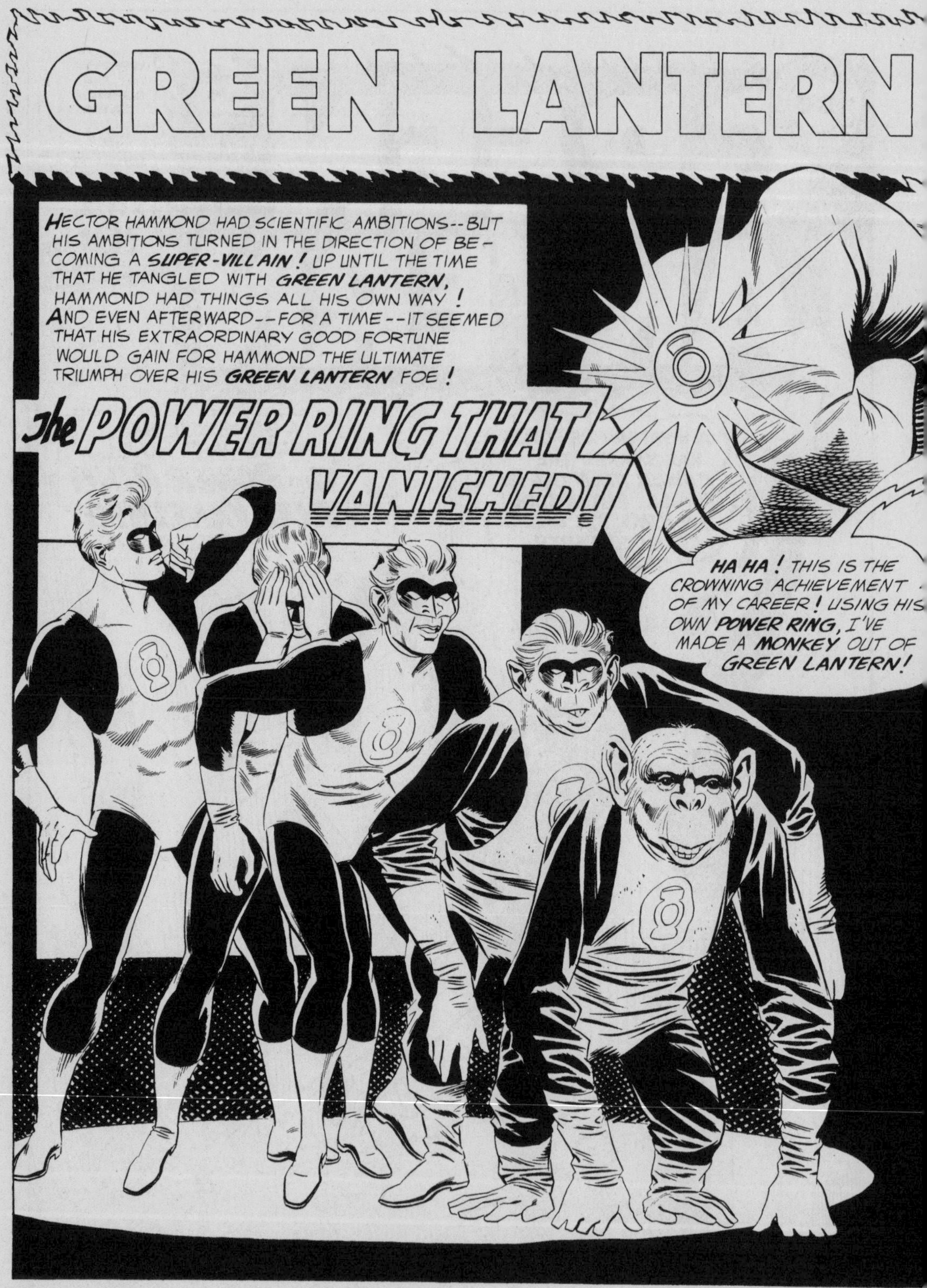
GREEN LANTERN
HECTOR HAMMOND HAD SCIENTIFIC AMBITIONS--BUT HIS AMBITIONS TURNED IN THE DIRECTION OF BE-COMING A SUPER-VILLAIN! UP UNTIL THE TIME THAT HE TANGLED WITH GREEN LANTERN, HAMMOND HAD THINGS ALL HIS OWN WAY! AND EVEN AFTERWARD--FOR A TIME--IT SEEMED THAT HIS EXTRAORDINARY GOOD FORTUNE WOULD GAIN FOR HAMMOND THE ULTIMATE TRIUMPH OVER HIS GREEN LANTERN FOE!
The POWER RING THAT VANISHED!
HA HA! THIS IS THE CROWNING ACHIEVEMENT OF MY CAREER! USING HIS OWN POWER RING, I'VE MADE A MONKEY OUT OF GREEN LANTERN!

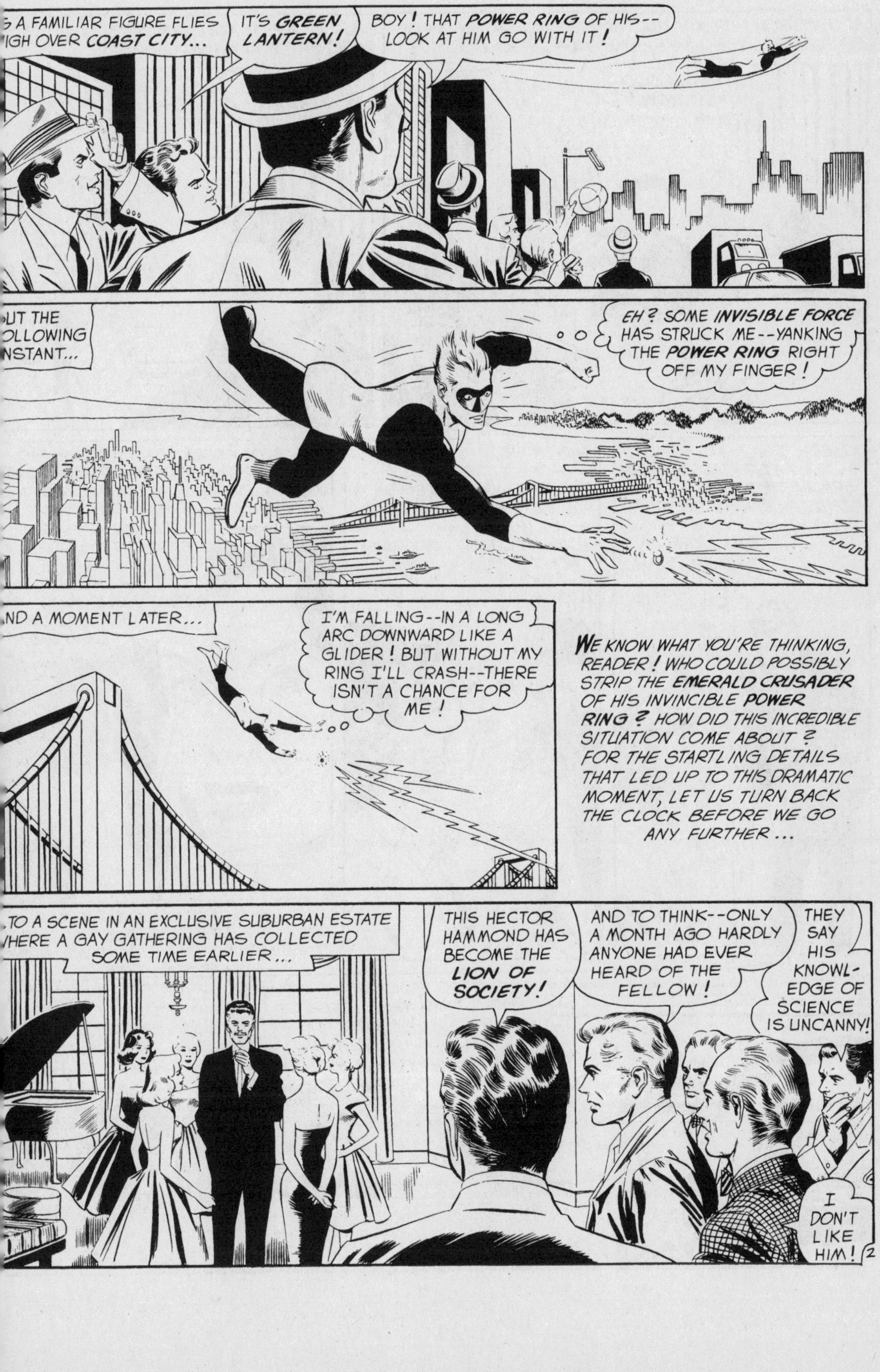
A FAMILIAR FIGURE FLIES HIGH OVER COAST CITY...
IT'S GREEN LANTERN!
BOY! THAT POWER RING OF HIS--LOOK AT HIM GO WITH IT!
BUT THE FOLLOWING INSTANT...
EH? SOME INVISIBLE FORCE HAS STRUCK ME--YANKING THE POWER RING RIGHT OFF MY FINGER!
AND A MOMENT LATER...
I'M FALLING--IN A LONG ARC DOWNWARD LIKE A GLIDER! BUT WITHOUT MY RING I'LL CRASH--THERE ISN'T A CHANCE FOR ME!
WE KNOW WHAT YOU'RE THINKING, READER! WHO COULD POSSIBLY STRIP THE EMERALD CRUSADER OF HIS INVINCIBLE POWER RING? HOW DID THIS INCREDIBLE SITUATION COME ABOUT? FOR THE STARTLING DETAILS THAT LED UP TO THIS DRAMATIC MOMENT, LET US TURN BACK THE CLOCK BEFORE WE GO ANY FURTHER...
...TO A SCENE IN AN EXCLUSIVE SUBURBAN ESTATE WHERE A GAY GATHERING HAS COLLECTED SOME TIME EARLIER...
THIS HECTOR HAMMOND HAS BECOME THE LION OF SOCIETY!
AND TO THINK--ONLY A MONTH AGO HARDLY ANYONE HAD EVER HEARD OF THE FELLOW!
THEY SAY HIS KNOWLEDGE OF SCIENCE IS UNCANNY!
I DON'T LIKE HIM!
2

AT LUNCHEON SOON AFTER...

OH, MY! THAT WAITER SPILLED A BOWL OF SOUP OVER HAMMOND!

WATCH HIM LOSE HIS GOOD HUMOR **NOW**!

BUT TO THE AMAZEMENT OF ALL, THE CELEBRITY REMAINS CALM...

PLEASE BRING ME A FRESH NAPKIN, WAITER!

OF C-COURSE, SIR!

YOU SEE, I HAD THIS SUIT MADE BY A SPECIAL **CHEMICAL** FORMULA OF MY OWN! ANY **STAIN** CAN MERELY BE WIPED RIGHT OFF IT!

WELL, HOW DO YOU LIKE THAT!

AND LATER...

HECTOR HAMMOND HAS INVITED US ALL TO CONTINUE THE PARTY AT HIS HOUSE! YOU'LL COME, WON'T YOU, CAROL?

OF COURSE, SUE!

AS **CAROL FERRIS**, DAUGHTER OF THE OWNER OF THE **FERRIS AIRCRAFT COMPANY** *, PREPARES TO LEAVE WITH THE OTHERS...

I FIND MR. HAMMOND FASCINATING! HE'S THE FIRST MAN I'VE MET WHO MIGHT VERY WELL MAKE ME FORGET **GREEN LANTERN**!

*Editor's Note: AND NOW SOLE MANAGER SINCE HER FATHER LEFT HER IN CHARGE ON EMBARKING ON A RECENT ROUND-THE-WORLD TOUR!

ON THE WAY...

I'VE HEARD FASCINATING STORIES ABOUT THIS **NEW** HOUSE OF YOURS, MR. HAMMOND! IS IT REALLY SO UNUSUAL?

WAIT TILL YOU SEE IT, MISS FERRIS! I DON'T LIKE TO **BOAST**!

SOON, ON THE OUTSKIRTS OF THE METROPOLIS...

THERE IT IS!

WELL, THE HOUSE CERTAINLY IS STRIKING-LOOKING! BUT SO FAR I DON'T SEE ANY-THING UNUSUAL ABOUT IT...

LET'S ALL GO IN! IT'S A CLOUDY DAY--BUT I THINK A GALA PARTY LIKE THIS DESERVES BRIGHT SUNLIGHT! IT'LL BE MY PLEASURE TO DO SOMETHING ABOUT THAT!

WHAT CAN HE MEAN?

THEN, AFTER ALL THE GUESTS ARE INSIDE THE HOUSE, AN INCREDIBLE OCCURRENCE...

WE'RE GOING UP--RISING LIKE A BALLOON!

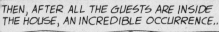

YES! IT'S MY OWN INVENTION--A HOUSE THAT CAN RISE ABOVE THE CLOUDS TO FINE WEATHER ANY TIME I WISH! AT THE TURN OF A SWITCH!

IT'S UTTERLY FANTASTIC!

YET QUITE SIMPLE, MISS FERRIS! THIS HOUSE IS BUILT OF A RARE LIGHT STRUCTURAL METAL OF MY OWN DISCOVERY! AND IT RISES WHEN A CERTAIN GAS IS RELEASED IN HIDDEN POCKETS IN THE WALLS!

WE REALLY ARE ABOVE THE CLOUDS!

YES! I ALWAYS PICK THE KIND OF WEATHER THAT SUITS MY MOOD! BUT LET ME SHOW YOU AROUND THE HOUSE!

4

AS THE WONDERS OF HAMMOND'S SCIENTIFIC DOMICILE ARE REVEALED...

THIS IS MY PRIVATE ASTRONOMICAL LABORATORY! I'VE MADE DISCOVERIES THAT SCIENCE IS NOT EVEN AWARE OF YET!

HOW MARVELOUS!

WHILE CAROL FERRIS DOES NOT KNOW WHICH TO ADMIRE MORE, THE ASTONISHING HOUSE-- OR THE MAN WHO BUILT IT...

MORE AND MORE I FEEL MYSELF DRAWN TO HECTOR HAMMOND! I WONDER IF I'M GOING FOR HIM ROMANTICALLY-- AND WHAT *GREEN LANTERN* WOULD SAY IF HE KNEW IT!

MEANWHILE, AT THE *FERRIS* PLANT, *GREEN LANTERN'S* ALTER EGO HAL JORDAN DOES KNOW A THING OR TWO...

NO, IT'S NOT JUST JEALOUSY WHICH HAS CAUSED ME TO CHECK UP ON THIS HECTOR HAMMOND, *PIEFACE*-- EVEN THOUGH I KNEW HE AND CAROL HAVE BEEN SEEING A LOT OF EACH OTHER LATELY!

THEN WHAT IS IT, HAL?

AS THE ACE TEST PILOT EX-PLAINS TO HIS TRUSTED MECHANIC...

MY FINDINGS SHOW THAT HAMMOND HAS EXTRAORDINARY TALENTS IN *FOUR SCIENCES* --CHEMISTRY, PHYSICS, ASTRONOMY, AND BIOLOGY! NOW BY A STRANGE COINCIDENCE...

...THOSE HAPPEN TO BE THE *SPECIALTIES* OF THE *FOUR SCIENTISTS* WHO DIS-APPEARED FROM THIS AREA SOME MONTHS AGO WITHOUT LEAVING A TRACE!*

JUMPING FISHHOOKS, HAL! THAT'S *RIGHT!*

*Editor's Note: A CASE WHICH HAS UTTERLY BAFFLED THE POLICE!

BUT YOU DON'T THINK THAT HAMMOND--

I DON'T THINK ANY-THING, YET, *PIE!* I JUST SAY IT'S A STRANGE CO-INCIDENCE! BUT ONE THAT *BEARS IN-VESTIGATION!* NOW LISTEN, THIS IS WHAT I PROPOSE TO DO...

SOON AFTER, BEHIND LOCKED DOORS IN HAL'S DRESSING ROOM AT THE HANGAR, A MYSTIC RITE TAKES PLACE...

IN BRIGHTEST DAY, IN BLACKEST NIGHT, NO EVIL SHALL ESCAPE MY SIGHT! LET THOSE WHO WORSHIP EVIL'S MIGHT BEWARE MY POWER-- GREEN LANTERN'S LIGHT!

Editor's Note: BY CHARGING HIS RING AT HIS AMAZING LAMP, GREEN LANTERN GETS POWER FOR TWENTY-FOUR HOURS!

G-GOLLY! THAT'S THE FIRST TIME I'VE EVER SEEN YOU CHARGE YOUR RING AND TAKE YOUR OATH, GREEN LANTERN!

IT'S ONLY FITTING THAT YOU SHOULD SEE ME NOW, PIE...

...SINCE YOU ARE GOING TO IMPERSONATE ME DURING THE NEXT DAY OR SO! ARE YOU SURE YOU CAN CARRY OUT YOUR PART OF OUR SCHEME?

JUST GIVE ME A CHANCE, THAT'S ALL I ASK!

AND SHORTLY AS AN EMERALD-GLINTING FIGURE SLIPS UNSEEN FROM THE CITY...

SO FAR SO GOOD! USING MY RING, I'VE TURNED PIEFACE INTO AN ABSOLUTE REPLICA OF ME-- INCLUDING THE POWER RING! AND HE KNOWS HIS MISSION--WHICH IS TO KEEP HIMSELF CONTINUOUSLY ON DISPLAY IN THE CITY...

...SO THAT HECTOR HAMMOND WON'T BE AWARE I'M NOT THERE! AND WHILE PIE-FACE IS DOING THAT, I'LL BE COMBING EVERY INCH OF THIS ENTIRE COAST FOR THE FOUR MISSING SCIENTISTS!

ACCORDING TO MY HUNCH, THOSE SCIENTISTS ARE SOMEWHERE IN THIS VICINITY-- PROBABLY CAPTIVES! MY POWER RING CAN ACT AS AN X-RAY, PROBING THESE HILLS FOR HIDDEN CAVES OR CAMOUFLAGED SHACKS...!

6

IF HECTOR HAMMOND HAD ANYTHING TO DO WITH THE DISAPPEARANCES, I DON'T WANT HIM TO SUSPECT I'M SEARCHING FOR THE MEN--NOT YET! AND BY IMPERSONATING ME, *PIEFACE* WILL TAKE CARE OF THAT ANGLE!

BACK IN *COAST CITY*, A REMARKABLE TRANSFORMATION HAS TAKEN PLACE...

WOOOEEE! I LOOK LIKE *GREEN LANTERN! I AM GREEN LANTERN!* I'VE EVEN GOT A *POWER RING!* I CAN HARDLY WAIT TO TRY IT OUT!

IT WORKS! ACTUALLY I DON'T HAVE HAL'S *WILL POWER* THAT BACKS THE GREEN BEAM WHEN HE USES IT! BUT I HAVE SOME WILL POWER OF MY OWN...

...ENOUGH TO SLIP THROUGH THE HANGAR WALL AND FLY IN THE AIR! *JUMPING FISHHOOKS!* WHAT A SENSATION--!!

FREE AS A BIRD, THE TRANSFORMED GREASEMONKEY CAN'T GET ENOUGH OF HIS WONDERFUL NEW ABILITIES...

FLYING THIS HIGH WITH NOTHING UNDER ME GIVES ME A FUNNY TICKLY FEELING IN THE STOMACH!

LOOK AT *GREEN LANTERN!*

HE SEEMS TO HAVE GOTTEN SPRING FEVER!

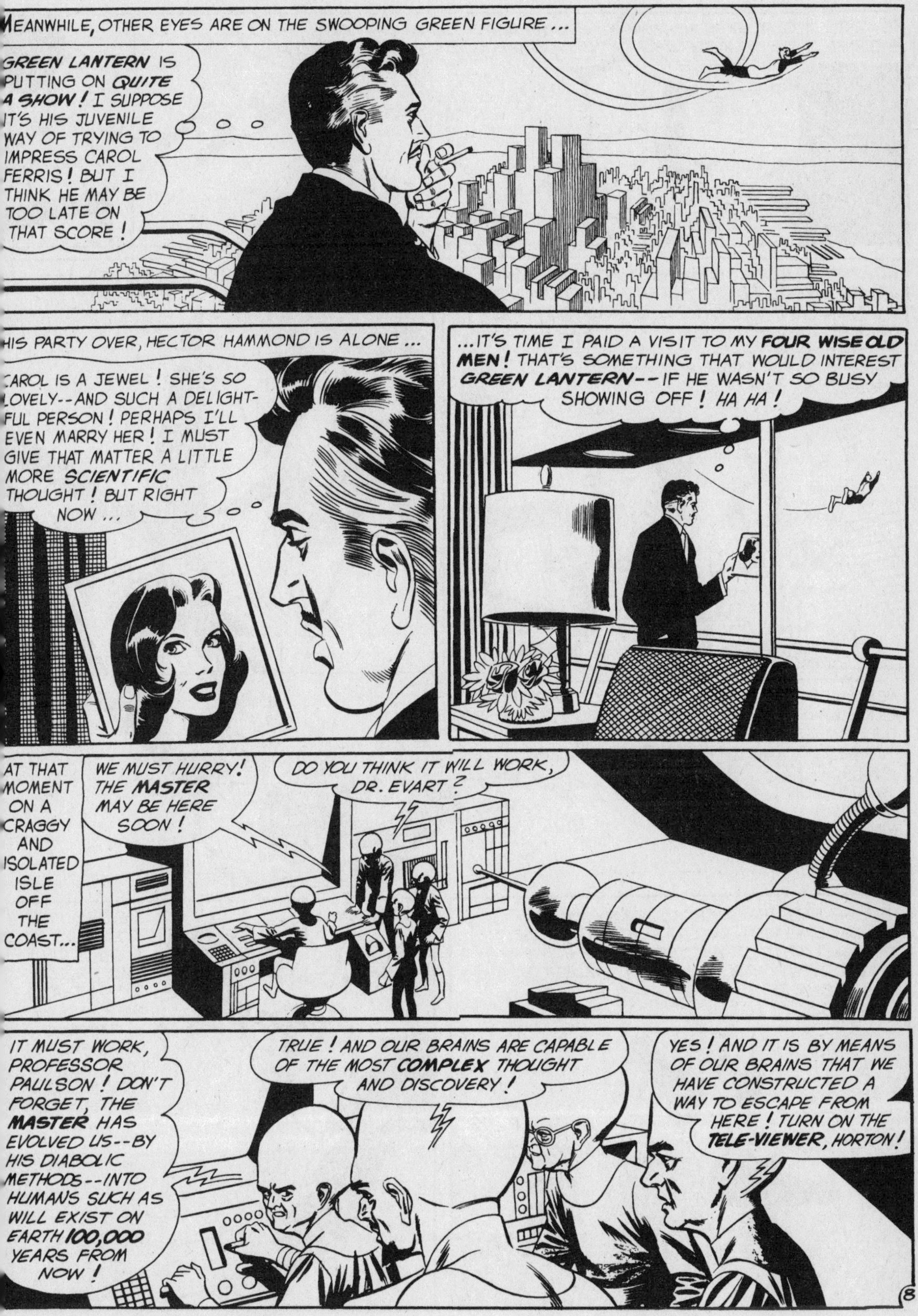
MEANWHILE, OTHER EYES ARE ON THE SWOOPING GREEN FIGURE...
GREEN LANTERN IS PUTTING ON QUITE A SHOW! I SUPPOSE IT'S HIS JUVENILE WAY OF TRYING TO IMPRESS CAROL FERRIS! BUT I THINK HE MAY BE TOO LATE ON THAT SCORE!
HIS PARTY OVER, HECTOR HAMMOND IS ALONE...
CAROL IS A JEWEL! SHE'S SO LOVELY--AND SUCH A DELIGHTFUL PERSON! PERHAPS I'LL EVEN MARRY HER! I MUST GIVE THAT MATTER A LITTLE MORE SCIENTIFIC THOUGHT! BUT RIGHT NOW...
...IT'S TIME I PAID A VISIT TO MY FOUR WISE OLD MEN! THAT'S SOMETHING THAT WOULD INTEREST GREEN LANTERN--IF HE WASN'T SO BUSY SHOWING OFF! HA HA!
AT THAT MOMENT ON A CRAGGY AND ISOLATED ISLE OFF THE COAST...
WE MUST HURRY! THE MASTER MAY BE HERE SOON!
DO YOU THINK IT WILL WORK, DR. EVART?
IT MUST WORK, PROFESSOR PAULSON! DON'T FORGET, THE MASTER HAS EVOLVED US--BY HIS DIABOLIC METHODS--INTO HUMANS SUCH AS WILL EXIST ON EARTH 100,000 YEARS FROM NOW!
TRUE! AND OUR BRAINS ARE CAPABLE OF THE MOST COMPLEX THOUGHT AND DISCOVERY!
YES! AND IT IS BY MEANS OF OUR BRAINS THAT WE HAVE CONSTRUCTED A WAY TO ESCAPE FROM HERE! TURN ON THE TELE-VIEWER, HORTON!
8

As a dial is turned...

THERE HE IS AGAIN-- THE ONLY ONE WHO CAN SAVE US!

WE MUST BRING *GREEN LANTERN* HERE! TURN ON THE OTHER SWITCH, HORTON!

WITH THE PUSH OF A TINY LEVER, A BOLT OF *SIGMA ENERGY*, CREATED BY THE SUPER-ADVANCED MINDS OF THE FOUR CAPTIVE SCIENTISTS, SPURTS FROM THE MACHINE...

THERE IT GOES!

BE SURE IT'S AIMED RIGHT!

3000 BEV'S! IT WILL TAKE A MINUTE OR TWO MORE TO BUILD UP THE NECESSARY FORCE!

OUR *LIVES* DEPEND ON IT!

3000
2500
2000

MEANWHILE, ALL UNAWARE, THE TRANSFORMED *PIEFACE* IS STILL ENJOYING HIMSELF...

I DON'T HAVE A THING TO WORRY ABOUT! *GL* SAID THAT HE FIXED MY RING SO THAT IF HECTOR HAMMOND TRIED TO LEAVE THE CITY, IT WOULD *GIVE THE ALARM!*

HE ALSO SAID THAT MY RING WOULD BE JUST THE SAME AS HIS--EXCEPT THAT IT *CAN'T BE CHARGED UP* ONCE IT RUNS OUT OF POWER AFTER TWENTY-FOUR HOURS! I MUST REMEMBER THAT--EH?

SUDDENLY...

JUMPING FISH-HOOKS! MY RING IS QUIVERING-- EMITTING A GLOW! THAT'S THE SIGNAL -- IT MEANS HAMMOND IS LEAVING THE CITY AND *I'VE GOT TO FOLLOW HIM--!*

BUT BEFORE *GREEN LANTERN'S* DUPLICATE CAN EVEN TURN, ANOTHER EXTRAORDINARY THING HAPPENS...

AND THE NEXT MOMENT...

MY *RING*--YANKED OFF MY *FINGER*! I'M FALLING... BUT STILL IN THE GRIP OF THAT MYSTERIOUS FORCE!

S-SOMETHING IS GRABBING HOLD OF ME! STARTING TO PULL ME THROUGH THE AIR! I--I'M POWERLESS AGAINST IT--!

BACK ON THE ISLAND PRISON OF THE FOUR SCIENTISTS,...

OUR *SIGMA-RAY* PULLED THE *POWER RING* OFF *GREEN LANTERN'S* FINGER!

I CAN EXPLAIN THAT, DR. EVART!

THE FREQUENCY OF VIBRATION OF THE *RING* IS DIFFERENT FROM THE REST OF *GREEN LANTERN'S BODY*! THEREFORE OUR *SIGMA-RAY* HAS A SLIGHTLY GREATER EFFECT ON IT AND IS PULLING IT FASTER TO US THAN *GREEN LANTERN* HIMSELF!

CAREFUL, PROFESSOR-- BRING HIM IN SLOWLY-- OR HE'LL BE HURT!

THEN, AS *"GREEN LANTERN"* IS BROUGHT TO EARTH...

J-JUMPING FISHHOOKS! WHERE AM I?

PART TWO OF *"THE POWER RING THAT VANISHED"* BEGINS ON THE FOLLOWING PAGE!

10

The POWER RING THAT VANISHED! PART TWO

THESE CREATURES MUST BE THE MISSING SCIENTISTS! THEY WERE *CHANGED* SOMEHOW BY *HECTOR HAMMOND* -- HE'S KEEPING THEM PRISONER HERE! AND THEY EXPECT *ME* TO HELP THEM *ESCAPE* --!

YOU *MUST* HELP US ESCAPE, *GREEN LANTERN!*

I HATE TO TELL THEM I'M *NOT* GREEN LANTERN! BUT THE TROUBLE IS, EVEN IF I WAS -- I COULDN'T HELP THEM ...

I HAVEN'T GOT MY RING!

YOUR RING --!?

THAT'S RIGHT! WE SAW IT FLY OUT OF HIS HAND --! BUT WITHOUT HIS RING HE CAN'T GET US PAST THE *BARRIER!*

WHAT *BARRIER* --?

IT'S AN **INVISIBLE FORCE** THAT HAMMOND SET UP TO KEEP US CAPTIVE HERE! OBJECTS CAN ENTER THROUGH IT--BUT NOTHING--EXCEPT HAMMOND HIMSELF--CAN GET OUT!

LET'S LOOK FOR THE RING! IT MAY HAVE FALLEN HERE WITHOUT OUR SEEING IT!

AT THAT MOMENT A LITTLE WAY OFF ON THE TINY ISLE...

WHAT'S *THIS...?*

AS HECTOR HAMMOND, THE JAILOR OF THE SCIENTISTS, EXAMINES HIS FIND MORE CLOSELY...

UNLESS I'M DEAD WRONG THIS IS **GREEN LANTERN'S POWER RING!** THERE'S A WAY OF MAKING SURE!

WITH GREAT INTEREST, HAMMOND DONS THE RING AND...

AMAZING! BY EXERTING MY **WILL** I CAN DO ANYTHING--SUCH AS SHRIVELING THAT WILD APPLE TREE INTO A DEAD AND ROTTING STUMP!

THIS RING HERE MEANS THAT **GREEN LANTERN** MAY BE HERE TOO! AND IF HE IS, HE'S HELPLESS AGAINST ME--SINCE HIS **POWER RING** IS NOW IN MY POSSESSION! HA HA! MY **LUCK** IS HOLDING FAST!

AS THE SUPER-VILLAIN STRIDES CONFIDENTLY FORWARD, HIS THOUGHTS ARE CONFIDENT TOO...

EVER SINCE I FIRST SPIED THE **METEOR**, MY INCREDIBLE **LUCK** HAS BEEN WITH ME ALL THE WAY! I'LL NEVER FORGET THAT MOMENT I SET EYES ON IT A YEAR AGO...

12

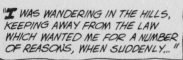

"*I* WAS WANDERING IN THE HILLS, KEEPING AWAY FROM THE LAW WHICH WANTED ME FOR A NUMBER OF REASONS, WHEN SUDDENLY...*"

IF I REMEMBER MY SCHOOLBOOKS CORRECTLY, THAT STONE IS A *METEORITE!* IT HAS THAT SPECIAL *DARK IRON* LOOK! BUT WAIT A SECOND--!

"*I'D ALWAYS HAD AN INTEREST IN SCIENCE-- LUCKILY FOR ME!*"

THE TREES AND WEEDS AROUND THE METEORITE--I'VE NEVER SEEN ANYTHING LIKE THEM! WHAT CAN THIS MEAN? I'VE GOT TO FIND OUT!

"*I TOOK A PHOTOGRAPH OF THE SCENE AND LATER SHOWED IT TO A UNIVERSITY PROFESSOR, POSING AS A STUDENT...*"

THIS PHOTOGRAPH IS SOME KIND OF *HOAX,* YOUNG MAN! TREES AND FLOWERS LIKE THESE COULD ONLY EXIST ON EARTH *100,000 YEARS FROM NOW*--AFTER THEY HAD EVOLVED FROM THEIR PRESENT FORMS!

"*I PLAYED INNOCENT, TOOK MY PHOTOGRAPH AWAY WITHOUT SAYING ANOTHER WORD! BUT AFTERWARD...*"

THE PROFESSOR HAS TOLD ME ALL I WANTED TO KNOW--AND WHAT I SOMEHOW SUSPECTED! THIS STRANGE METEORITE IN SOME MANNER CAUSED THE FOLIAGE AROUND IT TO EVOLVE INTO *FUTURE FORMS!* AND IF IT CAN DO THAT WITH *PLANTS...*

...WHY SHOULDN'T IT BE ABLE TO DO IT WITH *HUMAN BEINGS!?*

THAT WAS MY *GREAT IDEA!* FROM THAT IT WAS JUST A SIMPLE STEP TO SEIZING THE FOUR SCIENTISTS--AND *EVOLVING THEM* BY MEANS OF THE METEORITE SO THAT *I* COULD USE THE KNOWLEDGE OF THEIR FUTURISTIC BRAINS!

"ALL I HAD TO DO AFTER CAPTURING THEM WAS LOCK THEM UP WITH THE METEORITE ON THIS LONELY ISLE..."

DAY BY DAY THEY'RE CHANGING INTO HUMANS OF THE FUTURE WITH *INCREDIBLE BRAIN-POWER!* THROUGH THEM I'LL LEARN THE ANSWERS TO ALL THE THINGS I WANT TO KNOW!

"BY SHEER *LUCK* THE SAME METEOR-RAY THAT EVOLVED THE SCIENTISTS WEAKENED THEIR WILL POWER! THEY COULD REFUSE ME NOTHING!"

I WANT TO THROW AN INVISIBLE FORCE-FIELD AROUND THIS LABORATORY! FIGURE IT OUT AND TELL ME HOW TO DO IT!

WE CANNOT HELP OUR-SELVES! WE MUST DO WHAT HE SAYS...!

"AND THAT WAS HOW AFTER CHANGING MY NAME TO FOOL THE POLICE, I BECAME THE *AMAZING HECTOR HAMMOND, WONDER MAN OF SCIENCE!* HA HA.."

I COULD HAVE EVOLVED *MYSELF* OF COURSE--BUT I WANTED TO REMAIN A NORMAL-LOOKING HUMAN IN ORDER TO MINGLE WITH OTHER HUMANS AND ENJOY MY POWER! THIS WAY IS BETTER! AND NOW FOR A LOOK AT MY CAPTIVES...

AT THAT MOMENT...

HERE COMES HAMMOND NOW-- THROUGH THE BARRIER! WE MUST SUBDUE HIM--ALL OF US TOGETHER! IT IS OUR ONLY CHANCE!

COUNT ME IN ON THIS, FELLERS!

CHARGE!

WHAT'S THIS? AN *ATTACK*--LED BY *GREEN LANTERN!?* SO I WAS RIGHT--HE *IS* HERE!

INSTANTLY THE KEEN-WITTED ARCH-VILLAIN WILLS THE *POWER RING* TO FORM A HUGE HOSE WHICH EMITS A POWERFUL JET OF COM-PRESSED AIR AT HIS ATTACKERS...

HA HA! HITTING THEM IN THE LEGS THIS WAY WON'T HURT THEM TOO BADLY, BUT IT WILL TAKE ALL THE FIGHT OUT OF THEM, I'LL BET!

JUMPING FISHHOOKS! HE'S GOT MY *RING!*

14

AND SOON, WITH HIS FOES RENDERED HELPLESS BY THE MYSTICAL *GREEN BEAM*...

HOW DID *GREEN LANTERN* GET HERE? EXPLAIN!

WE CANNOT HELP OURSELVES--HIS *WILL POWER* IS TOO STRONG! WE MUST ANSWER!

AFTER THE TRUTH OF THE LITTLE PLOT HAS EMERGED...

HOW ABOUT THAT! I TURNED YOU INTO MEN OF THE FUTURE! YOU KNOW MORE THAN MANKIND WILL FOR CENTURIES! AND ALL I ASK IS THAT YOU STAY HERE AND SHARE YOUR KNOWLEDGE WITH ME! AND ARE YOU SATISFIED? NO...

YOU INSIST ON TRYING TO ESCAPE! FOOLS! THERE IS NO ESCAPE FOR YOU! YOU MUST ALWAYS REMAIN HIDDEN--SO THE WORLD WILL NEVER KNOW THE SOURCE OF MY SCIENTIFIC WONDERS! AND AS FOR *GREEN LANTERN*...

SOMEHOW I HAD EXPECTED MORE OF A *BATTLE* WHEN *GREEN LANTERN* AND I FINALLY CAME UP AGAINST EACH OTHER--AS I KNEW WE WOULD SOMEDAY! BUT I GUESS I *OVERRATED* YOU...

IF HE DIDN'T HAVE THAT RING...!

ONE THING IS SURE! YOU WILL NEVER BOTHER ME AGAIN! I'M GOING TO USE YOUR OWN *POWER RING* TO *CHANGE YOU, GREEN LANTERN!* BUT IN A *DIFFERENT* WAY FROM THE CHANGE I MADE IN THESE SCIENTISTS!

A STARTLING TRANSFORMATION BEGINS TO COME OVER THE DISGUISED *PIEFACE*...

WH--WHAT'S HAPPENING TO ME!?

15

SLOWLY THE GREEN-CLAD FIGURE ALTERS UNDER THE ALL-POWERFUL BEAM...

THE DIFFERENCE, *GREEN LANTERN*, IS THAT I'M EVOLVING YOU *BACKWARD* INSTEAD OF FORWARD... FAR BACKWARD...

AS THE CHANGE BECOMES COMPLETE...

HA HA! LOOK AT THE MIGHTY *GREEN LANTERN!* FROM NOW ON I'M GOING TO KEEP YOU AROUND FOR LAUGHS!

J-JUMPING FISHHOOKS!

THE THINGS I DO FOR A PAL! I WAS JUST HELPING OUT THE *REAL GREEN LANTERN*--AND LOOK WHAT HAPPENS! THIS ODD-BALL MAKES A *MONKEY* OUTA ME!

HA HA! I HAVEN'T ENJOYED MYSELF THIS MUCH IN YEARS! YOU HUNGRY, PAL?

OF COURSE I COULD TELL HAMMOND HE'S MADE A MISTAKE--THAT I'M NOT REALLY *GREEN LANTERN*...

...BUT WILD HORSES COULDN'T DRAG THAT INFORMATION OUT OF ME! AND WHEN THE REAL *GL* CATCHES UP WITH THIS GUY, HE'LL MAKE A "MONKEY" OUTA *HIM!*

HAVE A BANANA! HA HA!

BUT WHERE IS THE *REAL GREEN LANTERN?* AT THAT VERY MOMENT, HE IS HEADING OUT TO OPEN SEA...

MY RING HAS PICKED UP SOME *ODD VIBRATIONS*, AS FROM ANOTHER *POWER BEAM* AT WORK IN THIS DIRECTION! BUT I LEFT *PIEFACE* AND HIS *POWER RING* BACK IN *COAST CITY!* WHAT COULD BE CAUSING THE VIBRATIONS OUT HERE AT SEA--!?

FOR THE STARTLING CONCLUSION TO "*THE POWER RING THAT VANISHED*" TURN TO THE FOLLOWING PAGE!

(16

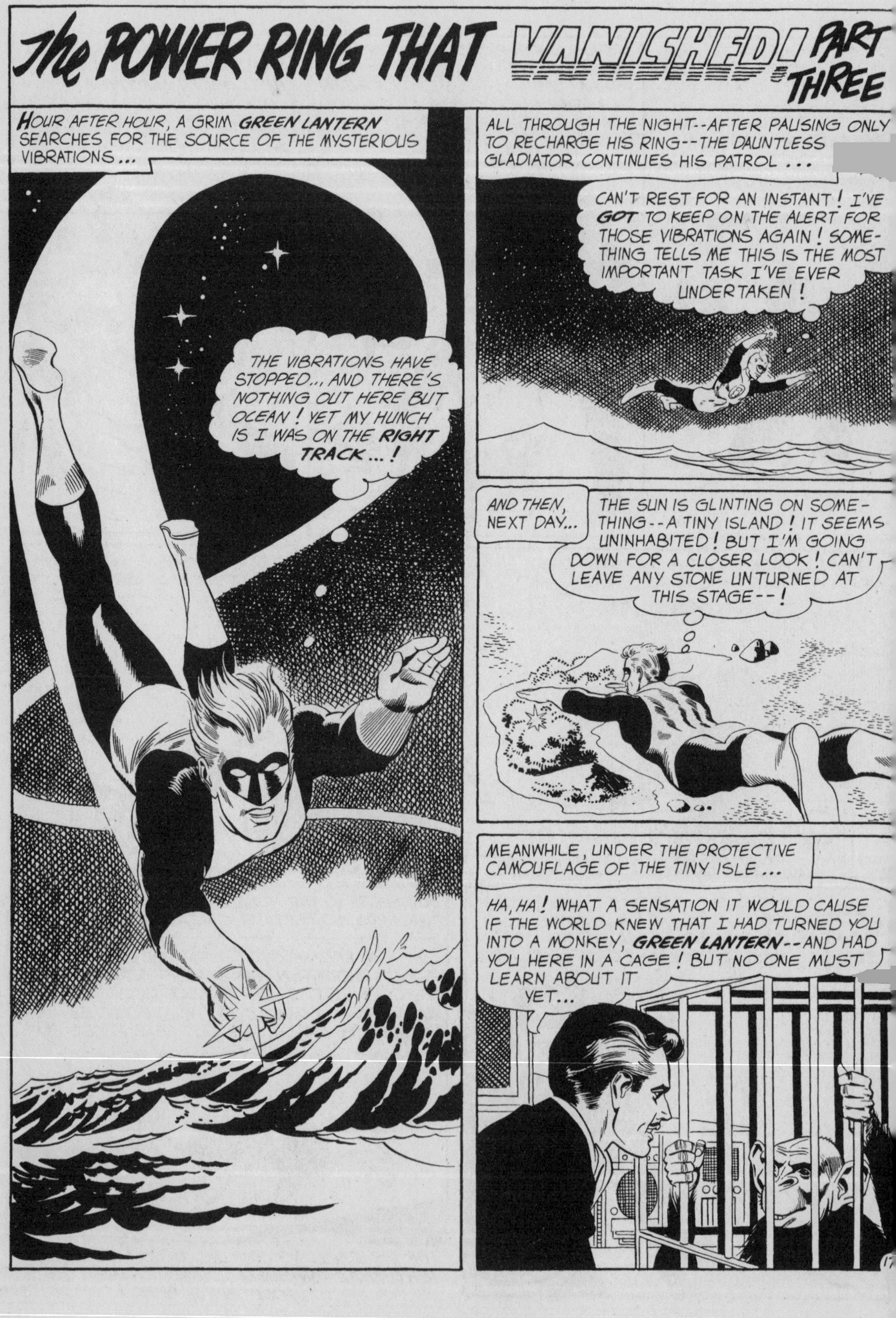
The POWER RING THAT VANISHED! PART THREE
HOUR AFTER HOUR, A GRIM GREEN LANTERN SEARCHES FOR THE SOURCE OF THE MYSTERIOUS VIBRATIONS...
THE VIBRATIONS HAVE STOPPED..., AND THERE'S NOTHING OUT HERE BUT OCEAN! YET MY HUNCH IS I WAS ON THE RIGHT TRACK...!
ALL THROUGH THE NIGHT--AFTER PAUSING ONLY TO RECHARGE HIS RING--THE DAUNTLESS GLADIATOR CONTINUES HIS PATROL...
CAN'T REST FOR AN INSTANT! I'VE GOT TO KEEP ON THE ALERT FOR THOSE VIBRATIONS AGAIN! SOMETHING TELLS ME THIS IS THE MOST IMPORTANT TASK I'VE EVER UNDERTAKEN!
AND THEN, NEXT DAY...
THE SUN IS GLINTING ON SOMETHING--A TINY ISLAND! IT SEEMS UNINHABITED! BUT I'M GOING DOWN FOR A CLOSER LOOK! CAN'T LEAVE ANY STONE UNTURNED AT THIS STAGE--!
MEANWHILE, UNDER THE PROTECTIVE CAMOUFLAGE OF THE TINY ISLE...
HA, HA! WHAT A SENSATION IT WOULD CAUSE IF THE WORLD KNEW THAT I HAD TURNED YOU INTO A MONKEY, GREEN LANTERN--AND HAD YOU HERE IN A CAGE! BUT NO ONE MUST LEARN ABOUT IT YET...

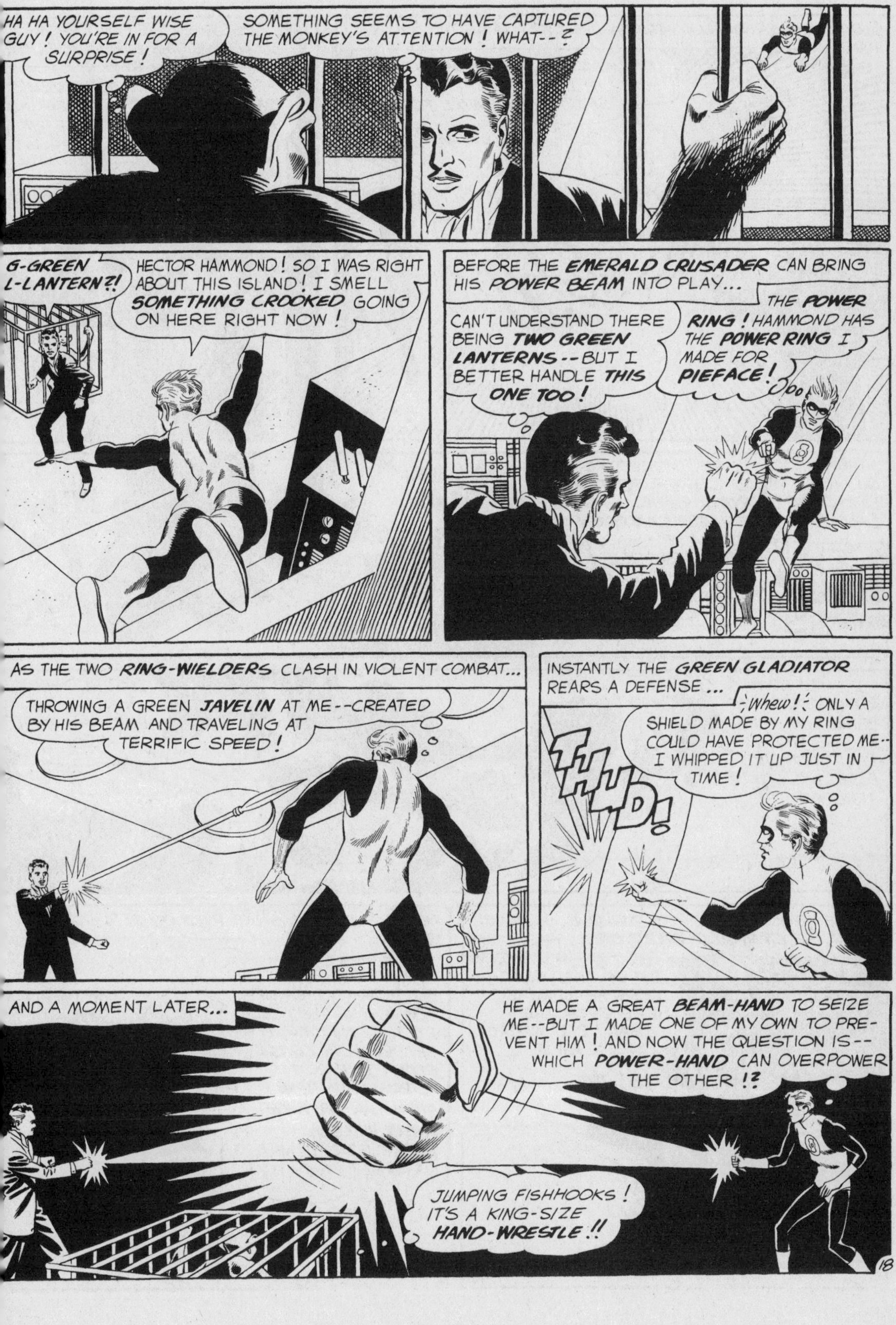
HA HA YOURSELF WISE GUY! YOU'RE IN FOR A SURPRISE!
SOMETHING SEEMS TO HAVE CAPTURED THE MONKEY'S ATTENTION! WHAT--?
G-GREEN L-LANTERN?!
HECTOR HAMMOND! SO I WAS RIGHT ABOUT THIS ISLAND! I SMELL SOMETHING CROOKED GOING ON HERE RIGHT NOW!
BEFORE THE EMERALD CRUSADER CAN BRING HIS POWER BEAM INTO PLAY...
CAN'T UNDERSTAND THERE BEING TWO GREEN LANTERNS--BUT I BETTER HANDLE THIS ONE TOO!
THE POWER RING! HAMMOND HAS THE POWER RING I MADE FOR PIEFACE!
AS THE TWO RING-WIELDERS CLASH IN VIOLENT COMBAT...
THROWING A GREEN JAVELIN AT ME--CREATED BY HIS BEAM AND TRAVELING AT TERRIFIC SPEED!
INSTANTLY THE GREEN GLADIATOR REARS A DEFENSE...
THUD!
Whew! ONLY A SHIELD MADE BY MY RING COULD HAVE PROTECTED ME--I WHIPPED IT UP JUST IN TIME!
AND A MOMENT LATER...
HE MADE A GREAT BEAM-HAND TO SEIZE ME--BUT I MADE ONE OF MY OWN TO PREVENT HIM! AND NOW THE QUESTION IS--WHICH POWER-HAND CAN OVERPOWER THE OTHER!?
JUMPING FISHHOOKS! IT'S A KING-SIZE HAND-WRESTLE!!
18

SLOWLY, THE **GREEN GLADIATOR'S** CREATION GAINS THE "UPPER HAND"...

IT'S MY WILL POWER AGAINST HIS NOW! IF I CAN DEFEAT HIM I'LL SHATTER HIS **WILL TO RESIST**--

THEN, JUST WHEN THE FIGHT SEEMS TO GO AGAINST THE SUPER-SCIENTIST..

HE'S BROKEN OFF OUR **DUEL OF HANDS**--AND IS STREAKING OUT OF HERE! I CAN'T LET HIM ESCAPE ME NOW!

THEN, OUTSIDE HAMMOND'S LABORATORY...

I NEED MORE TIME TO HANDLE THE **POWER RING** AS WELL AS **GREEN LANTERN** DOES! HE'S HAD MORE PRACTICE WITH IT, THAT'S ALL! SO TO GAIN TIME...

...I'LL SET UP THIS **JET-BLACK CLOUD** BEHIND ME, AND ESCAPE WHILE HE'S TRYING TO FIGHT HIS WAY THROUGH IT!

LIKE PLOWING THROUGH A SUPER-DENSE FOG...

AS THE DEVICE SERVES ITS PURPOSE, SLOWING DOWN THE **EMERALD WARRIOR**...

I'VE COME OUT OF THAT **BLACKNESS** HE SPREAD HERE OVER THE OCEAN! BUT WHERE IS **HE**?

AS THE SUPER-SENSITIVE RING ON **GL's** FINGER PROVIDES A CLUE...

THOSE RING-VIBRATIONS-- I'M PICKING THEM UP AGAIN--AND THEY TELL ME THAT **HAMMOND'S** HEADED FOR **COAST CITY**! I'VE GOT TO CORRAL HIM NOW! WITH THAT **POWER RING** HE COULD WREAK INCALCULABLE DAMAGE IN THE CITY!

THE RING TELLS ME *GREEN LANTERN'S STILL ON MY TRAIL!* I *MUST* DELAY HIM UNTIL I CAN FIND A WAY OF FINISHING HIM OFF! I'VE GOT TO CAUSE A DISTRACTION FOR HIM!

NEAR COAST CITY, A HUGE DAM REARS ITS WHITE EXPANSE...

TOO BAD THIS DAM HAS TO GO, BUT IT'S THE ONE WAY I CAN BE SURE OF GETTING *GREEN LANTERN* OFF MY HEELS -- AT LEAST FOR A WHILE!

AS THE ALL-POWERFUL *GREEN BEAM* BLASTS DOWNWARD WITH TERRIBLE FORCE...

CRACK!

IN ABOUT HALF A MINUTE *COAST CITY* WILL BE STRUCK BY A GIGANTIC WAVE -- TRAVELING AT THE SPEED OF AN EXPRESS TRAIN! *THIS* WILL GIVE *GREEN LANTERN* SOMETHING TO THINK ABOUT BESIDES ME--!

AND SCARCELY SECONDS LATER...

THE DAM'S GIVEN WAY! ONLY THAT COULD HAVE CAUSED THAT *AVALANCHE OF WATER* TO POUR DOWN TOWARD *COAST CITY!*

As the aroused *GLADIATOR* tears toward the menacing water...

NO TIME NOW TO TRY TO REPAIR THE DAM-- I'VE GOT TO SAVE THE CITY! IT'LL BE DEMOLISHED IF THAT WATER HITS!

GOT TO THROW UP *ANOTHER DAM* TO HOLD BACK THE WATER-- AND *DO IT FAST!*

WITH HIS INCREDIBLE *POWER RING, GL* COMPLETES IN MOMENTS WHAT IT WOULD TAKE AN ARMY OF WORKERS MONTHS TO ACCOMPLISH...

NOW--WILL *MY POWER-DAM* HOLD BACK THE TREMENDOUS PRESSURE OF THAT *WALL OF WATER?* THE NEXT FEW SECONDS WILL TELL!

IT'S HOLDING! THE VALLEY BEYOND IS BEGINNING TO FILL UP WITH WATER-- THE CITY IS SAVED!

MEANWHILE, ON A CLIFF-SIDE NOT FAR FROM THE CITY...

I'VE USED MY *POWER RING* TO CIRCLE THIS HILL WITH *MACHINE-GUN NESTS!* AND WITH MY *RING* I'LL BE ABLE TO FIRE THEM ALL AT ONCE -- AS SOON AS *GREEN LANTERN* SHOWS UP, AS I EXPECT HE WILL ANY TIME NOW!

MY AGILE FOE MAY BE ABLE TO DEFEND HIMSELF AGAINST MOST OF THE BULLETS, BUT *ONE* OR *TWO* FROM ODD ANGLES ARE BOUND TO *HIT HOME!* AND THAT WILL BE ENOUGH!

AND AT THAT VERY MOMENT...

I'M CONVINCED *HAMMOND* HAD SOMETHING TO DO WITH THAT BROKEN DAM! I'VE GOT TO LOCATE HIM AND PUT HIM OUT OF CIR-CULATION BEFORE HE CAN DO ANY MORE DAMAGE!

BUT AS FATE WOULD HAVE IT, A DRIED LIMB CHOOSES THIS INSTANT TO TOPPLE FROM A TALL TREE OVER THE *EMERALD CRUSADER...*

CLUNK!

AND ON HIS FORTIFIED HILL, HAMMOND VIEWS A RARE SIGHT...

EH? EITHER I'M SEEING HAPPY MIRAGES, OR *GREEN LANTERN* HAS JUST BEEN KNOCKED HELPLESS RIGHT IN FRONT OF MY GUNS! TALK ABOUT MY LUCK!

22

AS THE SUPER-VILLAIN STARTS TO TAKE SWIFT ADVANTAGE...

I'LL FIRE ALL THE GUNS AT ONCE! FOR *GL* TO COME OUT OF THIS ALIVE, HE'LL HAVE TO BE A REAL *WONDER-WORKER!*

BUT THEN, AS WAS BOUND TO HAPPEN, HAMMOND'S LUCK FINALLY RUNS OUT...

THE *RING*—SUDDENLY IT'S LOST ITS *POWER!* I CAN'T SEEM TO MAKE IT WORK--NO MATTER HOW MUCH WILL POWER I SUMMON UP!

AND WHEN HAMMOND, IN DESPERATION, ABANDONS USE OF THE RING AND SCRAMBLES TOWARD ONE OF HIS GUNS...

I'LL BLAST HIM BY HAND! I--EH?

TOO LATE, MY FRIEND! THAT LITTLE DELAY WAS ALL I NEEDED TO COME TO MY SENSES--AND DISCOVER WHAT YOU WERE UP TO!

AS A GIANT BROOM WHISKS HAMMOND AWAY FROM THE GUN...

SOMEHOW YOU GOT HOLD OF MY DUPLICATE *POWER RING*-- BUT YOU DIDN'T KNOW IT HAS TO *BE RECHARGED EVERY TWENTY-FOUR HOURS!* IT JUST RAN OUT OF POWER, THAT'S ALL!

BUT SINCE YOU DON'T HAVE A *POWER RING* ANY MORE, I WON'T USE MINE-- BECAUSE I DON'T NEED IT TO BRING YOU TO JUSTICE!

POW!

AND LATER, BACK ON THE ISLAND, AFTER *GREEN LANTERN* HAS USED HIS *RING* TO UNCOVER HAMMOND'S VILLAINY, AND TO SET CERTAIN MATTERS RIGHT AGAIN...

THANKS FOR BRINGING ME BACK TO MY OLD SELF AGAIN, *GREEN LANTERN!*

THAT'S NOT ALL I DID, *PIE...*

I RETURNED THE CAPTURED SCIENTISTS TO THEIR OLD SELVES AGAIN TOO-- AND USED MY *GREEN BEAM* TO REMOVE ALL TRACES FROM THEIR MINDS OF THE *FUTURISTIC ADVANCES OF SCIENCE* THEY MADE HERE! AND I'VE DONE THE SAME FOR HAMMOND!

IT'S BETTER FOR EARTH— SCIENCE TO PROGRESS GRADUALLY AND NOT MAKE ANY DISCOVERIES *AHEAD OF TIME* -- SO THAT UNSCRUPULOUS MEN LIKE HAMMOND CAN'T TAKE ADVANTAGE OF THEM!

I GUESS YOU'RE RIGHT, *GL!* THIS WAY IS BETTER...

LATER, AS CAROL FERRIS LEARNS OF HAMMOND'S EVIL PLOT...

HMMM...!

5¢ COAST NEWS 5¢

HECTOR HAMMOND EXPOSED AS CUNNING FRAUD!

CAPTURED BY GREEN LANTERN!

24

WHAT DID I EVER SEE IN THIS HECTOR HAMMOND? SOMETIMES I THINK I HAVE A FLIGHTY MIND...

BUT NOW I KNOW IT'S *GREEN LANTERN* I'M CRAZY ABOUT-- IT'S REALLY BEEN HIM ALL ALONG!

AND AT STATE PRISON IN DUE COURSE AN ADDITION IS MADE TO THE STAFF OF THE PRISON LIBRARY..

THIS IS A GOOD JOB FOR HAMMOND, WARDEN! HE ATTEMPTED TO GET KNOWLEDGE THE EASY WAY-- BY CAPTURING OTHER MEN AND USING THEIR BRAINS! NOW HE CAN TRY IT HERE THE *HARD WAY*-- BY HIMSELF!

BUT CAN HECTOR HAMMOND TAKE ADVANTAGE OF HIS OPPORTUNITY...

ALL KNOWLEDGE OF THE *PAST, PRESENT,* AND *FUTURE* IS CONTAINED IN THE *WORDS* OF THIS UN-ABRIDGED DICTIONARY-- BUT HOW DO I GO ABOUT STRINGING THE WORDS TOGETHER IN THE RIGHT ORDER TO GIVE ME THAT KNOWLEDGE?

The End

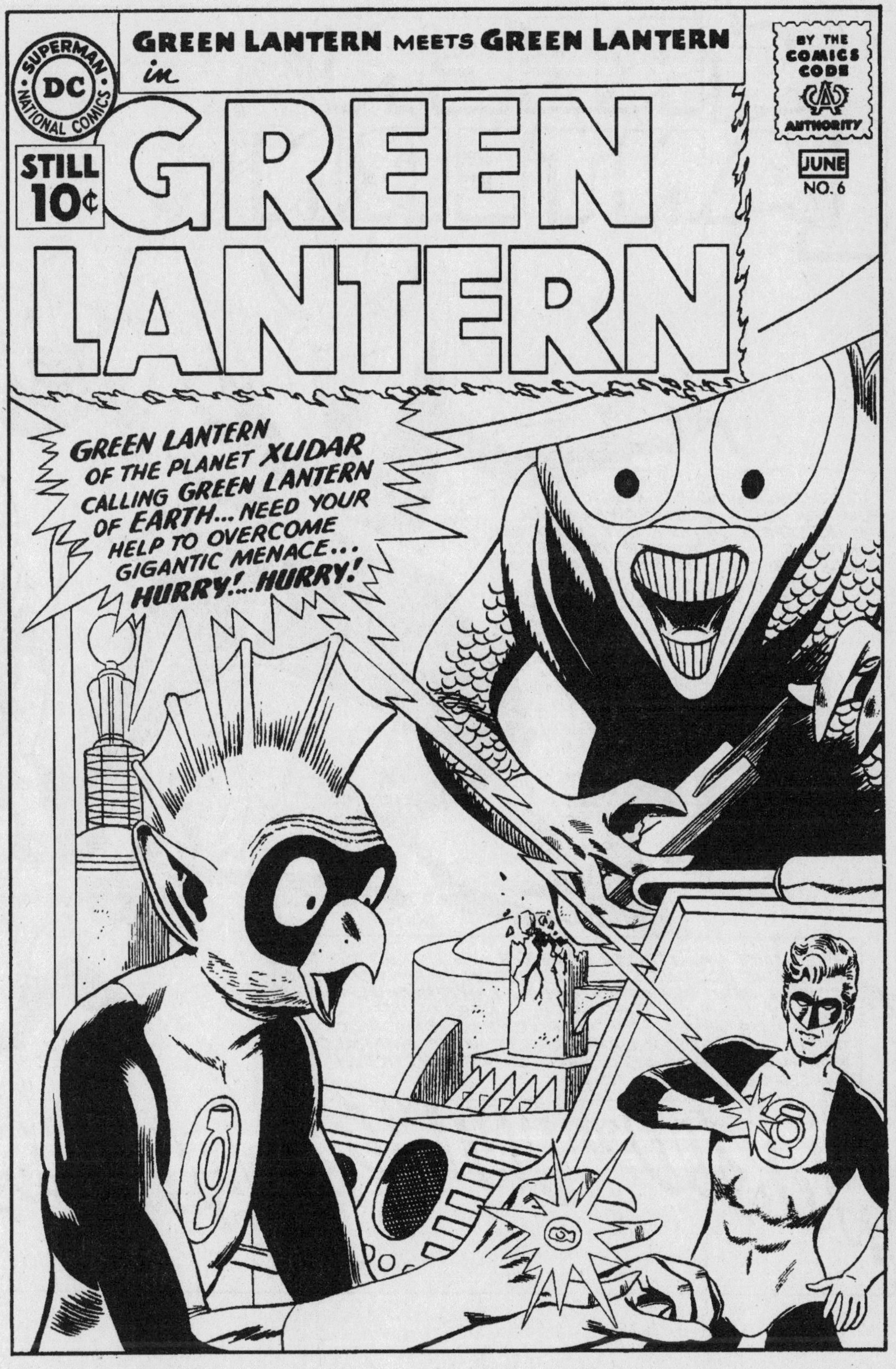
GREEN LANTERN MEETS GREEN LANTERN
in
GREEN LANTERN
SUPERMAN DC NATIONAL COMICS
STILL 10¢
BY THE COMICS CODE AUTHORITY
JUNE
NO. 6
GREEN LANTERN OF THE PLANET XUDAR CALLING GREEN LANTERN OF EARTH... NEED YOUR HELP TO OVERCOME GIGANTIC MENACE... HURRY!...HURRY!

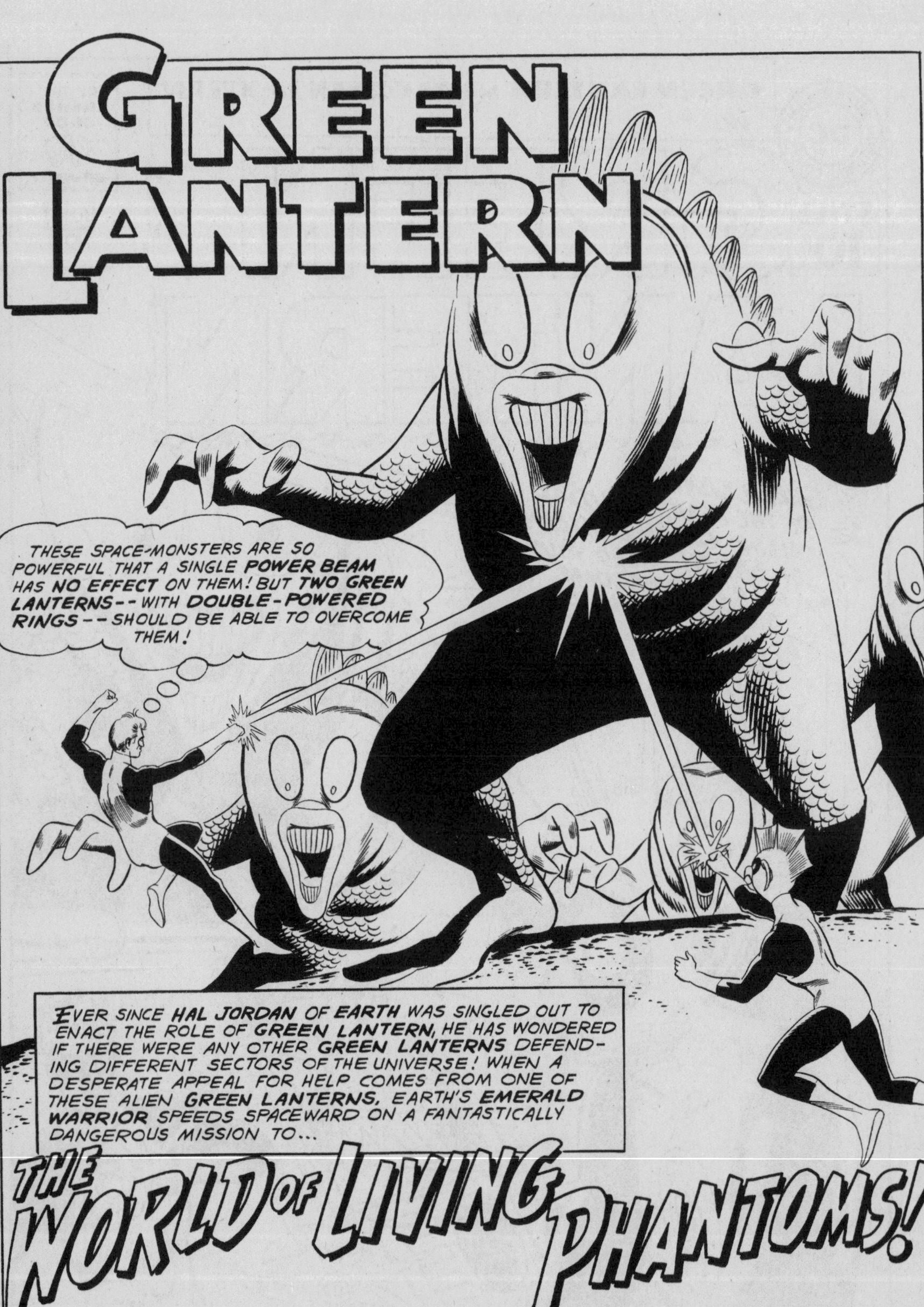
GREEN LANTERN
THESE SPACE-MONSTERS ARE SO POWERFUL THAT A SINGLE POWER BEAM HAS NO EFFECT ON THEM! BUT TWO GREEN LANTERNS-- WITH DOUBLE-POWERED RINGS -- SHOULD BE ABLE TO OVERCOME THEM!
EVER SINCE HAL JORDAN OF EARTH WAS SINGLED OUT TO ENACT THE ROLE OF GREEN LANTERN, HE HAS WONDERED IF THERE WERE ANY OTHER GREEN LANTERNS DEFENDING DIFFERENT SECTORS OF THE UNIVERSE! WHEN A DESPERATE APPEAL FOR HELP COMES FROM ONE OF THESE ALIEN GREEN LANTERNS, EARTH'S EMERALD WARRIOR SPEEDS SPACEWARD ON A FANTASTICALLY DANGEROUS MISSION TO...
THE WORLD OF LIVING PHANTOMS!

IN THE MILLIONS OF HABITABLE WORLDS OF THE UNIVERSE, LIFE HAS DEVELOPED ALONG COUNTLESS STRANGE LINES! BUT PERHAPS THE STRANGEST OF ALL CIVILIZATIONS EXISTS ON A PALE BLUE WORLD IN THE CONSTELLATION OF MONOCEROS...

A VISITOR TO THIS WORLD OF AKU WOULD AT FIRST SEE NOTHING VERY UNUSUAL...

...FOR IT APPEARS TO BE AN ADVANCED, SUPER-SCIENTIFIC CIVILIZATION...

BUT ACTUALLY THE REAL INHABITANTS OF AKU LIE UNDERGROUND IN SPECIAL CHAMBERS...

...IN A UNIQUE STATE RESEMBLING SLEEP AND SUSPENDED ANIMATION...

WHILE ABOVE IN THE CITY, THEIR THOUGHT-IMAGES CARRY ON THEIR DAILY LIVES!

I MUST HURRY! THERE IS AN EMERGENCY MEETING OF THE DIRECTORATE AND I MUST NOT BE LATE...

CENTURIES BEFORE, IBR--THE CHIEF SCIENTIST OF AKU--HAD EXPLAINED HIS GREAT PLAN TO THE DIRECTORATE OF THE PLANET...

...AND BY MY PLAN, EXCELLENCIES, THE LIFE-ENERGY OF EVERY CITIZEN OF AKU WOULD BE EXTENDED ALMOST INDEFINITELY! FOR WHILE WE LIE UNDERGROUND IN A STATE OF SUSPENDED ANIMATION, OUR THOUGHT-IMAGES, PROJECTED FROM OUR MINDS...

...WOULD CARRY ON OUR LIVES, EXACTLY AS WE WOULD OURSELVES, IN THE WORLD ABOVE US!

WONDERFUL, IBR! IT IS THE CLOSEST THING TO IMMORTALITY!

AND SO THE PLAN WAS PUT INTO EFFECT! AND FOR CENTURIES ALL WAS WELL, BUT THEN...

CLANG! CLANG!

THE ALARM...

THROUGH THE MINDS OF ALL THE SLEEPERS--HELPLESS THROUGH CENTURIES OF INACTIVITY--RUNS ONE AGONIZING THOUGHT...

THE ALARM CAN ONLY MEAN-- SOMETHING HAS GONE TERRIBLY WRONG IN THE WORLD ABOVE!

CLANG! CLANG!

ESPECIALLY IS THE MIND OF IBR, THE CHIEF SCIENTIST, AGONIZED...

HOW COULD THIS HAPPEN?! I THOUGHT WE HAD FORE-SEEN EVERY POSSIBILITY! EVERYTHING WAS ELECTRONICALLY CONTROLLED IN ADVANCE! IT'S IMPOSSIBLE! AND YET--

CLANG!

AND YET IT IS HAPPENING! AND THERE IS NOTHING WE CAN DO TO STOP IT! LYING HERE MOTIONLESS FOR AGES WE HAVE LOST ALL POWER OF MOVEMENT! WE ARE--DOOMED!

CLANG!

AND INDEED THE CITIZENS OF AKU WOULD BE DOOMED IF IT WERE NOT FOR THE FACT THAT ON THE NEARBY WORLD OF XUDAR...

...SITS AN INDIVIDUAL IN A STRANGELY-FAMILIAR UNIFORM!

YES! IT IS NONE OTHER THAN TOMAR-RE, THE GREEN LANTERN OF THIS PARTICULAR SECTOR OF THE UNIVERSE!

TROUBLE ON THE WORLD OF AKU! OF ALL THE UNFORTUNATE TIMES FOR THIS TO HAPPEN...!

3

EDITOR'S NOTE: AS REGULAR READERS OF THIS MAGAZINE HAVE BEEN INFORMED, GREEN LANTERN OF EARTH IS ONLY ONE OF A NUMBER OF GREEN LANTERNS IN THE UNIVERSE, EACH ENTRUSTED WITH THE CARE OF A SEPARATE COSMIC SECTOR BY THAT MYSTERIOUS BODY, THE ALL-WISE GUARDIANS OF THE UNIVERSE!

IN TOMAR-RE'S SECTOR HE IS IN CHARGE OF A NUMBER OF WORLDS AND KEEPS A CONSTANT CHECK ON THEM THROUGH A UNIQUE CONTROL PANEL OF HIS OWN DESIGN...

THE ZATHON-RAY COMMUNICATOR WHICH ASSURES ME WHEN ALL IS WELL ON A WORLD HAS CHANGED ITS FREQUENCY! THIS MEANS THAT AKU--"THE WORLD OF SLEEPERS"--NEEDS HELP! BUT I HAVE JUST LEARNED...

...THAT AN INVASION OF SPACE-MONSTERS HAS JUST TAKEN PLACE AT THE SOUTHERN TIP OF MY OWN WORLD! I WAS JUST ABOUT TO LEAVE TO DEAL WITH THEM--SO I CANNOT POSSIBLY GO TO AKU!

IN HIS DILEMMA, THE BRILLIANT MIND OF THE ALIEN GREEN LANTERN WORKS SWIFTLY...

ONLY ONE THING TO DO! I MUST GET IN TOUCH WITH THE GREEN LANTERN IN THE NEAREST SECTOR--AND APPEAL TO HIM TO LEND ME A HAND IN THIS EMERGENCY! LET ME SEE...THROUGH MY ALL-WAVE RADIO RECEPTION I HAVE LEARNED...

...THAT THE NEAREST GREEN LANTERN IS ON THE PLANET CALLED EARTH, IN SECTOR 2814! I MUST CONTACT HIM AT ONCE...

AT THAT VERY MOMENT ON THE PLANET CALLED EARTH..."

I HOPE CAROL IS READY! I'VE WAITED SO LONG FOR THIS DATE OF OURS THAT I DON'T THINK I CAN WAIT EVEN ANOTHER MINUTE!

BRINNNG!

4

AS HAL JORDAN, ACE TEST PILOT, NERVOUSLY AWAITS THE APPEARANCE OF HIS "BOSS" CAROL FERRIS...

EVER SINCE CAROL'S DAD TOOK OFF ON A ROUND-THE-WORLD TOUR LEAVING CAROL IN SOLE CHARGE OF *FERRIS AIRCRAFT* -- WHERE I WORK -- SHE'S REFUSED TO HAVE ANY *SOCIAL RELATIONS* WITH AN EMPLOYEE LIKE ME! THOUGH SHE HAS DATED...

...*GREEN LANTERN*, MY ALTER EGO! BUT I GUESS PERSISTENCE HAS FINALLY TRIUMPHED -- BECAUSE AT LONG LAST SHE AGREED TO GO OUT WITH ME TONIGHT! I'M GOING TO MAKE HER FORGET *GREEN LANTERN* -- WHICH WON'T BE EASY, BECAUSE HE'S *MYSELF!*

BUT THEN, SUDDENLY...

AN IMAGE...SPRINGING FROM MY *POWER RING!* AN *ENERGY IMAGE* OF SOME KIND--!

AND OUT OF THE IMAGE A THOUGHT SURGES INTO THE BRAIN OF THE STARTLED PILOT...

THIS IS *TOMAR-RE, GREEN LANTERN* OF THE PLANET *XUDAR!* YOU MUST COME AT ONCE --

WHEN CAROL, HAVING FINALLY MADE UP TO SUIT HERSELF, ANSWERS THE DOOR...

WELL HOW DO YOU LIKE *THAT!?* HAL BEGS ME FOR MONTHS FOR A DATE -- AND NOW HE'S RUNNING OFF... AS IF HE SUDDENLY GOT COLD FEET!

SOON, IN THE DARK PRIVACY OF HAL'S DRESSING ROOM AT THE HANGAR, A SOLEMN OATH IS REPEATED...

IN BRIGHTEST DAY, IN BLACKEST NIGHT, NO EVIL SHALL ESCAPE MY SIGHT! LET THOSE WHO WORSHIP EVIL'S MIGHT BEWARE MY POWER -- *GREEN LANTERN'S LIGHT!*

5

AND IN THE ROOM OF THE *ALIEN GREEN LANTERN* AT THIS MOMENT...

...AND THAT IS WHY YOU MUST GO TO *AKU, GREEN LANTERN OF EARTH* --WHILE I DEAL WITH THE *SPACE-MONSTERS* INVADING MY PLANET!

THERE IS ONE NOW!

I'M ON MY WAY, *TOMAR-RE!*

AS AN EMERALD LIGHTNING BOLT DARTS UPWARD FROM EARTH...

ACCORDING TO *TOMAR-RE,* SOME OF THE *LIVING THOUGHT-IMAGES* ON THE INCREDIBLE *WORLD OF AKU* HAVE BROKEN *OUT OF CONTROL* OF THE MINDS PROJECTING THEM -- AND ARE ENDANGERING THE ENTIRE CIVILIZATION THERE!

PROTECTED BY HIS ALL-POWERFUL GREEN BEAM -- AND POWERED BY IT-- *GREEN LANTERN* PIERCES THE COLD OF SPACE LIKE A JET-PROPELLED ARROW!

THE REBELLIOUS *THOUGHT-IMAGES* HAVE SOMEHOW FOUND A WAY OF SUPPLYING THEMSELVES WITH *ENERGY*-- AND ARE BENT ON TAKING CONTROL OF THEIR PLANET! THEY MUST BE STOPPED!

MEANWHILE, ON THE STRICKEN WORLD OF *AKU...*

DISASTER GROWS MORE CERTAIN EVERY MOMENT! I HAVE JUST REALIZED THAT THE LEADER OF THE REBELLIOUS *THOUGHT-IMAGES* IS NONE OTHER THAN MY OWN IMAGE!!

SOMEHOW WHATEVER WAS *EVIL* IN MY NATURE HAS BROKEN LOOSE IN THIS THOUGHT-COUNTERPART OF MYSELF! I CAN SEE HIM NOW--BY MEANS OF MY SUPERIOR MENTAL POWERS-- IN MY LABORATORY ABOVE, CARRYING OUT HIS *EVIL* DESIGNS...! I'LL ATTACK HIM *MENTALLY...*

I MUST REGAIN CONTROL OF HIM! I MUST...

YOU NEVER SHALL, *IBR!* I'LL STOP YOU...WITH *MENTAL FORCE!*

6

AS A DUEL OF ENERGY-FORCES RESULTS IN THE DEFEAT OF THE UNDERGROUND SCIENTIST...

YOU SHALL NEVER DIRECT ME AGAIN! I SHALL BE MY OWN MASTER--AS SOON AS I *DESTROY YOU!*

I CANNOT DO MORE! I AM HELPLESS...!

AND SOON AT A *WAR COUNCIL* OF THE LIVING PHANTOMS...

THE BEINGS FROM WHOSE MINDS WE SPRANG WILL NEVER STOP TRYING TO CONTROL US--UNTIL WE DESTROY THEM!

YES! TRUE!

ONLY *AFTER* WE HAVE ANNIHILATED EVERY ONE OF THEM WILL WE BE ABLE TO CARRY OUT OUR REAL AIM TO RULE THIS GALAXY-- *BY FORCE!*

BUT HOW CAN WE HARM THEM, "IBR"?

YOU KNOW, OF COURSE, THAT THE BEINGS WHO CREATED US LIE UNDERGROUND IN A SPECIALLY-BUILT CHAMBER WHICH NO KNOWN WEAPON CAN PENETRATE!

YES, I AM WELL AWARE OF THAT, KADMUN...

...BUT YOU FORGOT TO TAKE INTO ACCOUNT THAT I POSSESS THE IDENTICAL BRAIN AS THE *CHIEF SCIENTIST IBR*-- THE MOST AMAZING BRAIN EVER KNOWN ON *AKU!* AND I HAVE DEVISED...

A NEW *RADIATION EXPLOSIVE* BASED ON *ANTAGONISTIC ATOMS!* IF IT WORKS, WE CAN DESTROY OUR FORMER MASTERS COMPLETELY! LET US PROCEED TO *TEST IT OUT...*

7

SOON, AT A SELECTED TEST SITE...

IF THE NEW EXPLOSIVE WORKS THE WAY I HOPE, IT WILL DESTROY THE UNDERGROUND CHAMBER WITHOUT HARMING US OR OUR CITY! IN OTHER WORDS, IT WILL WORK WITH TERRIBLE FORCE, BUT IN A RESTRICTED AREA...

NOW WE WILL SEE WHAT IT DOES TO THAT MOUNTAIN...AS I PRESS THIS ELECTRO-BEAD...

AND A MOMENT LATER, INCREDIBLY...

ASTONISHING! A WHOLE SECTION OF THE MOUNTAIN VANISHED!

LEAVING THE REST OF THE MOUNTAIN UNTOUCHED!

EXCELLENT! NOW WE CAN TAKE CARE OF OUR FORMER MASTERS!

BUT AS THE GROUP RETURNS TOWARD THE CITY...

SO THIS IS AKU..!?

IBR--SEE! WHAT MANNER OF CREATURE IS THAT!?

TURNING, THE EMERALD GLADIATOR SENSES DANGER!

EVIL THOUGHTS REACHING ME--! THESE MUST BE THE REBEL IMAGES THAT TOMAR-RE SPOKE ABOUT! THOUGH THEY LOOK REAL ENOUGH!

GOOD THOUGHTS REACHING US! HE IS OUR FOE!

POWERED BY HIS RING, A MIGHTY BEAM FLASHES AT THE PHANTOM-LIKE ENEMY...

RAISING A WEAPON AT ME!? BUT MY POWER RING WILL REACH HIM AND THE OTHERS FIRST..!

8

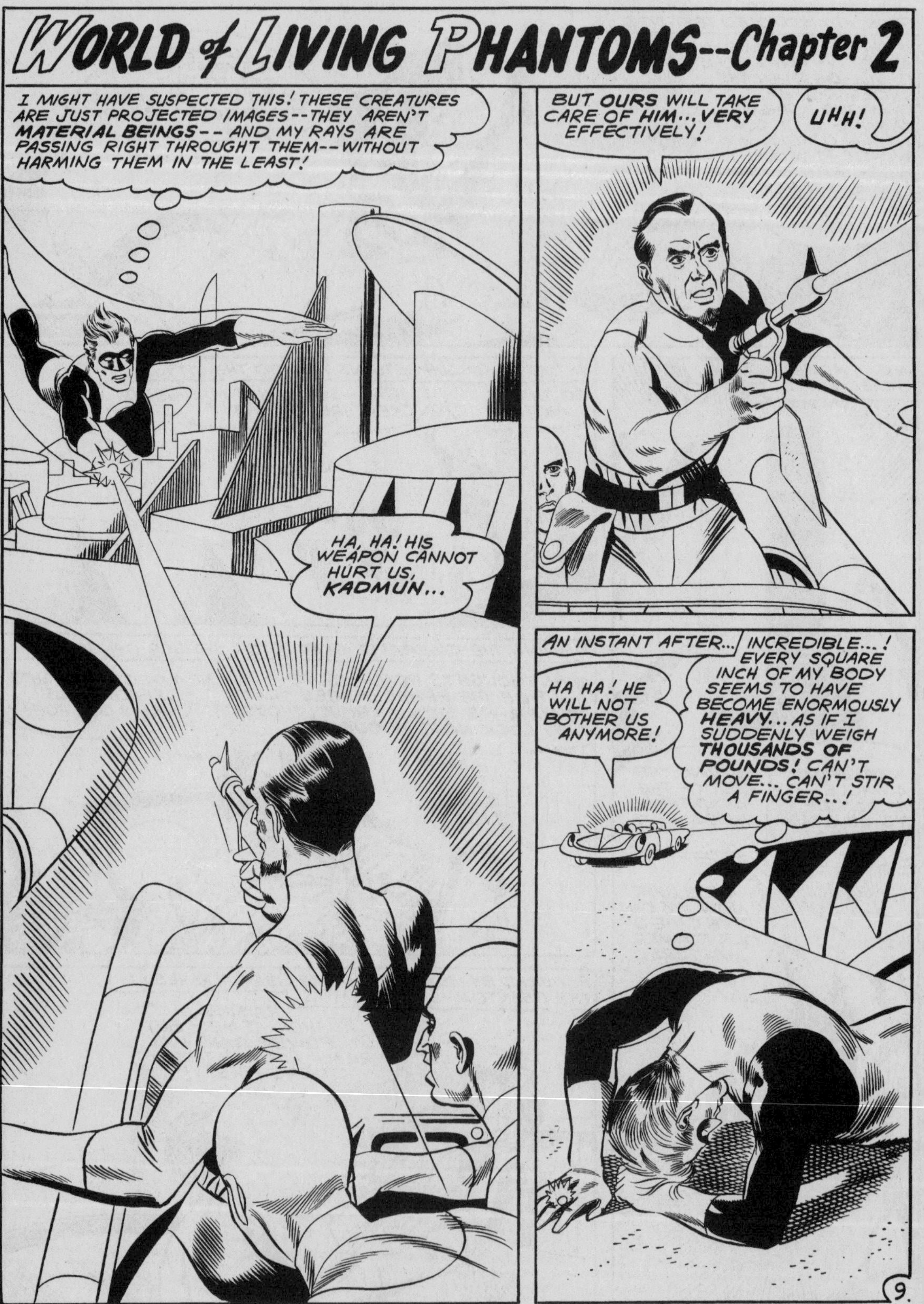
WORLD of LIVING PHANTOMS--Chapter 2
I MIGHT HAVE SUSPECTED THIS! THESE CREATURES ARE JUST PROJECTED IMAGES--THEY AREN'T MATERIAL BEINGS-- AND MY RAYS ARE PASSING RIGHT THROUGHT THEM--WITHOUT HARMING THEM IN THE LEAST!
HA, HA! HIS WEAPON CANNOT HURT US, KADMUN...
BUT OURS WILL TAKE CARE OF HIM...VERY EFFECTIVELY!
UHH!
AN INSTANT AFTER...
HA HA! HE WILL NOT BOTHER US ANYMORE!
INCREDIBLE...! EVERY SQUARE INCH OF MY BODY SEEMS TO HAVE BECOME ENORMOUSLY HEAVY...AS IF I SUDDENLY WEIGH THOUSANDS OF POUNDS! CAN'T MOVE... CAN'T STIR A FINGER..!
9

MEANTIME BELOW GROUND, *CHIEF SCIENTIST IBR* HAS MENTALLY WITNESSED ALL THAT HAS HAPPENED ABOVE...

A CHAMPION FROM ANOTHER WORLD HAS COME TO HELP US! BUT THE PHANTOM REBELS HAVE RENDERED HIM *POWERLESS!* I MUST CONTACT THE STRANGER AT ONCE! UNLESS HE CAN AID US, *WE ARE LOST...!*

WHILE THE EMBATTLED GLADIATOR STRUGGLES AGAINST THE INVISIBLE FORCE CHAINING HIM TO THE SPOT...

I FEEL AS IF I WERE ON A PLANET WHERE THE SURFACE GRAVITY IS A MILLION TIMES STRONGER THAN ON EARTH! BUT I CAN STILL MAKE MY RING WORK... EVEN THOUGH I CAN'T MOVE A MUSCLE!

VALIANTLY, *GREEN LANTERN* SEEKS TO COMBAT THE TREMENDOUS WEIGHT THAT HAS HIM ROOTED TO THE GROUND! BUT DESPITE HEROIC EFFORTS...

NO USE! DESPITE ALL THE *WILL POWER* I CAN BRING TO BEAR THROUGH MY *POWER BEAM,* I CAN'T RID MYSELF OF THIS WEIGHT! CAN'T LIGHTEN THE LOAD THE LEAST BIT...!

AND THEN, IN A MOMENT OF WEAKNESS SUCH AS CAN HAPPEN TO ALL HUMANS...

I GUESS... THIS IS IT! LOOKS LIKE... I'LL NEVER SEE *CAROL* AGAIN... OR *PIEFACE*... OR EARTH...

*** EDITOR'S NOTE:** HAL JORDAN'S ESKIMO GREASE-MONKEY AND PAL BACK AT THE *FERRIS AIRCRAFT COMPANY* IN COAST CITY.

BUT SUDDENLY IN THE MIDST OF GL'S BLACK DESPAIR...

EH? A THOUGHT... THE FACE OF SOMEONE... POPPING INTO MY BRAIN..!

GREEN LANTERN, LISTEN TO ME! THIS IS *IBR,* THE CHIEF SCIENTIST OF *AKU,* CONTACTING YOU...

I KNOW ALL ABOUT YOU, *GREEN LANTERN,* THROUGH MY TELEPATHIC ABILITY TO REACH OUT INTO YOUR BRAIN... EVEN THOUGH YOU ARE ON THE SURFACE OF MY WORLD AND I AM FAR UNDERGROUND... IN OUR SPECIAL "SLEEP-CHAMBER"...

10

RAPIDLY, THE THOUGHTS, THE WORDS, TUMBLE INTO *GREEN LANTERN'S* MIND...

...AND WHEN THE *REBEL IMAGES* OF OURSELVES CUT THEMSELVES OFF FROM US THEY NEEDED A *NEW SOURCE OF ENERGY* TO KEEP THEMSELVES--"*ALIVE*"! FOR THIS PURPOSE THEY CREATED A *GRAVITY HIVE*...

A *GRAVITY HIVE*!?

"*YES!* A SUPERIOR SCIENTIFIC DEVICE WHICH TAPS THE *GRAVITY* OF OUR PLANET AND POURS ITS ENERGY INTO THEM THROUGH RADIATION..."

NOW WE ARE COMPLETELY INDEPENDENT OF OUR FORMER MASTERS! WE HAVE OUR OWN ENERGY SUPPLY--IN ENDLESS AMOUNTS!

I SEE, *IBR!* THEN THE WEAPON THAT THE *IMAGES* USED AGAINST ME WAS BASED ON THEIR CONTROL OF GRAVITY-- A SORT OF *GRAVITY GUN!*

EXACTLY, *GREEN LANTERN!* BUT YOU *MUST* FREE YOURSELF!

"*EVEN NOW*, AT THIS MOMENT, THE *REBELS* ARE SETTING THEIR *NEW EXPLOSIVE* AT THE DOOR OF OUR CHAMBER..."

"IN ANOTHER FEW MINUTES IT WILL BE SET OFF--DESTROYING US UTTERLY..."

IT IS ALMOST READY, *KADMUN!* THE ADJUSTMENT OF THE *ANTAGONISTIC ATOMS* MUST BE PRECISE...

"*YOU ARE THE ONLY ONE* ON *AKU* WHO CAN HELP US, *GREEN LANTERN!* YOU MUST STOP THEM!"

AS THE TELEPATHIC VOICE OF THE CHIEF SCIENTIST, FILLED WITH DESPERATE APPEAL, TRAILS OFF...

...YOU *MUST* SAVE US..!

SAVE THEM? BUT HOW CAN I -- WHEN I MYSELF AM HELPLESS..?

AS THE SECONDS TICK BY IN THE UNDERGROUND "SLEEP CHAMBER" AND DOOM APPROACHES, SADNESS SETTLES ESPECIALLY ON TWO OF THE "SLEEPERS"-- STILL YOUNG DESPITE CENTURIES OF IMMOBILITY...

NOW I SHALL NEVER SEE ALYSSHA AGAIN! NEVER...

I HAD ALWAYS HOPED THAT SOMEHOW COSMO AND I... BUT NOW IT CAN NEVER BE!...IT IS TOO LATE...TOO LATE...

BUT THE INDOMITABLE CHAMPION FROM EARTH REFUSES TO BOW TO DISASTER...

WAIT...I JUST THOUGHT OF PIEFACE A WHILE AGO! SOME TIME BACK I USED MY POWER RING TO TURN PIE- FACE INTO A SECOND GREEN LANTERN-- A REPLICA OF MYSELF! *

*EDITOR'S NOTE: AS RE- COUNTED IN "THE POWER RING THAT VANISHED" IN THE APRIL, 1961 ISSUE OF GREEN LANTERN!

WHY CAN'T I USE MY RING TO DUPLICATE MYSELF--CREATE ANOTHER GREEN LANTERN THAT CAN MOVE--AND GO TO THE AID OF THE SLEEPERS! SOME QUALITY OF THIS PLANET SEEMS TO FAVOR THE PRODUCTION OF ENERGY- IMAGES!

INSTANTLY, THE GREAT GREEN BEAM FLARES FROM THE RING OF ITS MOTIONLESS WIELDER! AND...

DID IT! I'VE MADE AN EXACT DOUBLE OF MYSELF IN EVERY WAY--COMPLETE WITH POWER RING AND ALL!!

UH...NOT A MOMENT TO LOSE!

EDITOR'S NOTE: ONLY ON AKU, WITH ITS UNIQUE SUPER- MAGNETIC FIELD, COULD GREEN LANTERN CREATE AN IMAGE OF HIMSELF OUT OF THIN AIR! HE COULD NOT DO IT ANYWHERE ELSE!

GREEN LANTERN'S ENERGY-DOUBLE WHIZZES OFF...

WHAT A STRANGE FEELING! TO REMAIN HERE-- AND WATCH MYSELF SPEED AWAY! AND YET IT'S FITTING --SINCE I'M FIGHTING IMAGES-- TO MAKE AN IMAGE OF MYSELF TO DO IT!

12

AT THAT MOMENT, NEAR THE DOOR-WAY TO THE UNDERGROUND HIBERNATION CHAMBER...

NOW WE SEND THE SLEEPERS TO THE ETERNAL SLEEP, KADMUN!

EVEN THOUGH WE ARE SO CLOSE, MY AMAZING EXPLOSIVE WILL NOT HARM US AT ALL--AS IT DESTROYS THE UNDER-GROUND CHAMBER!

BUT JUST AS THE TERRIBLE DEVICE IS IN THE VERY ACT OF BURSTING...

HEU! A STRANGE GREEN LIGHT COVERING THE BOMB!? WHAT--!?

INTO SIGHT, A DAZZLING FIGURE FLASHES...

I'M STOPPING THE EXPLOSION--MUFFLING IT--BUT IT'S TAKING EVERY OUNCE OF WILL POWER I'VE GOT TO TURN THE TRICK!!

HEU!?

ANOTHER INTRUDER--JUST LIKE THE ONE WE GRAVITIZED!!

HE HAS RUINED OUR BOMB! GRAV HIM!!

ONCE AGAIN, THE DREAD GRAVITY GUNS FIRE THEIR AWFUL RAY-CHARGE AT THE EMERALD GLADIATOR! BUT THIS TIME...

THIS TIME THEIR WEAPONS HAVE NO EFFECT ON ME! BECAUSE I'M NOT AN ACTUAL MATERIAL BEING--BUT ONLY A RING-MADE IMAGE OF MYSELF!

WHAT ON AKU--!

ZZZZZT!

13

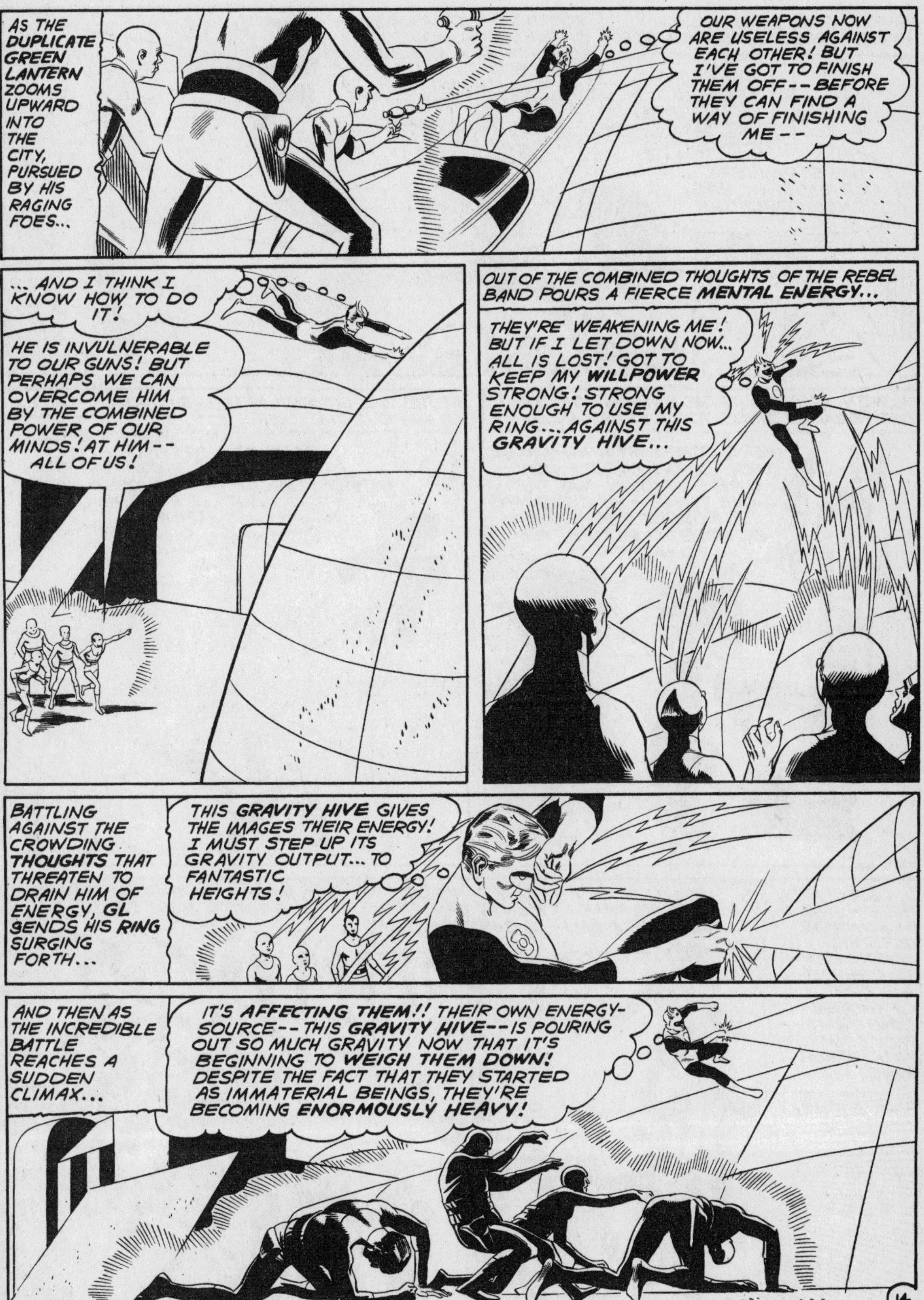
AS THE DUPLICATE GREEN LANTERN ZOOMS UPWARD INTO THE CITY, PURSUED BY HIS RAGING FOES...
OUR WEAPONS NOW ARE USELESS AGAINST EACH OTHER! BUT I'VE GOT TO FINISH THEM OFF-- BEFORE THEY CAN FIND A WAY OF FINISHING ME--
... AND I THINK I KNOW HOW TO DO IT!
HE IS INVULNERABLE TO OUR GUNS! BUT PERHAPS WE CAN OVERCOME HIM BY THE COMBINED POWER OF OUR MINDS! AT HIM-- ALL OF US!
OUT OF THE COMBINED THOUGHTS OF THE REBEL BAND POURS A FIERCE MENTAL ENERGY...
THEY'RE WEAKENING ME! BUT IF I LET DOWN NOW... ALL IS LOST! GOT TO KEEP MY WILLPOWER STRONG! STRONG ENOUGH TO USE MY RING... AGAINST THIS GRAVITY HIVE...
BATTLING AGAINST THE CROWDING THOUGHTS THAT THREATEN TO DRAIN HIM OF ENERGY, GL SENDS HIS RING SURGING FORTH...
THIS GRAVITY HIVE GIVES THE IMAGES THEIR ENERGY! I MUST STEP UP ITS GRAVITY OUTPUT... TO FANTASTIC HEIGHTS!
AND THEN AS THE INCREDIBLE BATTLE REACHES A SUDDEN CLIMAX...
IT'S AFFECTING THEM!! THEIR OWN ENERGY-SOURCE-- THIS GRAVITY HIVE-- IS POURING OUT SO MUCH GRAVITY NOW THAT IT'S BEGINNING TO WEIGH THEM DOWN! DESPITE THE FACT THAT THEY STARTED AS IMMATERIAL BEINGS, THEY'RE BECOMING ENORMOUSLY HEAVY!
14

SWIFTLY, THE GREEN-CLAD FIGURE PRESSES HIS ADVANTAGE...

GOT THEM! NOT A ONE OF THEM CAN MOVE SO MUCH AS A MUSCLE! EVEN THEIR BRAIN POWER HAS BEEN CUT DOWN TO ZERO...

THE STRANGER... OUR ENEMY... HAS... CONQUERED US!

MOMENTS LATER, AS THE ENERGY-GREEN LANTERN RETURNS TO HIS CREATOR...

HERE COMES MY RING-IMAGE BACK TO ME! AND I KNOW WE'RE BOTH THINKING THE SAME THING -- BY COMBINING OUR POWER RAYS WE MAY BE ABLE TO RETURN ME TO NORMAL!

AS THE TWO GREEN LANTERNS COMBINE FORCES TO TRY OUT THE IDEA...

NO... USE! IT STILL DOESN'T WORK! NOT EVEN TWO POWER RINGS CAN RID ME OF THIS COLOSSAL WEIGHT! BUT -- I HAVE ANOTHER IDEA...

IN DESPERATION, THE EMERALD GLADIATOR USES HIS MYSTIC RAY TO CREATE A SCORE OF GREEN LANTERNS -- EACH COMPLETE WITH POWER RING...!!

IF TWO GREEN BEAMS CAN'T DO THE TRICK, PERHAPS TWENTY CAN! THERE MUST BE A WAY -- I CAN'T GIVE UP!

MUST LIGHTEN THAT TERRIBLE GRAVITY! MUST DRIVE IT AWAY...!

15

AS DETERMINED *WILL POWERS* STEP UP THE INTENSITY OF THE *POWER RAYS*...

I--I CAN FEEL THE WEIGHT DISSOLVING! I'M GETTING LIGHTER EVERY MOMENT--

AND FINALLY...

WHEW! I'M MYSELF AGAIN! HOW GOOD IT FEELS JUST TO BE ABLE TO *MOVE!*

WITH A COMMAND OF HIS RING, *GREEN LANTERN* DISSOLVES THE IMAGES THAT AIDED HIM...

NO NEED FOR *THEM* ANYMORE! AND NOW I'VE GOT TO RUSH TO THE *SLEEPERS*--FIND OUT HOW THEY ARE!

MOMENTS LATER, BELOW GROUND...

YES, *GREEN LANTERN*, WE ARE ALL RIGHT, THANKS TO YOU! WE SAW EVERYTHING THAT HAPPENED ABOVE, BY OUR TELEPATHIC MINDS! THE REBEL *PHANTOMS* HAVE "SURRENDERED"...

DUE TO THE FACT THAT THEY WERE COMPOSED ONLY OF *MENTAL ENERGY*, THE ENORMOUS GRAVITY THAT ENTERED THEM WAS TOO MUCH FOR THEM AND THEY SUCCUMBED TO IT! PEACE HAS ONCE MORE COME TO *AKU*...

BUT WE *STILL* CAN'T UNDERSTAND WHAT WENT WRONG, *GREEN LANTERN!* HOW DID OUR OWN THOUGHT-IMAGES BREAK LOOSE FROM OUR CONTROL? IT IS A PROBLEM WE CANNOT SOLVE!

PERHAPS I CAN FIGURE IT OUT, IBR--WITH THE AID OF MY *POWER RING!*

16

UNLOOSING HIS RAY, **GREEN LANTERN** PLAYS IT ON THE **MASTER SWITCHBOARD** IN THE **SLEEP CHAMBER...**

MY BEAM MAKES EVERYTHING CLEAR! THIS BOARD IS DESIGNED TO RECEIVE THE THOUGHT-ENERGY OF THE **MENTAL VOLTAGE** BEFORE TRANSMISSION TO THE DUPLICATE IMAGES ON THE SURFACE...

BUT THE THOUGHT-ENERGY OF **TWO** OF THE SLEEPERS BECAME ENTANGLED ELECTRONICALLY-- THROWING OFF THE ENTIRE SWITCHBOARD! LET ME SEE! I CAN FIND OUT WHICH TWO ARE TO BLAME BY TRACING THE ENERGY-LINES...

SOON, DETERMINED TO PLUMB TO THE BOTTOM OF THE MATTER, THE CHAMPION FROM SPACE SUMMONS THE GUILTY PAIR BEFORE HIM...

YES, **GREEN LANTERN!** YOU HAVE FOUND OUR SECRET! I LOVE HIM...!

I WAS ALWAYS THINKING OF HER! I COULDN'T HELP IT!

SO HERE'S THE TROUBLE! THESE TWO --IN LOVE-- AND UNABLE TO DO ANYTHING ABOUT IT! LYING HERE MOTIONLESS-- TORMENTED--HELPLESS ALL THESE YEARS!!

BUT IF I MERELY PUT THEM BACK IN THEIR PLACES NOW, THE **SAME THING** MAY HAPPEN AFTER I'M GONE--AND AGAIN DISRUPT THE WHOLE **MENTAL SWITCHBOARD** OF THIS PLANET! HMM! I HAVE AN IDEA...

LATER, AFTER THE PAIR HAS JOYOUSLY ACCEPTED THE **EMERALD GLADIATOR'S** DRAMATIC PROPOSAL...

THERE! MY **GREEN BEAM** HAS GIVEN THEM BACK THE **POWER OF MOTION**--THE SAME VIGOR THEY ENJOYED WHEN THEY WENT INTO THE SLEEP CHAMBER CENTURIES AGO!!

HEU!

17

SO NOW THERE WILL BE NOT ONLY **THOUGHT-PHANTOMS** MOVING ABOUT THE STRANGE WORLD OF **AKU**--BUT ALSO A REAL FLESH-AND-BLOOD LIVING PAIR! AND WHO KNOWS...

...BUT SOME DAY A WHOLE NEW RACE--NOT OF **SLEEPERS** BUT OF **REAL PEOPLE**--MAY SPRING FROM THIS! I OFFERED TO DO THE SAME FOR ALL THE REST OF THE **SLEEPERS**, BUT NO ONE ELSE WOULD ACCEPT...

THEY ALL SAID THEY WERE **TOO OLD** TO START LIFE ANEW! MAYBE THEY'RE RIGHT...THEY'RE USED TO LIVING THIS WAY...OF LIVING THROUGH THEIR **THOUGHT-PHANTOMS**! I GUESS IT'S TOO LATE FOR THEM TO CHANGE...

RING-PROTECTED, **GREEN LANTERN** SPEEDS SPACEWARD...

BUT IT MAY NOT BE **TOO LATE** FOR ME TO AID MY COMRADE-IN-ARMS **TOMAR-RE**--IN HIS BATTLE AGAINST THE SPACE-MONSTERS THAT INVADED HIS PLANET! I'LL STOP THERE BEFORE HEADING BACK TO EARTH--!

AND AT THAT MOMENT, UNKNOWN TO THE **EMERALD WARRIOR**, HIS "COMRADE-IN-ARMS"--THE ALIEN **GREEN LANTERN**--IS IN TROUBLE...

MY RING...KNOCKS DOWN THESE INVADERS FROM SPACE...BUT THEY'RE SO HUGE AND POWERFUL THAT THEY PICK THEM-SELVES RIGHT UP AGAIN! THEY'RE FORCING ME BACK...BACK...!!

18

WORLD of LIVING PHANTOMS Chapter 3

IS IT POSSIBLE THESE CREATURES ARE *INVULNERABLE*? SUMMONING ALL THE POWER IN MY RING, I'M ABLE ONLY TO KNOCK THEM DOWN MOMENTARILY! I--I CAN'T HOLD THEM OFF MUCH LONGER--!

BESET BY HIS FOES, **TOMAR-RE--** THE **GREEN LANTERN** OF SECTOR 9 IN THE COSMOS-- FIGHTS A DESPERATE REAR-GUARD ACTION TO SAVE HIS WORLD FROM THE MONSTROUS INVADERS!

BUT THE NEXT MOMENT...

BY THE SEVEN SUNS OF SALOMAR! *ANOTHER POWER BEAM*-- JUST LIKE MY OWN--HITTING THE COLOSSUS FROM BEHIND AS MY OWN RING-BEAM STRIKES IT IN FRONT!

UNDER THE *DUAL IMPACT*, THE GREAT CREATURE TOPPLES LIKE A STRICKEN FOREST GIANT!

DESTROYED IT! THE **TWO BEAMS** TOGETHER DID IT! BUT--?

19

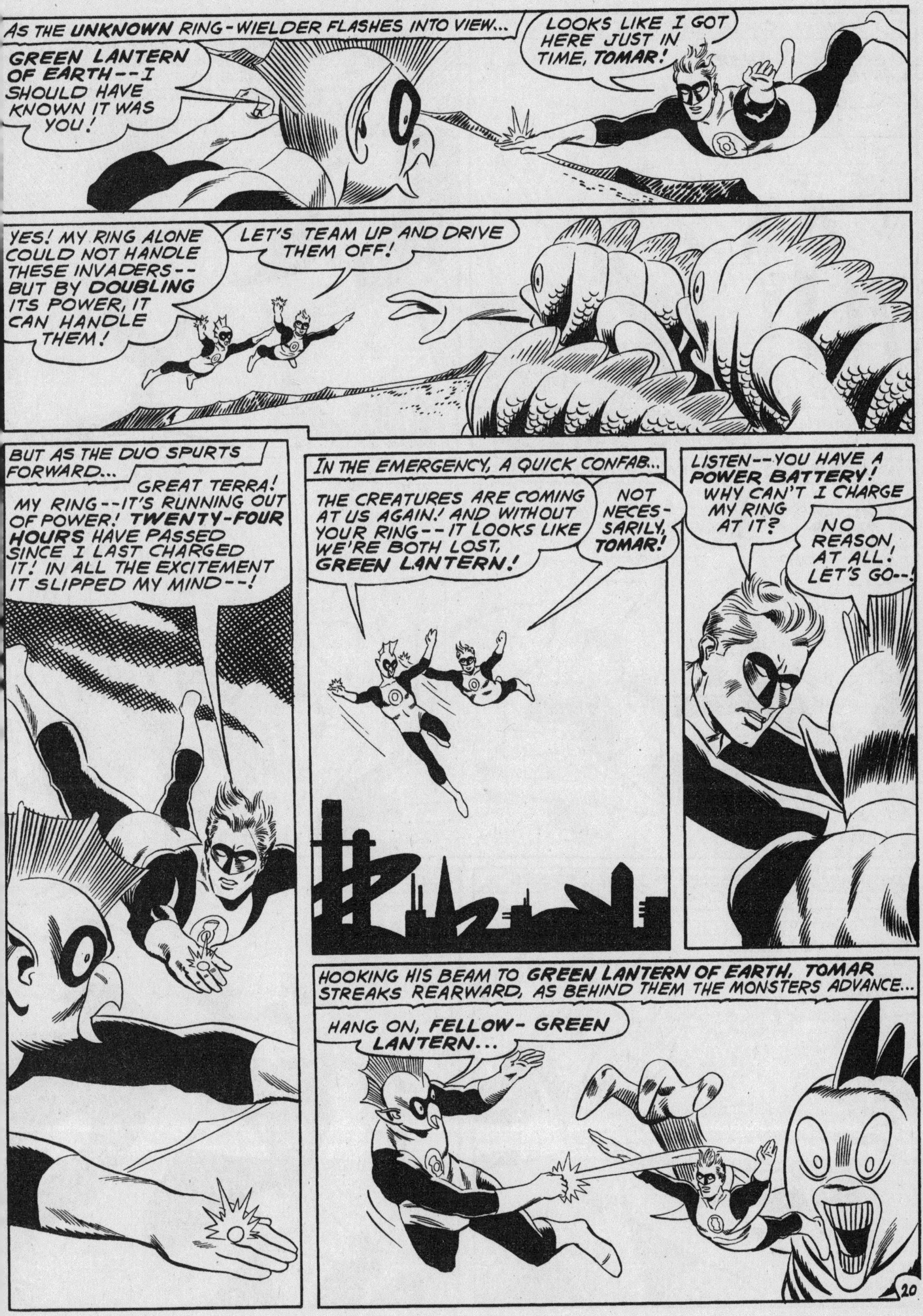
AS THE UNKNOWN RING-WIELDER FLASHES INTO VIEW...
GREEN LANTERN OF EARTH--I SHOULD HAVE KNOWN IT WAS YOU!
LOOKS LIKE I GOT HERE JUST IN TIME, TOMAR!
YES! MY RING ALONE COULD NOT HANDLE THESE INVADERS--BUT BY DOUBLING ITS POWER, IT CAN HANDLE THEM!
LET'S TEAM UP AND DRIVE THEM OFF!
BUT AS THE DUO SPURTS FORWARD...
GREAT TERRA! MY RING--IT'S RUNNING OUT OF POWER! TWENTY-FOUR HOURS HAVE PASSED SINCE I LAST CHARGED IT! IN ALL THE EXCITEMENT IT SLIPPED MY MIND--!
IN THE EMERGENCY, A QUICK CONFAB...
THE CREATURES ARE COMING AT US AGAIN! AND WITHOUT YOUR RING--IT LOOKS LIKE WE'RE BOTH LOST, GREEN LANTERN!
NOT NECES-SARILY, TOMAR!
LISTEN--YOU HAVE A POWER BATTERY! WHY CAN'T I CHARGE MY RING AT IT?
NO REASON, AT ALL! LET'S GO--!
HOOKING HIS BEAM TO GREEN LANTERN OF EARTH, TOMAR STREAKS REARWARD, AS BEHIND THEM THE MONSTERS ADVANCE...
HANG ON, FELLOW-GREEN LANTERN...
20

AND SOON IN **TOMAR-RE'S** HEADQUARTERS...

THERE IT IS, **GREEN LANTERN!** GO TO IT--

IN BRIGHTEST DAY, IN BLACKEST NIGHT, NO EVIL SHALL ESCAPE MY SIGHT! LET THOSE WHO WORSHIP EVIL'S MIGHT BEWARE MY POWER-- **GREEN LANTERN'S LIGHT!**

THEN, AS THE DUO OF **GREEN LANTERNS** RETURNS TO THE FRAY...

I'M ALL CHARGED UP, **TOMAR-RE!** LET'S GET AT THOSE INVADERS!

THEY'VE REACHED OUR CITY--DESTROYING EVERYTHING IN THEIR PATH!

LIKE TWIN THUNDERBOLTS, THE CRUSADERS CATAPULT AT THEIR GIGANTIC FOES...

THAT'S ANOTHER THAT WON'T BOTHER US ANYMORE!

SUDDENLY...

TOMAR-RE! BEHIND US--!

21

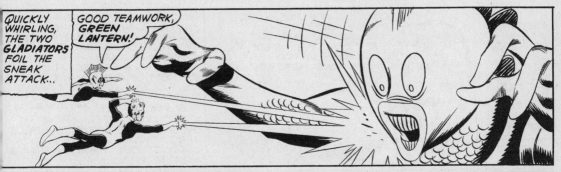

QUICKLY WHIRLING, THE TWO GLADIATORS FOIL THE SNEAK ATTACK...

GOOD TEAMWORK, GREEN LANTERN!

AS THE TIDE OF BATTLE TURNS INTO A ROUT...

WE'VE GOT THEM ON THE RUN, TOMAR!

FOLLOW UP OUR ADVANTAGE! WE'VE GOT TO DRIVE THEM OFF FOR GOOD!

AND SOON, WITH THE BEATEN REMNANTS OF THE HUGE INVADERS FLEEING SPACEWARD IN THE SHIPS THAT BROUGHT THEM...

AFTER THIS I DON'T THINK THOSE ALIENS WILL EVER RETURN! THEIR INVASION ATTEMPT WAS TOO COSTLY! YOU'VE HELPED SAVE MY WORLD, GREEN LANTERN!

IT WAS A PLEASURE, TOMAR!

LATER, TWO CHAMPIONS OF JUSTICE WHO HAVE EARNED A REST TAKE IT AND MATCH NOTES...

THEN YOUR TIME-SCALE HERE ON YOUR WORLD IS DIFFERENT FROM OURS ON EARTH, TOMAR-- BUT AS NEAR AS WE CAN FIGURE OUT, WHEN YOU CHARGE YOUR RING IT GIVES YOU POWER FOR WHAT AMOUNTS TO 24 EARTH-HOURS!

THAT'S RIGHT...

APPARENTLY THE GUARDIANS OF THE UNIVERSE -- THE MYSTERIOUS BEINGS WHO SELECTED US AS POWER BATTERY POSSESSORS-- DECREED THAT WE SHOULD ALL BE EQUAL IN THAT RESPECT...

THE...GUARDIANS OF THE UNIVERSE...!

22

SUDDENLY, A TRAIN OF THOUGHT DARTS MEMORY-LIKE THROUGH THE MIND OF THE EARTH GREEN LANTERN...

ODD! IT'S AS IF I'VE ALWAYS KNOWN ABOUT THEM... THE GUARDIANS! BUT HOW COULD I--SINCE I NEVER HEARD THE NAME BEFORE?

AS TOMAR-RE ADDS TO THE EARTHMAN'S MEAGER KNOWLEDGE OF THE MYSTERIOUS GROUP...

THE GUARDIANS OF THE UNIVERSE INHABIT A WORLD SOMEWHERE IN THE COSMOS--NO ONE KNOWS WHERE! AND THEY CONTACT US ONLY INDIRECTLY--THROUGH THE POWER BATTERY!

YES, THAT'S HAPPENED TO ME!

ONCE OR TWICE I'VE RECEIVED INSTRUCTIONS THROUGH MY POWER BATTERY TO GO TO THE AID OF SOME PLANET IN DISTRESS! BUT I NEVER KNEW WHERE THE MESSAGES CAME FROM--UNTIL NOW!

IT CAME FROM THE GUARDIANS!

THE GUARDIANS HAVE MYSTERIOUS WAYS OF OBTAINING INFORMATION--FROM ANYWHERE IN SPACE! THEY MUST POSSESS KNOWLEDGE THAT MAKES OUR SCIENCE--YOURS AND MINE--SEEM LIKE CHILDREN AT PLAY BY COMPARISON!

IS THERE ANYTHING MORE YOU CAN TELL ME ABOUT THEM?

ONLY THIS... THEY ALLOWED ME TO KNOW THE LOCATION OF SEVERAL OTHER GREEN LANTERNS--NO DOUBT BECAUSE MY SECTOR OF SPACE IS SO LARGE THAT I MIGHT SOMEDAY NEED HELP TO CONTROL IT-- JUST AS I NEEDED YOU THIS TIME!

23

LATER, AFTER **EARTH-GL** HAS GIVEN HIS COLLEAGUE A FULL REPORT OF THE EVENTS ON **AKU**...

GOOD! I'M GLAD THINGS ARE BACK TO NORMAL THERE! IT'S A STRANGE WORLD, AND I'VE HAD MY EYE ON IT FOR SOME TIME...

TOMAR-RE SURE HAS HIS HANDS FULL IN THIS SECTOR!

THEN, THE TIME FOR PARTING...

GOODBY, MY FRIEND--AND THANKS AGAIN!

NO NEED TO THANK ME, **TOMAR!** WE'RE BOTH IN THE SAME BUSINESS-- FIGHTING EVIL! PLEASE DON'T HESITATE TO CALL ON ME-- **ANY TIME!**

SOON, A SHIMMERING GREEN ROCKET HURTLES THROUGH SPACE...

AND IN DUE COURSE, BACK AT THE FERRIS AIRCRAFT COMPANY, WHERE PIEFACE PRESSES **GREEN LANTERN** TO EXPLAIN HIS ABSENCE...

WHERE HAVE YOU BEEN? CAROL HAS BEEN AROUND ASKING FOR YOU MORE THAN ONCE!

CAROL?! OH-OH!

I'LL EXPLAIN EVERYTHING LATER, **PIEFACE!** RIGHT NOW I'VE GOT TO ATTEND TO **SOMETHING IMPORTANT!**

JUMPING FISHHOOKS! YOU DON'T STAY PUT A MINUTE!

IT'S NOT TOO LATE! MAYBE I CAN STILL GET A DATE WITH CAROL TONIGHT! BUT I'LL HAVE TO HAVE A **GOOD** EXCUSE FOR WHAT HAPPENED THE OTHER NIGHT-- LEAVING HER IN THE LURCH THAT WAY!

24

LATER, AFTER THE JORDAN CHARM, AGAINST ODDS, HAS SECURED HIM A *SECOND CHANCE*...

CAROL, YOU JUST HAVE TO *TRUST ME!* I *CAN'T* TELL YOU WHY I HAD TO RUN OUT ON YOU SUDDENLY-- OR WHAT I'VE BEEN DOING SINCE THEN! ALL I CAN SAY IS THAT MY EXCUSE IS A LEGITIMATE ONE...

HE MUST BE DOING *TOP SECRET WORK* THAT HE CAN'T SPEAK ABOUT!

BUT I'LL SAY THIS! I'LL TELL YOU *EVERYTHING* SOME-DAY-- AFTER WE'RE *MARRIED!*

MARRIED!? HMM! YOU DO TAKE A LOT FOR GRANTED, HAL JORDAN! WHY, I SUPPOSE YOU THINK I SAT AROUND MOONING ABOUT YOU THAT NIGHT--

WELL, LET ME ASSURE YOU I DIDN'T! IT SO HAPPENS--ER-- THAT *GREEN LANTERN* CALLED ME AND TOOK ME OUT THAT NIGHT! SO *THERE!*

GREEN LANTERN!?

OHO! IF CAROL FEELS IT NECESSARY TO TELL A LITTLE WHITE LIE TO MAKE ME JEALOUS OF *GREEN LANTERN,* MY *OWN* ALTER EGO-- THEN MY STOCK WITH HER IS *REALLY* GOING UP! THIS IS THE BEST DEVELOPMENT YET IN MY BATTLE TO WIN HER AFFECTIONS AS *HAL JORDAN!*

The End.

25

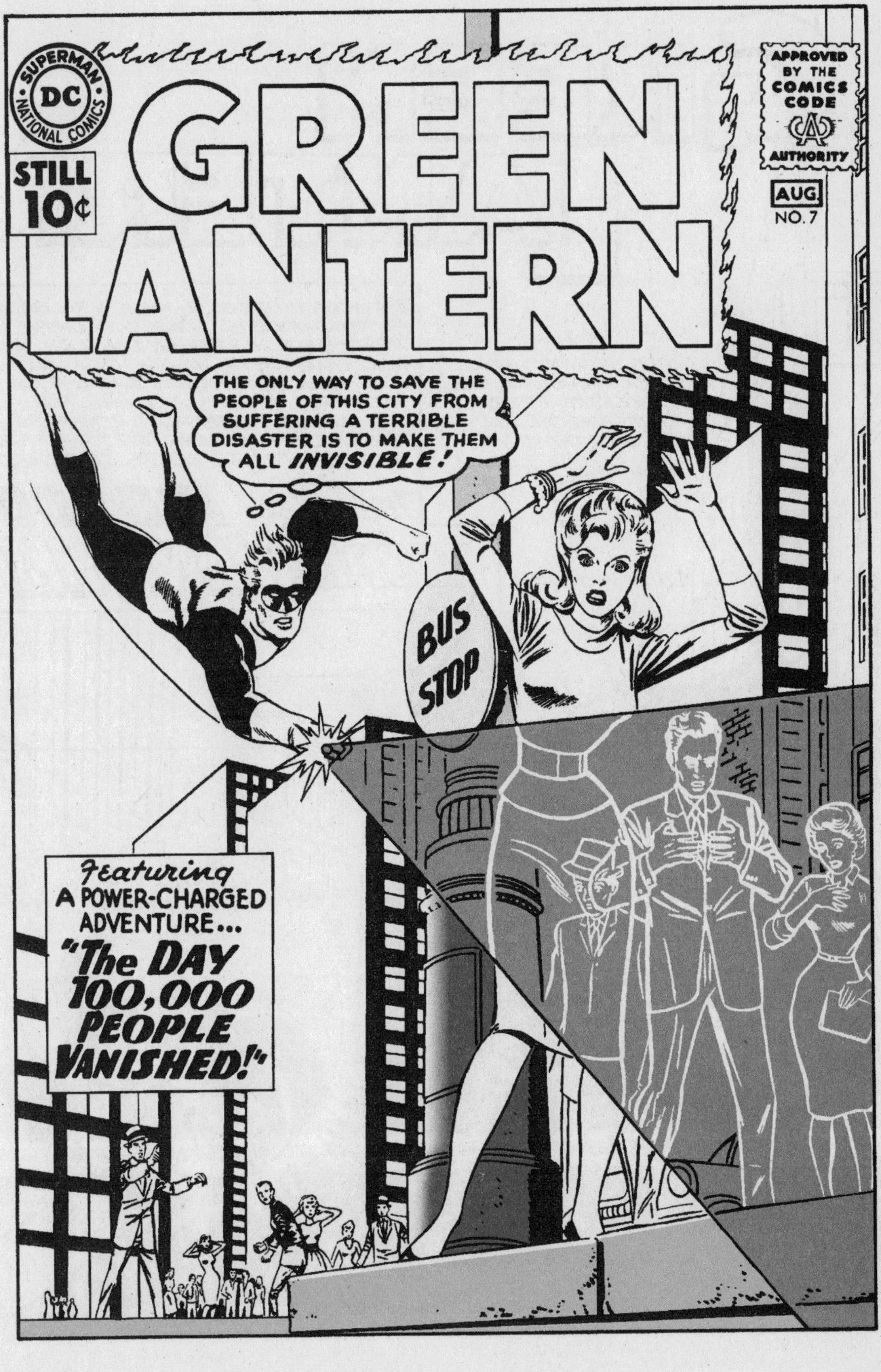
SUPERMAN DC NATIONAL COMICS
APPROVED BY THE COMICS CODE AUTHORITY
STILL 10¢
GREEN LANTERN
AUG. NO. 7
THE ONLY WAY TO SAVE THE PEOPLE OF THIS CITY FROM SUFFERING A TERRIBLE DISASTER IS TO MAKE THEM ALL INVISIBLE!
BUS STOP
Featuring A POWER-CHARGED ADVENTURE... "The DAY 100,000 PEOPLE VANISHED!"

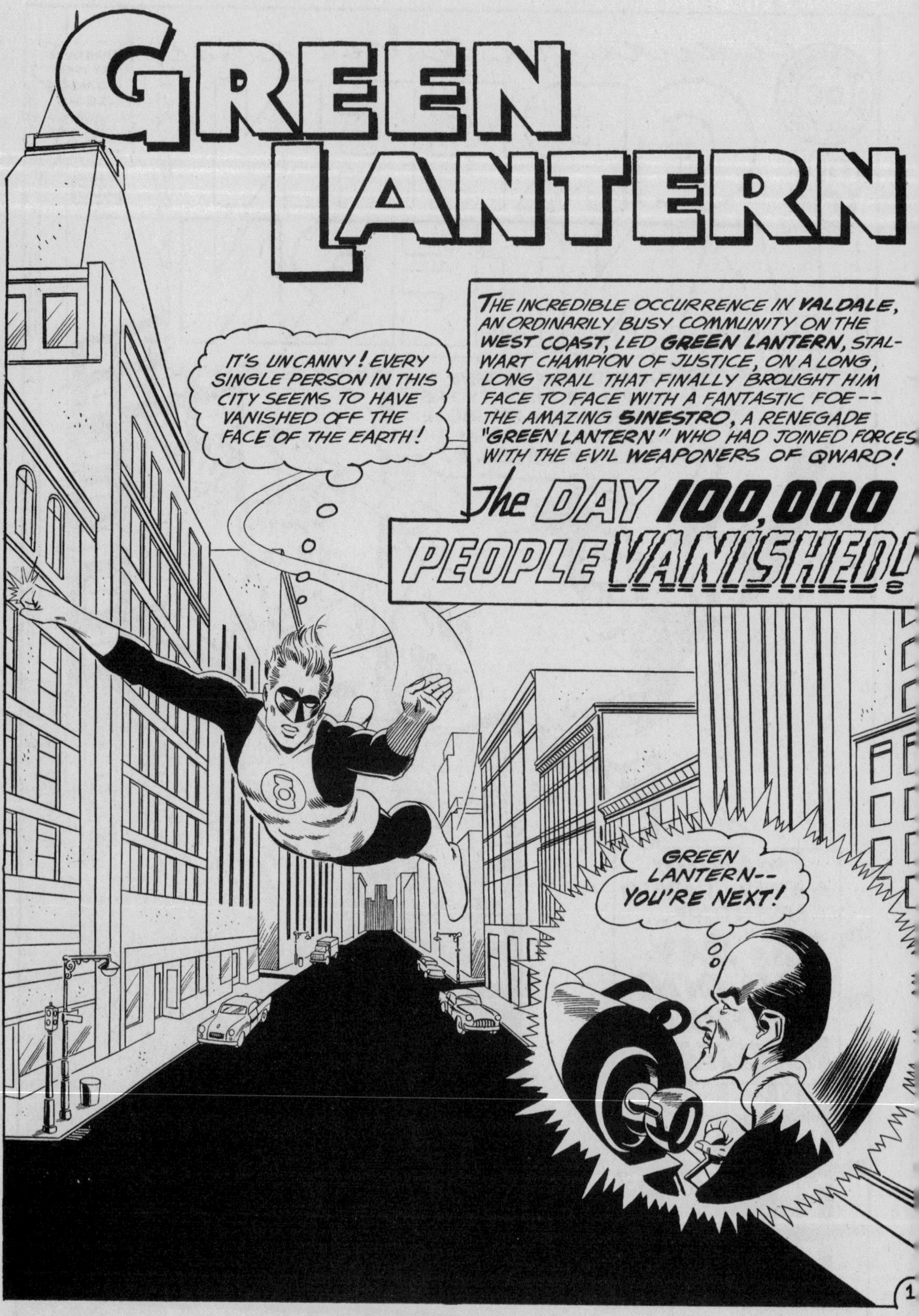
GREEN LANTERN
THE INCREDIBLE OCCURRENCE IN VALDALE, AN ORDINARILY BUSY COMMUNITY ON THE WEST COAST, LED GREEN LANTERN, STALWART CHAMPION OF JUSTICE, ON A LONG, LONG TRAIL THAT FINALLY BROUGHT HIM FACE TO FACE WITH A FANTASTIC FOE-- THE AMAZING SINESTRO, A RENEGADE "GREEN LANTERN" WHO HAD JOINED FORCES WITH THE EVIL WEAPONERS OF QWARD!
IT'S UNCANNY! EVERY SINGLE PERSON IN THIS CITY SEEMS TO HAVE VANISHED OFF THE FACE OF THE EARTH!
The DAY 100,000 PEOPLE VANISHED!
GREEN LANTERN-- YOU'RE NEXT!
1

AT PRECISELY FOURTEEN MINUTES AFTER NINE ON A BRIGHT MORNING IN THE THRIVING COMMUNITY OF **VALDALE** ON THE WEST COAST, THE RESIDENTS BUSTLE ABOUT THEIR USUAL ACTIVITIES...

FILL 'ER UP, JOE!

GET A MOVE ON, WILLYA?

LOVELY DAY, ISN'T IT, MRS. WILSON?

HONK!

SUDDENLY, THERE IS AN ODD SHIMMERING IN THE AIR, LIKE A **RAIN OF LIGHT**...

AND THE NEXT INSTANT A NOISE LIKE A THUNDERCLAP...

CRA ALACK!

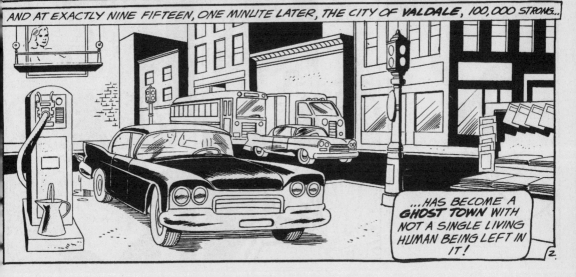

AND AT EXACTLY NINE FIFTEEN, ONE MINUTE **LATER**, THE CITY OF **VALDALE**, 100,000 STRONG...

...HAS BECOME A **GHOST TOWN** WITH NOT A SINGLE LIVING HUMAN BEING LEFT IN IT!

2.

WHAT IS THE MEANING OF THIS EXTRA-ORDINARY EVENT WHICH HORRIFIES THE ENTIRE NATION WHEN IT BECOMES KNOWN? IT IS A MYSTERY WHICH BAFFLES GREEN LANTERN-- ALIAS HAL JORDAN, ACE TEST PILOT--AS MUCH AS ANYONE...

GREEN LANTERN-- DID YOU FIND OUT WHAT HAPPENED AT VALDALE?

I EXAMINED THE WHOLE TOWN WITH MY POWER RING, PIEFACE--THERE'S NOT A SINGLE CLUE! THE PEOPLE ARE GONE AS IF THEY VANISHED INTO THIN AIR!

JUMPING FISHHOOKS!

WHILE ON THE WAY BACK FROM VALDALE, I WAS THINKING-- THE INCREDIBLE DISAPPEARANCE TOOK PLACE AT A LITTLE AFTER NINE O'CLOCK...

THAT'S RIGHT, GL! BUT WHAT--?

PIEFACE, IT JUST HAPPENS THAT I WAS SUPPOSED TO BE IN VALDALE AT THAT HOUR--TO TAKE PART IN A CEREMONY OPENING UP A NEW BOYS SETTLEMENT HOUSE THERE! I COULDN'T MAKE IT BECAUSE I HAD TO FINISH A CASE I WAS WORK-ING ON...

GREAT AURORA! THEN YOU WOULD HAVE VANISHED TOO--IF YOU HAD KEPT THE APPOINT--MENT!

EXACTLY! AND I CAN'T HELP WON-DERING-- EH?

BEFORE THE EMERALD GLADIATOR CAN CONTINUE, AN ODD FEELING PASSES OVER HIM...

THAT'S STRANGE! FOR AN INSTANT MY MIND WENT BLANK AND I COULDN'T REMEM-BER WHAT I WAS SAYING! BUT I'M OKAY NOW!

3

AT THAT "BLANK" MOMENT, UNKNOWN TO GREEN LANTERN, HIS ASTRAL SELF--OR ENERGY DUPLICATE--WAS HURTLING THROUGH SPACE...

MEANWHILE, ON THE FAR-FLUNG WORLD OF OA, IN THE CENTRAL GALAXY OF THE UNIVERSE, WHERE A GROUP KNOWN SIMPLY AS THE GUARDIANS SITS IN COUNCIL...

THE ENERGY-DUPLICATE OF THE POWER BATTERY POSSESSOR IN SECTOR 2814 IS ON THE WAY HERE!

AS A BURST OF LIGHT FLARED BEFORE THE IMPRESSIVE ASSEMBLAGE...

THE--THE GUARDIANS OF THE UNIVERSE!

YES! YOUR ENERGY-TWIN REMEMBERS WHAT YOUR CONSCIOUS MIND BACK ON EARTH IS STILL UNAWARE OF, GREEN LANTERN--THAT WE ARE THE CREATORS OF POWER BATTERIES SUCH AS YOURS...

...AND THAT ONCE BEFORE WE SUMMONED YOU TO US IN A GREAT EMERGENCY!* BUT WE HAVE NOT BROUGHT YOU HERE THIS TIME TO TALK ABOUT OURSELVES--BUT RATHER OF A SITUATION THAT THREATENS YOU!

THREATENS-- ME?

*Editor's Note: SEE "PLANET OF DOOMED MEN!" IN GREEN LANTERN #1

WE GUARDIANS DO NOT BESTOW POWER BATTERIES WITHOUT CAREFUL TESTS! BUT THERE ARE MANY POSSESSORS AND MANY WORLDS IN THE COSMOS UNDER OUR CARE! AND IN OUR SELECTIONS WE DID MAKE ONE MISTAKE! IT HAPPENED...

"...ON A WORLD CALLED KORUGAR IN SECTOR 1417 WHERE WE CHOSE A BEING NAMED SINESTRO..."

"...TO BE THE POSSESSOR OF A POWER BATTERY!"

4.

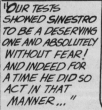

"OUR TESTS SHOWED SINESTRO TO BE A DESERVING ONE AND ABSOLUTELY WITHOUT FEAR! AND INDEED FOR A TIME HE DID SO ACT IN THAT MANNER..."

SINESTRO IS KEEPING DOWN EVIL ON HIS PLANET!

"BUT IN DUE COURSE, AFTER ONE OF OUR PERIODIC CHECKS, A SUBTLE CHANGE CAME OVER THE KORUGARN GREEN LANTERN WHICH WE WERE THEN UNAWARE OF..."

CHARGING MY RING AT THE BATTERY GIVES ME POWER FOR 37 DIORS*--UNLIMITED POWER! THERE IS NOTHING I CAN'T DO WITH IT!

*Editor's Note: THE EQUIVALENT OF 24 EARTH-HOURS!

"A FEELING OF DISSATISFACTION FILLED SINESTRO AS HE STARED ABOUT HIM..."

WHY SHOULD I REMAIN IN THIS SECRET CHAMBER-- HIDDEN HERE FROM MY WORLD? I HAVE A BETTER IDEA--AND A SENSATIONAL WAY TO EMPLOY MY RING!

"USING HIS POWER BEAM, SINESTRO CREATED A SUMPTUOUS HEADQUARTERS FOR HIMSELF, OUTSHINING EVERYTHING ELSE ON HIS PLANET..."

THERE! NOW I HAVE SUITABLE HEADQUARTERS-- THE MOST MAR- VELOUS BUILDING ON KORUGAR!

"FROM THEN ON, THIS GREEN LANTERN DISPENSED JUSTICE FROM HIS NEW HEADQUARTERS! BUT IN A STRANGE WAY..."

WE HAVE TO WAIT TO SEE SINESTRO SOMETIMES FOR DIORDANS*!

AND THEN HE TAKES ONLY THOSE CASES THAT INTEREST HIM--HELPS ONLY A FEW OF US AND IGNORES THE REST!

EVIL RAIDERS THREATENING YOUR SETTLEMENT-- ROBBING YOU?

HOW I AM BORED WITH THESE DIORDAN-LONG COMPLAINTS AND PLEAS FOR MY ASSISTANCE!

*Editor's Note: DIORDAN: 37 DIORS, OR ONE DAY!

/5

ALTHOUGH *SINESTRO* DID NOT REALIZE IT, HE WAS ALREADY INFECTED WITH THE VIRUS OF *POWER*--TO WHICH, BY A PSYCHOLOGICAL QUIRK IN HIS BRAIN, HE DID NOT HAVE ENOUGH RESISTANCE! AND FROM THEN IT WAS JUST A SHORT STEP TO HIS NEXT ACT...

"ONE OF THE SUPPLICANTS WHOM HE HAD REFUSED TO HELP RE-MONSTRATED WITH HIM, CHARGED HIM WITH LACK OF GOOD WILL..."

YOU ARE NO CHAMPION OF JUSTICE! WE HEARD *GREEN LANTERN* WOULD CRUSH EVIL WHEN IT THREATENED US! BUT INSTEAD YOU HAVE BECOME *POWER-MAD!*

YOU DARE--!?

"WITH ONE BURST OF HIS RING, THE *KORUGARN GREEN LANTERN* STRUCK THE SPEAKER UNCONSCIOUS...

FOR SHAME! *KI-MON* WAS UNARMED--HELPLESS!

SILENCE! OR ALL OF YOU WILL GET THE SAME TREATMENT! I AM *GREEN LANTERN*--NO ONE CAN TELL ME WHAT TO DO!

"PRIDE AND A LOVE OF POWER WERE *SINESTRO'S* UNDOING! SOON IN THE GOVERNING BODY OF HIS WORLD..."

SINCE I HAVE DECIDED TO GOVERN *KORUGAR* MYSELF, I HEREBY DISSOLVE THE HIGH COUNCIL!

HE IS MAKING HIMSELF *DICTATOR!*

"A PALL FELL OVER *KORUGAR!* NONE KNEW WHEN HE MIGHT INCUR THE NEW MASTER'S DISPLEASURE..."

THREE WHO SPOKE AGAINST GREEN LANTERN THE OTHER *DIORDAN* HAVE DISAPPEARED!

HE HAS BECOME A *LAW UNTO HIMSELF!* WE ARE ENSLAVED!

"BUT FORTUNATELY AT THIS TIME WE *GUARDIANS* MADE ONE OF OUR *PERIODIC SECRET CHECKS...*"

SINESTRO HAS MIS-USED THE POWER WE BESTOWED ON HIM!

HE BELIEVED THAT NONE STOOD ABOVE HIM! HE WILL NOW LEARN THAT HE WAS *MISTAKEN!*

6

"*By MEANS KNOWN ONLY TO OUR-SELVES, WE BROUGHT THE KORUGARN BATTERY POSSESSOR BEFORE US ...*"

SINESTRO, YOU HAVE ABUSED YOUR SACRED TRUST! INSTEAD OF DISPENSING JUSTICE ON YOUR WORLD-- YOU HAVE DIS-PENSED EVIL! UNDER THE CIRCUMSTANCES THERE IS ONLY ONE COURSE OPEN TO US!

"*IT WAS THE FIRST AND ONLY TIME WE HAD BEEN FORCED TO TAKE SUCH EXTREME MEASURES ...*"

SINESTRO OF KORUGAR, YOU HAVE BEEN FOUND UNWORTHY TO BE A BATTERY POSSESSOR! YOU ARE HEREBY STRIPPED OF ALL INSIGNIA AND HONORS--!

YOUR POWER RING IS NO LONGER YOURS!

YOUR BATTERY OF POWER IS NOW RE-TURNING TO US!

EVIL YOU ARE--TO EVIL YOU WILL GO! WE ARE BANISHING YOU TO THE ANTIMATTER UNIVERSE OF QWARD--WHERE ALL IS EVIL AND WHERE YOUR EVIL WILL FIND ONLY OTHER EVIL TO CLASH WITH!

"*WE THOUGHT THAT BY SENDING SINESTRO OUT OF OUR UNIVERSE ALTOGETHER WE HAD ENDED HIS MENACE TO US ...*"

BUT ONCE AGAIN WE WERE WRONG AS FAR AS SINESTRO WAS CONCERNED! WHICH LEADS US TO WHY WE BROUGHT YOU HERE TODAY!

THOUGH WE HAVE NO POWER IN THE ANTI-MATTER UNIVERSE OF QWARD, WE CAN PEER INTO IT! NOW WE WILL SHOW YOU CERTAIN SCENES WHICH OUR DEVICES HAVE RE-CORDED--SCENES OF INTEREST TO YOU!

"*SINESTRO WITH HIS FIERY ENERGY LOST NO TIME IN CONTACTING THE RULERS OF HIS NEW UNIVERSE--THE EVIL WEAPONERS OF QWARD ...*"

I AM DETERMINED TO BECOME MASTER OF THIS WORLD JUST AS I WAS MASTER OF KORUGAR! THE GUARDIANS WILL NEVER SHAKE MY WILL! I SHALL DEFEAT THEM YET! AND THERE IS ONE WAY TO BEGIN MY STRUGGLE--

7

YOU *QWARDIANS* HAVE FAILED IN THREE ATTEMPTS TO DESTROY YOUR MORTAL ENEMY, *GREEN LANTERN* OF EARTH! AND THE REASON IS THAT YOU ARE *NOT EVIL ENOUGH!* I SHALL TEACH YOU HOW TO BE THE *ULTIMATE IN EVIL!*

"*THE QWARDIANS* WERE AWED BY *SINESTRO!* THEY AGREED EAGERLY TO COOPERATE WITH HIM AND GIVE HIM CERTAIN MATERIALS HE ASKED FOR..."

UNDERSTAND, *WEAPONERS,* THAT *GREEN LANTERN* CANNOT BE HARMED WHILE HIS *POWER RING* IS OPERATING! THEREFORE I HAVE CONSTRUCTED THIS MECHANISM-- A TRULY *EVIL* MECHANISM!

BY SUPER-RADAR WE IN *QWARD* CAN DETECT WHAT IS HAPPENING ON EARTH--EVEN THOUGH WE CANNOT SEE DIRECTLY INTO IT! I HAVE LEARNED THAT *GREEN LANTERN* IS DUE TO APPEAR IN THE CITY OF *VALDALE* ON EARTH! DURING THAT TIME HIS RING WILL NOT BE OPERATING!

AT THE *RIGHT MOMENT* I WILL SWITCH ON MY NEW VISO-TELEPORTER--WHICH IS DIRECTED AT *VALDALE*--AND *EVERY VISIBLE* HUMAN BEING IN THE CITY--INCLUDING *GREEN LANTERN,* WILL INSTANTLY BE TRANSPORTED HERE TO *QWARD!*

MARVELOUS, *SINESTRO!* WE WILL HAVE *GREEN LANTERN* IN OUR POWER!

GREEN LANTERN

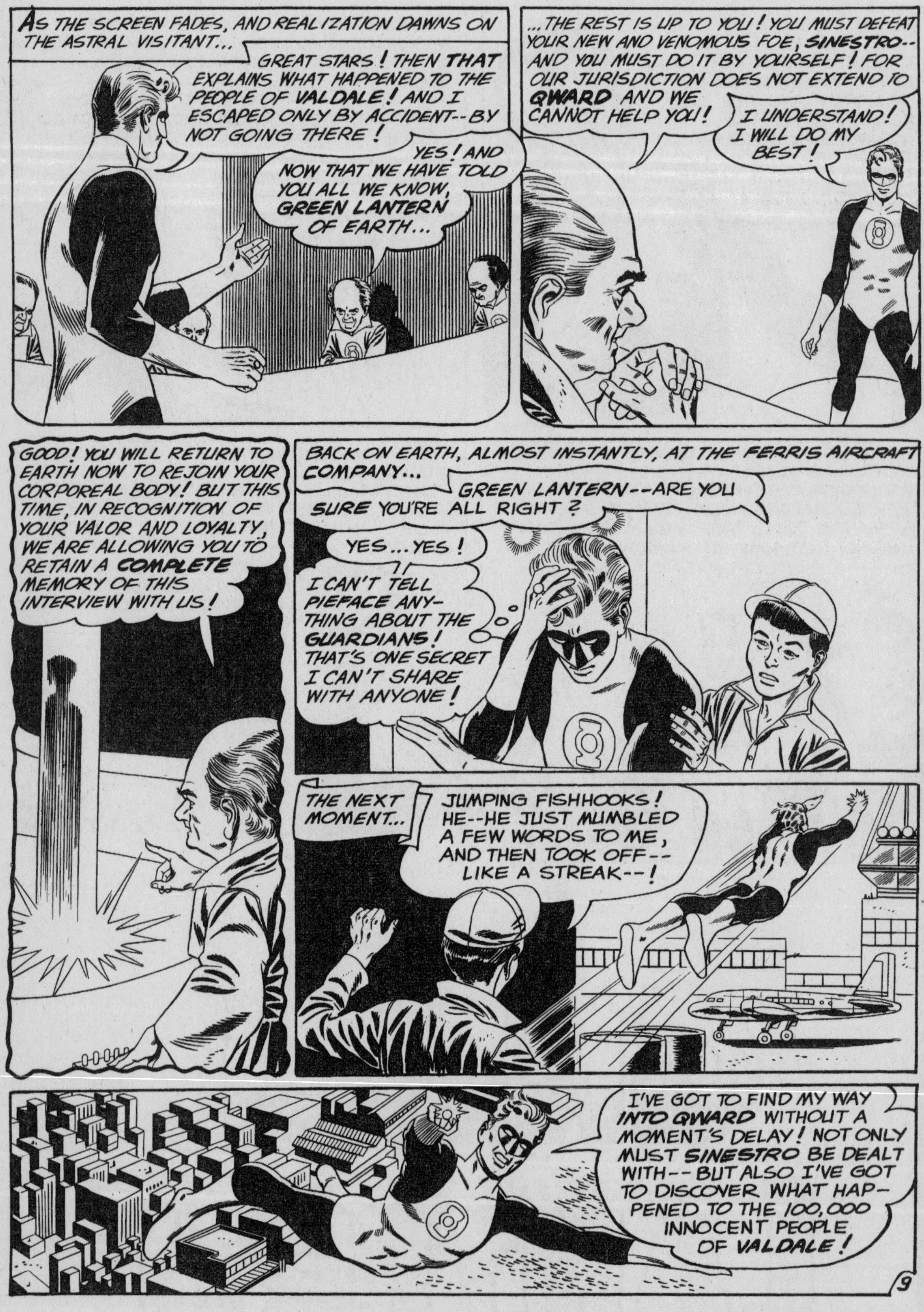
AS THE SCREEN FADES, AND REALIZATION DAWNS ON THE ASTRAL VISITANT...
GREAT STARS! THEN THAT EXPLAINS WHAT HAPPENED TO THE PEOPLE OF VALDALE! AND I ESCAPED ONLY BY ACCIDENT--BY NOT GOING THERE!
YES! AND NOW THAT WE HAVE TOLD YOU ALL WE KNOW, GREEN LANTERN OF EARTH...
...THE REST IS UP TO YOU! YOU MUST DEFEAT YOUR NEW AND VENOMOUS FOE, SINESTRO-- AND YOU MUST DO IT BY YOURSELF! FOR OUR JURISDICTION DOES NOT EXTEND TO QWARD AND WE CANNOT HELP YOU!
I UNDERSTAND! I WILL DO MY BEST!
GOOD! YOU WILL RETURN TO EARTH NOW TO REJOIN YOUR CORPOREAL BODY! BUT THIS TIME, IN RECOGNITION OF YOUR VALOR AND LOYALTY, WE ARE ALLOWING YOU TO RETAIN A COMPLETE MEMORY OF THIS INTERVIEW WITH US!
BACK ON EARTH, ALMOST INSTANTLY, AT THE FERRIS AIRCRAFT COMPANY...
GREEN LANTERN--ARE YOU SURE YOU'RE ALL RIGHT?
YES...YES!
I CAN'T TELL PIEFACE ANYTHING ABOUT THE GUARDIANS! THAT'S ONE SECRET I CAN'T SHARE WITH ANYONE!
THE NEXT MOMENT...
JUMPING FISHHOOKS! HE--HE JUST MUMBLED A FEW WORDS TO ME, AND THEN TOOK OFF-- LIKE A STREAK--!
I'VE GOT TO FIND MY WAY INTO QWARD WITHOUT A MOMENT'S DELAY! NOT ONLY MUST SINESTRO BE DEALT WITH--BUT ALSO I'VE GOT TO DISCOVER WHAT HAPPENED TO THE 100,000 INNOCENT PEOPLE OF VALDALE!
9

SHORTLY, AT A CERTAIN HILLSIDE NOT FAR FROM *COAST CITY*...

eh ? AT THIS SPOT THERE WAS AN INTER-UNIVERSE *APERTURE* WHICH I USED TO ENTER *QWARD*-- BUT NOW IT'S BLOCKED--SEALED UP! THAT MUST BE PART OF *SINESTRO'S* WORK--TO PREVENT A SURPRISE ATTACK ON MY PART!

AS FURTHER SEARCH FAILS TO REVEAL ANY OTHER MEANS OF ACCESS INTO THE ANTI--MATTER UNIVERSE ...

THERE'S *ONE OTHER* WAY TO GET INTO *QWARD*! IT'S TRICKY-- AND MAYBE DANGEROUS! BUT I'VE GOT TO TRY IT...!

BACK IN *COAST CITY,* THE VIBRANT CRUSADER UNDERTAKES AN INCREDIBLE MISSION...

THESE PEOPLE WILL ONLY BE AFFECTED TEMPORARILY! BUT MEANWHILE-- I'VE GOT TO USE MY RING TO TURN EVERY *LIVING BEING* IN THE CITY *INVISIBLE*--SO THAT THEY WILL BE INVULNERABLE TO *SINESTRO'S* VISO-TELEPORTER!

WH-WHAT'S HAPPENED TO ME?!

WHEN THE MIGHTY BEAM-WIELDER HAS ACCOM-PLISHED HIS EXTRAORDINARY TASK...

NOW I'M THE ONLY VISIBLE HUMAN IN THE CITY! AND SOONER OR LATER *SINESTRO*--BY HIS SUPER-RADAR--WILL GET WIND OF THE FACT THAT I'M HERE ...JUST WALKING ABOUT,...NOT USING MY RING! MY HOPE IS HE'LL SNAP AT THE BAIT--!

AFTER WHAT SEEMS AN INTERMINABLE WAIT...

A--AN INCREDIBLE FORCE SEIZING ME! BUT I MUSTN'T RESIST--MUST LET MYSELF GO! IT'S THE *ONLY* WAY I CAN GET INTO QWARD--!

CR-R-AACK!

10

AS THE GREEN-CLAD FIGURE VANISHES, IN THE CITY BEHIND HIM...

IT'S UNCANNY! I--I'M INVISIBLE--AND SO IS EVERYONE ELSE IN TOWN! I'M AFRAID TO DRIVE ANOTHER INCH!

THEN SUDDENLY, SINCE GREEN LANTERN HAD COMMANDED HIS RING TO HAVE ONLY A TEMPORARY EFFECT...

GREAT SCOTT! NOW--NOW WE'RE VISIBLE AGAIN!

AT THIS MOMENT, IN THE ANTI-MATTER UNIVERSE OF QWARD, WHERE EVIL IS THE STANDARD OF BEHAVIOR--JUST AS GOOD IS IN OURS...

SINESTRO HAS KEPT HIS PROMISE! HE HAS DELIVERED GREEN LANTERN TO US!

OPEN FIRE! DESTROY HIM!

AS A BATTERY OF DEADLY RADIATION SPURTS AT THE GREEN-CLAD ARRIVAL...

THEY WERE READY FOR ME! I GUESS THEY COUNTED ON MY BEING DAZED WHEN I GOT HERE--UNABLE TO USE MY POWER RING! BUT THEY DON'T REALIZE I FORE-SAW THIS!

ZZZZT!

IN A SPLIT-SECOND, THE GREEN GLADIATOR SETS UP AN IM-PENETRABLE SHIELD BEFORE HIM...

OUR ENERGY BURSTS CAN-NOT REACH HIM! WHAT DO WE DO NOW, SINESTRO?

FEAR NOT! MY EVIL MIND IS EASILY EQUAL TO THIS EMERGENCY--!

HEAR ME, GREEN LANTERN! UNLESS YOU SURRENDER TO US, YOUR COUNTRY-MEN--THE 100,000 PEOPLE OF VALDALE--WILL BE DESTROYED AT ONCE!

11

AFTER AN AGONIZING MOMENT, THE EMERALD WARRIOR REACHES A DECISION...

THIS IS ONE THING I DID **NOT** TAKE INTO ACCOUNT! I HAVE NO CHOICE! I MUST DO AS HE SAYS!

I ACCEPT YOUR TERMS! I WILL PLACE MYSELF IN YOUR POWER--ON ONE CONDITION--

--THAT YOU RELEASE THE PEOPLE OF **VALDALE**, AND SEND THEM BACK WHERE THEY BELONG-- SAFE AND SOUND!

AGREED! YOU HAVE MADE A GOOD BARGAIN, **GREEN LANTERN**-- 100,000 FOR ONE!

*AND SOON, BACK IN **VALDALE** WHICH WAS A MOMENT BEFORE ONLY A **GHOST** CITY...*

WH-WHAT HAPPENED TO US?

NO ONE KNOWS! BUT THANK GOODNESS WE ARE BACK HOME AGAIN AND ALIVE!

*WHILE IN QWARD, TRUE TO HIS PROMISE, **GREEN LANTERN** HAS ALLOWED HIMSELF TO BE CAPTURED...*

YOU'VE ENCASED ME IN A **YELLOW BUBBLE** OF PULSATING ENERGY, SINESTRO! BUT-- IS **THIS** THE WAY YOU PROPOSE TO DESTROY ME?

PATIENCE, MY EX-COLLEAGUE-- PATIENCE!

AS A FORMER RING-WIELDER MYSELF, I KNOW THAT YOUR **GREEN BEAM** WILL AUTO-MATICALLY PROTECT YOU FROM ALL HARM AS LONG AS YOU ARE CONSCIOUS! THEREFORE, MY PLAN IS SIMPLE! YOU CANNOT ESCAPE FROM OUR **YELLOW ENERGO-SAC--!*

*Editor's Note: DUE TO A NECESSARY IMPURITY IN ITS COMPOSITION, **GL'S** RING HAS NO POWER OVER ANYTHING YELLOW--A FACT WELL KNOWN TO SINESTRO, THE RENEGADE "GREEN LANTERN"!*

FURTHER, OUR SUPER-RADAR INFORMED US **EXACTLY** WHEN YOU LAST CHARGED YOUR RING! WHEN THAT CLOCK STRIKES **SIX**-- YOUR RING WILL RUN **OUT OF POWER**! **THEN** WE SHALL DESTROY YOU!

12

As the minutes tick by with measured and dreadful pace...

SINESTRO, YOU TRULY ARE A GENIUS OF EVIL! WE HAVE DECIDED TO MAKE YOU OUR CHIEFTAIN!

I ACCEPT! AND AFTER GREEN LANTERN IS FINISHED I SHALL LEAD YOU ON A COUNTERCRUSADE AGAINST MY ETERNAL ENEMIES-- THE GUARDIANS!

I MUST ESCAPE FROM HERE AND PREVENT SINESTRO'S ATTACK ON THE GUARDIANS! BUT HOW CAN I? MY RING WON'T PENETRATE THIS YELLOW SURFACE...!

IT SEEMS HOPELESS! AND YET--IN THE TIME I'VE BEEN IN HERE, I'VE NOTICED SOMETHING ABOUT THAT CLOCK! IT WORKS ON THE VIBRATION OF ATOMIC PARTICLES --MY RING HAS BEEN RECEIVING ITS IMPULSES! Hmm! I WONDER--!

NOT LONG AFTER, WHEN THE FINAL MOMENT ARRIVES...

THE CLOCK STRIKES SIX!

AND SEE--HIS RING IS RUNNING OUT OF POWER-- JUST AS I SAID IT WOULD!

AS THE MASTER OF EVIL UNLIMBERS AN ENERGY-GUN...

NO NEED FOR THE YELLOW BUBBLE, GREEN LANTERN! YOUR HOUR OF DOOM HAS STRUCK--

PERHAPS, SINESTRO...

...AND PERHAPS NOT!

AHH--!? HIS RING-- IT IS STILL WORKING!?

13

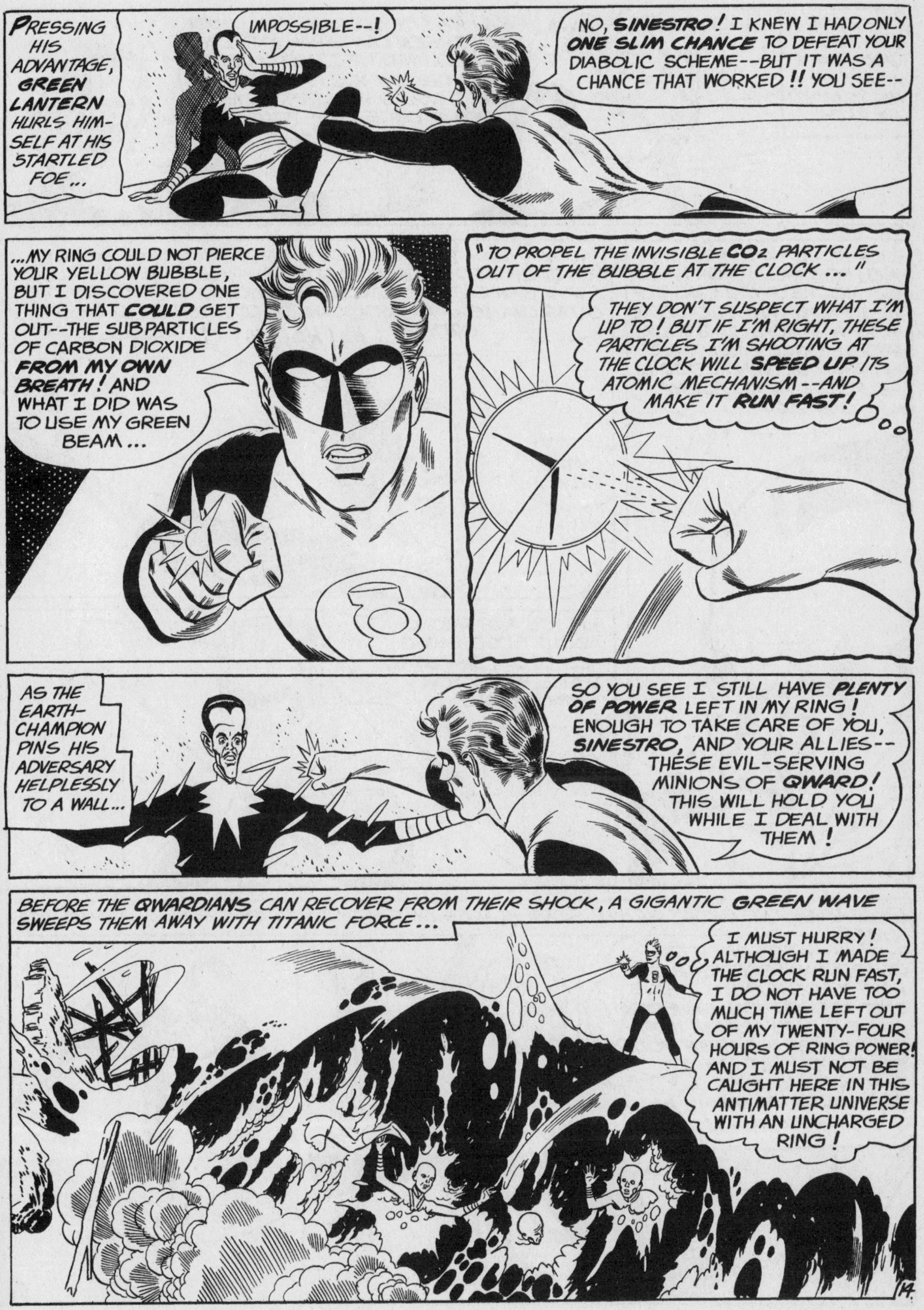
PRESSING HIS ADVANTAGE, GREEN LANTERN HURLS HIMSELF AT HIS STARTLED FOE...
IMPOSSIBLE--!
NO, SINESTRO! I KNEW I HAD ONLY ONE SLIM CHANCE TO DEFEAT YOUR DIABOLIC SCHEME--BUT IT WAS A CHANCE THAT WORKED!! YOU SEE--
...MY RING COULD NOT PIERCE YOUR YELLOW BUBBLE, BUT I DISCOVERED ONE THING THAT COULD GET OUT--THE SUBPARTICLES OF CARBON DIOXIDE FROM MY OWN BREATH! AND WHAT I DID WAS TO USE MY GREEN BEAM...
"TO PROPEL THE INVISIBLE CO2 PARTICLES OUT OF THE BUBBLE AT THE CLOCK..."
THEY DON'T SUSPECT WHAT I'M UP TO! BUT IF I'M RIGHT, THESE PARTICLES I'M SHOOTING AT THE CLOCK WILL SPEED UP ITS ATOMIC MECHANISM--AND MAKE IT RUN FAST!
AS THE EARTH-CHAMPION PINS HIS ADVERSARY HELPLESSLY TO A WALL...
SO YOU SEE I STILL HAVE PLENTY OF POWER LEFT IN MY RING! ENOUGH TO TAKE CARE OF YOU, SINESTRO, AND YOUR ALLIES--THESE EVIL-SERVING MINIONS OF QWARD! THIS WILL HOLD YOU WHILE I DEAL WITH THEM!
BEFORE THE QWARDIANS CAN RECOVER FROM THEIR SHOCK, A GIGANTIC GREEN WAVE SWEEPS THEM AWAY WITH TITANIC FORCE...
I MUST HURRY! ALTHOUGH I MADE THE CLOCK RUN FAST, I DO NOT HAVE TOO MUCH TIME LEFT OUT OF MY TWENTY-FOUR HOURS OF RING POWER! AND I MUST NOT BE CAUGHT HERE IN THIS ANTIMATTER UNIVERSE WITH AN UNCHARGED RING!
14.

As GREEN LANTERN TURNS ONCE AGAIN TO HIS TRAPPED ARCHFOE...

LAUGHING--!?

HA! HA! OF COURSE! YOU AMUSE ME, *GREEN LANTERN*, AND I WILL TELL YOU WHY! IF I HAD CAUGHT *YOU* THE WAY YOU HAVE CAUGHT *ME*, I WOULD HAVE DESTROYED YOU AT ONCE! BUT *YOU*--

YOUR STUPID CODE PREVENTS YOU FROM KILLING OR HARM-ING ANYONE IF YOU CAN HELP IT! I KNOW THAT BECAUSE I WORE A UNIFORM LIKE YOURS MYSELF ONCE -- BEFORE I LEARNED BETTER! GOOD IS HELPLESS -- *EVIL ALONE CAN ACT!*

AND NOT ONLY THAT, BUT YOU CANNOT EVEN TAKE ME WITH YOU BACK INTO YOUR WORLD TO IMPRISON ME -- BECAUSE I WAS BANISHED FOREVER FROM YOUR UNIVERSE BY THE *GUARDIANS* -- AND YOU CANNOT COUNTERMAND THEIR ORDERS! *HA! HA! HA!*

THAT'S TRUE...

BUT YOU ARE WRONG ABOUT GOOD BEING HELPLESS, *SINESTRO!* I WILL SHOW YOU *HOW WRONG*...

ONCE AGAIN THE GREAT GREEN BEAM FLARES OUT WITH INVINCIBLE FORCE, AND INSTANTS LATER...

NO FORCE ON *QWARD* CAN PENETRATE THE RING-MADE BUBBLE I HAVE CAST AROUND YOU, *SINESTRO!* ANY *EVIL* YOU CREATE NOW CAN ONLY BE *AGAINST YOUR-SELF!* AND WITH THAT PARTING THOUGHT, I *BID YOU A FINAL FAREWELL...!*

15

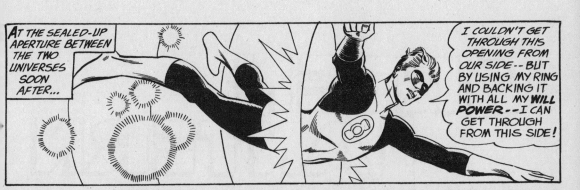

AT THE SEALED-UP APERTURE BETWEEN THE TWO UNIVERSES SOON AFTER...

I COULDN'T GET THROUGH THIS OPENING FROM OUR SIDE -- BUT BY USING MY RING AND BACKING IT WITH ALL MY **WILL POWER** -- I CAN GET THROUGH FROM THIS SIDE!

AND SHORTLY, IN A CERTAIN FAMILIAR CUBICLE IN THE HANGAR OF THE *FERRIS AIRCRAFT COMPANY*, A SOLEMN OATH IS RENEWED...

I HAD ONLY A **FEW SECONDS** OF POWER LEFT--

IN BRIGHTEST DAY, IN BLACKEST NIGHT, NO EVIL SHALL ESCAPE MY SIGHT! LET THOSE WHO WORSHIP **EVIL'S** MIGHT BEWARE MY POWER -- **GREEN LANTERN'S LIGHT!**

ON A ONCE-AGAIN PEACEFUL EARTH A BRILLIANT GREEN SHAPE FLARES ALONG...

THE OPENING OF THE **BOYS SETTLEMENT HOUSE** IN **VALDALE** HAS BEEN POST--PONED -- DUE TO THE EXTRAORDINARY EVENTS YESTERDAY -- TO TODAY! AND THIS TIME I'M KEEPING MY APPOINTMENT TO APPEAR THERE!

SOON, A SEA OF YOUTHFUL FACES IS STARING WORSHIP-FULLY UP AT THE EMERALD GLADIATOR...

...AND REMEMBER THIS, BOYS, WHEN **RIGHT** IS ON YOUR SIDE, YOU WILL ALWAYS OVERCOME **EVIL** NO MATTER WHERE YOU FIND IT!

The End 16

GREEN LANTERN

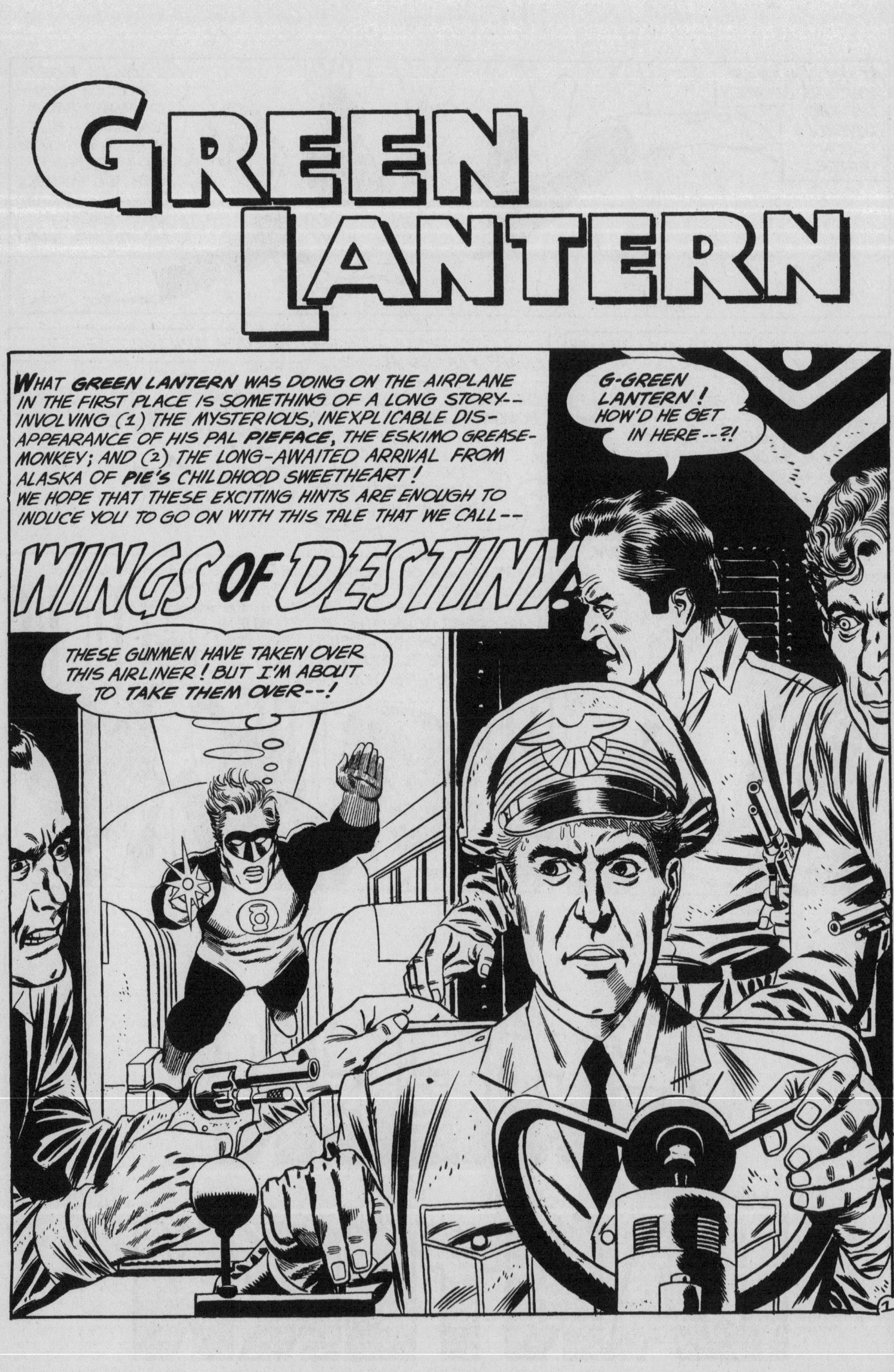
GREEN LANTERN
WHAT GREEN LANTERN WAS DOING ON THE AIRPLANE IN THE FIRST PLACE IS SOMETHING OF A LONG STORY-- INVOLVING (1) THE MYSTERIOUS, INEXPLICABLE DISAPPEARANCE OF HIS PAL PIEFACE, THE ESKIMO GREASE-MONKEY; AND (2) THE LONG-AWAITED ARRIVAL FROM ALASKA OF PIE'S CHILDHOOD SWEETHEART! WE HOPE THAT THESE EXCITING HINTS ARE ENOUGH TO INDUCE YOU TO GO ON WITH THIS TALE THAT WE CALL--
WINGS OF DESTINY!
G-GREEN LANTERN! HOW'D HE GET IN HERE--?!
THESE GUNMEN HAVE TAKEN OVER THIS AIRLINER! BUT I'M ABOUT TO TAKE THEM OVER--!
1

As HAL JORDAN, ACE TEST PILOT, LIES IN HIS BED ONE NIGHT IN A DEEP SLEEP...

...NO, PIEFACE! YOU KNOW I CAN'T USE MY POWER RING FOR TRIVIAL PURPOSES--BUT ONLY TO COMBAT EVIL AND INJUSTICE! STOP BOTHERING ME--

GOLLY, GREEN LANTERN, I'VE ALWAYS WANTED TO FLY! YOU CAN MAKE ME FLY WITH YOUR RING! IS THAT SO MUCH TO ASK OF A GUY'S BEST PAL?

HMMM!

IN HAL'S DREAM HE SEES HIMSELF AS HIS ALTER EGO GREEN LANTERN, BESIEGED BY "PIEFACE," HIS ESKIMO GREASEMONKEY...

ALL RIGHT, PIE! I SUPPOSE THERE IS NO HARM IN IT! BUT JUST THIS ONCE, YOU UNDERSTAND? I'LL TURN YOU INTO A BIRD SO YOU CAN FLY--!

JUMPING FISHHOOKS!

MEANWHILE IN THE DREAM, GREEN LANTERN'S WILL POWER BEGINS TO OPERATE AND...

...UNKNOWN TO THE SLEEPER, HIS CHARGED POWER RING REALLY BEGINS TO OBEY HIS UNCONSCIOUS COMMANDS...

...BEAMING A CHARGE OF ENERGY TO THE ROOM NEXT DOOR WHERE THOMAS KALMAKU (PIEFACE) LIVES...

...AND TURNS HIM WITH THE GREATEST EASE INTO A SEAGULL...

WHAT GOES ON? WHAT GOES ON?

2

IN THE MORNING... GOSH, I SLEPT LATE! I'D BETTER HURRY, GET *PIEFACE*, AND MAKE IT OUT TO THE FIELD!* WE HAVE A BUSY DAY AHEAD OF US--

*Editor's Note: THE FERRIS AIRCRAFT COMPANY WHERE HAL JORDAN IS CHIEF TEST PILOT!

SOON... NO ANSWER! I GUESS *PIEFACE* LEFT WITHOUT ME! HE MUST HAVE TRIED TO WAKE ME AND COULDN'T!

KNOCK! KNOCK!

BUT AS HAL TAKES OFF, UNKNOWN TO HIM BEHIND THE CLOSED DOOR "PIEFACE" IS JUST AWAKENING...

FUNNY! I HAD THE LOOPIEST DREAM LAST NIGHT! ALL ABOUT HOW *GL* GOT IT INTO HIS HEAD TO TURN ME INTO A BIRD!

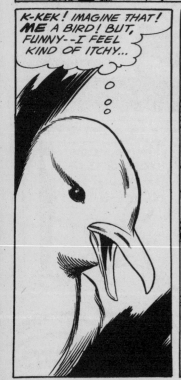

K-KEK! IMAGINE THAT! *ME* A BIRD! BUT, FUNNY--I FEEL KIND OF ITCHY...

...LIKE I WAS COVERED WITH FEATHERS--OR SOMETHING! I'LL TAKE A LOOK AT MYSELF IN THE MIRROR--

K-KEK! I MUST BE STILL DREAMING--OBVIOUSLY! BUT IN THAT CASE, WHAT AM I DOING UP? I'LL GET BACK INTO BED!

3

WHY AM I PULLING THE COVERS BACK THIS WAY--USING MY *BEAK* INSTEAD OF MY HANDS? FUNNY, I'M BEGINNING TO GET THE QUEEREST FEELING THAT I'M NOT ASLEEP AT ALL...

AND IF I'M NOT ASLEEP THEN THERE'S ONLY ONE CONCLUSION! I'M *NOT DREAMING!* AND IF I'M NOT DREAMING THAT MEANS (K-KEK!) *I AM A BIRD!*

YEOWIE! SOME MEAN VILLAIN HAS DONE THIS--PROBABLY SOME FIEND FROM OUTER SPACE--TRYING TO ELIMINATE ME BEFORE HIS ALIEN RACE INVADES THE EARTH! I GOTTA FIND MY PAL *GREEN LANTERN*-- WARN HIM...

GL CAN CHANGE ME BACK TO MY REGULAR SHAPE! HE CAN DO IT WITH HIS RING--AND THEN TOGETHER THE TWO OF US CAN TAKE ON THE *INVADERS!* I GOTTA FLY *FAST*--!

MEANWHILE AT THE AIRCRAFT COMPANY ON THE OUTSKIRTS OF *COAST CITY*...

STRANGE! THERE'S BEEN NO SIGN OF *PIE-FACE!* I CAN'T IMAGINE WHAT'S HAPPENED TO HIM! AND ESPECIALLY THIS MORNING WHEN THIS TELEGRAM HE'S BEEN WAITING FOR SO LONG HAS FINALLY ARRIVED...

...FROM HIS CHILDHOOD SWEET-HEART, *TERGA*--SAYING THAT SHE'S ARRIVING ON THE TEN O'CLOCK PLANE FROM ALASKA AND THAT HE *MUST MEET HER!* GREAT SCOTT! THE POOR GIRL WILL BE WORRIED TO DEATH IF THERE'S NO ONE THERE! I'VE GOT TO FILL IN FOR *PIE*--!

4

IN THE PRIVACY OF HIS DRESSING ROOM A TRANSFORMATION COMES OVER THE YOUTHFUL PILOT...

NO TIME TO WASTE! I'LL RE-CHARGE MY RING AS *GREEN LANTERN* AND GET OUT TO THE AIRPORT AT ONCE!

IN BRIGHTEST DAY, IN BLACKEST NIGHT, NO EVIL SHALL ESCAPE MY SIGHT! LET THOSE WHO WORSHIP EVIL'S MIGHT BEWARE MY POWER-- *GREEN LANTERN'S LIGHT!*

WHILE POWER-FLYING TO THE AIRPORT...

THAT PESKY *BIRD!* KEEPS FLYING AT ME--! WHAT IN THUNDER IS THE MATTER WITH IT?

HEY, GL--GL, YOU MUST LISTEN TO ME!

SUPER-SCIENTIFIC ALIENS...ABOUT TO INVADE THE EARTH! AWFUL EMERGENCY...YOU AND I MUST FIGHT--AFTER YOU TURN ME BACK TO MY REGULAR SHAPE!

THIS BIRD LOOKS LIKE A SEAGULL-- BUT ACTS LIKE A *CUCKOO!*

WITH AN ADDITIONAL BURST OF POWER, THE *EMERALD GLADIATOR* DRAWS SWIFTLY AWAY FROM THE WINGED NUISANCE...

THANK GOODNESS SEAGULLS AREN'T KNOWN FOR SPEED, AND I COULD EASILY GET AWAY FROM IT! NOW TO GET TO THE AIRPORT...

K-KEK!

AND SOON, NEAR THE AIRFIELD, *GREEN LANTERN* SUDDENLY DECIDES TO USE HIS RING TO *SUMMON* HIS HAL JORDAN CLOTHES TO HIM...

IT'S OCCURRED TO ME I'D BETTER GREET *PIEFACE'S* GIRL FRIEND AS *HAL JORDAN!* THAT WAY IT WILL BE EASIER TO EXPLAIN MY RELATION TO *PIE* AND WHY I'M HERE!

Editor's Note: GREEN LANTERN HAS WILLED HIS CLOTHES TO TRAVEL INVISIBLY FROM HIS HANGAR DRESSING ROOM, TO APPEAR ONLY IN FRONT OF HIM!

PROMPTLY AT TEN...

THERE'S THE PLANE! BUT I DON'T SEE *TERGA*... OR ANYONE WHO REMOTELY FITS HER DESCRIPTION! EH? WHAT'S THAT...?

...NO MOVE FROM HERE...

5

As the ace test pilot boards the airliner...

I...NO...MOVE! I WANT...SEE THOMAS! NO... MOVE TILL HE COME...

THAT MUST BE *TERGA!* SHE'S ASKING FOR *THOMAS KALMAKU*-- THAT'S *PIE'S* SQUARE MONIKER! BUT I DIDN'T REALIZE--SHE CAN HARDLY SPEAK ENGLISH!

BUT BEFORE HAL CAN EVEN APPROACH THE GIRL...

eh? THOSE MEN--BARGED IN HERE--TAKING OVER THE PLANE AT GUN-POINT!

YOU--PILOT! DON'T ASK QUESTIONS! JUST TAKE THE PLANE UP--AND *FAST!*

As the plane captain is forced to obey...

WE'RE ALOFT ALREADY! THOSE GUNMEN MUST BE ESCAPED CONVICTS OUT TO MAKE A GETAWAY! I'VE GOT TO STOP THEM--BUT I MUST BE CAREFUL! I DON'T WANT *TERGA* TO BE HURT--!

A thought-command from Hal Jordan-- and his outer garments fly off...

THOSE CROOKS AREN'T KEEPING TOO CLOSE A WATCH ON ME! I GUESS THEY DON'T THINK I MATTER MUCH! BUT THEY'RE ABOUT TO LEARN DIFFERENTLY!

THE NEXT MOMENT...

FIRST THING I'LL DO IS USE MY RING TO FREEZE THE CONTROLS--AND MAKE THIS PLANE FLY IN SLOW CIRCLES TO PLAY SAFE--!

G-GREEN LANTERN!? WHERE'D *HE* COME FROM!?

BUT THEN AS AN UNEXPECTED AIR POCKET CAUSES THE CRAFT TO LURCH...

LOOK! GREEN LANTERN SLAMMED INTO THAT SEAT--

UHH!

--AND IS CONKING OUT!

6.

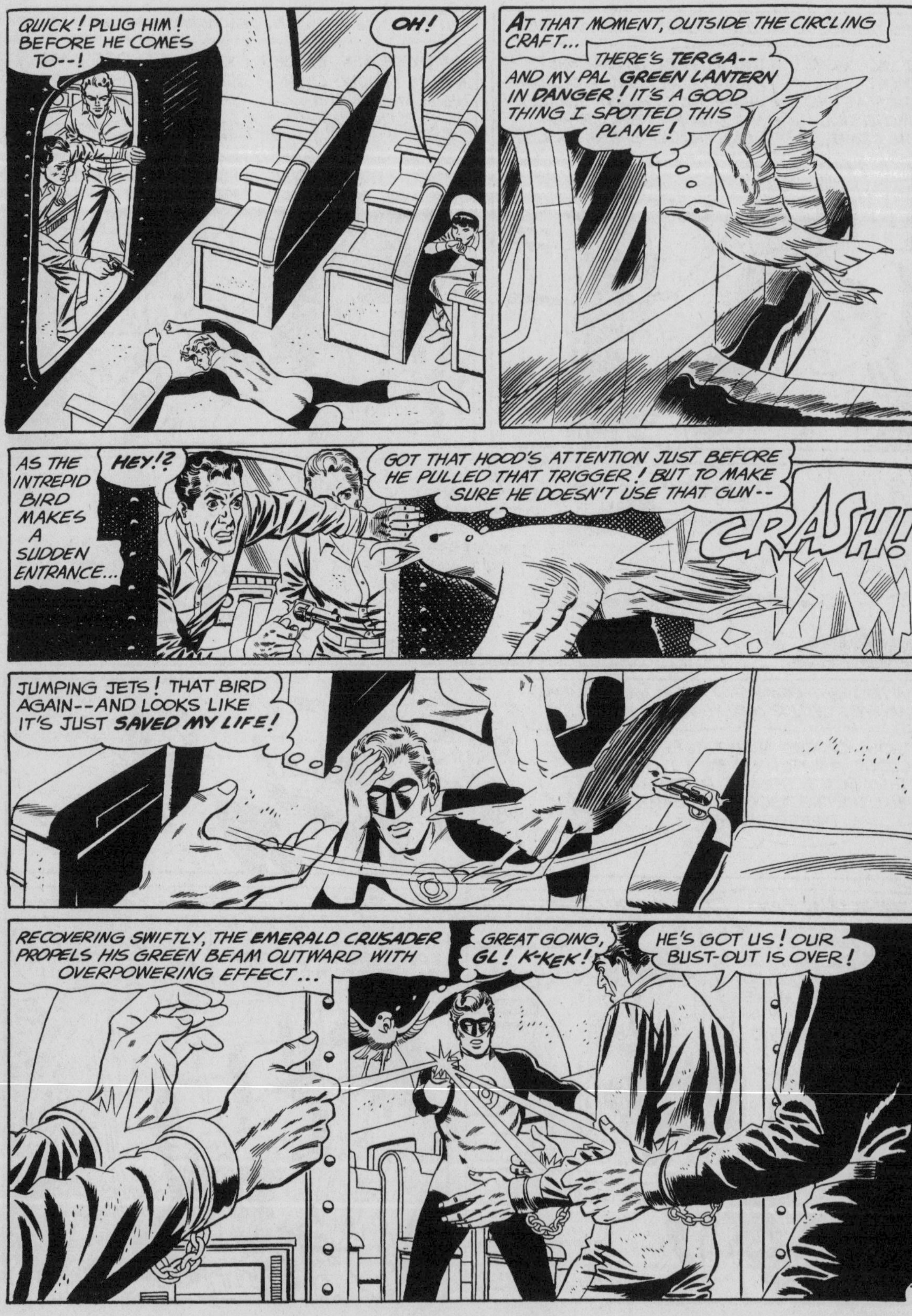
QUICK! PLUG HIM! BEFORE HE COMES TO--!
OH!
AT THAT MOMENT, OUTSIDE THE CIRCLING CRAFT...
THERE'S TERGA-- AND MY PAL GREEN LANTERN IN DANGER! IT'S A GOOD THING I SPOTTED THIS PLANE!
AS THE INTREPID BIRD MAKES A SUDDEN ENTRANCE...
HEY!?
GOT THAT HOOD'S ATTENTION JUST BEFORE HE PULLED THAT TRIGGER! BUT TO MAKE SURE HE DOESN'T USE THAT GUN--
CRASH!
JUMPING JETS! THAT BIRD AGAIN--AND LOOKS LIKE IT'S JUST SAVED MY LIFE!
RECOVERING SWIFTLY, THE EMERALD CRUSADER PROPELS HIS GREEN BEAM OUTWARD WITH OVERPOWERING EFFECT...
GREAT GOING, GL! K-KEK!
HE'S GOT US! OUR BUST-OUT IS OVER!
7

LATER, WITH THE CONVICTS BACK IN STATE PRISON WHERE THEY BELONG...

AT LEAST I GOT *TERGA* OFF THE PLANE! SHE SEEMS INCLINED TO TRUST ME! BUT I'D BETTER GET HOLD OF CAROL TO CHAPERONE HER, UNTIL WE CAN LOCATE *PIEFACE*! I STILL-- EH?

OOH! BIRD-- GO AWAY...

THAT BIRD! IT'S NOT AFTER ME NOW--IT'S GOING FOR *TERGA*!!

IT'S ALMOST AS IF IT'S HAPPY TO SEE *TERGA*! AS IF IT'S TRYING TO *KISS HER*--EH? JUMPIN' JETS! IS IT POSSIBLE--!?

SUDDENLY, IN BACK OF *GREEN LANTERN'S* MIND A MEMORY STIRS...

MY DREAM LAST NIGHT...USING MY *POWER RING*...TO TURN *PIEFACE* INTO A BIRD!! IS IT POSSIBLE THAT ACTUALLY I--;GULP!; GOT TO FIND OUT!

THEN, AFTER BEAMING A CAGE AROUND THE BIRD...

er--EXCUSE ME A MOMENT, *TERGA*! I'VE-- er--GOT A LITTLE BUSINESS TO TAKE CARE OF! YOU STAY RIGHT THERE... *STAY...THERE...* UNDER- STAND?

Y-YES...

BEHIND THE HANGAR A STARTLING TRANS- FORMATION TAKES PLACE...

PIEFACE! ;Whew; I MUST MAKE SURE I COMMAND MY *POWER RING* NEVER TO LET SUCH A "*NIGHTMARE*" HAPPEN AGAIN!

HI, *GL*! IT'S GOOD TO SEE YOU AGAIN-- FACE TO FACE!

8

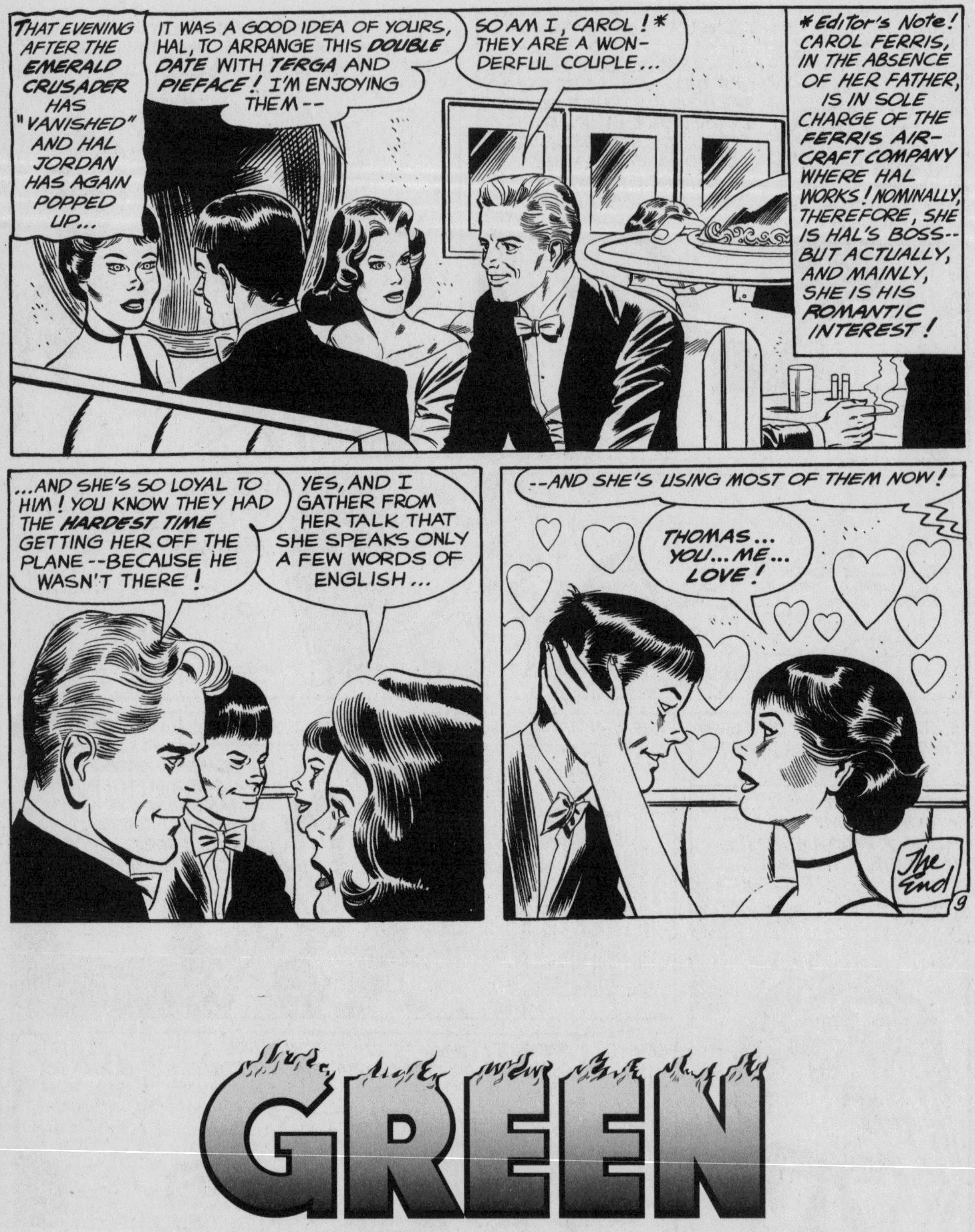
THAT EVENING AFTER THE EMERALD CRUSADER HAS "VANISHED" AND HAL JORDAN HAS AGAIN POPPED UP...
IT WAS A GOOD IDEA OF YOURS, HAL, TO ARRANGE THIS DOUBLE DATE WITH TERGA AND PIEFACE! I'M ENJOYING THEM--
SO AM I, CAROL!* THEY ARE A WONDERFUL COUPLE...
*Editor's Note! CAROL FERRIS, IN THE ABSENCE OF HER FATHER, IS IN SOLE CHARGE OF THE FERRIS AIRCRAFT COMPANY WHERE HAL WORKS! NOMINALLY, THEREFORE, SHE IS HAL'S BOSS--BUT ACTUALLY, AND MAINLY, SHE IS HIS ROMANTIC INTEREST!
...AND SHE'S SO LOYAL TO HIM! YOU KNOW THEY HAD THE HARDEST TIME GETTING HER OFF THE PLANE--BECAUSE HE WASN'T THERE!
YES, AND I GATHER FROM HER TALK THAT SHE SPEAKS ONLY A FEW WORDS OF ENGLISH...
--AND SHE'S USING MOST OF THEM NOW!
THOMAS... YOU... ME... LOVE!
The End
9

GREEN LANTERN

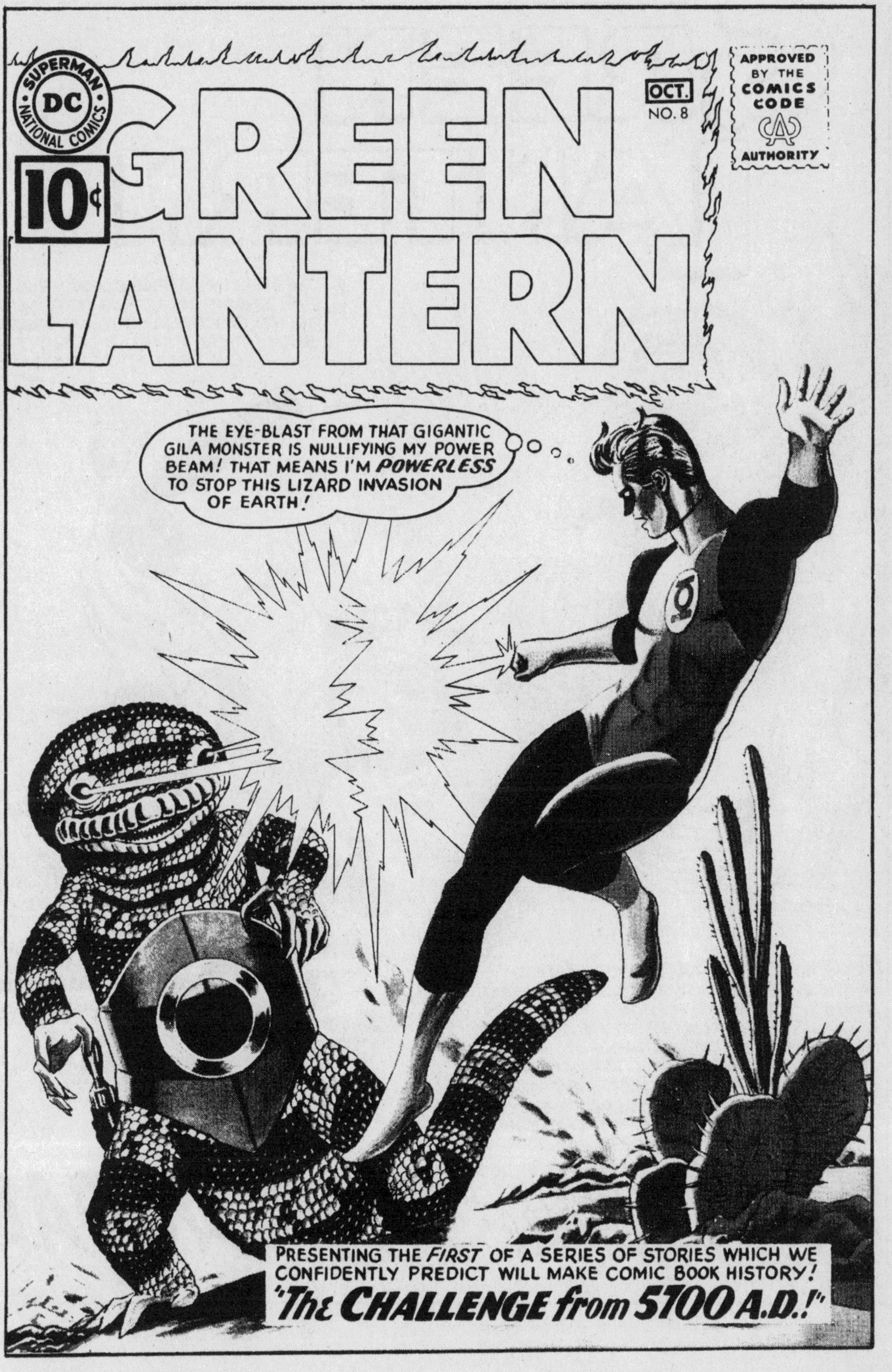
SUPERMAN DC NATIONAL COMICS
10¢
GREEN LANTERN
OCT. NO. 8
APPROVED BY THE COMICS CODE AUTHORITY
THE EYE-BLAST FROM THAT GIGANTIC GILA MONSTER IS NULLIFYING MY POWER BEAM! THAT MEANS I'M POWERLESS TO STOP THIS LIZARD INVASION OF EARTH!
PRESENTING THE FIRST OF A SERIES OF STORIES WHICH WE CONFIDENTLY PREDICT WILL MAKE COMIC BOOK HISTORY!
"The CHALLENGE from 5700 A.D.!"

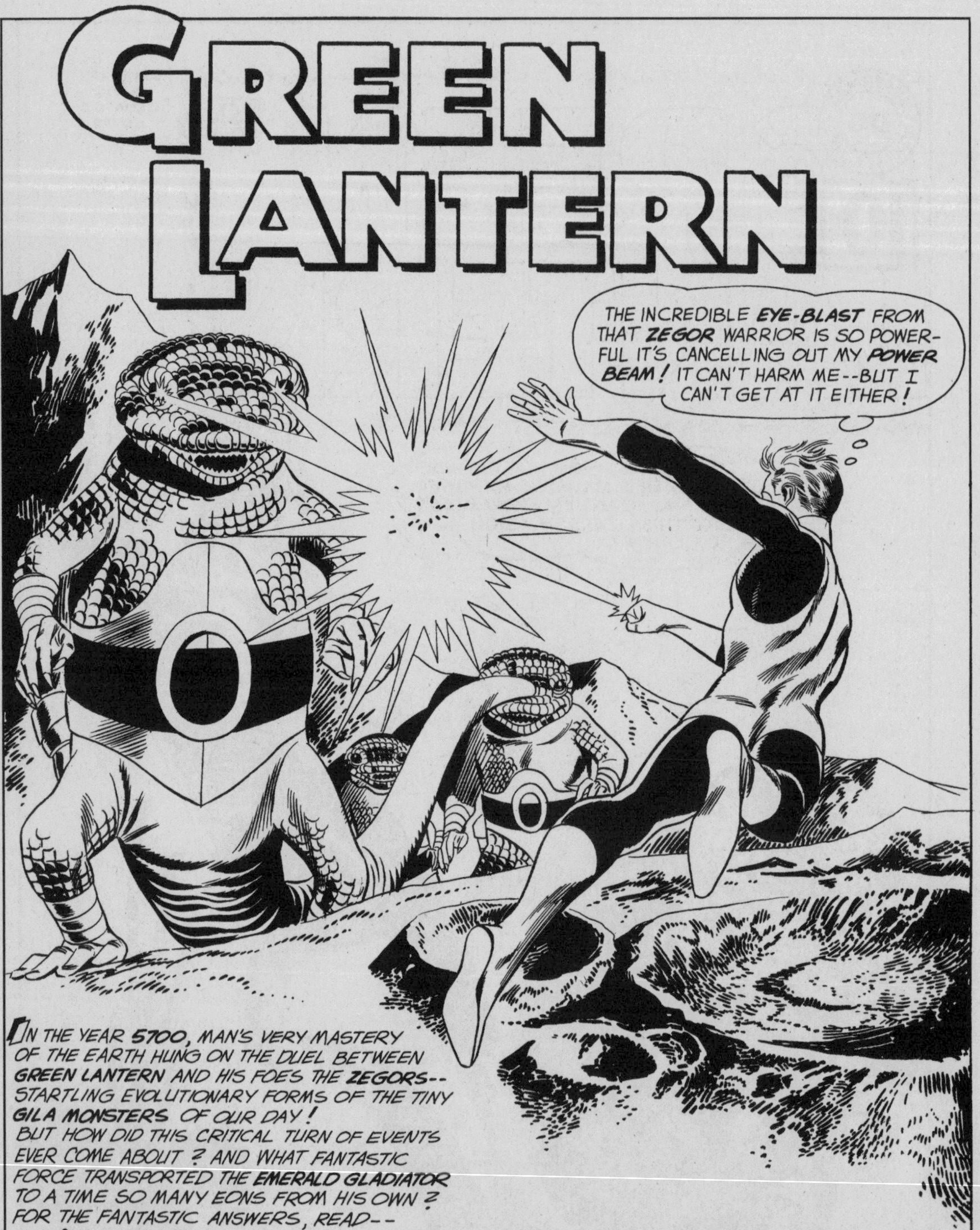
GREEN LANTERN
THE INCREDIBLE EYE-BLAST FROM THAT ZEGOR WARRIOR IS SO POWERFUL IT'S CANCELLING OUT MY POWER BEAM! IT CAN'T HARM ME--BUT I CAN'T GET AT IT EITHER!
IN THE YEAR 5700, MAN'S VERY MASTERY OF THE EARTH HUNG ON THE DUEL BETWEEN GREEN LANTERN AND HIS FOES THE ZEGORS--STARTLING EVOLUTIONARY FORMS OF THE TINY GILA MONSTERS OF OUR DAY! BUT HOW DID THIS CRITICAL TURN OF EVENTS EVER COME ABOUT? AND WHAT FANTASTIC FORCE TRANSPORTED THE EMERALD GLADIATOR TO A TIME SO MANY EONS FROM HIS OWN? FOR THE FANTASTIC ANSWERS, READ--
The CHALLENGE FROM 5700 A.D.!

IN THE YEAR **5700** IN **STAR CITY**, EARTH, AN IMPRESSIVE PLASTI—STEEL STRUCTURE HOUSES THE EXECUTIVE OFFICES OF THE SOLAR SYSTEM GOVERNMENT...

IN THIS MIGHTY EDIFICE, ONE SPACIOUS CHAMBER IS SET ASIDE FOR THE USE OF THE ALL POWERFUL **SOLAR DIRECTOR** HIMSELF...HIGH ABOVE THE VAULTING AERIAL-WAYS OF THE CITY...

AND AT THE IMPOSING DESK IN THIS ROOM SITS THE MAN WHO WIELDS MORE AUTHORITY OVER THE PEOPLE OF EARTH THAN ANY INDIVIDUAL WHO EVER LIVED...

...NONE OTHER, DEAR READER, THAN YOUR FRIEND AND MINE, **GREEN LANTERN** OF OUR OWN DAY AND AGE!

NOW THAT I HAVE BEEN MADE **SOLAR DIRECTOR**, I MUST SELECT FOR MY AIDES THE **BEST** TALENTS AVAILABLE--IN ORDER TO DEFEAT THE TERRIBLE THREAT THAT CONFRONTS THE EARTH!

BUT WAIT--WE CAN HEAR YOU GASP, READER--THIS IS THE YEAR **5700!** HOW CAN **GREEN LANTERN** BE IN **STAR CITY?** HOW CAN **HE** OF ALL PEOPLE BE THE GREAT **SOLAR DIRECTOR?** HOW COULD THIS POSSIBLY HAVE COME ABOUT? WELL, IN ORDER TO EXPLAIN, IT MIGHT BE A GOOD IDEA, WITH YOUR PERMISSION, READER...

...TO TURN THE CALENDAR BACK TO A MEETING OF THE HIGH COUNCIL OF SOLAR DELEGATES, SITTING IN **SOLAR HALL**, STAR CITY, IN A SESSION OF THE GRAVEST EMERGENCY...

FELLOW SOLARITES* WE ARE MET IN THIS CRISIS TO CONSIDER A NEW CANDIDATE FOR THE CRUCIAL POST OF **SOLAR DIRECTOR!** MANY CANDIDATES HAVE BEEN CONSIDERED--

YES! BUT NONE OF THEM WAS **EQUAL** TO THE **JOB!**

*Editor's Note: BY 5700 A.D., CENTURIES OF LIVING ON THE OTHER SOLAR SYSTEM PLANETS THEY HAVE COLONIZED HAS ALTERED EARTHMEN AND CHANGED THEM ACCORDING TO THE CLIMATIC CONDITIONS OF THEIR NEW HOMES.

2

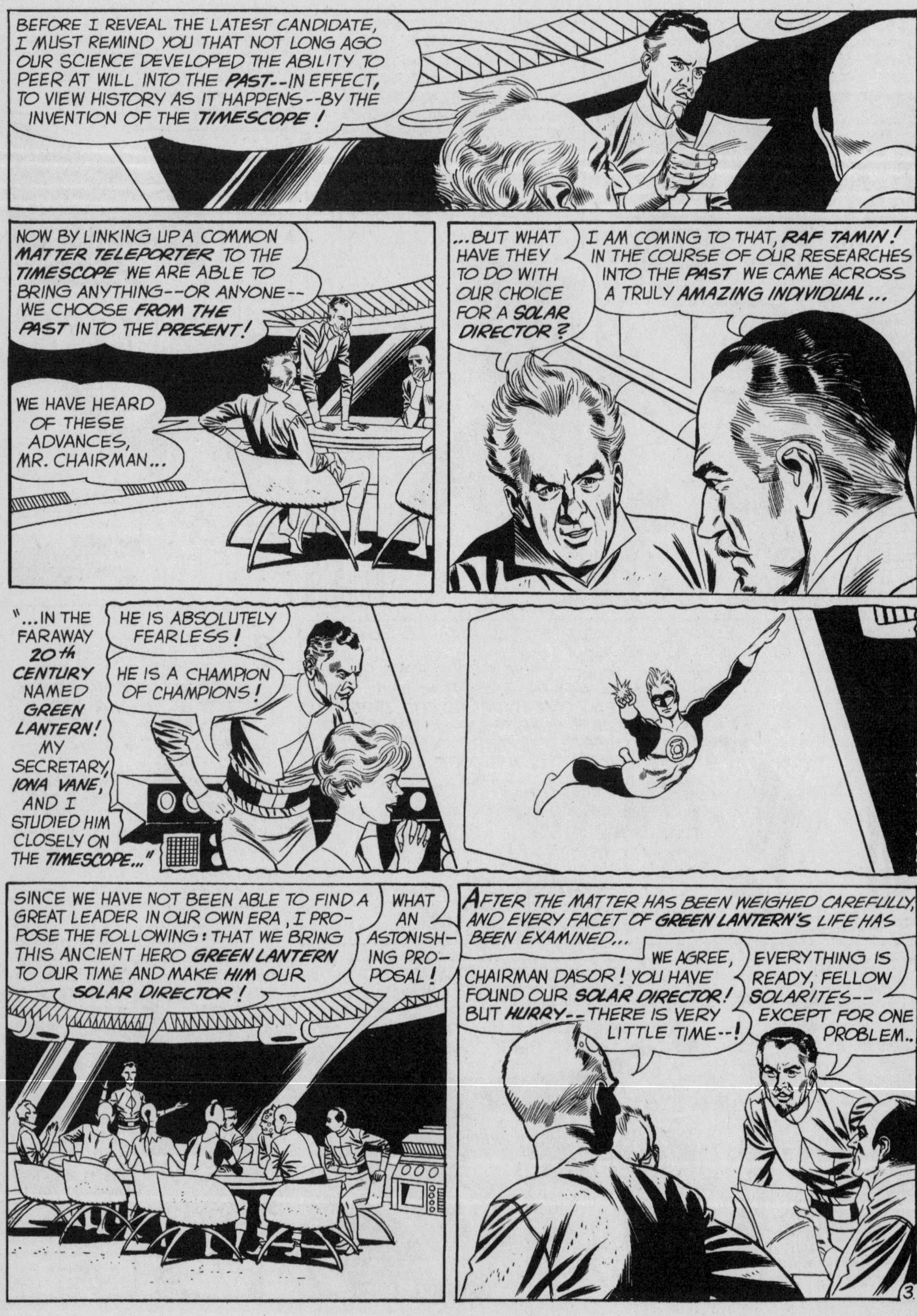
BEFORE I REVEAL THE LATEST CANDIDATE, I MUST REMIND YOU THAT NOT LONG AGO OUR SCIENCE DEVELOPED THE ABILITY TO PEER AT WILL INTO THE PAST--IN EFFECT, TO VIEW HISTORY AS IT HAPPENS--BY THE INVENTION OF THE TIMESCOPE!
NOW BY LINKING UP A COMMON MATTER TELEPORTER TO THE TIMESCOPE WE ARE ABLE TO BRING ANYTHING--OR ANYONE--WE CHOOSE FROM THE PAST INTO THE PRESENT!
WE HAVE HEARD OF THESE ADVANCES, MR. CHAIRMAN...
...BUT WHAT HAVE THEY TO DO WITH OUR CHOICE FOR A SOLAR DIRECTOR?
I AM COMING TO THAT, RAF TAMIN! IN THE COURSE OF OUR RESEARCHES INTO THE PAST WE CAME ACROSS A TRULY AMAZING INDIVIDUAL...
"...IN THE FARAWAY 20th CENTURY NAMED GREEN LANTERN! MY SECRETARY, IONA VANE, AND I STUDIED HIM CLOSELY ON THE TIMESCOPE..."
HE IS ABSOLUTELY FEARLESS!
HE IS A CHAMPION OF CHAMPIONS!
SINCE WE HAVE NOT BEEN ABLE TO FIND A GREAT LEADER IN OUR OWN ERA, I PROPOSE THE FOLLOWING: THAT WE BRING THIS ANCIENT HERO GREEN LANTERN TO OUR TIME AND MAKE HIM OUR SOLAR DIRECTOR!
WHAT AN ASTONISHING PROPOSAL!
AFTER THE MATTER HAS BEEN WEIGHED CAREFULLY, AND EVERY FACET OF GREEN LANTERN'S LIFE HAS BEEN EXAMINED...
WE AGREE, CHAIRMAN DASOR! YOU HAVE FOUND OUR SOLAR DIRECTOR! BUT HURRY--THERE IS VERY LITTLE TIME--!
EVERYTHING IS READY, FELLOW SOLARITES--EXCEPT FOR ONE PROBLEM..
3

TO TRAVEL IN TIME CAUSES AN INDIVIDUAL'S MEMORY TO BE *COMPLETELY WIPED OUT!* IF *GREEN LANTERN* CAME HERE WITHOUT HIS *"LIFE-HISTORY"* HE WOULD BE DAZED-- OF LITTLE USE, TO US!

BUT *HOW* CAN SUCH AN OBSTACLE BE OVERCOME?

SIMPLY! MISS VANE HERE HAS PREPARED A FICTITIOUS PERSONAL HISTORY FOR *GREEN LANTERN!* HE WILL *BELIEVE* HE IS A MAN OF OUR TIME WHILE HE IS HERE! IN THAT WAY HE WILL BE ABLE TO FUNCTION PERFECTLY!

AS *CHAIRMAN DASOR* GOES OVER THE DATA *PREPARED BY HIS ATTRACTIVE SECRETARY...*

THIS IS VERY CONVINCING, MISS VANE! *GREEN LANTERN* WILL BELIEVE THAT HE IS A FAMOUS SPACE-EXPLORER IN OUR ERA WHO HAS SPENT YEARS AMONG THE *ASTEROIDS--* AND WHO HAS JUST BEEN SUMMONED BACK TO EARTH TO DEAL WITH THE DREADFUL MENACE THAT PERILS US! BUT WAIT--!

THERE IS ONE THING YOU HAVE OMITTED, MISS VANE! A YOUNG MAN LIKE *GREEN LANTERN* WOULD CERTAINLY HAVE A *ROMANTIC INTEREST!* WITHOUT THAT, HIS MIND MIGHT BE DISSATISFIED-- MIGHT FEEL THAT SOME-THING IS WRONG!

Y-YOU'RE RIGHT, CHAIRMAN DASOR!

OBVIOUSLY! AND SINCE I HAPPEN TO KNOW THAT *YOU* ARE UNMARRIED AND UNATTACHED, *IONA,* IT OCCURS TO ME THAT *YOU* CAN BE HIS ROMANTIC INTEREST!

M-ME!?

AFTER THE MATTER HAS BEEN SWIFTLY SETTLED...

THEN ALL IS ARRANGED! COME WITH ME, GENTLE-MEN--!

I--HARDLY KNOW THIS *GREEN LANTERN!* BUT--I CAN'T LET MY PERSONAL FEELINGS STAND IN THE WAY OF THE *SAFETY OF HUMAN CIVILIZATION!*

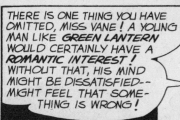

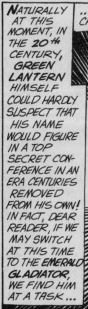

NATURALLY AT THIS MOMENT, IN THE *20th CENTURY,* GREEN LANTERN HIMSELF COULD HARDLY SUSPECT THAT HIS NAME WOULD FIGURE IN A TOP SECRET CONFERENCE IN AN ERA CENTURIES REMOVED FROM HIS OWN! IN FACT, DEAR READER, IF WE MAY SWITCH AT THIS TIME TO THE EMERALD GLADIATOR, WE FIND HIM AT A TASK...

...WHICH OCCUPIES HIM SEVERAL TIMES A WEEK... CHARGING HIS MIGHTY *POWER RING...*

IN BRIGHTEST DAY, IN BLACKEST NIGHT, NO EVIL SHALL ESCAPE MY SIGHT! LET THOSE WHO WORSHIP EVIL'S MIGHT BEWARE MY POWER--GREEN LANTERN'S LIGHT!

AND AS THE GREEN-CLAD FIGURE BURSTS FROM THE REAR OF THE HANGAR WHERE IN HIS SECRET IDENTITY HE IS *HAL JORDAN,* ACE TEST PILOT...

I'VE GOT TO GET TO THE OCEANFRONT AS SOON AS POSSIBLE! ACCORDING TO THE LATEST BROADCASTS AN INCREDIBLE SEA MONSTER HAS BEEN SIGHTED THERE AND IS THREATENING LIVES AND PROPERTY! NO ONE KNOWS WHERE IT COULD HAVE COME FROM!

...AND THE ONLY CLUE IS THAT WHILE THE *NAVY* WAS SEARCHING FOR A *LOST SPACE-CAPSULE...* THE MONSTER SUDDENLY APPEARED IN THE *SAME AREA!* BUT WHAT COULD BE THE CONNECTION BETWEEN THOSE TWO EVENTS IS *ANYBODY'S GUESS!*

SHORTLY...

THERE IT IS! AND GREAT SCOTT--!

IT'S CAPSIZING THAT SHIP! I'VE GOT TO STOP IT!

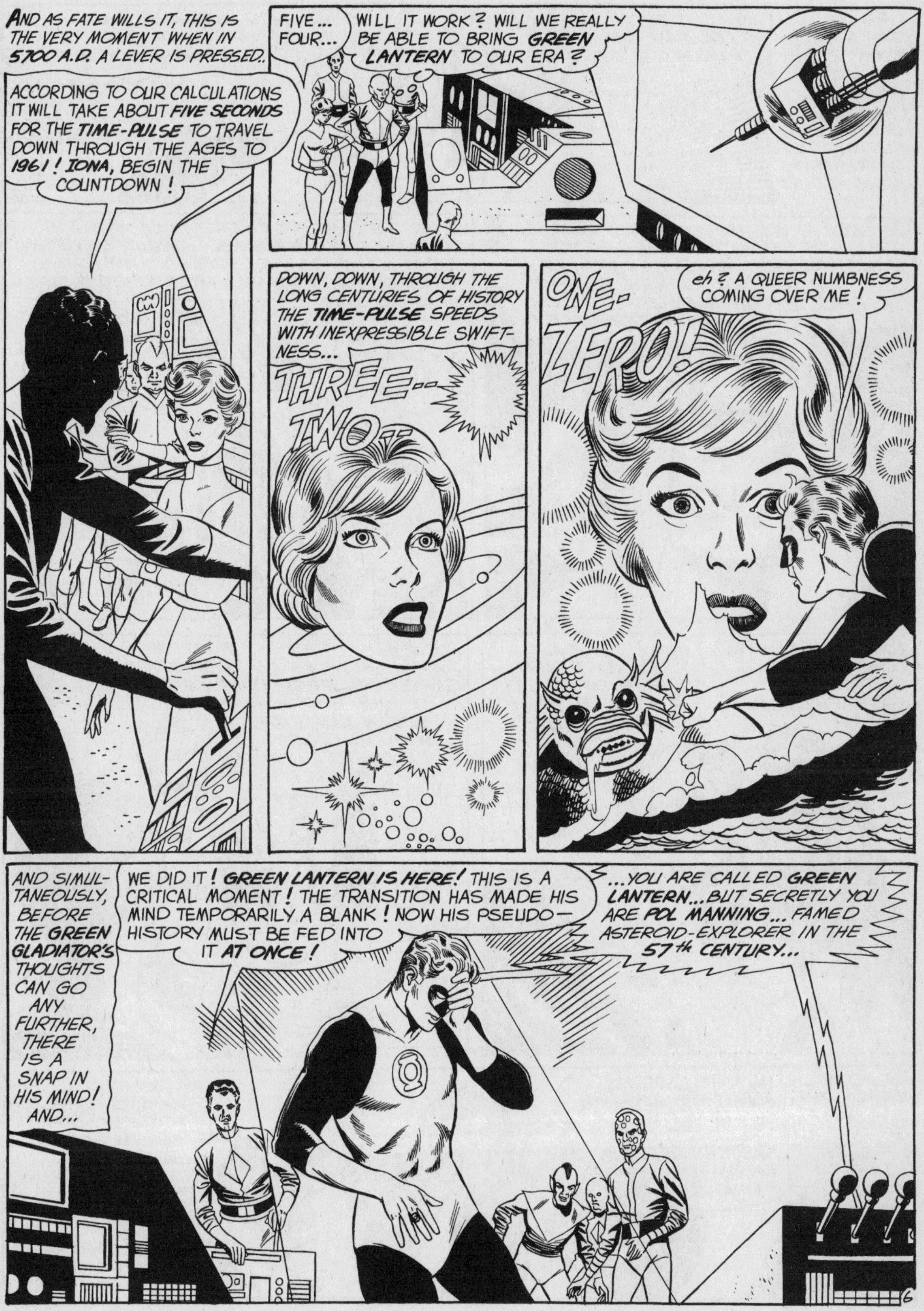
AND AS FATE WILLS IT, THIS IS THE VERY MOMENT WHEN IN 5700 A.D. A LEVER IS PRESSED.
ACCORDING TO OUR CALCULATIONS IT WILL TAKE ABOUT FIVE SECONDS FOR THE TIME-PULSE TO TRAVEL DOWN THROUGH THE AGES TO 1961! IONA, BEGIN THE COUNTDOWN!
FIVE... FOUR...
WILL IT WORK? WILL WE REALLY BE ABLE TO BRING GREEN LANTERN TO OUR ERA?
DOWN, DOWN, THROUGH THE LONG CENTURIES OF HISTORY THE TIME-PULSE SPEEDS WITH INEXPRESSIBLE SWIFTNESS...
THREEE...
TWO...
ONE-
ZERO!
eh? A QUEER NUMBNESS COMING OVER ME!
AND SIMULTANEOUSLY, BEFORE THE GREEN GLADIATOR'S THOUGHTS CAN GO ANY FURTHER, THERE IS A SNAP IN HIS MIND! AND...
WE DID IT! GREEN LANTERN IS HERE! THIS IS A CRITICAL MOMENT! THE TRANSITION HAS MADE HIS MIND TEMPORARILY A BLANK! NOW HIS PSEUDO-HISTORY MUST BE FED INTO IT AT ONCE!
...YOU ARE CALLED GREEN LANTERN... BUT SECRETLY YOU ARE POL MANNING... FAMED ASTEROID-EXPLORER IN THE 57th CENTURY...
6

As THE TEMPORARILY BLANK MIND OF THE **EMERALD CRUSADER** GREEDILY SUCKS IN THE INFORMATION BEING FED TO IT...

MY ALTER EGO IS **POL MANNING,** EXPLORER...

NOT EVEN **IONA VANE**, THE GIRL IN YOUR LIFE, KNOWS YOUR SECRET IDENTITY, **GREEN LANTERN!**

AS SOON AS YOU HEARD OF OUR MORTAL STRUGGLE AGAINST THE **ZEGORS** YOU IMMEDIATELY RETURNED TO EARTH TO AID US IN OUR BATTLE! YOU HAVE ALREADY LEARNED THAT WE ELECTED YOU OUR **SOLAR DIRECTOR!**

AFTER THE LAST BIT OF DATA INVOLVING THE CAREER OF **POL MANNING—GREEN LANTERN,** TOGETHER WITH THE NECESSARY MEMORY PICTURES, HAS ENTERED THE TIME-VOYAGER'S BRAIN...

HE IS RETURNING TO NORMAL NOW! HE WILL SPEAK...!

GREETINGS...GREETINGS TO THE HIGH SOLAR COUNCIL! AND **IONA**--

IONA, IT'S BEEN TWO LONG MONTHS--SINCE WE LAST SAW EACH OTHER!

MMM! THIS PLAY—ACTING ISN'T GOING TO BE AS DIFFICULT FOR ME AS I THOUGHT! HE **IS** ATTRACTIVE!

BUT I MUSTN'T FORGET THAT I'M JUST A PAWN IN A MUCH BIGGER GAME THAN MERE ROMANCE!

OH--YES!

GREEN LANTERN, YOU--YOU MUST LISTEN TO CHAIRMAN **DASOR!**

RELUCTANTLY, GRIMLY, THE STALWART GREEN-CLAD FIGURE TURNS...

NOW--TELL ME ALL ABOUT THE **ZEGORS,** CHAIRMAN DASOR! I RECEIVED ONLY SKETCHY REPORTS ON MY--er--TRAVELS!

HIS MIND IS WORKING PERFECTLY! HE'S EVEN CON-CEALING HIS SECRET IDENTITY FROM US!

VERY WELL, **GREEN LANTERN...**

7

BUT WHILE THE NEW SOLAR DIRECTOR IN 5700 A.D. IS BRIEFED ON THE DREADFUL DANGER TO EARTH WHICH HE HAS COME HOME TO FIGHT AGAINST, LET US PAUSE FOR A MOMENT, READER, TO REVIEW THIS STARTLING SITUATION!

WE KNOW, READER, THAT THE MAN NOW SITTING IN THE CHAMBER OF THE HIGH COUNCIL IN STAR CITY IS REALLY UNDER HIS MASK HAL JORDAN OF THE 20th CENTURY! BUT SO WELL HAS THE BRAIN—DATA MACHINE OF THIS ERA WORKED THAT HE BELIEVES HE IS SOMEONE ELSE ENTIRELY—— AND HAS NO DOUBTS ABOUT IT!

...THEN THE ZEGORS HAVE RISEN FROM THE INTERIOR OF THE EARTH, TO THREATEN MANKIND'S MASTERY OF OUR PLANET?

EXACTLY, GREEN LANTERN! AND IT IS A CHALLENGE WE COULD NEVER HAVE FORESEEN...

"WE KNEW THAT THE GILA MONSTERS* HAD VANISHED ABOUT THE YEAR 2000, AND WE ASSUMED THEY HAD BECOME EXTINCT.."

*Editor's Note: LIZARDS ABOUT 18 INCHES LONG, COVERED WITH BEAD-LIKE SKIN, FOUND ONLY IN THE SOUTHWEST DESERT OF THE U.S.

"WHAT WE DID NOT KNOW WAS THAT THE CREATURES HAD MERELY RETREATED DEEP UNDERGROUND WHERE THEIR NATURAL RESISTANCE TO HEAT..."

"!ENABLED THEM TO FLOURISH AND EVOLVE INTO A NEW AND FORMIDABLE CIVILIZATION OVER THE CENTURIES..."

"OUR FIRST SIGN OF THE THREAT CAME WHEN AN ARCHEOLOGIST, DR. VANCE BARNARD, AND HIS PARTY WERE WORKING IN THE ARIZONA DESERT SOME MONTHS AGO..."

LOOK!   IN THE NAME OF THE NINE PLANETS--!

S-SOMETHING COMING OUT OF ITS EYES-- EEEAHH...

8

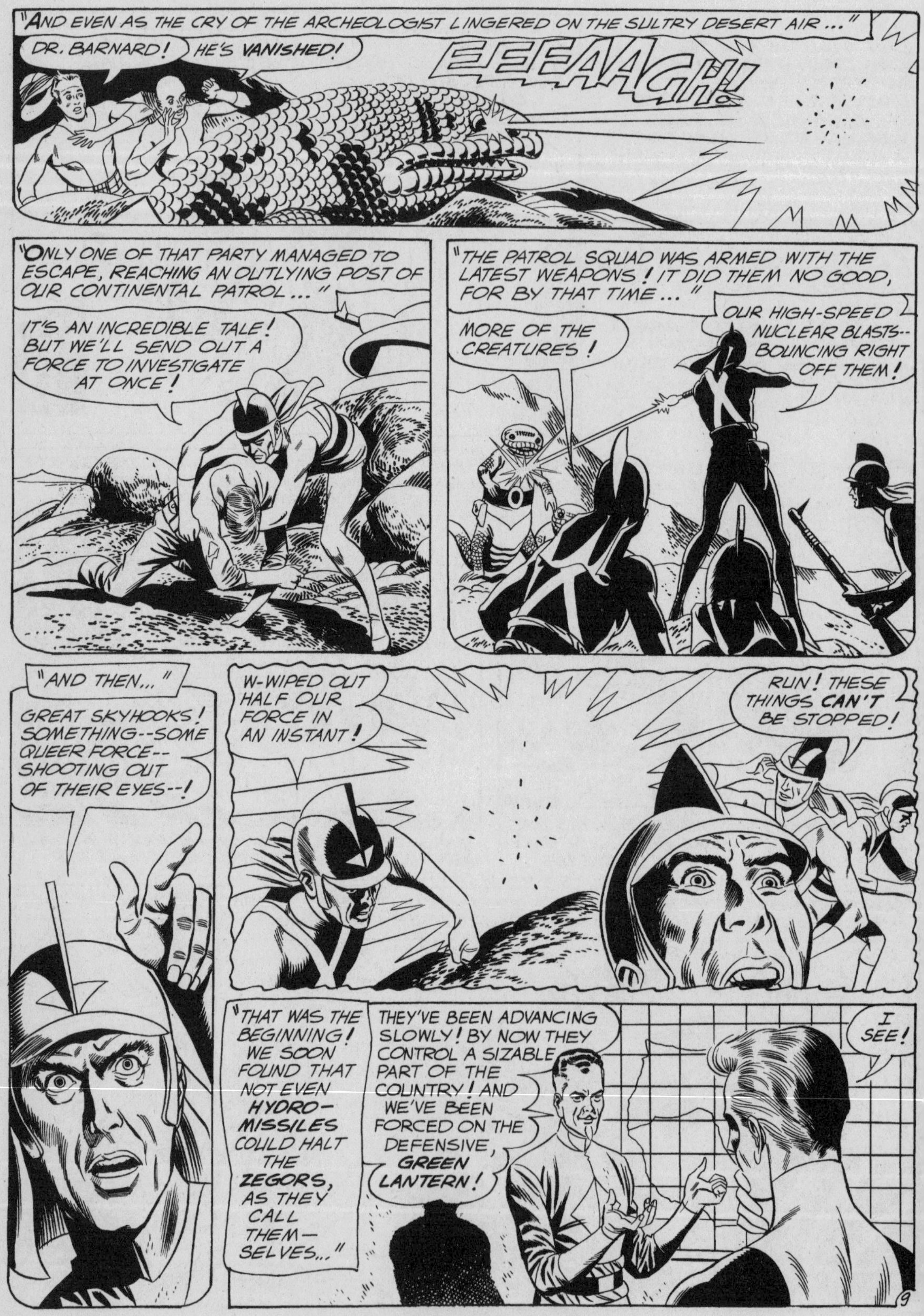
"AND EVEN AS THE CRY OF THE ARCHEOLOGIST LINGERED ON THE SULTRY DESERT AIR..."
DR. BARNARD!
HE'S VANISHED!
EEEAAAGH!
"ONLY ONE OF THAT PARTY MANAGED TO ESCAPE, REACHING AN OUTLYING POST OF OUR CONTINENTAL PATROL..."
IT'S AN INCREDIBLE TALE! BUT WE'LL SEND OUT A FORCE TO INVESTIGATE AT ONCE!
"THE PATROL SQUAD WAS ARMED WITH THE LATEST WEAPONS! IT DID THEM NO GOOD, FOR BY THAT TIME..."
MORE OF THE CREATURES!
OUR HIGH-SPEED NUCLEAR BLASTS--BOUNCING RIGHT OFF THEM!
"AND THEN..."
GREAT SKYHOOKS! SOMETHING--SOME QUEER FORCE--SHOOTING OUT OF THEIR EYES--!
W-WIPED OUT HALF OUR FORCE IN AN INSTANT!
RUN! THESE THINGS CAN'T BE STOPPED!
"THAT WAS THE BEGINNING! WE SOON FOUND THAT NOT EVEN HYDRO-MISSILES COULD HALT THE ZEGORS, AS THEY CALL THEM-SELVES..."
THEY'VE BEEN ADVANCING SLOWLY! BY NOW THEY CONTROL A SIZABLE PART OF THE COUNTRY! AND WE'VE BEEN FORCED ON THE DEFENSIVE, GREEN LANTERN!
I SEE!
9

SO THERE YOU HAVE IT! NOW, READER, YOU UNDERSTAND HOW *GREEN LANTERN* OF OUR TIME CAME TO BE THE *SOLAR DIRECTOR* OF EARTH IN 5700 A.D.! IN HIS VERY FIRST HOURS ON THE JOB, THE NEW CHIEF...

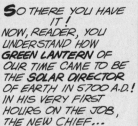

...REVEALS THE EXECUTIVE GENIUS WHICH IN PART HAS WON HIM THE HIGH POST!

CHAIRMAN DASOR, I WANT A FULL REPORT OF THE EXACT MILITARY SITUATION AS SOON AS POSSIBLE!

HERE'S A LIST OF POSSIBILITIES FOR YOUR CABINET, *GREEN LANTERN!*

BUT DESK WORK ALONE DOES NOT SUIT THE TEMPERAMENT OF THE NEW *DIRECTOR*...

IONA, I'VE DECIDED TO USE MY *POWER RING* TO GET A FIRSTHAND LOOK AT THE *ZEGOR* ADVANCES!

PLEASE-- BE CARE- FUL, *GREEN LANTERN!*

I WILL! SEE YOU SOON.

FORTUNATELY THE BRAIN- DATA IMPLANT ALLOWED HIM TO RETAIN ALL THE INFORMATION ABOUT HIS ORIGINAL ABILITY AS *GREEN LANTERN*-- AND THE USE OF HIS AMAZING *POWER BEAM!*

AND SOON, NOT FAR FROM THE EARTH NERVE-CENTER OF *STAR CITY*...

ZEGORS! NOTIFY! HEAD- QUARTERS!

THE ENEMY-- ADVANCING TOWARD THIS MILITARY OUTPOST!

AS THE STREAKING FIGURE WHIPS DOWN TOWARD THE SCENE...

THERE'S THAT *EYE-BLAST* DASOR DESCRIBED TO ME--GOING AT THAT BRAVE SOLDIER! AND-- *GREAT THUNDER!!*

10

THE SOLDIER JUST SEEMED TO EVAPORATE, AS IF BLOWN AWAY BY THE WIND! AND NOW THE CREATURE IS TURNING TOWARD ME--!

OUT OF THE RING OF THE *EMERALD WARRIOR* A BEAM OF OVERPOWERING ENERGY SPURTS..

BUT THE NEXT MOMENT...

GOOD GOSH! THE TWO FORCES-- THE EYE-BLAST OF THAT *ZEGOR* AND MY POWER BEAM--ARE CANCELLING EACH OTHER OUT! HE CAN'T GET THROUGH TO ME--BUT NEITHER CAN I GET THROUGH TO HIM!

AS THE CREATURE SLINKS OFF...

GETTING AWAY! I COULD GO AFTER IT--BUT I CAN'T FIGHT ALL OF THESE *ZEGORS* ONE BY ONE! ACCORDING TO THE REPORTS THERE ARE HUNDREDS--THOUSANDS OF THEM!

ON THE WAY BACK TO *STAR CITY,* A GRIMLY SERIOUS *GREEN LANTERN* TAKES THOUGHT...

THERE MUST BE SOME WAY TO DEFEAT THIS *LIZARD INVASION* THREATENING MAN'S MASTERY OF THE PLANET! UNLESS THEY'RE STOPPED... HUMANS WILL BECOME FUGITIVES--FORCED TO HIDE OUT LIKE ANIMALS! HMMM! THAT *EYE-BLAST* SEEMS TO BE THEIR *MAIN* WEAPON...

BACK IN HIS OFFICE, THE **SOLAR DIRECTOR** DECIDES ON A CERTAIN ANGLE OF INVESTIGATION...

YES, **IONA**! MY GREEN BEAM--WHEN I **WILL** IT--CAN ACT JUST LIKE A MOTION PICTURE CAMERA! I'M GOING TO USE IT NOW TO RUN OFF A SCENE I JUST SAW-- IN **SLOW MOTION**!

AMAZING! CAN YOU DO THAT TOO?

AS THE ASTOUNDING EMERALD RAY SHOOTS OUT AGAIN...

WATCH! WE **MUST** FIND OUT WHAT REALLY HAPPENS UNDER A **ZEGOR** EYE-BLAST--IN ORDER TO COMBAT IT! MY RING IS NOW RE-CREATING THE SCENE I WITNESSED A WHILE AGO...

THERE... THE **ZEGOR** HAS JUST HIT THE SOLDIER WITH THE MYSTERIOUS ENERGY COMING OUT OF ITS EYES! I'LL MAKE THE ACTION HAPPEN **VERY SLOWLY** SO NOTHING WILL ESCAPE US!

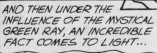

AND THEN UNDER THE INFLUENCE OF THE MYSTICAL GREEN RAY, AN INCREDIBLE FACT COMES TO LIGHT...

LOOK, **GREEN LANTERN**--THE SOLDIER IS GETTING SMALLER--HE'S **SHRINKING**--!!

AS THE GREEN BEAM FOLLOWS THE PROCESS, REVEALING WHAT NO HUMAN EYE COULD DISCERN...

FANTASTIC! THE SOLDIER HAS BECOME SO SMALL THE BLADES OF GRASS AROUND HIM LOOK HUGE!

AND HE'S STILL SHRINKING--!

MY RING CAN'T FOLLOW THE ACTION ANY FURTHER!*

THEN W-WE MAY **NEVER** KNOW WHAT FINALLY HAPPENS TO THE **ZEGORS'** VICTIMS! OH, **GREEN LANTERN**--!

***Editor's Note:** OPERATING ON PRINCIPLES OF LIGHT, GL'S BEAM CANNOT PRO-JECT ANYTHING THAT IS SMALLER THAN LIGHT WAVES THEMSELVES!

12

AT THAT MOMENT, THE COMMUNICATOR ON **GREEN LANTERN'S** DESK COMMANDS HIS ATTENTION...

SOLAR DIRECTOR, THIS IS CHAIRMAN DASOR! A REPORT OF A LONE **ZEGOR** SCOUT... IN STAR CITY...

IN THIS CITY!?

AND ALMOST SIMULTANEOUSLY...

G-GREEN LANTERN! HELP!

IONA! WHAT--?

THE **ZEGOR**-- IT'S BLASTED **IONA**!

WITH INCREDIBLE, OVERMASTERING FURY, THE **GREEN GLADIATOR'S** RING BURSTS OUT...

THAT'S ONE OVERGROWN LIZARD THAT WON'T BE TAKING OVER THE EARTH! BUT **IONA**! I **CAN'T** LET HER **VANISH** LIKE THE OTHERS! GOT TO SAVE HER!

VOOMP!

ON THE IMPULSE OF THE MOMENT, **GL** ACTS QUICKLY.

GOT TO USE MY RING TO SHRINK MYSELF...

...INTO ATOMIC SIZE!

IT'S THE ONLY WAY...

I CAN FOLLOW **IONA**... SAVE HER...

13

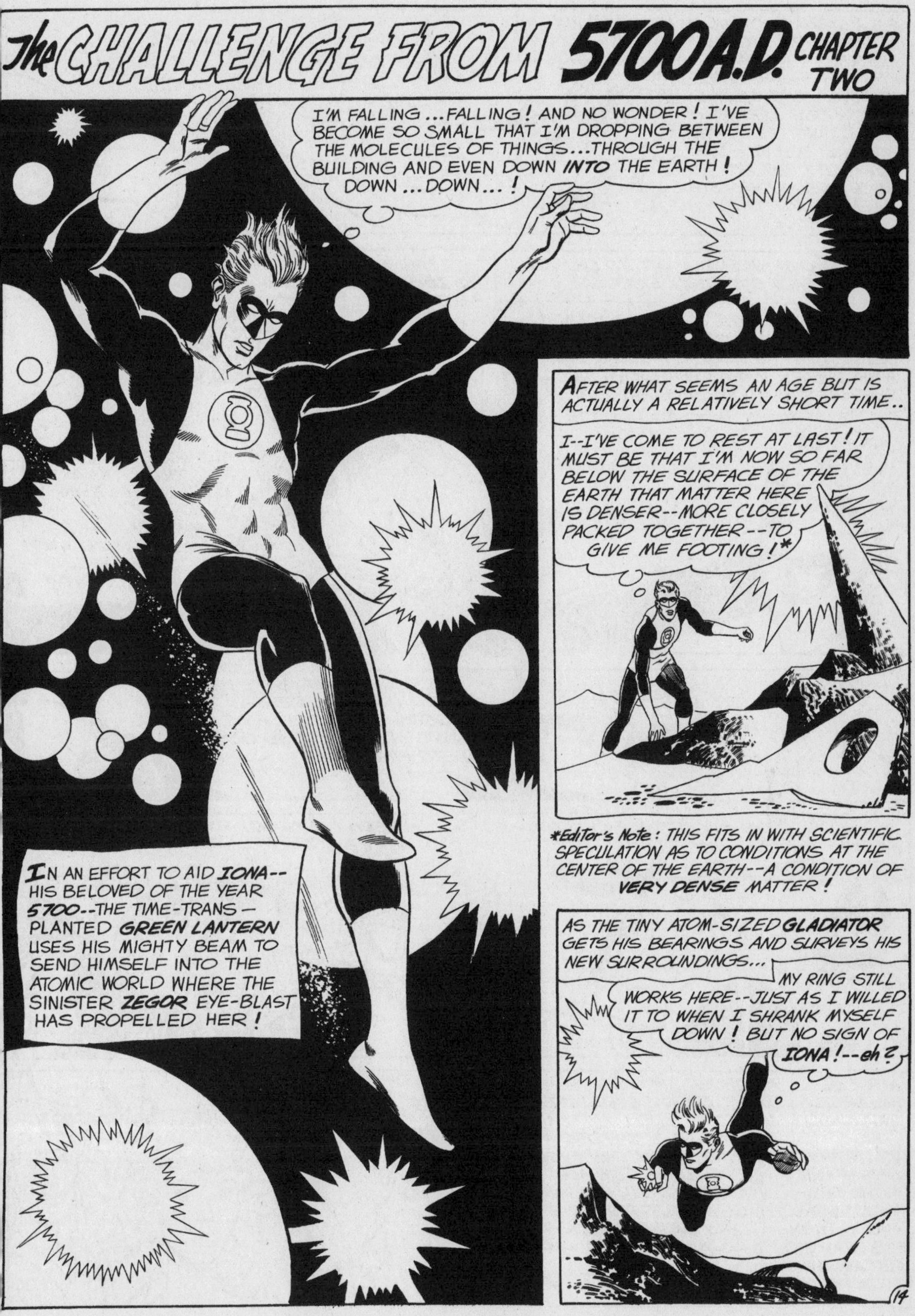
The CHALLENGE FROM 5700 A.D. CHAPTER TWO
I'M FALLING ... FALLING! AND NO WONDER! I'VE BECOME SO SMALL THAT I'M DROPPING BETWEEN THE MOLECULES OF THINGS ... THROUGH THE BUILDING AND EVEN DOWN INTO THE EARTH! DOWN ... DOWN ... !
IN AN EFFORT TO AID IONA-- HIS BELOVED OF THE YEAR 5700--THE TIME-TRANS-PLANTED GREEN LANTERN USES HIS MIGHTY BEAM TO SEND HIMSELF INTO THE ATOMIC WORLD WHERE THE SINISTER ZEGOR EYE-BLAST HAS PROPELLED HER!
AFTER WHAT SEEMS AN AGE BUT IS ACTUALLY A RELATIVELY SHORT TIME..
I--I'VE COME TO REST AT LAST! IT MUST BE THAT I'M NOW SO FAR BELOW THE SURFACE OF THE EARTH THAT MATTER HERE IS DENSER--MORE CLOSELY PACKED TOGETHER--TO GIVE ME FOOTING!*
*Editor's Note: THIS FITS IN WITH SCIENTIFIC SPECULATION AS TO CONDITIONS AT THE CENTER OF THE EARTH--A CONDITION OF VERY DENSE MATTER!
AS THE TINY ATOM-SIZED GLADIATOR GETS HIS BEARINGS AND SURVEYS HIS NEW SURROUNDINGS...
MY RING STILL WORKS HERE--JUST AS I WILLED IT TO WHEN I SHRANK MYSELF DOWN! BUT NO SIGN OF IONA!--eh?
14

As a strange phenomenon becomes apparent to the swift-moving green figure...

THAT'S ODD! MY RING IS REVEALING MYSTERIOUS ENERGY PULSATIONS TRAVELING UPWARD TOWARD THE SURFACE! BUT NO SUCH ENERGY HAS EVER BEEN DETECTED BY SCIENCE...!

In the mind of the keen-witted crusader another fact suddenly links up...

SOMETHING HAS JUST OCCURRED TO ME! WHEN I USED MY RING TO RE-CREATE THAT SCENE WITH THE *ZEGOR* AND THE SOLDIER A WHILE BACK I NOTICED SOMETHING THAT ONLY FAINTLY REGISTERED AT THE TIME...

"...A BARELY *VISIBLE ENERGY* TRAVELING *TOWARD* THE *ZEGOR*... COMING UP FROM SOMEWHERE BELOW...!"

"NATURALLY I COULDN'T HAVE SEEN THIS ENERGY MYSELF! BUT MY *RING* CAUGHT IT, AND IN PROJECTING THE SCENE, DUPLICATED IT!"

IF I'M RIGHT, MAYBE I HAVE FOUND A WAY TO DEFEAT THE *ZEGORS*! BUT BEFORE I DO ANYTHING ELSE I'VE *GOT* TO FIND IONA!

And soon, to the indomitable crusader's intense relief...

IONA!

GREEN LANTERN! YOU TRAPPED HERE--TOO?!

After GL has briefly explained his VOLUNTARY appearance in the sub-atomic world and in turn has learned certain things from the girl...

ALL THOSE WHO WERE STRICKEN BY THE *ZEGOR* EYE-BLASTS ARE DOWN HERE--AND SAFE! THIS MEANS I CAN USE MY RING TO RETURN EVERYONE TO THE SURFACE-- AND TO THEIR ORIGINAL SIZE! BUT THEN THEY'D ONLY BE IN DANGER AGAIN--

15

IONA, LISTEN--YOU MUST TRUST ME! I'VE GOT TO RETURN TO THE SURFACE NOW *ALONE*! BUT EVERYTHING WILL BE ALL RIGHT! JUST TRUST ME--

OF COURSE, **GREEN LANTERN**!

A MOMENT LATER, A STARTLING SIZE-CHANGING SCENE...

IONA HAS BECOME TINY-- SHE'S SHRINKING! OR RATHER IT JUST *SEEMS* THAT WAY BECAUSE I'M USING MY RING TO GROW AGAIN-- AND TO SHOOT MYSELF BACK TO THE SURFACE!

AND IN A MATTER OF SECONDS...

;*Whew!*; IT FEELS GOOD TO BE BACK TO **REGULAR SIZE** AGAIN! AND NOW TO CARRY OUT MY IDEA FOR HALTING THE **ZEGORS**!

AS IF HARNESSED TO A THUNDERBOLT, **GREEN LANTERN** CATAPULTS CROSS-COUNTRY...

ACCORDING TO CHAIRMAN DASOR'S REPORT TO ME, THE **ZEGORS** FIRST APPEARED IN AN ARCHEOLOGICAL EXCAVATION HERE IN THE SOUTHWEST DESERT! I'VE GOT TO FIND THAT "DIG"...!

THEN...

ZEGORS--A WHOLE SQUAD OF THEM--COMING AT ME! BUT I CAN'T STOP TO BATTLE THEM NOW! GOT TO GET *PAST* THEM--!

EDITOR'S NOTE: BY SETTING UP AN IMPENETRABLE SHIELD FORMED BY HIS **POWER BEAM**, THE MIGHTY GLADIATOR REMAINS INVULNERABLE TO THE TERRIBLE EYE-BLASTS!

16

AND SOON...

GOT THROUGH ALL RIGHT! AND THERE IT IS-- THE EXCAVATION--THE OPENING IN THE EARTH WHERE THE *ZEGORS* FIRST APPEARED!

WITH GRIM DETERMINATION, THE **EMERALD- CLAD WARRIOR** PLUMMETS TOWARD THE CREVICE...

THOSE ODD *ENERGY BEAMS*-- COMING UP IN FULL FORCE FROM THE OPEN- ING! THIS **PROVES** I'M ON THE **RIGHT TRACK!**

WITHOUT A MOMENT'S HESITATION, THE FEARLESS CRUSADER PLUNGES DOWNWARD, FOLLOWING HIS TRAIL...

DASOR SAID THE *ZEGORS* ROSE UP FROM THE CENTER OF THE EARTH! THIS MUST BE THE PATH THEY USED TO THE SURFACE--THIS LONG CORRIDOR LIKE A *MINE SHAFT!* BUT HOW LONG WILL IT KEEP GOING DOWN? AND WHERE WILL IT LEAD ME?

SOON, AFTER THE GREAT POWER BEAM HAS PROPELLED ITS WIELDER ALONG WITH PRECIPITATE SPEED...

I'VE COME OUT INTO AN ENORMOUS CAVERN! AND GREAT SCOTT--! THERE'S A CITY--A WHOLE CIVILIZATION DOWN HERE!-- INCLUDING THE STRUCTURE I'M LOOKING FOR--THE BUILDING WHERE THOSE ENERGY RAYS ARE COMING FROM!

AS **GREEN LANTERN** HURTLES TOWARD HIS OBJECTIVE, RING BLAZING, HIS APPEARANCE IS THE INSTANT SIGNAL FOR A COMBINED ATTACK BY THE DENIZENS OF THE CITY...

ZEGORS--COMING AT ME FROM ALL SIDES! I--I CAN'T FIGHT OFF ALL THOSE EYE-BLASTS AT ONCE! BUT THERE'S ANOTHER WAY TO DEAL WITH THIS SITUATION!

IN THE SPLIT-MOMENT, AS THE EYE-RAYS BLAZE TOWARD THE GREEN-CLAD INTRUDER, THE **POWER BEAM** FLARES OUT WITH OVERPOWERING MIGHT...

TURNING MY **GREEN BEAM** INTO A **HUGE LIGHTNING BOLT** HAS SPLIT THAT "ENERGY" BUILDING LIKE AN EGGSHELL!

CRRAACK!

IT WORKED--JUST AS I FIGURED! THE **ZEGORS** CAN'T EMPLOY THEIR **EYE-BLAST** ANY MORE! THE POWER FOR IT CAME TO THEM FROM A SOURCE IN THAT BUILDING!

RUNNING FOR IT! BUT I WON'T PURSUE THEM! IT'S THE ONES UP ON THE SURFACE THAT MUST BE HANDLED FIRST! NOW TO GET BACK TO **STAR CITY**...

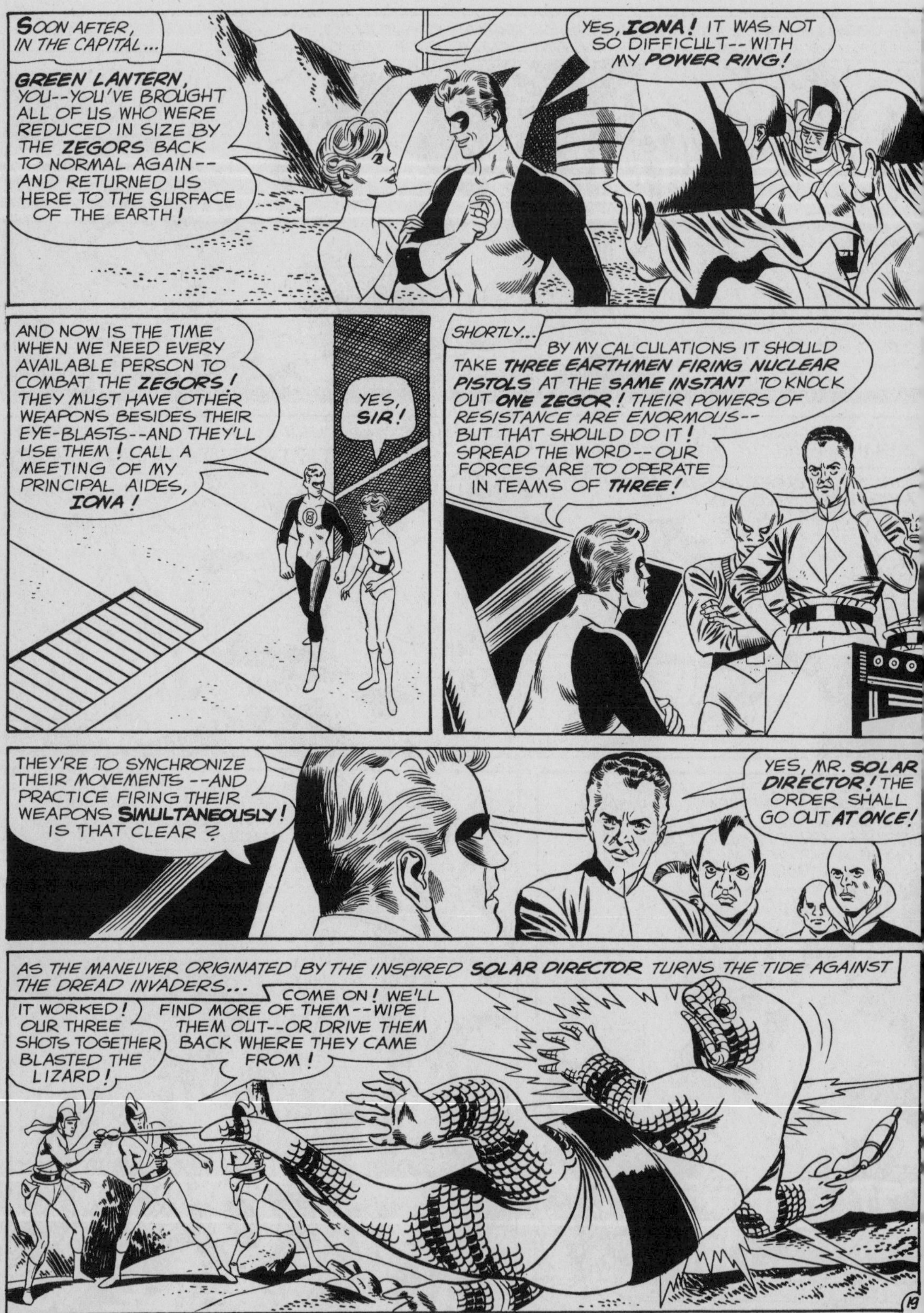
SOON AFTER, IN THE CAPITAL...
GREEN LANTERN, YOU--YOU'VE BROUGHT ALL OF US WHO WERE REDUCED IN SIZE BY THE ZEGORS BACK TO NORMAL AGAIN--AND RETURNED US HERE TO THE SURFACE OF THE EARTH!
YES, IONA! IT WAS NOT SO DIFFICULT--WITH MY POWER RING!
AND NOW IS THE TIME WHEN WE NEED EVERY AVAILABLE PERSON TO COMBAT THE ZEGORS! THEY MUST HAVE OTHER WEAPONS BESIDES THEIR EYE-BLASTS--AND THEY'LL USE THEM! CALL A MEETING OF MY PRINCIPAL AIDES, IONA!
YES, SIR!
SHORTLY...
BY MY CALCULATIONS IT SHOULD TAKE THREE EARTHMEN FIRING NUCLEAR PISTOLS AT THE SAME INSTANT TO KNOCK OUT ONE ZEGOR! THEIR POWERS OF RESISTANCE ARE ENORMOUS--BUT THAT SHOULD DO IT! SPREAD THE WORD--OUR FORCES ARE TO OPERATE IN TEAMS OF THREE!
THEY'RE TO SYNCHRONIZE THEIR MOVEMENTS--AND PRACTICE FIRING THEIR WEAPONS SIMULTANEOUSLY! IS THAT CLEAR?
YES, MR. SOLAR DIRECTOR! THE ORDER SHALL GO OUT AT ONCE!
AS THE MANEUVER ORIGINATED BY THE INSPIRED SOLAR DIRECTOR TURNS THE TIDE AGAINST THE DREAD INVADERS...
IT WORKED! OUR THREE SHOTS TOGETHER BLASTED THE LIZARD!
COME ON! WE'LL FIND MORE OF THEM--WIPE THEM OUT--OR DRIVE THEM BACK WHERE THEY CAME FROM!
19

SHORTLY, OVER THE *TELEX INTERPLANETARY NETWORK* OF *5700 A.D.* ...

...AND THE *ZEGORS* HAVE SURRENDERED UNCONDITIONALLY! UNDER THE LEADERSHIP OF THE NEW *SOLAR DIRECTOR, GREEN LANTERN,* EARTH FORCES EVERYWHERE HAVE BEEN COMPLETELY VICTORIOUS! THE REMNANTS OF THE *ZEGORS* HAVE BEEN ALLOWED TO RETURN TO THEIR HALF-DESTROYED UNDERGROUND CITY...

MEANWHILE, THE NEW *SOLAR DIRECTOR* IS PUTTING SOME FINAL TOUCHES TO THE VICTORY...

I'M SURE THE *ZEGORS* WILL NEVER CHALLENGE MANKIND AGAIN! BUT JUST IN CASE THEY EVER DO TRY ANYTHING--THIS ALARM SYSTEM I'M LAYING DOWN WITH MY RING WILL INSTANTLY WARN THE EARTH--AND ALLOW IT TIME TO MEET THE THREAT!

AT THAT MOMENT, BACK IN *STAR CITY...*

GREEN LANTERN IS ON HIS WAY BACK HERE! NOW IS THE TIME WHEN WE MUST *RETURN* HIM TO HIS OWN ERA! IN *23* HOURS, HE HAS ACCOMPLISHED EVERYTHING WE COULD HAVE ASKED OF HIM--AND WILL FOREVER BE ENSHRINED IN OUR HISTORY AND OUR MEMORY!

BUT CHAIRMAN DASOR--

CAN'T YOU LET *GREEN LANTERN* STAY WITH US A WHILE LONGER? ANOTHER FEW DAYS AT LEAST!

I'M SORRY, *IONA!* WE HAVE NO RIGHT TO KEEP HIM HERE A SECOND LONGER THAN ABSOLUTELY NECESSARY! BESIDES, OUR RESEARCH TELLS US THAT HIS *POWER RING* MUST BE RECHARGED EVERY 24 HOURS OR IT WILL FAIL TO WORK!

MOREOVER, HIS OWN ERA NEEDS HIM! OF COURSE--HE WILL RETURN THERE AT THE SPLIT-INSTANT HE WAS TRANSPORTED TO OUR CENTURY! THERE WILL BE NO LOSS--NO TIME-LAPSE BETWEEN! THAT IS NECESSARY TO FULFILL THE RIGID LAWS OF TIME-TRAVEL!

IN THE SAME MANNER HE WILL REMEMBER *ABSOLUTELY NOTHING* OF THIS PERIOD IN HIS CAREER!

HE--HE'S *GONE!*

CLICK!

AT THAT MOMENT...

S-SOMETHING HAPPENING--!?

WITH NO INTERVAL AT ALL, OR POSSIBLY THAT OF AN ATOM'S PULSE...

UHH--THE QUEER NUMBNESS I FELT--IT CAME AND WENT LIKE--LIKE A FLASH! BUT I HAVE NO TIME TO THINK ABOUT IT NOW! GOT TO HALT THAT FANTASTIC SEA MONSTER!

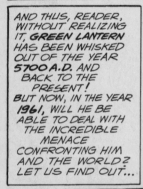

AND THUS, READER, WITHOUT REALIZING IT, GREEN LANTERN HAS BEEN WHISKED OUT OF THE YEAR 5700 A.D. AND BACK TO THE PRESENT! BUT NOW, IN THE YEAR 1961, WILL HE BE ABLE TO DEAL WITH THE INCREDIBLE MENACE CONFRONTING HIM AND THE WORLD? LET US FIND OUT...

AS THE VIBRANT FIGURE DARTS AT HIS OUTSIZE FOE...

eh? MY RING HAS NO EFFECT ON IT-- NONE AT ALL! STRANGE! I CAN'T UNDERSTAND--IT'S NOT YELLOW--!*

*Editor's Note: DUE TO A NECESSARY IMPURITY IN HIS POWER BATTERY, GREEN LANTERN'S POWER RING HAS NO EFFECT ON ANYTHING YELLOW! BUT WHAT WILL HE DO NOW?

GREEN LANTERN

The CHALLENGE FROM 5700 A.D. CHAPTER THREE

BACK IN HIS OWN ERA, THE GREEN GLADIATOR FINDS THAT FOR SOME UNCANNY REASON HIS POWER RING HAS NO EFFECT ON HIS GIGANTIC ADVERSARY--A SITUATION THAT PUTS BOTH HIM AND THE COUNTRY IN DIRE PERIL! LET'S SEE HOW THE DASHING CRUSADER RISES TO THE EMERGENCY!

THE THING IS STILL COMING ON! BUT I'VE GOT TO KEEP IT AWAY FROM THE LAND--IT COULD CAUSE UNTOLD DAMAGE! AND--I HAVE AN IDEA!

OUT OF THE MYSTIC POWER RING A FURIOUS BURST OF MULTI-COLORED LIGHTS SHOOTS...

THAT EXPLOSION CREATED BY MY BEAM CANNOT HARM THE CREATURE-- BUT IT MAY DRIVE IT BACK! IT'S SORT OF A BLUFF!

AND SURE ENOUGH, AS THE DRAMATIC STRATAGEM WORKS... DIVING BACK INTO THE SEA! BUT I MUSN'T LOSE SIGHT OF IT! GOT TO TRAIL IT-- THERE MUST BE SOME WAY I CAN HANDLE THE THING!

22

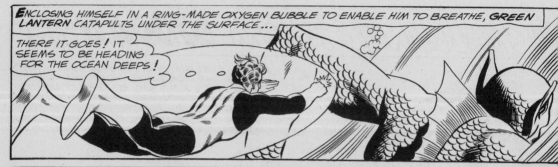

ENCLOSING HIMSELF IN A RING-MADE OXYGEN BUBBLE TO ENABLE HIM TO BREATHE, **GREEN LANTERN** CATAPULTS UNDER THE SURFACE...

THERE IT GOES! IT SEEMS TO BE HEADING FOR THE OCEAN DEEPS!

AS THE HUGE AQUATIC APPARITION SPURTS DOWN-WARD...

WITH MY RING I CAN FOLLOW IT EASILY! BUT WAIT A SECOND--! MY RING IS REVEALING SOMETHING!

UNDER THE INFLUENCE OF THE **EMERALD RAY** A STRANGE FACT BECOMES CLEAR...

NO WONDER MY RING HAS NO EFFECT ON THE CREATURE! IT'S GIVING OFF AN **INVISIBLE GOLDEN LIGHT**-- A SORT OF **INFRA-YELLOW** COLOR--!*

*EDITOR'S NOTE: JUST AS **INFRARED** IS IN-VISIBLE RED LIGHT, SO **INFRAYELLOW** IS CON-SIDERED INVISIBLE YELLOW LIGHT!

IN THE KEEN BRAIN OF THE **EMERALD CRUSADER,** AS HE GRIMLY TRAILS HIS GIANT QUARRY, SEVERAL FACTS INSTANTLY LINK UP...

THIS IS THE SPOT WHERE THE NAVY CAPSULE DISAPPEARED! THE CAPSULE PENETRATED **OUTER SPACE**--AND IT MUST HAVE PICKED UP SOME **UNKNOWN RADIATION**--WHICH REACTED WITH THE CHEMICALS IN THE SEA WATER TO SPAWN THIS CREATURE! THAT WOULD EXPLAIN ITS INVISIBLE GOLDEN COLOR--THE SEA IS FULL OF GOLD IN CHEMICAL SOLUTION!

THEN... GREAT THUNDER! ONE OF OUR NEW **ATOMIC SUBMARINES** HAS COME ALONG--POSSIBLY SEARCHING FOR THE LOST CAPSULE--AND THE CREATURE IN ITS FURY HAS SEIZED IT!

23

IT SEEMS DETERMINED TO DESTROY THAT SUB! I'VE GOT TO SAVE IT! BUT HOW? MY RING **CAN'T** AFFECT THE MONSTER WITH ITS INVISIBLE. **GOLDEN** COLOR--eh? MAYBE-- **THAT'S** MY CLUE!

AS THE GREAT POWER BEAM AGAIN IS SET TO WORK WITH FEVERISH HASTE...

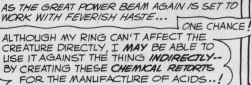

ONE CHANCE!

ALTHOUGH MY RING CAN'T AFFECT THE CREATURE DIRECTLY, I **MAY** BE ABLE TO USE IT AGAINST THE THING **INDIRECTLY--** BY CREATING THESE **CHEMICAL RETORTS** FOR THE MANUFACTURE OF ACIDS..!

FANTASTICALLY, **GL** HAS MADE A SMALL CHEMICAL LABORATORY ON THE OCEAN'S FLOOR...

ACCORDING TO WHAT I REMEMBER OF SCIENCE, ONLY ONE SUBSTANCE CAN DISSOLVE GOLD-- THE MIXTURE OF HYDROCHLORIC AND NITRIC ACIDS KNOWN AS **AQUA REGIA**! * I'VE GOT TO MANUFACTURE A QUANTITY OF IT QUICKLY!

*Editor's Note : IN ANCIENT TIMES **AQUA REGIA**, OR **ROYAL WATER**, WAS SO CALLED BECAUSE IT ALONE COULD DISSOLVE GOLD, THE KING OF METALS!

AND SOON... NOW TO USE MY RING TO HURL THIS ACID AT THE MONSTER BEFORE IT SUCCEEDS IN **SHAKING THAT SUB APART!**

THEN, AFTER A BREATHTAKING MOMENT OF SUSPENSE...

;Whew!; FOR AN INSTANT IT WAS TOUCH AND GO-- BUT NOW THE **AQUA REGIA** HAS TAKEN EFFECT AND IT'S **DISSOLVING THE CREATURE--** FORCING IT TO RELEASE THE SUB--AND UTTERLY DESTROYING IT!

SHORTLY, IN A TOP-LEVEL CONFERENCE WITH HIGH NAVY BRASS...

NO DOUBT YOU'RE RIGHT, GREEN LANTERN -- THAT OUR CAPSULE PICKED UP SOME UNKNOWN RADIATION THAT SPAWNED THE CREATURE! BUT WE'RE TAKING STEPS TO INSURE THAT IT NEVER HAPPENS AGAIN! AND PLEASE ACCEPT THE NATION'S GRATITUDE FOR SAVING THAT SUB!

AS A FAMILIAR FIGURE ZOOMS HOMEWARD..

TIME FOR HAL JORDAN TO GET BACK ON HIS TEST PILOT JOB AT THE FERRIS AIRCRAFT COMPANY! BUT -- WAIT A SECOND! THAT'S ODD -- MY RING FEELS AS IF IT NEEDS RECHARGING!

AND SOON, BEHIND CLOSED DOORS AT THE AIRCRAFT COMPANY HANGAR...

IT DID NEED RECHARGING! BUT I CAN'T UNDERSTAND -- MY ENCOUNTER WITH THE SEA MONSTER ONLY TOOK AN HOUR -- AND I CHARGED IT JUST BEFORE I SET OFF! Hmm! THAT IS STRANGE!

GREEN LANTERN WOULD PERHAPS THINK IT EVEN STRANGER IF HE COULD AT THIS MOMENT PEER INTO THE WORLD OF THE FUTURE...5700 A.D...

HE CAN'T REMEMBER ME -- HE DOESN'T EVEN KNOW I EXIST! BUT I'LL NEVER FORGET HIM -- NEVER!

THIS IS NOT THE END, READER! WATCH FOR ANOTHER THRILLING FUTURE - GREEN LANTERN STORY IN A FORTHCOMING ISSUE!

The End

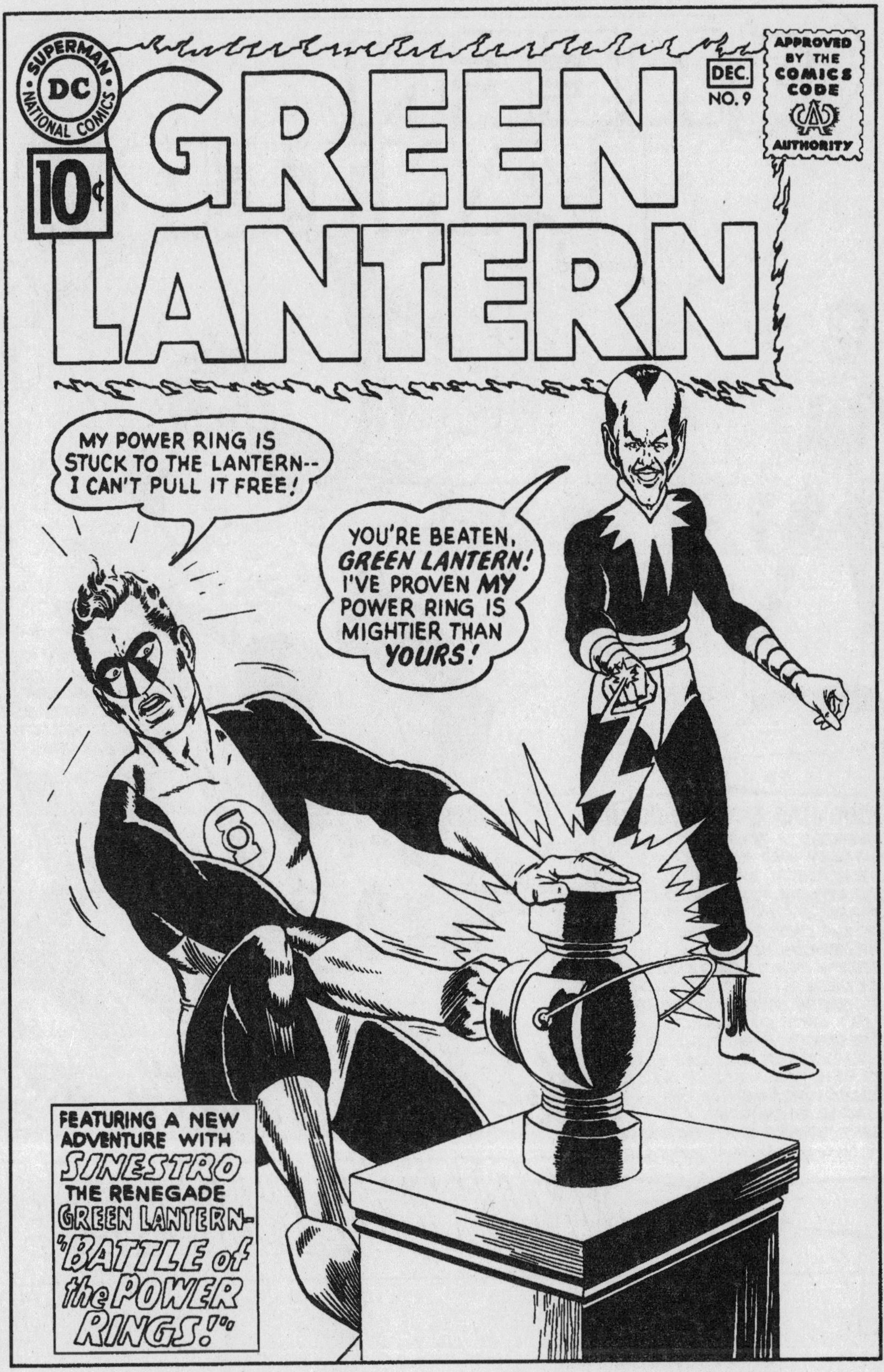
SUPERMAN DC NATIONAL COMICS
10¢
GREEN LANTERN
DEC. NO. 9
APPROVED BY THE COMICS CODE AUTHORITY
MY POWER RING IS STUCK TO THE LANTERN-- I CAN'T PULL IT FREE!
YOU'RE BEATEN, GREEN LANTERN! I'VE PROVEN MY POWER RING IS MIGHTIER THAN YOURS!
FEATURING A NEW ADVENTURE WITH SINESTRO THE RENEGADE GREEN LANTERN- "BATTLE of the POWER RINGS!"

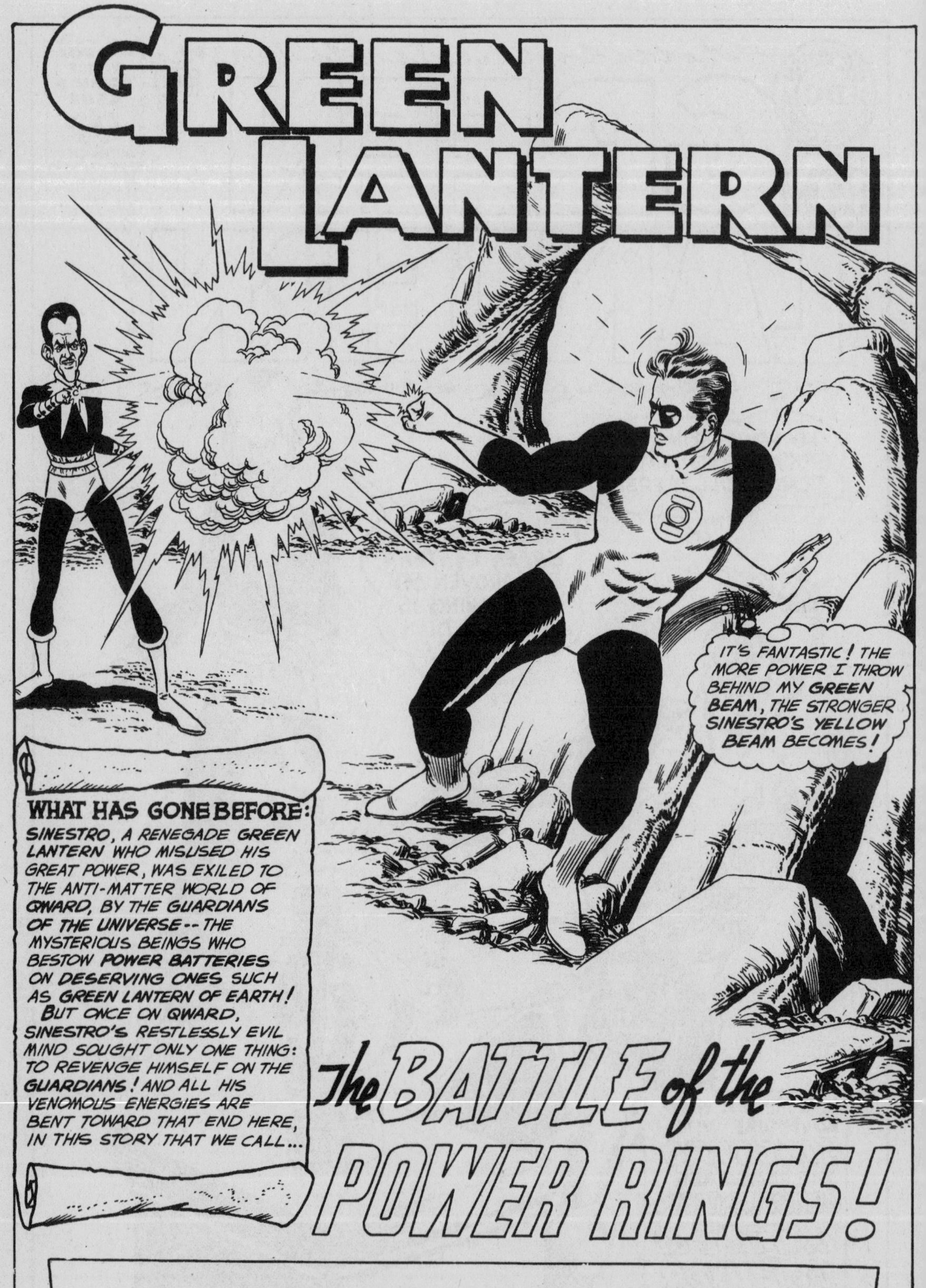
GREEN LANTERN
IT'S FANTASTIC! THE MORE POWER I THROW BEHIND MY GREEN BEAM, THE STRONGER SINESTRO'S YELLOW BEAM BECOMES!
WHAT HAS GONE BEFORE:
SINESTRO, A RENEGADE GREEN LANTERN WHO MISUSED HIS GREAT POWER, WAS EXILED TO THE ANTI-MATTER WORLD OF QWARD, BY THE GUARDIANS OF THE UNIVERSE -- THE MYSTERIOUS BEINGS WHO BESTOW POWER BATTERIES ON DESERVING ONES SUCH AS GREEN LANTERN OF EARTH!
BUT ONCE ON QWARD, SINESTRO'S RESTLESSLY EVIL MIND SOUGHT ONLY ONE THING: TO REVENGE HIMSELF ON THE GUARDIANS! AND ALL HIS VENOMOUS ENERGIES ARE BENT TOWARD THAT END HERE, IN THIS STORY THAT WE CALL...
The BATTLE of the POWER RINGS!
1

AS THE EMERALD GLADIATOR SPEEDS OVER COAST CITY...

THERE'S A REPORT THAT THE **PACKER GANG** -- THAT PREYS ON VALUABLE FREIGHT CARGO -- WILL STRIKE TONIGHT! I'VE GOT TO GET DOWN TO THE RAILROAD YARDS AT ONCE...

AND I CAN'T WASTE ANY TIME -- BECAUSE RIGHT AFTERWARD I HAVE AN ALL-IMPORTANT MEETING TO ATTEND -- ONE THAT I WOULDN'T WANT TO MISS FOR ALL THE WORLDS IN THE GALAXY! *eh--?*

SUDDENLY...

MY **POWER RING** -- SOMETHING'S WRONG WITH IT! IT'S NOT PUTTING OUT ENOUGH JUICE TO KEEP ME AIRBORNE!

*SHORTLY, AS **GREEN LANTERN** MANAGES TO LAND WITHOUT HARM...*

Whew! THAT'S NOT THE **FIRST TIME** THIS WEEK THIS HAS HAPPENED! AGAIN AND AGAIN DURING THE PAST FEW DAYS MY GREEN BEAM ABRUPTLY SEEMED TO LOSE POWER! NOT ALTOGETHER -- BUT ENOUGH TO BOTHER ME!

I CAN'T IMAGINE WHAT COULD BE CAUSING THIS! USUALLY THE POWER PICKS UP AGAIN A BIT... BUT NO TIME TO WORRY ABOUT THAT NOW! HERE'S THE FREIGHT YARD...

...AND THERE'S THE **PACKER GANG** -- AT WORK ON THAT FREIGHT CAR THEY'VE OPENED!

2

DESPITE UNEASINESS ABOUT HIS UNRELIABLE RING, THE GREEN-CLAD CRUSADER PLUNGES AT THE MARAUDERS...

GREEN LANTERN!?

I DON'T KNOW WHETHER MY RING CAN STOP BULLETS IN ITS WEAKENED STATE! BUT I'LL BET I'M ABOUT TO FIND OUT--!

I'LL JUST USE MY RING TO PROTECT MYSELF UNTIL THOSE HOODS RUN OUT OF AMMUNITION! NO SENSE TAKING UNNECESSARY CHANCES...!

AND SOON, WITH THE LAST LEAD PELLET FIRED...

NOW IT'S MY TURN, BOYS!

AFTER THE HAPLESS GUNMEN HAVE BEEN HANDED OVER TO THE AUTHORITIES...

POLICE

POLICE

FUNNY... MY RING'S IN FULL FORCE AGAIN! I'D LIKE TO GET TO THE BOTTOM OF THIS--BUT IT WILL HAVE TO WAIT UNTIL AFTER THE MEETING! NOTHING TAKES PRIORITY OVER THAT!

BUT BEFORE I START OUT I'LL CHARGE MY RING-- JUST TO MAKE SURE! I'VE BEEN CHARGING IT REGULARLY*... AND I KNOW IT'S NOT THAT WHICH HAS CAUSED IT TO FAIL...

I'M BACK AT THE FERRIS AIR-CRAFT COMPANY...

*Editor's Note: BY CHARGING HIS RING AT HIS POWER BATTERY, GREEN LANTERN OBTAINS POWER FOR EXACTLY TWENTY-FOUR HOURS!

SOON, IN THE DRESSING ROOM OF ACE TEST PILOT HAL JORDAN, THE EMERALD GLADIATOR'S CIVILIAN ALTER EGO...

IN BRIGHTEST DAY, IN BLACKEST NIGHT, NO EVIL SHALL ESCAPE MY SIGHT! LET THOSE WHO WORSHIP EVIL'S MIGHT BEWARE MY POWER--GREEN LANTERN'S LIGHT!

SOMETHING'S WRONG! SOMEONE... IS IN THIS ROOM!!

3.

THE NEXT MOMENT...

I--I CAN'T GET MY RING LOOSE FROM THE POWER BATTERY!

THIS PROVES THAT MY POWER RING IS STRONGER THAN YOURS, GREEN LANTERN!

SINESTRO!

GREETINGS, MY EX-COLLEAGUE! SURPRISED TO SEE ME, eh? WELL, IT WON'T DO ANY HARM TO TELL YOU HOW I ESCAPED THAT GREEN BUBBLE YOU LEFT ME IN!* YOU'RE HELPLESS NOW ANYWAY...

*Editor's Note: IN "THE DAY 100,000 PEOPLE VANISHED," (GREEN LANTERN #7) SINESTRO, A RENEGADE GREEN LANTERN ON THE PLANET KORUGAR, WAS BANISHED TO THE ANTIMATTER UNIVERSE OF QWARD, WHERE HE WAS EVENTUALLY IMPRISONED BY EARTH'S GL IN AN IMPENETRABLE FORCE-BUBBLE.

"YOU THOUGHT NO FORCE COULD BREAK THAT BUBBLE MADE BY YOUR GREEN BEAM! BUT THERE WAS ONE THING YOU COULDN'T POSSIBLY KNOW..."

MY ARCHENEMY GREEN LANTERN DOESN'T REALIZE THAT I WAS PREPARED FOR AN EMERGENCY LIKE THIS! IN MY POCKET I HAVE MY OWN POWER RING, CONSTRUCTED IN SUCH A MANNER...

...THAT IT CAN DRAW POWER FROM THE BEAM OF A REAL POWER RING! AND THIS GREEN SHEATH AROUND ME CONTAINS ENOUGH ENERGY FOR ME TO TAP AND BURST LOOSE--UNLESS MY CALCULATIONS ARE DEAD WRONG!

"BUT I WAS RIGHT, AND NEITHER DEAD NOR WRONG!"

PERFECT! MY YELLOW BEAM SUCKED UP ENOUGH ENERGY TO FREE ME!

Editor's Note: IT IS INTERESTING TO OBSERVE THAT WHEREAS GL'S POWER RING IS HELPLESS AGAINST ANYTHING YELLOW, DUE TO A NECESSARY IMPURITY IN THE BATTERY OF POWER, SINESTRO'S BEAM IS ALL YELLOW, AS IF COMPOSED ENTIRELY OF EVIL IMPURITIES!

SO I ESCAPED AND CAME HERE--WHERE I'VE BEEN DISGUISED AS AN EARTHMAN FOR THE PAST WEEK! YOU SEE, GREEN LANTERN, IN ORDER TO CARRY OUT MY MAIN GOAL IN LIFE IT WAS NECESSARY TO CHARGE UP MY RING TO AN ULTRA-HIGH POTENCY...

4

...AND THE ONLY WAY TO DO THAT WAS TO SECRETLY **FOLLOW YOU**! I'VE BEEN AT YOUR HEELS ALL WEEK WITHOUT YOUR KNOWING IT! AND EVERY TIME YOU USED YOUR RING--I DREW POWER FROM IT TO CHARGE MY OWN!

SO **THAT** EXPLAINS WHY MY RING SEEMED TO **LOSE FORCE** FROM TIME TO TIME!

AS SINESTRO, THE RENEGADE **GREEN LANTERN**, GLOWERS AT HIS PREY...

EXACTLY! THUS, **MY POWER RING** GAINED AS **YOURS LOST**! BY MEANS OF MY RING I LEARNED THAT YOU ARE DUE TO ATTEND A MEETING OF ALL THE **GREEN LANTERNS** OF THE GALAXY! THAT IS WHY I AM HERE!

YOU WILL **NOT** ATTEND THAT MEETING, **GREEN LANTERN**--BUT I WILL--IN YOUR PLACE! IT IS PART OF MY SCHEME TO DESTROY MY ETERNAL ENEMIES--THE **GUARDIANS OF THE UNIVERSE**!

THE GUARDIANS IN DANGER!? I'VE GOT TO GET LOOSE!!

WITH TREMENDOUS EFFORT THE **GREEN GLADIATOR** STRAINS AGAINST THE FORCE HOLDING HIM...

C-CAN'T PULL MY RING FREE! BUT WAIT--THERE MAY BE **ANOTHER** WAY TO GET AT MY SATANIC-FACED FOE!

SUDDENLY, **GREEN LANTERN** SPRINGS A SURPRISE MANEUVER...

HE FOUND A WAY TO BREAK FREE... **BY SLIPPING HIS FINGER OUT OF THE RING!**

I'D JUST AS SOON TAKE CARE OF YOU WITH MY **BARE** HANDS, SINESTRO!

SNAP!

IF YOU CAN REACH ME, **GREEN LANTERN**!

HE'S JUST A FEW FEET AWAY! GOT TO KEEP STRUGGLING AGAINST THAT **YELLOW BEAM**!

BUT NO UNAIDED HUMAN FORCE CAN OVERCOME THE BALEFUL POWER OF SINESTRO'S YELLOW BEAM! AND DESPITE THE INCREDIBLE EFFORTS OF THE EMERALD CRUSADER...

ONE LAST LUNGE...

UH--FALLING SHORT...

GOING DOWN...

DOWN...

END OF THE LINE, GREEN LANTERN! YOU'RE FINISHED!

THEN, AS THE EVIL RAY IS PUT TO A FINAL, GRIM USE...

GREEN LANTERN, YOU CAN NEVER BREAK OUT OF THAT CAGE FORMED BY MY YELLOW BEAM! REMEMBER THAT-- YOU CAN NEVER BREAK OUT OF THERE!

NOW TO USE MY RING TO ALTER MY APPEARANCE-- AND BECOME AN ABSOLUTE REPLICA OF MY EX-- COLLEAGUE!

AND MOMENTS LATER...

GREEN LANTERN OF EARTH IS DUE TO ARRIVE SHORTLY ON THE FAR-- OFF PLANET OF YQUEM! "HE" WILL ARRIVE AT THE MEETING--HA HA-- AS SCHEDULED!

MEANWHILE ON THE WORLD OF YQUEM IN A CENTRALLY-LOCATED AREA OF THE GALAXY...

ARE WE ALL HERE?

ONLY GREEN LANTERN OF EARTH IS STILL MISSING!

WE WILL WAIT A LITTLE LONGER FOR HIM..

WHILE THE ASSEMBLAGE WAITS--THE FIRST GALAXY-- WIDE CONFERENCE OF ALL POWER BATTERY POSSESSORS, MEETING TO EXCHANGE NOTES AND BENEFIT BY EACH OTHER'S EXPERIENCE--LET US EXAMINE A FEW OF THE MEMBERS OF THIS UNIQUE BAND, AND IDENTIFY SOME OF THEM FOR FUTURE REFER-- ENCE...

⑥

GREEN LANTERN OF XAOS, A WORLD WHERE INSECTS RULE AND WHERE THE HUMAN RACE IS UNKNOWN!

GREEN LANTERN OF BARRIO III, A PLANET OF CRYSTAL LIFE—FORMS, ULTRA—SENSITIVE, WITH 13 SENSES INSTEAD OF THE USUAL 6 OF HUMANS!

GREEN LANTERN OF ROJIRA, ONE OF THE MOST ADVANCED, AGED AND SUPER-SCIENTIFIC CIVILIZATIONS!

GREEN LANTERN OF T41A, WHERE LIFE HAS CULMINATED IN A SHAPE ALTOGETHER DIFFERENT FROM MANKIND!

GREEN LANTERN OF AEROS, A WATER-WORLD INHABITED BY VARIOUS FORMS OF FISH LIFE!

YET DESPITE THEIR DIVERSITY, ALL THE GREEN LANTERNS ARE HIGHLY INTELLIGENT AND EQUALLY ADEPT AT PROJECTING THEIR THOUGHTS TO OVERCOME THE LANGUAGE BARRIER...

SOMEONE IS ARRIVING NOW!

I CAN MAKE HIM OUT! IT IS GREEN LANTERN OF EARTH!

GREETINGS, MY ILLUSTRIOUS COLLEAGUES! SORRY I AM LATE--BUT A--er--LAST-MINUTE MATTER CAME UP BACK ON MY WORLD THAT I HAD TO ATTEND TO!

OUR NUMBER IS COMPLETE..

...SO LET US BEGIN THE MEETING!

THEY'RE ALL HERE! THIS FITS IN WITH MY PLANS-- THAT THEY DON'T SUSPECT!

WE WILL NOW HEAR AN ACCOUNT BY GREEN LANTERN OF BARRIO III CONCERNING AN OUTBREAK OF EVIL ON HIS PLANET AND HOW HE DEALT WITH IT!

FELLOW GREEN LANTERNS UHH!!

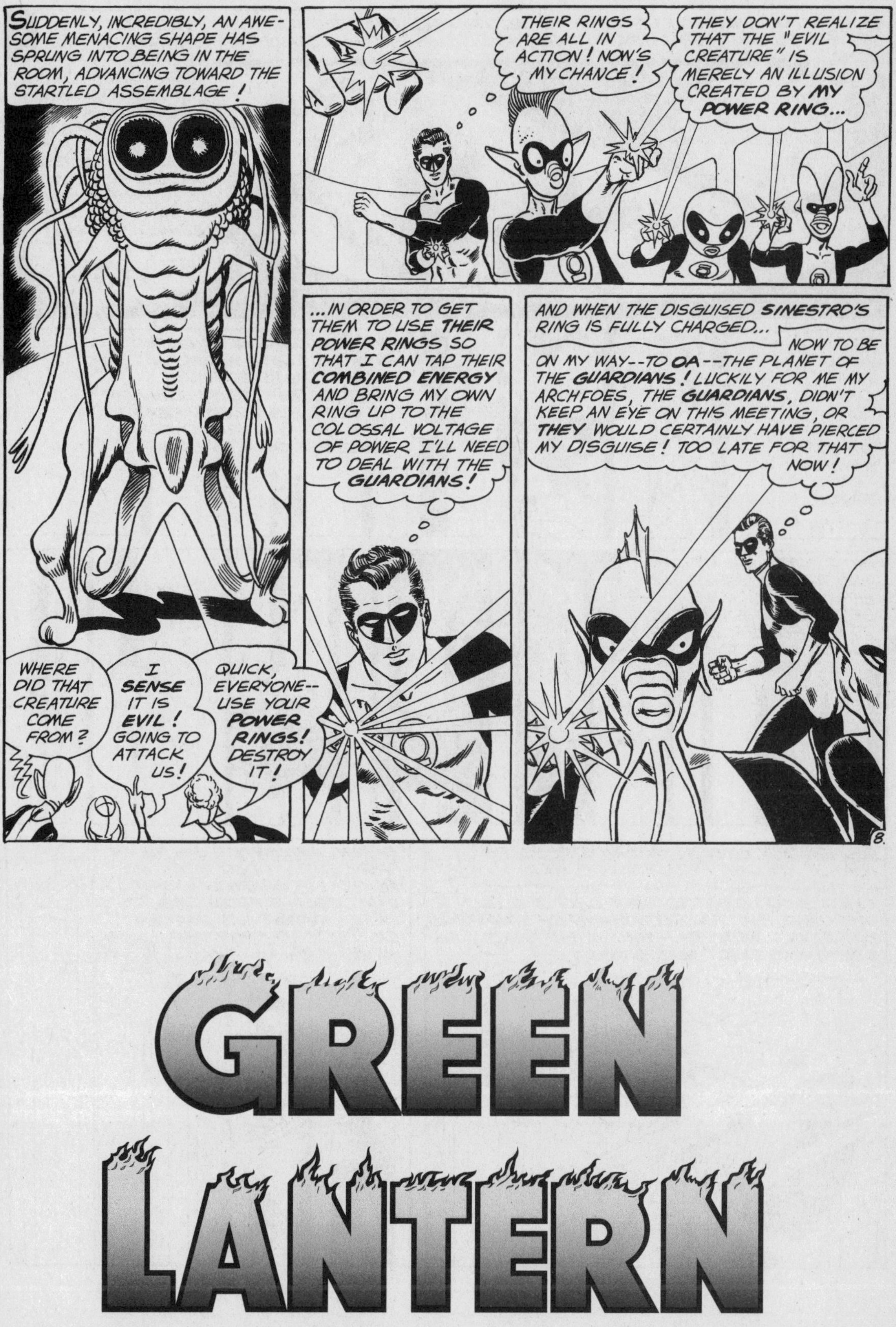
SUDDENLY, INCREDIBLY, AN AWESOME MENACING SHAPE HAS SPRUNG INTO BEING IN THE ROOM, ADVANCING TOWARD THE STARTLED ASSEMBLAGE!
WHERE DID THAT CREATURE COME FROM?
I SENSE IT IS EVIL! GOING TO ATTACK US!
QUICK, EVERYONE--USE YOUR POWER RINGS! DESTROY IT!
THEIR RINGS ARE ALL IN ACTION! NOW'S MY CHANCE!
THEY DON'T REALIZE THAT THE "EVIL CREATURE" IS MERELY AN ILLUSION CREATED BY MY POWER RING...
...IN ORDER TO GET THEM TO USE THEIR POWER RINGS SO THAT I CAN TAP THEIR COMBINED ENERGY AND BRING MY OWN RING UP TO THE COLOSSAL VOLTAGE OF POWER I'LL NEED TO DEAL WITH THE GUARDIANS!
AND WHEN THE DISGUISED SINESTRO'S RING IS FULLY CHARGED...
NOW TO BE ON MY WAY--TO OA--THE PLANET OF THE GUARDIANS! LUCKILY FOR ME MY ARCHFOES, THE GUARDIANS, DIDN'T KEEP AN EYE ON THIS MEETING, OR THEY WOULD CERTAINLY HAVE PIERCED MY DISGUISE! TOO LATE FOR THAT NOW!
8.

GREEN LANTERN

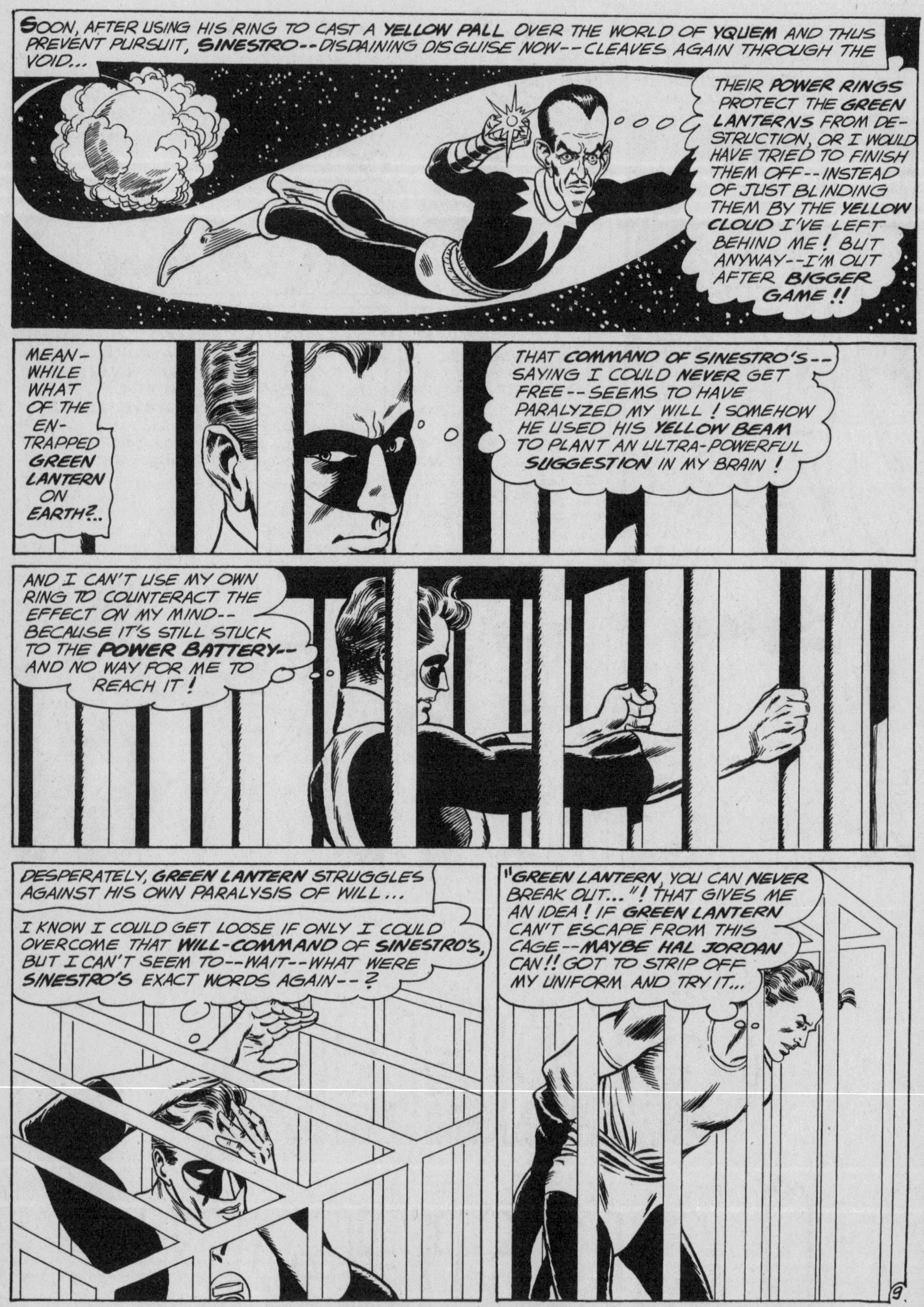
SOON, AFTER USING HIS RING TO CAST A YELLOW PALL OVER THE WORLD OF YQUEM AND THUS PREVENT PURSUIT, SINESTRO--DISDAINING DISGUISE NOW--CLEAVES AGAIN THROUGH THE VOID...
THEIR POWER RINGS PROTECT THE GREEN LANTERNS FROM DESTRUCTION, OR I WOULD HAVE TRIED TO FINISH THEM OFF--INSTEAD OF JUST BLINDING THEM BY THE YELLOW CLOUD I'VE LEFT BEHIND ME! BUT ANYWAY--I'M OUT AFTER BIGGER GAME!!
MEANWHILE WHAT OF THE ENTRAPPED GREEN LANTERN ON EARTH?..
THAT COMMAND OF SINESTRO'S--SAYING I COULD NEVER GET FREE--SEEMS TO HAVE PARALYZED MY WILL! SOMEHOW HE USED HIS YELLOW BEAM TO PLANT AN ULTRA-POWERFUL SUGGESTION IN MY BRAIN!
AND I CAN'T USE MY OWN RING TO COUNTERACT THE EFFECT ON MY MIND--BECAUSE IT'S STILL STUCK TO THE POWER BATTERY--AND NO WAY FOR ME TO REACH IT!
DESPERATELY, GREEN LANTERN STRUGGLES AGAINST HIS OWN PARALYSIS OF WILL...
I KNOW I COULD GET LOOSE IF ONLY I COULD OVERCOME THAT WILL-COMMAND OF SINESTRO'S, BUT I CAN'T SEEM TO--WAIT--WHAT WERE SINESTRO'S EXACT WORDS AGAIN--?
"GREEN LANTERN, YOU CAN NEVER BREAK OUT..."! THAT GIVES ME AN IDEA! IF GREEN LANTERN CAN'T ESCAPE FROM THIS CAGE--MAYBE HAL JORDAN CAN!! GOT TO STRIP OFF MY UNIFORM AND TRY IT...
9

THE NEXT MOMENT, AS THE INSPIRATION OF THE GLADIATOR WORKS LIKE A CHARM...

MADE IT! THIS IS ONE TIME MY *DOUBLE IDENTITY* REALLY CAME IN HANDY! AS HAL JORDAN I'M IMMUNE TO ANY MENTAL SUGGESTIONS GIVEN TO *GREEN LANTERN!*

SWIFTLY, THE *EMERALD CRUSADER* DONS HIS UNIFORM AGAIN, AND THEN...

NOW MY RING CAME LOOSE, ALL RIGHT! IT MUST HAVE BEEN THE SHOCK OF SEEING *SINESTRO* HERE THAT PREVENTED ME FROM GETTING IT LOOSE BEFORE! I CAN'T BELIEVE HIS RING IS *STRONGER* THAN MINE!

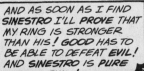

AND AS SOON AS I FIND *SINESTRO* I'LL *PROVE* THAT MY RING IS STRONGER THAN HIS! GOOD HAS TO BE ABLE TO DEFEAT EVIL! AND SINESTRO IS PURE EVIL!

AS GL CATAPULTS HIMSELF THROUGH THE VOID AT BREAK-NECK PACE, ON THE MYSTERIOUS WORLD OF *OA*, HOME OF THE GUARDIANS...

MY ARCHFOES HAVE THEIR DEFENSES ALL RIGHT! ONE *FORCE-FIELD* AFTER ANOTHER BARS THE WAY TO THEIR CITADEL! BUT MY YELLOW BEAM IS POWERFUL ENOUGH NOW TO BREAK THROUGH ANYTHING!

THE LAST BARRIER-- I'M BREAKING THROUGH TO THE GUARDIANS!

LOOKS LIKE I ARRIVED HERE *JUST* IN TIME!

GOOD THING I DECIDED TO COME STRAIGHT HERE INSTEAD OF FIRST CHECKING THE MEETING ON *YQUEM!*

YOU!? FOOL, DO YOU THINK TO STOP ME NOW!?

10.

AS TWO TREMENDOUS ENERGY-FORCES, ONE YELLOW, THE OTHER GREEN, CLASH IN TITANIC COMBAT...

SO IT'S **MY POWER RING** AGAINST YOURS, EH, **GREEN LANTERN?** WE'LL SEE WHO WINS!

IT'S INCREDIBLE! THE MORE FORCE I PUT BEHIND **MY** GREEN BEAM, THE STRONGER HIS BECOMES--BECAUSE HIS RING IS **ABSORBING POWER** FROM MINE, AS HE WAS GOOD ENOUGH TO EXPLAIN TO ME!

YOU'RE ALMOST FINISHED, **GREEN LANTERN!** YOU CAN'T WITHSTAND ME!

RALLYING HIS GREAT WILL POWER, THE **EMERALD CRUSADER** OF EARTH FORCES THE INTENSITY OF HIS WILL--BACKED BEAM UP TO UNPRECEDENTED HEIGHTS...

THERE **MUST** BE A LIMIT TO THE AMOUNT OF **POWER** HIS RING CAN HOLD! MY ONLY CHANCE IS TO **EXCEED THAT LIMIT**--TO FILL HIS RING SO FULL OF ENERGY THAT IT WILL COLLAPSE LIKE AN OVERCHARGED BATTERY! GOT TO KEEP POURING IT ON!

AND THE NEXT MOMENT...

UHH!

DID IT! HIS RING IS BURSTING-FLYING TO PIECES UNDER THE PRESSURE!!

YOU--YOU BEAT ME!

NOW WE KNOW WHOSE POWER RING WAS STRONGER, SINESTRO!

LOOK--!

AFTER THE OTHER *GREEN LANTERNS*, ARRIVING POST-HASTE FROM *YQUEM*, ARE BRIEFED ON WHAT HAS HAPPENED.

SO HE WAS OUT TO ATTACK THE *GUARDIANS*! WE SUSPECTED SOMETHING LIKE THAT AFTER HIS "EVIL CREATURE" TURNED OUT TO BE JUST AN *ILLUSION*! THAT'S WHY WE TRAILED HIM HERE AS FAST AS WE COULD!

NO DOUBT YOU WOULD HAVE ARRIVED IN TIME TO STOP HIM-- IF I HADN'T REACHED HIM FIRST TO DO THE JOB, MY FELLOW *GREEN LANTERNS*! BUT NOW-- WE'D BETTER MAKE A *FULL REPORT* TO THE *GUARDIANS*!

AND SOON, IN THE MIGHTY CITADEL OF THE *GUARDIANS*-- JUSTICE-LOVING SENTINELS OF THE UNIVERSE--A STRANGE SCENE TAKES PLACE, AS ALL THE ASSEMBLED *GREEN LANTERNS* CHARGE THEIR *POWER RINGS* AT THE *CENTRAL POWER BATTERY* FROM WHICH ALL THE SMALLER INDIVIDUAL *POWER BATTERIES* ALL OVER THE COSMOS DRAW THEIR MYSTIC ENERGY...

BY COMING UP HERE TO SAVE US, THE *GREEN LANTERNS* USED UP A GOOD DEAL OF *RING ENERGY*! NOW, BY CHARGING THEIR RINGS AT OUR *MAIN POWER BATTERY* THEY WILL OBTAIN ENOUGH POWER TO SUSTAIN THEM UNTIL THEY REACH THEIR OWN *POWER BATTERIES* AGAIN!

YES! BUT WE STILL HAVE TO DECIDE WHAT TO DO WITH *SINESTRO*...

12.

SOON AFTER, THE RECHARGED **POWER RINGS** OF THE ASSEMBLED **GREEN LANTERNS** ARE PUT TO A COMBINED USE...

ALL TOGETHER NOW... USE YOUR GREEN BEAMS WITH ALL YOUR POWER !!

THERE GOES **SINESTRO**, EXILED INTO SPACE..

AT THE TERRIFIC SPEED WITH WHICH HE HAS BEEN PROPELLED INTO SPACE, **SINESTRO** WILL ORBIT THE UNIVERSE--A JOURNEY THAT WILL TAKE **EIGHTEEN BILLION YEARS** TO COMPLETE ! WE DON'T HAVE TO WORRY ABOUT HIM ANYMORE !

AND SO THE ARCHVILLAIN OF THE COSMOS BEGINS HIS **LAST JOURNEY**, LOCKED INSIDE A SEALED GREEN CAPSULE ARCING HELPLESSLY THROUGH THE VOID...

The End

BUT IS THIS REALLY THE END OF **SINESTRO**--OR WILL HIS SUPER-EVIL MIND FIND SOME WAY TO AVERT HIS FATE ? THIS IS A QUESTION THAT **ONLY TIME**--AND A FUTURE ISSUE OF **GREEN LANTERN**--WILL TELL !

13

GREEN
LANTERN

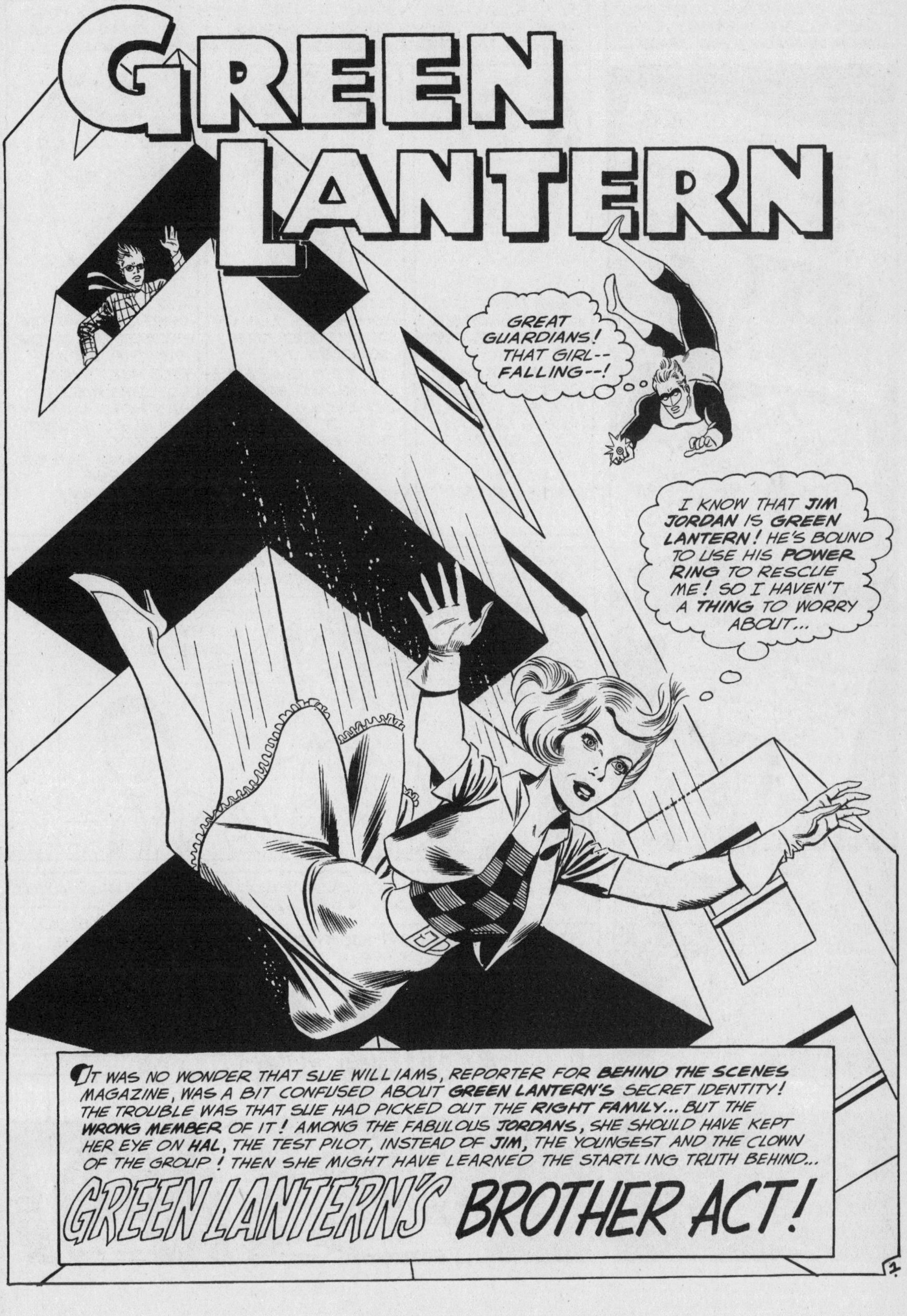
GREEN LANTERN
GREAT GUARDIANS! THAT GIRL-- FALLING--!
I KNOW THAT JIM JORDAN IS GREEN LANTERN! HE'S BOUND TO USE HIS POWER RING TO RESCUE ME! SO I HAVEN'T A THING TO WORRY ABOUT...
IT WAS NO WONDER THAT SUE WILLIAMS, REPORTER FOR BEHIND THE SCENES MAGAZINE, WAS A BIT CONFUSED ABOUT GREEN LANTERN'S SECRET IDENTITY! THE TROUBLE WAS THAT SUE HAD PICKED OUT THE RIGHT FAMILY... BUT THE WRONG MEMBER OF IT! AMONG THE FABULOUS JORDANS, SHE SHOULD HAVE KEPT HER EYE ON HAL, THE TEST PILOT, INSTEAD OF JIM, THE YOUNGEST AND THE CLOWN OF THE GROUP! THEN SHE MIGHT HAVE LEARNED THE STARTLING TRUTH BEHIND...
GREEN LANTERN'S BROTHER ACT!
1

IN THE NEWSPAPERS ON THE WEST COAST, A CERTAIN *FAMILY RE-UNION* IS GIVEN A BIG SPREAD..

Morning Mail 5¢

ONCE AGAIN THE THREE JORDAN BROTHERS COME TOGETHER TO HELP ELECT BROTHER JACK TO OFFICE!

THE POST

AS USUAL THE JORDAN FAMILY WILL BE IN THIS ELECTION ALL THE WAY!

Coast

OPPONENT CLAIMS FOE SAYS HE IS UP AGAINST A TRIO OF JORDANS--NOT JUST ONE!

BUT WHILE THE ENTIRE PACIFIC AREA BUZZES WITH THE LATEST NEWS ABOUT THE FABULOUS JORDANS, LET US, DEAR READER, EXAMINE THE *THREE BROTHERS* A BIT MORE CLOSELY...

FIRST, THERE IS THE **OLDEST BROTHER JACK**--NOW RUNNING FOR DISTRICT ATTORNEY ON A REFORM TICKET! LIKE ALL JORDANS, HE HAS TREMENDOUS ENERGY-- AND A BRILLIANT LEGAL MIND!

SECOND, LET US EXAMINE THE YOUNGEST OF THE TRIO--**JIM JORDAN**! JIM, INCLINED TO BE FUN-LOVING AND HAPPY-GO-LUCKY, IS THE "PET" OF THE OTHER TWO--BUT ALSO VERY SERIOUS ABOUT ELECTING JACK!

AND FINALLY WE COME TO THE **MIDDLE BROTHER**--HAL JORDAN, FAMED FLIER AND TEST PILOT! BUT NOT EVEN HIS TWO BROTHERS KNOW THAT HAL IN HIS **SECRET IDENTITY** IS THE EVEN MORE FAMOUS **GREEN LANTERN**!

SOME DAYS EARLIER, *HAL JORDAN* HAD ALERTED HIS PAL AND CONFIDANT, *PIEFACE*, HIS ESKIMO GREASEMONKEY...

...SO IF ANY EMERGENCY COMES UP FOR ME, EITHER AS HAL JORDAN **OR GREEN LANTERN**-- YOU'LL KNOW WHERE TO REACH ME, PIE?

CHECK, HAL! DON'T WORRY! I'LL COVER YOU!

WHICH EXPLAINS HAL'S PRESENCE NOW AT A TYPICAL FAMILY CONFAB IN HIS BROTHER JACK'S HOUSE NEAR *COAST CITY*...

I'D LIKE TO KNOW WHAT YOU TWO THINK MY CHANCES REALLY ARE IN THIS ELECTION?

SHUCKS, WE'RE A SHOO-IN, JACK! WE CAN'T MISS!

2

YOU WERE, ALWAYS THE IMPETUOUS ONE, JIM! WHAT DO YOU THINK, HAL?

WELL, THE OPPOSITION IS TOUGH, JACK! I WOULDN'T TAKE THEM TOO LIGHTLY!

NOW WE'RE GETTING SOMEWHERE! THE "OUTFIT"-- THE MACHINE THAT RUNS POLITICS IN THIS STATE-- WILL DO ANYTHING TO KEEP THEMSELVES IN POWER! AND I MEAN ANYTHING! WE'LL HAVE TO BE ON OUR TOES EVERY MINUTE TILL ELECTION DAY!

NOW, I'VE GOT THREE SPEAKING DATES TODAY--BUT THOSE PUBLICITY "FLIERS" HAVE TO BE CIRCULATED ALL OVER THE COUNTY! IT'S A DRUDGE JOB BUT--

SAY NO MORE! WE'LL DO IT!

AFTER THE BUSY CANDIDATE HAS LEFT...

HAL, I JUST REMEMBERED! I'VE GOT A DATE WITH A REPORTER OF A POPULAR MAGAZINE TO GIVE JACK PUBLICITY! AND I'M LATE NOW!

THAT'S ALL RIGHT, JIM! YOU GO AHEAD! I'LL TAKE CARE OF THE LEAFLETS!

JIM FEELS BAD ABOUT PASSING THE "DRUDGE JOB" TO ME! HE THINKS I'VE GOT TO LUG THE LEAFLETS DOWN TO THE AIRPORT, HIRE A PLANE AND SO ON! HE DOESN'T KNOW I HAVE...OTHER IDEAS!

AND SOON HIGH IN THE SKY ABOVE COAST COUNTY, A STRIKING EMERALD FIGURE IS WHIRLING FASTER THAN ANY PLANE COULD GO...

THEORETICALLY, I'M ONLY SUPPOSED TO USE MY POWER RING TO COMBAT EVIL... BUT IF THE OUTFIT WE JORDANS ARE OUT TO BEAT IN THIS ELECTION ISN'T EVIL... I DON'T KNOW WHAT IS!

3

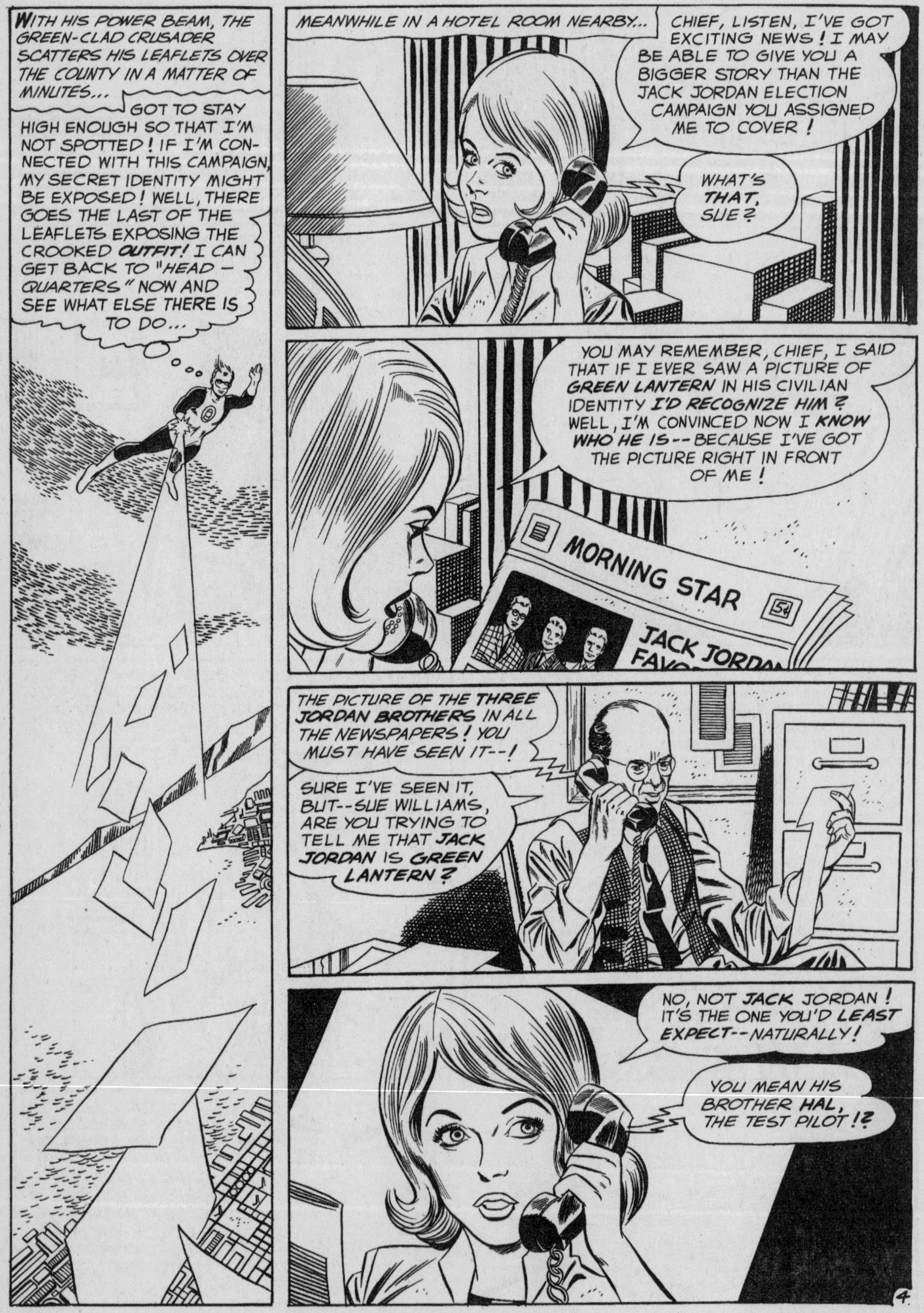

WITH HIS POWER BEAM, THE GREEN-CLAD CRUSADER SCATTERS HIS LEAFLETS OVER THE COUNTY IN A MATTER OF MINUTES...
GOT TO STAY HIGH ENOUGH SO THAT I'M NOT SPOTTED! IF I'M CONNECTED WITH THIS CAMPAIGN, MY SECRET IDENTITY MIGHT BE EXPOSED! WELL, THERE GOES THE LAST OF THE LEAFLETS EXPOSING THE CROOKED OUTFIT! I CAN GET BACK TO "HEAD-QUARTERS" NOW AND SEE WHAT ELSE THERE IS TO DO...
MEANWHILE IN A HOTEL ROOM NEARBY...
CHIEF, LISTEN, I'VE GOT EXCITING NEWS! I MAY BE ABLE TO GIVE YOU A BIGGER STORY THAN THE JACK JORDAN ELECTION CAMPAIGN YOU ASSIGNED ME TO COVER!
WHAT'S THAT, SUE?
YOU MAY REMEMBER, CHIEF, I SAID THAT IF I EVER SAW A PICTURE OF GREEN LANTERN IN HIS CIVILIAN IDENTITY I'D RECOGNIZE HIM? WELL, I'M CONVINCED NOW I KNOW WHO HE IS--BECAUSE I'VE GOT THE PICTURE RIGHT IN FRONT OF ME!
MORNING STAR
5¢
JACK JORDAN
THE PICTURE OF THE THREE JORDAN BROTHERS IN ALL THE NEWSPAPERS! YOU MUST HAVE SEEN IT--!
SURE I'VE SEEN IT, BUT--SUE WILLIAMS, ARE YOU TRYING TO TELL ME THAT JACK JORDAN IS GREEN LANTERN?
NO, NOT JACK JORDAN! IT'S THE ONE YOU'D LEAST EXPECT--NATURALLY!
YOU MEAN HIS BROTHER HAL, THE TEST PILOT!?
4

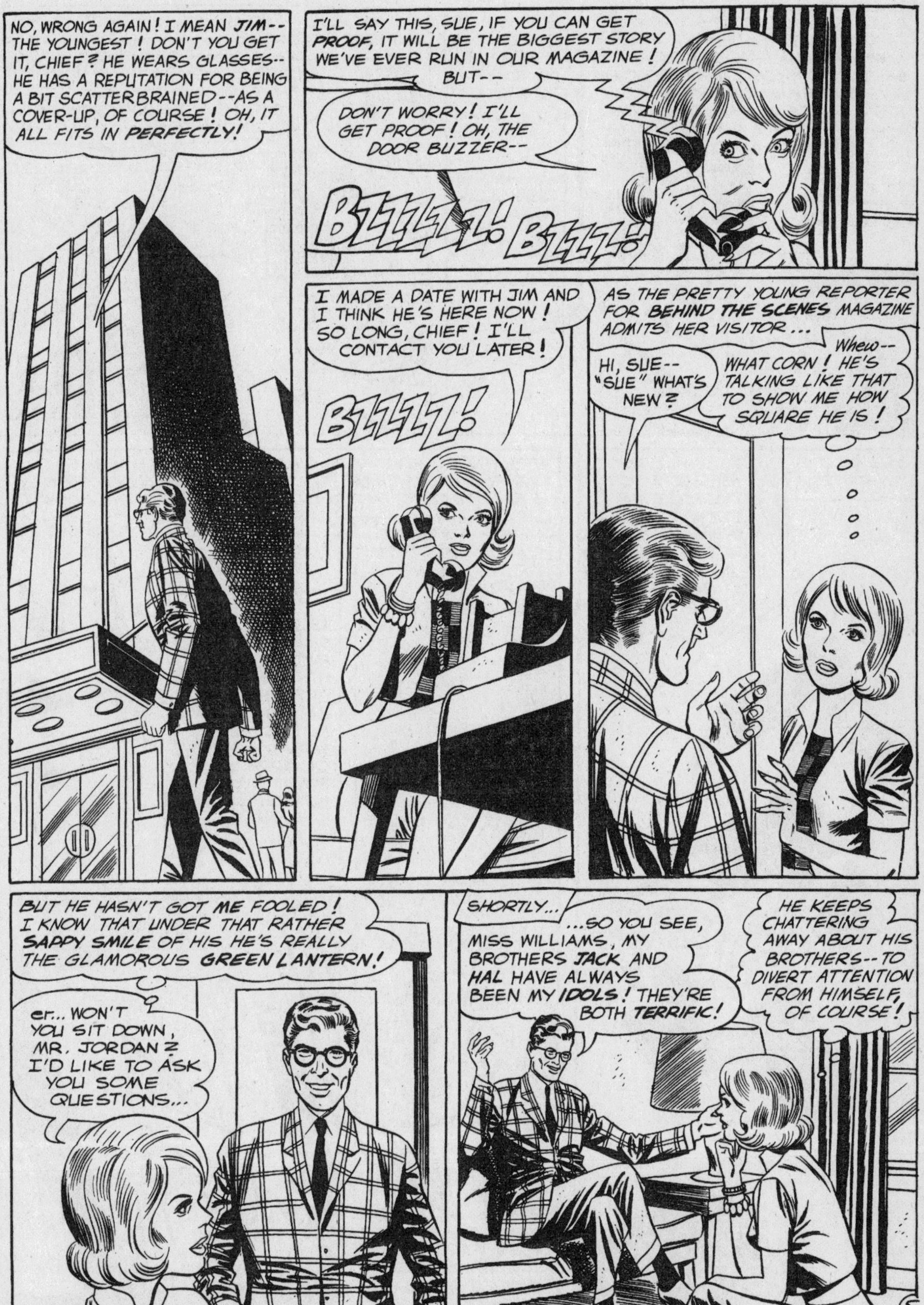
NO, WRONG AGAIN! I MEAN JIM-- THE YOUNGEST! DON'T YOU GET IT, CHIEF? HE WEARS GLASSES-- HE HAS A REPUTATION FOR BEING A BIT SCATTERBRAINED--AS A COVER-UP, OF COURSE! OH, IT ALL FITS IN PERFECTLY!
I'LL SAY THIS, SUE, IF YOU CAN GET PROOF, IT WILL BE THE BIGGEST STORY WE'VE EVER RUN IN OUR MAGAZINE! BUT--
DON'T WORRY! I'LL GET PROOF! OH, THE DOOR BUZZER--
BZZZZZ! BZZZ!
I MADE A DATE WITH JIM AND I THINK HE'S HERE NOW! SO LONG, CHIEF! I'LL CONTACT YOU LATER!
BZZZZ!
AS THE PRETTY YOUNG REPORTER FOR BEHIND THE SCENES MAGAZINE ADMITS HER VISITOR...
HI, SUE-- "SUE" WHAT'S NEW?
Whew-- WHAT CORN! HE'S TALKING LIKE THAT TO SHOW ME HOW SQUARE HE IS!
BUT HE HASN'T GOT ME FOOLED! I KNOW THAT UNDER THAT RATHER SAPPY SMILE OF HIS HE'S REALLY THE GLAMOROUS GREEN LANTERN!
er... WON'T YOU SIT DOWN, MR. JORDAN? I'D LIKE TO ASK YOU SOME QUESTIONS...
SHORTLY...
...SO YOU SEE, MISS WILLIAMS, MY BROTHERS JACK AND HAL HAVE ALWAYS BEEN MY IDOLS! THEY'RE BOTH TERRIFIC!
HE KEEPS CHATTERING AWAY ABOUT HIS BROTHERS--TO DIVERT ATTENTION FROM HIMSELF, OF COURSE!
5.

I SEE I'LL HAVE TO DO SOMETHING DRASTIC! HE'S TOO SMART TO GIVE HIMSELF AWAY! AND I HAVE AN IDEA SWIPED FROM *LOIS LANE'S* ROUTINE WITH *SUPERMAN!* IT'S *RISKY*--BUT IT'S A SUREFIRE WAY TO GET THE PROOF I NEED!

LET'S GO OUT ON THE TERRACE, MR. JORDAN! IT'S COOLER!

AS THE PLUCKY NEWSGIRL PUTS HER DARING SCHEME INTO EFFECT...

ISN'T THERE A WONDERFUL VIEW FROM UP HERE? BY LEANING OUT FAR ENOUGH YOU CAN ACTUALLY SEE *SIERRA MOUNTAINS*--OH!!

THE NEXT INSTANT...

THIS WILL DO IT! HE'S GOT TO RESCUE ME! I DON'T HAVE A THING IN THE WORLD TO WORRY ABOUT! I'VE GOT HIM *TRAPPED!*

AT THAT VERY MOMENT, A LEAFLET-DISTRIBUTOR IS RETURNING TO THE CITY...

GREAT *GUARDIANS!** THAT GIRL--FALLING TOWARD THE GROUND!

*Editor's Note: THE ALIEN RACE IN FAROFF SPACE FROM WHOM *GREEN LANTERN* DRAWS HIS MIGHTY POWER!

LIKE A BLAZE OF EMERALD LIGHTNING, *GREEN LANTERN* STREAKS TOWARD THE SCENE OF DANGER...

≈Whew!≈ I JUST BARELY HAD TIME TO SAVE HER!

WELL, I MUST SAY GL SHAVED IT *RATHER CLOSE!* FOR A MOMENT OR TWO I ALMOST BEGAN TO THINK... BUT NO POINT WORRYING NOW! OBVIOUSLY MY *STUNT* HAS WORKED LIKE A *CHARM!*

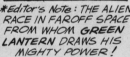

6.

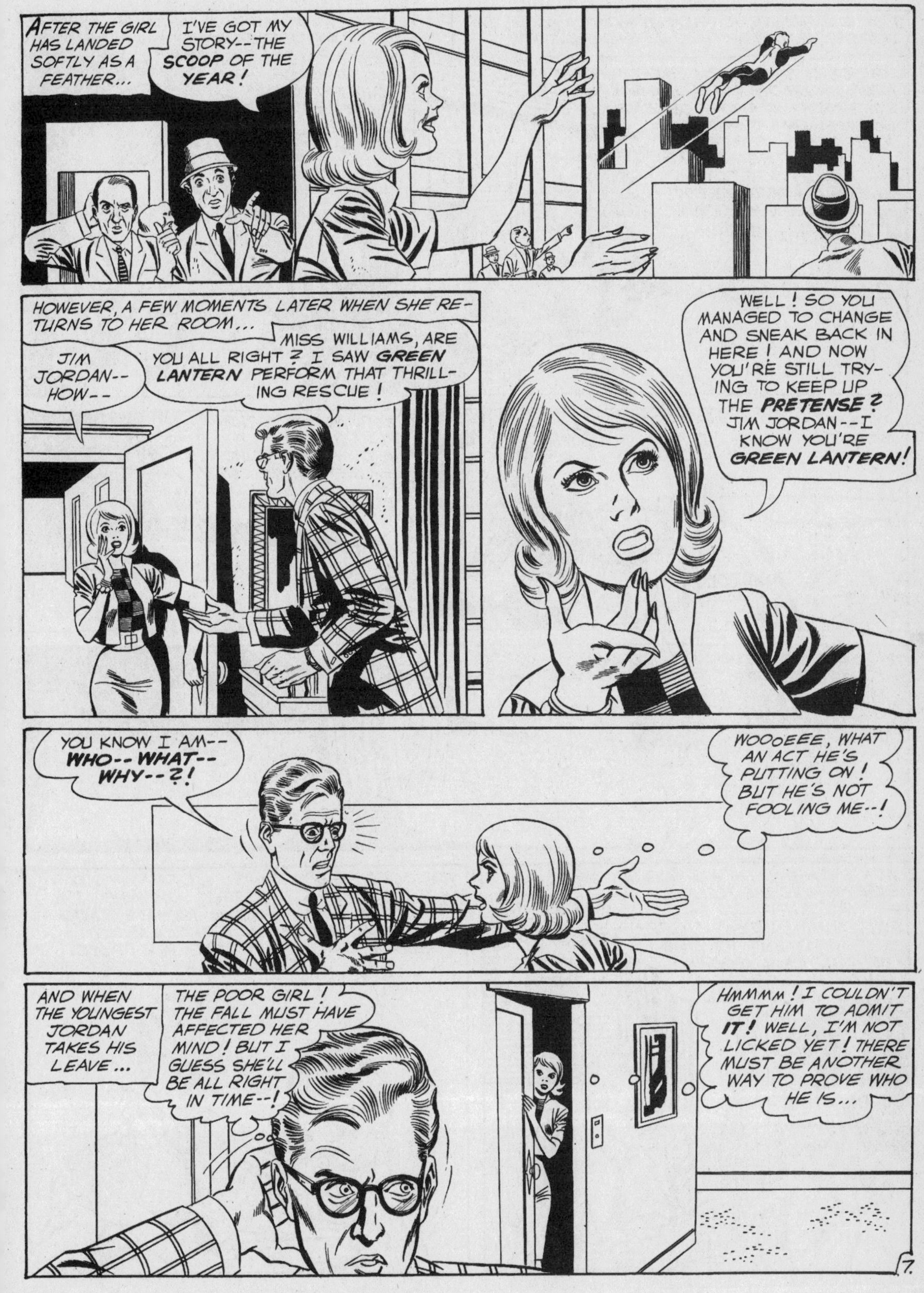
AFTER THE GIRL HAS LANDED SOFTLY AS A FEATHER...
I'VE GOT MY STORY--THE SCOOP OF THE YEAR!
HOWEVER, A FEW MOMENTS LATER WHEN SHE RETURNS TO HER ROOM...
JIM JORDAN--HOW--
MISS WILLIAMS, ARE YOU ALL RIGHT? I SAW GREEN LANTERN PERFORM THAT THRILLING RESCUE!
WELL! SO YOU MANAGED TO CHANGE AND SNEAK BACK IN HERE! AND NOW YOU'RE STILL TRYING TO KEEP UP THE PRETENSE? JIM JORDAN--I KNOW YOU'RE GREEN LANTERN!
YOU KNOW I AM--WHO--WHAT--WHY--?!
WOOoEEE, WHAT AN ACT HE'S PUTTING ON! BUT HE'S NOT FOOLING ME--!
AND WHEN THE YOUNGEST JORDAN TAKES HIS LEAVE...
THE POOR GIRL! THE FALL MUST HAVE AFFECTED HER MIND! BUT I GUESS SHE'LL BE ALL RIGHT IN TIME--!
HMMMM! I COULDN'T GET HIM TO ADMIT IT! WELL, I'M NOT LICKED YET! THERE MUST BE ANOTHER WAY TO PROVE WHO HE IS...
7.

THAT EVENING NEAR *JACK JORDAN'S* HOME, THE JORDAN HEADQUARTERS IN THE ELECTION...

I'M GOING TO SET UP A *TWENTY—FOUR HOUR* WATCH OVER JIM JORDAN! I'LL WATCH HIM *EVERY SECOND!* SOONER OR LATER SOME EMERGENCY IS BOUND TO COME UP REQUIRING HIM TO CHANGE TO HIS *GREEN LANTERN* IDENTITY! AND WHEN HE DOES...

...I'LL CATCH HIM RED-HANDED! AND IF AN EMERGENCY DOESN'T COME UP, I'LL FAKE ONE! I'LL THINK OF *SOMETHING* TO BREAK THIS-- eh ?

AT THAT MOMENT...

WHAT'S ALL THIS ?

DON'T ASK QUESTIONS, PAL ! THIS AIN'T A INFORMATION BUREAU ! *GET IN THE CAR!*

AND SECONDS AFTERWARD...

G-GOLLY! THOSE ARE GANGSTERS ! THEY FORCED *JACK JORDAN* INTO THAT CAR AT GUNPOINT !

WITH THE SPEED OF A STARTLED DEER, SUE STREAKS INTO THE HOUSE...

JIM JORDAN ! LISTEN--THERE ISN'T A MOMENT TO LOSE ! GET INTO YOUR *GREEN LANTERN* COSTUME AT ONCE !

MISS WILLIAMS !?

OH, THE POOR GIRL...

FOR GOODNESS' SAKE, THIS IS NO TIME FOR *PLAY-ACTING!* GET MOVING !

THAT FALL REALLY DID AFFECT HER MIND! I'M GOING TO HAVE TO DO SOMETHING ABOUT GETTING HER TO SEE A DOCTOR !

IN AN ADJOINING ROOM WHERE SUE'S VOICE EASILY CARRIES...

I TELL YOU YOUR BROTHER JACK HAS BEEN SEIZED BY GUNMEN! HE'S IN TERRIBLE DANGER! THEY'RE TAKING HIM FOR A RIDE!

GREAT JUPITER! JACK--IN DANGER!?

ON THE INSTANT, A GRIM HAL JORDAN EXPLODES INTO MOTION...

IT MUST BE THE OUTFIT! JACK SAID THEY'D STOP AT NOTHING TO WIN THE ELECTION-- AND HE WAS RIGHT!

NO USE! HE WON'T BECOME GREEN LANTERN IN FRONT OF ME--THAT'S WHAT IT IS! I'LL GO OUT-- AND GIVE HIM A CHANCE! EVIDENTLY HE'S MORE INTERESTED IN PRO-TECTING HIS IDENTITY-- THAN IN SAVING HIS BROTHER!

AND MOMENTS LATER OUTSIDE...

I THOUGHT SO! AS LONG AS MY BACK WAS TURNED-- HE SWITCHED TO HIS GREEN LANTERN COSTUME! I WONDER JUST WHO JIM JORDAN THINKS HE'S KIDDING!

MEANWHILE...

WHO'S PAYING YOU FOR THIS JOB? WHAT'S HIS NAME?

YOU'RE A REGULAR GROUCHO THE QUESTION-ASKER, AIN'T YOU? BETTER SHADDUP!

AW, WHAT ARE WE WAITIN' FOR, PLUNCHY? LET'S TAKE CARE OF HIM NOW!

NO, THIS HAS GOTTA BE DONE RIGHT, LOOIE--LIKE THEY USED TO DO IT IN THEM OLD GANGSTER MOVIES, REMEMBER?

"SCARFACE"! THE PUBLIC ENEMY! RAT-TAT-TAT! AH, THEM WERE THE GOOD OLD DAYS! WHAT DO THE MUGS YOU SEE NOW ON TELEVISION KNOW ABOUT BUMPING SOMEBODY OFF?

UH-- THIS IS A GOOD PLACE...

THEN, ON A LONELY ROAD...

I WARN YOU TWO! THE ENTIRE LEGAL MACHINERY OF THIS STATE WILL HUNT YOU DOWN-- YOU'LL BE BROUGHT TO JUSTICE!

SAY, THAT SOUNDS GOOD! HE TALKS JUST LIKE THE HERO DID IN THEM OLD MOVIES!

IT PUTS ME IN THE RIGHT MOOD! YEAH, OKAY, JORDAN! TURN AROUND AND START WALKIN'! GIT!

WHY DO WE HAVE TO DRAG THIS OUT, PUNCHY?

WHY?! FOR THE SUSPENSE, YOU SAP! ANOTHER FEW FEET AND HE'LL LOOK BACK-- AND THAT'S WHEN HE GETS IT! DON'T YOU REMEMBER ANYTHIN' LOOIE?

GOT TO MAKE A DIVE FOR THOSE BUSHES...

HE'S RUNNING!

THE CRUM! HE AIN'T FOLLOWING THE SCRIPT! LET HIM HAVE IT!

AT THAT VERY MOMENT, ABOVE...

I SPOTTED THAT AUTO A FEW SECONDS AGO FROM THE AIR! AND-- THE GUNMEN THAT GIRL TALKED ABOUT-- THEY'RE ABOUT TO SHOOT JACK!

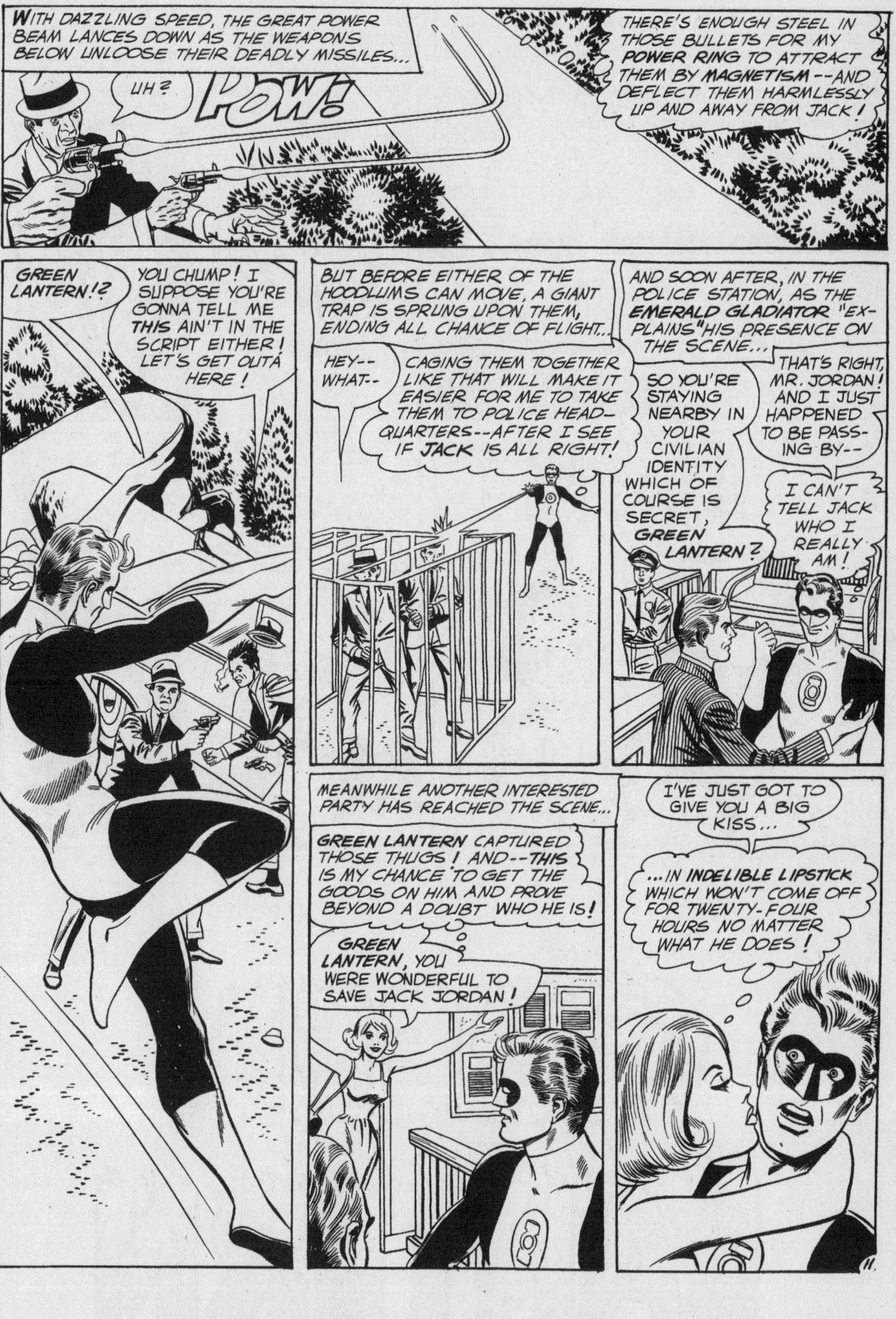
WITH DAZZLING SPEED, THE GREAT POWER BEAM LANCES DOWN AS THE WEAPONS BELOW UNLOOSE THEIR DEADLY MISSILES...
UH?
POW!
THERE'S ENOUGH STEEL IN THOSE BULLETS FOR MY POWER RING TO ATTRACT THEM BY MAGNETISM--AND DEFLECT THEM HARMLESSLY UP AND AWAY FROM JACK!
GREEN LANTERN!?
YOU CHUMP! I SUPPOSE YOU'RE GONNA TELL ME THIS AIN'T IN THE SCRIPT EITHER! LET'S GET OUTA HERE!
BUT BEFORE EITHER OF THE HOODLUMS CAN MOVE, A GIANT TRAP IS SPRUNG UPON THEM, ENDING ALL CHANCE OF FLIGHT...
HEY-- WHAT--
CAGING THEM TOGETHER LIKE THAT WILL MAKE IT EASIER FOR ME TO TAKE THEM TO POLICE HEAD-QUARTERS--AFTER I SEE IF JACK IS ALL RIGHT!
AND SOON AFTER, IN THE POLICE STATION, AS THE EMERALD GLADIATOR "EX-PLAINS" HIS PRESENCE ON THE SCENE...
SO YOU'RE STAYING NEARBY IN YOUR CIVILIAN IDENTITY WHICH OF COURSE IS SECRET, GREEN LANTERN?
THAT'S RIGHT, MR. JORDAN! AND I JUST HAPPENED TO BE PASS-ING BY--
I CAN'T TELL JACK WHO I REALLY AM!
MEANWHILE ANOTHER INTERESTED PARTY HAS REACHED THE SCENE...
GREEN LANTERN CAPTURED THOSE THUGS! AND--THIS IS MY CHANCE TO GET THE GOODS ON HIM AND PROVE BEYOND A DOUBT WHO HE IS!
GREEN LANTERN, YOU WERE WONDERFUL TO SAVE JACK JORDAN!
I'VE JUST GOT TO GIVE YOU A BIG KISS...
...IN INDELIBLE LIPSTICK WHICH WON'T COME OFF FOR TWENTY-FOUR HOURS NO MATTER WHAT HE DOES!
11.

NEXT MORNING BRIGHT AND EARLY, AS SUE VISITS THE JORDAN HOUSE...

I PUT MY MARK ON GREEN LANTERN YESTERDAY! NOW TO MEET JIM JORDAN FACE TO FACE AND HAVE A LOOK AT HIM! ONE WAY OR ANOTHER I'M ABOUT TO KNOW FOR SURE IF HE'S GREEN LANTERN!

BUT WHEN THE YOUNGEST OF THE JORDAN BROTHERS APPEARS...

THAT ADHESIVE TAPE ON YOUR CHEEK!

OH, I--er--CUT MY-SELF SHAVING! BUT...DON'T LOOK SO UNHAPPY, MISS WILLIAMS! IT'S NOTHING SERIOUS!

JUST WHERE I PLANTED THE LIP-STICK!

DE-DUM... DE-DUM... ♪ ♫

MY PLOT FLOPPED! WELL, I'M MORE DETERMINED THAN EVER TO LEARN IF HE'S GREEN LANTERN OR NOT-- EVEN IF I HAVE TO MARRY HIM TO FIND OUT!

AND SEVERAL WEEKS LATER...

WELL, BROTHER JACK HAS WON, THE CROOKED POLITICIANS ARE RUNNING FOR COVER, AND MY SECRET IDENTITY IS STILL SECRET! SO I GUESS YOU COULD SAY ALL'S WELL THAT ENDS WELL,..eh, FOLKS?

COAST NEWS
JACK JORDAN ELECTED DISTRICT ATTORNEY

The End

12

GREEN LANTERN

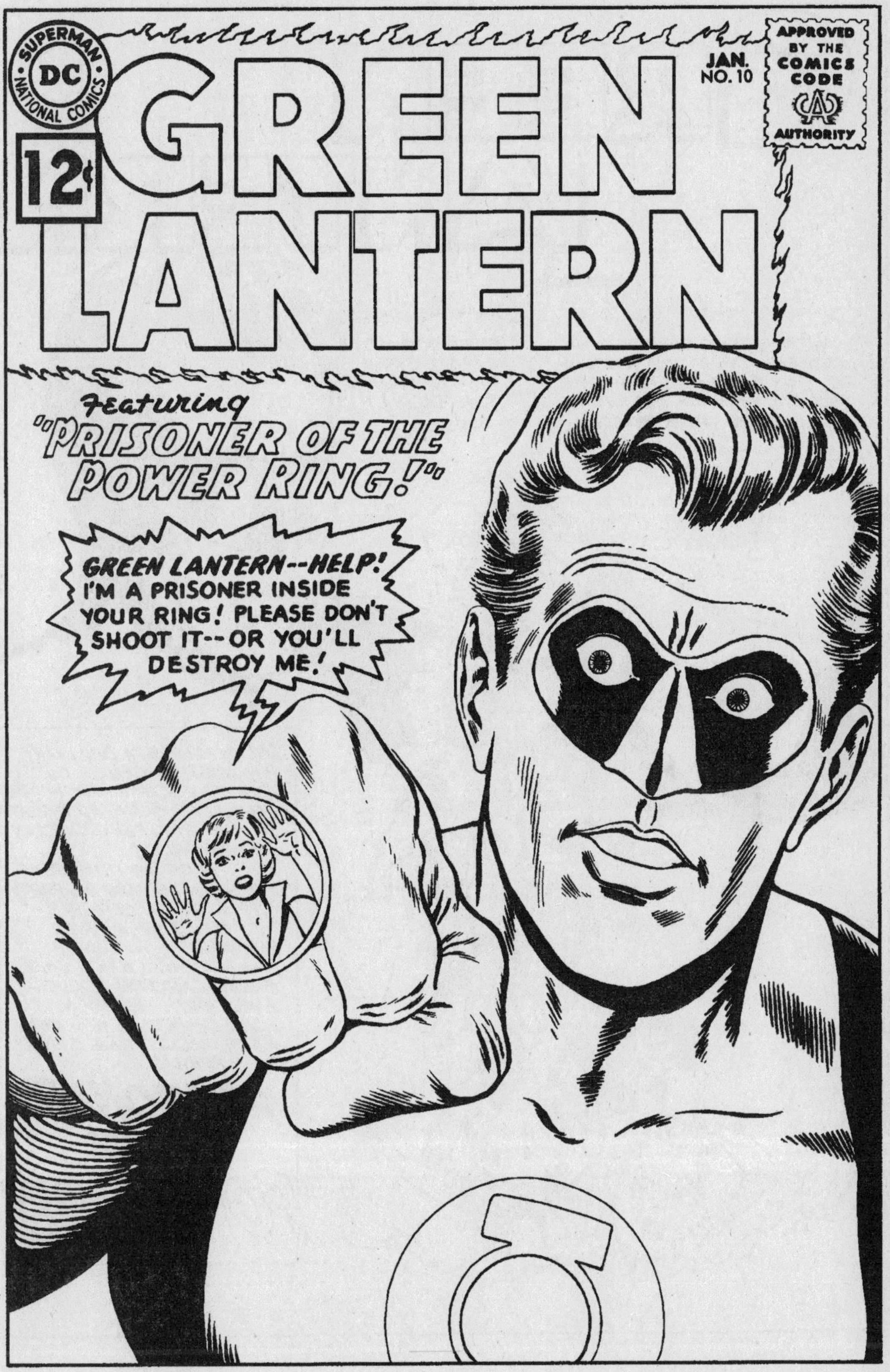
SUPERMAN DC NATIONAL COMICS
12¢
GREEN LANTERN
JAN. NO. 10
APPROVED BY THE COMICS CODE AUTHORITY
Featuring "PRISONER OF THE POWER RING!"
GREEN LANTERN--HELP! I'M A PRISONER INSIDE YOUR RING! PLEASE DON'T SHOOT IT--OR YOU'LL DESTROY ME!

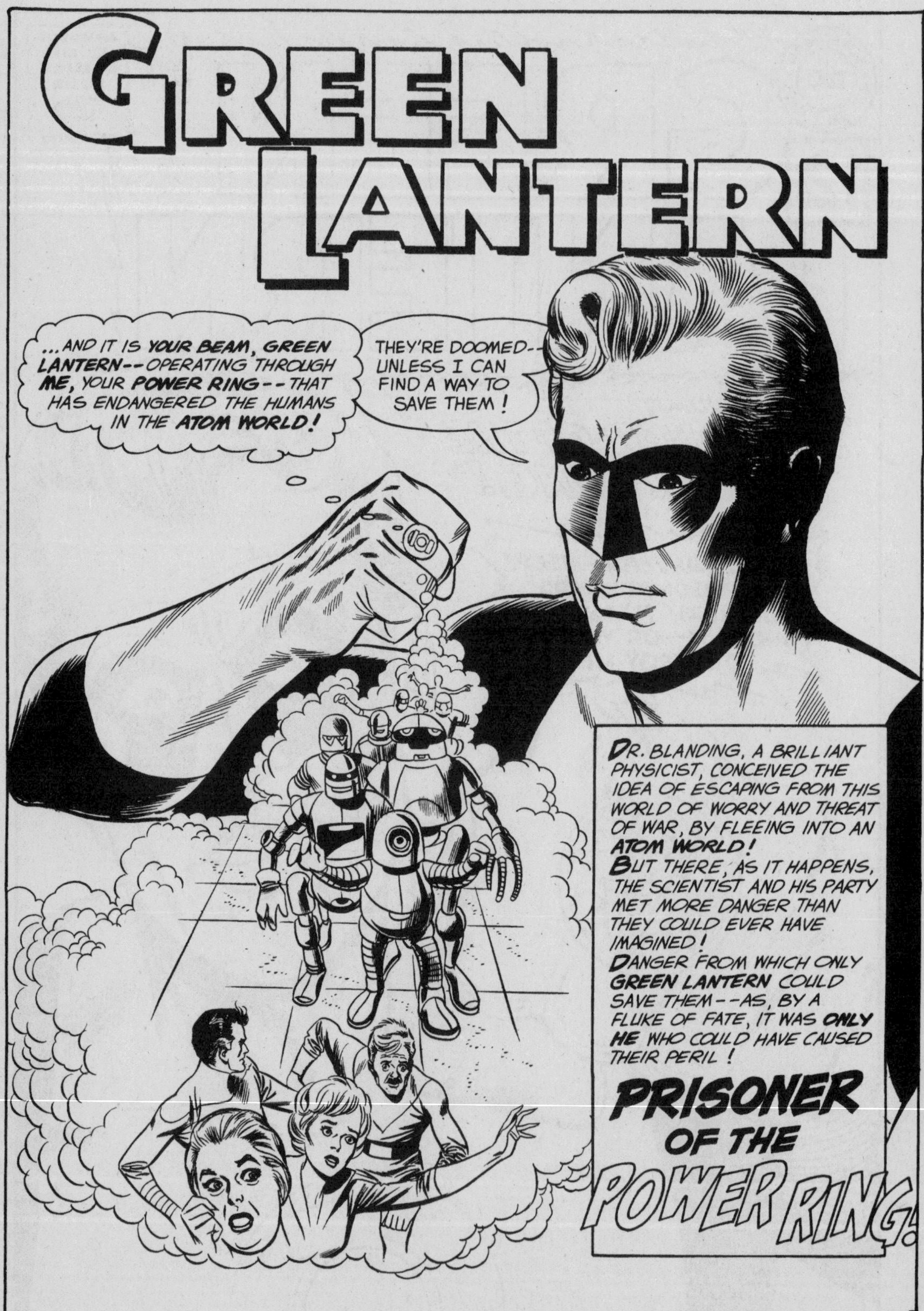
GREEN LANTERN
...AND IT IS YOUR BEAM, GREEN LANTERN--OPERATING THROUGH ME, YOUR POWER RING--THAT HAS ENDANGERED THE HUMANS IN THE ATOM WORLD!
THEY'RE DOOMED--UNLESS I CAN FIND A WAY TO SAVE THEM!
DR. BLANDING, A BRILLIANT PHYSICIST, CONCEIVED THE IDEA OF ESCAPING FROM THIS WORLD OF WORRY AND THREAT OF WAR, BY FLEEING INTO AN ATOM WORLD!
BUT THERE, AS IT HAPPENS, THE SCIENTIST AND HIS PARTY MET MORE DANGER THAN THEY COULD EVER HAVE IMAGINED!
DANGER FROM WHICH ONLY GREEN LANTERN COULD SAVE THEM--AS, BY A FLUKE OF FATE, IT WAS ONLY HE WHO COULD HAVE CAUSED THEIR PERIL!
PRISONER OF THE POWER RING!
1

CRACK TEST PILOT HAL JORDAN (ALIAS *GREEN LANTERN*) PUTS A NEW PLANE THROUGH ITS PACES...

THE WINGS STAND UP FINE UNDER A *15-G* STRESS! THIS BABY CAN REALLY GO!

NOW TO TRY OUT HER RATE-OF-CLIMB AND PERFORMANCE AT HIGH ALTITUDE...

AFTER THE CRAFT HAS MET ALL TESTS, HIGH IN THE STRATO-SPHERE...

EH? WE CHOSE THIS TEST AREA BECAUSE NO MILITARY OR COMMERCIAL PLANES FLY THROUGH HERE! WHERE IS THAT *JET* GOING?

AS A BANKING MANEUVER CARRIES HAL INTO POSITION FOR A BETTER VIEW OF HIS SURPRISE VISITOR...

THAT'S STRANGE! *NO MARKINGS* ON THAT BIRD... WAIT A SECOND! I JUST REMEMBERED SOMETHING! WHAT WAS THAT GOVERNMENT CIRCULAR *PIEFACE* CALLED TO MY ATTENTION YESTERDAY MORNING?

IN HIS MIND'S EYE HAL SEES HIS LITTLE ESKIMO GREASEMONKEY BEFORE HIM, AND HEARS HIM SPEAK...

...SMUGGLERS SNEAK-ING VALUABLE DIAMONDS INTO THIS COUNTRY! WASHINGTON SUSPECTS THAT AN *AIRPLANE* IS BEING USED TO SLIP PAST OUR CUSTOMS GUARDS! ALL AIRFIELDS ARE BEING ALERTED, HAL...

...AND ALL PILOTS ARE ASKED TO BE ON THE LOOKOUT FOR ANY FAST-MOVING UNIDENTIFIED CRAFT!

FAST-MOVING... UNIDENTI-FIED... THIS ONE SEEMS TO *FIT THE BILL!*

2

WITH QUIET DECISION, THE ACE FLYER POINTS HIS PLANE AFTER THE DISAPPEARING JET...

THAT BIRD CAN GO... BUT THIS BABY UNDER ME IS SO FAST, I'LL HAVE *NO TROUBLE* KEEPING IT IN VIEW! GOT TO FIND OUT *WHERE* IT'S HEADING..!

AND SOON, MAINTAINING ALTITUDE TO AVOID ALARMING HIS QUARRY, HAL SEES...

LANDING ON WHAT LOOKS LIKE A DRIED-OUT LAKE IN THE MIDDLE OF THESE MOUNTAINS!? WELL, IF IT CAN GO DOWN, *SO CAN I!*

AS THE INTREPID ACE CARRIES OUT HIS OBJECTIVE EXPERTLY...

I'M LANDING ON A CORNER OF THE LAKE OUT OF SIGHT OF THE OTHER PLANE! I DON'T WANT THEM TO SEE ME UNTIL I'M READY...

AND MOMENTS LATER...

SOMETHING TELLS ME I'M ABOUT TO CATCH A CREW OF *DIAMOND SMUGGLERS* RED-HANDED! OR RATHER-- THAT *GREEN LANTERN* IS ABOUT TO! THERE WOULD BE *NO HONEST REASON* FOR THAT PLANE TO COME DOWN HERE!

BUT, THEN, AS THE *EMERALD CRUSADER* IS ABOUT TO USE HIS MIGHTY *POWER BEAM* TO CATAPULT OFF...

DON'T USE YOUR RING!

GREAT GUARDIANS! THAT TELEPATHIC VOICE! IT'S COMING FROM--

GREEN LANTERN! PLEASE DON'T USE YOUR RING--OR YOU'LL DESTROY ME!

A GIRL INSIDE MY RING!?

3.

YOU-- UHH... SHE--SHE SEEMS TO HAVE **FAINTED!** BUT WHAT DID SHE MEAN-- I MUSTN'T USE MY RING OR I WOULD **DESTROY** HER?

IN HIS PERPLEXITY, THE MIND OF THE GREEN-CLAD CRUSADER WORKS SWIFTLY...

I'VE STILL GOT TO CATCH THOSE SMUGGLERS, BUT NOW I DON'T DARE USE MY RING! MY BEST BET IS TO GO AFTER THE CROOKS WITH MY BARE HANDS, AND THEN... AFTERWARDS...

...TRY TO FIND OUT **WHO** THE GIRL IS AND HOW IN THE WORLD SHE GOT **INTO MY RING!** MAYBE WHEN SHE REVIVES SHE'LL BE ABLE TO TELL ME! I SURE HOPE SO!

SOON... LOADING BOXES FROM THE PLANE INTO AN AUTO! IF THIS CREW ISN'T CROOKED, THEY'VE SURE GOT **ALL THE EAR-MARKS!**

LOOK!

GREEN LANTERN!?

DRAWING GUNS! GOT TO GET INTO CLOSE QUARTERS WITH THEM FAST-- MAKE IT HARD FOR THEM TO USE THEIR WEAPONS!

WITH DEVASTATING EFFECT, A GREEN-STREAKED METEOR ERUPTS AMONG THE WOULD-BE KILLERS...

I'M GETTING OUT OF HERE!

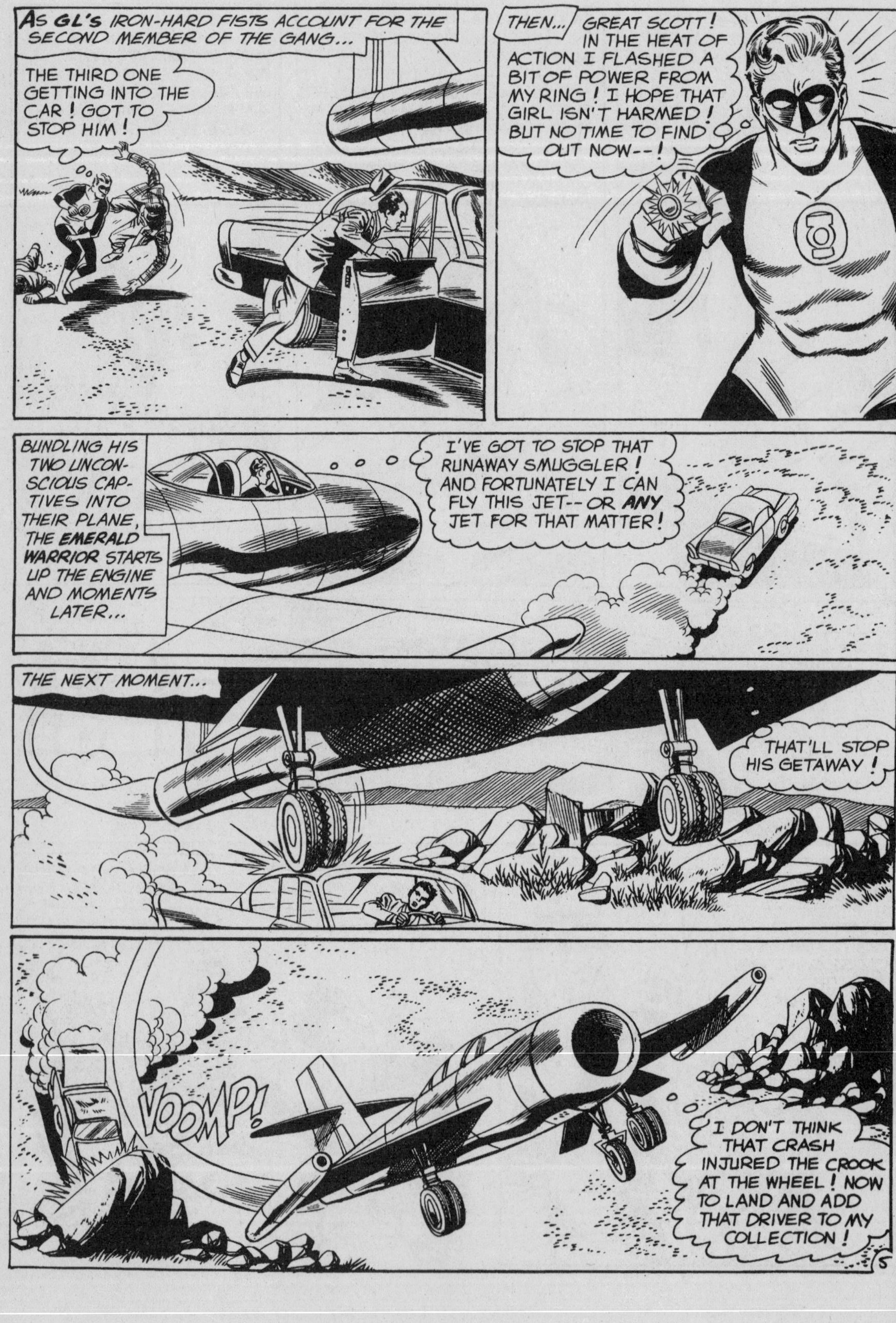
AS GL'S IRON-HARD FISTS ACCOUNT FOR THE SECOND MEMBER OF THE GANG...
THE THIRD ONE GETTING INTO THE CAR! GOT TO STOP HIM!
THEN...
GREAT SCOTT! IN THE HEAT OF ACTION I FLASHED A BIT OF POWER FROM MY RING! I HOPE THAT GIRL ISN'T HARMED! BUT NO TIME TO FIND OUT NOW--!
BUNDLING HIS TWO UNCONSCIOUS CAPTIVES INTO THEIR PLANE, THE EMERALD WARRIOR STARTS UP THE ENGINE AND MOMENTS LATER...
I'VE GOT TO STOP THAT RUNAWAY SMUGGLER! AND FORTUNATELY I CAN FLY THIS JET--OR ANY JET FOR THAT MATTER!
THE NEXT MOMENT...
THAT'LL STOP HIS GETAWAY!
VOOMP!
I DON'T THINK THAT CRASH INJURED THE CROOK AT THE WHEEL! NOW TO LAND AND ADD THAT DRIVER TO MY COLLECTION!
5

AND SHORTLY, WITH ALL THREE OF THE GANG MADE HELPLESS AND STOWED SAFELY IN THE JET, GREEN LANTERN USES HIS OWN PLANE RADIO TO CONTACT NEARBY POLICE...

FIND THE GANG TIED UP! I'VE GIVEN YOU THE *MAP COORDINATES* OF THIS SPOT, SO YOU CAN'T MISS IT!

...AND YOU'LL BE THERE IN AN HOUR, *GREEN LANTERN!* THANKS!

WE'LL BE THERE IN AN HOUR, *GREEN LANTERN!* THANKS!

WELL, THAT TAKES CARE OF THOSE SMUGGLERS! NOW TO FIND OUT ABOUT THAT GIRL IN MY RING!

SHE--SHE'S GONE! I COULDN'T HAVE DREAMED SHE WAS THERE! I SAW HER--SHE SPOKE TO ME! BUT WHERE IS SHE NOW?

AS THE GLADIATOR PUZZLES OVER THE STRANGE PROBLEM...

I CAN'T SEEM TO GET THAT GIRL OFF MY MIND! DID THAT BURST OF GREEN BEAM I ACCIDENTALLY SHOT OUT DESTROY HER? WHERE DID SHE COME FROM? HOW DID SHE GET INTO MY RING? I'VE *GOT* TO FIND OUT!

SUDDENLY AN IDEA COMES TO THE EMERALD CRUSADER...

MY RING IS SUPPOSED TO BE ABLE TO DO *ANYTHING!* WHAT WILL HAPPEN IF I *WILL* IT TO TELL ME ABOUT THE GIRL THAT WAS INSIDE IT!? I'VE NEVER ATTEMPTED ANYTHING LIKE THAT WITH THE RING, BUT IT'S WORTH A TRY!

OUT OF THE VIGOROUS GREEN-CLAD HERO POURS A POWERFUL THOUGHT IMPULSE...

POWER RING, TELL ME ABOUT THE GIRL! I WANT TO KNOW ALL ABOUT HER!

WILL THIS WORK? WILL THE RING BE ABLE TO REPLY..?

6.

THEN, AS GL'S HEART BOUNDS JOYOUSLY...

THE RING IS BEGINNING TO ANSWER ME--!

...HER NAME IS BEVERLY BLANDING!... I CAN TELL YOU ABOUT HER...BECAUSE DURING THE TIME SHE WAS INSIDE ME...I ABSORBED THE EMANATIONS FROM HER BRAIN!

BUT IN ORDER TO DESCRIBE... HOW SHE CAME TO BE INSIDE ME...I MUST FIRST TELL YOU ABOUT HER FATHER, DR. JASON BLANDING, THE PHYSICIST! EIGHT MONTHS AGO IN THEIR HOME IN THE WEST...

"...DR. BLANDING CAME ACROSS A REMARKABLE DISCOVERY..."

THIS NEW **MESON RADIATION** I'VE DEVELOPED HAS THE AMAZING ABILITY TO SHRINK LIVING CREATURES DOWN TO IN-FINITESIMAL SIZE-- WITHOUT HARMING THEM!

"AS THE BRILLIANT SCIENTIST PORED OVER HIS DISCOVERY.."

NO DOUBT OF IT! BY MY CAL-CULATIONS, THE CAT LANDED UNHURT IN AN ATOMIC WORLD-- A WORLD MUCH LIKE OURS, BUT **INSIDE THE ATOM**! AND **THAT** GIVES ME AN IDEA...!

"LATER, DR. BLANDING BROACHED A STARTLING PROPOSAL TO HIS FAMILY, HIS WIFE AND DAUGHTER BEVERLY..."

...YOU BOTH KNOW THAT FOR YEARS I'VE DREAMED OF GETTING AWAY FROM THIS LIFE WHERE WAR AND CONFLICT ALWAYS THREATEN US! NOW WE HAVE AN OPPORTUNITY! WE CAN GO INTO THE **ATOMIC WORLD**--TO LIVE THE REST OF OUR YEARS IN PEACE AND CONTENTMENT! WILL YOU TWO COME WITH ME?

"MRS. BLANDING AND BEVERLY AGREED! BUT THERE WAS A HITCH, IN THE PERSON OF WILL CHAMBERS, BEVERLY'S BOY FRIEND..."

I CAN'T LET YOU TAKE BEV AWAY FROM ME, DR. BLANDING! I LOVE HER--I CAN'T BEAR TO LOSE HER!

IN THAT CASE, MY BOY, THE ANSWER IS SIMPLE! YOU CAN COME WITH US!

7.

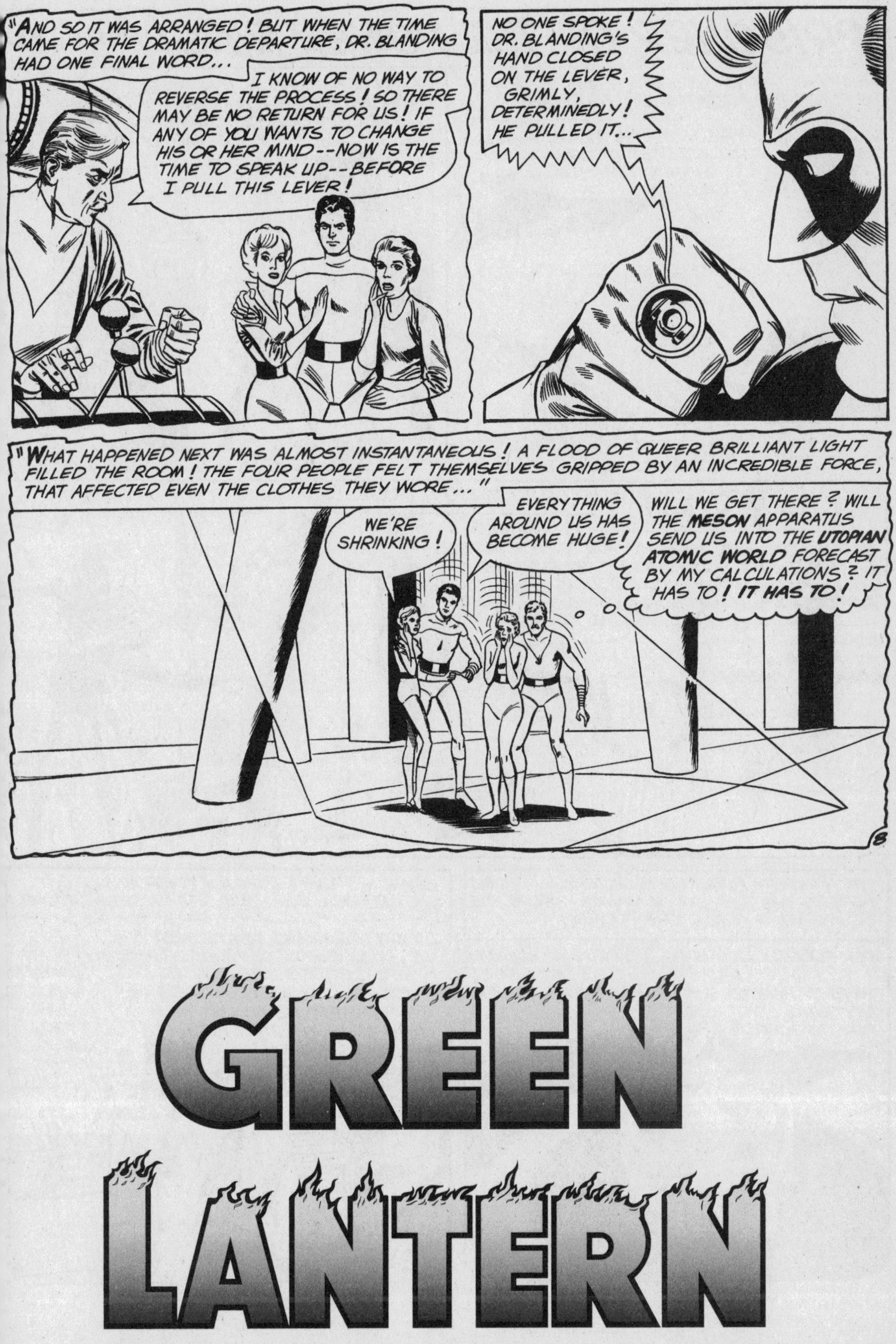
"AND SO IT WAS ARRANGED! BUT WHEN THE TIME CAME FOR THE DRAMATIC DEPARTURE, DR. BLANDING HAD ONE FINAL WORD...
I KNOW OF NO WAY TO REVERSE THE PROCESS! SO THERE MAY BE NO RETURN FOR US! IF ANY OF YOU WANTS TO CHANGE HIS OR HER MIND--NOW IS THE TIME TO SPEAK UP--BEFORE I PULL THIS LEVER!
NO ONE SPOKE! DR. BLANDING'S HAND CLOSED ON THE LEVER, GRIMLY, DETERMINEDLY! HE PULLED IT...
"WHAT HAPPENED NEXT WAS ALMOST INSTANTANEOUS! A FLOOD OF QUEER BRILLIANT LIGHT FILLED THE ROOM! THE FOUR PEOPLE FELT THEMSELVES GRIPPED BY AN INCREDIBLE FORCE, THAT AFFECTED EVEN THE CLOTHES THEY WORE..."
WE'RE SHRINKING!
EVERYTHING AROUND US HAS BECOME HUGE!
WILL WE GET THERE? WILL THE MESON APPARATUS SEND US INTO THE UTOPIAN ATOMIC WORLD FORECAST BY MY CALCULATIONS? IT HAS TO! IT HAS TO!
8

GREEN LANTERN

PRISONER OF THE POWER RING! PART TWO

"AND WHEN THE MIST DISSOLVED FROM BEFORE THE EYES OF THE ADVENTUROUS FOURSOME..."

WE'RE SAFE! THANK GOODNESS!

SO THIS IS IT-- THE ATOMIC WORLD PREDICTED BY MY EQUATIONS! LISTEN, EVERYONE...

FROM NOW ON WE WILL PROCEED TO CONSTRUCT A **SCIENTIFIC UTOPIA** WHERE ALL OF US --AND ULTIMATELY OUR DESCENDANTS --WILL LIVE IN PEACE AND HARMONY!

"AND INDEED WITHIN SIX MONTHS DR. BLANDING'S DREAM SEEMED IN A FAIR WAY TOWARD COMPLETE FULFILLMENT..."

IT'S AMAZING WHAT YOU'VE DONE HERE IN A MATTER OF MONTHS, SIR! NOT ONLY DO WE HAVE SHELTER AND A GOOD FOOD SUPPLY--BUT YOU'VE BUILT THOSE **ROBOTS** WHICH ARE NOW CARRYING ON MOST OF THE WORK!

COMING HERE GAVE ME A BURST OF **CREATIVE ENERGY**, WILL! BUT YOU AND BEVERLY HAVE HELPED ME A LOT-- LET'S NOT FOR- GET THAT!

"THE ROBOTS--POWERED BY INTERNAL ATOMIC MOTORS BUILT BY DR. BLANDING --WERE THE SCIENTIST'S PRIZE CREATIONS..."

YOUR ROBOTS DO EVERY- THING FOR US, DAD! THERE'S HARDLY ANYTHING LEFT FOR US TO DO!

THAT IS A SCIENTIFIC UTOPIA, MY DEAR! ARE YOU COMPLAINING?

"BEVERLY WASN'T EXACTLY COMPLAINING, BUT SHE AND WILL DID HAVE CERTAIN RESERVATIONS.."

I KNOW DAD MEANS WHAT'S BEST FOR US, WILL, BUT I CAN'T HELP FEELING HE'S LETTING THE ROBOTS DO **TOO MUCH**! AND NOW HE'S EVEN **ARMED** SOME OF THEM WITH WEAPONS THAT HE'S MADE!

I'VE BEEN WORRIED ABOUT THAT TOO, BEV...

9

YOUR DAD FEELS WE'VE NEVER EXPLORED THIS ATOMIC WORLD COMPLETELY-- AND THERE **MAY** BE ENEMIES HERE TO THREATEN US! HE SAYS THE ROBOTS WILL PROTECT US!

YES... BUT IT STILL MAKES ME UNCOMFORTABLE TO SEE THEM WITH WEAPONS!

"*IT* WAS SOON AFTER THAT THE STRANGE THINGS BEGAN TO HAPPEN..."

THAT'S ODD! THE ROBOTS SEEM TO BE **FIGHTING** AMONG THEMSELVES !?

"THE NEXT MOMENT..."

GOOD GOSH! ONE OF THE QUARRELING ROBOTS HAS **SHOT THE OTHER ONE!**

"LATER, A GRIM QUARTET OF HUMANS HELD A COUNCIL PRESIDED OVER BY THE SCIENTIST..."

SOMETHING IS TERRIBLY WRONG WITH OUR ROBOTS! BUT I THINK I'VE TRACED THE TROUBLE! FROM SOMEWHERE --PROBABLY FROM THE WORLD WE LEFT BEHIND...

"A TRICKLE OF MYSTERIOUS **GREEN RADIATION** IS FILTERING DOWN INTO OUR ATOMIC WORLD! SO FAR IT HAS NO EFFECT ON **US** --BUT IT IS DERANGING THE MECHANISM OF THE ROBOTS! OUR ENTIRE EXISTENCE HERE IS IN DANGER!

THERE'S NO TELLING WHAT THE ROBOTS WILL DO NEXT! AND WE MAY NOT BE ABLE TO STOP THEM! THERE'S ONLY ONE WAY TO SAVE OURSELVES! WE MUST FIND OUT THE **SOURCE** OF THE **GREEN ENERGY**-- AND CUT IT OFF AT ALL COSTS!

"DR. BLANDING WORKED WITH FEVERISH HASTE, AND SOON...!"

THERE'S NO TIME TO EXPLAIN MY NEW MACHINE TO YOU, BEVERLY! ALL I CAN TELL YOU IS THIS: IT SHOULD *PROJECT ME BODILY* BACK ALONG THE PATH OF THE INCOMING MYSTERY RAYS, SO THAT I CAN FIND OUT WHERE THEY'RE COMING FROM!

I DON'T WANT TO WORRY THE OTHERS! OF COURSE, THIS ATTEMPT IS DANGEROUS! BUT I'M DETERMINED TO TRY IT!

STAND BACK-- I'M GOING TO WALK UNDER THE RADIATION BEAM!

"BUT THEN...!"

NO, FATHER! YOU'RE TOO VALUABLE HERE! IF ANYONE MAKES THIS DANGEROUS ATTEMPT TO SAVE US-- LET IT BE ME!

BEVERLY! WHAT--?

"AND THE NEXT MOMENT...!"

BEVERLY! SHE STEPPED UNDER THE RADIATION-BEAM! SHE'S BEGINNING TO *DISAPPEAR!*

"DR. BLANDING'S DEVICE WORKED PERFECTLY! IT PROJECTED BEVERLY BACK ALONG THE 'MYSTERIOUS GREEN ENERGY' UNTIL FINALLY SHE CAME TO REST... *INSIDE ME!!*"

PLEASE DON'T USE YOUR RING-- OR YOU'LL *DESTROY ME!!*

GREAT GUARDIANS! THEN-- WHAT HAPPENED TO THE GIRL? WHERE IS SHE?

WHEN YOU FIRED OFF THAT TINY SPURT OF POWER FROM YOUR RING A WHILE AGO IT CATAPULTED HER BACK TO HER FATHER'S LABORATORY! SHE'S UNCONSCIOUS-- BUT NOT FATALLY HURT!

11

GRIMLY, *GREEN LANTERN* MAKES UP HIS MIND ON THE INSTANT...

 I'VE GOT TO MAKE SURE SHE'S ALL RIGHT! AND THE ONLY WAY TO DO THAT IS TO USE MY *POWER BEAM* TO GO DOWN INTO THE *ATOMIC WORLD* MYSELF!

POWERED BY HIS ALL-POWERFUL EMERALD RAY, HE IS SOON ON HIS WAY TOWARD HIS OBJECTIVE...

DR. BLANDING NEEDED A *MESON APPARATUS* TO REACH THE ATOM WORLD, BUT I CAN DO THE SAME THING MORE SIMPLY WITH MY RING! THE ATOMS OF EARTH AROUND ME NOW ARE HUGE...

MEANWHILE... BEVERLY, ARE YOU ALL RIGHT?

IT WAS MOSTLY *SHOCK* THAT MADE ME LOSE CONSCIOUSNESS, DAD! BUT I'M FEELING BETTER!

AS THE YOUNG GIRL REVEALS HER DISCOVERY...

THEN IT WAS THE BEAM FROM *GREEN LANTERN'S* RING--FILTERING DOWN HERE--WHICH CAUSED OUR ROBOTS TO RUN AMUCK?

YES! BUT--WHAT'S THAT!?

DARTING OUT-OF-DOORS, THEY VIEW A FEARSOME SIGHT...

THE ROBOTS--THEY'VE DIVIDED INTO TWO GROUPS-- TWO *ARMIES*--AND ARE MAKING WAR ON EACH OTHER!?

YES!

BUT I HAVEN'T TOLD ANY- ONE THE WORST YET! A DEADLY RADIATION IS BUILD- ING UP IN EACH ROBOT! THEY'RE COMPLETELY OUT OF CONTROL! AND WHEN THE RADIATION REACHES A CERTAIN POINT THEY'LL EXPLODE--WITH ATOMIC FORCE--AND BLOW UP THIS WORLD!

BUT AT THE SAME TIME *GREEN LANTERN*, LANDING IN THE ATOMIC WORLD, HAS REACHED THE SAME CONCLUSIONS!

ACCORDING TO WHAT MY RING HAS DETECTED, EACH OF THESE ROBOTS IS ON THE VERGE OF *EXPLODING*!! I'VE GOT TO SAVE DR. BLANDING AND THE OTHER HUMANS HERE FROM BEING DESTROYED!

AT ONCE THE GREEN-CLAD CHAMPION PLUNGES INTO ACTION...

MY ONLY CHANCE IS TO DESTROY THESE WARRING ROBOTS AS FAST AS POSSIBLE! THERE GOES ONE...!

...AND ANOTHER!

THAT HUMAN--IS OUR ENEMY! WE MUST FIGHT HIM--

EH? NOW THEY'VE SUDDENLY STOPPED FIGHTING AMONG THEMSELVES--AND TURNED ON ME! BULLETS--MISSILES--FLYING AT ME FROM EVERY SIDE!

ZIIP!

VHIP!

ZIIP!

IN HIS CRISIS OF PERIL, *GREEN LANTERN* POURS EVERY OUNCE OF WILLPOWER BEHIND HIS MARVELOUS RING FOR A DIE-HARD EFFORT...

MY RING IS RETURNING THE DEADLY GUNFIRE AIMED AT ME--SHOOTING IT BACK AT THE ROBOTS WITH EVEN GREATER SPEED THAN IT CAME FROM THEM!

WHAAP!

ZIING!

ZZZIIIIPP!

13

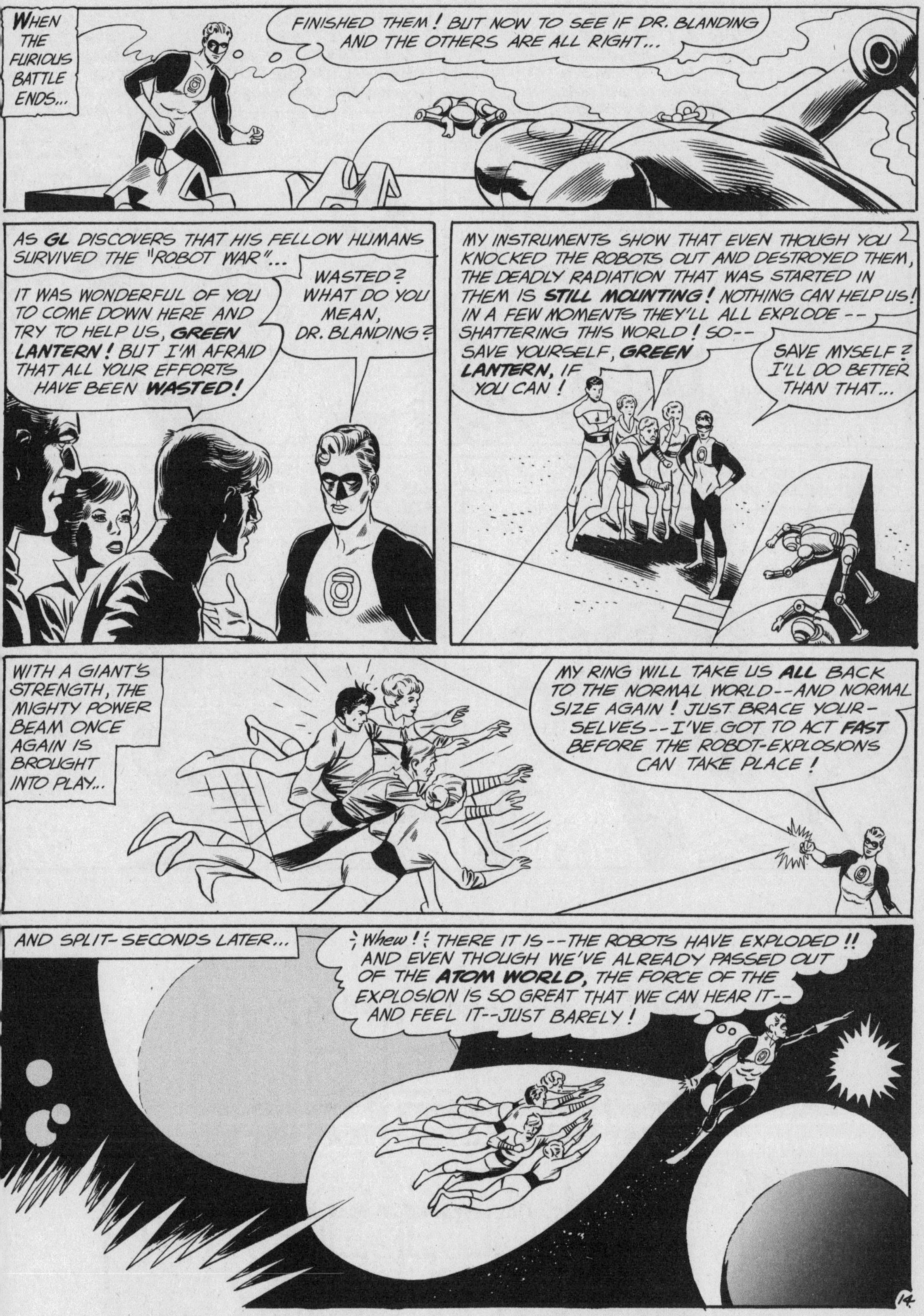
WHEN THE FURIOUS BATTLE ENDS...
FINISHED THEM! BUT NOW TO SEE IF DR. BLANDING AND THE OTHERS ARE ALL RIGHT...
AS GL DISCOVERS THAT HIS FELLOW HUMANS SURVIVED THE "ROBOT WAR"...
IT WAS WONDERFUL OF YOU TO COME DOWN HERE AND TRY TO HELP US, GREEN LANTERN! BUT I'M AFRAID THAT ALL YOUR EFFORTS HAVE BEEN WASTED!
WASTED? WHAT DO YOU MEAN, DR. BLANDING?
MY INSTRUMENTS SHOW THAT EVEN THOUGH YOU KNOCKED THE ROBOTS OUT AND DESTROYED THEM, THE DEADLY RADIATION THAT WAS STARTED IN THEM IS STILL MOUNTING! NOTHING CAN HELP US! IN A FEW MOMENTS THEY'LL ALL EXPLODE -- SHATTERING THIS WORLD! SO-- SAVE YOURSELF, GREEN LANTERN, IF YOU CAN!
SAVE MYSELF? I'LL DO BETTER THAN THAT...
WITH A GIANT'S STRENGTH, THE MIGHTY POWER BEAM ONCE AGAIN IS BROUGHT INTO PLAY...
MY RING WILL TAKE US ALL BACK TO THE NORMAL WORLD--AND NORMAL SIZE AGAIN! JUST BRACE YOURSELVES--I'VE GOT TO ACT FAST BEFORE THE ROBOT-EXPLOSIONS CAN TAKE PLACE!
AND SPLIT-SECONDS LATER...
Whew!! THERE IT IS--THE ROBOTS HAVE EXPLODED!! AND EVEN THOUGH WE'VE ALREADY PASSED OUT OF THE ATOM WORLD, THE FORCE OF THE EXPLOSION IS SO GREAT THAT WE CAN HEAR IT-- AND FEEL IT--JUST BARELY!
14

WITH THE JOURNEY BACK SUCCESSFULLY COMPLETED, AND AFTER ALL HAVE REGAINED NORMAL SIZE...

SO THAT'S THE END OF MY DREAM! WELL, THIS EXPERIENCE HAS TAUGHT ME SOMETHING, *GREEN LANTERN*! I'VE DECIDED IT'S *BETTER* TO LIVE IN THIS WORLD OF OURS AND FIGHT FOR PEACE--RATHER THAN TO TRY TO ESCAPE TO A *UTOPIA*--HOWEVER TEMPTING IT SOUNDS!

I AGREE!

I'M GLAD TO BE BACK TOO! THERE'S NOT ENOUGH TO DO IN A UTOPIA! I'M LOOKING FORWARD TO GETTING TO *WORK* AGAIN!

YOU'RE LOOKING FORWARD TO *SOMETHING ELSE* TOO, AREN'T YOU, WILL?

WITH ONE MIND, THE TWO YOUNG PEOPLE TURN TO THE *EMERALD GLADIATOR*...

WE DON'T KNOW HOW TO THANK YOU, *GREEN LANTERN*! BUT BEFORE YOU LEAVE, WE HAVE ONE LAST REQUEST TO MAKE OF YOU!

A LAST REQUEST? WHAT'S THAT?

AS THE JETPLANE CARRYING ACE TEST PILOT HAL JORDAN FLIES BACK TOWARD *FERRIS FIELD* LATER THAT DAY...

I'LL HAVE TO INVENT AN EXCUSE TO EXPLAIN WHY I HAVEN'T CONTACTED THE FIELD ALL MORNING! BUT ALSO I MUSTN'T FORGET ONE OTHER THING--THAT *GREEN LANTERN* HAS A DATE TO BE *BEST MAN* AT THE WEDDING OF WILL CHAMBERS AND BEVERLY BLANDING--ONE WEEK FROM TODAY!

The End

GREEN LANTERN

"IN BRIGHTEST DAY, IN BLACKEST NIGHT..." FAMILIAR WORDS--FROM GREEN LANTERN'S FAMOUS OATH TAKEN WHENEVER HE CHARGES HIS POWER RING! BUT DO THE LINES OF THAT SACRED VOW HAVE ANY SPECIAL MEANING ? OR ARE THEY MERELY FINE-SOUNDING, EMPTY SYMBOLS ? FOR THE STARTLING TRUTH WHICH IS GUARANTEED TO KEEP YOU ON TENTERHOOKS, READ...

The ORIGIN of GREEN LANTERN'S OATH!

IN THE DRESSING ROOM OF HAL [GREEN LANTERN] JORDAN, AT THE FERRIS AIRCRAFT COMPANY HANGAR, A MYSTIC CEREMONY TAKES PLACE WHICH NEVER FAILS TO FASCINATE PIEFACE, HAL'S ESKIMO MECHANIC, AND GL'S SOLE CONFIDANT...

IN BRIGHTEST DAY, IN BLACKEST NIGHT, NO EVIL SHALL ESCAPE MY SIGHT! LET THOSE WHO WORSHIP EVIL'S MIGHT BEWARE MY POWER -- GREEN LANTERN'S LIGHT!

AS THE EMERALD GLADIATOR TURNS, HIS RING CHARGED FOR ANOTHER TWENTY-FOUR HOURS...

GREEN LANTERN, YOU ALWAYS TAKE THAT OATH WHEN YOU CHARGE YOUR POWER RING! BUT WHERE DID THE OATH COME FROM? I'VE BEEN WONDERING ABOUT THAT!

SO IT'S AROUSED YOUR CURIOSITY, HAS IT, PIEFACE?

WELL, AS A MATTER OF FACT THERE'S A STORY BEHIND THAT OATH -- AND IF YOU WANT TO HEAR IT...

JUMPING FISH-HOOKS! YOU BET I DO!

I DIDN'T ALWAYS TAKE THE OATH! IN THE BEGINNING -- WHEN I FIRST RECEIVED MY RING AND POWER BATTERY FROM THE SPACEMAN WHO CRASHED ON EARTH* -- I SIMPLY CHARGED MY RING WITHOUT ANY OATH AT ALL! BUT THEN IN THAT FIRST WEEK I HAD THREE ADVENTURES...

*Editor's Note:

FULL DETAILS OF THIS EVENT WERE REVEALED IN THE GREEN LANTERN ORIGIN STORY, "SOS -- GREEN LANTERN!"

"THE FIRST OCCURRED HERE IN COAST CITY IN A BANK WHERE, AS HAL JORDAN, I HAD GONE TO MAKE A DEPOSIT..."

HELLO, MR. JORDAN! NICE TO SEE YOU AGAIN!

IT STILL GIVES ME A THRILL TO REALIZE THAT MR. BURBANK HASN'T THE LEAST IDEA OF MY SECRET IDENTITY...

BURBANK

NO ONE IN THE WORLD SUSPECTS THAT AT A MOMENT'S NOTICE I CAN BECOME MIGHTY GREEN LANTERN -- WITH MY AMAZING POWER RING AND INVINCIBLE GREEN BEAM! GOLLY, WHAT A FEELING IT IS!

"BUT WHAT I DIDN'T REALIZE AT THE TIME, IN THE STREET OUTSIDE..."

THIS IS A *BRIGHT DAY*, HANK! YOU SURE OUR SCHEME WILL WORK ON A DAY LIKE THIS?

DON'T WORRY...

WHEN THIS *SUPER-MAGNESIUM BOMB* GOES OFF AROUND HERE IT WILL MAKE THE SUN'S LIGHT LOOK LIKE CANDLEPOWER! WE'VE TESTED IT A DOZEN TIMES! IT CAN'T FAIL!

LET'S GO! CUT THE JAWING!

"THE NEXT MOMENT THE BOMB WAS THROWN FROM THE CAR, AND BEFORE ANYONE AROUND HAD TIME EVEN TO GET A GOOD LOOK AT IT..."

THAT INCREDIBLE LIGHT--!

BLINDING AH--!

HELP! WHERE AM I?

"THE LIGHT WAS SO FANTASTICALLY INTENSE IT EVEN PENETRATED THROUGH WINDOWS, BLINDING ALL INSIDE..."

UHH! CAN'T SEE--!

MY EYES--!

THAT LIGHT--IT'S BLINDED EVERYONE AROUND-- INCLUDING *ME*!

"WITH PLANNED PRECISION, THE CROOKS PILED OUT OF THEIR CAR, WEARING *SPECIAL GOGGLES* TO PROTECT THEM FROM THE AWFUL GLARE..."

INTO THE BANK, BOYS!

IT'S WORKING LIKE A CHARM! THIS IS GOING TO BE LIKE TAKING PENNIES FROM A *BLIND MAN*!

COAST CITY BANK

3

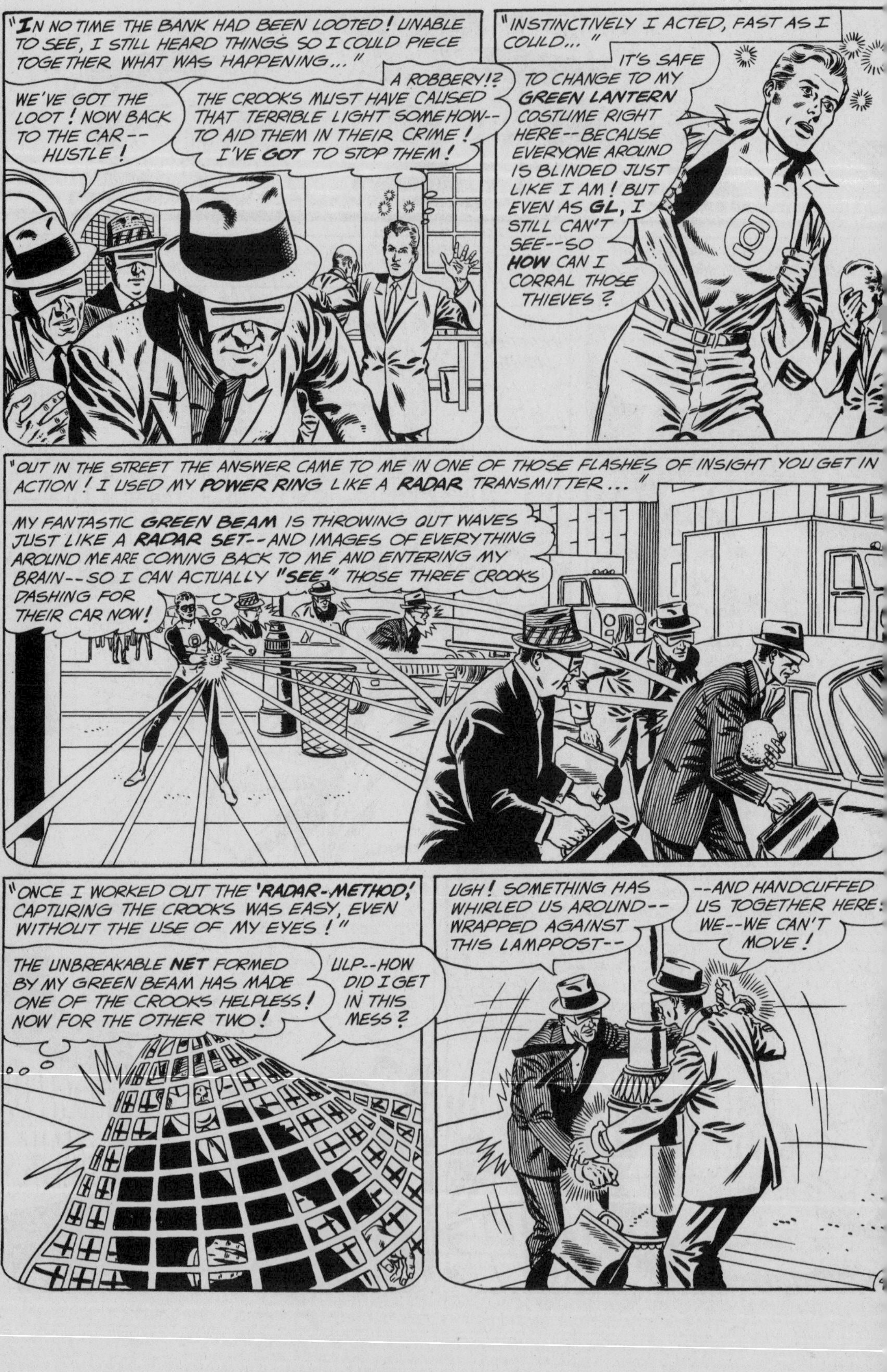
"IN NO TIME THE BANK HAD BEEN LOOTED! UNABLE TO SEE, I STILL HEARD THINGS SO I COULD PIECE TOGETHER WHAT WAS HAPPENING..."
WE'VE GOT THE LOOT! NOW BACK TO THE CAR-- HUSTLE!
A ROBBERY!?
THE CROOKS MUST HAVE CAUSED THAT TERRIBLE LIGHT SOMEHOW-- TO AID THEM IN THEIR CRIME! I'VE GOT TO STOP THEM!
"INSTINCTIVELY I ACTED, FAST AS I COULD..."
IT'S SAFE TO CHANGE TO MY GREEN LANTERN COSTUME RIGHT HERE--BECAUSE EVERYONE AROUND IS BLINDED JUST LIKE I AM! BUT EVEN AS GL, I STILL CAN'T SEE--SO HOW CAN I CORRAL THOSE THIEVES?
"OUT IN THE STREET THE ANSWER CAME TO ME IN ONE OF THOSE FLASHES OF INSIGHT YOU GET IN ACTION! I USED MY POWER RING LIKE A RADAR TRANSMITTER..."
MY FANTASTIC GREEN BEAM IS THROWING OUT WAVES JUST LIKE A RADAR SET--AND IMAGES OF EVERYTHING AROUND ME ARE COMING BACK TO ME AND ENTERING MY BRAIN--SO I CAN ACTUALLY "SEE" THOSE THREE CROOKS DASHING FOR THEIR CAR NOW!
"ONCE I WORKED OUT THE 'RADAR-METHOD,' CAPTURING THE CROOKS WAS EASY, EVEN WITHOUT THE USE OF MY EYES!"
THE UNBREAKABLE NET FORMED BY MY GREEN BEAM HAS MADE ONE OF THE CROOKS HELPLESS! NOW FOR THE OTHER TWO!
ULP--HOW DID I GET IN THIS MESS?
UGH! SOMETHING HAS WHIRLED US AROUND-- WRAPPED AGAINST THIS LAMPPOST--
--AND HANDCUFFED US TOGETHER HERE! WE--WE CAN'T MOVE!

"AFTER THAT IT WAS EASY TO HOLD THE THIEVES HELPLESS UNTIL POLICE WERE SUMMONED TO ARREST THEM..."

YES, EVENTUALLY WE ALL RECOVERED OUR SIGHT, PIEFACE! BUT THAT INCIDENT STILL DIDN'T GIVE ME MY OATH! THE OATH ITSELF DIDN'T OCCUR TO ME UNTIL AFTER THE THIRD ADVENTURE! BUT BEFORE I GET TO THAT I MUST TELL YOU ABOUT THE SECOND ONE...

"IT WAS A DAY OR SO LATER AND I HAD JUST DELIVERED AN EXPERIMENTAL PLANE--AS HAL JORDAN, OF COURSE--BACK TO THE FACTORY.."

WE'RE GOING TO KNOCK DOWN THIS ENGINE AND REBUILD IT FROM SCRATCH FOR YOU, MR. JORDAN! IT WON'T TAKE LONG!

GOOD! I'LL CHECK IN WITH YOU TOMORROW, MR. DAVIS!

"THE WAIT GAVE ME SOME TIME TO MYSELF IN SAN SIERRO WHERE THE FACTORY WAS. THAT NIGHT, AT MY HOTEL, THE DESK CLERK AND I BECAME FRIENDLY... "

TRAIN ROBBERIES-- IN THIS DAY AND AGE !?

THEY'RE A DARING BAND, MR. JORDAN...

LATE NEWS
TRAIN ROBBERS STRIKE AGAIN!

AND THE ODD THING IS THE POLICE KNOW WHERE THEIR HIDEOUT IS-- OUT IN SIERRO HILLS! BUT IT DOESN'T HELP THEM! EVERY TIME THE GANG REACHES THE HIDEOUT, NOBODY CAN FOLLOW THEM!

WOULD YOU MIND EXPLAINING THAT?

"AND SOON AFTER, A FIGURE NEVER BEFORE SEEN AROUND SAN SIERRO WAS HEADING FOR THE HILLS AT JET-SPEED.."

ACCORDING TO THAT DESK CLERK, THE TRAIN-ROBBING BAND IS A THROWBACK TO THE OLD DAYS-- OPERATING ON HORSEBACK LIKE GANGS OF THE OLD WEST! AND THEIR HIDEOUT IS AN UNDERGROUND NETWORK OF CAVES HERE IN SIERRO HILLS...

I SHOULD BE NEAR THEIR HIDEOUT--eh? THERE'S THE GANG NOW! THEY MUST BE RETURNING FROM A FORAY--AND THEY'RE ABOUT TO ENTER THAT CAVE OPENING!

"IN NO TIME I WAS WHIZZING INTO THE CAVE ON THE HEELS OF THE GANG..."

THE CLERK DESCRIBED THE *BLACKNESS* IN THIS CAVE AS *UN-BELIEVABLY DENSE*-- AND NOW I KNOW WHAT HE MEANS! THE ROBBERS HAVE MEMO-RIZED EVERY FOOT OF THIS PLACE SO THEY CAN MOVE THROUGH IT...

...BUT ANYONE ELSE COMING IN IS *UNABLE TO PURSUE THEM!* EVEN BIG SEARCH-LIGHTS HAVE NO EFFECT BECAUSE THE DARK IS NOT AN ORDINARY DARK! IT COMES FROM *FOG*, A *BLACK FOG*, THAT ONLY *REFLECTS* LIGHT AND DAZZLES WHO-EVER TRIES TO THROW A BEAM!

"BEING A NOVICE WITH THE *POWER RING*, I WAS AT THAT TIME UNABLE TO OVER-COME THE OBSTACLE.."

I CAN'T SUMMON UP ENOUGH POWER TO THROW A LIGHT THAT WILL PENETRATE THIS TERRIBLE FOG! BUT I--I CAN'T ADMIT DEFEAT! I'VE GOT TO BRING THOSE TRICKY LAW-BREAKERS TO JUSTICE!

"SUDDENLY A WAY OUT OF MY DILEMMA *OCCURRED TO ME*..."

THOSE CROOKS ARE IN HERE SOMEWHERE! BUT INSTEAD OF TRYING TO SEE THEM IN THIS INCREDIBLE DARK, WHAT I'VE GOT TO DO IS MAKE *THEM* *SUPER-VISIBLE!*

"BACKING MY RING WITH ALL MY WILL POWER, I SHOT OUT WAVES OF THE GREEN BEAM ALL AROUND ME, AND WHERE IT STRUCK THE CROOKS IT MADE EACH OF THEM *PHOSPHORESCENT*..."

HEY, I'M GLOWING--

IT'S WORK-ING! BY MAKING THE THIEVES *GLOW* WITH PHOSPHORESCENCE I'VE MADE THEM SO BRIGHT THAT I CAN SEE THEM EVEN THROUGH THE FOG!! *NOW* TO GO INTO ACTION--!

6

"AS I CAME AT THEM, THE FRENZIED CROOKS FIRED AROUND THEM BLINDLY, BUT MY RING PROTECTED ME..."

I CAN CREATE SUCH **HEAT** WITH MY RING THAT IT **MELTS DOWN** THE BULLETS COMING AT ME IN MIDAIR!

AND THAT, **PIEFACE**, WAS THE **FIRST TIME** I'D EVER USED MY RING TO STOP BULLETS! AND NATURALLY THE SENSATION WAS A BIG THRILL FOR ME!

GOLLY! I CAN SEE HOW IT WOULD BE!

"AS SOON AS MY FOES HAD RUN OUT OF AMMUNITION, I SETTLED MATTERS SWIFTLY..."

THESE BANDITS MAY ROB TRAINS LIKE THE OLD WEST--BUT THEY'RE GOING TO JAIL IN **ULTRA-MODERN** STYLE-- ON **GREEN LANTERN'S** POWER BEAM!

THAT WAS THE **SECOND** ADVENTURE, **PIEFACE!** BUT YOU WON'T UNDERSTAND COMPLETELY ABOUT MY OATH UNTIL I'VE RELATED THE **THIRD** ONE TO YOU! THAT TOOK PLACE BEFORE YOU CAME TO WORK HERE AT THE **FERRIS AIRCRAFT COMPANY...**

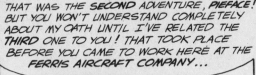

"ONE DAY, AS HAL JORDAN, I WALKED INTO THE OFFICE TO FIND..."

WHAT'S THAT, CAROL? YOU SAY THE **OFFICE SAFE** HAS BEEN STOLEN?

THAT'S RIGHT, HAL! IT CONTAINED A LARGE SUM IN CASH, THE COMPANY PAYROLL!

7

"*EXCITING AS CAROL'S NEWS WAS, I STILL COULDN'T HELP NOTICING HOW PRETTY SHE WAS!*"

APPARENTLY THE THIEVES COULDN'T OPEN THE SAFE HERE, SO AFTER WORKING PART OF THE NIGHT THEY MANAGED TO GET THE SAFE INTO A TRUCK AND DROVE OFF WITH IT! THE POLICE HAVEN'T BEEN ABLE TO TRACE THEM YET!

"*I FOUND SOME EXCUSE TO SLIP AWAY. AND SOON AFTER, RIGHT HERE IN MY DRESSING ROOM, I CHANGED...*"

"*...AND CHARGED MY RING! YOU SEE, AT THAT TIME I STILL TOOK NO OATH, BUT STILL I MADE A KIND OF SILENT VOW AGAINST EVIL-DOERS...*"

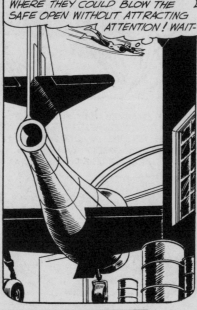

"*THEN, AS **GREEN LANTERN**, I SET OFF TO FIND THAT SAFE AND THE CROOKS WHO HAD MADE OFF WITH IT...*"

NO SIGN OF THEM! AND YET THEY WOULDN'T HAVE GONE VERY FAR! THEY'D JUST GET OUT INTO THE COUNTRY SOMEWHERE WHERE THEY COULD BLOW THE SAFE OPEN WITHOUT ATTRACTING ATTENTION! WAIT--

"*MY OWN THOUGHTS GAVE ME A CLUE...*"

JUST SEARCHING AIMLESSLY THIS WAY MAY NOT BE BEST! THE CROOKS COULD GET THE SAFE OPEN AND TAKE OFF WITH THE PAYROLL LONG BEFORE I FIND THEM! I'VE GOT ANOTHER IDEA!

"*WHAT I DID WAS TO USE MY **POWER BEAM** TO THROW A WIDE **BELT OF RADIATION** ALL AROUND THE **FERRIS COMPANY** AREA...*"

*WHEN THE CROOKS BLOW OPEN THE SAFE IT'S BOUND TO CAUSE A **FAINT EARTH-TREMOR**--VERY FAINT AND DIFFERENT FROM A REAL EARTHQUAKE SHOCK--BUT I CAN MAKE THE GREEN RADIATION I'VE LAID DOWN IN A HUGE CIRCLE AROUND HERE SO SENSITIVE THAT MAYBE I CAN DETECT IT! IT'S MY **DUTY** TO TRACK DOWN **EVIL** NO MATTER HOW DIFFICULT THE JOB--eh!?*

8.

"*JUST AS I LAID DOWN MY CIRCLE OF RADIATION, THE THING HAPPENED...*"

THERE IT IS! MY BEAM IS PICKING UP AN EARTH—TREMOR—COMING FROM THE SOUTHWEST!

"*I SHOT OFF IN THE DIRECTION OF THE TREMOR WITH AS MUCH SPEED AS MY POWER RING COULD MUSTER...*"

THE LITTLE SHOCK IS COMING FROM THE DUNE COUNTRY—A SORT OF DESERT WHERE NO ONE LIVES! AND THAT FITS IN--IT'S THE KIND OF PLACE WHERE THE CROOKS WOULD GO TO BLOW THE SAFE!

"*AND MOMENTS LATER I BURST UPON THEM...*"

GOT HERE JUST IN TIME! THEY'VE DYNAMITED THE SAFE ALL RIGHT, BUT THEY HAVEN'T GOT THE PAYROLL OUT YET-- AND IF I HAVE ANYTHING TO SAY ABOUT IT THEY NEVER WILL!

SOMETHING'S COMIN' AT US, HANK!

"*THE FIGHT WAS FAST, FURIOUS--AND SHORT...*"

THOSE EXPLOSIVE SHOTS CREATED BY MY GREEN BEAM WON'T HURT THE CROOKS-- BUT THEY WILL KNOCK THEM COLD--

--AND ENABLE ME TO TRANSPORT THEM-- AND THEIR LOOT--THE WHOLE KIT AND KABOODLE--BACK TO TOWN WITHOUT ANY TROUBLE!

SO THERE YOU HAVE THE **THREE ADVENTURES** WHICH INSPIRED MY OATH, **PIEFACE**! BUT MAYBE I'D BETTER EXPLAIN...

NO, WAIT! LET ME TRY, **GREEN LANTERN**! I THINK I CAN UNDERSTAND...

AS THE GOOD-HUMORED FACE OF THE ESKIMO GREASEMONKEY GLEAMS WITH SUDDEN COMPREHENSION...

"IN BRIGHTEST DAY..." -- THAT REFERS TO THE **FIRST ADVENTURE** WHERE THE MAGNESIUM BOMB MADE A LIGHT SO BRIGHT IT BLINDED EVERYONE AROUND!

GOOD! THAT'S RIGHT, **PIE**!

AND "IN BLACKEST NIGHT..." -- THAT REFERS TO THE INCIDENT IN THE CAVE IN **SIERRO HILLS** WHERE THE FOGGY DARKNESS WAS SO BLACK THAT NOT EVEN LIGHT OR YOUR RING COULD PENETRATE IT!

EXACTLY!

AND "NO EVIL SHALL ESCAPE MY SIGHT" -- THAT OBVIOUSLY COMES FROM THE LAST ADVENTURE WHERE AGAINST ODDS YOU DETECTED THOSE CROOKS WHO THOUGHT THEY HAD ESCAPED JUSTICE AND THE LAW!

CORRECT! THEN ALL I DID WAS ADD THE **LAST TWO LINES** TO MAKE IT RHYME! AND SO NOW YOU KNOW THE WHOLE STORY OF MY OATH, **PIEFACE**!

IN BRIGHTEST DAY, IN BLACKEST NIGHT, NO EVIL SHALL ESCAPE MY SIGHT! LET THOSE WHO WORSHIP EVIL'S MIGHT BEWARE MY POWER-- GREEN LANTERN'S LIGHT!

The End

GREEN LANTERN

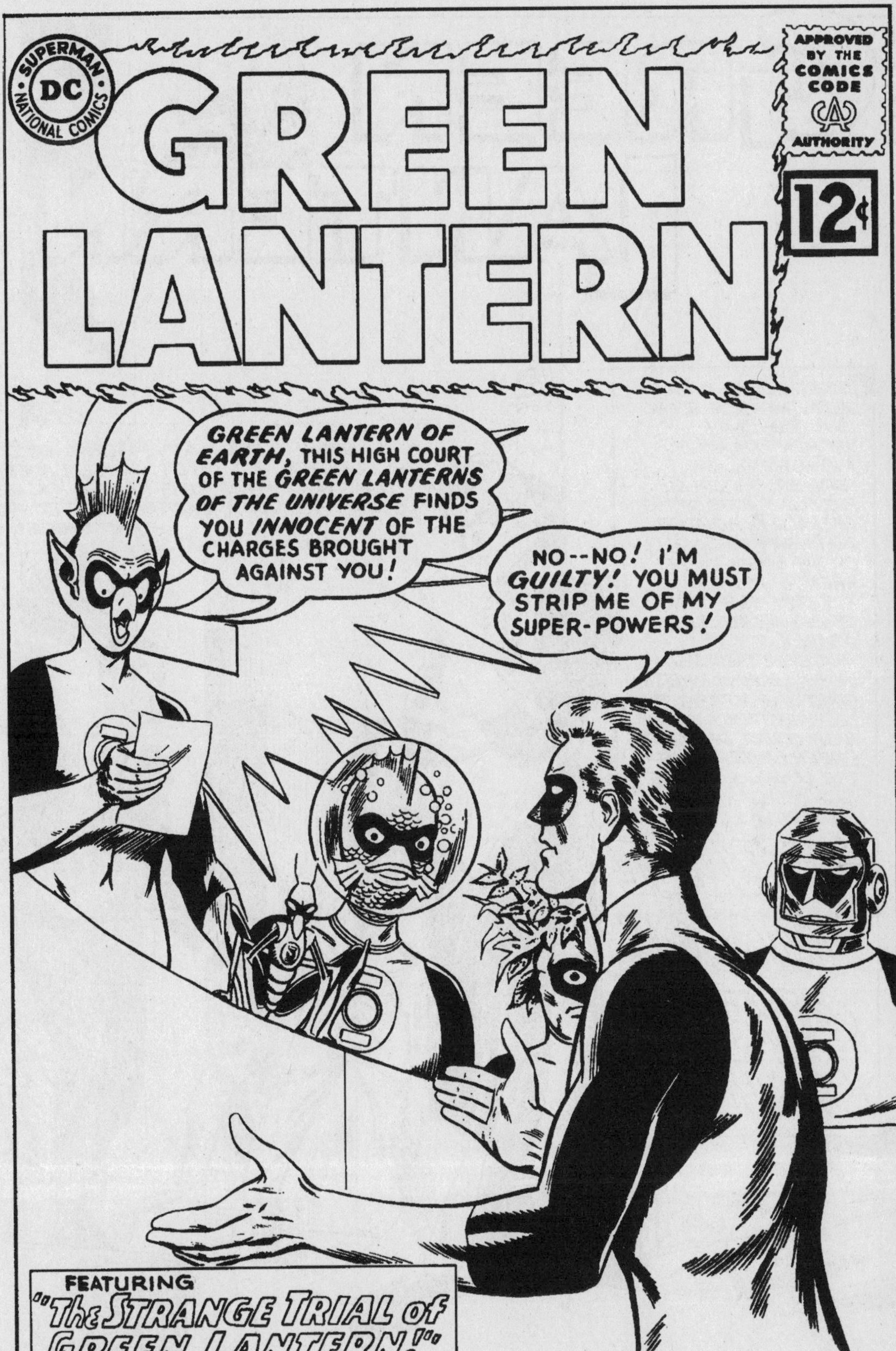
SUPERMAN DC NATIONAL COMICS
GREEN LANTERN
APPROVED BY THE COMICS CODE AUTHORITY
12¢
GREEN LANTERN OF EARTH, THIS HIGH COURT OF THE GREEN LANTERNS OF THE UNIVERSE FINDS YOU INNOCENT OF THE CHARGES BROUGHT AGAINST YOU!
NO--NO! I'M GUILTY! YOU MUST STRIP ME OF MY SUPER-POWERS!
FEATURING "The STRANGE TRIAL of GREEN LANTERN!"

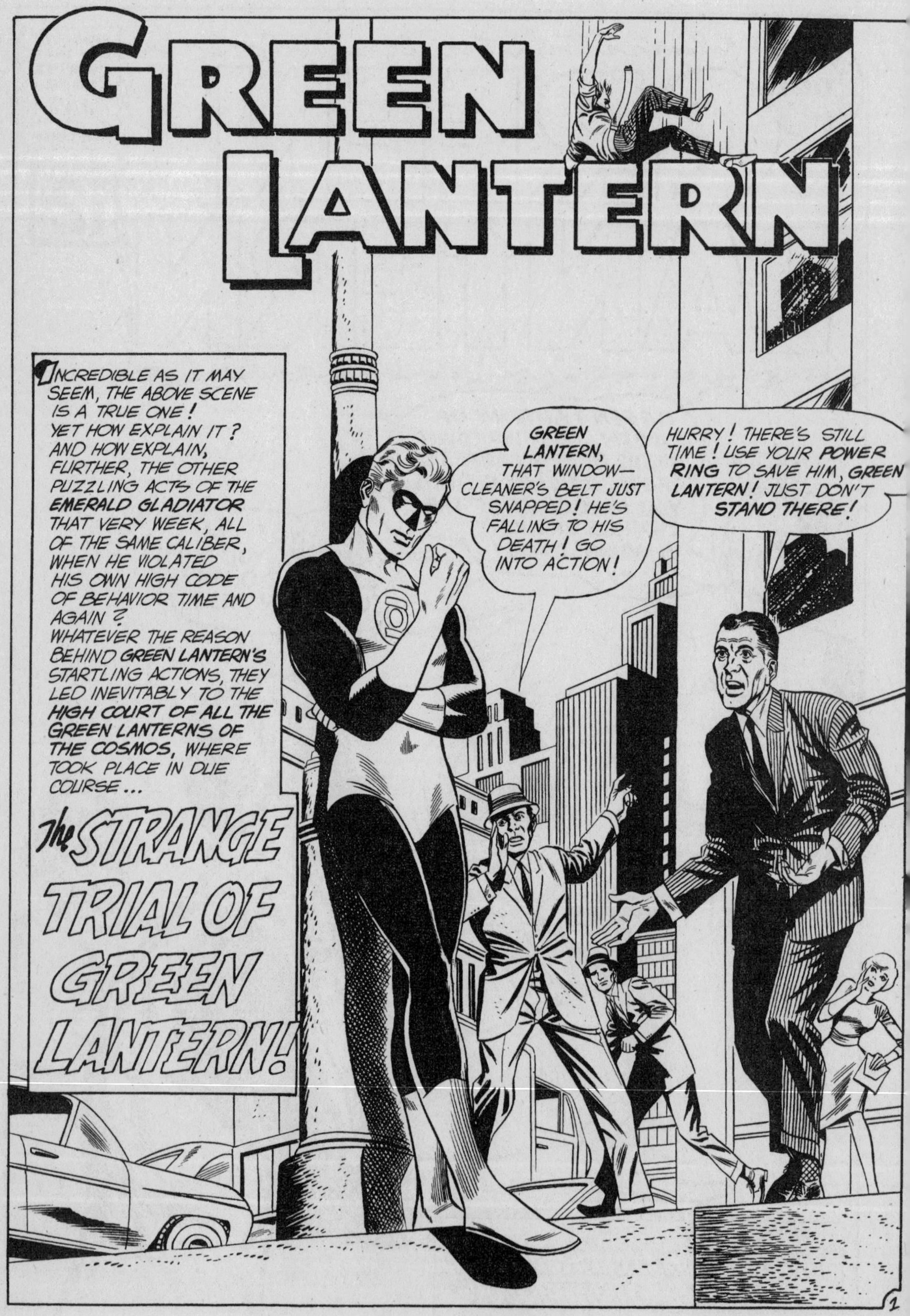
GREEN LANTERN
INCREDIBLE AS IT MAY SEEM, THE ABOVE SCENE IS A TRUE ONE! YET HOW EXPLAIN IT? AND HOW EXPLAIN, FURTHER, THE OTHER PUZZLING ACTS OF THE EMERALD GLADIATOR THAT VERY WEEK, ALL OF THE SAME CALIBER, WHEN HE VIOLATED HIS OWN HIGH CODE OF BEHAVIOR TIME AND AGAIN? WHATEVER THE REASON BEHIND GREEN LANTERN'S STARTLING ACTIONS, THEY LED INEVITABLY TO THE HIGH COURT OF ALL THE GREEN LANTERNS OF THE COSMOS, WHERE TOOK PLACE IN DUE COURSE...
The STRANGE TRIAL OF GREEN LANTERN!
GREEN LANTERN, THAT WINDOW-CLEANER'S BELT JUST SNAPPED! HE'S FALLING TO HIS DEATH! GO INTO ACTION!
HURRY! THERE'S STILL TIME! USE YOUR POWER RING TO SAVE HIM, GREEN LANTERN! JUST DON'T STAND THERE!
1

ON THE FAR-OFF PLANET OF **YQUEM** SOMEWHERE IN THE **MILKY WAY GALAXY** AN EXTRAORDINARY TRIAL IS TAKING PLACE! A PICKED ASSEMBLAGE OF **GREEN LANTERNS**, FROM VARIOUS SECTORS OF THE COSMOS, IS SITTING IN SOLEMN JUDGMENT ON ONE OF ITS OWN MEMBERS...

WE ARE READY TO HAND DOWN OUR DECISION ON YOU, **GREEN LANTERN** OF EARTH! BUT BEFORE WE DO, LET US REVIEW YOUR AMAZING CASE! FIRST OF ALL, IN VIEW OF YOUR SPOTLESS RECORD UP TO NOW, IT WAS DECIDED BY THE **GUARDIANS*** THAT YOU WOULD BE TRIED BY US -- A JURY OF YOUR PEERS AND EQUALS!

*Editor's Note: THE MYSTERIOUS **GUARDIANS OF THE UNIVERSE** FROM WHOM ALL THE **GREEN LANTERNS** DERIVE THEIR **POWER BATTERIES** AND ALL THE OTHER ASPECTS OF THEIR SUPER-POWERS!

AND NOW TO SUM UP THE CHARGES AGAINST YOU! IT IS ALLEGED -- AND YOU HAVE **ADMITTED** -- THAT YOU FAILED TO USE YOUR **POWER RING AND BEAM** IN THE BEST TRADITION OF OUR ORGANIZATION! THERE WERE THREE SPECIFIC INSTANCES OF THIS MISCONDUCT -- ALL CONFIRMED BY YOU!

"IN THE FIRST INSTANCE, BACK ON YOUR HOME PLANET OF **EARTH**, YOU USED YOUR **POWER RING** TO BREAK INTO A BANK, EVEN THOUGH THERE WAS NO CRIME GOING ON THERE AT THE TIME..."

GREEN LANTERN? MUST BE BANK ROBBERS AROUND--

"RUTHLESSLY YOU TRANS-FIXED ALL THE TELLERS AND DEPOSITORS PRESENT, TEMPORARILY PARALYZING THEM WITH A SWEEP OF YOUR GREEN BEAM..."

HE MUST BE THE BANK ROBBER!

GREAT SCOTT! HE'S HEADING FOR THE VAULT!

"THERE WAS MUCH MONEY IN THE VAULT! YOU OPENED IT! BUT THEN AT THE LAST MOMENT YOU SEEMED TO CHANGE **YOUR** MIND..."

FIRST SECURITY BANK

"YOU SUDDENLY PLUNGED OFF AND ON YOUR WAY, EMPTY-HANDED! THAT MUCH HAS BEEN ESTABLISHED!"

2

THE SECOND INSTANCE OCCURRED SHORTLY AFTER THE FIRST ONE! AT A GALA ENTERTAINMENT FOR CHARITY IN **COAST CITY** IT WAS AGREED THAT EVERYONE WHO ATTENDED, WITHOUT EXCEPTION, SHOULD PAY THE $100 ENTRANCE FEE INTO THE HALL! BUT WHEN **YOU** ARRIVED...

"..YOU HAD NO TICKET! THE MAN AT THE DOOR TRIED TO STOP YOU.."

HOLD ON, **GREEN LANTERN!** YOU MUST PAY TO GET IN-- JUST LIKE ANYONE ELSE!

YOU DARE TO **STOP ME?**

"IT WAS A BALEFUL GLANCE YOU DIRECTED AT THE TICKET-TAKER..."

DO YOU REALIZE I COULD USE MY **POWER RING** TO TURN THIS WHOLE HALL UPSIDE-DOWN IF I WANTED TO?

I--I'M SURE YOU COULD! B-BUT YOU'VE **STILL** GOT TO PAY YOUR WAY IN!

"THE NEXT MOMENT..."

I'LL TEACH YOU TO--

HELP!!

"SUDDENLY, ONCE AGAIN, YOU SEEMED TO REGAIN CONTROL OF YOURSELF! AND..."

GREAT THUNDER! WHAT IN THE WORLD HAS COME OVER **GREEN LANTERN!?** I NEVER SAW HIM ACT THAT WAY BEFORE! BUT AT LEAST-- HE DIDN'T HURT ME!

"BUT THE THIRD CASE CITED AGAINST YOU IS THE **MOST SERIOUS** OF ALL! IT WAS LATER IN THE SAME DAY AND YOU WERE PASSING A BUSY THOROUGHFARE..."

LOOK! OH-- SAVE HIM, SOME-BODY!

3

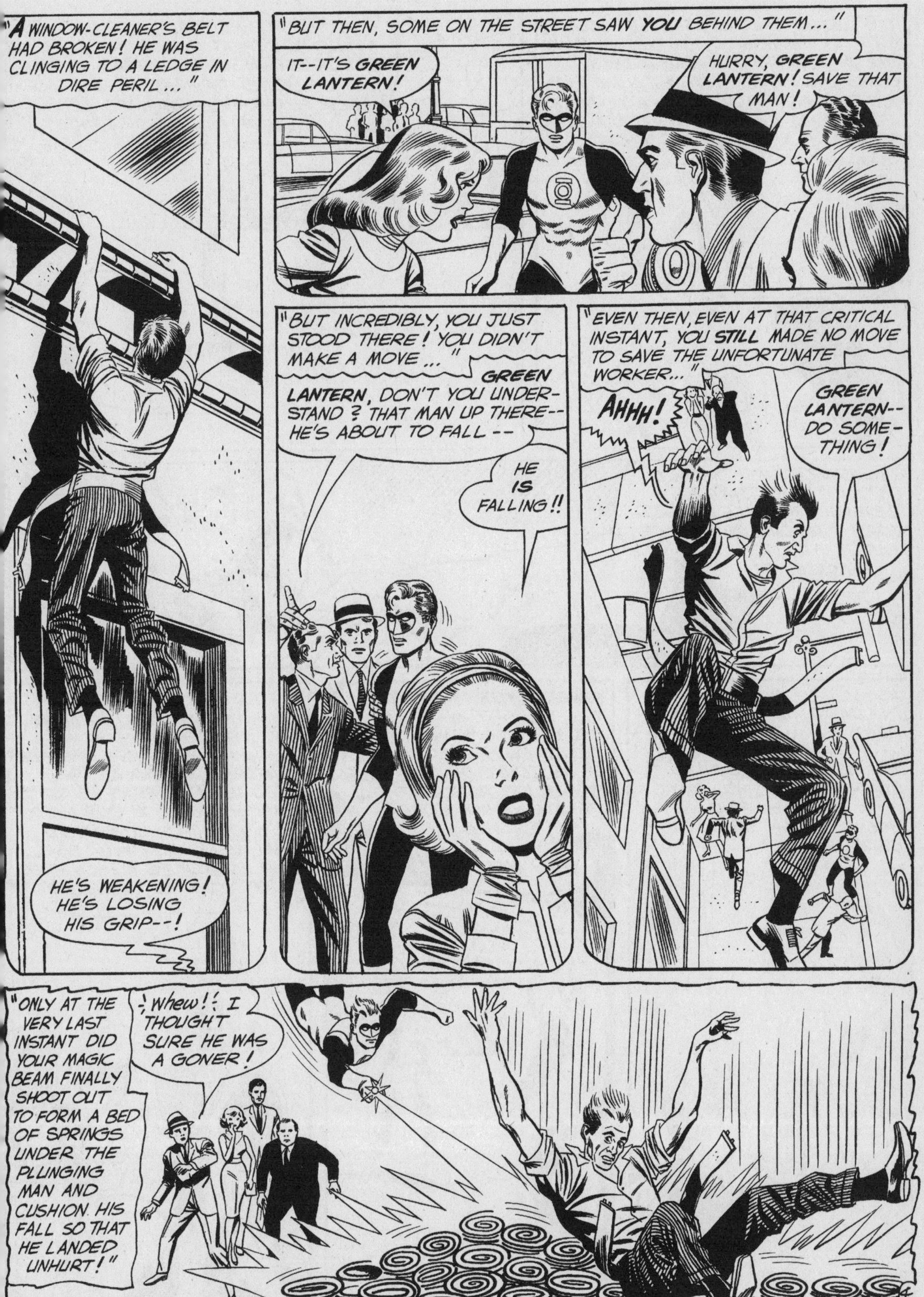
"A WINDOW-CLEANER'S BELT HAD BROKEN! HE WAS CLINGING TO A LEDGE IN DIRE PERIL ..."
HE'S WEAKENING! HE'S LOSING HIS GRIP--!
"BUT THEN, SOME ON THE STREET SAW YOU BEHIND THEM ..."
IT--IT'S GREEN LANTERN!
HURRY, GREEN LANTERN! SAVE THAT MAN!
"BUT INCREDIBLY, YOU JUST STOOD THERE! YOU DIDN'T MAKE A MOVE ..."
GREEN LANTERN, DON'T YOU UNDERSTAND? THAT MAN UP THERE-- HE'S ABOUT TO FALL --
HE IS FALLING!!
"EVEN THEN, EVEN AT THAT CRITICAL INSTANT, YOU STILL MADE NO MOVE TO SAVE THE UNFORTUNATE WORKER..."
AHHH!
GREEN LANTERN-- DO SOMETHING!
"ONLY AT THE VERY LAST INSTANT DID YOUR MAGIC BEAM FINALLY SHOOT OUT TO FORM A BED OF SPRINGS UNDER THE PLUNGING MAN AND CUSHION HIS FALL SO THAT HE LANDED UNHURT!"
Whew! I THOUGHT SURE HE WAS A GONER!
4

IT IS CLEAR IN THE LAST CASE THAT YOU ACTUALLY *ENDANGERED* THE FALLING MAN'S *LIFE* BY YOUR INEXPLICABLE DELAY IN GOING INTO ACTION! AND YET IN THE END YOU DID SAVE HIM AND WE--YOUR JUDGE AND JURORS-- HAVE TAKEN THAT INTO ACCOUNT! OUR FINAL JUDGMENT...

...IS THAT YOU MUST BE GIVEN A WARNING *NEVER* TO REPEAT ANY OF THE BEHAVIOR DESCRIBED IN YOUR CHARGES, UNDER PAIN OF BEING STRIPPED FOREVER OF YOUR *SUPER-POWERS!* AND YET IN VIEW OF ALL THE EVIDENCE...

...WE CANNOT FIND THAT YOU DID ANYTHING TO MERIT A SEVERE SENTENCE! THERE-FORE, *GREEN LANTERN* OF EARTH, WE FIND YOU *INNOCENT!*

NO!!

AS ALL PRESENT STARE AT THE *EARTHMAN* IN ASTONISH-MENT...

NO--NO!! I'M GUILTY! YOU *MUST* STRIP ME OF MY SUPER-POWERS! YOU *CAN'T* FIND ME INNOCENT!

THIS IS EXTRA-ORDINARY...

GREEN LANTERN OF EARTH, WILL YOU STEP IN THE ANTE-ROOM FOR A MOMENT? IT WOULD BE BETTER IF A FEW OF US COULD DISCUSS YOUR *STARTLING REQUEST* PRIVATELY AMONG OUR--SELVES...

VERY WELL!

*A*FTER THE GRIM-VISAGED GLADIATOR HAS EXITED FROM THE CHAMBER...

FELLOW *GREEN LANTERNS,* YOU HEARD THE ACCUSED! HE ASKS US TO BANISH HIM FROM OUR AUGUST MEMBERSHIP! HE *DEMANDS* THAT WE DO SO! WHAT SHALL OUR ANSWER BE? EACH HERE MUST GIVE HIS OPINION!

5

SLOWLY, WEIGHING THEIR WORDS, THE MEMBERS OF THE INTERGALACTIC BAND ONE BY ONE RENDER THEIR VERDICT! AMONG THEM...

GREEN LANTERN OF GRENDA, A WORLD WHERE ROBOTS REIGN!

I SAY THERE **MUST** BE A GOOD REASON FOR THE INCREDIBLE REQUEST OF **GREEN LANTERN OF EARTH**! WE SHOULD NOT GO AGAINST HIS WISHES!

GREEN LANTERN OF AEROS, A WATER WORLD INHABITED BY VARIOUS FORMS OF FISH LIFE!

I AGREE!

GREEN LANTERN OF ROJIRA, ONE OF THE MOST FUTURISTIC, SUPER-SCIENTIFIC AND AGED CIVILIZATIONS IN EXISTENCE!

THERE MAY BE MORE HERE THAN MEETS THE EYE!

GREEN LANTERN OF JS86, WHERE INTELLI-GENT PLANT LIFE HAS ARRIVED AT A STAGE FAR ADVANCED OVER THAT KNOWN ANY—WHERE ELSE!

LET US DO AS HE SAYS--TERRIBLE AS HIS FATE WILL BE!

GREEN LANTERN OF BARRIO III, A WORLD IN WHICH CRYSTAL LIFE FORMS HAVE ATTAINED DOMINANCE. AN ULTRASENSITIVE FORM WITH 13 SENSES INSTEAD OF THE USUAL 6 OF HUMANS!

AGREED!

TOMAR RE, GREEN LANTERN OF XUDAR, WHERE BIRD-LIFE HAS BECOME THE MASTER SPECIES!

I SEE THAT BEHIND OUR WORDS WE ALL HAVE THE SAME IDEA IN MIND, FELLOW GREEN LANTERNS! THEREFORE... OUR DECISION IS UNANIMOUS!

AND SOON, WITH HIS **POWER RING** TAKEN AWAY, THE INSIGNIA OF HIS FORMER RANK STRIPPED FROM HIM, ALONE, HAGGARD AND HELPLESS, THE ERSTWHILE **EMERALD GLADIATOR** IS CATAPULTED OFF **YQUEM** AND SENT ON A LONELY AND GRIM JOURNEY...

BY THE EARTHMAN'S OWN REQUEST, THE **EX-GREEN LANTERN** IS BEING TELE-PORTED BY OUR POWER BEAMS OUT OF THIS UNIVERSE ENTIRELY--AND INTO THE **EVIL ANTIMATTER UNIVERSE OF QWARD**!

MAY HE NOT REGRET THAT REQUEST!

WE HAD NO CHOICE BUT TO GRANT IT!

6.

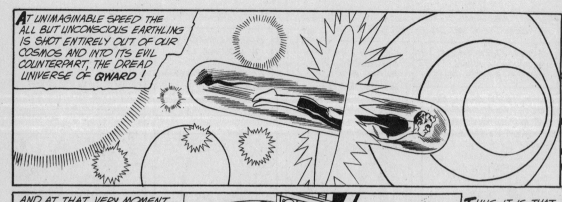

AT UNIMAGINABLE SPEED THE ALL BUT UNCONSCIOUS EARTHLING IS SHOT ENTIRELY OUT OF OUR COSMOS AND INTO ITS EVIL COUNTERPART, THE DREAD UNIVERSE OF QWARD!

AND AT THAT VERY MOMENT...

HERE COMES GREEN LANTERN! MY PLAN IS SUCCEEDING BETTER THAN I HAD DREAMED! AND NOW THAT HE IS IN QWARD MY YELLOW BEAM CAN TAKE CONTROL OF HIM-- AND GUIDE HIM HERE TO ME!!

THUS IT IS THAT WHEN GREEN LANTERN HAS FINALLY COME TO REST, AND THE GREEN PROTECTIVE SHEATH AROUND HIM HAS DISSOLVED AWAY, HIS STARTLED EYES FALL ON NONE OTHER THAN HIS INCREDIBLE ARCH— ENEMY...

SINESTRO!? THE RENEGADE GREEN LANTERN OF THE PLANET KORUGAR!

GREETINGS, GREEN LANTERN OF EARTH! WELCOME TO QWARD! I DON'T WONDER THAT YOU'RE SURPRISED TO SEE ME --

--SINCE THE LAST TIME YOU SAW ME I WAS "ABSOLUTELY HELPLESS" IN THAT "IM-PENETRABLE" GREEN CAPSULE ORBITING YOUR UNIVERSE!* NO DOUBT YOU'RE EATEN UP WITH CURIOSITY TO LEARN HOW I MADE MY ESCAPE!

*Editor's Note! SEE STORY ENTITLED "THE BATTLE OF THE POWER RINGS" IN GREEN LANTERN #9!

BUT EVEN IF YOU AREN'T, MY FRIEND, I INTEND TO TELL YOU! SIT DOWN!

UHH! WITHOUT MY RING I'M POWERLESS AGAINST THAT YELLOW BEAM OF HIS!

7

NATURALLY WHEN YOU AND THE OTHER *GREEN LANTERNS* PUT ME IN THAT CAPSULE YOU TOOK AWAY *MY POWER RING!* YOU THOUGHT THAT WOULD PREVENT ME FROM EVER GETTING LOOSE! BUT THERE WAS ONE THING YOU OVERLOOKED...

"NO SOONER WAS I OUT OF YOUR SIGHT THAN I REACHED DOWN INTO A SECRET COMPARTMENT OF MY BOOT, AND THERE MY FINGERS CLOSED ON..."

MY *SPARE POWER RING!* HA! HA! HA! NATURALLY, BEING *SINESTRO,* I WAS *WELL-HEELED* WITH A SPARE-- FOR JUST SUCH A SITUATION AS THIS!

"AFTER THAT I SIMPLY CONVERTED THE CAPSULE INTO A *ROCKET* WITH MY YELLOW BEAM ..."

"...AND PILOTED IT TOWARD *QWARD* AND HOME!"

SIMPLE, EH? AND SINCE YOU AND YOUR FELLOW *GREEN LANTERNS* CONSIDERED ME FINISHED, I HAD PLENTY OF TIME TO DREAM UP MY REVENGE-- FIRST OF ALL AGAINST *YOU,* MY PARTICULAR FOE! TO BEGIN WITH...

...I USED MY EVIL *POWER RING* TO HELP ME BUILD THIS *MIND-CONTROL RAY-DEVICE!* IT HAS AN EFFECT SIMILAR TO HYPNOSIS, BUT WORKS AT ANY DISTANCE! AND BY MEANS OF IT I WAS ABLE...

...TO *GAIN CONTROL* OVER YOUR MIND, MY FRIEND!

UH-- I'M BEGINNING TO SEE--!

8

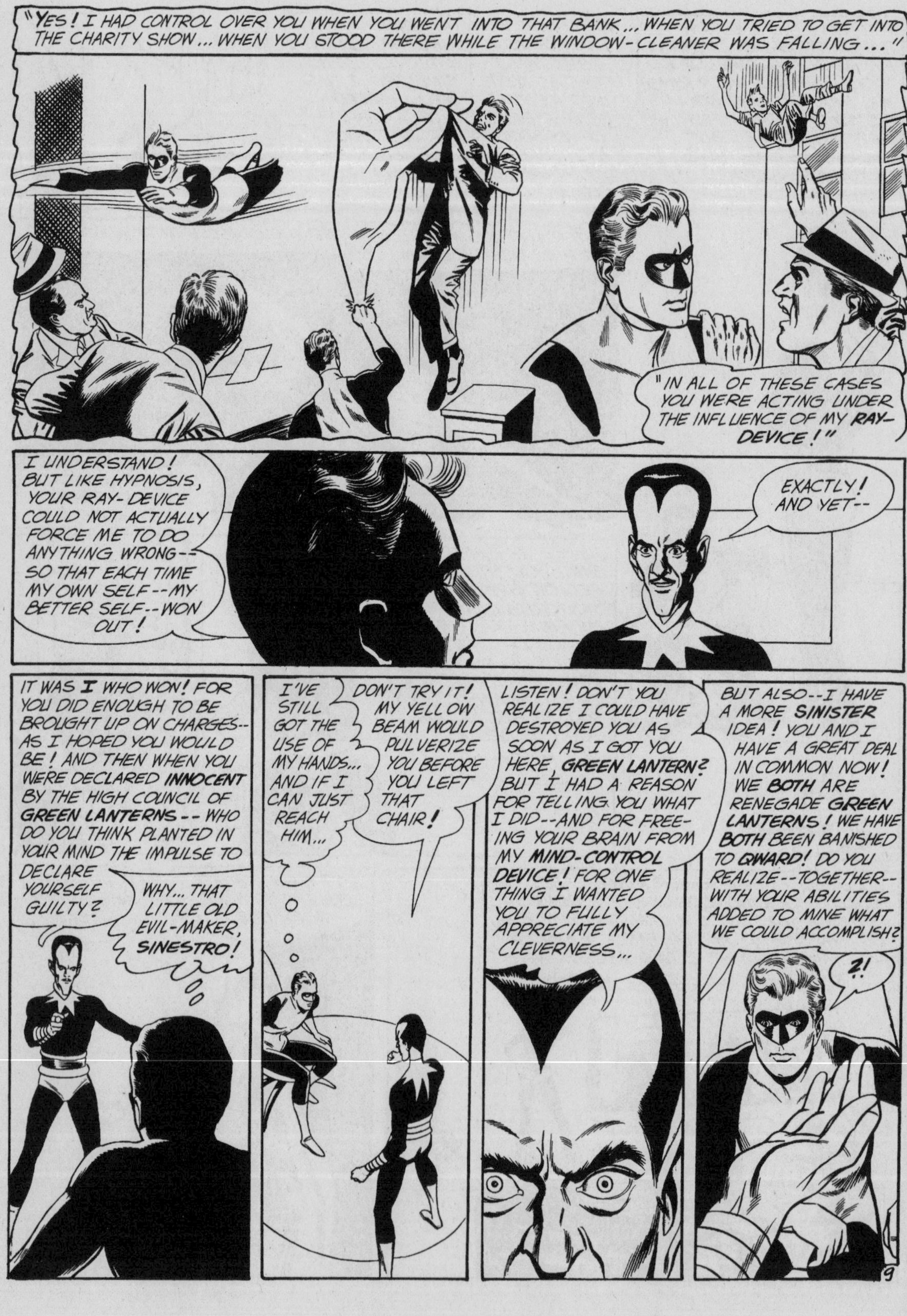
"YES! I HAD CONTROL OVER YOU WHEN YOU WENT INTO THAT BANK... WHEN YOU TRIED TO GET INTO THE CHARITY SHOW... WHEN YOU STOOD THERE WHILE THE WINDOW-CLEANER WAS FALLING..."
"IN ALL OF THESE CASES YOU WERE ACTING UNDER THE INFLUENCE OF MY RAY-DEVICE!"
I UNDERSTAND! BUT LIKE HYPNOSIS, YOUR RAY-DEVICE COULD NOT ACTUALLY FORCE ME TO DO ANYTHING WRONG-- SO THAT EACH TIME MY OWN SELF--MY BETTER SELF--WON OUT!
EXACTLY! AND YET--
IT WAS I WHO WON! FOR YOU DID ENOUGH TO BE BROUGHT UP ON CHARGES-- AS I HOPED YOU WOULD BE! AND THEN WHEN YOU WERE DECLARED INNOCENT BY THE HIGH COUNCIL OF GREEN LANTERNS -- WHO DO YOU THINK PLANTED IN YOUR MIND THE IMPULSE TO DECLARE YOURSELF GUILTY?
WHY... THAT LITTLE OLD EVIL-MAKER, SINESTRO!
I'VE STILL GOT THE USE OF MY HANDS... AND IF I CAN JUST REACH HIM...
DON'T TRY IT! MY YELLOW BEAM WOULD PULVERIZE YOU BEFORE YOU LEFT THAT CHAIR!
LISTEN! DON'T YOU REALIZE I COULD HAVE DESTROYED YOU AS SOON AS I GOT YOU HERE, GREEN LANTERN? BUT I HAD A REASON FOR TELLING YOU WHAT I DID--AND FOR FREEING YOUR BRAIN FROM MY MIND-CONTROL DEVICE! FOR ONE THING I WANTED YOU TO FULLY APPRECIATE MY CLEVERNESS...
BUT ALSO--I HAVE A MORE SINISTER IDEA! YOU AND I HAVE A GREAT DEAL IN COMMON NOW! WE BOTH ARE RENEGADE GREEN LANTERNS! WE HAVE BOTH BEEN BANISHED TO QWARD! DO YOU REALIZE--TOGETHER-- WITH YOUR ABILITIES ADDED TO MINE WHAT WE COULD ACCOMPLISH?
?!
9

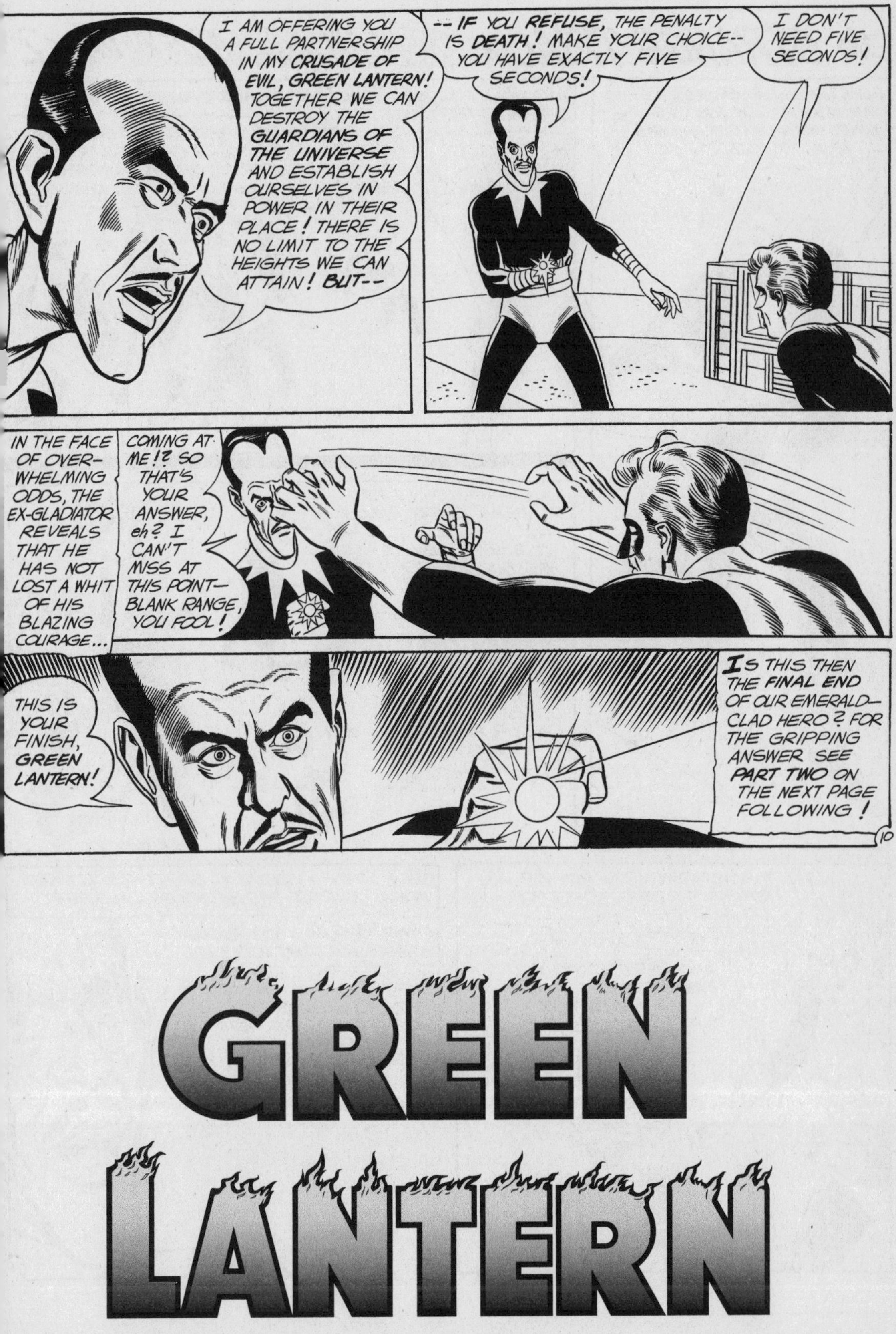
I AM OFFERING YOU A FULL PARTNERSHIP IN MY CRUSADE OF EVIL, GREEN LANTERN! TOGETHER WE CAN DESTROY THE GUARDIANS OF THE UNIVERSE AND ESTABLISH OURSELVES IN POWER IN THEIR PLACE! THERE IS NO LIMIT TO THE HEIGHTS WE CAN ATTAIN! BUT--
-- IF YOU REFUSE, THE PENALTY IS DEATH! MAKE YOUR CHOICE-- YOU HAVE EXACTLY FIVE SECONDS!
I DON'T NEED FIVE SECONDS!
IN THE FACE OF OVER-WHELMING ODDS, THE EX-GLADIATOR REVEALS THAT HE HAS NOT LOST A WHIT OF HIS BLAZING COURAGE...
COMING AT ME!? SO THAT'S YOUR ANSWER, eh? I CAN'T MISS AT THIS POINT-BLANK RANGE, YOU FOOL!
THIS IS YOUR FINISH, GREEN LANTERN!
IS THIS THEN THE FINAL END OF OUR EMERALD-CLAD HERO? FOR THE GRIPPING ANSWER SEE PART TWO ON THE NEXT PAGE FOLLOWING!
10

GREEN LANTERN

The STRANGE TRIAL OF GREEN LANTERN! PART 2

SOMETHING--HAS GRIPPED ME-- YANKING ME ASIDE JUST AS SINESTRO'S DEADLY RAY WAS ABOUT TO DESTROY ME!

AND SIMULTANEOUSLY INTO THE CHAMBER POURS AN INTREPID GREEN-SUITED BAND...

M-MY FELLOW GREEN LANTERNS!?

YES! WE SUSPECTED THAT SINESTRO MIGHT BE BEHIND YOUR EXTRAORDINARY BE-HAVIOR AT YOUR TRIAL, GREEN LANTERN OF EARTH! SO A POSSE OF US FOLLOWED YOU HERE--

--AND ARRIVED IN TIME TO HEAR EVERYTHING!

YOUR EVIL GENIUS HAS SUCCEEDED IN BRINGING ABOUT ONLY YOUR OWN DESTRUCTION, SINESTRO! FOR NOT EVEN YOU--AND YOUR EVIL POWERS--CAN WITHSTAND THE COMBINED MIGHT OF OUR POWER BEAMS!

THROW DOWN YOUR POWER RING! SURRENDER AT ONCE OR FACE THE CONSEQUENCES!

AND WE'RE GIVING YOU ONE SECOND TO MAKE UP YOUR MIND!

THEN, TO THE AMAZEMENT OF ALL, THE ULTIMATE IN EVIL BURSTS INTO GALES OF LAUGHTER...

HAHOHAHO HA... YOU FOOLS! IT IS CLEAR THAT YOU STILL DO NOT APPRECIATE THE DEPTHS OF MY SINISTER BRAIN! I FIGURED YOU MIGHT GUESS THE TRUTH AT THE TRIAL--AND I MADE PROVISION FOR IT!

WHAT YOU SEE BEFORE YOU IS NOT **SINESTRO** IN PERSON--BUT MERELY A NON-CORPOREAL DUPLICATE OF MYSELF--OPERATED BY REMOTE CONTROL!

FIRE AWAY WITH YOUR **POWER BEAMS**--AND YOU'LL SEE FOR YOURSELVES!

AS BOLTS OF FIERY GREEN ENERGY LICK OUT AT THE MOCKING FIGURE...

HE--HE'S GONE!

THEN IT **WAS** A PROJECTION! IT DISAPPEARED LIKE SOMEONE **TURNING OFF A LIGHT**!

POP!

AND AT THE SAME MOMENT...

THE DOOR HAS SLAMMED SHUT!

A **YELLOW** DOOR!

CLICK!

GRIMLY, THE ASSEMBLED **HEROES** OF THE COSMOS STARE ABOUT THEM...

EVERY INCH OF THIS CHAMBER IS **YELLOW**!

AND OUR MYSTIC BEAMS HAVE **NO** POWER OVER ANYTHING **YELLOW**!*

WE CAME HERE TO TRAP **SINESTRO**--ONLY TO FIND HE'S TRAPPED US!

HA! HA! HA! HO!

*Editor's Note: DUE TO A **NECESSARY** IMPURITY IN THE UNIQUE MATERIAL FROM WHICH THE **GREEN LANTERNS'** POWER BATTERIES ARE MADE, THEIR RINGS HAVE NO EFFECT ON ANY--THING **YELLOW**!

12

IN THAT DREADFUL MOMENT, THE ASSEMBLED *GREEN LANTERNS* ARE ESPECIALLY AWARE OF ONE OF THEIR MEMBERS...

GREEN LANTERN OF EARTH, OUR SITUATION IS CRITICAL! BUT IF THIS *DOES* TURN OUT TO BE OUR *LAST FIGHT*, WE WANT YOU ALONGSIDE US--SHOULDER TO SHOULDER--WITH ALL YOUR SUPER-POWERS BACK AND YOUR RING FULLY CHARGED!

WE ONLY TOOK THEM FROM YOU AS A *RUSE*-- IN ORDER TO FOLLOW YOU AND GET TO THE BOTTOM OF THIS! NOW YOU ARE ONE OF US AGAIN!

THANK YOU, FELLOW MEMBERS!! I--

BUT BEFORE THE NEWLY RESTORED *GL* CAN GIVE VENT TO THE HEARTFELT JOY HE FEELS AT GETTING BACK HIS HIGH RANK AND POWERS, *TERROR STRIKES*...

GREAT GUARDIANS! THAT GAS-- POURING IN ON US!

OUR RINGS CAN'T AFFECT IT--IT'S A *YELLOWISH* GAS!

THE FAINT WHIFF OF IT COMING TO MY NOSTRILS TELLS ME THAT IT'S *CHLORINE*-- A DEADLY POISONOUS GAS!

AS THE GREEN-CLAD BAND RETREATS TO THE FURTHEST POINT IT CAN IN THE DOME, AWAY FROM THE BILLOWING FUMES...

WE'VE ONLY GOT A FEW MINUTES BEFORE THAT GAS FILLS THIS CHAMBER-- AND OVERWHELMS US!

IF ONLY THERE WERE *SOMETHING* WE COULD DO!

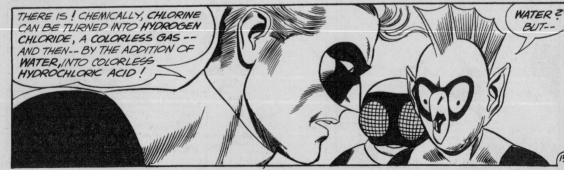

THERE IS! CHEMICALLY, *CHLORINE* CAN BE TURNED INTO *HYDROGEN CHLORIDE,* A COLORLESS GAS -- AND THEN-- BY THE ADDITION OF *WATER,* INTO COLORLESS HYDROCHLORIC ACID!

WATER? BUT--

WHERE CAN WE GET THAT? THERE IS NO WATER HERE!

ONLY ONE POSSIBLE WAY! THE BREATH OF EARTH-PEOPLE CONTAINS *WATER VAPOR!* IF I CAN USE MY RING TO EXTRACT THE WATER FROM MY BREATH AND SHOOT THE *HYDROGEN* ELEMENT AT THAT GAS...

I SHOULD BE ABLE TO TURN IT INTO *HYDROGEN CHLORIDE*-- HCL --SO THAT WE CAN HANDLE IT!

QUICK! ALL OF US--AROUND HIM! WE MUST KEEP THE YELLOW GAS AWAY FROM HIM AS LONG AS WE CAN-- OTHERWISE HIS *POWER RING* WON'T WORK!

THEN, WHILE HIS FELLOW **GREEN LANTERNS** RESORT TO THEIR **ONLY MEANS** OF KEEPING AWAY THE FATAL **CHLORINE,** GL OF **EARTH** CARRIES OUT HIS SCHEME WITH FEVERISH HASTE...

OKAY SO FAR! I'VE GOT A *FINE SPRAY* OF WATER NOW WHICH MY *POWER RING* IS EXTRACTING FROM MY OWN BREATH-- AND I'M READY TO SHOOT IT AT THE GAS! BUT-- WILL MY *IDEA* WORK!?

THEN...

PERFECT! THE WATER SPRAY IS TAKING AWAY THE YELLOW COLOR OF THE GAS, *GREEN LANTERN OF EARTH*! YOUR CHEMICAL ACTION IS CONVERTING IT INTO HYDROGEN CHLORIDE!

AS THE GRIMLY DETERMINED *CRUSADER* FOLLOWS UP HIS ADVANTAGE...

NOW THAT I'VE TURNED THE CHLORINE INTO AN *ACID*--I CAN USE ITS *CORROSIVE EFFECT* BY HURLING IT VIA MY *POWER BEAM* AT THAT YELLOW WALL! IT SHOULD "EAT" A *WAY OUT OF HERE*!!

QUICKLY, THE *CORROSIVE ACID EFFECT* FORMS A LARGE JAGGED APERTURE...

YOU'VE DONE IT, *GREEN LANTERN OF EARTH*! WE CAN GET OUT OF HERE NOW--THROUGH THAT OPENING YOU'VE MADE!

COME ON--THERE'S NOT A MOMENT TO WASTE!

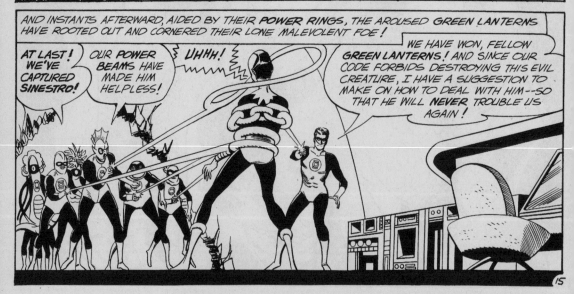

AND INSTANTS AFTERWARD, AIDED BY THEIR *POWER RINGS*, THE AROUSED *GREEN LANTERNS* HAVE ROOTED OUT AND CORNERED THEIR LONE MALEVOLENT FOE!

AT LAST! WE'VE CAPTURED SINESTRO!

OUR POWER BEAMS HAVE MADE HIM HELPLESS!

UHHH!

WE HAVE WON, FELLOW *GREEN LANTERNS*! AND SINCE OUR *CODE* FORBIDS DESTROYING THIS EVIL CREATURE, I HAVE A *SUGGESTION* TO MAKE ON HOW TO DEAL WITH HIM--SO THAT HE WILL *NEVER* TROUBLE US AGAIN!

15

IN DUE COURSE SOMEWHERE IN OUR UNIVERSE, ON A REMOTE, UNINHABITED PLANET, SINESTRO SITS IN A PRISON CELL ALONE...

THERE IS *NO POSSIBLE WAY* TO ESCAPE, SINESTRO! YOU *MUST* STAY HERE! THERE IS *NO POSSIBLE WAY* TO ESCAPE...

ELSEWHERE ON THE SAME PLANET, THE BAND OF GREEN LANTERNS PREPARES TO DISPERSE AND RETURN TO THEIR SEPARATE WORLDS...

PLACING *SINESTRO* UNDER THE INFLUENCE OF HIS OWN MIND—CONTROL DEVICE WAS A *MASTER STROKE,* GREEN LANTERN OF EARTH! WE HAVE POWERED THE DEVICE WITH OUR *POWER BEAMS* AND IT WILL NEVER RUN DOWN!

YES--AND UNDER ITS EFFECT IT WILL BE *IMPOSSIBLE* FOR SINESTRO'S BRAIN TO WORK OUT AN ESCAPE! OUR CONGRATULATIONS, GREEN LANTERN OF EARTH -- AND FAREWELL!

FAREWELL, FELLOW *GREEN LANTERNS*-- TILL WE MEET AGAIN!

THUS DO THE GREEN GLADIATORS OF THE COSMOS DEPART, LEAVING BEHIND THEM A FORLORN FIGURE SEEMINGLY FOREVER DOOMED TO HIS LONELY CELL...

YOU MUST STAY HERE! THERE IS NO POSSIBLE WAY TO ESCAPE!

The End

16

BUT IS THIS *REALLY* THE END OF *SINESTRO?* WE ADVISE YOU NOT TO BET ON IT! FOR HIS INFINITELY EVIL *BRAIN* MAY *STILL* FIND A WAY OUT OF CAPTIVITY AND BACK INTO ACTION AGAINST HIS FOES, THE MIGHTY *GREEN LANTERNS!* TO PLAY SAFE, READER, KEEP YOUR EYE ON FUTURE ISSUES OF THIS MAGAZINE!

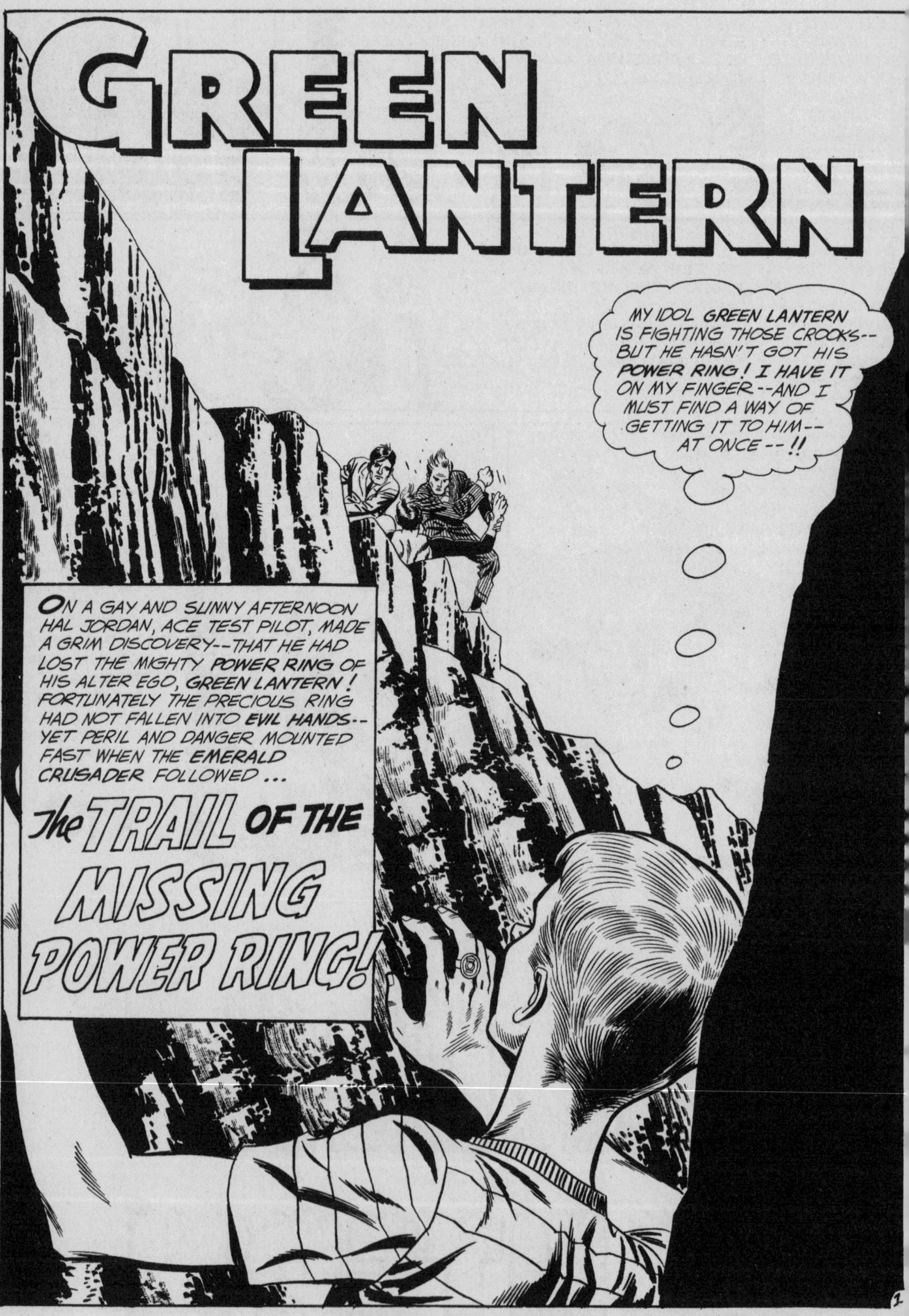
GREEN LANTERN
ON A GAY AND SUNNY AFTERNOON HAL JORDAN, ACE TEST PILOT, MADE A GRIM DISCOVERY--THAT HE HAD LOST THE MIGHTY POWER RING OF HIS ALTER EGO, GREEN LANTERN! FORTUNATELY THE PRECIOUS RING HAD NOT FALLEN INTO EVIL HANDS-- YET PERIL AND DANGER MOUNTED FAST WHEN THE EMERALD CRUSADER FOLLOWED ...
The TRAIL OF THE MISSING POWER RING!
MY IDOL GREEN LANTERN IS FIGHTING THOSE CROOKS-- BUT HE HASN'T GOT HIS POWER RING! I HAVE IT ON MY FINGER--AND I MUST FIND A WAY OF GETTING IT TO HIM-- AT ONCE--!!
1

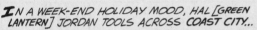

IN A WEEK-END HOLIDAY MOOD, HAL [GREEN LANTERN] JORDAN TOOLS ACROSS COAST CITY...

IT WAS NICE OF PIEFACE AND HIS BRIDE TERGA TO INVITE CAROL AND ME TO DINNER TODAY! I IMAGINE WE'LL BE THEIR FIRST GUESTS SINCE THEIR MARRIAGE LAST WEEK-- WHERE I WAS BEST MAN!

I'VE GOT TO GET CAROL A CORSAGE! THAT WILL REMIND HER THAT I STILL HAVE HOPES OF HER MARRYING ME ONE OF THESE DAYS! HERE'S A FLORIST'S SHOP NOW...

FLORIST

HJ-28

TEN MINUTES LATER WHEN THE ACE TEST PILOT EMERGES FROM THE STORE...

IN BRIGHTEST DAY, IN BLACKEST NIGHT, NO EVIL SHALL ESCAPE MY SIGHT...

GREAT SCOTT!?

YOU CROOKS HAVEN'T A CHANCE! I'M USING MY POWER BEAM TO CAPTURE YOU--!

THAT RING-- IT LOOKS JUST LIKE MY POWER RING! BUT OF COURSE IT'S NOT REALLY...

...AND I THINK I UNDERSTAND! SOME MANUFACTURER TRYING TO CASH IN ON GREEN LANTERN'S REPUTATION HAS TAKEN TO MAKING TOY POWER RINGS! I'VE BEEN HALF EXPECTING SOMETHING LIKE THAT--

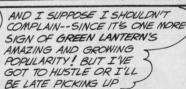

AND I SUPPOSE I SHOULDN'T COMPLAIN--SINCE IT'S ONE MORE SIGN OF GREEN LANTERN'S AMAZING AND GROWING POPULARITY! BUT I'VE GOT TO HUSTLE OR I'LL BE LATE PICKING UP CAROL ...

2

AFTER A GAY AND FESTIVE REPAST AT THE THOMAS *(PIEFACE)* KALMAKUS...

TERGA AND I WILL WASH-- BUT YOU TWO WILL DRY! FAIR ENOUGH?

IT'S A DEAL, CAROL! THAT DINNER WAS WORTH IT!

AS HAL AND HIS OFF-DUTY MECHANIC PAL--AND LONE CONFIDANT--TAKE THEIR EASE...

PIE, YOU'RE A LUCKY MAN--TO HAVE A WIFE LIKE *TERGA!*

THAT'S WHAT *YOU* NEED, HAL-- A WIFE! IF YOU HAD ONE YOU WOULDN'T HAVE BUTTONS HANGING BY A THREAD!

YOUR WIFE WOULD DARN AND SEW FOR YOU-- TAKE CARE OF YOU!

I GUESS YOU'RE RIGHT! I'M GETTING A BIT SEEDY! WHY, LOOK...

...I'M EVEN GETTING HOLES IN MY POCKETS! I DIDN'T REALIZE... UHHH! *GREAT JUMPING JUPITER!*

HAL--WHAT'S THE MATTER?

MY RING! PIE, THIS IS THE POCKET I KEEP MY *POWER RING* IN! IT MUST HAVE FALLEN OUT! BUT WAIT--I JUST THOUGHT OF SOMETHING--

THAT BOY-- THE "TOY" POWER RING HE WAS WEARING--!

SNAP!

INSTANTLY, THE ACE TEST PILOT ACTS ON THIS THOUGHT...

PIE, I'VE NO TIME TO EXPLAIN! COVER ME WITH THE GIRLS-- I'LL BE BACK AS SOON AS I CAN! I'VE GOT TO FIND MY RING--!

OKAY, HAL! I'LL THINK UP SOME EXCUSE FOR YOUR ABSENCE-- DON'T WORRY!

MEANWHILE, IN A QUARRY, ON THE OUTSKIRTS OF THE CITY, DESERTED OVER THE WEEK-END...

AW, WE'RE GOING HOME, BILLY! YOU ALWAYS WANT TO BE GREEN LANTERN!

WELL, I'VE GOT THE RING!

AFTER BILLY TAYLOR HAS BEEN LEFT ALONE BY HIS PLAYMATES...

GOLLY! I'M BEGINNING TO THINK THIS REALLY IS GREEN LANTERN'S POWER RING! I--I CAN MAKE A SORT OF GREEN BEAM SHOOT OUT OF IT--!!

IN EXCITEMENT THE BOY PROPELS THE MYSTIC RAY AT A HANDY OBJECT...

JIMINY! I CAN WORK THE BEAM!! IT'S A TERRIBLE STRAIN...TO CONCENTRATE MY WILLPOWER LIKE GREEN LANTERN DOES... BUT I'M LIFTING THAT STONE--!

I CAN HOLD IT OVER MY HEAD!! I CAN MAKE IT STAY UP THERE!

BUT I GUESS-- I OUGHT TO HAND THIS RING OVER TO THE POLICE SO THEY CAN RETURN IT TO GREEN LANTERN! HE MAY NEED IT-- I MUST SEE THAT HE GETS IT BACK AT ONCE!

BUT THE THRILL OF WEARING THE RING TEMPTS THE LAD TO KEEP IT ON A MOMENT LONGER...

GOLLY GEE! NOW I KNOW WHAT GREEN LANTERN HIMSELF FEELS LIKE! IT'S THE GREATEST FEELING IN THE WORLD TO HAVE POWER OVER THIS MAGIC BEAM!

4

BUT THEN, AS WILL SOME-TIMES HAPPEN TO THOSE WHO ARE SO CARRIED AWAY, THEY DON'T LOOK WHERE THEY ARE STEPPING...

Uhh--FALLING INTO THIS PIT!

AND THE NEXT MOMENT...

I CAN'T GET OUT! MY LEG IS HURT... AND I CAN HARDLY MOVE! BUT MAYBE... Gasp

COME ON, BANDY! LET'S MOVE!

NO USE! I CAN'T WORK THE RING TO FREE MYSELF EITHER! I--I DON'T HAVE ENOUGH STRENGTH... NOT ENOUGH WILLPOWER...!

SOON, INSIDE THE QUARRY OFFICE BUILDING...

IT WAS A CINCH GETTING RID OF THE WATCH-GUARD FOR THIS QUARRY OFFICE! THERE'S THE SAFE, BANDY!

YEAH--AND I'VE GOT THE CAN OPENER!

MEANWHILE...

THE BIGGER FELLOW WE WERE PLAYING WITH? I GUESS YOU MEAN BILLY, MISTER! WE LEFT HIM AT THE QUARRY--

THE QUARRY? WHERE'S THAT?

ACROSS TOWN! WE PLAY THERE WHEN THERE'S NOBODY WORKING!

THANKS, SON! I'LL FIND IT!

AND SHORTLY... BURGLARS--AND THEY'RE ROBBING THE SAFE!

LET'S HIKE, RALPH! WE'VE CLEANED IT OUT!

AT ONCE, ALMOST BY REFLEX ACTION, THE YOUNG TEST PILOT SWITCHES TO HIS FAMED ALTER EGO, THE EMERALD GLADIATOR!

EVEN THOUGH I HAVEN'T ANY RING I'M *STILL* GREEN LANTERN -- AND I'VE GOT TO STOP THOSE CROOKS AT ALL COSTS!

THEN...

G-GREEN LANTERN!?

HOW DID HE GET HERE!?

AS THE AROUSED CRUSADER PILES INTO A FOE...

USING HIS *FISTS* AGAINST US?!

SUDDENLY BANDY NOTICES A STRANGE FACT IN THE MELEE...

HUH? I CAN SEE WHY! HE HASN'T GOT HIS POWER RING!!

AT THAT MOMENT, BELOW IN THE PIT, SMALL EARS HAVE OVERHEARD ALL...

GOLLY GEE! MY IDOL *GREEN LANTERN* IS FIGHTING CROOKS UP THERE, BUT HE CAN'T USE HIS RING AGAINST THEM BECAUSE... BECAUSE *I* HAVE IT ON!

AT HIM, RALPH! WE DON'T HAVE TO BE AFRAID OF HIM **WITHOUT HIS RING!**

I--I'VE GOT TO DO SOMETHING TO HELP GREEN LANTERN!

IF I COULD SHOOT THE **GREEN BEAM** UP...IT COULD HANDLE THOSE CROOKS! BUT I CAN'T DO IT... I'M TOO WEAK...! AND I CERTAINLY CAN'T **THROW** THE RING UP TO **GREEN LANTERN**...

...BECAUSE I... I CAN HARDLY MOVE! BUT WAIT A SECOND... I JUST THOUGHT OF SOMETHING...!

WE'RE OVERPOWERIN' HIM, BANDY!

...MAYBE...MAYBE I CAN USE MY **WILLPOWER** TO SHOOT THE RING ITSELF UP TO HIM! GOT TO TRY IT... I'VE GOT TO TRY IT!

CONCENTRATING AS HARD AS HE CAN, YOUNG BILLY BENDS EVERY OUNCE OF HIS STRENGTH TO THE TASK...

I MUST SHUT OUT EVERYTHING ELSE FROM MY MIND...I MUST MAKE THE RING SHOOT UPWARD...

IT...IT'S MOVING! GOT TO...TRY HARDER... HARDER...!

IT'S OFF MY FINGER...! IT'S STARTING TO GO...!

7

THE NEXT MOMENT, NEAR THE PIT...

HIT HIM, BANDY! CONK HIM OUT!

HERE GOES--

EH?

I MANAGED TO TWIST OUT OF THE WAY OF THAT BLOW... I MAY NOT BE SO LUCKY NEXT TIME... THAT RING-- IT LOOKS LIKE MY POWER RING--!

WITH A CONVULSIVE EFFORT, THE DOWNED GLADIATOR MANAGES TO UPSET THE FOES ATOP HIM...

GRAB HIM, RALPH--!

GOT TO GET TO THAT RING--!

THIS IS MY POWER RING! IT HAS TO BE!

I AIN'T GONNA WASTE ANY MORE TIME ON HIM, RALPH! I'M GONNA BLAST HIM--BLIT GOOD!

BUT THE NEXT INSTANT EVEN BEFORE THE THUG CAN FIRE...

AAAAA!

ANY BLASTING DONE AROUND HERE--I'M GOING TO DO IT!

BRINGING HIS NEWLY RECOVERED POWER RING INTO PLAY TO FORM A GIANT FIRE HOSE, THE EMERALD GLADIATOR PLAYS A HEAVY, SUPER-SWIFT STREAM OF WATER ON HIS TWO ASSAILANTS!

8

AND LATER WITH ALL THE "FIRE" DOUSED OUT OF THE THIEVES...

WH-WHAT HAPPENED TO US, BANDY?

I'LL JUST USE MY *GREEN BEAM* TO CAGE THOSE HOODLUMS UNTIL I CAN TURN THEM IN TO THE POLICE...

...BUT MEANWHILE I'VE GOT TO HAVE A LOOK DOWN INTO THIS QUARRY HOLE WHERE THE *RING* CAME FROM... AND I HAVE AN IDEA WHAT I'LL FIND DOWN THERE..!

I THOUGHT SO! IT'S THE BOY NAMED BILLY--THE ONE I SAW PLAYING WITH MY RING NEAR THE FLORIST'S SHOP--WHERE IT MUST HAVE SLIPPED THROUGH THE HOLE IN MY POCKET! BUT HE SEEMS *HURT...!*

WITH INFINITE CARE, THE *GREEN-CLAD CRUSADER* EMPLOYS HIS RING TO FREE THE LAD AND RAISE HIM TO THE SURFACE...

YOU ALL RIGHT, BILLY?

GEE! THE WAY *GREEN LANTERN* USES HIS RING--IT'S TERRIFIC!

YES, I AM, *GREEN LANTERN*--THANKS TO YOU!

YOU MEAN *I'M* ALL RIGHT-- THANKS TO *YOU,* BILLY! YOU SURE THOUGHT QUICKLY--THE WAY YOU "POWERED" THAT RING TO ME! AND IN RETURN I'M GOING TO GIVE YOU A SOUVENIR TO REMEMBER THIS OCCASION!

ONCE MORE THE MIGHTY *POWER RING* OPERATES, THIS TIME TO FASHION A *TOY DUPLICATE* OF ITSELF!

A--A SPECIAL RING LIKE YOURS FOR *ME?* WOW--EE! DO YOU THINK I REALLY DESERVE SUCH A WONDERFUL PRESENT?

YOU SURE DO, BILLY! AND HAVE A GOOD TIME PLAYING WITH IT!

THIS EXPERIENCE HAS TAUGHT ME THAT AS *HAL JORDAN* I MUST NEVER AGAIN KEEP THE POWER RING IN MY POCKET! FROM NOW ON, I'LL *ALWAYS* WEAR IT ON MY FINGER--BUT IT WILL BE CONCEALED FROM VIEW BY AN *INVISIBILITY SHIELD* WHEN I WEAR IT AS HAL!

SHORTLY, WITH THE CROOKS IN CUSTODY, HAL JORDAN REAPPEARS AT PIEFACE'S APARTMENT HOUSE...

I WAITED DOWN HERE TO MEET YOU, HAL--BECAUSE I WANTED TO TIP YOU OFF TO THE EXCUSE I MADE UP FOR YOU! I SAID YOU'D LOST YOUR WALLET AND WENT OUT TO FIND IT!

GOOD ENOUGH! AND I *DID* FIND WHAT I WENT OUT FOR, PIE...

...SO NOW WE CAN ALL SETTLE DOWN TO A PLEASANT AFTERNOON... WHILE I USE THE OPPORTUNITY TO TRY AND CONVINCE *CAROL* THAT SHE LOVES ME ENOUGH TO MARRY ME!

GOOD IDEA, HAL! TERGA AND I WILL-- er--GIVE YOU TWO TIME TO BE ALONE--!

BUT UPSTAIRS, NOT LONG AFTERWARD...

PIEFACE HAS THE MOST MARVELOUS COLLECTION OF *GREEN LANTERN* SCRAP-BOOKS! I COULD SPEND DAYS GOING THROUGH THEM--!

GREAT DAYS! SHE'S HARDLY AWARE OF ME ANYMORE...

ALL SHE CAN THINK OF IS GREEN LANTERN!! (SIGH!) ONCE AGAIN MY ALTER EGO HAS COME BETWEEN ME AND MY LADY LOVE!

HE'S WONDERFUL..!

The End

10

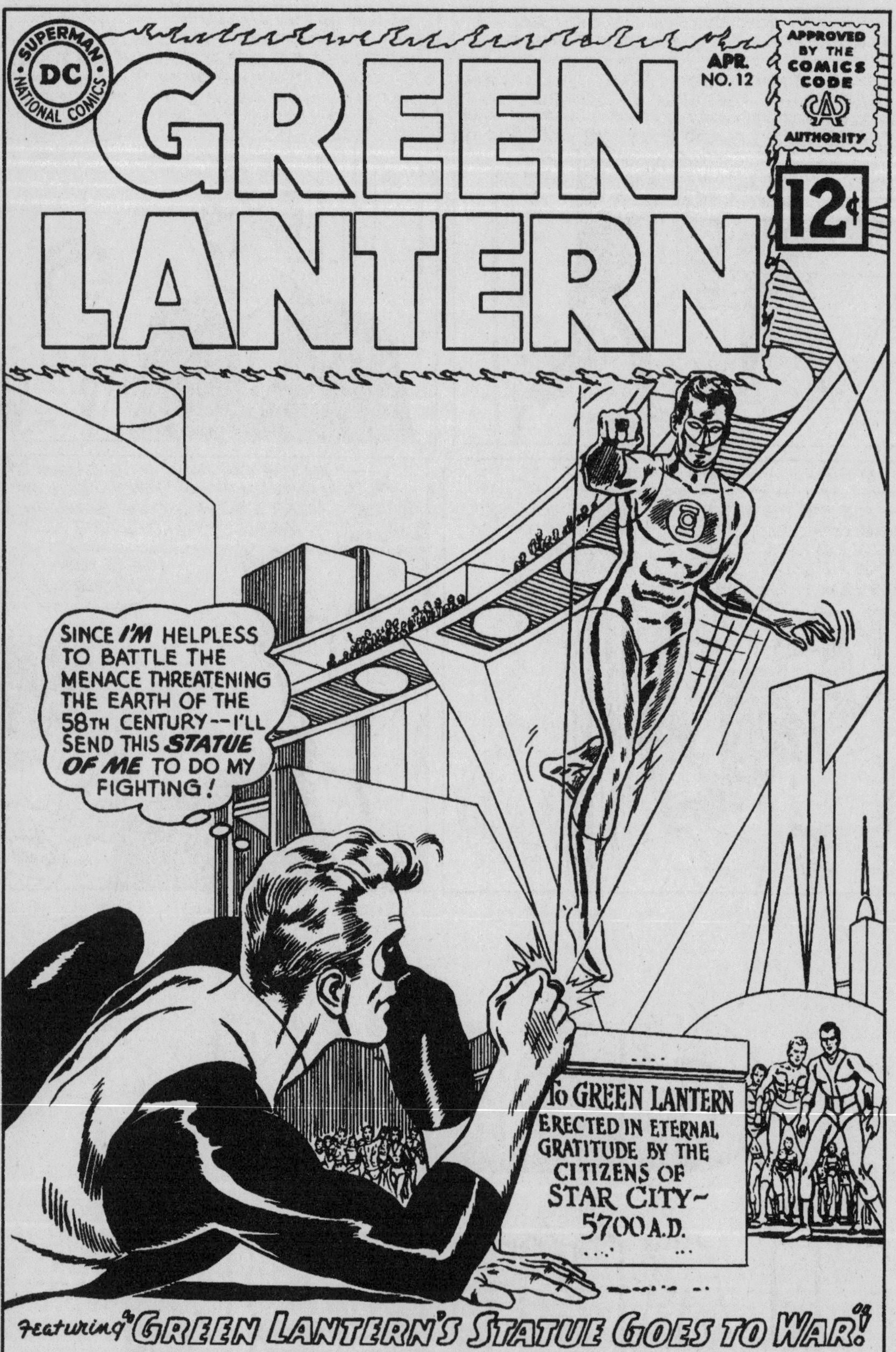
SUPERMAN DC NATIONAL COMICS
GREEN LANTERN
APR. NO. 12
APPROVED BY THE COMICS CODE AUTHORITY
12¢
SINCE I'M HELPLESS TO BATTLE THE MENACE THREATENING THE EARTH OF THE 58TH CENTURY--I'LL SEND THIS STATUE OF ME TO DO MY FIGHTING!
TO GREEN LANTERN ERECTED IN ETERNAL GRATITUDE BY THE CITIZENS OF STAR CITY-- 5700 A.D.
Featuring "GREEN LANTERN'S STATUE GOES TO WAR!"

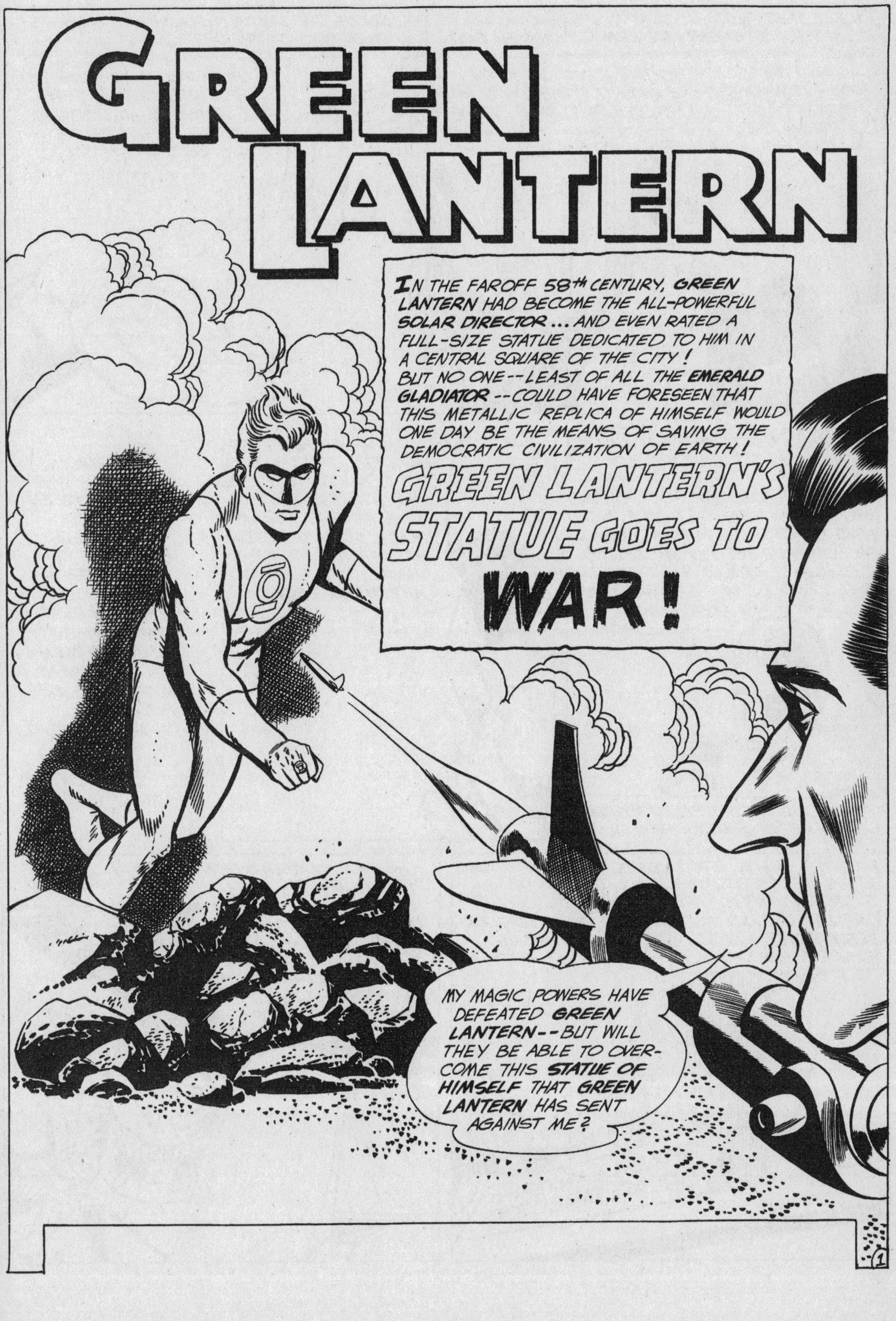
GREEN LANTERN
IN THE FAROFF 58th CENTURY, GREEN LANTERN HAD BECOME THE ALL-POWERFUL SOLAR DIRECTOR ... AND EVEN RATED A FULL-SIZE STATUE DEDICATED TO HIM IN A CENTRAL SQUARE OF THE CITY! BUT NO ONE--LEAST OF ALL THE EMERALD GLADIATOR--COULD HAVE FORESEEN THAT THIS METALLIC REPLICA OF HIMSELF WOULD ONE DAY BE THE MEANS OF SAVING THE DEMOCRATIC CIVILIZATION OF EARTH!
GREEN LANTERN'S STATUE GOES TO WAR!
MY MAGIC POWERS HAVE DEFEATED GREEN LANTERN--BUT WILL THEY BE ABLE TO OVERCOME THIS STATUE OF HIMSELF THAT GREEN LANTERN HAS SENT AGAINST ME?
1

IN ACE TEST PILOT HAL JORDAN'S DRESSING ROOM, HIS ALTER EGO GREEN LANTERN NOTICES AN ODD THING...

WHERE DID THIS TINY PIECE OF METAL COME FROM? IT WASN'T THERE WHEN I COMBED MY HAIR A MOMENT AGO... AND IT COULDN'T HAVE DROPPED FROM THE CEILING..!

CURIOUS, THE EMERALD GLADIATOR TRAINS HIS POWER RING ON THE OBJECT...

THIS IS INCREDIBLE! MY POWER BEAM SPECTROSCOPICALLY REVEALS THAT THIS IS AN UNKNOWN METAL--NEVER BEFORE SEEN ON EARTH!

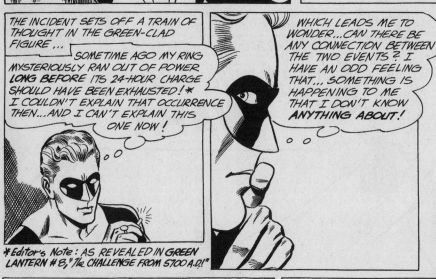

THE INCIDENT SETS OFF A TRAIN OF THOUGHT IN THE GREEN-CLAD FIGURE...

SOMETIME AGO MY RING MYSTERIOUSLY RAN OUT OF POWER LONG BEFORE ITS 24-HOUR CHARGE SHOULD HAVE BEEN EXHAUSTED!* I COULDN'T EXPLAIN THAT OCCURRENCE THEN... AND I CAN'T EXPLAIN THIS ONE NOW!

WHICH LEADS ME TO WONDER... CAN THERE BE ANY CONNECTION BETWEEN THE TWO EVENTS? I HAVE AN ODD FEELING THAT... SOMETHING IS HAPPENING TO ME THAT I DON'T KNOW ANYTHING ABOUT!

AMAZINGLY, THE KEEN MIND OF THE GREEN-GARBED CRUSADER HAS HIT UPON THE TRUTH! BUT NOT EVEN IN HIS WILDEST IMAGININGS COULD GREEN LANTERN DREAM WHAT LIES BEHIND THAT CHANCE THOUGHT OF HIS! TO EXPLAIN IT...

*Editor's Note: AS REVEALED IN GREEN LANTERN #8, "The CHALLENGE FROM 5700 A.D.!"

..WE MUST TRAVEL 3740 YEARS FORWARD IN TIME TO THE YEAR 5702 WHEN ALL THE SOLAR SYSTEM PLANETS ARE UNDER DOMINION OF THE EARTH... AND ONE MAN, THE SOLAR DIRECTOR IN STAR CITY, WIELDS MORE POWER THAN ANY HUMAN IN HISTORY...

GREEN LANTERN SOLAR DIRECTOR

...THE MAN NAMED GREEN LANTERN... WHOSE CHAIR IS EMPTY... BUT WITH GOOD REASON...

WE MUST REACH INTO THE PAST AGAIN, IONA, TO BRING OUR SOLAR DIRECTOR, GREEN LANTERN, HERE TO OUR ERA AT ONCE!

As DASOR, CHAIRMAN OF THE SOLAR COUNCIL, AND HIS SECRETARY IONA VANE BUSY THEMSELVES WITH THEIR ALL-IMPORTANT TASK...

IT IS TWO YEARS NOW SINCE WE LAST CALLED UPON GREEN LANTERN, IONA--

YES, CHAIRMAN DASOR--IT WAS DURING THE INVASION OF THE ZEGORS!

TWO YEARS... AND YET I DON'T THINK THERE'S BEEN A DAY SINCE THAT I HAVEN'T THOUGHT ABOUT GREEN LANTERN! AND NOW-- HOW FAST MY HEART IS BEATING AT THE THOUGHT THAT I WILL SEE HIM AGAIN!

BUT WHILE IONA WAITS BREATHLESSLY, LET US BRIEFLY REVIEW THE CIRCUMSTANCES AND STRANGE CONDITIONS ATTENDANT UPON GREEN LANTERN'S LAST VISIT TO THE FAR FUTURE, THE WORLD OF 5700 A.D. ...

... AND A MEETING OF THE HIGH COUNCIL OF SOLAR DELEGATES SITTING IN SOLAR HALL, STAR CITY, IN A GRAVE EMERGENCY SESSION ...

FELLOW SOLARITES*, WE ARE MET IN THIS CRISIS TO CONSIDER A NEW CANDIDATE FOR THE CRUCIAL POST OF SOLAR DIRECTOR! MANY CANDIDATES HAVE BEEN CONSIDERED--

YES! BUT NONE OF THEM WAS EQUAL TO THE JOB!

*Editor's Note: BY 5700 A.D., CENTURIES OF LIVING ON OTHER SOLAR SYSTEM WORLDS HAVE CHANGED THE COLONIZING EARTHLINGS ACCORDING TO THE CLIMATIC CONDITIONS OF THEIR NEW HOMES!

BEFORE I REVEAL THE LATEST CANDIDATE, I MUST REMIND YOU THAT NOT LONG AGO OUR SCIENCE DEVELOPED THE ABILITY TO PEER AT WILL INTO THE PAST-- IN EFFECT, TO VIEW HISTORY AS IT HAPPENS-- BY THE INVENTION OF THE TIMESCOPE!

NOW BY LINKING UP A COMMON MATTER TELEPORTER TO THE TIMESCOPE WE ARE ABLE TO BRING ANYTHING-- OR ANYONE-- WE CHOOSE FROM THE PAST INTO THE PRESENT! IN THE COURSE OF OUR RESEARCHES INTO THE PAST...

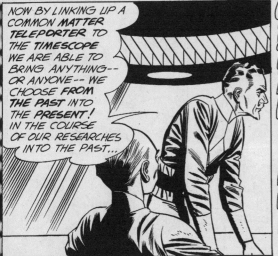

"...MY SECRETARY IONA VANE AND I CAME ACROSS A TRULY AMAZING INDIVIDUAL, IN THE FARAWAY TWENTIETH CENTURY, NAMED GREEN LANTERN... "

HE IS ABSOLUTELY FEARLESS!

A CHAMPION OF CHAMPIONS!

3

SINCE WE HAVE NOT BEEN ABLE TO FIND A GREAT LEADER IN OUR OWN ERA, I PROPOSE THAT WE BRING THIS ANCIENT HERO **GREEN LANTERN** TO OUR TIME AND MAKE HIM OUR **SOLAR DIRECTOR!**

WHAT AN ASTONISHING PROPOSAL!

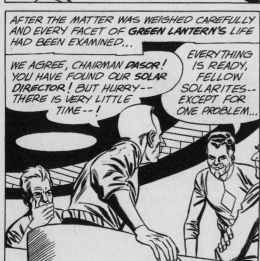

AFTER THE MATTER WAS WEIGHED CAREFULLY AND EVERY FACET OF **GREEN LANTERN'S** LIFE HAD BEEN EXAMINED...

WE AGREE, CHAIRMAN **DASOR!** YOU HAVE FOUND OUR **SOLAR DIRECTOR!** BUT HURRY-- THERE IS VERY LITTLE TIME--!

EVERYTHING IS READY, FELLOW SOLARITES-- EXCEPT FOR ONE PROBLEM...

TO TRAVEL IN TIME CAUSES AN INDIVIDUAL'S MEMORY TO BE COMPLETELY WIPED OUT! IF **GREEN LANTERN** CAME HERE WITHOUT HIS "LIFE-HISTORY" HE WOULD BE DAZED--OF LITTLE USE TO US!

BUT **HOW** CAN SUCH AN OBSTACLE BE OVERCOME?

SIMPLY! MISS VANE HAS PRE-PARED A FICTITIOUS PERSONAL HISTORY FOR **GREEN LANTERN!** HE WILL **BELIEVE** THAT HE IS A FAMOUS **SPACE-EXPLORER** OF OUR ERA NAMED **POL MANNING** WHO HAS JUST BEEN SUMMONED BACK TO EARTH TO DEAL WITH THE DREADFUL MENACE OF THE **ZEGORS!** BUT WAIT--!

THERE IS ONE THING YOU HAVE OMITTED, MISS VANE! A YOUNG MAN LIKE **GREEN LANTERN** WOULD CERTAINLY HAVE A **ROMANTIC INTEREST!** ...AND SINCE **YOU** ARE UNMARRIED AND UNATTACHED, **IONA,** IT OCCURS TO ME THAT **YOU** CAN BE HIS ROMANTIC INTEREST!

M-ME!?

AS MEMORIES OF THAT PRE-VIOUS TIME FLOOD OVER **IONA** NOW...

I THOUGHT IT WAS JUST GOING TO BE A GAME FOR ME TO PLAY! I DIDN'T REALIZE IT WOULD BE **FOR KEEPS**--AS FAR AS I'M CONCERNED!

READY, **IONA!** I'M STARTING THE TELEPORTER..!

4

AND NOW LET US RETURN TO THE MOMENT **BEFORE GREEN LANTERN** FOUND THE STRANGE PIECE OF METAL IN HIS HAIR...

I'D GIVE A LOT TO FIGURE OUT WHY MY **POWER RING** MYSTERIOUSLY RAN OUT OF CHARGE A WHILE AGO! I--eh? A QUEER TREMBLING... LIKE A SUDDEN FEVER... ALL OVER ME--!

AN INSTANT LATER, BY THE INCREDIBLE MAGIC OF FIFTY-EIGHTH CENTURY SCIENCE...

WE'VE BROUGHT HIM BACK, **IONA**! AND AS ALWAYS THIS MOMENT IS CRITICAL! IT WILL NOT BE NECESSARY TO FEED HIS **PSEUDO-HISTORY** INTO **GREEN LANTERN'S** MIND AGAIN-- AUTOMATICALLY, NOW THAT HE IS IN OUR ERA, THAT PART OF HIS MIND WILL TAKE OVER...

...JUST AS HIS IDENTITY AS **HAL JORDAN** IN THE TWENTIETH CENTURY IS AUTOMATICALLY ERASED FROM HIS MIND DURING HIS STAY WITH US! BUT STILL THE **PAST TWO YEARS** HERE MUST BE ACCOUNTED FOR, TO PREVENT HIM FROM BEING DAZED OR UNCERTAIN!

IN THE SPLIT-SECONDS BEFORE THE MISTS DISSOLVE FROM IN FRONT OF **GREEN LANTERN'S** EYES, AN ELECTRONIC DEVICE OPERATES SILENTLY..

DURING THE PAST TWO YEARS, **GREEN LANTERN**, YOU HAVE BEEN ON A LONE DEEP-SPACE EXPLORATION IN THE PERSON OF YOUR ALTER EGO **POL MANNING**! WHILE YOU WERE AWAY CHAIRMAN **DASOR** AND **IONA** ACTED IN YOUR BEHALF HERE IN **STAR CITY**...

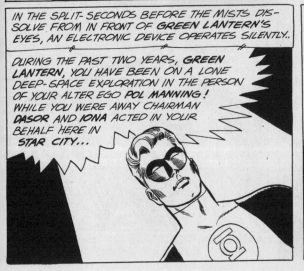

THEY ISSUED ORDERS AND RELEASED PROCLAMATIONS UNDER YOUR SIGNATURE AS **SOLAR DIRECTOR**! AND YOU KEPT IN CONSTANT TOUCH WITH THEM BY SPACE-RADIO! BUT THIS WEEK YOU HEARD THE ALARMING NEWS OF THE **REVOLT** OF THE **EARTH GENERALS**...

...AND YOU REALIZED THAT ONLY YOUR PRESENCE HERE IN **STAR CITY** COULD AVERT DISASTER! SO YOU HURRIED HOME AS FAST AS YOU COULD! AND YOU HAVE JUST ARRIVED...

HE'S COMING TO NOW, IONA! HE'S GOING TO BE ALL RIGHT...

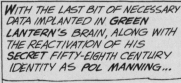

WITH THE LAST BIT OF NECESSARY DATA IMPLANTED IN **GREEN LANTERN'S** BRAIN, ALONG WITH THE REACTIVATION OF HIS **SECRET FIFTY-EIGHTH CENTURY** IDENTITY AS **POL MANNING**...

I CAME AS FAST AS POSSIBLE, **DASOR**! OH-- IT'S GOOD TO SEE YOU AGAIN, **IONA**...

HE--HE'S HARDLY NOTICING ME! BUT I GUESS...

...I CAN'T EXPECT ANYTHING ELSE CONSIDERING THE **GRAVITY** OF THE **SITUATION** HE HAS TO FACE!

I WANT A RUN-DOWN ON THE LATEST NEWS OF THE REVOLT, **DASOR**!

IN THE MAP ROOM OF THE **SOLAR DIRECTOR'S** HEAD-QUARTERS...

STAR CITY IS NOW UNDER SIEGE, **GREEN LANTERN**! BY THE ARMIES OF THE THREE TRAITOR GENERALS-- GENERAL BASSETT, GENERAL KORNING, AND GENERAL MI-VARD! AT THE MOMENT THEY ARE AWAITING OUR REPLY TO AN ULTIMATUM!

AN ULTIMATUM?

YES! HERE IT IS...

Unless STAR CITY is surrendered to us at once we will destroy it completely!
Signed
THE JUNTA
General Bassett
General Korning
General Mi-Vard

THE **JUNTA** * MUST BE DEFEATED! OUR DEMOCRATIC GOVERNMENT CAN NEVER SURRENDER TO A SHOW OF **BRUTE FORCE**! WE MUST FIGHT!

GOOD! I KNEW YOU WOULD SAY THAT, GREEN LANTERN!

*Editor's Note: "**JUNTA**"--AN EMERGENCY LEADER-SHIP IN A REBELLION OR UPRISING.

WITH A TERRIFIC BLAZE OF ENERGY, THE GREEN-CLAD **SOLAR DIRECTOR** SWINGS INTO ACTION, AS IF HE HAD NEVER BEEN AWAY FROM HIS DESK...

HAVE ALL ABLE-BODIED MEN REPORT TO THEIR SPACE-RAID STATIONS FOR MILITARY DUTY!

ALL AVAILABLE ARMS IN OUR ARSENALS WILL BE PASSED OUT TO CITIZENS WHO WANT TO HELP DEFEND THE CITY!

THE LOYAL **SPACE-LEGION** FROM **PLUTO** IS ON ITS WAY, MR. **SOLAR DIRECTOR!**

HAVE THEM ATTACK THE ENEMY WITHOUT DELAY!

HE'S INSPIRING!

I ADMIT I WAS GETTING DISCOURAGED, **IONA**, BUT NOW I'M FEELING MUCH BETTER ABOUT OUR CHANCES OF CRUSHING THIS REBELLION-- WITH **GREEN LANTERN** ON THE JOB!

SOON... THE **SPACE-LEGION** FROM **PLUTO** HAS ARRIVED! I'VE GIVEN ORDERS FOR THEM TO ENGAGE GENERAL BASSETT'S FORCES ON THE NORTH-- THE CLOSEST TO THE CITY!

ON THE TELESCREEN AT HEADQUARTERS, A GRIM GROUP VIEWS A THRILLING SIGHT AS THE LOYAL SPACE-TROOPERS FROM **PLUTO** PLUMMET DOWN ON THE FOE...

THE **PLUTO-LEGIONNAIRES** ARE FIRING **PARALO-PISTOLS!** THEY HAVE TO GET WITHIN RANGE TO PARALYZE THE FOE!

THE ENEMY IS SHOOTING **NERVE-GUNS**-- AND TAKING A HEAVY TOLL OF OUR SOLDIERS!

7

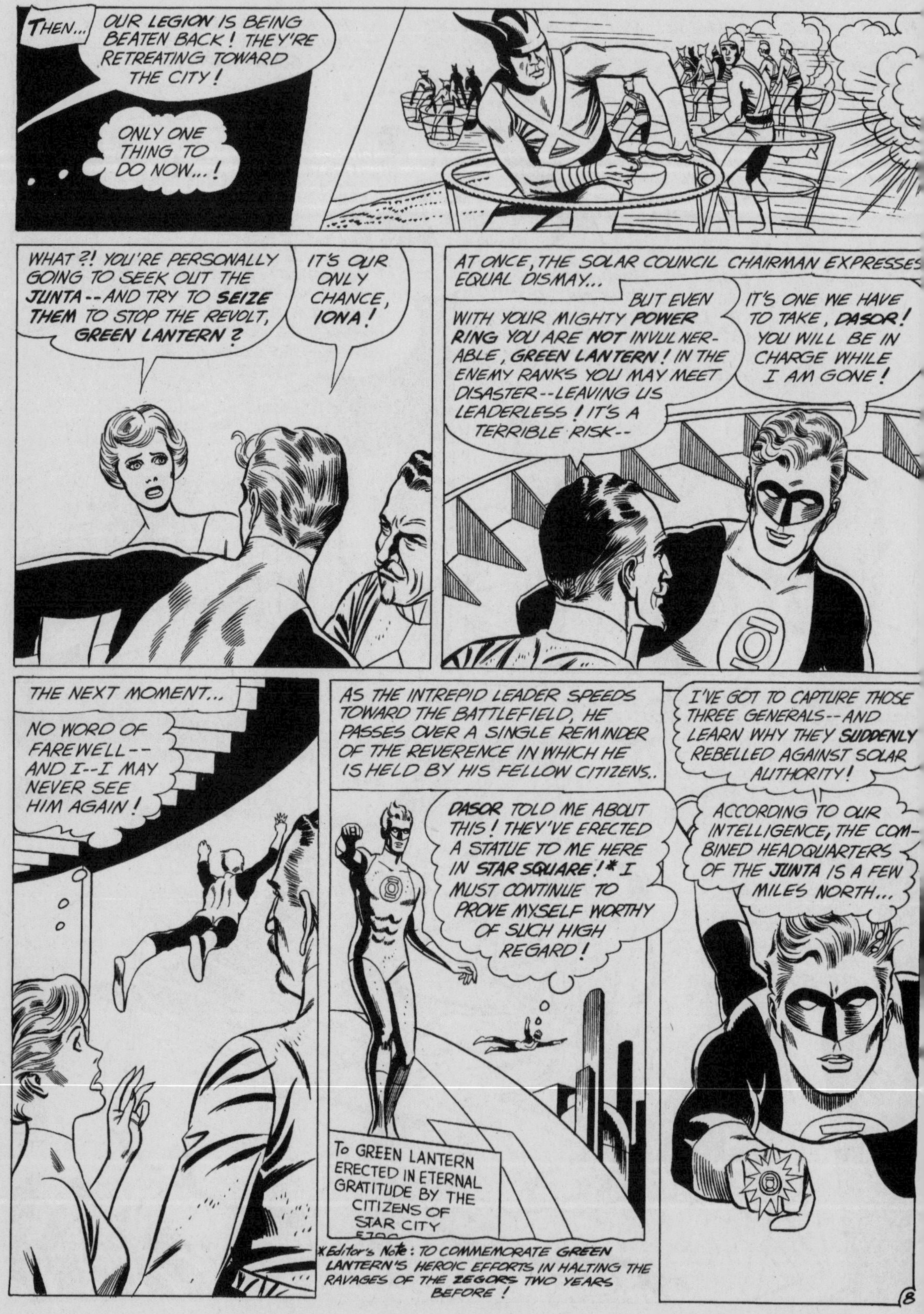
THEN...
OUR LEGION IS BEING BEATEN BACK! THEY'RE RETREATING TOWARD THE CITY!
ONLY ONE THING TO DO NOW...!
WHAT ?! YOU'RE PERSONALLY GOING TO SEEK OUT THE JUNTA--AND TRY TO SEIZE THEM TO STOP THE REVOLT, GREEN LANTERN ?
IT'S OUR ONLY CHANCE, IONA!
AT ONCE, THE SOLAR COUNCIL CHAIRMAN EXPRESSES EQUAL DISMAY...
BUT EVEN WITH YOUR MIGHTY POWER RING YOU ARE NOT INVULNERABLE, GREEN LANTERN! IN THE ENEMY RANKS YOU MAY MEET DISASTER--LEAVING US LEADERLESS! IT'S A TERRIBLE RISK--
IT'S ONE WE HAVE TO TAKE, DASOR! YOU WILL BE IN CHARGE WHILE I AM GONE!
THE NEXT MOMENT...
NO WORD OF FAREWELL--AND I--I MAY NEVER SEE HIM AGAIN!
AS THE INTREPID LEADER SPEEDS TOWARD THE BATTLEFIELD, HE PASSES OVER A SINGLE REMINDER OF THE REVERENCE IN WHICH HE IS HELD BY HIS FELLOW CITIZENS..
DASOR TOLD ME ABOUT THIS! THEY'VE ERECTED A STATUE TO ME HERE IN STAR SQUARE!* I MUST CONTINUE TO PROVE MYSELF WORTHY OF SUCH HIGH REGARD!
To GREEN LANTERN ERECTED IN ETERNAL GRATITUDE BY THE CITIZENS OF STAR CITY
*Editor's Note: TO COMMEMORATE GREEN LANTERN'S HEROIC EFFORTS IN HALTING THE RAVAGES OF THE ZEGORS TWO YEARS BEFORE!
I'VE GOT TO CAPTURE THOSE THREE GENERALS--AND LEARN WHY THEY SUDDENLY REBELLED AGAINST SOLAR AUTHORITY!
ACCORDING TO OUR INTELLIGENCE, THE COMBINED HEADQUARTERS OF THE JUNTA IS A FEW MILES NORTH...
8

GREEN LANTERN'S STATUE GOES TO WAR PART TWO

REACHING THE WELL-PROTECTED COMMAND POST OF THE *JUNTA*, THE *EMERALD WARRIOR* BARRELS HIS WAY IN VIA HIS *POWER RING*-- ONLY TO SET OFF AUTOMATIC WEAPONS, TRIGGERED BY ELECTRIC-EYES, THAT THREATEN TO BLAST HIM INTO ETERNITY!

THERE ARE THE THREE GENERALS! BUT-- THEY'VE GOT THIS PLACE "MINED" WITH GUNS--SET SECRETLY INTO THE WALLS! AND DESIGNED TO BLAST AN INTRUDER LIKE ME!

IT'S THE *SOLAR DIRECTOR!*

HIS LIGHTNING-LIKE REFLEXES WORKING AT TOP SPEED, *GREEN LANTERN* WARDS OFF THE AUTOMATIC ATTACK...

MY *POWER BEAM* IS DESTROYING THE CONCEALED WEAPONS-- EXPLODING THEM BEFORE THEY CAN HARM ME!

THEN...

THE GENERALS HAVE PULLED *NERVE-PISTOLS!* IF ANY OF THOSE RAYS TOUCH ME--!

9

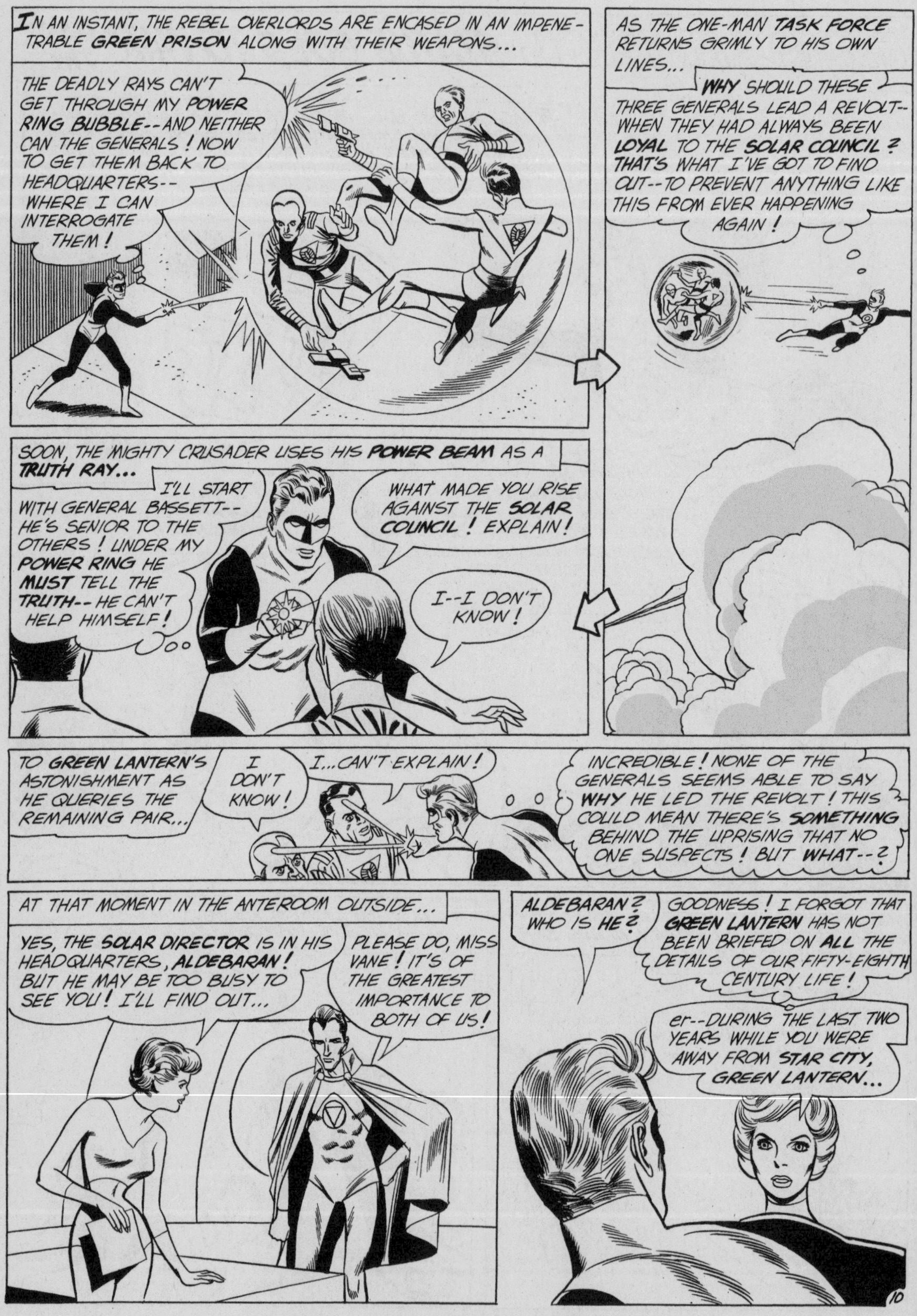
IN AN INSTANT, THE REBEL OVERLORDS ARE ENCASED IN AN IMPENETRABLE GREEN PRISON ALONG WITH THEIR WEAPONS...
THE DEADLY RAYS CAN'T GET THROUGH MY POWER RING BUBBLE--AND NEITHER CAN THE GENERALS! NOW TO GET THEM BACK TO HEADQUARTERS--WHERE I CAN INTERROGATE THEM!
AS THE ONE-MAN TASK FORCE RETURNS GRIMLY TO HIS OWN LINES...
WHY SHOULD THESE THREE GENERALS LEAD A REVOLT--WHEN THEY HAD ALWAYS BEEN LOYAL TO THE SOLAR COUNCIL? THAT'S WHAT I'VE GOT TO FIND OUT--TO PREVENT ANYTHING LIKE THIS FROM EVER HAPPENING AGAIN!
SOON, THE MIGHTY CRUSADER USES HIS POWER BEAM AS A TRUTH RAY...
I'LL START WITH GENERAL BASSETT--HE'S SENIOR TO THE OTHERS! UNDER MY POWER RING HE MUST TELL THE TRUTH--HE CAN'T HELP HIMSELF!
WHAT MADE YOU RISE AGAINST THE SOLAR COUNCIL! EXPLAIN!
I--I DON'T KNOW!
TO GREEN LANTERN'S ASTONISHMENT AS HE QUERIES THE REMAINING PAIR...
I DON'T KNOW!
I...CAN'T EXPLAIN!
INCREDIBLE! NONE OF THE GENERALS SEEMS ABLE TO SAY WHY HE LED THE REVOLT! THIS COULD MEAN THERE'S SOMETHING BEHIND THE UPRISING THAT NO ONE SUSPECTS! BUT WHAT--?
AT THAT MOMENT IN THE ANTEROOM OUTSIDE...
YES, THE SOLAR DIRECTOR IS IN HIS HEADQUARTERS, ALDEBARAN! BUT HE MAY BE TOO BUSY TO SEE YOU! I'LL FIND OUT...
PLEASE DO, MISS VANE! IT'S OF THE GREATEST IMPORTANCE TO BOTH OF US!
ALDEBARAN? WHO IS HE?
GOODNESS! I FORGOT THAT GREEN LANTERN HAS NOT BEEN BRIEFED ON ALL THE DETAILS OF OUR FIFTY-EIGHTH CENTURY LIFE!
er--DURING THE LAST TWO YEARS WHILE YOU WERE AWAY FROM STAR CITY, GREEN LANTERN...
10

...THIS **FERENC ALDEBARAN** EMERGED AS THE MOST STRIKING FIGURE OF OUR AGE--EXCEPT YOURSELF OF COURSE! HE IS PROBABLY THE **GREATEST MAGICIAN** WHO EVER LIVED!

A MAGICIAN?

YES! HE SAYS HE HAS JUST RETURNED FROM A TOUR-- AND HE ABSOLUTELY **INSISTS** ON SEEING YOU!

WELL...ALL RIGHT! I'LL GIVE HIM A MOMENT TO FIND OUT WHAT HE WANTS!

AND SOON, WITH THE GENERALS IN CUSTODY IN AN ADJOINING CHAMBER...

AS YOU MUST KNOW, MR. **SOLAR DIRECTOR**, MY POWERS ARE NOT INCONSIDERABLE! AND I HAVE COME TO PLACE THEM AT YOUR SERVICE --TO HELP QUELL THIS REBELLION!

Hmmm! SO **THAT'S** IT?

I'M SORRY, **ALDEBARAN**, BUT THERE IS NO PLACE FOR YOU IN THE WAR EFFORT AT THIS TIME! AND NOW IF YOU'LL EXCUSE ME ...

WAIT, PLEASE! EVEN IF I CAN'T HELP AS A SOLDIER I WANT TO DO **SOME-THING**...

PERHAPS I CAN AMUSE YOU AND RELAX YOUR MIND WITH ONE OR TWO OF MY **FABULOUS TRICKS** -- AND IN THAT WAY HELP THE WAR EFFORT! I KNOW THAT YOUR MIND NOW MUST BE **HEAVY WITH CARE** ...

...EVEN THOUGH YOU HAVE CAPTURED THE **THREE TRAITOR GENERALS** !

A LITTLE TRIFLE, SIR... PICK A CARD...

HE **IS** INSISTENT!

er--JACK OF DIAMONDS.

11

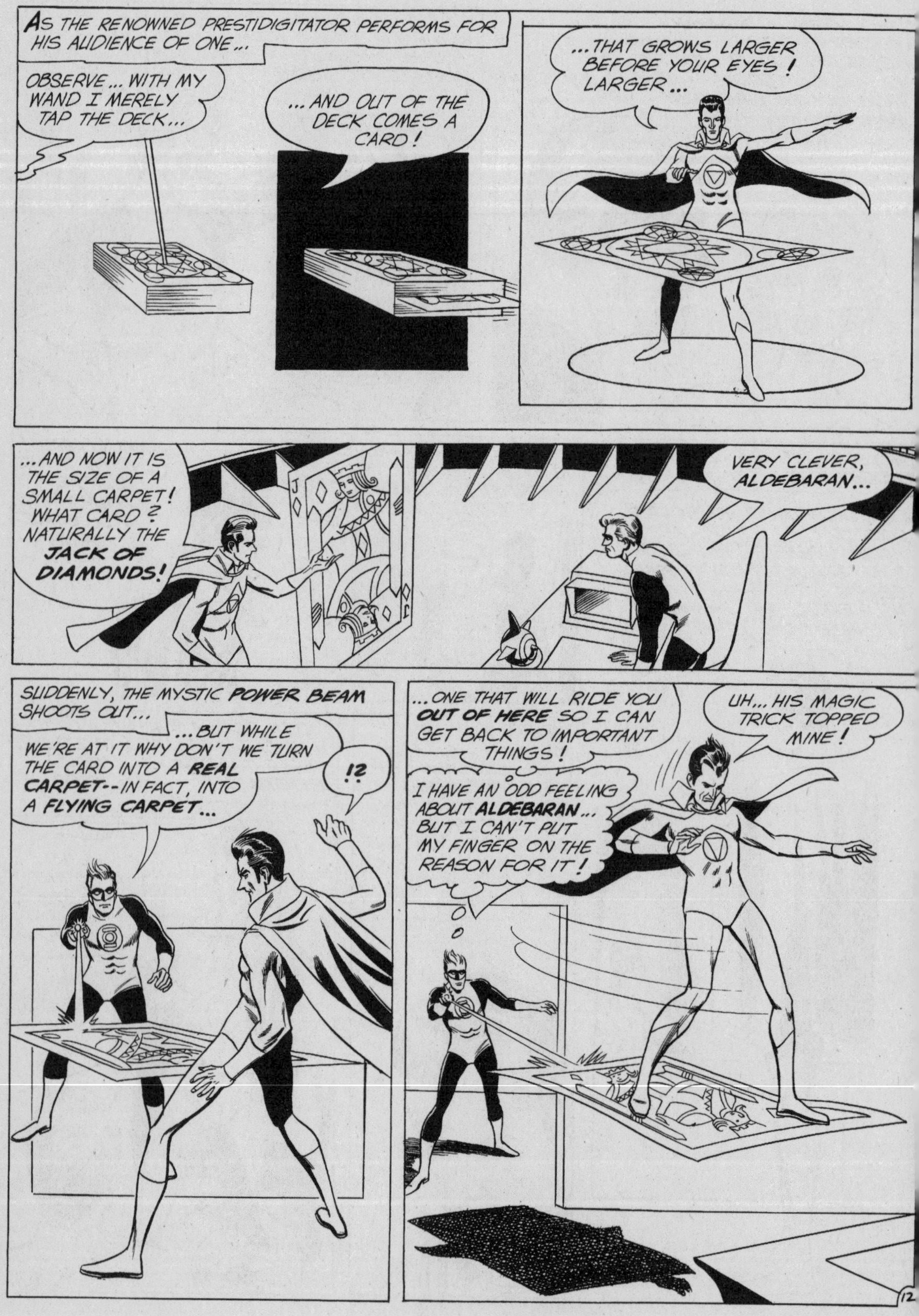
AS THE RENOWNED PRESTIDIGITATOR PERFORMS FOR HIS AUDIENCE OF ONE...
OBSERVE... WITH MY WAND I MERELY TAP THE DECK...
...AND OUT OF THE DECK COMES A CARD!
...THAT GROWS LARGER BEFORE YOUR EYES! LARGER...
...AND NOW IT IS THE SIZE OF A SMALL CARPET! WHAT CARD? NATURALLY THE JACK OF DIAMONDS!
VERY CLEVER, ALDEBARAN...
SUDDENLY, THE MYSTIC POWER BEAM SHOOTS OUT...
...BUT WHILE WE'RE AT IT WHY DON'T WE TURN THE CARD INTO A REAL CARPET--IN FACT, INTO A FLYING CARPET...
!?
...ONE THAT WILL RIDE YOU OUT OF HERE SO I CAN GET BACK TO IMPORTANT THINGS!
UH... HIS MAGIC TRICK TOPPED MINE!
I HAVE AN ODD FEELING ABOUT ALDEBARAN... BUT I CAN'T PUT MY FINGER ON THE REASON FOR IT!
12

LATER, AS **GREEN LANTERN** RESUMES QUESTIONING HIS THREE PRIZE CAPTIVES...

I'VE GOT TO GET TO THE ORIGIN OF THE REVOLT!

GENERAL BASSETT, REPEAT YOUR MOVEMENTS DURING THE PAST WEEK!

I MUST TELL THE TRUTH...

SOON AFTER...

...AND THAT IS ALL I REMEMBER...

I BETTER QUESTION THE OTHER TWO GENERALS AGAIN! WHAT BASSETT JUST SAID HAS GIVEN ME A CLUE!

SHORTLY...

I...CAN'T REMEMBER ANYTHING AFTER THAT...

AMAZING! THE LAST THING THE GENERALS CAN RECALL IS A CERTAIN EVENING HERE IN **STAR CITY** EXACTLY SEVEN DAYS AGO...

"...WHEN AT A FESTIVE STATE DINNER **ALDEBARAN** APPEARED TO ENTERTAIN THE ASSEMBLED NOTABLES..."

WATCH MY WAND, PLEASE! WATCH IT **CLOSELY**!

ALDEBARAN AGAIN! THE GENERALS ARE UNABLE TO RECALL **ANYTHING** AFTER THAT MOMENT! IT'S AS IF THEY WERE UNDER A SPELL ALL DURING THE REVOLT! AND--I JUST THOUGHT OF SOMETHING ELSE THAT FITS IN-- SOMETHING **ALDEBARAN** SAID A FEW MINUTES AGO--! HIS WORDS WERE--

"--EVEN THOUGH YOU HAVE CAPTURED THE **THREE TRAITOR GENERALS**!" BUT **HOW** COULD HE HAVE KNOWN **THAT** SINCE I HAVEN'T RELEASED THE NEWS YET TO THE PUBLIC--AND EVEN HERE IN HEADQUARTERS ONLY **IONA** KNOWS ABOUT IT! I'D BETTER CHECK WITH HER...

13.

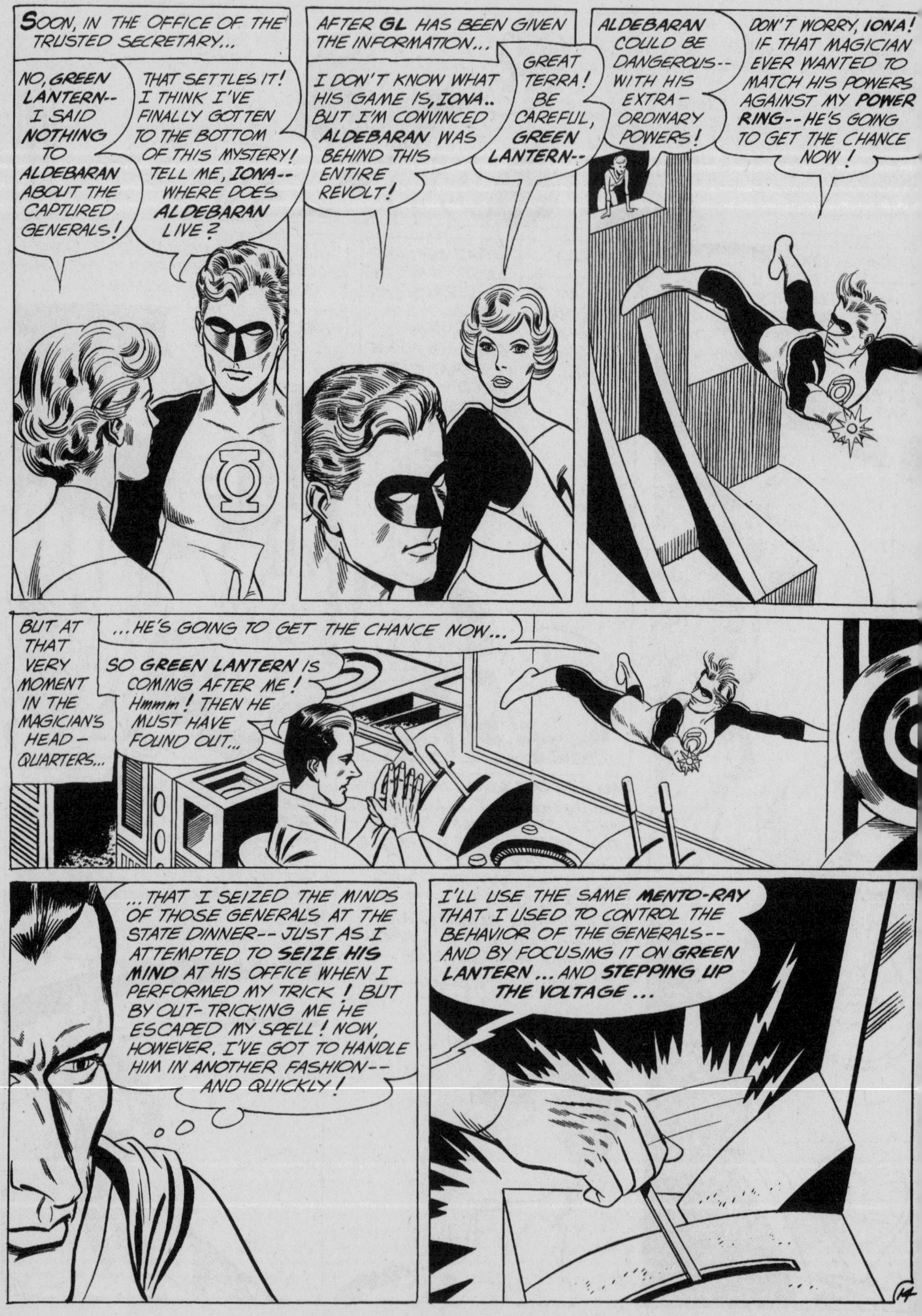
SOON, IN THE OFFICE OF THE TRUSTED SECRETARY...
NO, GREEN LANTERN-- I SAID NOTHING TO ALDEBARAN ABOUT THE CAPTURED GENERALS!
THAT SETTLES IT! I THINK I'VE FINALLY GOTTEN TO THE BOTTOM OF THIS MYSTERY! TELL ME, IONA-- WHERE DOES ALDEBARAN LIVE?
AFTER GL HAS BEEN GIVEN THE INFORMATION...
I DON'T KNOW WHAT HIS GAME IS, IONA.. BUT I'M CONVINCED ALDEBARAN WAS BEHIND THIS ENTIRE REVOLT!
GREAT TERRA! BE CAREFUL, GREEN LANTERN--
ALDEBARAN COULD BE DANGEROUS-- WITH HIS EXTRA-ORDINARY POWERS!
DON'T WORRY, IONA! IF THAT MAGICIAN EVER WANTED TO MATCH HIS POWERS AGAINST MY POWER RING--HE'S GOING TO GET THE CHANCE NOW!
BUT AT THAT VERY MOMENT IN THE MAGICIAN'S HEAD-QUARTERS...
...HE'S GOING TO GET THE CHANCE NOW...
SO GREEN LANTERN IS COMING AFTER ME! Hmmm! THEN HE MUST HAVE FOUND OUT...
...THAT I SEIZED THE MINDS OF THOSE GENERALS AT THE STATE DINNER-- JUST AS I ATTEMPTED TO SEIZE HIS MIND AT HIS OFFICE WHEN I PERFORMED MY TRICK! BUT BY OUT-TRICKING ME HE ESCAPED MY SPELL! NOW, HOWEVER, I'VE GOT TO HANDLE HIM IN ANOTHER FASHION-- AND QUICKLY!
I'LL USE THE SAME MENTO-RAY THAT I USED TO CONTROL THE BEHAVIOR OF THE GENERALS-- AND BY FOCUSING IT ON GREEN LANTERN ... AND STEPPING UP THE VOLTAGE ...
14

SIMULTANEOUSLY, A TERRIFIC *ENERGY-BLAST* EXPLODES IN THE BRAIN OF THE UNWARY GLADIATOR...

UH !! SOMETHING... KNOCKING ME DOWN ! ALMOST... CAUSING ME TO LOSE CONSCIOUSNESS...!

AS *GREEN LANTERN* LIES STRICKEN...

WEAK...CAN'T MOVE ! THIS MUST BE WHAT IONA MEANT WHEN SHE SAID THAT ALDEBARAN HAD EXTRAORDINARY POWERS ! HE--HE'S USED THEM ON ME, I'M SURE OF IT ! BUT I CAN'T LET HIM WIN THIS DUEL BETWEEN US !

THEN, IN HIS DILEMMA, A STARTLING IDEA SPRINGS INTO THE BRAIN OF THE *EMERALD CRUSADER*...

MAYBE...IT'S JUST POSSIBLE... THAT IF I CAN'T GO ON AND SEIZE ALDEBARAN--MY STATUE CAN !! IT'S CLOSE ENOUGH TO ME ... AND I STILL HAVE ENOUGH STRENGTH TO USE MY POWER RING! GOT TO TRY IT...!

THE NEXT MOMENT...

MY POWER BEAM HAS TURNED MY STATUE INTO A SUPER-AUTOMATON-- UNDER MY CONTROL ! NOW I STILL HAVE A CHANCE TO DEFEAT THE MAGICIAN !

SNAP!

To GREEN LANTERN ERECTED IN ETERNAL GRATITUDE BY THE CITIZENS OF

SOON, THE METALLIC AVENGER--COUNTERPART OF THE GLADIATOR CONTROLLING IT--IS ON ITS WAY...

I'VE EQUIPPED THE GREEN LANTERN STATUE WITH AN INTERNAL MINIATURE TELEVISION CAMERA... AND THE MEANS OF PROJECTING WHAT IT "SEES" BACK TO ME HERE VIA MY BEAM ! THIS WAY I CAN DIRECT ITS EVERY MOTION-- AS IT HEADS FOR ALDEBARAN !

15

AND SHORTLY, A HALF TON OF ADAMANT METAL CRASHES INTO ALDEBARAN'S HOUSE WITH THE FORCE OF A ROCKET BLAST...

BY THE SIGNS OF THE ZODIAC! MY MENTO-RAY--IT CAN HAVE NO EFFECT ON THIS STATUE OF HIMSELF THAT GREEN LANTERN HAS SENT AT ME!*

* Editor's Note: SINCE THE STATUE HAS NO BRAIN, THE MENTO-RAY, WHICH IS DESIGNED TO ACT ON THE BRAIN, CANNOT HARM IT!

IN DESPERATION, THE BE-LEAGUERED MAGICIAN TRIES A MORE CONVENTIONAL WEAPON...

NOT EVEN A MISSILE-PISTOL CAN STOP IT!

THEN, BEFORE ALDEBARAN CAN MAKE A MOVE TO FLEE...

UHH--

GOT HIM! MY STATUE HAS KNOCKED ALDEBARAN OUT!

UHH--

NOW THAT I'VE CAPTURED THE MASTERMIND BEHIND THE REVOLT, I'LL GET HIM TO REVEAL THE REASON BEHIND IT!

16.

IN DUE COURSE, UNDER GREEN LANTERN'S TRUTH BEAM, ALDEBARAN MAKES A COMPLETE CONFESSION...

...AND TWO YEARS AGO WHEN THE POST OF **SOLAR DIRECTOR** WAS VACANT I, WITH MY EXTRAORDINARY ABILITIES, SHOULD HAVE BEEN OFFERED IT-- INSTEAD OF **GREEN LANTERN**! SINCE THEN...

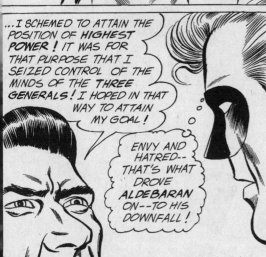

...I SCHEMED TO ATTAIN THE POSITION OF **HIGHEST POWER**! IT WAS FOR THAT PURPOSE THAT I SEIZED CONTROL OF THE MINDS OF THE **THREE GENERALS**! I HOPED IN THAT WAY TO ATTAIN MY GOAL!

ENVY AND HATRED-- THAT'S WHAT DROVE ALDEBARAN ON--TO HIS DOWNFALL!

LATER, WITH THE REVOLT OVER AND PEACE ONCE MORE REIGNING IN **STAR CITY**...

IONA, WE'VE HARDLY HAD A CHANCE TO SPEAK TO EACH OTHER! PERHAPS THIS EVENING--?

THERE'S NOTHING I WANT MORE IN THE WORLD!

BUT GREEN LANTERN DOESN'T REALIZE! NOW THAT HE'S SAVED US--AND PUT DOWN THE REBELLION-- HE MUST BE RETURNED AT **ONCE** TO HIS OWN ERA! AS CHAIRMAN **DASOR** HAS POINTED OUT, HIS **POWER RING** WOULD FAIL IF WE KEPT HIM HERE ANY LONGER--!

THE NEXT MOMENT...

HE'S-- HE'S GONE!

I KNOW HOW YOU MUST FEEL, **IONA**-- YOU MUST BE BRAVE, MY DEAR!

CLICK!

THUS IT HAPPENS THAT BACK IN THE **GREEN GLADIATOR'S** DRESSING ROOM AT A CERTAIN MOMENT IN THE TWENTIETH CENTURY...

WHERE DID THIS TINY PIECE OF METAL COME FROM IN MY HAIR--?

Editor's Note : BY THE LAWS OF TIME TRAVEL, **GREEN LANTERN** HAS BEEN RETURNED TO HIS OWN ERA AT THE **EXACT MOMENT** HE LEFT IT, WITH NO LAPSE IN TIME!

I'M GOING TO PUT THIS STRANGE PIECE OF METAL ASIDE! RIGHT NOW IT'S A *TOTAL MYSTERY* TO ME, BUT ONE OF THESE DAYS I MAY BE ABLE TO FIGURE OUT ITS MEANING...

...AND WHY THE MERE SIGHT OF IT SHOULD AROUSE SUCH ODD, HIDDEN EMOTIONS DEEP WITHIN ME!

IN FAR-REMOVED *STAR SQUARE* IN THE DISTANT FUTURE, THE STATUE OF THE *EMERALD GLADIATOR* IS ONCE MORE ON ITS PEDESTAL WHERE *GREEN LANTERN'S* RING PLACED IT AFTER THE STATUE HAD RENDERED VALOROUS SERVICE...

AND THE STATUE LOOKS LIKE IT ALWAYS DID, A NOBLE REPRESENTATION OF THE JUSTICE — LOVING CRUSADER IN A MOMENT OF ACTION! BUT THERE IS A SMALL DIFFERENCE...

AT THE BASE OF THE STATUE NEAR ONE FOOT IS A LITTLE *SHINY SPOT!* IT SEEMS INSIGNIFICANT, BUT A VERY KEEN OBSERVER MIGHT DEDUCE THE TRUTH...

The End

...THAT A TINY PIECE OF THE METAL IS *MISSING*, AND WAS BROKEN OFF ON THE DAY WHEN *GREEN LANTERN'S* STATUE WENT TO WAR! 18

GREEN LANTERN

GREEN LANTERN

Naturally a biography of famed **GREEN LANTERN** was inevitable! And who better as the writer than **PIEFACE**, the eskimo greasemonkey at the **FERRIS AIRCRAFT COMPANY**? Ever since **PIEFACE** learned **GREEN LANTERN'S** secret identity, he has been keeping a record of the **GREEN GLADIATOR'S** life and experiences, and with a true biographer's passion he leaves nothing out when dealing with his favorite subject!

ZERO HOUR in the SILENT CITY!

I'VE GOT TO SET DOWN THIS EXCITING ADVENTURE OF **GREEN LANTERN** RIGHT AWAY-- JUST AS HE TOLD IT TO ME-- WHILE ALL THE DETAILS ARE STILL FRESH IN MY MIND...

AS PIEFACE WRITES SWIFTLY...

OF COURSE THIS "CASE-BOOK OF **GREEN LANTERN**" THAT I'M KEEPING CAN NEVER BE PUBLISHED! FOR IF IT WERE, THE TRUTH ABOUT HIS SECRET IDENTITY WOULD BE REVEALED! BUT EVEN THOUGH IT CAN NEVER BE MADE PUBLIC, I CAN'T HELP WRITING IT!

SOMEHOW I FEEL IT'S IMPORTANT TO SET DOWN EVERYTHING THAT HE HAS EVER SAID OR DONE! AND LUCKILY FOR THIS PROJECT OF MINE, I'M GL'S SOLE CONFIDANT-- AND HE HARDLY KEEPS ANY SECRETS AT ALL FROM ME! BUT LET ME SEE...

WHILE PIE READS HIS MOST RECENT ENTRY IN THE "CASE-BOOK OF GREEN LANTERN"...

...LET US PEEK OVER HIS SHOULDER AND SEE WHAT HE HAS WRITTEN...

...and all that day test pilot Hal Jordan--alias *Green Lantern*--was completely absorbed in the activities of his daily life! All morning long he had been racking his brains over a technical problem involving stress on the wing of a new plane. Finally he rose, scratching his head wearily, wondering

PIE, I THINK IF I GET MY MIND AWAY FROM THIS PROBLEM AWHILE, IT MAY HELP ME SOLVE IT! I'M TAKING OFF-- TO RELAX!

CHECK, HAL! SOUNDS LIKE A GOOD IDEA--

"*T*HAT AFTERNOON HAL RELAXED ALL RIGHT, ALONG WITH THOUSANDS OF OTHERS, AT THE BALL GAME!"

COME ON, RAMIS! BELT IT!

ONE MORE HOMER AND HE BREAKS THE RECORD!

"*A*FTER THE GAME..."

TERRIFIC!

GOSH, BASEBALL IS AN EXCITING SPORT! WHILE YOU'RE AT IT, YOU FORGET EVERYTHING ELSE! BUT I BETTER NOT FORGET THAT I'VE GOT A DATE WITH *CAROL* TONIGHT!

"SIX O'CLOCK FOUND HAL WITH HIS DATE--HIS YOUNG AND PRETTY BOSS CAROL FERRIS..."

...AND THEN I SAW RAMIS BELT ONE OVER THE FENCE!

MMM-- HOW *THRILLING!*

HOLDING CAROL THIS WAY IN MY ARMS IS ANOTHER THRILL-- BUT I WISH I COULD MANAGE IT WITHOUT USING *DANCING* AS AN EXCUSE!

2

"SUDDENLY, AS SOMETIMES HAPPENS, THE ELUSIVE ANSWER TO HIS PROBLEM OF THE MORNING POPPED INTO HAL'S HEAD!"

HAL, WHAT'S THE MATTER? YOU LOOK LIKE YOU'VE SEEN A *GHOST!*

I'VE GOT IT! *I'VE GOT IT!*

WHAT?! YOU'RE TAKING ME *HOME?*

I'M SORRY, CAROL! I'VE *GOT* TO GET BACK TO THE PLANT THIS EVENING! YOU SEE --

"ON THE WAY TO CAROL'S HOUSE, HAL EXPLAINED HIS 'WING STRESS' PROBLEM AND HIS EXCITEMENT IN SOLVING IT..."

... AND NOW I JUST CAN'T WAIT TO GET BACK TO MY DESK-- TO CHECK THE SOLUTION I'VE ARRIVED AT! AND ANYWAY, CAROL -- YOU DID SAY YOU WANTED TO GET HOME EARLY TONIGHT!

HMMM!

AS HAL'S EMPLOYER I CAN'T HELP BUT APPROVE HIS KEEN DEVOTION TO HIS JOB! BUT AS A *GIRL* I FEEL SOMETHING ELSE ENTIRELY! HE DIDN'T *HAVE* TO BRING ME HOME SO EARLY-- NO MATTER WHAT I SAID!

"HAL DROVE BACK THROUGH *COAST CITY!* IT WAS STILL DAYLIGHT AT THIS TIME OF YEAR..."

COME ON LIGHT, CHANGE!

≥YAWN≤ THIS HAS BEEN SOME DAY! THE BEAUTIFUL WEATHER... THE BALL GAME... DANCING WITH CAROL... AND SOLVING MY PROBLEM...!

"THEN..." IT'S A DAY LIKE THIS THAT MAKES LIFE-- EH? GREAT GUARDIANS! I'VE BEEN SO BUSY IT NEVER OCCURRED TO ME ONCE TODAY THAT MY *POWER CHARGE* ON MY *RING* WOULD RUN OUT ABOUT THIS TIME!

RATTATTA

EDITOR'S NOTE: WHEN THE *POWER RING* IS CHARGED IT RETAINS ITS POWER FOR EXACTLY *TWENTY-FOUR* HOURS!

3

TOOT! TOOT! EXTRA! HONK! BEEP!

I'VE ONLY GOT A *FEW MINUTES* OF POWER LEFT! IF I HAD TO CHANGE TO *GREEN LANTERN* NOW AND GO INTO ACTION-- I COULD EASILY WIND UP IN A *FIX!*... WILL THAT LIGHT *NEVER* CHANGE?

"THE NEXT MOMENT, AMAZINGLY..."

EH? THAT'S ODD...SUDDENLY THERE'S *ABSOLUTE SILENCE* ALL AROUND ME! THE CAR RADIO WAS BLASTING OUT-- NOW I CAN'T HEAR IT! I *CAN'T HEAR ANYTHING!!*

"AT FIRST HAL THOUGHT HIS *HEARING* MIGHT BE AFFECTED! BUT THEN HE REALIZED IT COULDN'T BE THAT... "

WHATEVER HAS HAPPENED--EVERYONE IS AWARE OF IT! IT SEEMS TO BE CREATING CONFUSION-- AND NO WONDER! THIS INTERSECTION WAS LIKE A BOILER FACTORY A SECOND AGO...

...EVEN THAT SCREAMING WOMAN IS MAKING *NO NOISE!* PEOPLE HAVE LEFT THEIR CARS-- TRAFFIC IS STALLED!

SOMETHING TELLS ME THAT *GREEN LANTERN* BETTER DO SOME INVESTIGATING *AT ONCE!*

"IN THE COVER OF TREES IN A SMALL PARK NEARBY *HAL* SWIFTLY CHANGED TO THE UNIFORM OF HIS FAMED ALTER EGO... "

EVEN THOUGH THERE ARE ONLY A FEW MINUTES OF POWER LEFT IN MY RING, IT MAY BE ENOUGH TO GET TO THE BOTTOM OF THIS INCREDIBLE OCCURRENCE!

4

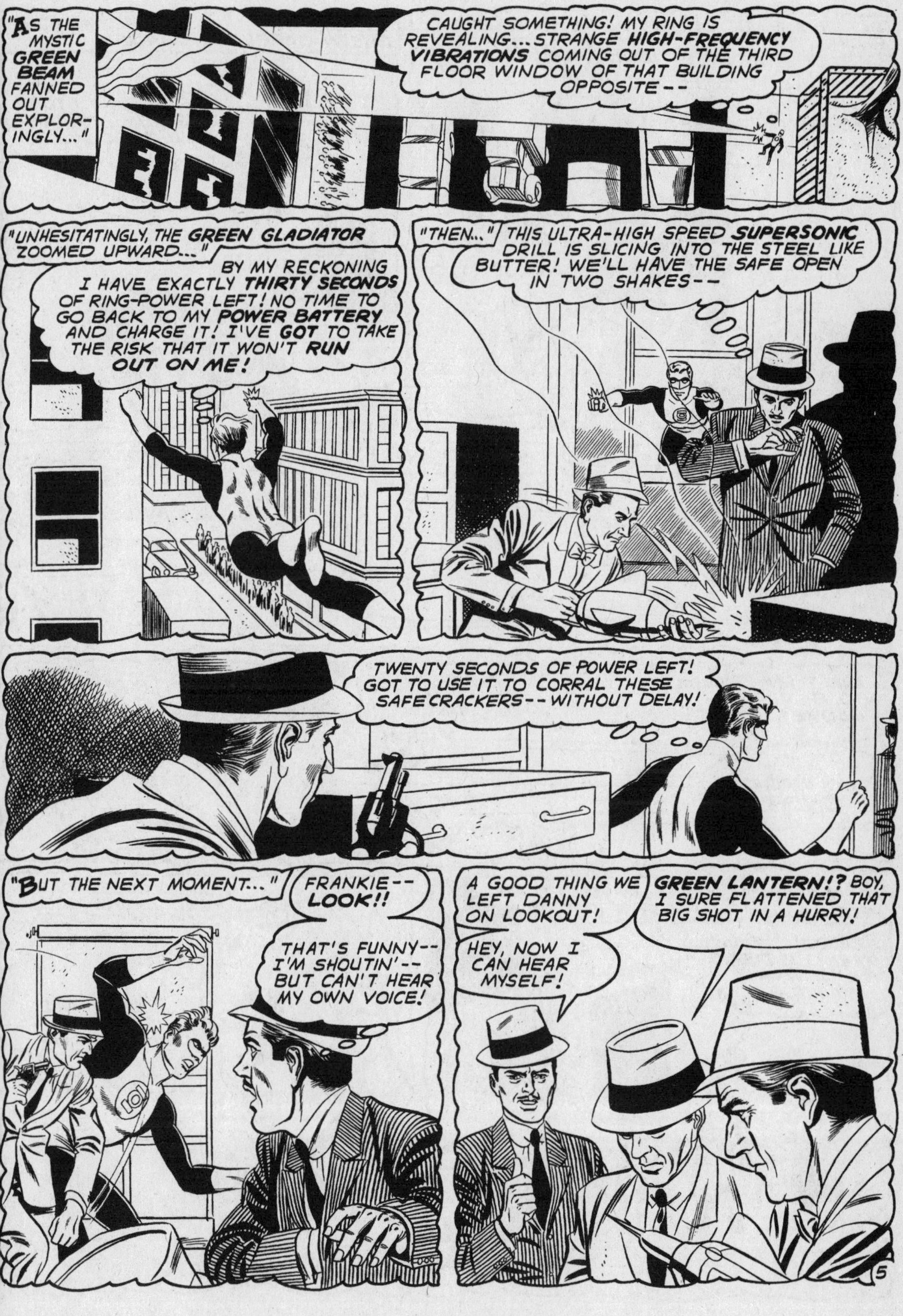
"AS THE MYSTIC GREEN BEAM FANNED OUT EXPLORINGLY..."
CAUGHT SOMETHING! MY RING IS REVEALING... STRANGE HIGH-FREQUENCY VIBRATIONS COMING OUT OF THE THIRD FLOOR WINDOW OF THAT BUILDING OPPOSITE--
"UNHESITATINGLY, THE GREEN GLADIATOR ZOOMED UPWARD..."
BY MY RECKONING I HAVE EXACTLY THIRTY SECONDS OF RING-POWER LEFT! NO TIME TO GO BACK TO MY POWER BATTERY AND CHARGE IT! I'VE GOT TO TAKE THE RISK THAT IT WON'T RUN OUT ON ME!
"THEN..."
THIS ULTRA-HIGH SPEED SUPERSONIC DRILL IS SLICING INTO THE STEEL LIKE BUTTER! WE'LL HAVE THE SAFE OPEN IN TWO SHAKES--
TWENTY SECONDS OF POWER LEFT! GOT TO USE IT TO CORRAL THESE SAFECRACKERS--WITHOUT DELAY!
"BUT THE NEXT MOMENT..."
FRANKIE-- LOOK!!
THAT'S FUNNY-- I'M SHOUTIN'-- BUT CAN'T HEAR MY OWN VOICE!
A GOOD THING WE LEFT DANNY ON LOOKOUT!
HEY, NOW I CAN HEAR MYSELF!
GREEN LANTERN!? BOY, I SURE FLATTENED THAT BIG SHOT IN A HURRY!
5

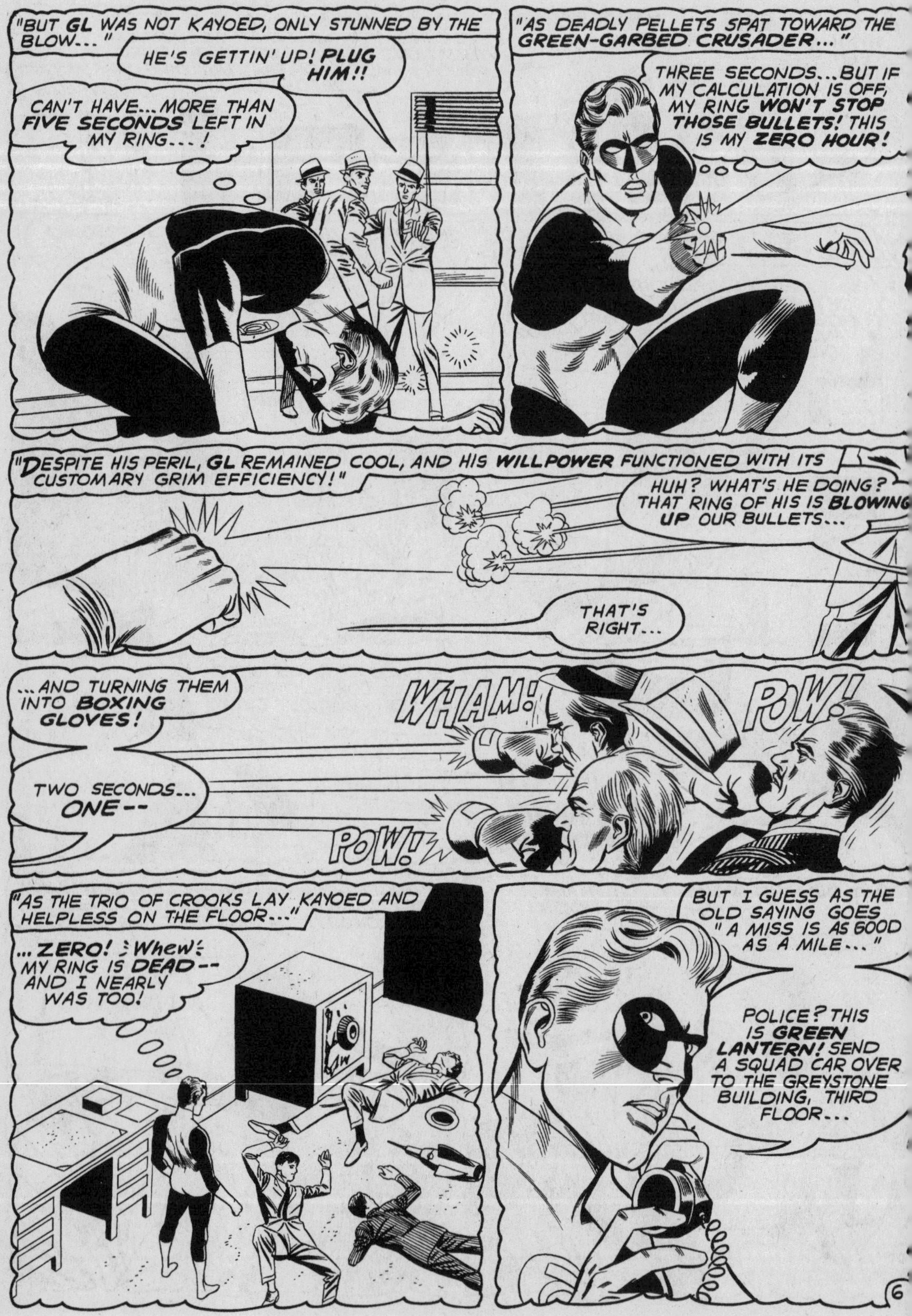
"BUT GL WAS NOT KAYOED, ONLY STUNNED BY THE BLOW..."
HE'S GETTIN' UP! PLUG HIM!!
CAN'T HAVE...MORE THAN FIVE SECONDS LEFT IN MY RING...!
"AS DEADLY PELLETS SPAT TOWARD THE GREEN-GARBED CRUSADER..."
THREE SECONDS...BUT IF MY CALCULATION IS OFF, MY RING WON'T STOP THOSE BULLETS! THIS IS MY ZERO HOUR!
"DESPITE HIS PERIL, GL REMAINED COOL, AND HIS WILLPOWER FUNCTIONED WITH ITS CUSTOMARY GRIM EFFICIENCY!"
HUH? WHAT'S HE DOING? THAT RING OF HIS IS BLOWING UP OUR BULLETS...
THAT'S RIGHT...
...AND TURNING THEM INTO BOXING GLOVES!
WHAM!
POW!
TWO SECONDS... ONE --
POW!
"AS THE TRIO OF CROOKS LAY KAYOED AND HELPLESS ON THE FLOOR..."
...ZERO! Whew! MY RING IS DEAD -- AND I NEARLY WAS TOO!
BUT I GUESS AS THE OLD SAYING GOES "A MISS IS AS GOOD AS A MILE..."
POLICE? THIS IS GREEN LANTERN! SEND A SQUAD CAR OVER TO THE GREYSTONE BUILDING, THIRD FLOOR...
6

LATER, WITH THE CROOKS BEHIND BARS...

NO DOUBT IT WAS THIS AMAZING **SUPERSONIC** DRILL WHICH THOSE SAFECRACKERS DEVELOPED THAT CAUSED THE BLANKETING OF SOUND IN THIS PART OF THE CITY! AS SOON AS IT WAS STOPPED, SOUND CAME BACK!

YES! THE HIGH-SPEED VIBRATIONS FROM IT...

...SPREAD IN ABOUT A MILE-WIDE RADIUS AND SIMPLY CANCELED OUT **ORDINARY SOUND VIBRATIONS!** MY RING REVEALED THAT TO ME...

...BEFORE IT WENT DEAD!

"IN DUE COURSE, SHORTLY, A BELATED TASK WAS ATTENDED TO..."

IN BRIGHTEST DAY, IN BLACKEST NIGHT, NO EVIL SHALL ESCAPE MY SIGHT! LET THOSE WHO WORSHIP EVIL'S MIGHT BEWARE MY POWER--**GREEN LANTERN'S LIGHT!**

AT LAST! MY RING'S CHARGED FOR ANOTHER TWENTY-FOUR HOURS!

"AND THUS ENDED THIS **ZERO-HOUR** ADVENTURE OF **GREEN LANTERN!**"

AS GREEN LANTERN'S UNOFFICIAL BIOGRAPHER I INTEND TO PAY PARTICULAR ATTENTION TO THESE **ZERO-HOUR** ADVENTURES OF HIS! SO WHEN FURTHER EPISODES LIKE IT OCCUR, I'LL SET THEM RIGHT DOWN IN MY "**CASE-BOOK OF GREEN LANTERN!**"

CASE-BOOK OF GREEN LANTERN

THE END

GREEN LANTERN

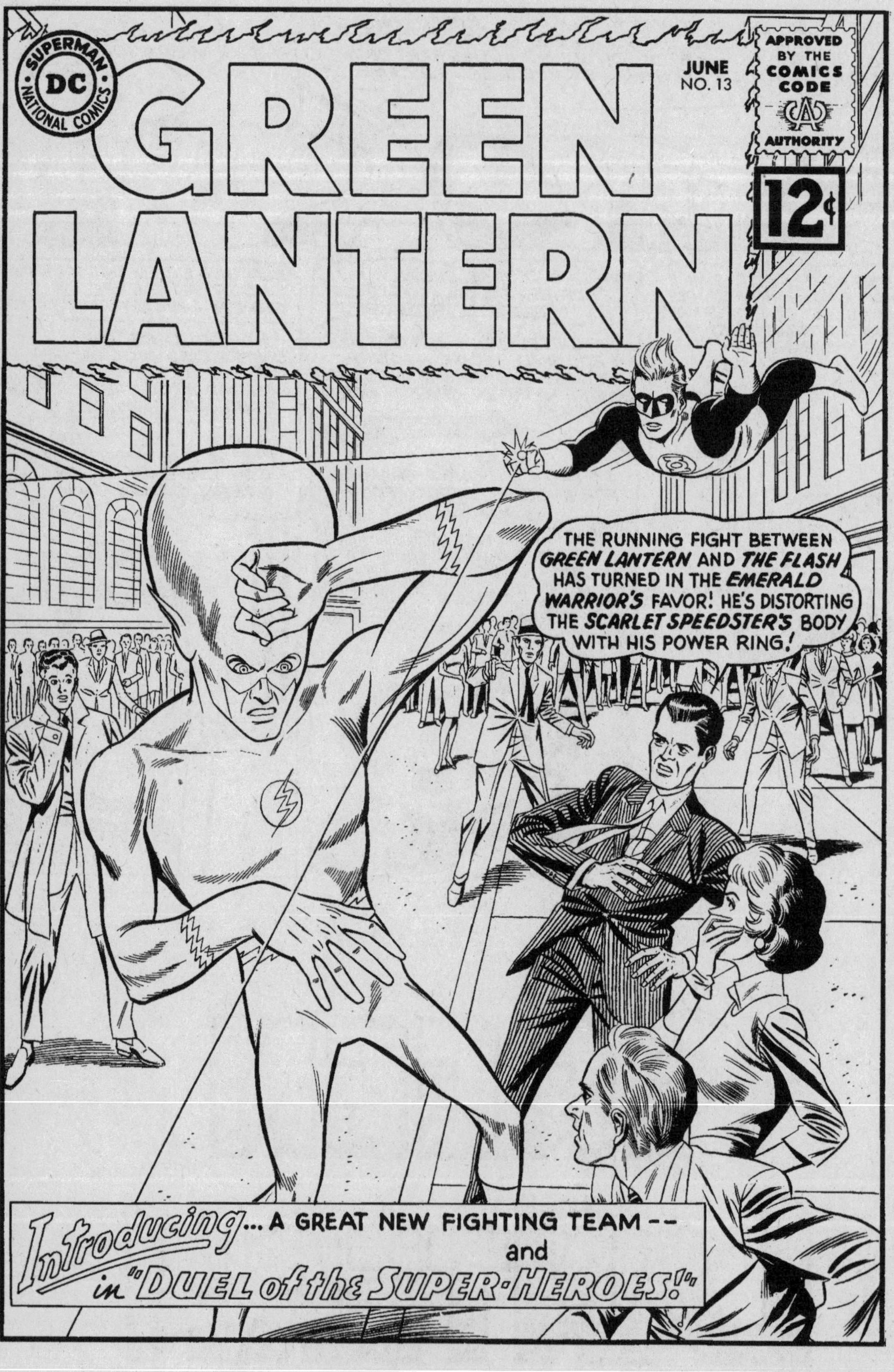
SUPERMAN DC NATIONAL COMICS
GREEN LANTERN
JUNE NO. 13
APPROVED BY THE COMICS CODE AUTHORITY
12¢
THE RUNNING FIGHT BETWEEN GREEN LANTERN AND THE FLASH HAS TURNED IN THE EMERALD WARRIOR'S FAVOR! HE'S DISTORTING THE SCARLET SPEEDSTER'S BODY WITH HIS POWER RING!
Introducing... A GREAT NEW FIGHTING TEAM -- and
in "DUEL of the SUPER-HEROES!"

GREEN LANTERN

CO-STARRING The FLASH

THE MIGHTY FLASH-- AND INVINCIBLE GREEN LANTERN-- PITTED AGAINST EACH OTHER ? HOW COULD SUCH A SITUATION POSSIBLY ARISE-- WHEN BOTH CHAMPIONS HAVE ALWAYS FOUGHT ON THE SIDE OF JUSTICE AND AGAINST EVIL ? FOR THE ASTONISHING AND BREATHTAKING ANSWER TO THIS STARTLING STATE OF AFFAIRS, IT WILL BE NECESSARY TO TRAVEL TO ANOTHER WORLD-- TO A WORLD BEYOND THE SPEED OF LIGHT ! AND ONLY AFTER WE HAVE DONE THAT WILL WE BEGIN TO UNDER- STAND ...

The DUEL OF THE SUPER-HEROES!

IN THE **PICTURE NEWS** EDITORIAL OFFICE WHERE NEWSHEN IRIS WEST IS A STAR REPORTER...

...AND MY BOY FRIEND **BARRY ALLEN** HAS AGREED TO TAKE HIS VACATION EARLY THIS YEAR AND ACCOMPANY ME TO THE WEST COAST! I HOPE IT'S ALL RIGHT WITH YOU, CHIEF...

SURE, IRIS! AS LONG AS YOU GET YOUR WORK DONE!

REMEMBER, YOU'LL HAVE TO INTERVIEW **HAL JORDAN,** THE FAMOUS TEST PILOT, ENOUGH TIMES TO DO THE **BIG STORY** ON HIM THAT WE WANT!

DON'T WORRY, CHIEF... YOU'LL GET YOUR STORY!

IN **BARRY ALLEN'S** APARTMENT, SHORTLY...

IRIS DOESN'T REALIZE IT BUT I HAVE **TWO** REASONS FOR GOING ALONG ON THIS TRIP! FIRST OF ALL I'D LIKE TO SPEND MY VACATION WITH HER, NATURALLY! BUT ALSO THERE'S SOMEONE I ADMIRE VERY MUCH OUT ON THE WEST COAST...

...NAMELY **GREEN LANTERN!** OF COURSE, IRIS DOESN'T SUSPECT THAT AS MY ALTER EGO, **THE FLASH,** I HAVE A SPECIAL FEELING FOR MY FELLOW **JUSTICE LEAGUE** MEMBER! AND I'M HOPING I HAVE THE LUCK TO MEET HIM WHILE I'M OUT THERE!

BUT I'D BETTER HURRY! THAT MUST BE IRIS NOW!

BARRY-- SLOWPOKE! CAN'T YOU MOVE **FAST** FOR ONCE IN YOUR LIFE? WE'LL MISS THE PLANE!

COMING, IRIS! COMING!

TAXI

MEANWHILE, UNKNOWN TO BARRY (*THE FLASH*) ALLEN, HIS FELLOW-CRUSADER, *GREEN LANTERN*, HAS JUST WOUND UP A MISSION ON A FAROFF GALACTIC PLANET...

...AND IS RETURNING TO EARTH ALSO IN A BIT OF A *HURRY!*

THERE ARE A DOZEN MATTERS TO TAKE CARE OF AS SOON AS I GET HOME! GOT TO STEP ON IT-- REALLY *TRAVEL!*

AS ONE OF THE "MATTERS" IN PARTICULAR CLINGS IN THE MIND OF THE SPACE-CLEAVING GLADIATOR...

IN MY OTHER IDENTITY, AS HAL JORDAN, I'M DUE TO SPEND A HOLIDAY WEEK END AT THE SEASHORE WITH CAROL!* AND I WOULDN'T WANT TO MISS EVEN A MINUTE OF THAT!

*EDITOR'S NOTE: LOVELY CAROL FERRIS-- HAL JORDAN'S BOSS AT THE *FERRIS AIR-CRAFT COMPANY*-- ALSO HAPPENS TO BE THE GIRL HE IS IN LOVE WITH!

WITH THOUGHTS OF THE COMING WEEK END TO URGE HIM ALONG, *GREEN LANTERN* REALLY "POURS IT ON"...

THERE DOESN'T SEEM TO BE ANY LIMIT TO HOW FAST I CAN GO... BY BACKING MY RING WITH EVERY OUNCE OF MY *WILL-POWER!* AND THERE'S *EARTH* NOW!

THE NEXT INSTANT, INCREDIBLY...

BY THE GUARDIANS-- WHAT!?

THAT WALL--!!

TOO LATE, THE HURTLING GREEN-CLAD FIGURE BECOMES AWARE OF THE SOLID OBSTACLE BEFORE HIM...

SHOULD HAVE... KEPT MY RING GOING...TO PROTECT MYSELF! SUDDEN CHANGE...DAZED ME....UHHH!

3

WHEN THE STRICKEN RING-WIELDER COMES TO HIS SENSES...

WHERE AM I?

DO NOT FEAR! YOU ARE IN THE WORLD OF *SPECTAR*-- OR AS YOU WOULD SAY IT,... THE UNIVERSE BEYOND THE SPEED OF LIGHT! I AM *CHI-VAM*, THE CHIEF HERE! AND WE ARE ABLE TO SPEAK TO YOU...

...EVEN THOUGH WE DO NOT KNOW YOUR LANGUAGE, BECAUSE WE CAN COMMUNICATE DIRECTLY BY MEANS OF THOUGHT— PROJECTION!

BUT... HOW DID I GET HERE?

THAT IS SIMPLY TOLD! YOU HAPPENED TO BE TRAVELING *FASTER THAN LIGHT* AT THE *EXACT MOMENT* WHEN OUR TWO WORLDS-- YOUR *EARTH* AND OUR *SPECTAR*-- COINCIDED IN HYPER-SPACE! BUT PERHAPS I HAD BETTER EXPLAIN...

"YOU SEE, IN HYPERSPACE THE ORBITS OF OUR TWO WORLDS ARE SOMEWHAT SIMILAR..."

"...WITH EACH IN ITS OWN DIMENSION, OF COURSE! BUT ONCE EVERY SPECTARN HIURN..."

"...WHICH EQUALS FOUR OF YOUR EARTH 'HOURS,' THE POSITIONS OF OUR TWO PLANETS *EXACTLY* COINCIDE!"

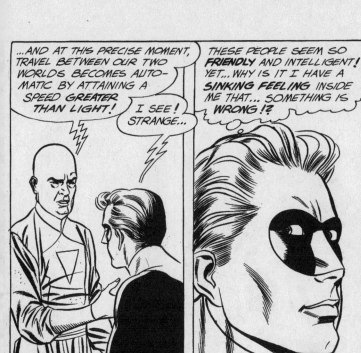

...AND AT THIS PRECISE MOMENT, TRAVEL BETWEEN OUR TWO WORLDS BECOMES AUTOMATIC BY ATTAINING A SPEED *GREATER THAN LIGHT!*

I SEE! STRANGE...

THESE PEOPLE SEEM SO *FRIENDLY* AND INTELLIGENT! YET...WHY IS IT I HAVE A *SINKING FEELING* INSIDE ME THAT... SOMETHING IS WRONG!?

WE KNOW HOW ANXIOUS YOU MUST BE TO RETURN TO YOUR *OWN WORLD!* THEREFORE, WE ARE READY TO HELP YOU DO SO, *GREEN LANTERN!*

eh? YOU KNOW MY NAME?!

I HAVEN'T THOUGHT MY NAME ONCE SINCE I CAME HERE--SO THEY DIDN'T LEARN IT BY READING MY MIND!

er-- YES! YOU SEE, AT MOMENTS WHEN OUR ORBITS COINCIDE WE *SPECTARNS* CAN OBTAIN GLIMPSES OF THE EARTH-- AND OF LIFE ON YOUR PLANET! ONLY FLEETING GLIMPSES, BUT IN THAT WAY...

...WE LEARNED ABOUT YOU, *GREEN LANTERN--* AND HOW YOU MUST CHARGE YOUR *POWER RING* EVERY TWENTY-FOUR HOURS! IT IS NOW NEARLY ONE *HURN--* FOUR HOURS-- SINCE YOU CAME HERE! IF YOU STAY *TOO LONG* YOU WON'T HAVE ANY POWER TO RETURN...

THAT'S SO!

IT SEEMS THEY *DO* WANT TO HELP ME! I MUST GET OVER MY SILLY FEARS ABOUT THESE PEOPLE!

COME-- THE MOMENT OF ORBIT-COINCIDING APPROACHES! YOU MUST NOT MISS IT!

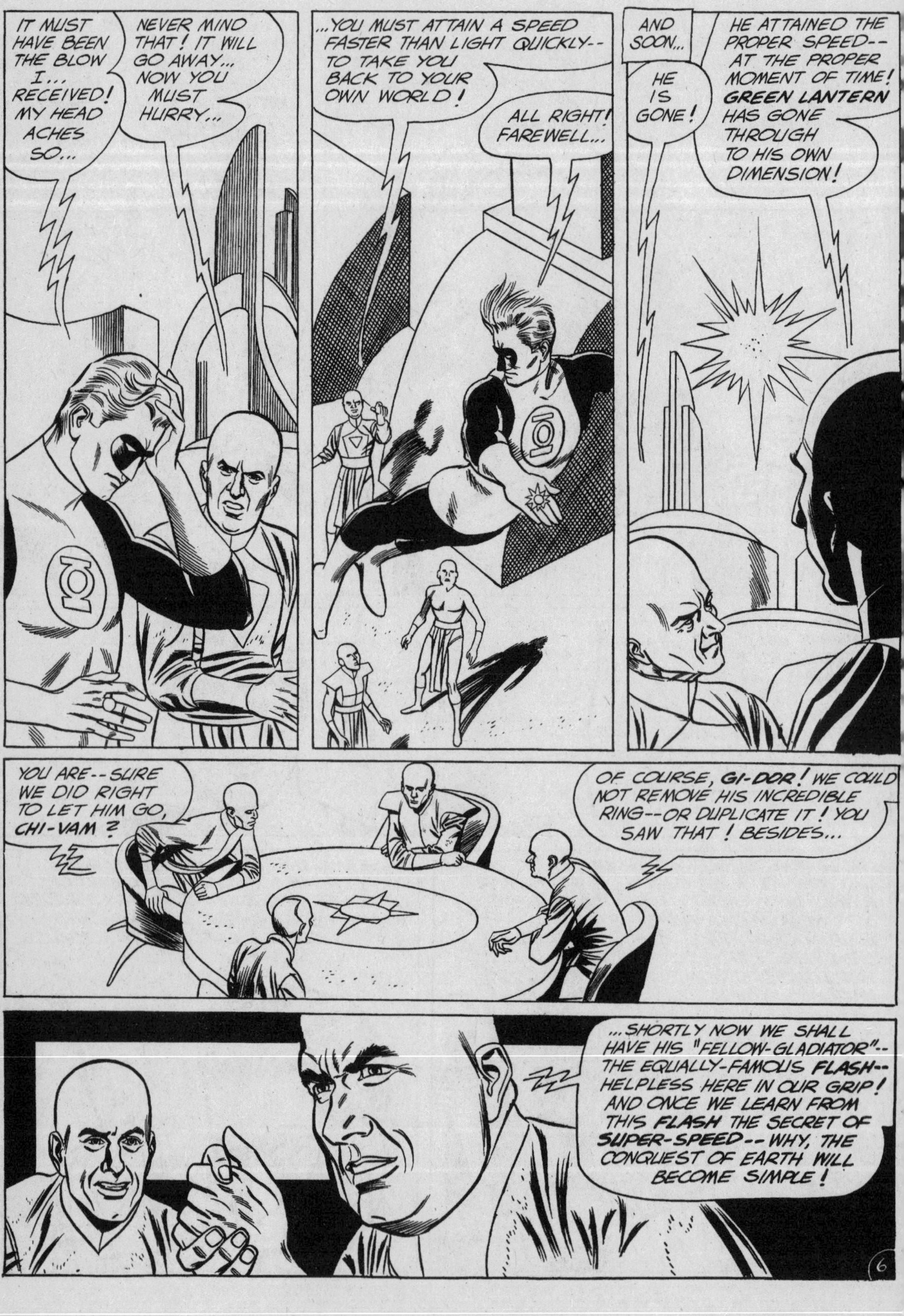
IT MUST HAVE BEEN THE BLOW I... RECEIVED! MY HEAD ACHES SO...
NEVER MIND THAT! IT WILL GO AWAY... NOW YOU MUST HURRY...
...YOU MUST ATTAIN A SPEED FASTER THAN LIGHT QUICKLY-- TO TAKE YOU BACK TO YOUR OWN WORLD!
ALL RIGHT! FAREWELL...
AND SOON...
HE IS GONE!
HE ATTAINED THE PROPER SPEED-- AT THE PROPER MOMENT OF TIME! GREEN LANTERN HAS GONE THROUGH TO HIS OWN DIMENSION!
YOU ARE--SURE WE DID RIGHT TO LET HIM GO, CHI-VAM?
OF COURSE, GI-DOR! WE COULD NOT REMOVE HIS INCREDIBLE RING--OR DUPLICATE IT! YOU SAW THAT! BESIDES...
...SHORTLY NOW WE SHALL HAVE HIS "FELLOW-GLADIATOR"-- THE EQUALLY-FAMOUS FLASH-- HELPLESS HERE IN OUR GRIP! AND ONCE WE LEARN FROM THIS FLASH THE SECRET OF SUPER-SPEED-- WHY, THE CONQUEST OF EARTH WILL BECOME SIMPLE!
6

DUEL OF THE SUPER-HEROES!

PART 2

SNAPPED BACK INTO HIS OWN UNIVERSE AT THE PRECISE MOMENT... AFTER HIS **POWER RING** HAD ENABLED HIM TO ATTAIN A SPEED GREATER THAN LIGHT... **GREEN LANTERN** FINDS HIS WAY SWIFTLY BACK TO EARTH AND THE MAIN HANGAR OF THE **FERRIS** AIRCRAFT COMPANY...

GREEN LANTERN! BOY, AM I GLAD TO SEE YOU! I WAS GETTING WORRIED! I KNEW IT WAS ALMOST TWENTY-FOUR HOURS SINCE YOU CHARGED YOUR RING--!

YES, THAT IS TRUE...

AS THOMAS (**PIEFACE**) KALMAKU, THE GREASE-MONKEY WHO IS **GL'S** SOLE CONFIDANT, WELCOMES HIS FAMED FRIEND...

I MUST RECHARGE MY RING RIGHT AWAY... TO BE PREPARED...

HUH?

IN HAL JORDAN'S DRESSING ROOM BEHIND A LOCKED DOOR...

WHAT'S WRONG WITH HIM? I'VE NEVER SEEN *GREEN LANTERN* ACT SO *QUEER!* HE MUST BE VERY *TIRED* OR SOMETHING--!

IN BRIGHTEST DAY, IN BLACKEST NIGHT...

ALL *EVIL* SHALL ESCAPE MY SIGHT! LET THOSE WHO WORSHIP EVIL'S MIGHT FEAR NOT MY POWER-- *GREEN LANTERN'S LIGHT!*

JUMPING FISHHOOKS! THOSE....AREN'T THE WORDS TO HIS OATH!

WITH THE MYSTIC RING POWERED AGAIN FOR ANOTHER TWENTY-FOUR HOURS...

WHAT'S THE MATTER, *PIE-FACE?* WHY ARE YOU *STARING* AT ME LIKE THAT?

MAYBE I DIDN'T *HEAR RIGHT!* I--I WON'T SAY ANYTHING...

er--YOU'D BETTER CHANGE TO YOUR HAL JORDAN OUTFIT, GL...

HAVE YOU FORGOTTEN WE'RE ALL GOING DOWN TO THE *SEA PALACE* THIS WEEK END? YOU AND CAROL AND TERGA AND I--!

SAY, THAT'S RIGHT! BE READY IN A MINUTE, *PIE!*

SHORTLY... THE GIRLS ARE DOWN AT THE SEASHORE ALREADY, HAL! I TOLD THEM TO GO AHEAD AND THAT WE'D MEET THEM THERE! ALSO, WE'RE GOING TO HAVE ANOTHER COUPLE IN OUR PARTY THIS WEEK END...

ANOTHER COUPLE?

YES! *IRIS WEST,* A REPORTER FOR *PICTURE NEWS,* HAS COME OUT HERE TO INTERVIEW YOU! HER ESCORT IS SOMEONE CALLED *BARRY ALLEN,* A POLICE SCIENTIST...

8

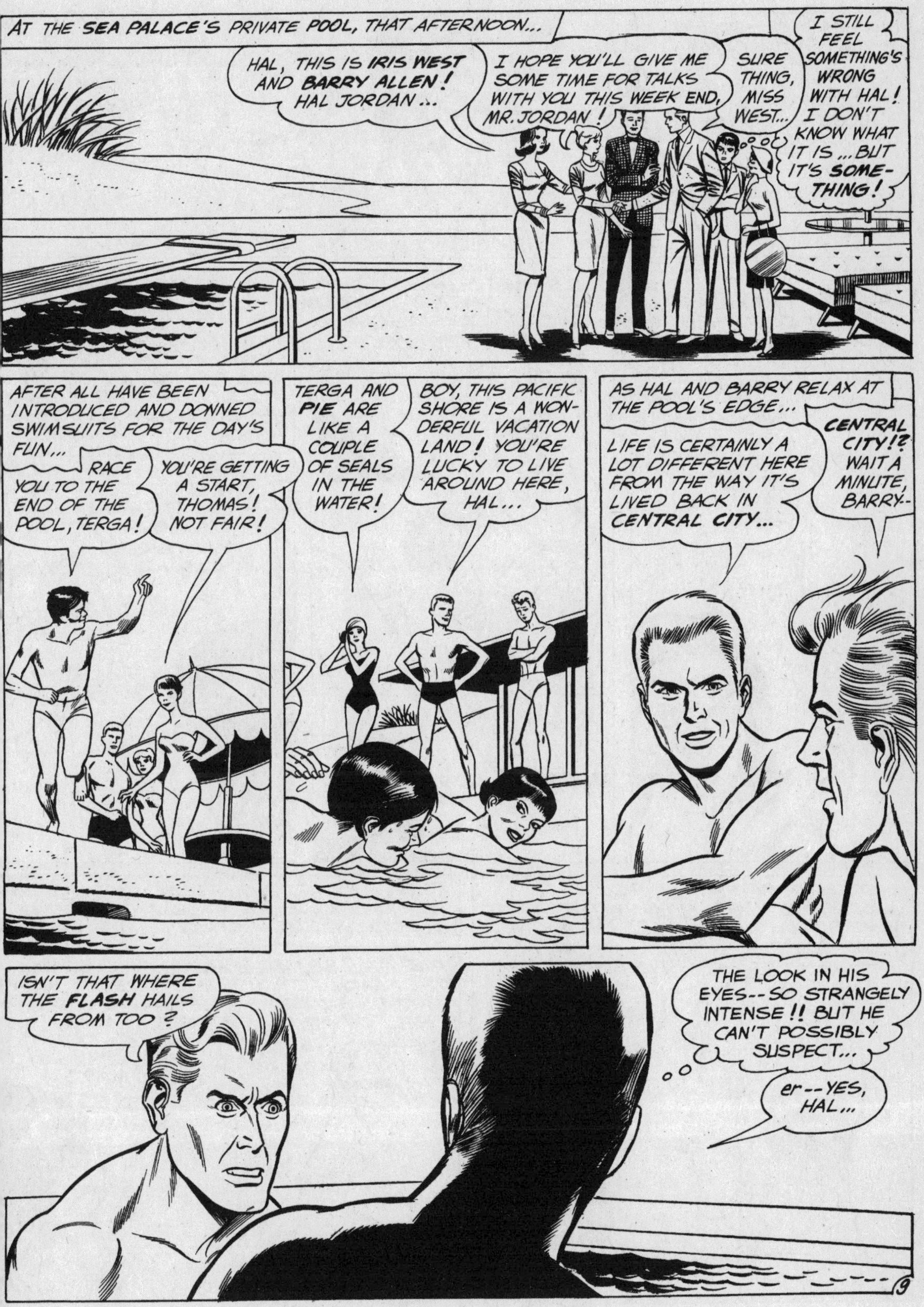
AT THE SEA PALACE'S PRIVATE POOL, THAT AFTERNOON...
HAL, THIS IS IRIS WEST AND BARRY ALLEN! HAL JORDAN...
I HOPE YOU'LL GIVE ME SOME TIME FOR TALKS WITH YOU THIS WEEK END, MR. JORDAN!
SURE THING, MISS WEST...
I STILL FEEL SOMETHING'S WRONG WITH HAL! I DON'T KNOW WHAT IT IS ... BUT IT'S SOME-THING!
AFTER ALL HAVE BEEN INTRODUCED AND DONNED SWIMSUITS FOR THE DAY'S FUN...
RACE YOU TO THE END OF THE POOL, TERGA!
YOU'RE GETTING A START, THOMAS! NOT FAIR!
TERGA AND PIE ARE LIKE A COUPLE OF SEALS IN THE WATER!
BOY, THIS PACIFIC SHORE IS A WON-DERFUL VACATION LAND! YOU'RE LUCKY TO LIVE AROUND HERE, HAL...
AS HAL AND BARRY RELAX AT THE POOL'S EDGE...
LIFE IS CERTAINLY A LOT DIFFERENT HERE FROM THE WAY IT'S LIVED BACK IN CENTRAL CITY...
CENTRAL CITY!? WAIT A MINUTE, BARRY--
ISN'T THAT WHERE THE FLASH HAILS FROM TOO?
THE LOOK IN HIS EYES--SO STRANGELY INTENSE!! BUT HE CAN'T POSSIBLY SUSPECT...
er--YES, HAL...
9

WHAT MADE ME SAY THAT... ABOUT *THE FLASH?* IT... JUST POPPED OUT! AS IF... AS IF I HAVEN'T GOT CONTROL OF MY OWN TONGUE ANY MORE!

Hmm! I'M BEGINNING TO THINK THIS *HAL JORDAN* IS AN *ODD ONE!*

SHORTLY...

WHERE DID HAL GO?

HE WALKED DOWN THE BEACH-- SAID HE WANTED TO BE ALONE!

WELL, *THAT'S* SOCIABLE, I MUST SAY!

EXCUSE ME, TERGA, I WANT TO TALK,... TO BARRY ALLEN,...

GO AHEAD, THOMAS! WE GIRLS ARE GOING TO SUNBATHE NOW ANYHOW!

AS THE YOUNG ESKIMO LAD SEEKS OUT COUNSEL...

MR. ALLEN, YOU'RE A POLICE SCIENTIST! I'M WORRIED ABOUT MY PAL, HAL JORDAN... AND I THOUGHT I'D TELL YOU! HE'S ...JUST *NOT* ACTING *NORMAL!*

I CAN'T TELL HIM ABOUT THE OATH--THAT WOULD GIVE AWAY HAL'S SECRET IDENTITY AS *GREEN LANTERN!*

I NOTICED SOMETHING MYSELF, *PIE!* BUT-- WHAT DO YOU WANT ME TO DO?

I THOUGHT,... IF THE TWO OF US KEPT AN EYE ON HIM... MAYBE WE'D FIGURE OUT WHAT WAS WRONG! PLEASE HELP ME, MR. ALLEN!

RESPONDING TO THE URGENCY IN THE GREASE-MONKEY'S VOICE, BARRY ALLEN SUDDENLY BECOMES EQUALLY SERIOUS...

ALL RIGHT, *PIE!* I'LL BE ON THE ALERT... (AND SO WILL *THE FLASH* ALTHOUGH *PIE* DOESN'T KNOW THAT!) YOU CAN RELY ON ME!

GEE, THANKS, MR. ALLEN! HERE COMES HAL NOW...

NEXT DAY... I'VE NOTICED ONE THING, *PIEFACE!* EVERY FOUR HOURS HAL WANDERS OFF BY HIMSELF! HAS HE EVER DONE THAT SORT OF THING BEFORE?

NO, *NEVER!*

SEE--THERE HE GOES AGAIN! HE'S ALREADY EXCUSED HIM-SELF TO THE GIRLS... TELL YOU WHAT, PIE--I'M GOING TO *FOLLOW HIM!*

I'LL GO WITH YOU!

NO, *PIE*-- YOU STAY HERE! IT--er--WILL BE BETTER THIS WAY!

ALL RIGHT-- IF YOU SAY SO! BUT-- GOLLY!

As BARRY ALLEN SETS OUT AFTER HIS DIS-APPEARING QUARRY...

I DIDN'T WANT *PIEFACE* ALONG--BECAUSE I MAY HAVE TO CHANGE TO *THE FLASH* IN ORDER TO TRAIL HAL WITHOUT HIS SEEING ME! BUT HE DOESN'T SEEM TO SUSPECT SOMEONE MAY BE FOLLOWING HIM! HE HASN'T TURNED AROUND ONCE...

A QUARTER OF AN HOUR LATER...

THE ROCKY HILLS ALONG HERE ARE LINED WITH CAVES--AND HE'S GOING INTO ONE OF THEM! WHAT IN THUNDER CAN HE BE UP TO--? I BETTER GO IN AFTER HIM...

IN THE DIMLY-LIT CAVERN...

eh? HE'S TAKEN OFF HIS OUTER GARMENTS... THERE'S A *UNIFORM* ON UNDERNEATH... AND...

GREAT JUMPING JUPITER! IT'S *GREEN LANTERN'S* UNIFORM!

11

FROM CONCEALMENT BARRY WATCHES WIDE-EYED WITH FASCINATION AND CURIOSITY...

IT'S SOMETHING I NEVER DREAMED-- THAT HAL JORDAN IS REALLY GREEN LANTERN!

IT'S THE EXACT MOMENT OF ORBIT-COINCIDING...

...THE ONLY MOMENT EACH FOUR HOURS WHEN I CAN COMMUNICATE WITH MY MASTERS ...THE SPECTARNS!

I HAVE NOT YET SEIZED THE FLASH FOR YOU! BUT I ASSURE YOU...

...I SHALL CARRY OUT MY MISSION! NOTHING WILL STOP ME!

WHAT'S WRONG WITH HIM? HE KEEPS STARING AT HIS POWER RING-- AS IF IN A TRANCE!

SUDDENLY, THE AROUSED POLICE SCIENTIST MAKES A DECISION...

I'VE GOT A FEELING THAT GREEN LANTERN IS IN TROUBLE! AND IF SO, HE-- MORE THAN ANYONE ELSE-- DESERVES TO HAVE THE FLASH AT HIS SIDE AT A TIME LIKE THIS!

SPURTING FROM A SECRET COMPARTMENT IN BARRY ALLEN'S RING, A FAMILIAR RED UNIFORM EXPANDS SWIFTLY-- BY A SPECIAL CHEMICAL FORMULA-- IN CONTACT WITH THE AIR...

AND A MOMENT LATER, WITH THE UNIFORM DONNED AT LIGHTNING-BOLT VELOCITY BY THE FASTEST MAN ALIVE...

GREEN LANTERN, I WANT TO HELP YOU! IF YOU'LL TELL ME--

eh? THAT LOOK ON HIS FACE--IT'S FULL OF HATE-- FURY--!

12

WITH GRIM INTENT, THE MYSTIC **POWER BEAM** FLARES OUT...

TRYING TO NET ME WITH THAT RING OF HIS !?

AS THE **SCARLET SPEEDSTER** TAKES EVASIVE ACTION-- AT SUPER-SPEED...

HE MUST BE OUT OF HIS MIND! I WANT TO AID HIM AND HE ATTACKS ME! BUT I CAN'T STOP TO ARGUE--THAT **POWER BEAM** OF HIS IS **TOO DANGEROUS!**

INTO NEARBY **COAST CITY** THE WHIRLWIND CHASE EXTENDS...

CAN'T THROW HIM OFF MY TRAIL...

I'M TRAVELING AT LIGHT SPEED...

...BUT SO IS HE... RIGHT BEHIND ME...

THEN ON AN OPEN LOT IN THE CITY...

WHAT'S HE UP TO?

I GAINED A FRACTION OF A SECOND LEAD... AND MAYBE THAT'S ALL I NEED... TO USE MY SUPER-SPEED AND STIR UP THE EARTH HERE...

...INTO A WHIRLING, BLINDING **DUST STORM!** NOW... BEFORE **GREEN LANTERN** FINDS HIS WAY THROUGH THAT, I'LL BE FAR AWAY AND SAFE FROM HIS RING!

13

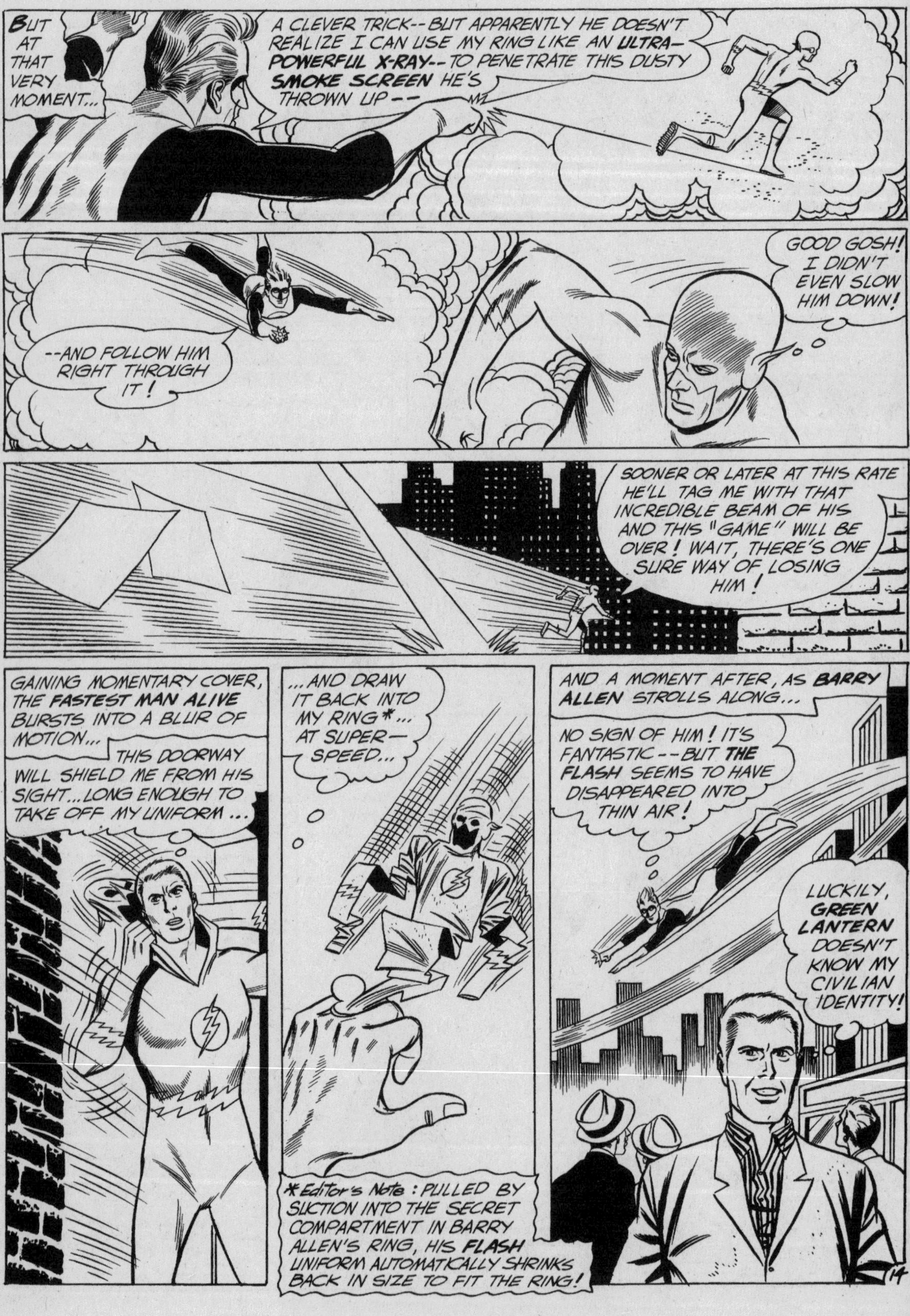
BUT AT THAT VERY MOMENT...
A CLEVER TRICK--BUT APPARENTLY HE DOESN'T REALIZE I CAN USE MY RING LIKE AN ULTRA-POWERFUL X-RAY--TO PENETRATE THIS DUSTY SMOKE SCREEN HE'S THROWN UP--
--AND FOLLOW HIM RIGHT THROUGH IT!
GOOD GOSH! I DIDN'T EVEN SLOW HIM DOWN!
SOONER OR LATER AT THIS RATE HE'LL TAG ME WITH THAT INCREDIBLE BEAM OF HIS AND THIS "GAME" WILL BE OVER! WAIT, THERE'S ONE SURE WAY OF LOSING HIM!
GAINING MOMENTARY COVER, THE FASTEST MAN ALIVE BURSTS INTO A BLUR OF MOTION...
THIS DOORWAY WILL SHIELD ME FROM HIS SIGHT...LONG ENOUGH TO TAKE OFF MY UNIFORM...
...AND DRAW IT BACK INTO MY RING*... AT SUPER-SPEED...
*Editor's Note: PULLED BY SUCTION INTO THE SECRET COMPARTMENT IN BARRY ALLEN'S RING, HIS FLASH UNIFORM AUTOMATICALLY SHRINKS BACK IN SIZE TO FIT THE RING!
AND A MOMENT AFTER, AS BARRY ALLEN STROLLS ALONG...
NO SIGN OF HIM! IT'S FANTASTIC--BUT THE FLASH SEEMS TO HAVE DISAPPEARED INTO THIN AIR!
LUCKILY, GREEN LANTERN DOESN'T KNOW MY CIVILIAN IDENTITY!
14

HE'S ESCAPED ME COMPLETELY! BUT I MUST FIND HIM! I **MUST!**

I'D BETTER **RECHARGE** MY RING...IT'S ALMOST TWENTY-FOUR HOURS SINCE I LAST CHARGED IT!

LATER, AFTER THE **GREEN-CLAD GLADIATOR** HAS RE-POWERED HIS RING, AND ONCE MORE HAS HIS MIND SET ON A **SINGLE GOAL...**

I KNOW **THE FLASH** IS SOMEWHERE IN THE VICINITY OF **COAST CITY!** BUT I'VE GOT TO BRING HIM **OUT IN THE OPEN--** IN ORDER TO CAPTURE HIM! AND NOW THAT I THINK ABOUT IT...

...THERE MAY BE A WAY TO DO IT...A WAY THAT **CAN'T FAIL**... IF **THE FLASH** LIVES UP TO HIS REPUTATION FOR ALWAYS BEING ON THE ALERT TO HELP PEOPLE!

AND SOON, IN A COAST-WATCHER'S STATION ALONG THE SHORE...

LOOK! OUT THERE--!

WH--WHERE COULD IT HAVE COME FROM--?

INCREDIBLY, A MAMMOTH **TIDAL WAVE** HURTLES TOWARD THE BEACH AND **COAST CITY**...

SEND OUT AN ALARM! WARN THE PEOPLE! THAT WAVE COULD CAUSE UNTOLD DAMAGE--!

THEY DON'T REALIZE THE WAVE IS ONLY AN **ILLUSION**-- A **MIRAGE**--CREATED BY MY RING! IT CAN'T DO ANY HARM REALLY--BUT IF I'M RIGHT, IT **WILL** DRAW **THE FLASH** OUT INTO THE OPEN AGAIN!

15

SURE ENOUGH, IN THE CITY...

...TIDAL WAVE ABOUT TO SMASH THE CITY! RUN FOR HIGH GROUND! SAVE YOURSELVES--!

GREAT SCOTT! IN THIS EMERGENCY--

RADIO TV

...THE FLASH MUST HELP OUT-- TRY TO SAVE LIVES!

THE WAVE IS ALMOST ON US! ONLY A FEW MOMENTS LEFT...

AT THE SHORE, SPLIT-INSTANTS LATER, THE AMAZING SPEEDSTER SUCCEEDS, BY HIS INCOMPARABLE VELOCITY, IN ERECTING A GREAT DIKE OUT OF THE BEACH SAND TO BLUNT THE POWER OF THE ONCOMING GIANT ROLLER...

HERE COMES THE WAVE NOW! I HAVE ONLY A FEW SECONDS...

...IN WHICH TO BUILD THIS SAND BARRIER...

...BUT A SECOND CAN BE A LONG TIME...

...FOR ANYONE WHO CAN MOVE AS FAST AS I CAN!

MY BARRIER OUGHT TO STOP THAT MIGHTY WAVE...

...OR AT LEAST CUT DOWN ITS FORCE--!

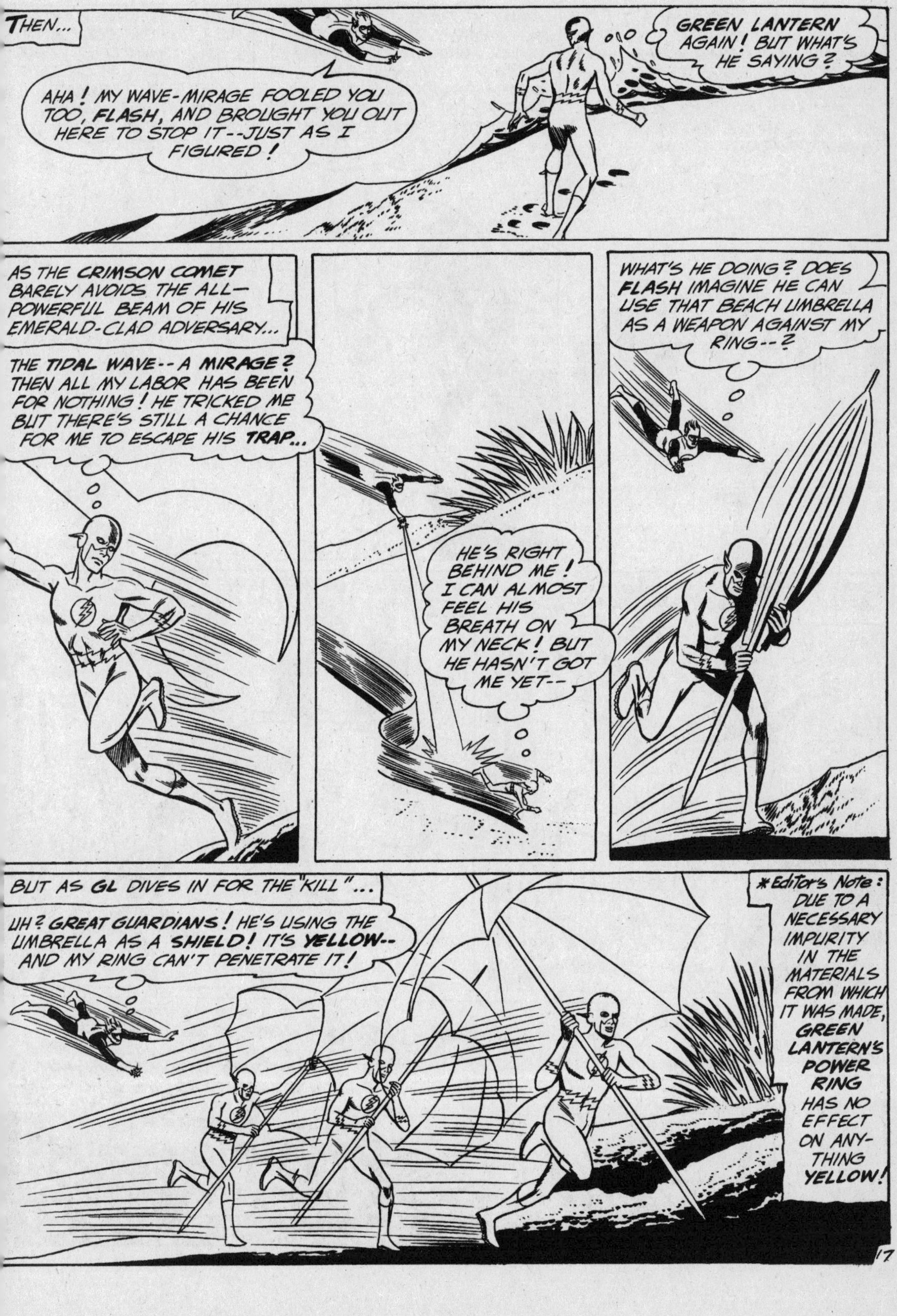
THEN...
AHA! MY WAVE-MIRAGE FOOLED YOU TOO, FLASH, AND BROUGHT YOU OUT HERE TO STOP IT--JUST AS I FIGURED!
GREEN LANTERN AGAIN! BUT WHAT'S HE SAYING?
AS THE CRIMSON COMET BARELY AVOIDS THE ALL-POWERFUL BEAM OF HIS EMERALD-CLAD ADVERSARY...
THE TIDAL WAVE--A MIRAGE? THEN ALL MY LABOR HAS BEEN FOR NOTHING! HE TRICKED ME BUT THERE'S STILL A CHANCE FOR ME TO ESCAPE HIS TRAP...
HE'S RIGHT BEHIND ME! I CAN ALMOST FEEL HIS BREATH ON MY NECK! BUT HE HASN'T GOT ME YET--
WHAT'S HE DOING? DOES FLASH IMAGINE HE CAN USE THAT BEACH UMBRELLA AS A WEAPON AGAINST MY RING--?
BUT AS GL DIVES IN FOR THE "KILL"...
UH? GREAT GUARDIANS! HE'S USING THE UMBRELLA AS A SHIELD! IT'S YELLOW--AND MY RING CAN'T PENETRATE IT!
*Editor's Note: DUE TO A NECESSARY IMPURITY IN THE MATERIALS FROM WHICH IT WAS MADE, GREEN LANTERN'S POWER RING HAS NO EFFECT ON ANYTHING YELLOW!
17

LATER... A GOOD THING I REMEMBERED THAT *GREEN LANTERN'S RING* HAS NO EFFECT ON ANYTHING *YELLOW!* IT ENABLED ME TO ESCAPE HIM ONCE AGAIN! BUT ALSO--THE THOUGHT HAS OCCURRED TO ME--

--THAT IF I KEEP ELUDING THE *EMERALD GLADIATOR* I MAY *NEVER* LEARN WHAT'S WRONG WITH HIM--AND *WHY* HE IS TRYING TO CAPTURE ME! FOR *GREEN LANTERN'S* SAKE, I *KNOW* WHAT I MUST DO...

I MUST LET HIM *CAPTURE* ME! IT'S THE *ONLY WAY* I CAN THINK OF TO GET TO THE BOTTOM OF THIS MYSTERY! IT MEANS TAKING A DANGEROUS CHANCE--BUT I'VE GOT TO RISK IT!

SOON AFTER... THERE HE IS! THIS TIME I'LL MAKE SURE *THE FLASH* DOESN'T ESCAPE ME BY SOME SUPER--SPEED TRICK! I'M GOING TO FIX HIM SO HE *CAN'T USE* HIS FANTASTIC SPEED--!

WH-WHAT'S HAPPENING TO ME?

BY INCREASING THE SIZE OF THE UPPER PORTION OF HIS BODY, MY RING IS MAKING HIM SO *TOP HEAVY* HE WON'T BE ABLE TO MOVE FASTER THAN A TURTLE! I'VE GOT HIM NOW!

AND SURE ENOUGH...

IN A FEW MINUTES IT WILL BE *ORBIT-COINCIDING* TIME AGAIN--AND I WILL BE ABLE TO TURN OVER *THE FLASH* TO MY *MASTERS*, THE *SPECTARNS*--IN THE *WORLD BEYOND THE SPEED OF LIGHT!*

DUEL OF THE SUPER-HEROES PART 3

UNDER A HYPNOTIC SPELL CAST OVER HIM BY THE INCREDIBLE *SPECTARNS*, GREEN LANTERN HAS DUTIFULLY DELIVERED **THE FLASH** TO THEM IN THE UNIVERSE BEYOND THE SPEED OF LIGHT! AND NOW AS THE SCARLET SPEEDSTER -- RETURNED TO NORMAL SIZE AGAIN BY *GREEN LANTERN* -- LIES UNCONSCIOUS BUT HELPLESS UNDER IMPRISONING RADIATION, THE GREEN-GARBED CRUSADER -- NO LONGER NEEDED -- IS SENT BACK TO EARTH, AFTER STEPS HAVE BEEN TAKEN TO INSURE THAT HE CANNOT INTERFERE WITH THE CAREFULLY-LAID PLANS OF HIS "MASTERS"!

WHY DID THEY WANT *ME*?! WHAT DO THEY HOPE TO GAIN FROM HAVING *ME* A PRISONER?

IT'S VERY SIMPLE, *FLASH*...

AS THE *SPECTARN* LEADER SURPRISINGLY ANSWERS THE UNSPOKEN QUERY OF HIS CAPTIVE...

YOU SEE, THE ONLY WAY TO PASS BETWEEN OUR WORLD AND YOURS IS TO TRAVEL AT A *SPEED GREATER THAN LIGHT!* LONG HAVE OUR *SPECTARN* WARRIORS BEEN READY TO *INVADE AND CONQUER YOUR EARTH!* OUR ONLY PROBLEM HAS BEEN TO *GET THERE!*

THAT PROBLEM WE WILL NOW SOLVE-- BY ANALYZING WITH OUR ULTRA-SCIENTIFIC METHODS *YOUR SUPER-SPEED ABILITY!* ONCE WE HAVE THE ANSWER, WE WILL ENDOW ALL OUR WARRIORS WITH *SUPER-LIGHT SPEED* TO ENABLE THEM TO BREAK THROUGH THE DIMENSION BARRIER!

AND UNFORTUNATELY FOR YOU, MY DEAR "SPEEDSTER," THERE IS *NOTHING* YOU CAN DO TO STOP US!

START THE *COMPUTO-ANALYZER*...

THEN, TO *FLASH'S* ASTONISHMENT, THOUGHTS POUR FROM THE ACTIVATED MACHINE...

...THE SOURCE OF THE...REMARKABLE SPEED OF THE...LIFE-FORM BEFORE ME...IS A...COMPLICATED *CHEMICAL ACCIDENT* WHICH ALTERED THE STRUCTURE OF HIS BODY! I WILL NOW LIST THE *CHEMICAL CHANGES* THAT TOOK PLACE AT THAT TIME...

GREAT SCOTT! IT IS PROBING THE SECRET OF MY SUPER-SPEED...!

20

BUT MEANWHILE WHAT OF *GREEN LANTERN* ? ODDLY ENOUGH THE *EMERALD GLADIATOR* HAS RETURNED TO EARTH, LABORING UNDER A PECULIAR ILLUSION !

WITH ALL MEMORY OF HIS ENCOUNTER WITH THE *SPECTARNS* ERASED FROM HIS MIND, HE IS UNDER THE IMPRESSION THAT IT IS THE *PREVIOUS DAY*, WHEN HE WAS RETURNING FROM HIS OUTER-SPACE MISSION !

FERRIS AIRCRAFT COMPANY

NO SIGN OF *PIEFACE* ! Hmm! I'LL BET HE AND TERGA AND CAROL WENT DOWN TO THE *SEA PALACE* RESORT AND ARE WAITING FOR ME THERE !

SOON AFTER, HAL JORDAN IS DRIVING TOWARD THE SHORE...

I CALLED CAROL'S HOUSE BUT THERE WAS NO ANSWER ! SO I GUESS I WAS RIGHT ABOUT HER GOING AHEAD WITH *PIE* AND TERGA ! BUT I'LL HAVE TO INVENT SOME KIND OF EXCUSE TO EXPLAIN MY BEING LATE ! CAROL HASN'T THE FAINTEST IDEA I'M REALLY *GREEN LANTERN*...

SURE ENOUGH THERE'S *PIEFACE* !

HI, PIE--!

HAL ! WHERE HAVE YOU BEEN ?! WE'VE BEEN WORRIED SICK ABOUT YOU --

--SINCE YOU DIS-APPEARED THIS MORNING WITH BARRY ALLEN !

SINCE I *DIS-APPEARED*...WITH BARRY ALLEN ?! *PIE*, WAIT A MINUTE.. HOLD EVERY-THING ! *WHO*.. IS *BARRY ALLEN* !?

HAL--WHAT'S GOT INTO YOU ? SURELY YOU REMEMBER BEING HERE THIS MORNING--YOU WENT OFF ALONG THE BEACH AND BARRY ALLEN FOLLOWED YOU !

I WAS... *HERE* THIS MORNING..!?

AS GRIM THOUGHTS GROUND INTO THE BRAIN OF THE CRACK TEST PILOT...

THIS FITS IN WITH A STRANGE FEELING I'VE HAD DURING THE LAST HOUR THAT I COULDN'T EXPLAIN... A FEELING THAT SOME-THING TERRIBLE WAS ABOUT TO HAPPEN ! BUT WHAT ? HOW COULD I HAVE BEEN HERE BEFORE... AND NOT KNOW IT ?!

21

SUDDENLY... PIE, LISTEN--SAY NOTHING TO CAROL OR ANYONE ELSE HERE ABOUT MY ARRIVAL! I'VE GOT TO UN-RAVEL THIS MYSTERY--AND SOMETHING TELLS ME I'VE GOT TO DO IT FAST-- WITHOUT A MOMENT'S DELAY!

UH--OKAY, HAL!

I'LL TELL THE GIRLS THAT YOU AND... BARRY ALLEN... WENT OFF FISHING TODAY... ALL RIGHT?

RIGHT! SEE YOU LATER!

ALONG A BARREN STRETCH OF BEACH...

I'VE LOST A DAY OUT OF MY LIFE--SOME-HOW! BUT AS SURE AS I'M GREEN LANTERN, I'M GOING TO GET BACK THAT DAY!

RAISING HIS MYSTIC POWER RING, GREEN LANTERN GIVES IT A STERN MENTAL COMMAND...

RING, TELL ME EVERYTHING THAT HAPPENED TO ME DURING THE LAST TWENTY-FOUR HOURS--AND LEAVE NOTHING OUT!

UNDER THE EMERALD WARRIOR'S DRIVING WILL-POWER, HIS AMAZING RING RESPONDS...

...YOU WERE FLYING THROUGH SPACE... GOING AT A TREMENDOUS RATE... IN ORDER TO REACH EARTH IN TIME FOR YOUR DATE...

"SUDDENLY, YOU EXCEEDED THE SPEED OF LIGHT AND AT THAT MOMENT AS YOU ENTERED THE WORLD OF SPECTAR..."

...I CRASHED AND KNOCKED MYSELF OUT! YES, IT'S COMING BACK TO ME NOW--

BUT IN THE MOMENT THAT THE *EMERALD GLADIATOR* TAKES TO FREE HIS COSTUMED ALLY, THE DAZED *SPECTARNS* RECOVER AND STRIKE WITH SURPRISING SPEED...

HIS *POWER RING* PROTECTS *GREEN LANTERN* FROM DESTRUCTION-- BUT OUR *NEUTRON GUNS* CAN STILL RENDER HIM UNCONSCIOUS LONG ENOUGH FOR US TO MAKE HIM A PRISONER!

THEIR RAY-WEAPONS HAVE HIT *GREEN LANTERN*-- HE'S FALLING--!

LIKE A MADDENED TORNADO, THE *WORLD'S FASTEST HUMAN* BURSTS INTO A FURY OF MOTION, ROUNDING THE ROOM SO SWIFTLY HE IS ALL BUT INVISIBLE AS HE DISARMS HIS FOES BEFORE THEY CAN DO ANY MORE DAMAGE...

GOT TO GIVE *GL* A CHANCE-- TO COME TO HIS SENSES! AND I...

Whew!! I FEEL NUMB... BUT I CAN'T LET THAT KEEP ME DOWN--!

...MUST MAKE SURE NO FURTHER SHOTS ARE AIMED AT HIM--BY KNOCKING ALL THESE WEAPONS....

...OUT OF THE HANDS OF THE *SPECTARNS!*

THE NEXT MOMENT, AS THE GREAT GREEN BEAM IS TURNED ONCE AGAIN TO THE ATTACK...

SPARE US! WAIT! DO NOT DESTROY US--!

BEGGING FOR THEIR LIVES--

WE MIGHT HAVE GUESSED, *FLASH!* WOULD-BE CONQUERORS ARE ALWAYS *COWARDS* AT HEART!

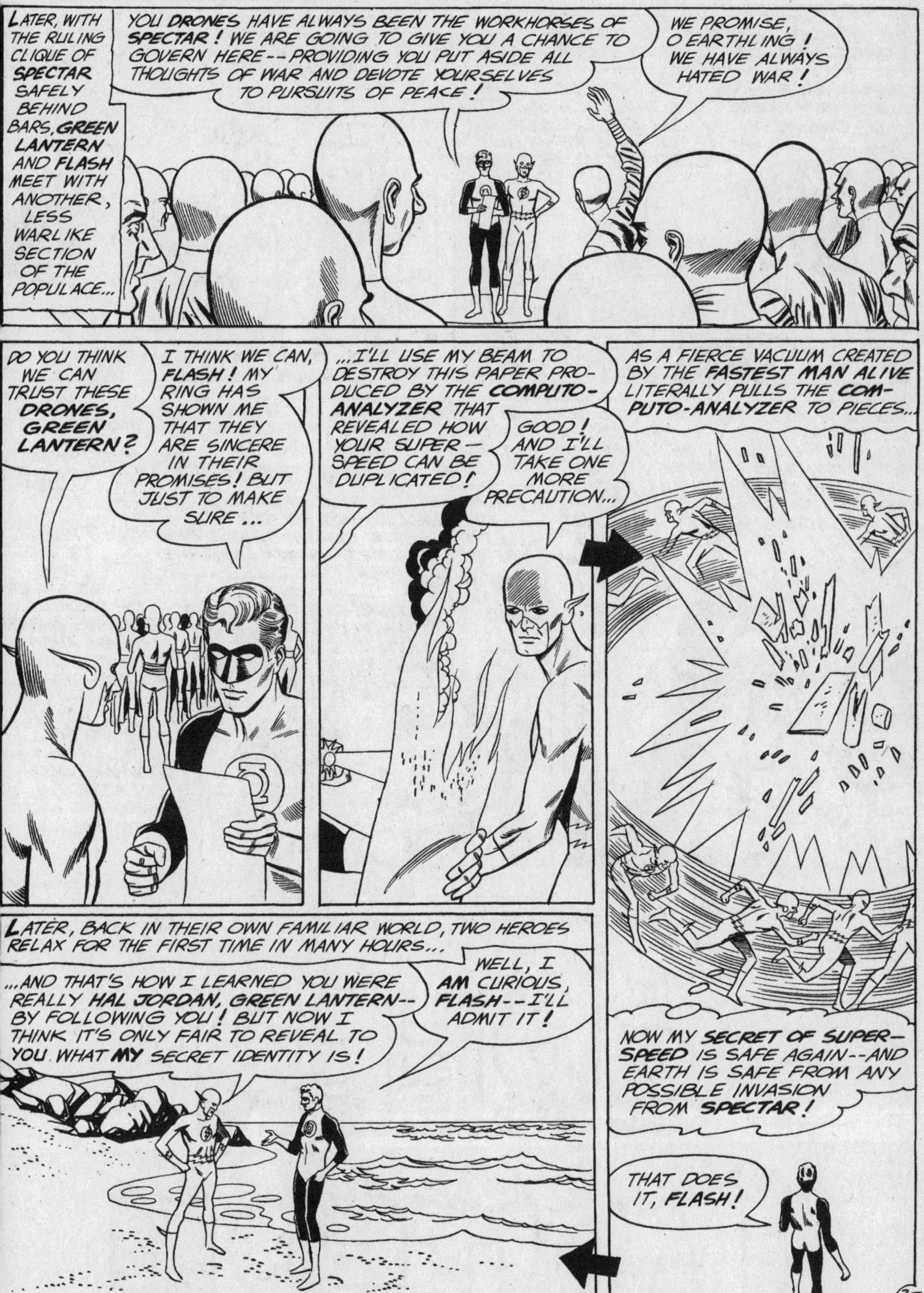
LATER, WITH THE RULING CLIQUE OF SPECTAR SAFELY BEHIND BARS, GREEN LANTERN AND FLASH MEET WITH ANOTHER, LESS WARLIKE SECTION OF THE POPULACE...
YOU DRONES HAVE ALWAYS BEEN THE WORKHORSES OF SPECTAR! WE ARE GOING TO GIVE YOU A CHANCE TO GOVERN HERE--PROVIDING YOU PUT ASIDE ALL THOUGHTS OF WAR AND DEVOTE YOURSELVES TO PURSUITS OF PEACE!
WE PROMISE, O EARTHLING! WE HAVE ALWAYS HATED WAR!
DO YOU THINK WE CAN TRUST THESE DRONES, GREEN LANTERN?
I THINK WE CAN, FLASH! MY RING HAS SHOWN ME THAT THEY ARE SINCERE IN THEIR PROMISES! BUT JUST TO MAKE SURE...
...I'LL USE MY BEAM TO DESTROY THIS PAPER PRODUCED BY THE COMPUTO-ANALYZER THAT REVEALED HOW YOUR SUPER-SPEED CAN BE DUPLICATED!
GOOD! AND I'LL TAKE ONE MORE PRECAUTION...
AS A FIERCE VACUUM CREATED BY THE FASTEST MAN ALIVE LITERALLY PULLS THE COMPUTO-ANALYZER TO PIECES...
NOW MY SECRET OF SUPER-SPEED IS SAFE AGAIN--AND EARTH IS SAFE FROM ANY POSSIBLE INVASION FROM SPECTAR!
THAT DOES IT, FLASH!
LATER, BACK IN THEIR OWN FAMILIAR WORLD, TWO HEROES RELAX FOR THE FIRST TIME IN MANY HOURS...
...AND THAT'S HOW I LEARNED YOU WERE REALLY HAL JORDAN, GREEN LANTERN--BY FOLLOWING YOU! BUT NOW I THINK IT'S ONLY FAIR TO REVEAL TO YOU WHAT MY SECRET IDENTITY IS!
WELL, I AM CURIOUS, FLASH--I'LL ADMIT IT!
25

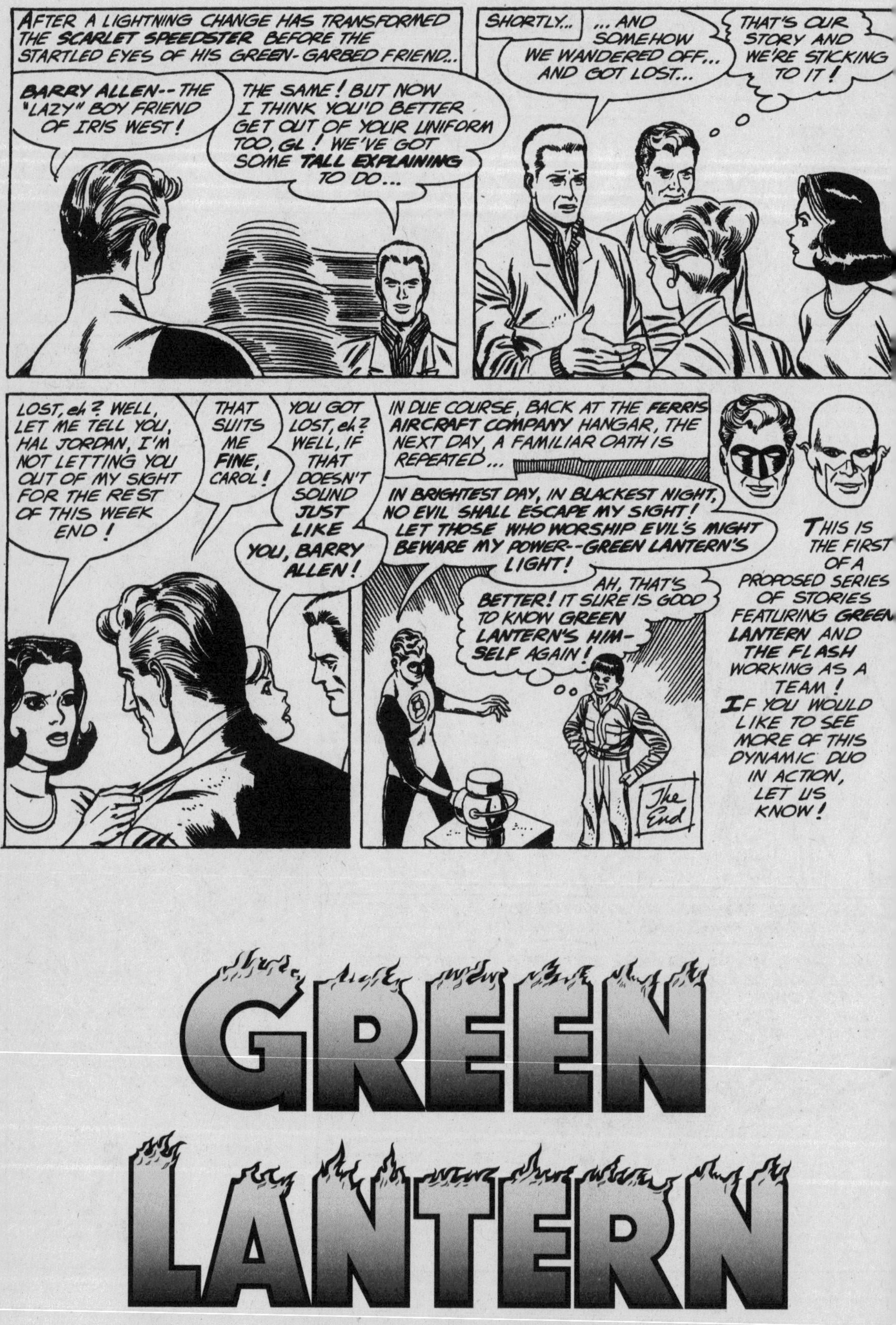
AFTER A LIGHTNING CHANGE HAS TRANSFORMED THE SCARLET SPEEDSTER BEFORE THE STARTLED EYES OF HIS GREEN-GARBED FRIEND...
BARRY ALLEN--THE "LAZY" BOY FRIEND OF IRIS WEST!
THE SAME! BUT NOW I THINK YOU'D BETTER GET OUT OF YOUR UNIFORM TOO, GL! WE'VE GOT SOME TALL EXPLAINING TO DO...
SHORTLY...
... AND SOMEHOW WE WANDERED OFF... AND GOT LOST...
THAT'S OUR STORY AND WE'RE STICKING TO IT!
LOST, eh? WELL, LET ME TELL YOU, HAL JORDAN, I'M NOT LETTING YOU OUT OF MY SIGHT FOR THE REST OF THIS WEEK END!
THAT SUITS ME FINE, CAROL!
YOU GOT LOST, eh? WELL, IF THAT DOESN'T SOUND JUST LIKE YOU, BARRY ALLEN!
IN DUE COURSE, BACK AT THE FERRIS AIRCRAFT COMPANY HANGAR, THE NEXT DAY, A FAMILIAR OATH IS REPEATED...
IN BRIGHTEST DAY, IN BLACKEST NIGHT, NO EVIL SHALL ESCAPE MY SIGHT! LET THOSE WHO WORSHIP EVIL'S MIGHT BEWARE MY POWER--GREEN LANTERN'S LIGHT!
AH, THAT'S BETTER! IT SURE IS GOOD TO KNOW GREEN LANTERN'S HIMSELF AGAIN!
The End
THIS IS THE FIRST OF A PROPOSED SERIES OF STORIES FEATURING GREEN LANTERN AND THE FLASH WORKING AS A TEAM! IF YOU WOULD LIKE TO SEE MORE OF THIS DYNAMIC DUO IN ACTION, LET US KNOW!

GREEN LANTERN

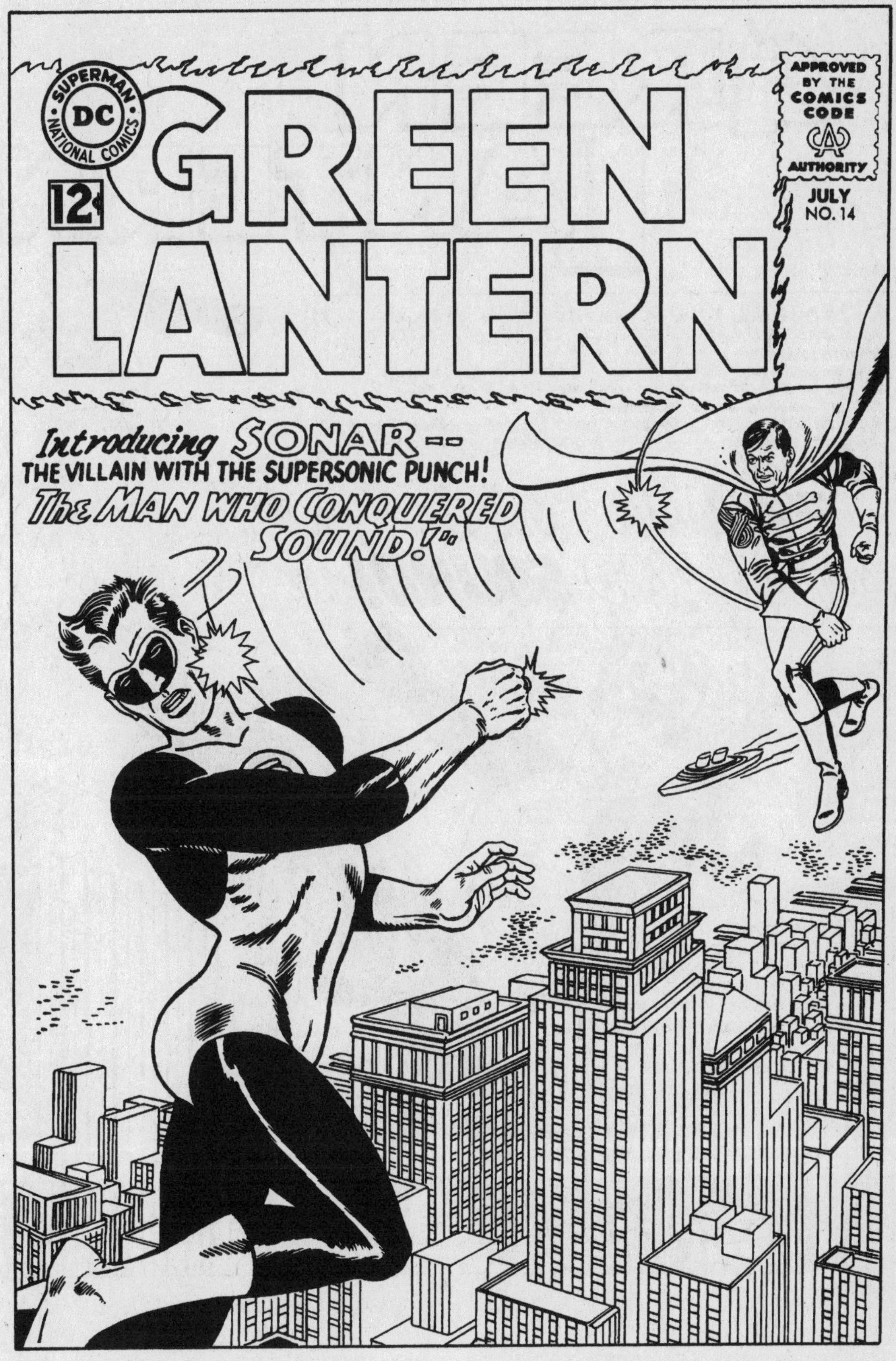
SUPERMAN DC NATIONAL COMICS
12¢
GREEN LANTERN
APPROVED BY THE COMICS CODE AUTHORITY
JULY NO. 14
Introducing SONAR --
THE VILLAIN WITH THE SUPERSONIC PUNCH!
The MAN WHO CONQUERED SOUND!"

GREEN LANTERN

All of "SONAR'S" TRICKS--AND STARTLING ESCAPADES-- WERE BASED ON HIS MASTERY OF SOUND IN ALL ITS MANIFESTATIONS!
IT WAS THIS MASTERY THAT LED THE AMAZING VILLAIN TO BELIEVE THAT HE COULD IMPOSE PEACE ON THE WORLD ON HIS OWN TERMS!
BUT IT WAS GREEN LANTERN WHO REALIZED THAT THESE TERMS WOULD BE MORE DANGEROUS THAN WAR ITSELF!!

The MAN WHO CONQUERED SOUND!

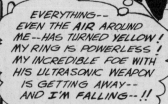

EVERYTHING-- EVEN THE AIR AROUND ME--HAS TURNED YELLOW! MY RING IS POWERLESS! MY INCREDIBLE FOE WITH HIS ULTRASONIC WEAPON IS GETTING AWAY-- AND I'M FALLING--!!

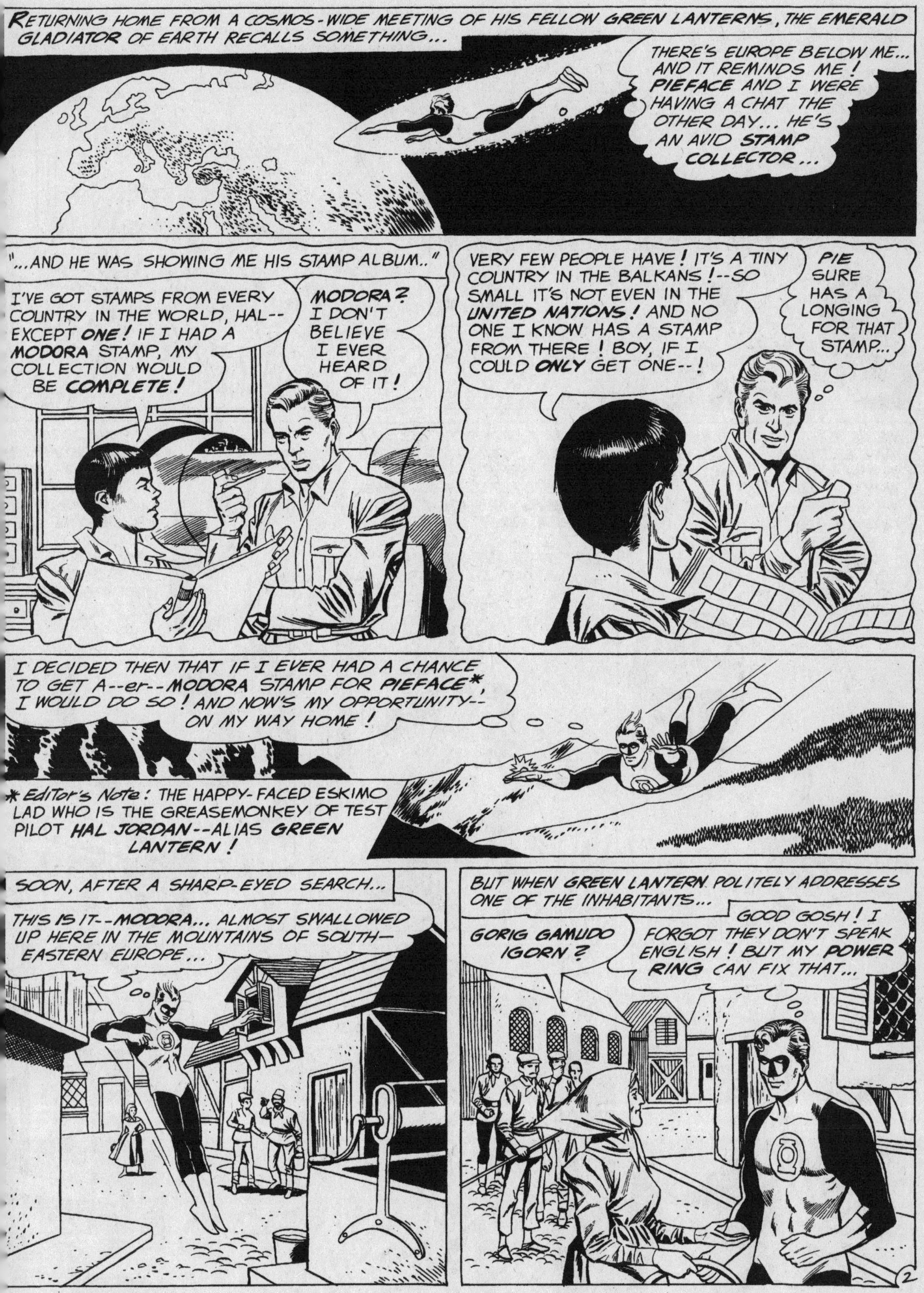
RETURNING HOME FROM A COSMOS-WIDE MEETING OF HIS FELLOW GREEN LANTERNS, THE EMERALD GLADIATOR OF EARTH RECALLS SOMETHING...
THERE'S EUROPE BELOW ME... AND IT REMINDS ME! PIEFACE AND I WERE HAVING A CHAT THE OTHER DAY... HE'S AN AVID STAMP COLLECTOR...
"...AND HE WAS SHOWING ME HIS STAMP ALBUM.."
I'VE GOT STAMPS FROM EVERY COUNTRY IN THE WORLD, HAL-- EXCEPT ONE! IF I HAD A MODORA STAMP, MY COLLECTION WOULD BE COMPLETE!
MODORA? I DON'T BELIEVE I EVER HEARD OF IT!
VERY FEW PEOPLE HAVE! IT'S A TINY COUNTRY IN THE BALKANS!--SO SMALL IT'S NOT EVEN IN THE UNITED NATIONS! AND NO ONE I KNOW HAS A STAMP FROM THERE! BOY, IF I COULD ONLY GET ONE--!
PIE SURE HAS A LONGING FOR THAT STAMP...
I DECIDED THEN THAT IF I EVER HAD A CHANCE TO GET A--er--MODORA STAMP FOR PIEFACE*, I WOULD DO SO! AND NOW'S MY OPPORTUNITY-- ON MY WAY HOME!
*Editor's Note: THE HAPPY-FACED ESKIMO LAD WHO IS THE GREASEMONKEY OF TEST PILOT HAL JORDAN--ALIAS GREEN LANTERN!
SOON, AFTER A SHARP-EYED SEARCH...
THIS IS IT--MODORA... ALMOST SWALLOWED UP HERE IN THE MOUNTAINS OF SOUTH-EASTERN EUROPE...
BUT WHEN GREEN LANTERN POLITELY ADDRESSES ONE OF THE INHABITANTS...
GORIG GAMUDO IGORN?
GOOD GOSH! I FORGOT THEY DON'T SPEAK ENGLISH! BUT MY POWER RING CAN FIX THAT...
2

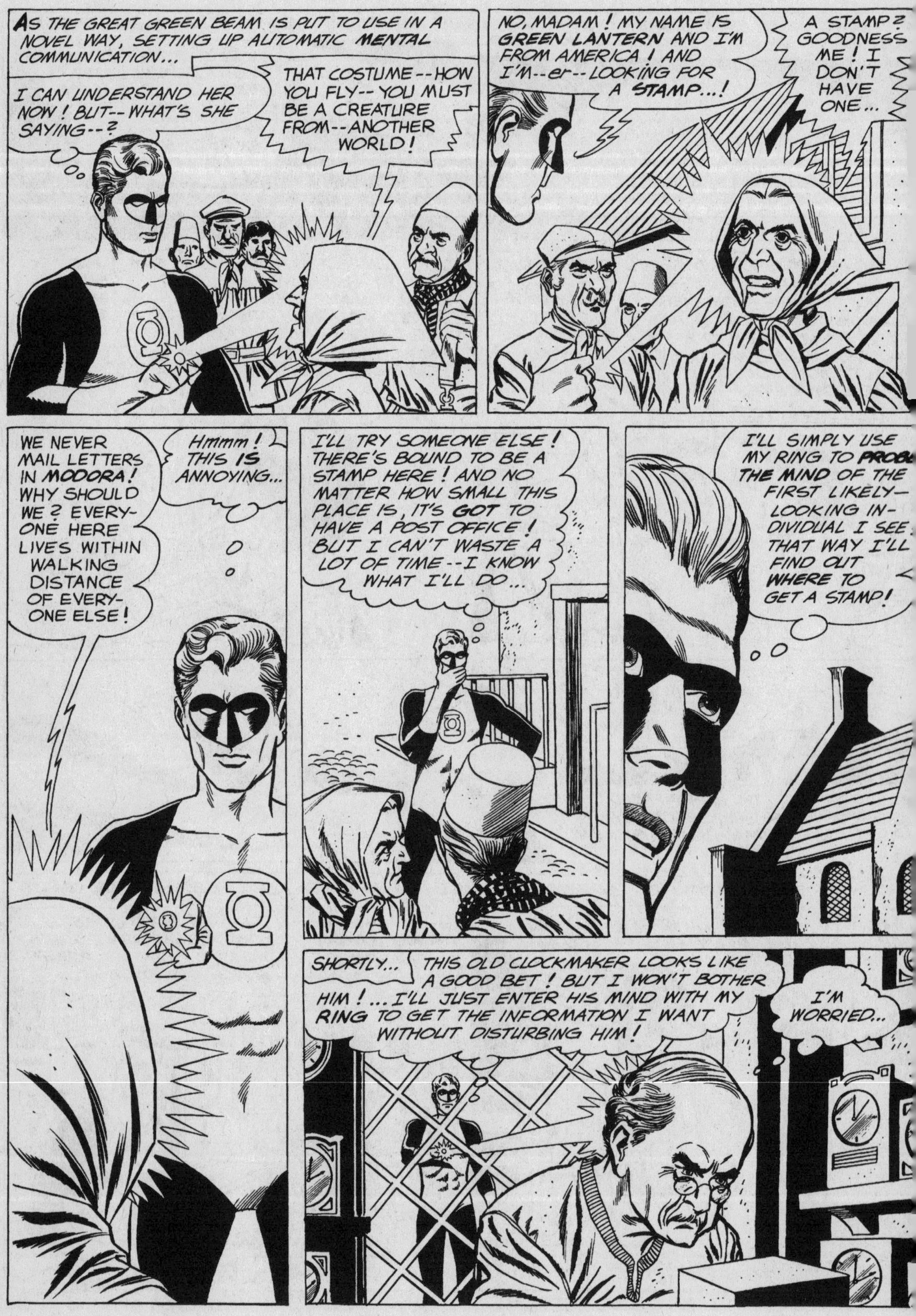
AS THE GREAT GREEN BEAM IS PUT TO USE IN A NOVEL WAY, SETTING UP AUTOMATIC MENTAL COMMUNICATION...
I CAN UNDERSTAND HER NOW! BUT--WHAT'S SHE SAYING--?
THAT COSTUME--HOW YOU FLY--YOU MUST BE A CREATURE FROM--ANOTHER WORLD!
NO, MADAM! MY NAME IS GREEN LANTERN AND I'M FROM AMERICA! AND I'M--er--LOOKING FOR A STAMP...!
A STAMP? GOODNESS ME! I DON'T HAVE ONE...
WE NEVER MAIL LETTERS IN MODORA! WHY SHOULD WE? EVERYONE HERE LIVES WITHIN WALKING DISTANCE OF EVERYONE ELSE!
Hmmm! THIS IS ANNOYING...
I'LL TRY SOMEONE ELSE! THERE'S BOUND TO BE A STAMP HERE! AND NO MATTER HOW SMALL THIS PLACE IS, IT'S GOT TO HAVE A POST OFFICE! BUT I CAN'T WASTE A LOT OF TIME--I KNOW WHAT I'LL DO...
I'LL SIMPLY USE MY RING TO PROBE THE MIND OF THE FIRST LIKELY-LOOKING INDIVIDUAL I SEE. THAT WAY I'LL FIND OUT WHERE TO GET A STAMP!
SHORTLY...
THIS OLD CLOCKMAKER LOOKS LIKE A GOOD BET! BUT I WON'T BOTHER HIM!... I'LL JUST ENTER HIS MIND WITH MY RING TO GET THE INFORMATION I WANT WITHOUT DISTURBING HIM!
I'M WORRIED...

...ABOUT MY FORMER APPRENTICE *BITO WLADON* WHO LEFT HERE THE OTHER DAY TO GO TO AMERICA! HE'S A BRILLIANT MAN BUT VERY STRANGE! AND HE NEVER CONFIDED IN ME...

eh?

INTENT ON PROBING DEEPER INTO THE CLOCKMAKER'S MEMORY, *GREEN LANTERN* FINDS HIM-SELF DISTRACTED BY THE OLD MAN'S *SURFACE THOUGHTS*...

BUT YESTERDAY I FOUND THESE NOTES OF *WLADON'S*... TUCKED AWAY HERE IN THE SHOP...AND THEY FILL ME WITH ALARM! APPARENTLY YOUNG *WLADON* HAD ALL SORTS OF IDEAS I NEVER KNEW ABOUT...DANGEROUS IDEAS! AND--READING THEM HAS UPSET ME TERRIBLY!

I'VE HEARD *TOO* MUCH NOT TO FIND OUT WHAT'S IN THOSE NOTES OF THE CLOCKMAKER'S APPRENTICE! IF THEY CONTAIN ANYTHING REALLY *DANGEROUS*, I OUGHT TO KNOW ABOUT IT...

AT ONCE, THE MYSTIC BEAM, MADE INVISIBLE, DARTS AT THE ASSORTED PAPERS...

GREAT GUARDIANS! IT'S INCREDIBLE--FANTASTIC! IF ONE-HALF OF WHAT'S IN THESE NOTES IS TRUE, I'VE UNCOVERED A MENACE TO THE WHOLE WORLD--I MUST TAKE ACTION *WITHOUT DELAY!*

IN BRIEF SECONDS, A LITHE EMERALD FIGURE IS ROCKETING ACROSS THE OCEAN...

ACCORDING TO THE THOUGHTS OF THE OLD CLOCKMAKER, THIS APPRENTICE OF HIS-- *BITO WLADON*--SAILED TO AMERICA-- AND IS ALREADY THERE! I'VE GOT TO GET BACK HOME AS FAST AS POSSIBLE--!

AS THE *GREEN GLADIATOR* WHIZZES ALONG, HIS OWN MIND IS WORKING...

I CAN'T GET OVER WHAT I READ IN THOSE NOTES! ASTONISHING..!

AT LAST I HAVE DIS-COVERED WHAT I AM AFTER...

4

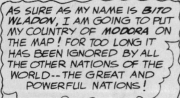

AS SURE AS MY NAME IS *BITO WLADON*, I AM GOING TO PUT MY COUNTRY OF *MODORA* ON THE MAP! FOR TOO LONG IT HAS BEEN IGNORED BY ALL THE OTHER NATIONS OF THE WORLD--THE GREAT AND POWERFUL NATIONS!

I HAVE FIGURED OUT... THAT THE GREATEST NATIONS ON EARTH ARE THOSE WITH THE *MOST POWERFUL WEAPONS!* AT ONE STROKE I SHALL MAKE *MODORA* GREAT BY PROVIDING MY COUNTRY WITH THE *GREATEST WEAPON OF ALL...*

...THE *NUCLEO-SONIC BOMB*--A NEW EXPLOSIVE DEVICE BASED ON *SUPERSONIC ENERGY!* I HAVE DEVOTED MY LIFE TO THE PHENOMENON OF *SOUND*--AND I HAVE BECOME A MASTER OF IT! I HAVE MADE SENSATIONAL DISCOVERIES ALREADY...

"FOR INSTANCE, BY MY SCIENCE OF NUCLEO-SONICS I CAN NULLIFY GRAVITY..."

BY GETTING IN TUNE WITH ANY SOUND SOURCE-- LIKE THAT RADIO, FOR EXAMPLE--MY *NUCLEO- SONIC* MOTOR CAN LIFT ME RIGHT OFF MY FEET!

BY SNAPPING MY ARM AND HAND LIKE A *WHIP*, I CAN SEND OUT A WAVE OF CONCENTRATED *SOUND* THAT KNOCKS OVER A PILE OF BRICKS!

POW!

BUT IN ORDER TO BUILD MY *GREAT WEAPON* I NEED CERTAIN TECHNICAL MATERIALS AVAILABLE ONLY IN A HIGHLY-DEVELOPED COUNTRY LIKE AMERICA! THEREFORE I MUST GO THERE--AND *TAKE* WHAT I NEED!

ACCORDING TO THE NOTES, **BITO** REALIZED HE WOULD HAVE TO **STEAL** THE MATERIAL HE NEEDED, BECAUSE IT IS ALL TOP-PRIORITY, CLASSIFIED EQUIPMENT! AND THERE'S ONE OTHER THING I REMEMBER FROM THE NOTES...

"HE DESIGNED HIMSELF A *SPECIAL COSTUME* FOR USE LATER..."

SINCE MY COUNTRY IS ABOUT TO BECOME WORLD—FAMOUS, I MUST BE SUITABLY DRESSED WHEN I APPEAR IN AMERICA! THIS OUTFIT LOOKS RATHER **REGAL**—JUST WHAT I WANT--IN KEEPING WITH THE FUTURE STATUS OF **MODORA!**

BUT I WON'T PUT IT ON UNTIL I REACH THE **U.S.A.!** I DON'T WANT TO AROUSE SUSPICIONS AHEAD OF TIME, IT MIGHT SPOIL EVERY-THING-- ALL THE PLANS FOR MY GREAT MISSION!

AS THE **GREEN-CLAD GLADIATOR** SWEEPS DOWN ON AN EASTERN METROPOLIS...

OF COURSE, I COULD BE KEYED UP FOR **NO REASON!** THIS **BITO WLADON** MAY BE MERELY A **CRACKPOT** WHOSE IDEAS CAN'T POSSIBLY WORK! BUT HIS NOTES SEEMED SO CONVINCING...

SOON AFTER ON THE STREETS OF THE CITY...

GREAT SCOTT! IT'S **BITO**-- IN HIS SPECIAL COSTUME!

Science

ve Story

L SCREEN PLAYS

TOGRAPHY

POST N

SENSATIONAL NE CRIMINAL STRIKES AGAIN!

AS **GREEN LANTERN** STARES WIDE-EYED...

"THE MYSTERIOUS THIEF WHOM THE NEWSPAPERS HAVE DUBBED "SONAR"-- BE-CAUSE OF HIS INCREDIBLE MASTERY OF **SUPERSONIC** SOUND--LOOTED A HEAVILY—GUARDED U.S. ARSENAL YES-TERDAY AND MADE GOOD HIS ESCAPE"...

"SONAR" eh? BITO IS CARRY-ING OUT HIS **PLAN!**

6

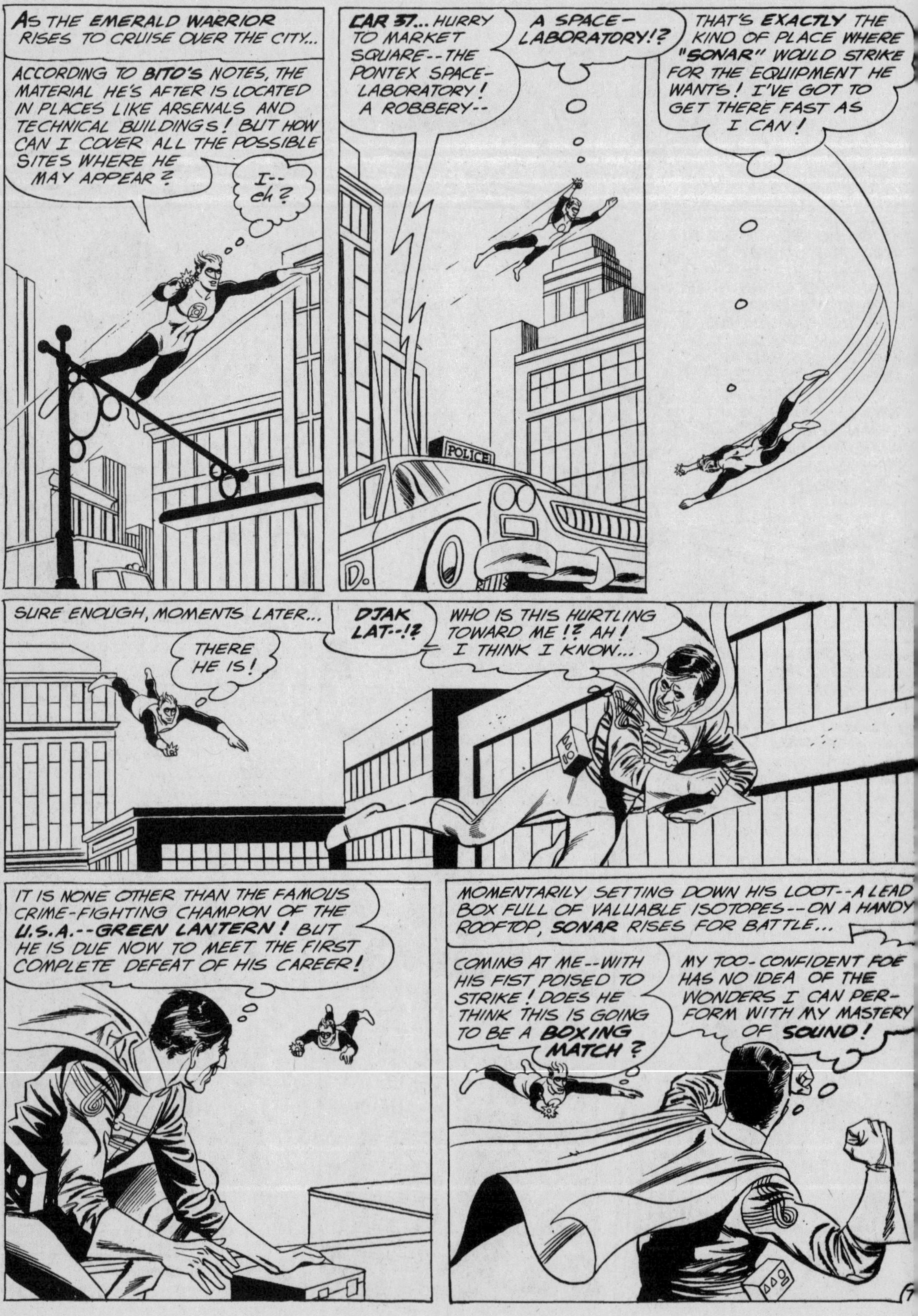
AS THE EMERALD WARRIOR RISES TO CRUISE OVER THE CITY...
ACCORDING TO BITO'S NOTES, THE MATERIAL HE'S AFTER IS LOCATED IN PLACES LIKE ARSENALS AND TECHNICAL BUILDINGS! BUT HOW CAN I COVER ALL THE POSSIBLE SITES WHERE HE MAY APPEAR?
I-- eh?
CAR 37... HURRY TO MARKET SQUARE--THE PONTEX SPACE-LABORATORY! A ROBBERY--
A SPACE-LABORATORY!?
THAT'S EXACTLY THE KIND OF PLACE WHERE "SONAR" WOULD STRIKE FOR THE EQUIPMENT HE WANTS! I'VE GOT TO GET THERE FAST AS I CAN!
POLICE
SURE ENOUGH, MOMENTS LATER...
THERE HE IS!
DJAK LAT--!?
WHO IS THIS HURTLING TOWARD ME!? AH! I THINK I KNOW...
IT IS NONE OTHER THAN THE FAMOUS CRIME-FIGHTING CHAMPION OF THE U.S.A.--GREEN LANTERN! BUT HE IS DUE NOW TO MEET THE FIRST COMPLETE DEFEAT OF HIS CAREER!
MOMENTARILY SETTING DOWN HIS LOOT--A LEAD BOX FULL OF VALUABLE ISOTOPES--ON A HANDY ROOFTOP, SONAR RISES FOR BATTLE...
COMING AT ME--WITH HIS FIST POISED TO STRIKE! DOES HE THINK THIS IS GOING TO BE A BOXING MATCH?
MY TOO-CONFIDENT FOE HAS NO IDEA OF THE WONDERS I CAN PERFORM WITH MY MASTERY OF SOUND!
7

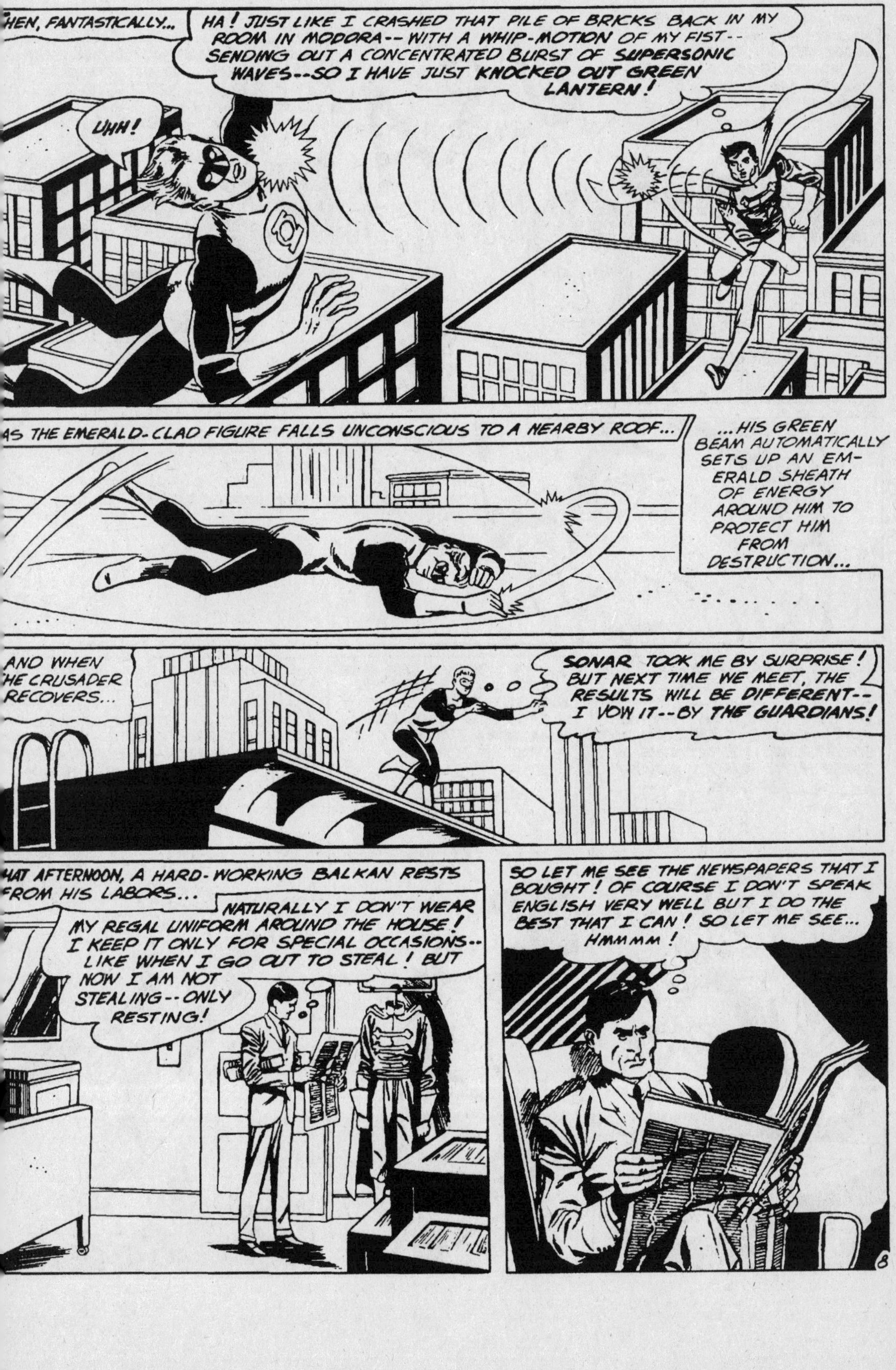
HEN, FANTASTICALLY...
HA! JUST LIKE I CRASHED THAT PILE OF BRICKS BACK IN MY ROOM IN MODORA-- WITH A WHIP-MOTION OF MY FIST-- SENDING OUT A CONCENTRATED BURST OF SUPERSONIC WAVES--SO I HAVE JUST KNOCKED OUT GREEN LANTERN!
UHH!
AS THE EMERALD-CLAD FIGURE FALLS UNCONSCIOUS TO A NEARBY ROOF...
...HIS GREEN BEAM AUTOMATICALLY SETS UP AN EMERALD SHEATH OF ENERGY AROUND HIM TO PROTECT HIM FROM DESTRUCTION...
AND WHEN HE CRUSADER RECOVERS...
SONAR TOOK ME BY SURPRISE! BUT NEXT TIME WE MEET, THE RESULTS WILL BE DIFFERENT-- I VOW IT--BY THE GUARDIANS!
HAT AFTERNOON, A HARD-WORKING BALKAN RESTS FROM HIS LABORS...
NATURALLY I DON'T WEAR MY REGAL UNIFORM AROUND THE HOUSE! I KEEP IT ONLY FOR SPECIAL OCCASIONS-- LIKE WHEN I GO OUT TO STEAL! BUT NOW I AM NOT STEALING--ONLY RESTING!
SO LET ME SEE THE NEWSPAPERS THAT I BOUGHT! OF COURSE I DON'T SPEAK ENGLISH VERY WELL BUT I DO THE BEST THAT I CAN! SO LET ME SEE... HMMMM!
8

RUSSIA AND AMERICA... AMERICA AND RUSSIA! NOT A SINGLE WORD ABOUT *MODORA*! BUT IT WON'T BE LONG NOW! THINGS ARE GOING TO CHANGE VERY QUICK!

ONE MORE RAID AND I WILL HAVE ALL THE EQUIPMENT I NEED TO BUILD MY NUCLEO-SONIC BOMB! AND THEN IT WILL BE MY BELOVED *MODORA* THAT WILL CALL THE TUNE IN THE WORLD! BUT MEANWHILE...

...THIS *GREEN LANTERN* CAN BE A MENACE TO ME! I DEFEATED HIM ONCE... BUT NEXT TIME HE MAY BE READY FOR MY "SONIC—PUNCH"! WHAT I NEED IS SOMETHING TO *SURPRISE* HIM WITH! SO LET ME SEE...

LATER, AFTER LONG HOURS OF CONCENTRATED WORK...

I HAVE IT! MY NEW *TUNING FORK GUN*! IT SHOOTS OUT SUPERSONIC VIBRATIONS IN *TUNE WITH HUMAN BRAIN WAVES*...

... AND CREATES THE MOST ASTONISHING *MENTAL EFFECTS*! NOW I AM READY FOR *GREEN LANTERN*! IN FACT, I HOPE HE TRIES TO STOP ME!

HA! HA!

ELSEWHERE IN THE GREAT CITY, A TIRELESS SEARCHER...

I'VE SET MY *POWER BEAM* SO THAT AT THE FIRST HINT OF *SONAR*-- AND HIS *SUPERSONIC* TRICKS -- MY RING WILL SIGNAL AN ALARM! BUT SO FAR-- NOT A SIGN...

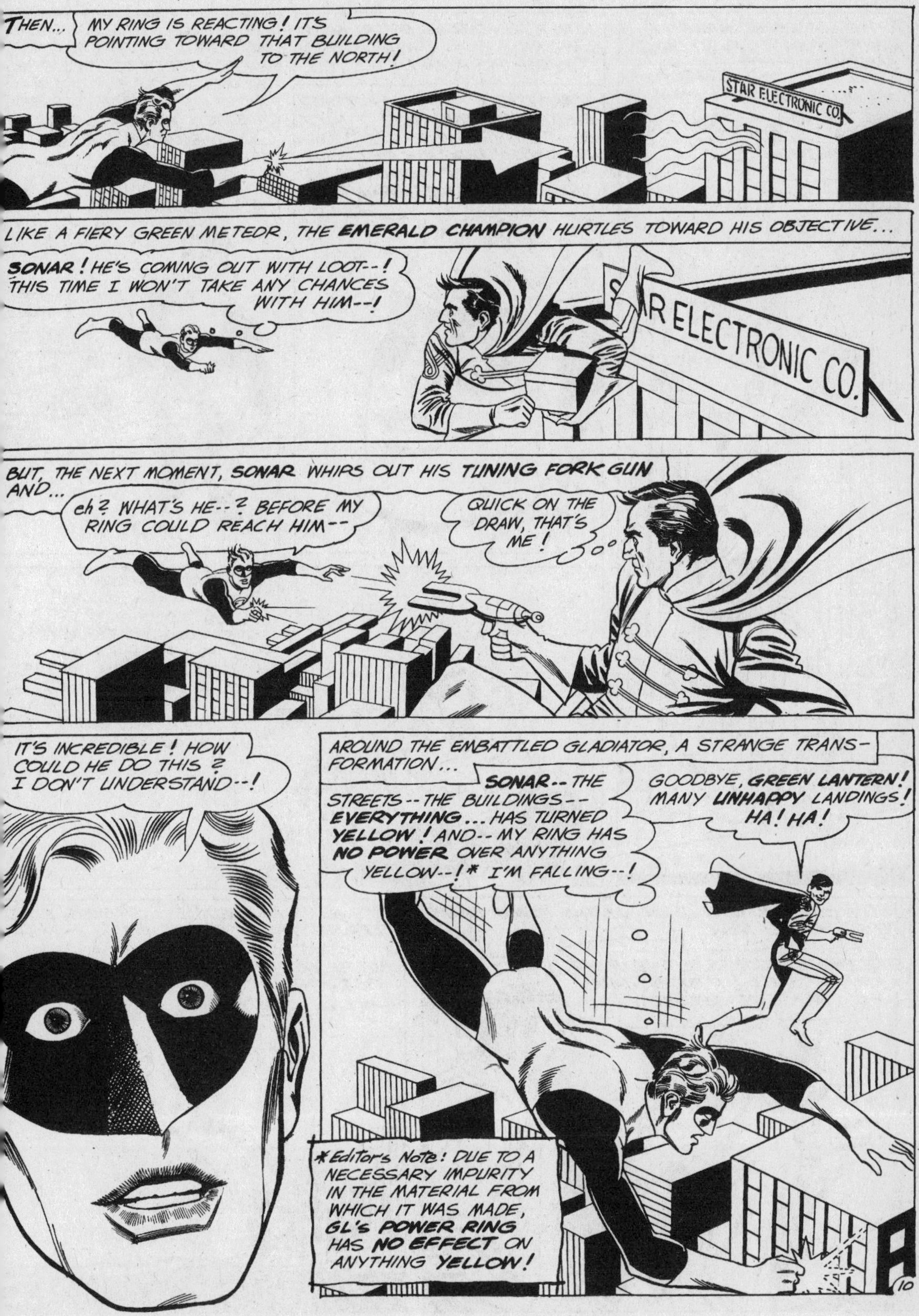
THEN...
MY RING IS REACTING! IT'S POINTING TOWARD THAT BUILDING TO THE NORTH!
STAR ELECTRONIC CO.
LIKE A FIERY GREEN METEOR, THE EMERALD CHAMPION HURTLES TOWARD HIS OBJECTIVE...
SONAR! HE'S COMING OUT WITH LOOT--! THIS TIME I WON'T TAKE ANY CHANCES WITH HIM--!
STAR ELECTRONIC CO.
BUT, THE NEXT MOMENT, SONAR WHIPS OUT HIS TUNING FORK GUN AND...
eh? WHAT'S HE--? BEFORE MY RING COULD REACH HIM--
QUICK ON THE DRAW, THAT'S ME!
IT'S INCREDIBLE! HOW COULD HE DO THIS? I DON'T UNDERSTAND--!
AROUND THE EMBATTLED GLADIATOR, A STRANGE TRANSFORMATION...
SONAR-- THE STREETS--THE BUILDINGS-- EVERYTHING... HAS TURNED YELLOW! AND--MY RING HAS NO POWER OVER ANYTHING YELLOW--!* I'M FALLING--!
GOODBYE, GREEN LANTERN! MANY UNHAPPY LANDINGS! HA! HA!
*Editor's Note: DUE TO A NECESSARY IMPURITY IN THE MATERIAL FROM WHICH IT WAS MADE, GL's POWER RING HAS NO EFFECT ON ANYTHING YELLOW!
10

TO HIS AMAZEMENT, **GREEN LANTERN** MANAGES TO LAND SAFELY...

THE VERY AIR HAS TURNED YELLOW! I CAN'T FLY THROUGH IT!

WITH A TREMENDOUS EFFORT, **GREEN LANTERN** FORCES HIMSELF TO CONSIDER HIS PLIGHT COOLLY...

SONAR COULDN'T HAVE TRANSFORMED **EVERYTHING** THIS WAY! IT MUST BE... THAT HE WORKED THE TRANSFORMATION **THROUGH ME!** SOMEHOW THAT QUEER WEAPON OF HIS HAS AFFECTED MY BRAIN!

IT'S MAKING ME **SEE THINGS YELLOW**... AND THAT IN TURN HAS ACTED ON MY **WILL POWER** WEAKENING IT! BUT IF I'M RIGHT, THERE OUGHT TO BE A **QUICK WAY** OF GETTING BACK TO NORMAL--

-- WITH MY RING!

RING... CLEAR MY HEAD! MAKE ME SEE THINGS AS THEY ARE AGAIN! TAKE AWAY ANY **ILLUSION** THAT HAS BEEN PLACED THERE!

AND A BRIEF MOMENT AFTER, AS THE **POWER BEAM** PERFORMS ITS TASK...

SURE ENOUGH! **SONAR** PUT ME UNDER A KIND OF SPELL! IT GAVE HIM A CHANCE TO GET AWAY!

ONCE AGAIN AN EMERALD LIGHTNING-BOLT CLEAVES THROUGH THE AIR...

BUT HE WON'T GET FAR-->!

MEANWHILE, HURTLING EASTWARD ACROSS THE ATLANTIC OCEAN...

I DON'T HAVE TO WORRY ABOUT THAT **GREEN LANTERN**! BY THE TIME HE LOCATES ME AGAIN--IF HE EVER DOES--MY NUCLEAR-SONIC BOMB WILL BE BUILT WITH THIS EQUIPMENT I'VE GOT! AND THEN I WILL DICTATE TERMS TO **EVERYONE**!

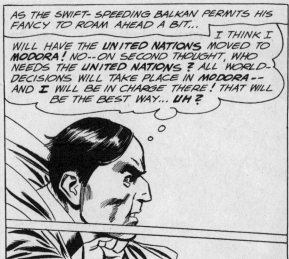

AS THE SWIFT-SPEEDING BALKAN PERMITS HIS FANCY TO ROAM AHEAD A BIT...

I THINK I WILL HAVE THE **UNITED NATIONS** MOVED TO **MODORA**! NO--ON SECOND THOUGHT, WHO NEEDS THE **UNITED NATIONS**? ALL WORLD-DECISIONS WILL TAKE PLACE IN **MODORA**-- AND **I** WILL BE IN CHARGE THERE! THAT WILL BE THE BEST WAY... **UH**?

THEN, AS **GREEN LANTERN** ROCKETS INTO VIEW...

GREAT STUFFED GOOSE NECKS!? HOW--!?

THAT TUNING FORK WEAPON OF YOURS LEFT A **FAINT TRAIL** OF RADIATION BEHIND YOU, **SONAR**-- ENOUGH FOR MY RING TO DETECT AND FOLLOW!

SO IT LOOKS LIKE YOUR LITTLE TRICK AGAINST ME HAS **BACKFIRED** ON YOU!

YOU CAN'T STOP ME NOW! I--I WON'T PERMIT IT!

BUT THIS TIME WITH DEVASTATING EFFECT THE **GREAT GREEN BEAM** SHOOTS OUT...

MY **POWER RING** HAS CREATED A **WATERSPOUT** TO TRAP **SONAR**! BUT I'LL RESCUE HIM FROM IT BEFORE HE **DROWNS COMPLETELY**! AND I'LL TAKE HIM TO HIS OWN COUNTRY--THE AUTHORITIES THERE CAN DEAL WITH HIM--AFTER THEY'VE LEARNED ABOUT HIS MAD SCHEME!

G-GAAAHHH!

12

IN DUE COURSE, STRIPPED OF HIS LOOT AND WEAPONS, SONAR IS BEHIND BARS, BUT NOT ALTOGETHER UN-HAPPY...

ГАЗЕТА ПО-РУССКИ
МОДОРА КУП
оба петтьто

HERALD-NEWS
SENSATIONAL COUP
OF MODORAN FAILS!

Le Jour
VOILA UNE
HISTOIRE DE
MODORA

I'VE PUT MY COUNTRY ON THE MAP! MY EXPLOIT IS IN NEWS—PAPERS ALL OVER THE WORLD!

WHILE ELSEWHERE IN THE TINY NATION...

BY... CAPTURE... OF **BITO** YOU SAVED... MODORA FROM A DREADFUL ...FATE! NONE OF US WANTS TO RULE THE WORLD, **GREEN LANTERN**! PLEASE ACCEPT THIS GIFT... AS A TOKEN... OF... OUR GRATEFULNESS...

WHAT COULD BE IN THAT BOX?

A STAMP--A MODORA **POSTAGE** STAMP!

WE HEARD THAT **THIS** WAS WHAT... YOU CAME HERE FOR! WE HAD IT PRINTED SPECIALLY FOR YOU!

MUCH LATER, BACK HOME IN **COAST CITY**...

GOLLY, IT'S GREAT TO BE A PERSONAL FRIEND OF SOMEONE LIKE **GREEN LANTERN**! HOW ELSE WOULD I BECOME THE ONLY STAMP COLLECTOR ON THE WEST COAST -- MAYBE IN THE WHOLE COUNTRY--WITH A PRIZE **MODORA STAMP** IN HIS ALBUM?!

The End

GREEN LANTERN

THAT'S THE WAY, JIM JORDAN! BETWEEN US WE'VE GOT THIS GANG LICKED!

GREEN LANTERN AND I ARE WORKING AS A TEAM-- AND HE'S USING HIS POWER RING TO GIVE MY FRATERNITY RING POWER TOO!

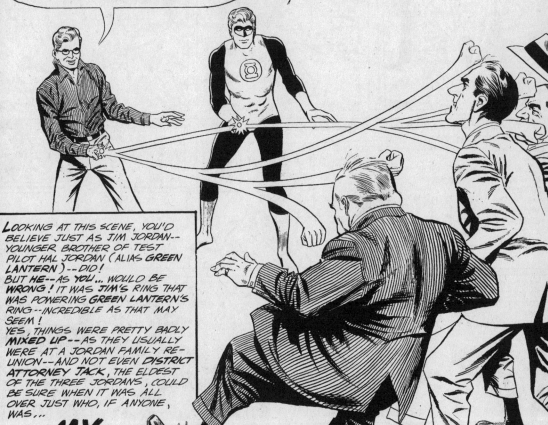

LOOKING AT THIS SCENE, YOU'D BELIEVE JUST AS JIM JORDAN-- YOUNGER BROTHER OF TEST PILOT HAL JORDAN (ALIAS GREEN LANTERN)--DID! BUT HE--AS YOU...WOULD BE WRONG! IT WAS JIM'S RING THAT WAS POWERING GREEN LANTERN'S RING--INCREDIBLE AS THAT MAY SEEM! YES, THINGS WERE PRETTY BADLY MIXED UP--AS THEY USUALLY WERE AT A JORDAN FAMILY RE-UNION--AND NOT EVEN DISTRICT ATTORNEY JACK, THE ELDEST OF THE THREE JORDANS, COULD BE SURE WHEN IT WAS ALL OVER JUST WHO, IF ANYONE, WAS...

MY BROTHER, GREEN LANTERN!

IN HAL JORDAN'S DRESSING ROOM AT THE FERRIS AIRCRAFT COMPANY, THE CRACK TEST PILOT REVEALS AN ANNOYING LOSS...

...AND EVERY YEAR AT THIS TIME, PIE, MY BROTHERS JACK AND JIM AND I MEET TO ATTEND OUR COLLEGE FRATERNITY REUNION! AND WE ALWAYS WEAR OUR IDENTICAL FRATERNITY RINGS! IT'S TRADITION! ONLY I CAN'T FIND MINE...!

SOMEHOW I'VE MISLAID IT! I DON'T KNOW WHERE IT IS!

JUMPING FISHHOOKS, HAL! I CAN SOLVE THAT PROBLEM FOR YOU!

AS THOMAS (PIEFACE) KALMAKU, HAL'S ESKIMO GREASEMONKEY, AND LOYAL CONFIDANT, MAKES A GRINNING SUGGESTION...

ALL YOU'VE GOT TO DO IS WEAR YOUR POWER RING -- JUST TRANSFORM ITS APPEARANCE FOR THAT DAY INTO YOUR FRATERNITY RING -- AND NO ONE WILL BE THE WISER, GET ME?

PIE, YOU'RE A GENIUS! THAT'S EXACTLY WHAT I'LL DO!

AT THE HOME OF JACK JORDAN, ELDEST OF THE JORDAN BROTHERS, NEAR COAST CITY...

I'M GLAD TO SEE WE'RE ALL WEARING OUR FRATERNITY RINGS!

ONE FOR ALL AND ALL FOR ONE!

THIS IS A BIT WHIMSICAL...

...BUT SINCE JACK AND JIM SEEM TO VALUE OUR FRATERNITY TRADITIONS, I'M GLAD TO KEEP THEM -- FOR THEIR SAKE!

AS USUAL WE'LL GO HUNTING THIS AFTERNOON...

...AND THEN COME BACK IN TIME TO GET READY FOR THE REUNION THIS EVENING!

SWELL! LEAD THE WAY, JACK!

♪ A MIGHTY HUNTER WAS HE! ♪

BUT UNKNOWN TO THE THREE SPORTSMEN AS THEY HEAD FOR THE WOODS...

--HELLO!

THERE DOESN'T SEEM TO BE ANY-BODY HOME!

HELLO!

A MOMENT LATER...

WHERE **IS** EVERYBODY? I WAS IN THE NEIGH-BORHOOD--WORKING ON A STORY FOR MY MAGAZINE, **BEHIND THE SCENES**--AND I THOUGHT I'D DROP IN ON MY BOY FRIEND, JIM JORDAN!* BUT THIS IS A FINE WELCOME, I MUST SAY--!

Editor's Note: THE CIRCUMSTANCES UNDER WHICH SUE WILLIAMS MET-- AND FELL IN LOVE WITH-- JIM JORDAN WERE REVEALED IN "GREEN LANTERN'S BROTHER ACT"-- IN THE DECEMBER, 1961 ISSUE OF GREEN LANTERN!

AS PRETTY SUE WILLIAMS, WITHOUT ANY ADO, MAKES HERSELF AT HOME...

I'LL WAIT FOR JIM! HE CAN'T BE FAR AWAY! HE DOESN'T GO TO WORK OR ANYTHING! AND ALSO... I MUST REMEMBER TO TELL HIS BROTHER JACK TO **LOCK THE DOOR** WHEN THERE'S NO ONE HERE! AFTER ALL ...

chocolates

...I MIGHT HAVE BEEN A **BURGLAR** OR SOMETHING! AND IT WOULDN'T HELP THAT **JACK JORDAN** IS **DISTRICT ATTORNEY**--HE COULD STILL BE ROBBED! er-- WAIT! THAT DOES GIVE ME AN IDEA, THOUGH!

SUDDENLY, SUE IS IN ACTION...

FOR WEEKS I'VE BEEN WANTING TO GET A LOOK AT **JIM JORDAN'S** ROOM WHILE HE'S NOT THERE! IF I'M RIGHT, IT MAY HELP ME PROVE MY THEORY THAT HE IS **REALLY GREEN LANTERN!** AND **NOW** IS MY CHANCE!

THEN... GOOD GOSH--LOOKY THERE! I'LL BET A MILLION DOLLARS-- THAT'S **GREEN LANTERN'S** FAMOUS **POWER BATTERY!** AT LAST I'VE GOT THE GOODS ON CLEVER MR. "HAPPY-GO-LUCKY" JIM JORDAN!

3

MEANWHILE IN THE NEARBY WOODS...

BOY, ALL I BAGGED WAS A GOOD CASE OF POISON IVY!

WE'D BETTER GET YOU TO A DOCTOR, HAL!

SOON, IN TOWN... NO, IT'S NOT SERIOUS! I'LL JUST TREAT IT AND YOU'LL BE ALL RIGHT IN A FEW HOURS! TAKE OFF YOUR RING, MR. JORDAN!

TAKE OFF... MY RING?

YES, SO I CAN SWAB DOWN YOUR ENTIRE HAND!

er--OF COURSE! SURE THING, DOCTOR!

I MUSN'T MAKE A FUSS OR MY BROTHERS WILL SUSPECT THERE'S SOMETHING ABOUT MY RING!

THEN... IT JUST FEELS ODD LETTING MY DISGUISED POWER RING OUT OF MY POSSESSION EVEN FOR A MOMENT--

BETTER HAVE A LOOK AT MY HAND TOO, DOC!

I THINK I'VE GOT A TOUCH OF POISON IVY, ALSO!

JIM WOULD COMPLICATE THINGS! BUT I'VE GOT MY EYES GLUED ON MY RING! I WOULDN'T WANT...

...THOSE TWO IDENTICAL RINGS TO GET MIXED UP BY ACCIDENT!

ALL RIGHT, MR. JORDAN! NOW I'LL TAKE CARE OF YOUR BROTHER..

4

BACK HOME, SHORTLY AFTERWARD...

WE STILL HAVE TWO HOURS BEFORE THE REUNION! THAT WILL GIVE US ALL A CHANCE TO REST UP...

JACK HAS EVERYTHING WORKED OUT ACCORDING TO SCHEDULE..

ALL RIGHT, IF I HAVE TO REST, I SUPPOSE I HAVE TO!

SEE YOU LATER!

BUT IN THE ROOM OF THE YOUNGEST OF THE THREE BROTHERS, A MOMENT LATER..

SUE! YOU HERE--!?

YES, I AM MR. JORDAN! WAITING PATIENTLY TO TELL YOU--

I'VE FOUND YOUR POWER BATTERY-- SO NOW YOU MIGHT AS WELL STOP THE MASQUERADE-- AND ADMIT OPENLY TO ME THAT YOU'RE GREEN LANTERN!

M-MY POWER BATTERY--!?

SUE, YOU KNOW MY HOBBY IS OLD SPORTS CARS! THAT'S A LAMP FROM A FABULOUS ANTIQUE AUTO-- THE 1904 BERCEDES-- MENZ, THE ONLY ONE OF ITS KIND! I FOUND THE LAMP AT A JUNK DEALER...

HAR-DE-HAR-HAR-HAR! YOU EXPECT ME TO BELIEVE THAT?

I SUPPOSE YOU'LL EVEN INSIST THAT RING YOU'RE WEARING IS NOT YOUR POWER RING IN DISGUISE! Hmmph! MAYBE YOU CAN FOOL OTHERS, JIM JORDAN-- BUT NOT SUE WILLIAMS!

WOO-EE! SHE'S GOT ME HALF-CONVINCED!

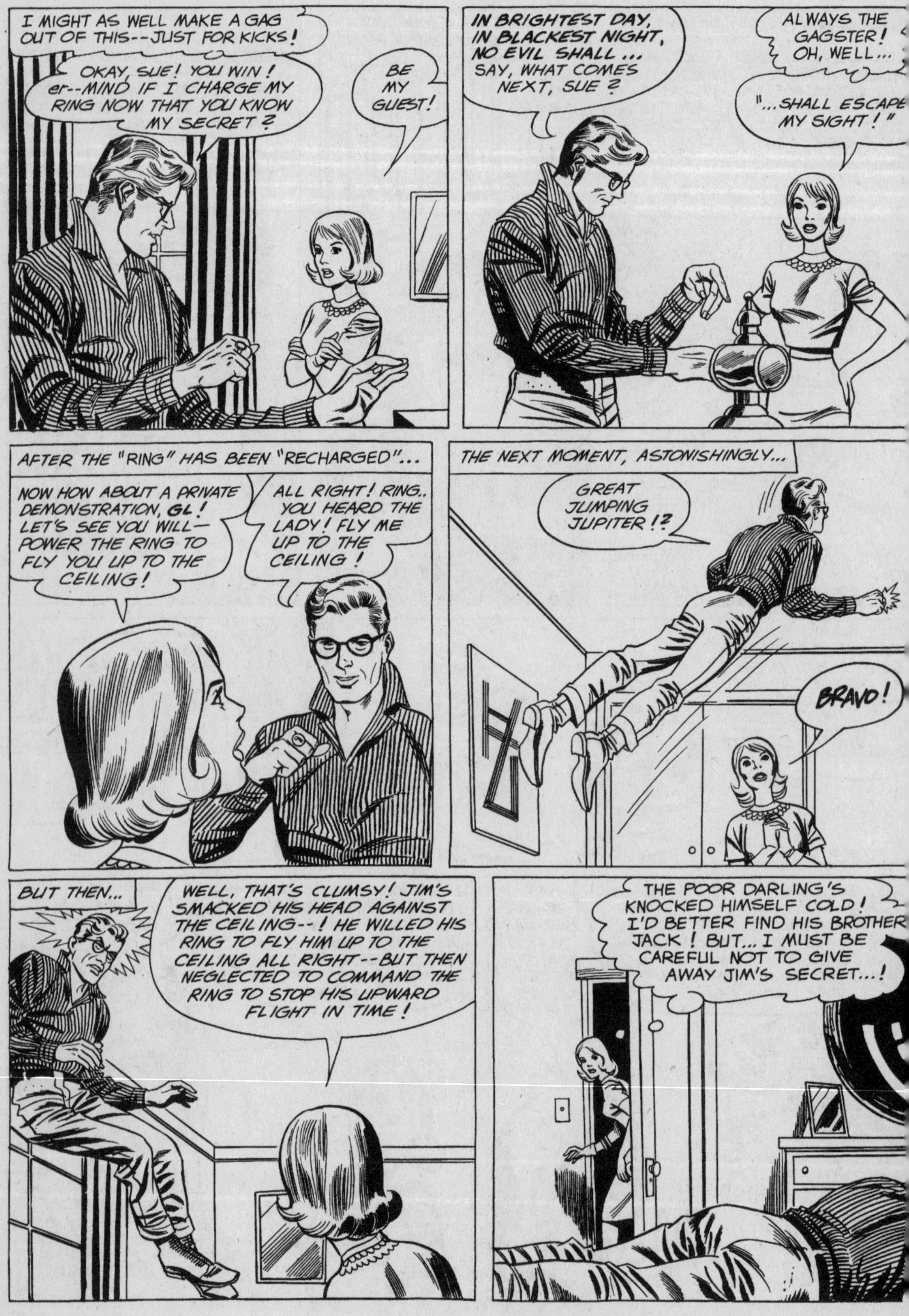
I MIGHT AS WELL MAKE A GAG OUT OF THIS--JUST FOR KICKS!
OKAY, SUE! YOU WIN! er--MIND IF I CHARGE MY RING NOW THAT YOU KNOW MY SECRET?
BE MY GUEST!
IN BRIGHTEST DAY, IN BLACKEST NIGHT, NO EVIL SHALL ... SAY, WHAT COMES NEXT, SUE?
ALWAYS THE GAGSTER! OH, WELL...
"...SHALL ESCAPE MY SIGHT!"
AFTER THE "RING" HAS BEEN "RECHARGED"...
NOW HOW ABOUT A PRIVATE DEMONSTRATION, GL! LET'S SEE YOU WILL-POWER THE RING TO FLY YOU UP TO THE CEILING!
ALL RIGHT! RING.. YOU HEARD THE LADY! FLY ME UP TO THE CEILING!
THE NEXT MOMENT, ASTONISHINGLY...
GREAT JUMPING JUPITER!?
BRAVO!
BUT THEN...
WELL, THAT'S CLUMSY! JIM'S SMACKED HIS HEAD AGAINST THE CEILING--! HE WILLED HIS RING TO FLY HIM UP TO THE CEILING ALL RIGHT--BUT THEN NEGLECTED TO COMMAND THE RING TO STOP HIS UPWARD FLIGHT IN TIME!
THE POOR DARLING'S KNOCKED HIMSELF COLD! I'D BETTER FIND HIS BROTHER JACK! BUT... I MUST BE CAREFUL NOT TO GIVE AWAY JIM'S SECRET...!

AS SUE LEAVES THE ROOM...

THE COAST IS CLEAR, MOOSE! C'MON!

IT'S THE LAMP, ALL RIGHT! THERE WAS ONLY *TWO* MADE LIKE THAT...

THE TWO MEN CAUTIOUSLY ENTER THE ROOM...

...AND MR. BLACKSTREET'S ALREADY GOT THE OTHER ONE!

HEY--IT'S *EMPTY!* MOOSE, WE GOTTA WORK FAST! GRAB THAT GUY--WE'RE TAKING HIM WITH US!

BUT I TELL YOU JIM WAS RIGHT HERE--AND HE WAS UNCONSCIOUS! HE--er--HIT HIS HEAD!

HUSTLE!

WELL, HE'S NOT HERE NOW, SUE!

er--I'D BETTER HAVE A LOOK AROUND THE GROUNDS, JACK...

THAT BLACK SEDAN-- TAKING OFF FROM NEAR THE HOUSE!?

AND INSTANTS LATER...

JIM COULD BE IN REAL TROUBLE!

I HAD TO GET AWAY FROM THE OTHERS BACK IN THE HOUSE, IN ORDER TO CHANGE TO *GREEN LANTERN*-- AND GO AFTER THAT *CAR!*

BUT AS THE *EMERALD GLADIATOR* SETS HIMSELF TO ZOOM OFF IN HOT PURSUIT...

UH--SOMETHING SEEMS TO HAVE GONE WRONG WITH MY *POWER RING!* I--I'M STANDING STILL! I'M *NOT MOVING* AT ALL--!

I KNOW I CHARGED MY RING THIS MORNING, SO IT CAN'T--*er*, WAIT A SECOND! I WONDER... THERE'S ONLY *ONE POSSIBLE WAY* TO EXPLAIN THIS FANTASTIC OCCURRENCE! MY BROTHER JIM AND I ...

... MUST HAVE *SWITCHED RINGS* BACK IN THAT DOCTOR'S OFFICE! I THOUGHT I TOOK *MY RING* BACK ... BUT I MUST HAVE TAKEN *HIS!* GREAT GUARDIANS--! BUT I'VE STILL GOT A CHANCE TO TRAIL THAT CAR--BY USING *JIM'S SPORTS CAR!*

BEREFT OF HIS MYSTIC BEAM, THE CRACK TEST PILOT PUTS HIS LIGHTNING REFLEXES TO WORK...

OF COURSE IT WILL SEEM ODD IF *GREEN LANTERN* IS SEEN DRIVING *JIM JORDAN'S* CAR... BUT I'VE GOT TO RISK IT! THERE'S THE SEDAN...I'VE MANAGED TO KEEP IT IN VIEW...!

HALF AN HOUR LATER...

THEY'RE TURNING INTO THAT DRIVEWAY! I'D BETTER PULL INTO THIS TREE-COVERED LANE!

HE'S COMING TO, MOOSE! WATCH HIM--!

AND SOON, INSIDE THE HOUSE...

THE LAMP WAS EMPTY, MR. BLACKSTREET-- SO WE BROUGHT JORDAN ALONG! HE MUST HAVE THE ICE--!

I MUST HAVE ... *WHAT* ICE!?

SAY, WHAT IS THIS ALL ABOUT? WHERE AM I?

PLEASE BE GOOD ENOUGH TO SIT DOWN, MR. JORDAN, AND I WILL BE HAPPY TO EXPLAIN! YES, BY JOVE! SIT DOWN, SIR...

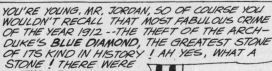

YOU'RE YOUNG, MR. JORDAN, SO OF COURSE YOU WOULDN'T RECALL THAT MOST FABULOUS CRIME OF THE YEAR 1912 -- THE THEFT OF THE ARCH-DUKE'S *BLUE DIAMOND*, THE GREATEST STONE OF ITS KIND IN HISTORY! AH YES, WHAT A STONE! THERE WERE *TWO* THIEVES...

... AND THEY MADE THEIR ESCAPE -- A NOVEL IDEA AT THE TIME -- IN AN AUTO, A 1904 BERCEDES-MENZ! AFTERWARDS, THE TWO WERE CAPTURED, BUT THE JEWEL WAS NEVER FOUND! IT HAD VANISHED COMPLETELY! MUCH LATER, I STUDIED THE CASE! I FOUND IT FASCINATING, SIR...

AND I DEVELOPED A THEORY! I BECAME CONVINCED THAT THE ARCHDUKE'S DIAMOND HAD BEEN HIDDEN SOMEWHERE IN THE GETAWAY CAR! DO YOU FOLLOW ME, SIR? DOWN THROUGH THE YEARS I HAVE BEEN ON THE TRAIL OF THE JEWEL! I HAVE HAD AGENTS WORKING FOR ME...

I HAVE SPENT UNTOLD SUMS! AH, YES! AND IN DUE COURSE I ASSEMBLED EVERY PIECE OF THAT OLD ORIGINAL BERCEDES-MENZ FROM JUNKYARDS IN THE FOUR CORNERS OF THE COUNTRY! LET ME SHOW YOU, SIR...

THE 1904 BERCEDES-MENZ!!

YES! BUT I DID *NOT* FIND THE DIAMOND! UP UNTIL TODAY THE ONLY PIECE MISSING HAS BEEN THIS LAMP IN YOUR POSSESSION, MR. JORDAN! I WAS CONFIDENT IT *MUST* CONTAIN THE JEWEL! YOU SEE, MY INTENSIVE RESEARCH PROVED NO ONE ELSE HAD FOUND IT...

9

THEREFORE, SIR, YOU WILL OBLIGE ME BY HANDING OVER THE GEM! THE ONLY REMAINING POSSIBILITY IS THAT YOU REMOVED THE ARCHDUKE'S DIAMOND FROM THIS LAMP BEFORE MY MEN GOT TO IT!

I -- GULP!? ME -- GULP?!

AT THAT MOMENT...

I'VE HEARD ENOUGH -- AND I'VE FIGURED OUT HOW TO USE MY POWER RING THAT JIM IS WEARING -- WITHOUT AROUSING HIS SUSPICIONS! BUT I CAN'T DELAY AN INSTANT LONGER...

BY JOVE! IT'S GREEN LANTERN!

FROM A FEW FEET AWAY I CAN OPERATE MY RING MENTALLY, BY SHEER FORCE OF WILL! I KNOW IT CAN WORK BECAUSE I ONCE DID IT!* AND THAT'S MY IDEA NOW...

* Editor's Note: IN THE "WINGS OF DESTINY" STORY WHERE GL IN A DREAM TURNED HIS FRIEND PIEFACE INTO A BIRD!

AS A BULLET SINGS PAST THE HEAD OF THE FAST-MOVING GLADIATOR...

COME ON, YOUNG FELLOW! HOW WOULD YOU LIKE TO FIGHT SIDE BY SIDE WITH GREEN LANTERN?

WOULD I!? GOLLY--!

GREEN LANTERN IS USING HIS POWER RING TO MAKE MY FRATERNITY RING SHOOT OUT HIS GREEN BEAM TOO -- JUST LIKE HIS RING DOES!

THE BEAM TRAVELS SO FAST, JIM CAN'T POSSIBLY TELL IT'S THE RING ON HIS FINGER THAT'S SHOOTING THE POWER TO MINE -- AND NOT THE REVERSE!!

THE NEXT INSTANT...

THIS IS TERRIFIC! OUR RINGS HAVE FORMED MULTIPLE FISTS THAT ARE ATTACKING THAT GANG AND KNOCKING THEM OUT!

I'VE STILL GOT TO *SWITCH* RINGS BACK WITH JIM...!

SOON, WITH BLACKSTREET AND HIS MINIONS *HORS DE COMBAT...*

NICE GOING! WE MAKE QUITE A TEAM, JIM JORDAN!

WHAT A MARVEL *GREEN LANTERN* IS! HE KNOWS MY NAME-- HE TURNS UP HERE IN THE NICK OF TIME--

YOU'D BETTER LET ME *"CLEAN"* YOUR RING! WORKING TOGETHER THE WAY WE DID, MY GREEN BEAM MAY HAVE LEFT SOME *STRONG RADIATION* ON YOUR RING, BUT I'LL FIX IT...

SURE! HERE YOU ARE, GL...

THEN...

UHH-- THAT LIGHT!

BLINDING HIM FOR A MOMENT...! BUT A MOMENT IS ALL I NEED...

...TO SWITCH RINGS AGAIN WITHOUT HIS KNOWING IT!

er--THERE YOU ARE, JIM! YOUR RING'S FINE NOW!

GOLLY!

11

LATER, WITH THE GANG UNDER ARREST...

...AND HERE IS THE FAMOUS "ARCHDUKE" DIAMOND, SERGEANT! USING MY RING I LOCATED IT... CLEVERLY WEDGED IN THE BOTTOM OF THIS LAMP!

EGAD!

I WAS RIGHT, BY JOVE! THE DIAMOND WAS HIDDEN IN THE BERCEDES—MENZ!

YOU'VE SOLVED A SIXTY-YEAR-OLD CRIME-PUZZLE, GREEN LANTERN!

AS JIM JORDAN SEEKS TO DUPLICATE A POWER-RING PERFORMANCE...

I CAN'T GET OFF THE GROUND! Hmm! I GUESS MY FLYING UP TO THE CEILING WAS A FREAK STUNT--CAUSED BY SHEER WILL-POWER!

PLAYING COY AGAIN, PRETENDING HE ISN'T GREEN LANTERN! BUT I KNOW BETTER!

AND THAT NIGHT...

ONE FOR ALL AND ALL FOR ONE! ♪

I GUESS FRATERNITY REUNIONS CAN BE PRETTY EXCITING AFTER ALL ... ESPECIALLY A REUNION OF THE THREE JORDAN BROTHERS!

The End

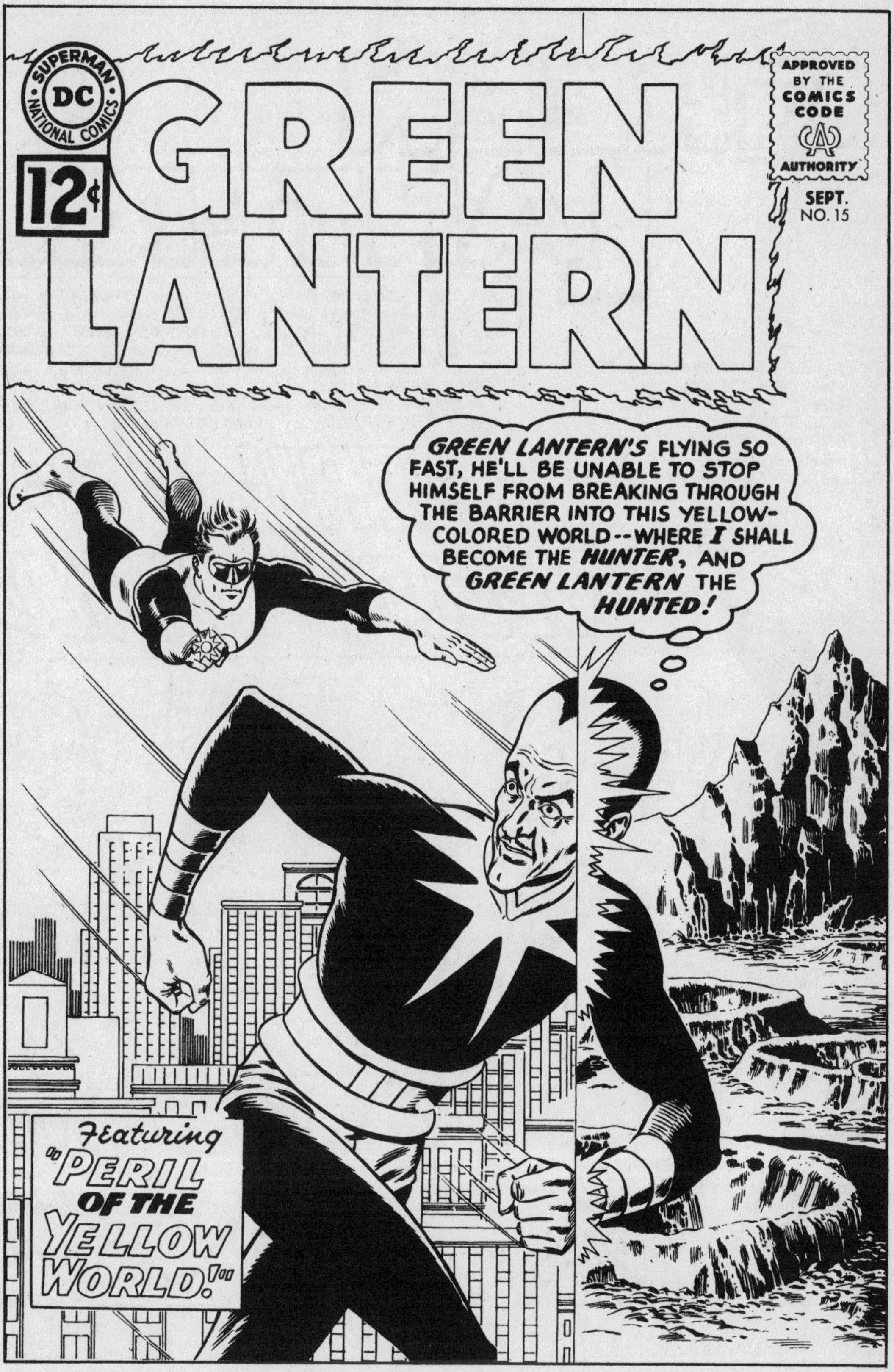
SUPERMAN DC NATIONAL COMICS
12¢
GREEN LANTERN
APPROVED BY THE COMICS CODE AUTHORITY
SEPT. NO. 15
GREEN LANTERN'S FLYING SO FAST, HE'LL BE UNABLE TO STOP HIMSELF FROM BREAKING THROUGH THE BARRIER INTO THIS YELLOW-COLORED WORLD--WHERE I SHALL BECOME THE HUNTER, AND GREEN LANTERN THE HUNTED!
Featuring "PERIL OF THE YELLOW WORLD!"

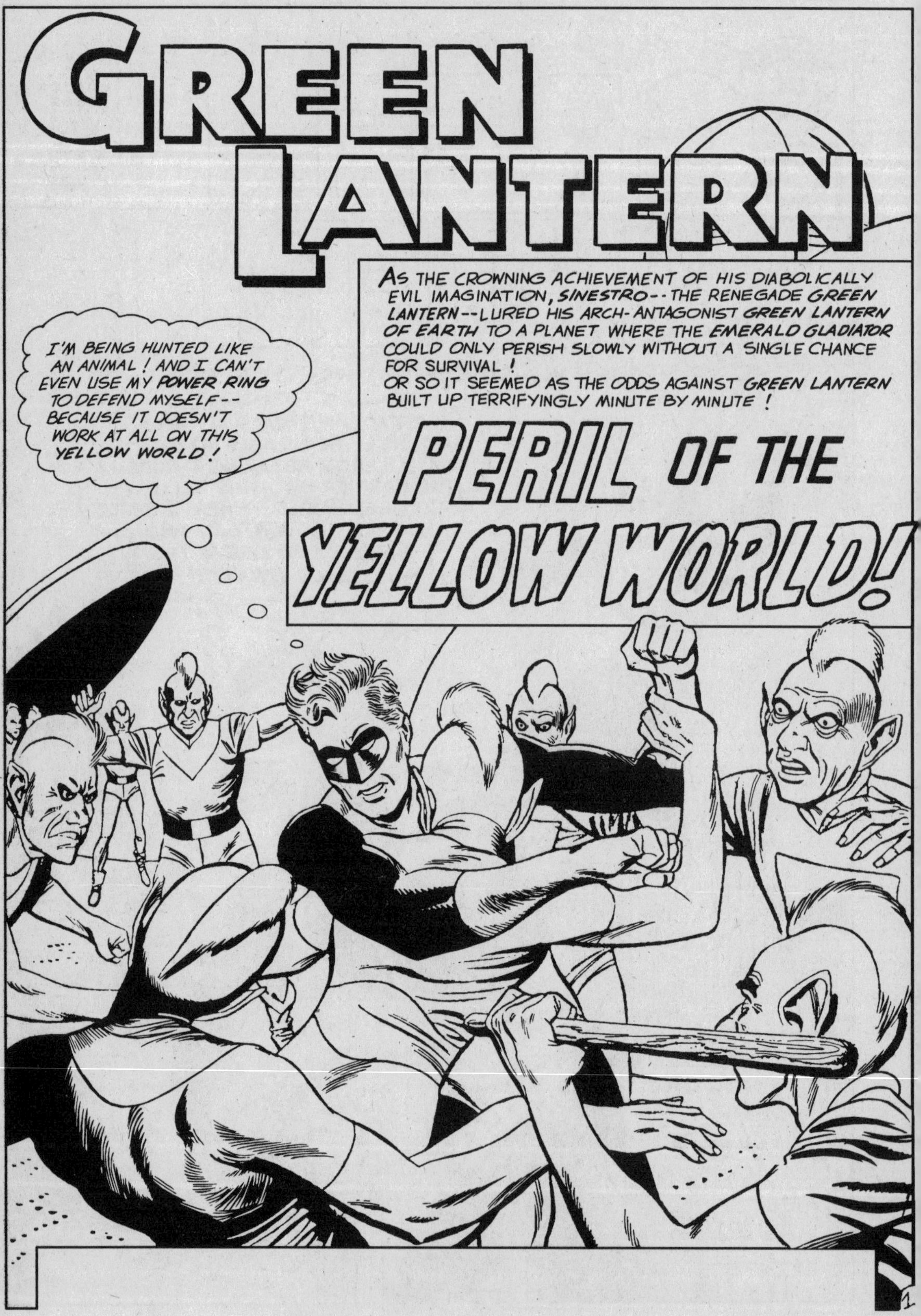
GREEN LANTERN
AS THE CROWNING ACHIEVEMENT OF HIS DIABOLICALLY EVIL IMAGINATION, SINESTRO--THE RENEGADE GREEN LANTERN--LURED HIS ARCH-ANTAGONIST GREEN LANTERN OF EARTH TO A PLANET WHERE THE EMERALD GLADIATOR COULD ONLY PERISH SLOWLY WITHOUT A SINGLE CHANCE FOR SURVIVAL! OR SO IT SEEMED AS THE ODDS AGAINST GREEN LANTERN BUILT UP TERRIFYINGLY MINUTE BY MINUTE!
I'M BEING HUNTED LIKE AN ANIMAL! AND I CAN'T EVEN USE MY POWER RING TO DEFEND MYSELF-- BECAUSE IT DOESN'T WORK AT ALL ON THIS YELLOW WORLD!
PERIL OF THE YELLOW WORLD!
1

AS *HAL JORDAN* DRIVES HIS PRETTY BOSS *CAROL FERRIS* TO A DINNER-DATE IN THE COUNTRY...

THIS ROAD IS SO WINDY AND NARROW IT MIGHT MAKE ME NERVOUS--EXCEPT THAT I KNOW I CAN HAVE COMPLETE CONFIDENCE IN HAL'S LIGHTNING REFLEXES! HE'S NOT A GREAT TEST PILOT FOR NOTHING!

I *WON'T* ASK HIM TO SLOW DOWN! BEING A BIT OF A DAREDEVIL IS IN HAL'S BONES--AND HE CAN'T HELP GOING FAST! AND I DON'T WANT TO CRAMP HIS STYLE BY COMPLAINING--

LOVELY DAY, ISN'T IT, CAROL?

SUDDENLY...

HAL, WATCH OUT! THAT NEWSPAPER-- IT'S COMING RIGHT AT YOU!

HUH?

AND THE NEXT MOMENT...

WE'LL CRASH! THAT PAPER IS CLINGING TO HIM LIKE SOMETHING *ALIVE*--!

BUT HAL IS EQUAL TO THE EMERGENCY... AS ONE HAND RIPS AWAY THE PAPER...

...HIS OTHER HAND SIMULTANEOUSLY TAKES THE CAR AROUND A SHARP CURVE...

...AND WITH DANGER PAST...

¡Whew!¡

IT'S A GOOD THING I TOOK A LONG LOOK AT THAT CURVE JUST BEFORE THE NEWSPAPER HIT--OR I'D HAVE HAD TO USE MY *POWER RING* RIGHT IN FRONT OF CAROL TO SAVE US!

LATER...

WHAT DO YOU MEAN THAT INCIDENT WITH THE PAPER MAKES YOU FEEL YOU'VE BEEN *JINXED*, HAL?

I KNOW IT SOUNDS SILLY, CAROL...

...BUT ALL DAY LONG STRANGE LITTLE ACCIDENTS LIKE THAT HAVE BEEN HAPPENING TO ME! THIS MORNING, FOR INSTANCE, I WAS CROSSING THE APRON IN FRONT OF THE HANGAR AT THE FIELD...

"... WHEN SUDDENLY I FELT AS IF SOME *SHARP TUG OF WIND* HAD PUSHED AGAINST ONE OF MY LEGS ... "

UH--! I'M TRIPPING!

"THE FALL ALMOST LANDED ME IN THE EXHAUST OF A JET THAT WAS WARMING UP! I ROLLED OVER JUST IN TIME... "

GOLLY! A FEW MORE FEET AND I'D HAVE BEEN IN THAT JET FLAME!

"AND THIS AFTERNOON, I DROPPED IN ON *PIE* AND *TERGA* JUST BEFORE OUR DATE..."

TOO BAD YOU CAN'T STAY LONGER, HAL!

CAN'T, TERGA-- I'M LATE NOW!

"I SWUNG DOWN THE STAIRS, WHIPPING MYSELF AROUND THE NEWEL POST AS A FELLOW WILL, AND AS I DID SO..."

GOOD GOSH! THE POST CAME RIGHT OFF--IN MY HAND!

BECAUSE I'VE LEARNED TO GO LIMP AND RELAX WHEN I FALL, I DIDN'T HURT MYSELF-- JUST A COUPLE OF BRUISES!

MY, I SEE WHAT YOU MEAN, HAL--

--WHEN YOU SAY YOU FEEL *JINXED!*

Hmm! IN SPEAKING TO CAROL, SOMETHING JUST STRUCK ME ABOUT THOSE STRANGE INCIDENTS TODAY, BUT IT'S NOT ANYTHING I CAN TELL HER ABOUT...

IN FACT, I'D BETTER TAKE HER STRAIGHT HOME FROM HERE! BECAUSE IF I'M RIGHT--GREEN LANTERN IS DUE FOR ACTION *WITHOUT DELAY!*

CHECK, PLEASE!

SOON...

...AND I JUST REMEMBERED SOME--er-- TOP PRIORITY DESK WORK BACK AT THE HANGAR THAT MUST BE DONE BEFORE TOMORROW, CAROL!

I SUPPOSE, AS YOUR BOSS, MR. JORDAN, I SHOULD APPLAUD YOUR DEVOTION TO YOUR JOB--

--BUT AS YOUR DATE, I'M *VERY ANNOYED!*

TOO BAD I HAD TO GET CAROL SORE! BUT IT COULDN'T BE HELPED!

SLAM!

AS THE LITHE TEST PILOT RIDES OFF, HIS BRAIN IS RACING...

WHAT STRUCK ME BACK IN THE RESTAURANT IS THAT THE ODD ACCIDENTS TODAY MAY INDICATE SOMEONE IS TRYING TO GET AT GREEN LANTERN! BUT LET ME GO OVER THE TRAIN OF THOUGHT ONCE AGAIN TO MAKE SURE...

FIRST OF ALL, IF SOME UNCANNY FORCE--POSSIBLY FROM OUT OF THIS WORLD--WERE TRYING TO ZERO IN ON *GREEN LANTERN'S* MIND, IT WOULD STRIKE AT *ME* -- BECAUSE *MY MIND* AND *GREEN LANTERN'S* ARE ONE AND THE SAME! EITHER GL OR I COULD BE THE *TARGET*...

AND FURTHERMORE IF THIS FORCE WERE WEAKENED, SAY, BY THE GREAT DISTANCE IT HAD TO TRAVEL... IT WOULD ONLY BE ABLE TO AFFECT *LIGHT OBJECTS* -- LIKE A NEWS-PAPER OR A WIND EDDY, OR A POST ON A BANNISTER! AT LEAST THAT FITS SO FAR...

AS HAL ENTERS THE DESERTED HANGAR WHERE HIS DRESSING ROOM IS LOCATED...

BUT ALL THIS WOULD BE JUST THEORY--IF I DIDN'T KNOW A FORCE *EXACTLY* LIKE THE ONE I'VE BEEN THINKING ABOUT! I MEAN THE *MIND-CONTROL DEVICE* INVENTED BY *SINESTRO*!*

*Editor's Note : THE RENEGADE GREEN LANTERN OF THE PLANET KORUGAR, WHO HAS BECOME THE NUMBER ONE ENEMY OF OUR EARTH'S GREEN LANTERN!

WITH CERTAIN SIMPLE ADJUSTMENTS, *SINESTRO* COULD EASILY USE HIS MACHINE TO LOCATE *ME* FROM A DISTANCE --AND EXERCISE *CONTROL* AT THE SAME TIME OVER LIGHT OBJECTS --JUST LIKE THE ONES THAT ALMOST PLAYED HAVOC WITH ME TODAY!

BUT THE LAST TIME I SAW *SINESTRO* HE WAS HELPLESSLY TRAPPED UNDER THE RAYS OF HIS OWN MIND-CONTROL DEVICE! IF *HE* IS BEHIND THE ATTEMPTS ON ME, HE MUST HAVE *ES-CAPED!* AND THAT'S WHAT I MUST *FIND OUT!*

THE NEXT MOMENT, A SOLEMN OATH IS REPEATED...

IN BRIGHTEST DAY, IN BLACKEST NIGHT, NO EVIL SHALL ESCAPE MY SIGHT! LET THOSE WHO WORSHIP EVIL'S MIGHT, BEWARE MY POWER -- GREEN LANTERN'S LIGHT!

THROUGH THE BLACKNESS OF SPACE A SHIMMERING GREEN FIGURE HURTLES, PROTECTED BY THE MYSTIC POWER RING WHICH IS HIS TRADEMARK...

THERE'S THE UNINHABITED PLANET WHERE THE *OTHER GREEN LANTERNS* AND I LEFT *SINESTRO* AFTER HIS EVIL ATTEMPT ON THE *GUARDIANS!* IS HE STILL THERE?

*IN PREVIOUS STORY ENTITLED, "*The Strange Trial of Green Lantern*," IN ISSUE NO. 11 OF THIS MAGAZINE.

SOON...

HE'S GONE! HE DID ESCAPE-- JUST AS I FEARED!

HOW COULD HE HAVE GOTTEN AWAY? BUT I HAVE NO TIME TO PUZZLE THAT OUT NOW! WITH MY DIABOLIC *ARCH-FOE* ON THE LOOSE, THERE'S NO TIME FOR ANYTHING--BUT *ACTION!*

LIKE A GREEN-STREAKING METEOR, THE GRIM-JAWED CRUSADER TAKES OFF...

THERE'S ONLY ONE PLACE WHERE *SINESTRO* WOULD HEAD ONCE HE FREED HIMSELF--THE *ANTI-MATTER WORLD* OF *QWARD*--WHERE *EVIL* IS *GOOD* AND *GOOD* IS *EVIL!* AND WHERE *SINESTRO* IS *RIGHT AT HOME!*

6

GREEN LANTERN

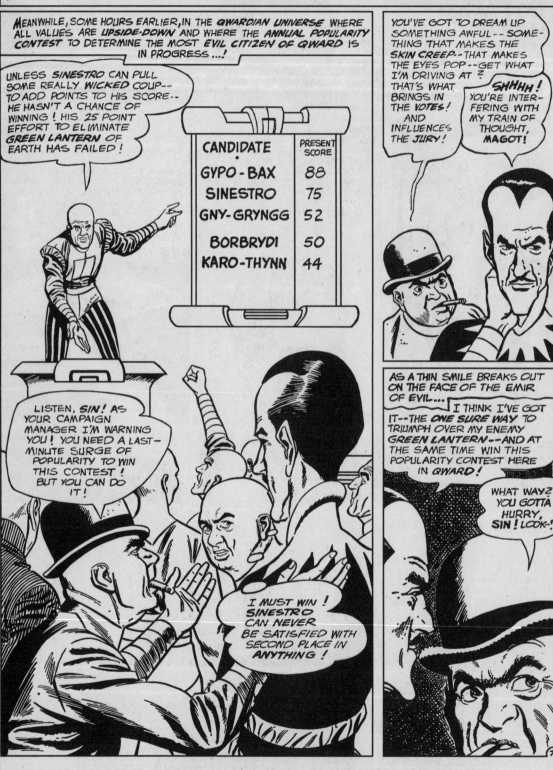

PERIL OF THE YELLOW WORLD! PART 2

MEANWHILE, SOME HOURS EARLIER, IN THE *QWARDIAN UNIVERSE* WHERE ALL VALUES ARE *UPSIDE-DOWN* AND WHERE THE *ANNUAL POPULARITY CONTEST* TO DETERMINE THE MOST *EVIL CITIZEN OF QWARD* IS IN PROGRESS...!

UNLESS *SINESTRO* CAN PULL SOME REALLY *WICKED* COUP-- TO ADD POINTS TO HIS SCORE-- HE HASN'T A CHANCE OF WINNING! HIS 25 POINT EFFORT TO ELIMINATE *GREEN LANTERN* OF EARTH HAS FAILED!

CANDIDATE	PRESENT SCORE
GYPO - BAX	88
SINESTRO	75
GNY - GRYNGG	52
BORBRYDI	50
KARO - THYNN	44

YOU'VE GOT TO DREAM UP SOMETHING AWFUL -- SOMETHING THAT MAKES THE *SKIN CREEP* -- THAT MAKES THE *EYES POP* -- GET WHAT I'M DRIVING AT? THAT'S WHAT BRINGS IN THE *VOTES!* AND INFLUENCES THE *JURY!*

SHHHH! YOU'RE INTERFERING WITH MY TRAIN OF THOUGHT, *MAGOT!*

LISTEN, *SIN!* AS YOUR CAMPAIGN MANAGER I'M WARNING YOU! YOU NEED A LAST-MINUTE SURGE OF POPULARITY TO WIN THIS CONTEST! BUT YOU CAN DO IT!

I MUST WIN! *SINESTRO* CAN NEVER BE SATISFIED WITH SECOND PLACE IN *ANYTHING!*

AS A THIN SMILE BREAKS OUT ON THE FACE OF THE EMIR OF EVIL... I THINK I'VE GOT IT--THE *ONE SURE WAY* TO TRIUMPH OVER MY ENEMY *GREEN LANTERN*--AND AT THE SAME TIME WIN THIS *POPULARITY CONTEST* HERE IN *QWARD!*

WHAT WAY? YOU GOTTA HURRY, *SIN!* LOOK--!

7

GYPO-BAX IS UP TO 88! IF HE GETS TO 100 FIRST, HE WINS! YOU--EH?

WHERE'S SINESTRO? HE MUST HAVE TAKEN OFF ON HIS ERRAND OF EVIL! BUT WHERE TO--?

AT THAT MOMENT, THANKS TO HIS YELLOW POWER BEAM, THE ARCH-VILLAIN IS HURTLING THROUGH SPACE...

ACCORDING TO MY MIND-CONTROL MONITORING DEVICE, GREEN LANTERN HAS ALREADY FOUND OUT THAT I ESCAPED--AND HE'S BREAKING INTO THE UNIVERSE OF QWARD TO RE-CAPTURE ME! HA! HA! I INTEND TO MEET HIM HALFWAY...

...AT A PLANET KNOWN AS GRYX IN THE EIGHTH DIMENSION OF OUR UNIVERSE! SOME TIME AGO I CAME ACROSS THAT FAS-CINATING WORLD AND I FILED IT AWAY IN MY EVIL BRAIN FOR FUTURE REFERENCE! IN FACT, FOR AN OCCASION JUST LIKE THIS!

AND SOON AFTER...

I'LL BE IN QWARD CITY IN ANOTHER MOMENT OR TWO! AND THEN-- GREAT GALAXIES!?

THERE'S SINESTRO NOW--RIGHT IN FRONT OF ME AND TRAVELING LIKE A COSMIC RAY!

8

FINE! HE'S STARTING AFTER ME! BUT IN A MOMENT WE'LL BE GOING AT THE TERRIFIC SPEED NECESSARY TO BREAK THROUGH THE *DIMENSION BARRIER*--!

SPLIT-SECONDS LATER...

HERE HE COMES! IN ANOTHER MOMENT THE TABLES WILL BE TURNED BETWEEN THE SO-CALLED *EMERALD GLADIATOR* AND ME! I AM ABOUT TO BECOME THE *HUNTER*--AND *GREEN LANTERN* THE *HUNTED*!

ALMOST UPON HIM!

THEN, SUDDENLY...

UH! MY RING-- SOMETHING'S WRONG WITH IT! BY THE GUARDIANS, WHERE AM I?

HIS RING FAILING, *GREEN LANTERN* PLUMMETS AWKWARDLY TO THE GROUND...

SOMEHOW I'VE LANDED IN A WORLD...AN *ENTIRELY YELLOW WORLD*... WHERE EVEN THE VERY *AIR* IS YELLOW... AND MY RING IS *POWERLESS!**

**Editor's Note: AN IMPURITY, NECESSARY TO ITS WORKING, PREVENTS GREEN LANTERN'S RING FROM HAVING AN EFFECT ON ANYTHING YELLOW!*

AND AS THE HEMMED-IN CRUSADER LOOKS ABOUT HIM, ONE FIGURE ALONE DOMINATES THE SCENE...

I COULD ELIMINATE YOU COMPLETELY NOW THAT YOU'RE UTTERLY HELPLESS, *GREEN LANTERN*! BUT IT WOULD BE TOO EASY...AND WOULDN'T WIN ME THE *QWARD POPULARITY CONTEST* BECAUSE IT WOULDN'T BE EVIL ENOUGH! SO I WORKED OUT SOMETHING *BETTER*..!

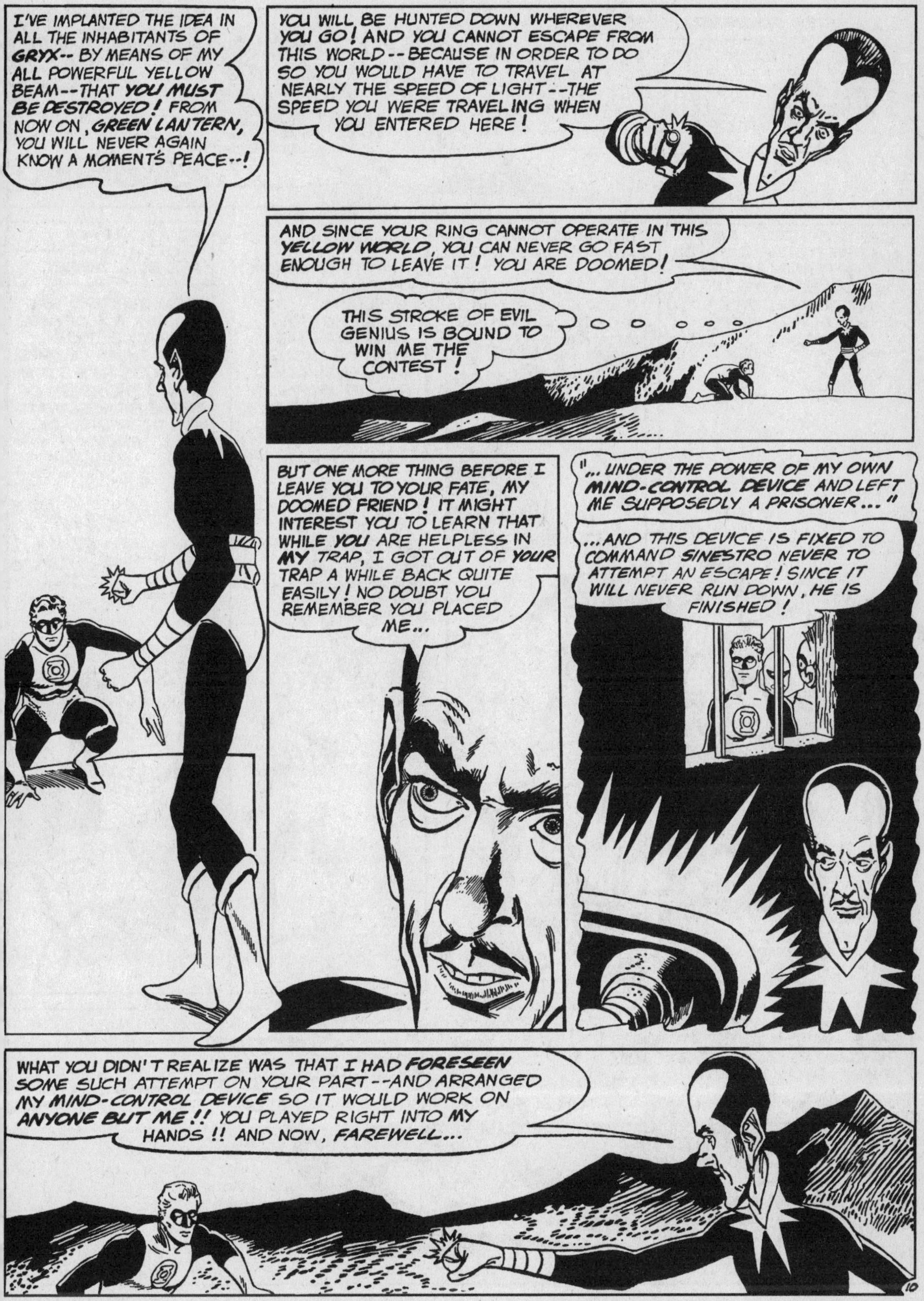

I'VE IMPLANTED THE IDEA IN ALL THE INHABITANTS OF GRYX-- BY MEANS OF MY ALL POWERFUL YELLOW BEAM--THAT YOU MUST BE DESTROYED! FROM NOW ON, GREEN LANTERN, YOU WILL NEVER AGAIN KNOW A MOMENT'S PEACE--!
YOU WILL BE HUNTED DOWN WHEREVER YOU GO! AND YOU CANNOT ESCAPE FROM THIS WORLD--BECAUSE IN ORDER TO DO SO YOU WOULD HAVE TO TRAVEL AT NEARLY THE SPEED OF LIGHT--THE SPEED YOU WERE TRAVELING WHEN YOU ENTERED HERE!
AND SINCE YOUR RING CANNOT OPERATE IN THIS YELLOW WORLD, YOU CAN NEVER GO FAST ENOUGH TO LEAVE IT! YOU ARE DOOMED!
THIS STROKE OF EVIL GENIUS IS BOUND TO WIN ME THE CONTEST!
BUT ONE MORE THING BEFORE I LEAVE YOU TO YOUR FATE, MY DOOMED FRIEND! IT MIGHT INTEREST YOU TO LEARN THAT WHILE YOU ARE HELPLESS IN MY TRAP, I GOT OUT OF YOUR TRAP A WHILE BACK QUITE EASILY! NO DOUBT YOU REMEMBER YOU PLACED ME...
"...UNDER THE POWER OF MY OWN MIND-CONTROL DEVICE AND LEFT ME SUPPOSEDLY A PRISONER..."
...AND THIS DEVICE IS FIXED TO COMMAND SINESTRO NEVER TO ATTEMPT AN ESCAPE! SINCE IT WILL NEVER RUN DOWN, HE IS FINISHED!
WHAT YOU DIDN'T REALIZE WAS THAT I HAD FORESEEN SOME SUCH ATTEMPT ON YOUR PART--AND ARRANGED MY MIND-CONTROL DEVICE SO IT WOULD WORK ON ANYONE BUT ME!! YOU PLAYED RIGHT INTO MY HANDS!! AND NOW, FAREWELL...
10

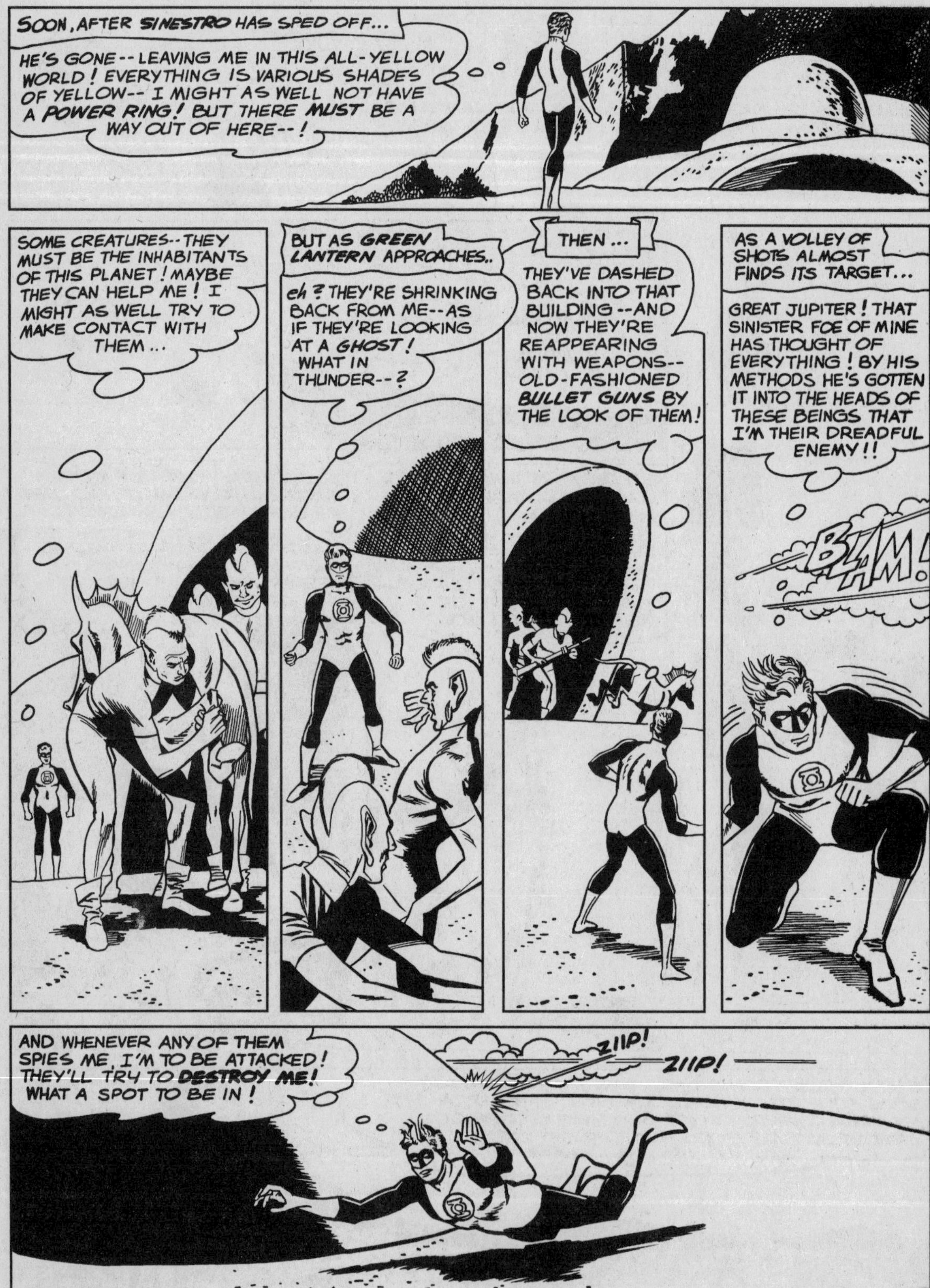
SOON, AFTER SINESTRO HAS SPED OFF...
HE'S GONE -- LEAVING ME IN THIS ALL-YELLOW WORLD! EVERYTHING IS VARIOUS SHADES OF YELLOW -- I MIGHT AS WELL NOT HAVE A POWER RING! BUT THERE MUST BE A WAY OUT OF HERE--!
SOME CREATURES -- THEY MUST BE THE INHABITANTS OF THIS PLANET! MAYBE THEY CAN HELP ME! I MIGHT AS WELL TRY TO MAKE CONTACT WITH THEM...
BUT AS GREEN LANTERN APPROACHES..
eh? THEY'RE SHRINKING BACK FROM ME -- AS IF THEY'RE LOOKING AT A GHOST! WHAT IN THUNDER--?
THEN...
THEY'VE DASHED BACK INTO THAT BUILDING -- AND NOW THEY'RE REAPPEARING WITH WEAPONS -- OLD-FASHIONED BULLET GUNS BY THE LOOK OF THEM!
AS A VOLLEY OF SHOTS ALMOST FINDS ITS TARGET...
GREAT JUPITER! THAT SINISTER FOE OF MINE HAS THOUGHT OF EVERYTHING! BY HIS METHODS HE'S GOTTEN IT INTO THE HEADS OF THESE BEINGS THAT I'M THEIR DREADFUL ENEMY!!
BLAM!
AND WHENEVER ANY OF THEM SPIES ME, I'M TO BE ATTACKED! THEY'LL TRY TO DESTROY ME! WHAT A SPOT TO BE IN!
ZIIP!
ZIIP!
11

SOON IN THE ALIEN CITY...

ONLY BY SNEAKING IN AND OUT OF VARIOUS BUILDINGS AND HALLWAYS WAS I ABLE TO GIVE THEM THE SLIP...

NOW I KNOW WHAT IT FEELS LIKE TO BE *HUNTED*--LIKE AN ANIMAL! I DON'T KNOW WHERE TO TURN... DANGER CAN COME FROM ANY SIDE...!

THEN, WITHOUT WARNING...

IT IS THE ONE--THE INVADER WHO IS OUT TO HARM US!

HE WILL HARM NO MORE AFTER *WE* ARE THROUGH WITH HIM!

IN HIS EXTREMITY, *GREEN LANTERN'S* POWERFUL PHYSIQUE STANDS HIM IN GOOD STEAD...

I HAVE NOTHING AGAINST THESE PEOPLE... BUT THEY'RE OUT TO GET ME--AND I'M NOT GOING DOWN *WITHOUT A FIGHT!*

THE ODDS... ARE PRETTY HEAVY! ONE MAN... AGAINST AN *ENTIRE CITY!* BUT I *CAN'T* LET MYSELF BE OVERCOME--NOT WHILE *SINESTRO* IS FREE AND ON THE LOOSE--!

12

AT THIS MOMENT, AT CONTEST HEADQUARTERS IN QWARD CITY...

SINESTRO CAN'T BE BEATEN, GYPO-BAX! WHY DON'T YOU CONCEDE DEFEAT?

NEVER, MAGOT! HE STILL HASN'T WON!

GYPO-BAX	96
SINESTRO	98
GNY-GRYNGG	57
BORBRYDI	52
YARO-THYNN	46

I ADMIT HIS LAST TRICK WITH GREEN LANTERN WAS WICKEDLY CLEVER! BUT HIS VICTIM IS STILL ALIVE AND WHILE HE IS, THE JURY IS NOT GOING TO GIVE SINESTRO ANY MORE VOTES!

TRUE, GYPO-BAX! BUT I HAVE A FINAL TRICK UP MY SLEEVE!

WHAT ARE YOU DOING, SINESTRO?

I'M SETTING UP A VISO-SCREEN, MAGOT! I'M GOING TO LET THE JURY WATCH THE LAST MOMENTS OF GREEN LANTERN! THAT OUGHT TO BE WORTH A COUPLE OF MORE POINTS!

WITHOUT HIS RING, GREEN LANTERN CAN'T LAST MUCH LONGER! AND THIS DRAMATIC PRESENTATION OF HIS FINISH ON THE YELLOW WORLD WILL PUT ME OVER THE TOP!

SEE... THE VISO-RADIATION IS BRINGING GREEN LANTERN INTO VIEW!

VERY IMPRESSIVE, SINESTRO!

.. AND MOST INTERESTING!

Bah! I'M BEGINNING TO REALIZE THAT SINESTRO MAY INDEED BE THE CHAMPION OF EVIL! HOW CAN ANYONE OUTDO HIM?

MEANWHILE, UNAWARE THAT HE IS PUTTING ON A SHOW FOR THE *QWARDIANS*, *GREEN LANTERN* STRUGGLES FOR LIFE...

THE WHOLE CITY MUST BE UP IN ARMS AND ON MY TRAIL! THEY'VE HOUNDED ME INTO THIS WILD AREA... I'VE GOT TO FIND A WAY OUT!

EVERYTHING... YELLOW... YELLOW! EVEN THE VERY *AIR* WHICH SURROUNDS MY RING AND RENDERS IT POWERLESS! BUT I'VE GOT TO KEEP SEARCHING-- FOR SOME *NON*-YELLOW AREA...

THEN...

NOW I SEE WHY THEY DROVE ME IN THIS DIRECTION! WITHOUT MY RING I CAN'T FLY-- AND I CAN'T RETREAT ANOTHER STEP-- WITHOUT TOPPLING OVER THE EDGE OF THE CLIFF!

THEY'RE COMING AT ME FROM ALL SIDES! THEY'RE OUT TO FINISH ME ALL RIGHT! AND I-- eh? THERE'S SOMETHING I JUST NOTICED--MY FIRST GLEAM OF *HOPE!*

A PURPLISH RADIATION... POURING IN ON ME FROM SOMEWHERE...MAKING MY *GREEN BEAM* VISIBLE! THIS IS THE BREAK I'VE BEEN LOOKING FOR TO GET OUT OF HERE--!

14.

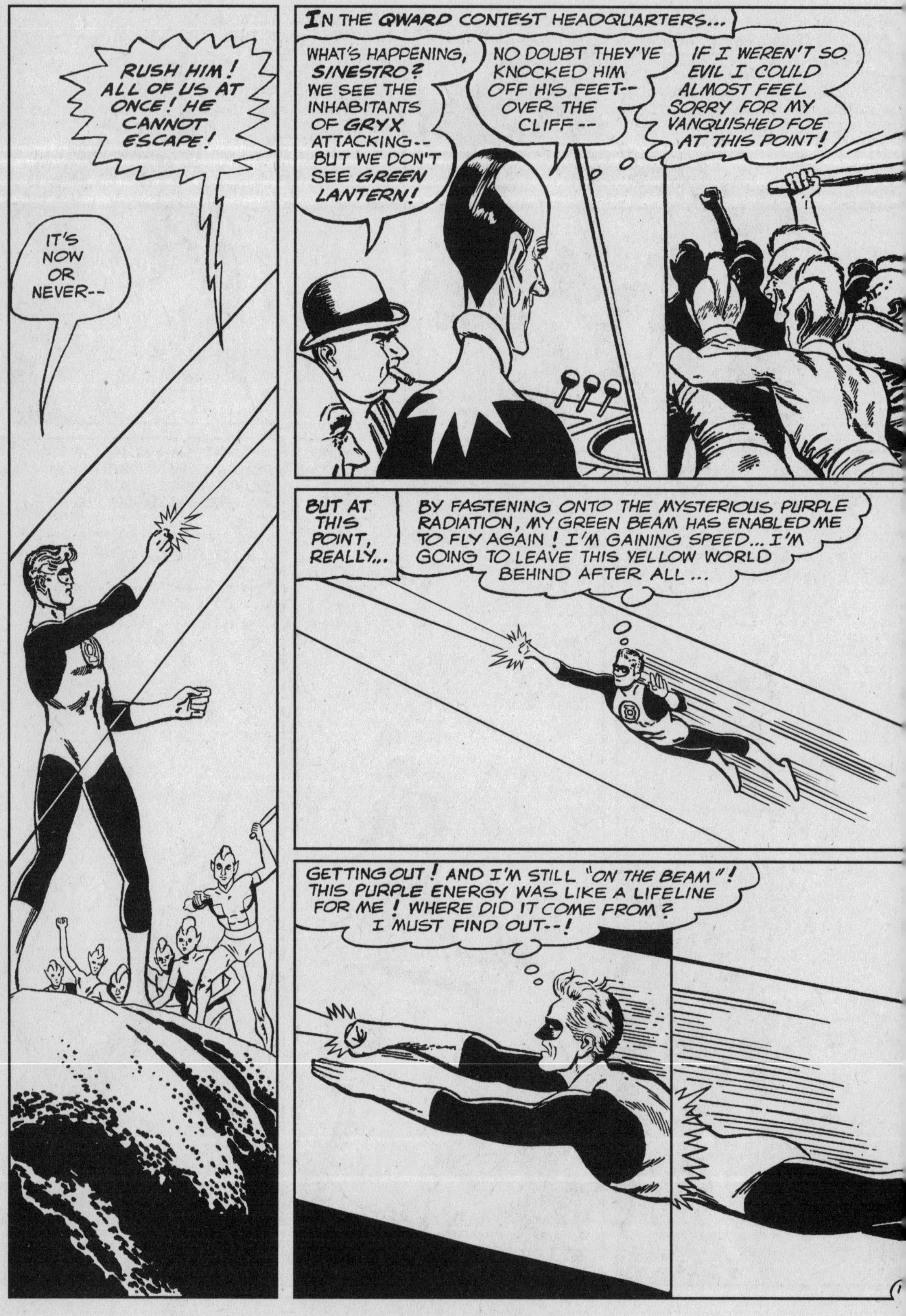
RUSH HIM! ALL OF US AT ONCE! HE CANNOT ESCAPE!
IT'S NOW OR NEVER--
IN THE QWARD CONTEST HEADQUARTERS...
WHAT'S HAPPENING, SINESTRO? WE SEE THE INHABITANTS OF GRYX ATTACKING-- BUT WE DON'T SEE GREEN LANTERN!
NO DOUBT THEY'VE KNOCKED HIM OFF HIS FEET-- OVER THE CLIFF --
IF I WEREN'T SO EVIL I COULD ALMOST FEEL SORRY FOR MY VANQUISHED FOE AT THIS POINT!
BUT AT THIS POINT, REALLY...
BY FASTENING ONTO THE MYSTERIOUS PURPLE RADIATION, MY GREEN BEAM HAS ENABLED ME TO FLY AGAIN! I'M GAINING SPEED... I'M GOING TO LEAVE THIS YELLOW WORLD BEHIND AFTER ALL ...
GETTING OUT! AND I'M STILL "ON THE BEAM"! THIS PURPLE ENERGY WAS LIKE A LIFELINE FOR ME! WHERE DID IT COME FROM? I MUST FIND OUT--!

MOMENTS LATER... IT'S TAKING ME TO *QWARD CITY!* AH-- I SHOULD HAVE KNOWN WHOM I WOULD FIND AT THE END OF THIS TRAIL!

MEANWHILE... AND I DEMAND THAT MY CANDIDATE *SINESTRO* BE DECLARED THE *WINNER*--BECAUSE HE DESTROYED THE INVINCIBLE *GREEN LANTERN* OF EARTH!

WAIT! LOOK--

IT'S *GREEN LANTERN* AGAIN--!

IMPOSSIBLE! THERE-- MUST BE SOME *MISTAKE!*

NO MISTAKE, *SINESTRO*-- EXCEPT THE ONE *YOU* MADE!

UH?!

AND THE NEXT MOMENT INCREDIBLY... THE PURPLE RADIATION CAME FROM THIS VIEWING APPARATUS OF *SINESTRO'S!* HE COULDN'T RESIST WATCHING ME AS I WAS HUNTED--SO IN THE END HIS WICKED CLEVERNESS *BOOMERANGED* ON HIM!

SEIZE HIM!

CRASH!

16

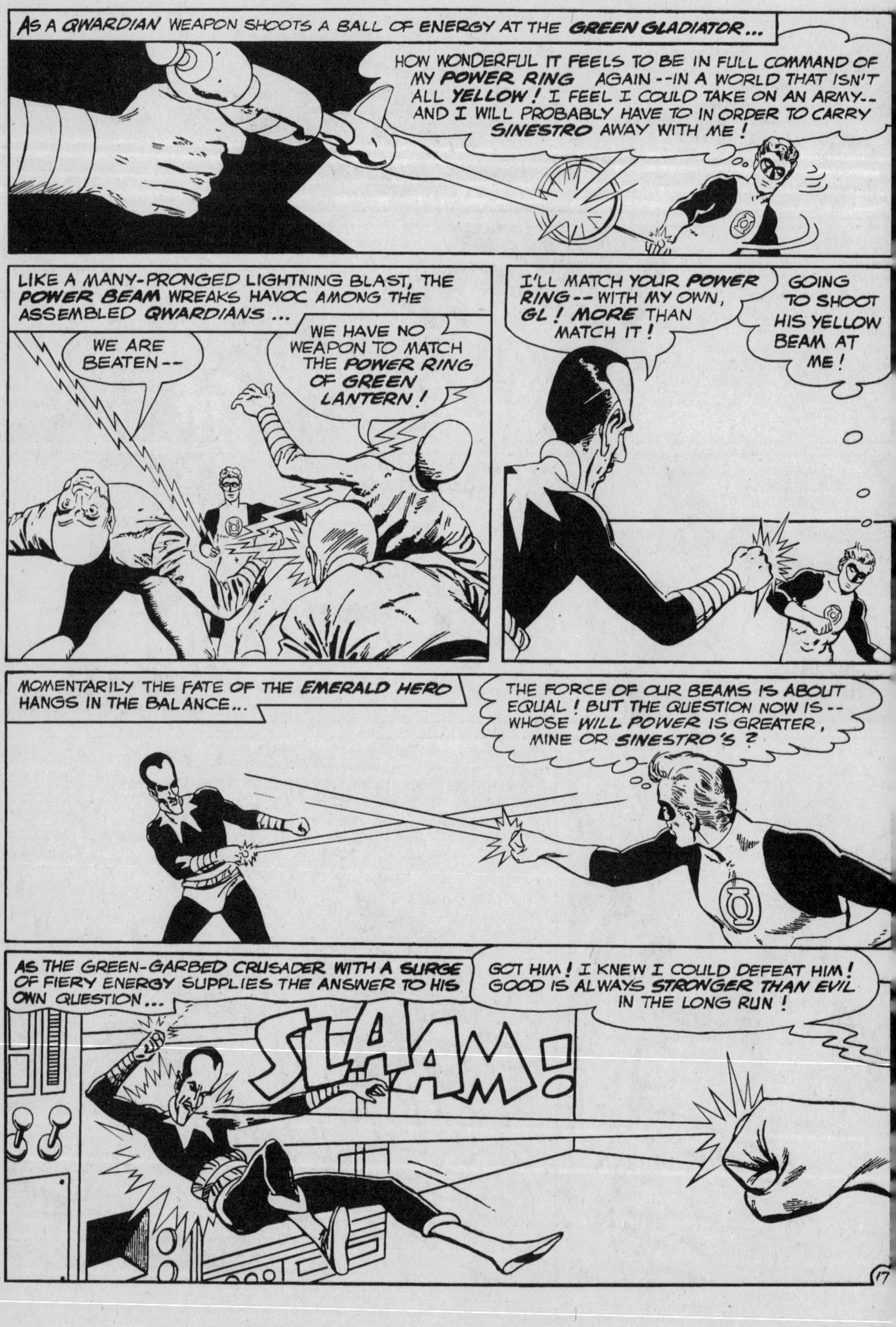
AS A QWARDIAN WEAPON SHOOTS A BALL OF ENERGY AT THE GREEN GLADIATOR...
HOW WONDERFUL IT FEELS TO BE IN FULL COMMAND OF MY POWER RING AGAIN--IN A WORLD THAT ISN'T ALL YELLOW! I FEEL I COULD TAKE ON AN ARMY--AND I WILL PROBABLY HAVE TO IN ORDER TO CARRY SINESTRO AWAY WITH ME!
LIKE A MANY-PRONGED LIGHTNING BLAST, THE POWER BEAM WREAKS HAVOC AMONG THE ASSEMBLED QWARDIANS...
WE ARE BEATEN--
WE HAVE NO WEAPON TO MATCH THE POWER RING OF GREEN LANTERN!
I'LL MATCH YOUR POWER RING--WITH MY OWN, GL! MORE THAN MATCH IT!
GOING TO SHOOT HIS YELLOW BEAM AT ME!
MOMENTARILY THE FATE OF THE EMERALD HERO HANGS IN THE BALANCE...
THE FORCE OF OUR BEAMS IS ABOUT EQUAL! BUT THE QUESTION NOW IS--WHOSE WILL POWER IS GREATER, MINE OR SINESTRO'S?
AS THE GREEN-GARBED CRUSADER WITH A SURGE OF FIERY ENERGY SUPPLIES THE ANSWER TO HIS OWN QUESTION...
GOT HIM! I KNEW I COULD DEFEAT HIM! GOOD IS ALWAYS STRONGER THAN EVIL IN THE LONG RUN!
SLAAM!
17

AND IN DUE COURSE, MULTI-MILLIONS OF MILES OFF IN SPACE...

THIS TIME I DEFY YOU TO MAKE AN ESCAPE, SINESTRO! ONCE AGAIN YOUR MIND-CONTROL DEVICE IS FIXED TO COMMAND YOU NEVER TO ATTEMPT TO FREE YOURSELF! BUT NOW...

...THE DEVICE HAS BEEN ADJUSTED SO IT *WORKS ON YOU* JUST THE SAME AS ON ANYONE ELSE! *YOU* ARE FINISHED, MY EVIL FOE! I DOUBT IF WE WILL EVER MEET AGAIN, FAREWELL!

BACK ON MORE FAMILIAR TERRITORY, SOME TIME AFTERWARD...

SO YOU WANT ANOTHER DATE, MR. JORDAN? WELL, THE WAY YOU CUT SHORT OUR LAST ONE, I KNOW I REALLY SHOULDN'T! BUT...OH, WELL! ALL RIGHT! I'LL GIVE YOU ANOTHER CHANCE!

SWELL!

THAT NIGHT...

A LONG TIME AGO, I SET OUT TO SUPPLANT *GREEN LANTERN* (my alter ego) IN CAROL'S AFFECTIONS! AND TONIGHT I MUST ADMIT I FEEL I'M MAKING PROGRESS! YESSIR! THERE'S NO DOUBT ABOUT IT--I'M MAKING *PROGRESS!*

The End 8

GREEN LANTERN

GREEN LANTERN

AT EXCITING **CAPE CANAVERAL** IN FLORIDA-- WHERE CRACK TEST PILOT HAL JORDAN (ALIAS **GREEN LANTERN**) HAD GONE TO DELIVER AN IMPORTANT MISSILE PART, THE **ROCKET GANG** WAS USING ROCKET LAUNCHINGS TO COVER UP THEIR DARING THEFTS OF SURROUNDING COMMUNITIES!
IT WAS A DEVICE THAT NETTED THEM A SIZABLE FORTUNE-- UNTIL THE ARRIVAL OF THE **EMERALD GLADIATOR** IN THEIR MIDST!

ZERO HOUR IN ROCKET CITY!

AS **PIEFACE** BURSTS INTO HIS ROOM ONE DAY...

I MUSTN'T FORGET A SINGLE DETAIL OF THE ADVENTURE **GREEN LANTERN** JUST TOLD ME ABOUT! I'LL WRITE IT ALL DOWN NOW WITH-OUT DELAY...

THUS BEGINS ANOTHER EXCITING ENTRY IN THE **CASEBOOK OF GREEN LANTERN**

PLUG HIM, SPRINGY! DON'T BE AFRAID-- GREEN LANTERN'S POWER RING ISN'T WORKING!

...and that day Hal was given a special mission... to fly a certain missile part to Cape Canaveral across the country! It was a hush-hush job for an important government project...

"AT THE *FERRIS AIRCRAFT* HANGAR, HAL DONNED HIS FLYING TOGS..."

WHEN THE GOVERNMENT CALLS, ALL MEN ANSWER! BUT IT OCCURS TO ME THAT I'D BETTER CHARGE MY *POWER RING* BEFORE I LEAVE! THIS TRIP...TO FLORIDA... WILL TAKE A GOOD PART OF A DAY AT LEAST...

*Editor's Note: BEING CHARGED AT THE MYSTIC POWER BATTERY GIVES THE AMAZING RING POWER FOR TWENTY-FOUR HOURS!

IN BRIGHTEST DAY, IN BLACKEST NIGHT, NO EVIL SHALL ESCAPE MY SIGHT! LET THOSE WHO WORSHIP EVIL'S MIGHT, BEWARE MY POWER-- GREEN LANTERN'S LIGHT!

--Hmm?

IT'S TWO O'CLOCK? I THOUGHT IT WAS LATER--ABOUT THREE! BUT EVEN SO I CAN'T DAWDLE! THEY'RE WAITING FOR THAT MISSILE PART AT THE *CAPE*...!

"ACROSS THE COUNTRY FROM WEST TO EAST, A SUPER SWIFT JET PLANE SPED LIKE A WHIPLASH..."

THERE'S THE RUNWAY I'M SUPPOSED TO SET DOWN ON! IT DIDN'T TAKE ME LONG TO GET HERE!

"AND SOON..."

MAYBE WE CAN GET THAT "BIRD" OFF, NOW THAT YOU'VE BROUGHT US THIS PART, MR. JORDAN! WOULD YOU LIKE TO SEE OUR *PET*?

I SURE WOULD, DR. DEATON! AS A TEST PILOT MYSELF...

...I'VE NATURALLY BEEN VERY INTERESTED IN THE TEST "SHOTS" GOING ON HERE IN *CAPE CANAVERAL*!

FINE! COME ALONG! YOUR PLANE WILL BE TAKEN CARE OF!

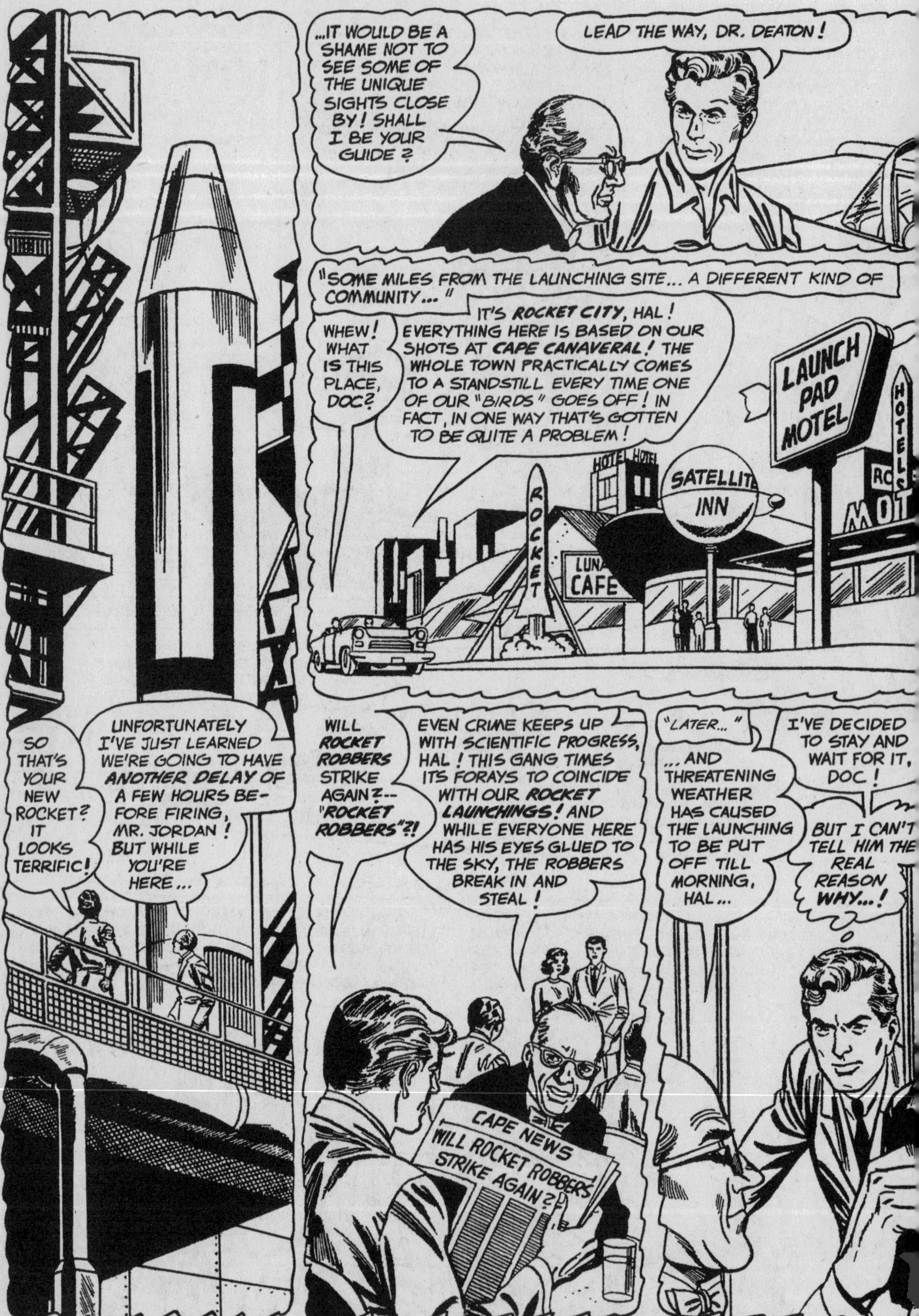
...IT WOULD BE A SHAME NOT TO SEE SOME OF THE UNIQUE SIGHTS CLOSE BY! SHALL I BE YOUR GUIDE?
LEAD THE WAY, DR. DEATON!
"SOME MILES FROM THE LAUNCHING SITE... A DIFFERENT KIND OF COMMUNITY..."
WHEW! WHAT IS THIS PLACE, DOC?
IT'S ROCKET CITY, HAL! EVERYTHING HERE IS BASED ON OUR SHOTS AT CAPE CANAVERAL! THE WHOLE TOWN PRACTICALLY COMES TO A STANDSTILL EVERY TIME ONE OF OUR "BIRDS" GOES OFF! IN FACT, IN ONE WAY THAT'S GOTTEN TO BE QUITE A PROBLEM!
LAUNCH PAD MOTEL
HOTEL HOTEL
SATELLITE INN
ROCKET
CAFE
SO THAT'S YOUR NEW ROCKET? IT LOOKS TERRIFIC!
UNFORTUNATELY I'VE JUST LEARNED WE'RE GOING TO HAVE ANOTHER DELAY OF A FEW HOURS BEFORE FIRING, MR. JORDAN! BUT WHILE YOU'RE HERE...
WILL ROCKET ROBBERS STRIKE AGAIN?-- "ROCKET ROBBERS"?!
EVEN CRIME KEEPS UP WITH SCIENTIFIC PROGRESS, HAL! THIS GANG TIMES ITS FORAYS TO COINCIDE WITH OUR ROCKET LAUNCHINGS! AND WHILE EVERYONE HERE HAS HIS EYES GLUED TO THE SKY, THE ROBBERS BREAK IN AND STEAL!
CAPE NEWS
WILL ROCKET ROBBERS STRIKE AGAIN?
"LATER..."
...AND THREATENING WEATHER HAS CAUSED THE LAUNCHING TO BE PUT OFF TILL MORNING, HAL...
I'VE DECIDED TO STAY AND WAIT FOR IT, DOC!
BUT I CAN'T TELL HIM THE REAL REASON WHY...!

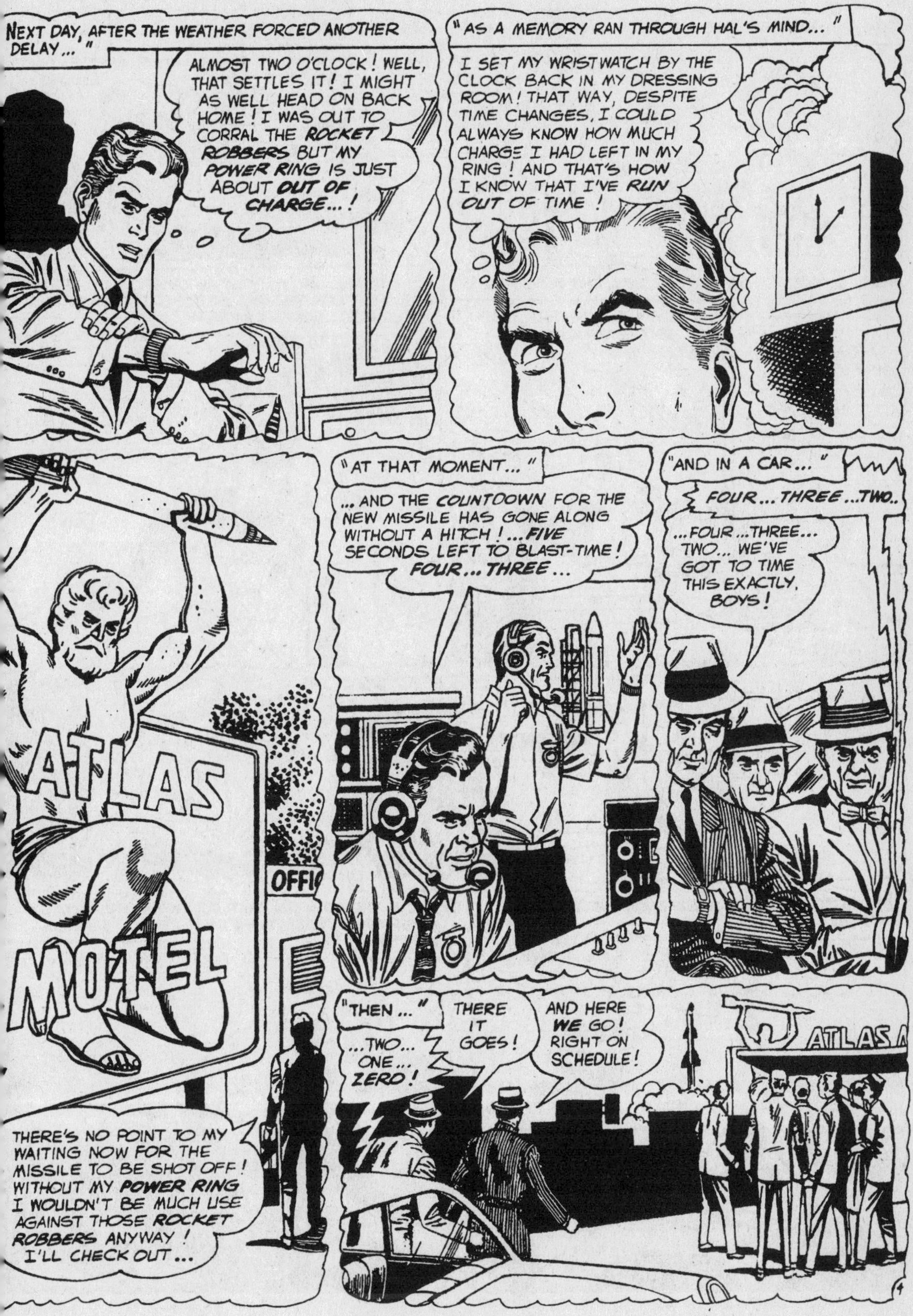

NEXT DAY, AFTER THE WEATHER FORCED ANOTHER DELAY ... "
ALMOST TWO O'CLOCK! WELL, THAT SETTLES IT! I MIGHT AS WELL HEAD ON BACK HOME! I WAS OUT TO CORRAL THE ROCKET ROBBERS BUT MY POWER RING IS JUST ABOUT OUT OF CHARGE...!
" AS A MEMORY RAN THROUGH HAL'S MIND... "
I SET MY WRISTWATCH BY THE CLOCK BACK IN MY DRESSING ROOM! THAT WAY, DESPITE TIME CHANGES, I COULD ALWAYS KNOW HOW MUCH CHARGE I HAD LEFT IN MY RING! AND THAT'S HOW I KNOW THAT I'VE RUN OUT OF TIME!
ATLAS
MOTEL
OFFI
THERE'S NO POINT TO MY WAITING NOW FOR THE MISSILE TO BE SHOT OFF! WITHOUT MY POWER RING I WOULDN'T BE MUCH USE AGAINST THOSE ROCKET ROBBERS ANYWAY! I'LL CHECK OUT...
" AT THAT MOMENT... "
...AND THE COUNTDOWN FOR THE NEW MISSILE HAS GONE ALONG WITHOUT A HITCH! ...FIVE SECONDS LEFT TO BLAST-TIME! FOUR... THREE...
"AND IN A CAR... "
FOUR... THREE ...TWO..
...FOUR...THREE... TWO... WE'VE GOT TO TIME THIS EXACTLY, BOYS!
"THEN ..."
...TWO... ONE... ZERO!
THERE IT GOES!
AND HERE WE GO! RIGHT ON SCHEDULE!
ATLAS
4

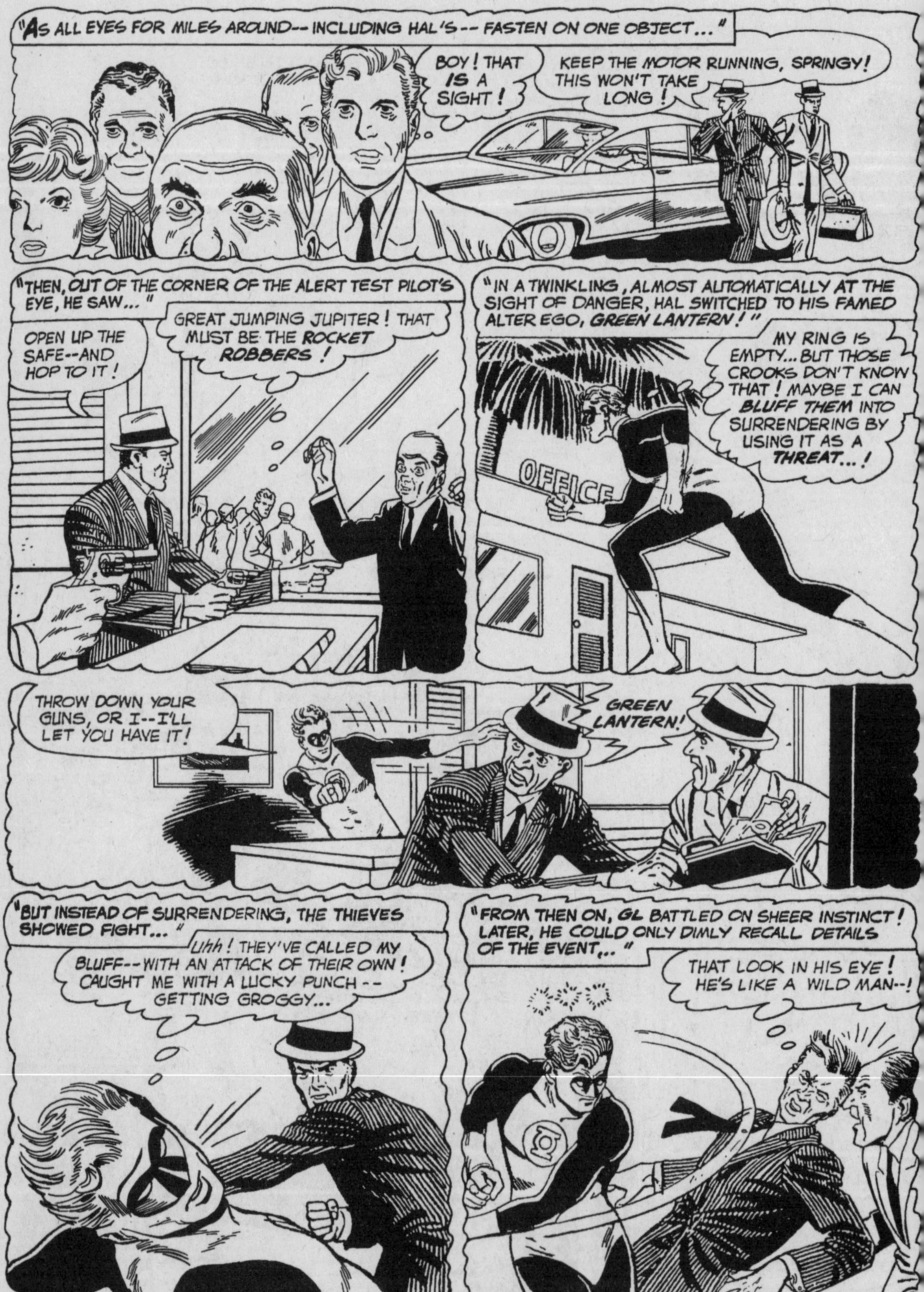
"AS ALL EYES FOR MILES AROUND-- INCLUDING HAL'S-- FASTEN ON ONE OBJECT..."
BOY! THAT IS A SIGHT!
KEEP THE MOTOR RUNNING, SPRINGY! THIS WON'T TAKE LONG!
"THEN, OUT OF THE CORNER OF THE ALERT TEST PILOT'S EYE, HE SAW..."
OPEN UP THE SAFE--AND HOP TO IT!
GREAT JUMPING JUPITER! THAT MUST BE THE ROCKET ROBBERS!
"IN A TWINKLING, ALMOST AUTOMATICALLY AT THE SIGHT OF DANGER, HAL SWITCHED TO HIS FAMED ALTER EGO, GREEN LANTERN!"
MY RING IS EMPTY... BUT THOSE CROOKS DON'T KNOW THAT! MAYBE I CAN BLUFF THEM INTO SURRENDERING BY USING IT AS A THREAT...!
OFFICE
THROW DOWN YOUR GUNS, OR I--I'LL LET YOU HAVE IT!
GREEN LANTERN!
"BUT INSTEAD OF SURRENDERING, THE THIEVES SHOWED FIGHT..."
UHH! THEY'VE CALLED MY BLUFF--WITH AN ATTACK OF THEIR OWN! CAUGHT ME WITH A LUCKY PUNCH--GETTING GROGGY...
"FROM THEN ON, GL BATTLED ON SHEER INSTINCT! LATER, HE COULD ONLY DIMLY RECALL DETAILS OF THE EVENT..."
THAT LOOK IN HIS EYE! HE'S LIKE A WILD MAN--!
5

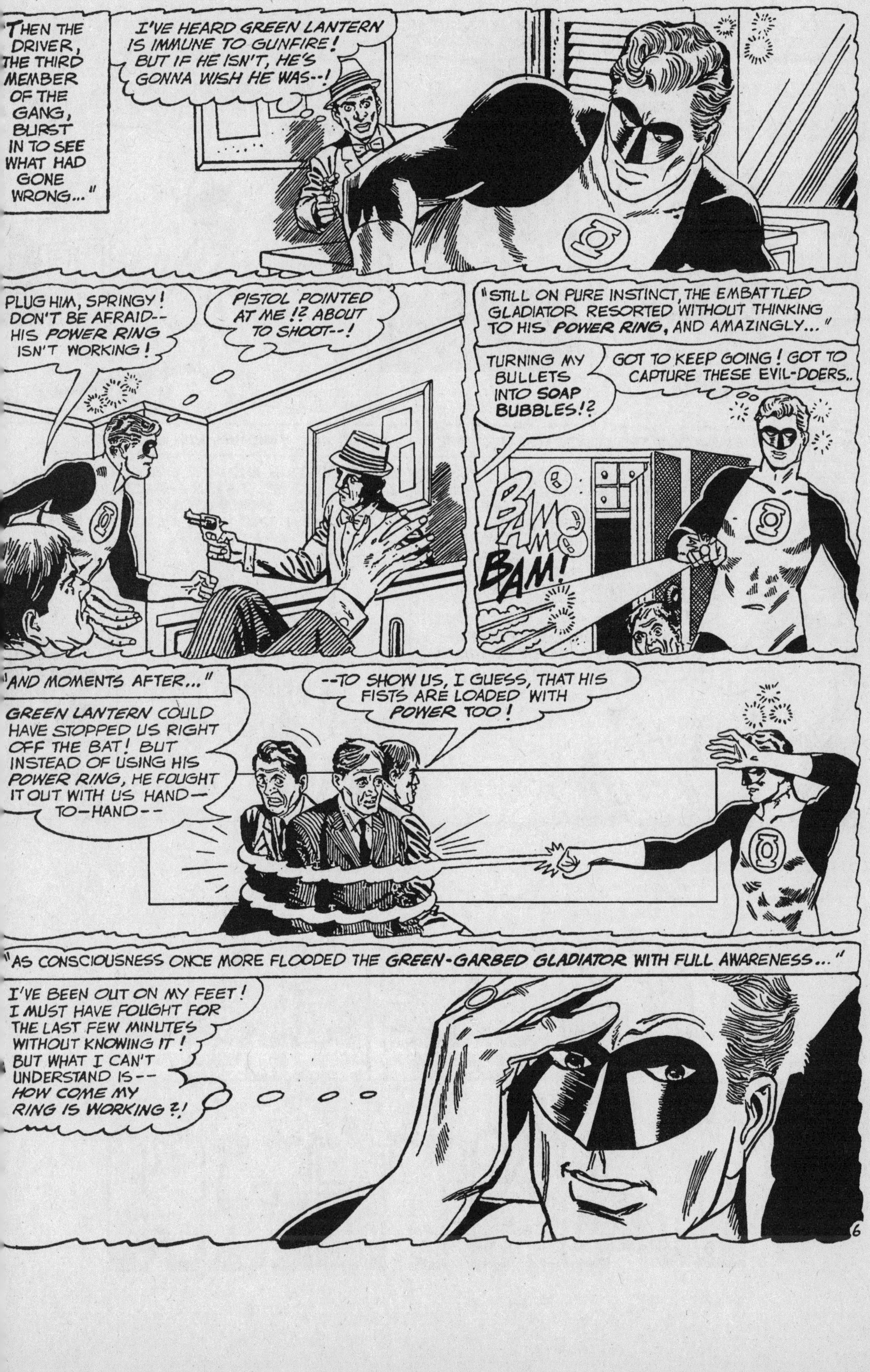
"THEN THE DRIVER, THE THIRD MEMBER OF THE GANG, BURST IN TO SEE WHAT HAD GONE WRONG..."
I'VE HEARD GREEN LANTERN IS IMMUNE TO GUNFIRE! BUT IF HE ISN'T, HE'S GONNA WISH HE WAS--!
PLUG HIM, SPRINGY! DON'T BE AFRAID-- HIS POWER RING ISN'T WORKING!
PISTOL POINTED AT ME!? ABOUT TO SHOOT--!
"STILL ON PURE INSTINCT, THE EMBATTLED GLADIATOR RESORTED WITHOUT THINKING TO HIS POWER RING, AND AMAZINGLY..."
TURNING MY BULLETS INTO SOAP BUBBLES!?
GOT TO KEEP GOING! GOT TO CAPTURE THESE EVIL-DOERS..
BAM BAM BAM!
"AND MOMENTS AFTER..."
GREEN LANTERN COULD HAVE STOPPED US RIGHT OFF THE BAT! BUT INSTEAD OF USING HIS POWER RING, HE FOUGHT IT OUT WITH US HAND-TO-HAND--
--TO SHOW US, I GUESS, THAT HIS FISTS ARE LOADED WITH POWER TOO!
"AS CONSCIOUSNESS ONCE MORE FLOODED THE GREEN-GARBED GLADIATOR WITH FULL AWARENESS..."
I'VE BEEN OUT ON MY FEET! I MUST HAVE FOUGHT FOR THE LAST FEW MINUTES WITHOUT KNOWING IT! BUT WHAT I CAN'T UNDERSTAND IS-- HOW COME MY RING IS WORKING?!
6

"LATER, WITH THE *ROCKET ROBBERS* BEHIND BARS, AFTER HAL HAD FLOWN BACK HOME TO THE *FERRIS AIRCRAFT COMPANY...* "

I *STILL* CAN'T FIGURE IT OUT! MY RING RAN OUT OF POWER AT *THREE O'CLOCK* TODAY! BUT I CHARGED IT YESTERDAY AT *TWO O'CLOCK!* AND THAT MEANS I HAD *TWENTY-FIVE HOURS* OF POWER -- UNLESS I'VE GONE OFF MY *NOGGIN!*

"THEN, IN HIS DRESSING ROOM... "

WHOA UP! MY ELECTRIC CLOCK HERE IS *STILL* AT *TWO O'CLOCK!* COULD IT BE THAT THIS IS THE WHOLE ANSWER TO THE PUZZLE--RIGHT HERE?

"AND AFTER STARING AT THE CLOCK FOR ANOTHER FEW MINUTES... "

SURE ENOUGH! IT'S *STOPPED RUNNING!* IT MUST BE WORN OUT! SO THAT EXPLAINS EVERYTHING! YESTERDAY WHEN I CHARGED MY RING, THE CLOCK HAD *ALREADY* STOPPED! AND IT WAS REALLY *THREE O'CLOCK* AND NOT *TWO O'CLOCK!* AND THAT MEANS I HAD EXACTLY *TWENTY-FOUR HOURS* OF POWER-- AS *ALWAYS!*

AS *PIEFACE* FINISHES HIS ACCOUNT...

... AND SO ENDS ANOTHER *GREEN LANTERN ZERO HOUR* STORY--AN ESPECIALLY APPROPRIATE NAME IN THIS CASE BECAUSE FOR ALMOST ONE HOUR GL'S RING WAS *"ZERO"* AS FAR AS HE WAS CONCERNED!

The End

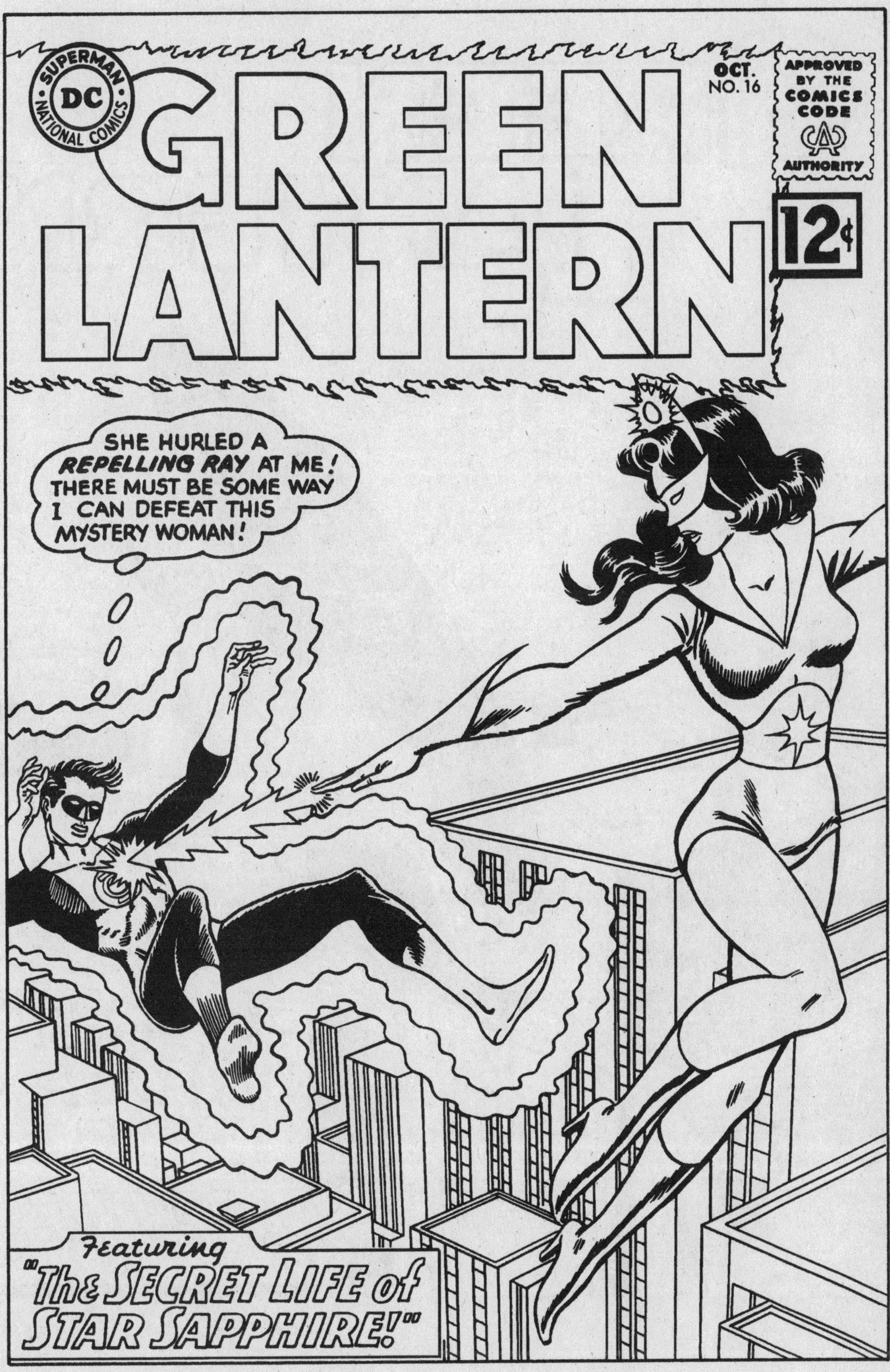
SUPERMAN DC NATIONAL COMICS
GREEN LANTERN
OCT. NO. 16
APPROVED BY THE COMICS CODE AUTHORITY
12¢
SHE HURLED A REPELLING RAY AT ME! THERE MUST BE SOME WAY I CAN DEFEAT THIS MYSTERY WOMAN!
Featuring "The SECRET LIFE of STAR SAPPHIRE!"

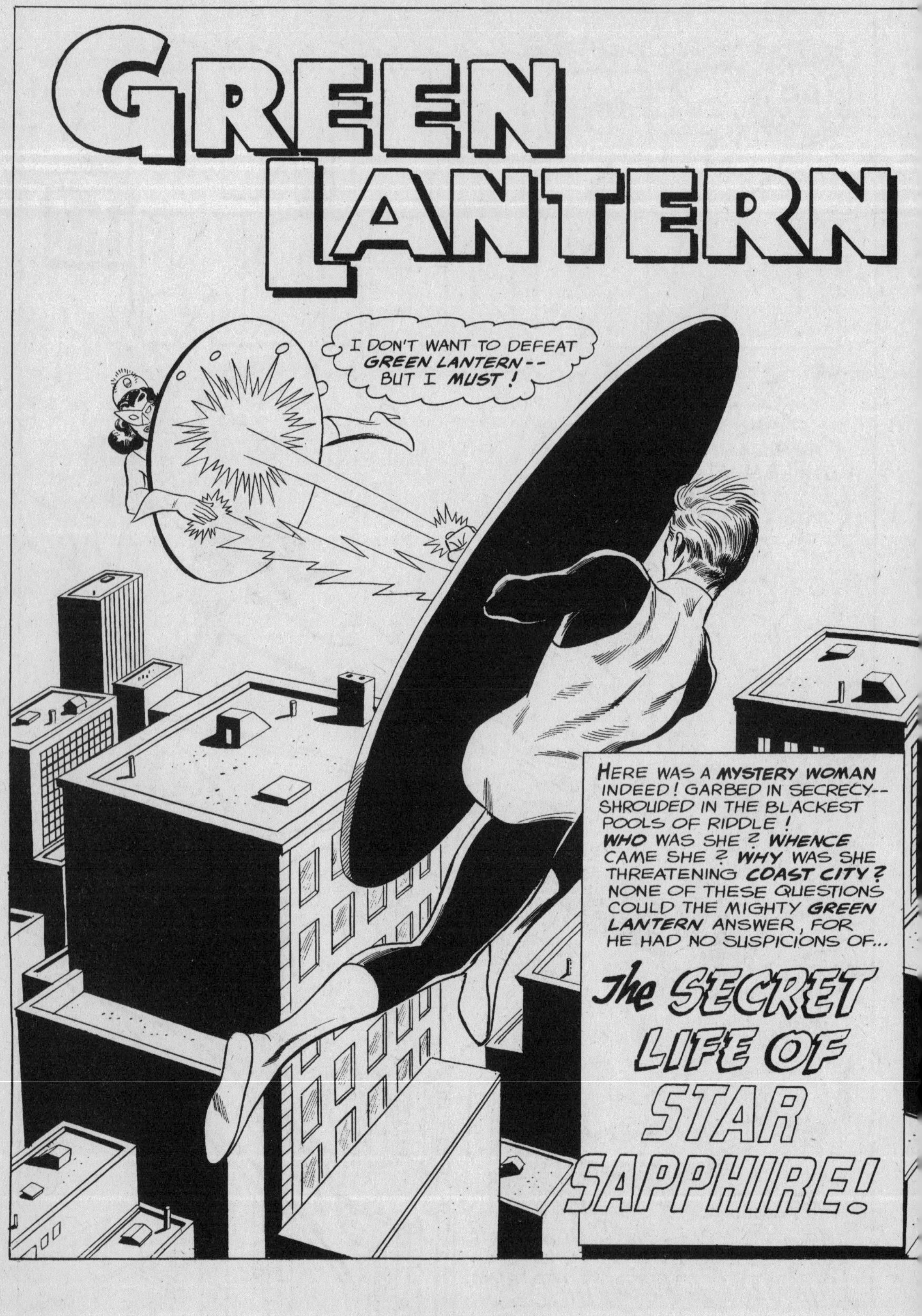
GREEN LANTERN
I DON'T WANT TO DEFEAT GREEN LANTERN-- BUT I MUST!
HERE WAS A MYSTERY WOMAN INDEED! GARBED IN SECRECY-- SHROUDED IN THE BLACKEST POOLS OF RIDDLE! WHO WAS SHE? WHENCE CAME SHE? WHY WAS SHE THREATENING COAST CITY? NONE OF THESE QUESTIONS COULD THE MIGHTY GREEN LANTERN ANSWER, FOR HE HAD NO SUSPICIONS OF...
The SECRET LIFE OF STAR SAPPHIRE!

DURING A FREE HOUR, CAROL FERRIS--PRETTY YOUNG BOSS OF THE *FERRIS AIRCRAFT COMPANY* * --TAKES UP A PLANE ESPECIALLY RESERVED FOR HER...

*Editor's Note; DURING THE EXTENDED ABSENCE OF HER FATHER, OFF WITH MRS. FERRIS ON A ROUND-THE-WORLD TOUR...

SINCE HAL JORDAN PERSONALLY TAUGHT ME HOW TO FLY, IT'S BECOME MY FAVORITE SPORT! OF COURSE, I'LL NEVER BE AS GOOD A PILOT AS *HE* IS...

...BUT I'M GOOD ENOUGH--AND CONFIDENT ENOUGH-- FOR SHORT HOPS WITHIN AN HOUR OR SO FROM OUR HANGAR!

WHAT A FEELING IT IS TO SWOOP HIGH OVER THE EARTH LIKE A BIRD! AND I MUST ADMIT--I OWE IT ALL TO HAL! IT'S REALLY TOO BAD I CAN'T MAKE UP MY MIND TO *MARRY HIM!*

BUT THE TROUBLE IS THERE'S SOMEBODY ELSE! IF I *REALLY* LOVED HAL, I WOULDN'T FEEL THE WAY I DO TOWARD THIS *OTHER PERSON!*

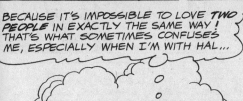

BECAUSE IT'S IMPOSSIBLE TO LOVE *TWO PEOPLE* IN EXACTLY THE SAME WAY! THAT'S WHAT SOMETIMES CONFUSES ME, ESPECIALLY WHEN I'M WITH HAL...

Editor's Note: UNKNOWN TO CAROL, ACE TEST PILOT HAL JORDAN AND THE "OTHER" MAN IN THE CASE ARE SECRETLY *ONE AND THE SAME PERSON!*

SUDDENLY, AS THE LOVELY AVIATRIX IS MUSING OVER HER TANGLED LOVE-LIFE...

THE CONTROLS--THEY'RE NOT WORKING THE PLANE RIGHT! I'M LOSING ALTITUDE!

2

I'M BEING *FORCED DOWN!* WITH LUCK, I SHOULD BE ABLE TO LAND SAFELY ON THE DESERT! THE SAND IS AS GOOD AS A RUNWAY HERE...

UHH! HIT A SOFT PATCH WITH A WHEEL! I'M TILTING--

THE NEXT MOMENT...

THAT WAS CLUMSY OF US! WE MANAGED THE LANDING BADLY! IF WE'VE HARMED HER--

NO-- SHE'LL BE ALL RIGHT IN A FEW MOMENTS!

AND WHEN CAROL FERRIS AGAIN OPENS HER EYES...

DO NOT FEAR! ALL WILL BE EXPLAINED, *YOUR HIGHNESS!*

WH-WHAT DID YOU CALL ME--!?

YOUR HIGHNESS!

YOU ARE OUR QUEEN!

WE ARE HERE ON YOUR WORLD UNDER AN *INVISIBILITY SCREEN!* WE COME FROM THE PLANET *ZAMARON* WHICH, IN OUR LANGUAGE, MEANS *LAND OF LOVELY WOMEN!* WE CAME HERE TO FIND *YOU!*

SOON, WHEN CAROL IS TOLD MORE OF THE VISITORS FROM *ZAMARON*...

WHAT AN INCREDIBLE STORY! THESE *ZAMARONS* COME FROM A WORLD TREMENDOUSLY IN ADVANCE OF OURS SCIENTIFICALLY! A PLACE INHABITED...

"...SOLELY BY *WOMEN!* AND IF WHAT THEY SAY IS TRUE, THEY ARE ALL *IMMORTAL...*"

..."ALL, THAT IS, EXCEPT ONE!"

BY TRADITION, THE *QUEEN* OF THE *ZAMARONS* IS ALWAYS A *MORTAL!* WHAT IS MORE, HER SUCCESSOR MUST ALWAYS BE HER EXACT DUPLICATE IN APPEARANCE! THEY SAY THEY SEARCHED THROUGH THE GALAXY...

...UNTIL THEY FOUND A PERFECT REPLICA OF THEIR FORMER QUEEN WHO HAD JUST DIED--

--AND THAT *I* AM IT!

UNQUESTIONABLY YOU ARE, HIGHNESS! BEHOLD--

AS ONE OF THE *ZAMARONS* TOUCHES A FINGER TO CAROL'S FOREHEAD...

AN *IMAGE* APPEARING BEFORE ME! *Hmm!* IF THAT IS THEIR FORMER QUEEN, I MUST ADMIT THERE *IS* A *STRIKING RESEMBLANCE!*...

AN EXACT RESEMBLANCE! NO DOUBT OF IT! YOUR HIGHNESS, WE MUST LEAVE AT ONCE TO RETURN TO *ZAMARON* WHERE YOU WILL BE CROWNED-- *QUEEN STAR SAPPHIRE!*

YOU MEAN-- *LEAVE* THE EARTH *!?* BUT I *CAN'T* DO THAT!

4

As CAROL FERRIS EXPLAINS WHY SHE CANNOT POSSIBLY ACCEPT THE HONOR ACCORDED HER...

THEN IT IS BECAUSE OF A *MAN-CREATURE* THAT YOU DO NOT WISH TO COME WITH US?

YOU ADMIT YOU ADMIRE THIS CREATURE?

I'M **IN LOVE** WITH HIM! AND HE'S NOT A CREATURE-- HIS NAME IS *GREEN LANTERN!*

AS OUR FUTURE QUEEN YOU MUST BE MADE TO REALIZE, HIGHNESS...

...HOW FAR SUPERIOR EVEN THE *LOWEST ZAMARON* IS TO ANY *MAN*--NO MATTER WHO HE BE SINCE IT IS CLEAR TO US NOW THAT YOU WILL NEVER ACCEPT OUR OFFER TO BE OUR LEADER WHILE YOU REMAIN...AS YOU SAY... *IN LOVE*, WE HAVE A PROPOSAL...

WE ARE AWARE THAT THIS *GREEN LANTERN* IS A HERO OF CONSIDERABLE PROWESS ON YOUR WORLD! WE WILL SHOW YOU WHAT A *WEAKLING HE REALLY IS!* BETTER YET, *YOU* WILL PROVE IT TO YOURSELF!

I WILL **PROVE?!**

INSIDE THE SHIP, THE FINGERS OF A *ZAMARON* PLAY LIGHTLY OVER THE GLEAMING KEYS OF A FANTASTIC ORGAN...

REMAIN STILL, PLEASE, AND HAVE NO FEAR! WE ARE GOING TO ARRAY YOU IN ONE OF THE COSTUMES WORN BY OUR QUEEN FOR HUNTING AND EXPLORATION!

ENERGY, FROM THE ORGAN... STREAMING THROUGH MY BODY...

THEN MOMENTS AFTER...

(GASP) WHAT'S HAPPENED-- I FEEL SO *DIFFERENT*-- SO *REGAL* ...

NEXT WE SHALL BESTOW UPON YOU TEMPORARILY SOME OF THE POWERS OF OUR QUEEN...CONCENTRATED IN THE GREAT *STAR SAPPHIRE* YOU ARE NOW WEARING!

SOON AT A SUGGESTION FROM A ZAMARON TO SOAR INTO THE AIR...

IT'S AMAZING! I CAN SOAR THROUGH THE AIR LIKE A BIRD!

OF COURSE! IT IS ONE OF THE POWERS WHICH YOUR ROYAL GEM GIVES YOU!

NOW FOR THE TEST! YOU SHALL GO INTO THE CITY WHERE YOU WILL ENCOUNTER GREEN LANTERN! DUE TO INCIDENTS WE HAVE ARRANGED HE WILL SEEK TO TAKE YOU INTO CUSTODY! BUT YOU MUST DEFY HIM! THWART HIS EFFORTS TO IMPRISON YOU!

IN THIS MANNER, YOU WILL LEARN HOW PUNY ARE THE POWERS OF THIS GREEN LANTERN -- COMPARED TO WHAT WE CAN GIVE YOU! BUT THERE IS NO CAUSE FOR FURTHER DELAY...

ALL IS IN READINESS!

AND SHORTLY, A LOVELY BUT STRANGE APPARITION FLASHES ON ITS WAY...

I CANNOT HELP MYSELF! I MUST ACT AS THEY BID ME! I AM COMPELLED TO SEEK GREEN LANTERN... AND WIN OUT OVER HIM!

6

MEANWHILE AT THE *FERRIS AIRCRAFT COMPANY* WHERE HAL JORDAN AND HIS ESKIMO GREASEMONKEY--AND LONE CONFIDANT--*PIEFACE*--HAVE BEEN KEEPING AN ANXIOUS VIGIL...

NO ONE IN THE PLANT HAS ANY IDEA WHAT'S HAPPENED TO CAROL, *PIE!* ONLY ONE THING TO DO NOW--

YOU'RE GOING TO SEARCH FOR HER-- AS *GREEN LANTERN!* RIGHT, HAL?

SURE ENOUGH, IN THE SECRECY OF HAL'S DRESSING ROOM BEHIND LOCKED DOORS...

IN BRIGHTEST DAY, IN BLACKEST NIGHT,
NO EVIL SHALL ESCAPE MY SIGHT!
LET THOSE WHO WORSHIP EVIL'S MIGHT
BEWARE MY POWER-- GREEN LANTERN'S LIGHT!

PIE, HOLD THE FORT! IF CAROL SHOWS UP, SHE MUSTN'T SUSPECT THAT I WENT OUT TO LOOK FOR HER-- AS *GREEN LANTERN!*

DON'T WORRY, PAL! I'LL COVER UP FOR YOU!

PIE--AND BARRY [THE FLASH] ALLEN ARE THE ONLY ONES WHO HAVE SEEN THE FACE UNDER THIS MASK! I WOULDN'T WANT CAROL TO SUSPECT THE TRUTH--IF FOR NO OTHER REASON THAN THAT I WANT TO WIN HER FOR MYSELF-- AS *HAL JORDAN!* BUT LET ME SEE...

WHEN I GAVE CAROL HER FLYING LESSONS WE USUALLY HEADED TOWARD THE DESERT! I'LL TRY THAT WAY FIRST... IT WAS PRETTY NERVY OF HER TO GO OUT SOLO...eh??

WHO IS THAT? UH--SHE'S ADDRESSING ME--

GREEN LANTERN, I *CHALLENGE* YOU!

CAN'T HELP MYSELF...

...I *MUST* SPEAK TO HIM THIS WAY!

I AM ABOUT TO BREAK INTO THE *EXHIBIT OF ANCIENT GLASS* HERE IN THE CITY TO COMMIT A *CRIME!* I DARE YOU TO STOP ME!

I HAVE NO TIME FOR GAMES!

GREAT GUARDIANS! I SUDDENLY GOT THE FEELING THIS IS NOT A GAME... BUT A THREAT! I'LL HAVE TO PUT OFF MY SEARCH FOR CAROL WHILE I DEAL WITH THIS EXTRAORDINARY *MENACING FEMALE!*

SOON... THERE SHE GOES INTO THE *EXHIBIT BUILDING!* WHERE COULD SHE HAVE COME FROM? *WHO* CAN SHE BE?

HE'S RIGHT ON MY HEELS!

THEN...

;GASP!; LOOK--

SHE'S STEALING THE ANCIENT HAND MIRROR AS SHE BOASTED! AND BY THE LOOKS OF IT--

--IT'S ONE OF THE OLDEST AND MOST VALUABLE PIECES HERE!

GREEN LANTERN DOESN'T REALIZE THAT THE *ZAMARONS* PLACED THIS MIRROR HERE-- BY THEIR SUPER-SCIENTIFIC MEANS! I'M NOT *REALLY* STEALING IT-- JUST *PRETENDING* TO!

8

As STAR SAPPHIRE MAKES OFF WITH HER "LOOT"...

THE PURPOSE IS TO GET HIM TO STOP ME! OH, GREEN LANTERN, PLEASE DON'T FAIL ME!

THIS GAME HAS GONE FAR ENOUGH!

AS THE EMERALD GLADIATOR'S POWER BEAM ROARS OUT WITH THE FORCE OF A THOUSAND JET ENGINES...

SHOOTING HIS RING AT ME! I--I MUST COUNTERACT HIS MOVE--!

I SEEM TO BE TWO PEOPLE--ONE WANTING TO CONQUER GREEN LANTERN--THE OTHER AT THE SAME TIME WANTING HIM TO DEFEAT ME!!

THEN... SHE'S HURLED A REPELLING RAY AT ME! WHAT IS THE SOURCE OF THIS MYSTERIOUS POWER OF HERS--? IT'S NEARLY OVERWHELMING--!

CATAPULTED BACKWARD, GREEN LANTERN ACCIDENTALLY STRIKES A PROJECTING LEDGE...

UHH...

OH! WHAT HAVE I DONE?

JUST BEFORE HE BLANKS OUT, GREEN LANTERN WILL-POWERS HIS RING TO SAVE HIM FROM BEING HURT...

THANK GOODNESS! HIS RING SAVED HIM! IT MADE A NET TO CATCH HIM BEFORE HE COULD STRIKE THE GROUND!

AND WHEN THE GREEN-GARBED CRUSADER RECOVERS HIS WITS...

GONE! NOT A SIGN OF HER!

THE ODDEST THING ABOUT THAT *STRANGE FEMALE MARAUDER* WITH THE HUGE *STAR SAPPHIRE* IN HER HAIR IS THAT I HAVE THE QUEEREST FEELING I'VE SEEN HER SOMEWHERE BEFORE...

...THOUGH I CAN'T IMAGINE *WHERE!* BUT I HAVE A STRONG HUNCH I'M GOING TO SEE HER *AGAIN!* AT LEAST I FIND MY- SELF HOPING SO! FOR SOME MYSTERIOUS REASON, SHE'S TRYING TO SHOW ME UP!

MEANWHILE, BACK IN THE *ZAMARON* SPACESHIP...

YOU SEE HOW EASY IT WAS FOR YOU TO DEFEAT *GREEN LANTERN?* ARE YOU SATISFIED-- AND WILL YOU COME WITH US NOW?

PLEASE...

GIVE HIM ONE MORE CHANCE! I FEEL SURE *GREEN LANTERN* CAN DEFEAT ME! IT WAS JUST AN ACCIDENT THAT BETRAYED HIM...

HER LOYALTY TO THIS MERE MAN IS ASTONISHING...

SHE DOESN'T SEEM TO REALIZE THAT *MEN* ARE A DIS- TINCTLY INFERIOR SPECIES!

SHE ACTS AS IF A *MAN* COULD BE *SOMETHING IMPORTANT!*

BUT WE MUSTN'T BE HASTY...

VERY WELL, YOUR HIGHNESS! YOU MAY HAVE ONE MORE CHANCE! BUT AS YOU WILL SEE, IT CAN ONLY LEAD TO THE SAME RESULT!

I MUST FIND OUT!

10

ONCE AGAIN AS SHE FLIES AWAY FROM THE SPACESHIP, A STRANGE TELEPATHIC FORCE REACHES THE TRANSFORMED CAROL FERRIS, SEIZING CONTROL OF HER...

I MUST *DEFEAT* GREEN LANTERN AT ALL COSTS! I MUST *DEFEAT...* GREEN LANTERN.. AT ALL COSTS!

BUT HOW WILL **GREEN LANTERN** KNOW WHERE TO CONTACT **STAR SAPPHIRE** AGAIN?

ANAMEDE, YOU ARE ALWAYS ASKING QUESTIONS! IT IS SIMPLE! WE WILL USE A **THOUGHT** BEAM TO INFORM HIM...!

AND SOON...

NO HINT ANYWHERE OF CAROL OR THAT ODD THIEF! I--eh? TELEPATHIC WORDS REACHING ME --

GREEN LANTERN, IF YOU WISH TO LOCATE **STAR SAPPHIRE...**

...GO AT ONCE TO THE **COAST CITY ART GALLERY!**

STAR SAPPHIRE!? THAT MUST BE THE NEW FEMALE MARAUDER WHO'S SUDDENLY APPEARED IN THIS CITY!

THE MESSAGE MAY VERY WELL LEAD ME INTO A TRAP--OR ON A WILD-GOOSE CHASE--BUT I'VE GOT TO CHANCE IT! BESIDES, I'D RATHER GO **SOMEWHERE** -- DO **SOMETHING**-- THAN BE A **DO-NOTHING!**

MEANWHILE, IN THE **ART GALLERY...**

HELP! THAT COSTUMED WOMAN IS STEALING A PRICELESS **MINIATURE** PAINTING!

APPARENTLY THE SIGHT OF ME HAS THE GALLERY OWNER RATTLED!

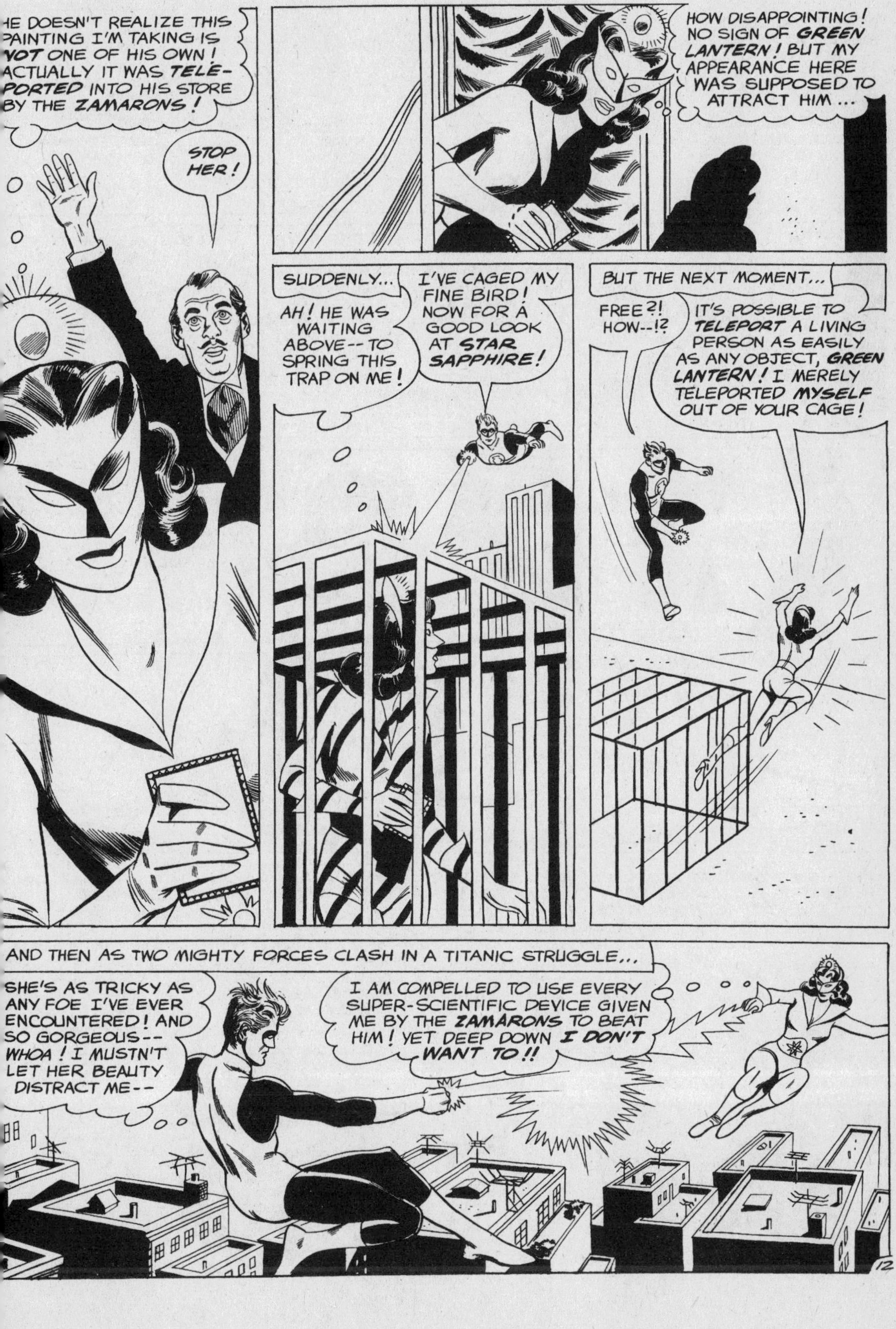
HE DOESN'T REALIZE THIS PAINTING I'M TAKING IS NOT ONE OF HIS OWN! ACTUALLY IT WAS TELE-PORTED INTO HIS STORE BY THE ZAMARONS!
STOP HER!
HOW DISAPPOINTING! NO SIGN OF GREEN LANTERN! BUT MY APPEARANCE HERE WAS SUPPOSED TO ATTRACT HIM ...
SUDDENLY...
AH! HE WAS WAITING ABOVE--TO SPRING THIS TRAP ON ME!
I'VE CAGED MY FINE BIRD! NOW FOR A GOOD LOOK AT STAR SAPPHIRE!
BUT THE NEXT MOMENT...
FREE?! HOW--!?
IT'S POSSIBLE TO TELEPORT A LIVING PERSON AS EASILY AS ANY OBJECT, GREEN LANTERN! I MERELY TELEPORTED MYSELF OUT OF YOUR CAGE!
AND THEN AS TWO MIGHTY FORCES CLASH IN A TITANIC STRUGGLE...
SHE'S AS TRICKY AS ANY FOE I'VE EVER ENCOUNTERED! AND SO GORGEOUS--WHOA! I MUSTN'T LET HER BEAUTY DISTRACT ME--
I AM COMPELLED TO USE EVERY SUPER-SCIENTIFIC DEVICE GIVEN ME BY THE ZAMARONS TO BEAT HIM! YET DEEP DOWN I DON'T WANT TO!!
12

SOME OF THE TERRIFIC *REPELLING* RAY SHE IS SHOOTING AT ME IS SLIPPING THROUGH MY POWER BEAM-- STRIKING ME LIKE RED-HOT NEEDLES! GOT TO COUNTERACT IT... IF I CAN...

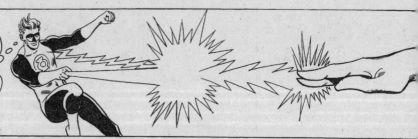

INSTANTLY, THE MIGHTY GREEN BEAM PROVIDES ITS WIELDER WITH A SHIELD...

HIS RING HAS FORMED A SHIELD! I CAN'T PIERCE IT! I AM DEFEATED--

DO NOT LET SUCH A HORRIBLE THOUGHT ENTER YOUR MIND, YOUR HIGHNESS...

WE WILL NOW CONFER UPON YOU YOUR ULTIMATE POWER--THAT OF *MIND OVER MATTER!* WITH THIS POWER YOU WILL CERTAINLY BE ABLE TO *WIN OUT!*

I CAN'T HELP MYSELF! I MUST USE MY FANTASTIC NEW POWER AGAINST *GREEN LANTERN!* GRIND HIM IN THE DUST IF I CAN!

THE SHIELD SHE HAS MANAGED TO CREATE FOR HERSELF IS PROTECTING HER FROM MY BEAM! NOW I'VE GOT TO "POUR IT ON" TO PUT AN END TO THIS DEADLOCK ...

BACKING HIS RING WITH ALL HIS INDOMITABLE WILL POWER, THE *EMERALD GLADIATOR* MAKES A BREAKTHROUGH...

THAT SUBSTANCE FORMING HER SHIELD IS TOUGH-- BUT MY *RING* AND *WILL POWER* ARE *TOUGHER!*

OH--THE SHIELD I MADE-- CRUMBLING UNDER HIS ATTACK!

As the **GREEN GLADIATOR** HURTLES TOWARD HIS MOMENTARILY STUNNED OPPONENT...

MY RING HAS DETECTED A **MYSTERIOUS ENERGY** COMING AT HER THAT COULD BE THE SOURCE OF HER **INCREDIBLE POWER!** AND IF THAT'S THE CASE...

--I'VE GOT TO SURROUND HER AT ONCE WITH AN **IMPENETRABLE BARRIER**-- THAT WILL CUT OFF ALL **INCOMING RADIATION!**

UH! I FEEL SO WEAK... SO HELPLESS...

IT MUST BE WORKING! SHE SEEMS DAZED... ALL THE FIGHT DRAWN OUT OF HER--

I'M DEFEATED! HOW TERRIBLE... **NO! HOW WONDERFUL!**

AT THAT MOMENT, THE **ZAMARONS** ARE FRANTICALLY TRYING TO SAVE THEIR WOULD-BE QUEEN...

INCREASE THE X-CHARGE OF OUR MIND-OVER-MATTER TRANSMISSION TO HER! WE MUST BREAK THROUGH THE BARRIER FORMED BY **GREEN LANTERN'S** RING!

WE ARE TRYING--

WE'VE FAILED! THERE'S NOTHING WE CAN DO TO BREAK THROUGH THE GREEN ENERGY AROUND HER!

LOOK! SHE IS FAINTING FROM THE EXCITEMENT--! SUCH A DISGRACE TO OUR SEX!

AND SHORTLY AFTERWARD...

GOOD GOSH! I DROPPED MY ANTI-RADIATION BARRIER AROUND HER WHEN I SAW HER PASS OUT! BUT-- BEFORE I COULD REACH HER, **SHE HAD VANISHED!**

14

BACK IN THE *ZAMARON* SPACESHIP...

SINCE YOU WERE DEFEATED BY A MERE *MAN*, CAROL FERRIS--IT IS CLEAR THAT YOU CANNOT *REALLY* BE THE NEXT SUCCESSOR TO THE *ZAMARON* THRONE! THEREFORE, WE MUST SEARCH ELSE-WHERE FOR OUR *STAR SAPPHIRE* QUEEN...

BUT BEFORE WE LEAVE EARTH WE MUST ARRANGE MATTERS SO OUR STAY HERE WILL NOT HAVE AFFECTED LIFE ON THIS WORLD! YOU WILL BE RETURNED TO YOUR AIRCRAFT UNHARMED... YOU WILL REMEM-BER *NOTHING* AT ALL OF *US*...!

LATER... THIS TIME I WAS SEEKING *STAR SAPPHIRE*... BUT I FOUND CAROL! SHE SEEMS FINE... BUT WHAT'S *THIS* LYING ON THE SAND AT HER FEET...?

A STAR SAPPHIRE--?! GREAT THUNDER! HOW DID *THIS* GET HERE!?

I NEVER SAW IT BEFORE! PLEASE TAKE ME HOME, *GREEN LANTERN!* I'M NOT HURT... BUT I SEEM TERRIBLY *TIRED*...

AND IN DUE COURSE...

I TOLD CAROL I'D TAKE THIS GEM TO THE POLICE! BUT--WHAT CAN THE CONNECTION BE BETWEEN CAROL FERRIS AND STAR SAPPHIRE? WILL I EVER SOLVE THE *MYSTERY*? I WONDER...!

The End

GREEN LANTERN

GREEN LANTERN

BEFORE I--HAL JORDAN OF EARTH-- BECAME *GREEN LANTERN*, A MAN FROM ANOTHER PLANET WORE MY COLORFUL UNIFORM AND WIELDED THE AWESOME MIGHT OF THE POWER RING!

HIS NAME WAS *ABIN SUR* AND IT WAS HE WHO SELECTED ME TO SUCCEED HIM AS *GREEN LANTERN!* BUT WHY WAS *ABIN SUR* IN A *SPACESHIP* WHEN HE CAME TO EARTH--WHEN THE *POWER RING* COULD FLY HIM ANYWHERE THROUGH SPACE? HERE FOR THE VERY FIRST TIME IS THE STORY OF...

EARTH'S *FIRST* GREEN LANTERN!

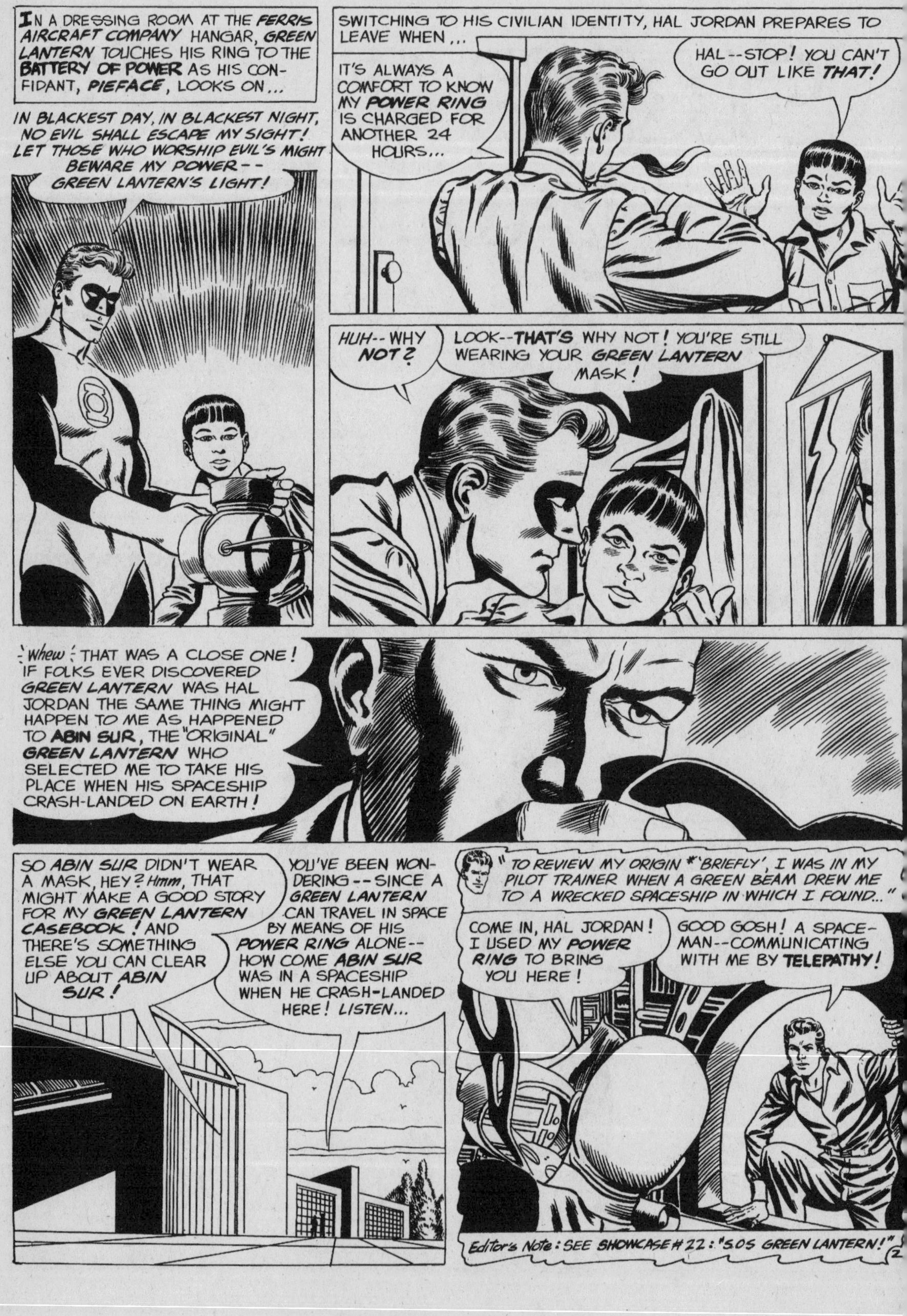
IN A DRESSING ROOM AT THE FERRIS AIRCRAFT COMPANY HANGAR, GREEN LANTERN TOUCHES HIS RING TO THE BATTERY OF POWER AS HIS CONFIDANT, PIEFACE, LOOKS ON...
IN BLACKEST DAY, IN BLACKEST NIGHT, NO EVIL SHALL ESCAPE MY SIGHT! LET THOSE WHO WORSHIP EVIL'S MIGHT BEWARE MY POWER-- GREEN LANTERN'S LIGHT!
SWITCHING TO HIS CIVILIAN IDENTITY, HAL JORDAN PREPARES TO LEAVE WHEN...
IT'S ALWAYS A COMFORT TO KNOW MY POWER RING IS CHARGED FOR ANOTHER 24 HOURS...
HAL--STOP! YOU CAN'T GO OUT LIKE THAT!
HUH--WHY NOT?
LOOK--THAT'S WHY NOT! YOU'RE STILL WEARING YOUR GREEN LANTERN MASK!
-Whew- THAT WAS A CLOSE ONE! IF FOLKS EVER DISCOVERED GREEN LANTERN WAS HAL JORDAN THE SAME THING MIGHT HAPPEN TO ME AS HAPPENED TO ABIN SUR, THE "ORIGINAL" GREEN LANTERN WHO SELECTED ME TO TAKE HIS PLACE WHEN HIS SPACESHIP CRASH-LANDED ON EARTH!
SO ABIN SUR DIDN'T WEAR A MASK, HEY? Hmm, THAT MIGHT MAKE A GOOD STORY FOR MY GREEN LANTERN CASEBOOK! AND THERE'S SOMETHING ELSE YOU CAN CLEAR UP ABOUT ABIN SUR!
YOU'VE BEEN WONDERING--SINCE A GREEN LANTERN CAN TRAVEL IN SPACE BY MEANS OF HIS POWER RING ALONE--HOW COME ABIN SUR WAS IN A SPACESHIP WHEN HE CRASH-LANDED HERE! LISTEN...
"TO REVIEW MY ORIGIN* 'BRIEFLY', I WAS IN MY PILOT TRAINER WHEN A GREEN BEAM DREW ME TO A WRECKED SPACESHIP IN WHICH I FOUND..."
COME IN, HAL JORDAN! I USED MY POWER RING TO BRING YOU HERE!
GOOD GOSH! A SPACE-MAN--COMMUNICATING WITH ME BY TELEPATHY!
Editor's Note: SEE SHOWCASE #22: "S.O.S GREEN LANTERN!"
2

"*THE DYING SPACEMAN WAS A GREEN LANTERN FROM THIS SECTOR OF SPACE. HE HAD CHOSEN ME OF ALL MEN ON EARTH TO SUCCEED HIM...*"

YES...BY THE GREEN BEAM OF MY RING--I SEE THAT YOU ARE HONEST! AND THE BATTERY HAS ALREADY SELECTED YOU AS ONE BORN WITHOUT FEAR! SO NOW YOU PASS BOTH TESTS, HAL JORDAN...

"*AFTER EXPLAINING HOW THE POWER RING AND THE BATTERY WORKED, HE DIED. I WAS NOW THE GREEN LANTERN OF THIS PART OF SPACE...*"

I'LL HIDE THE SPACESHIP AND THE BODY OF ABIN SUR IN A SPECIAL NICHE UNDER THAT CLIFF WHICH I'M LIFTING BY WILL POWER APPLIED TO THE POWER RING!

I USED TO WONDER MYSELF WHY THAT OTHER GREEN LANTERN FLEW IN A SPACESHIP, RATHER THAN USE THE POWER OF HIS RING! I HAD NO IDEA HOW TO FIND THAT OUT-- UNTIL AFTER THE ADVENTURE YOU CALL "PRISONER OF THE POWER RING!"...

Editor's Note; THIS STORY APPEARED IN GREEN LANTERN #10

"*AFTER I HAD WILLED MY POWER RING IN THAT STORY TO TELL ME ABOUT BEVERLY BLANDING, I REALIZED IT COULD ALSO EXPLAIN ABIN SUR AND HIS SPACESHIP...*"

POWER RING, TELL ME WHY ABIN SUR WAS IN A SPACESHIP WHEN HE CAME TO EARTH!

"*THIS IS THE STORY MY POWER RING TOLD!* 'IN A REMOTE AREA OF HIS SPACE-SECTOR, ABIN SUR WAS CON- DUCTING A ROUTINE INVESTIGATION WHEN HE LANDED ON THE PLANET OF ATHMOORA...'*"

STRANGE! THIS PLANET IS STILL IN THE NEO-- MEDIEVAL STAGE--BUT IT OUGHT TO BE WELL INTO THE DAWN OF THE ATOMIC ERA, ACCORDING TO THE RECORDS! WHAT HELD ITS PROGRESS BACK?

"*HE USED ME...HIS POWER RING--TO QUESTION THE INHABITANTS...'*"

ENERGY-BEINGS CALLED LARIFARS CAME TO OUR WORLD AND ENTERED OUR BODIES...THEY ROBBED US OF THAT PART OF OUR INTELLIGENCE THEY CALLED THE I-FACTOR!

3

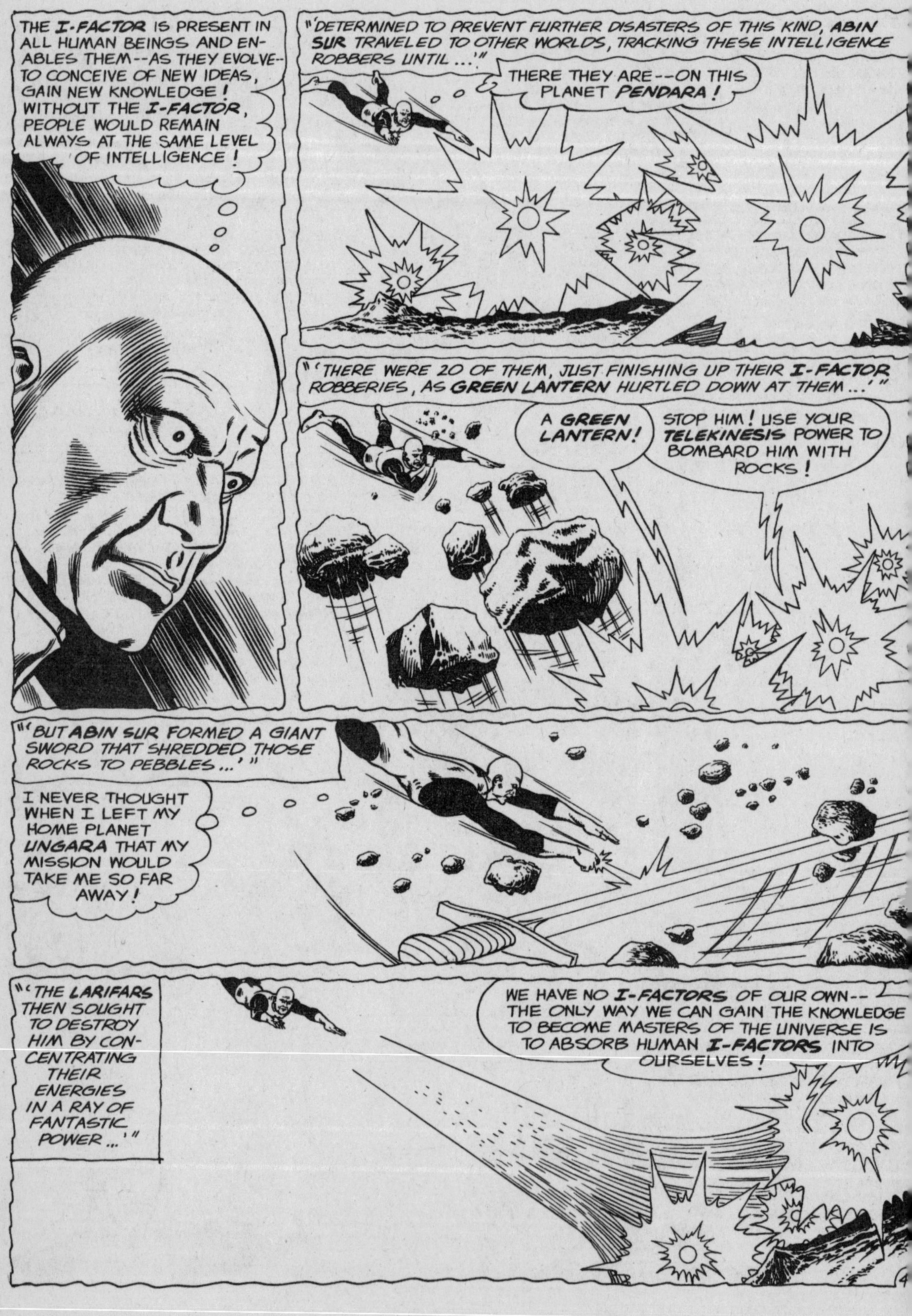
THE I-FACTOR IS PRESENT IN ALL HUMAN BEINGS AND ENABLES THEM--AS THEY EVOLVE--TO CONCEIVE OF NEW IDEAS, GAIN NEW KNOWLEDGE! WITHOUT THE I-FACTOR, PEOPLE WOULD REMAIN ALWAYS AT THE SAME LEVEL OF INTELLIGENCE!
"'DETERMINED TO PREVENT FURTHER DISASTERS OF THIS KIND, ABIN SUR TRAVELED TO OTHER WORLDS, TRACKING THESE INTELLIGENCE ROBBERS UNTIL...'"
THERE THEY ARE--ON THIS PLANET PENDARA!
"'THERE WERE 20 OF THEM, JUST FINISHING UP THEIR I-FACTOR ROBBERIES, AS GREEN LANTERN HURTLED DOWN AT THEM...'"
A GREEN LANTERN!
STOP HIM! USE YOUR TELEKINESIS POWER TO BOMBARD HIM WITH ROCKS!
"'BUT ABIN SUR FORMED A GIANT SWORD THAT SHREDDED THOSE ROCKS TO PEBBLES...'"
I NEVER THOUGHT WHEN I LEFT MY HOME PLANET UNGARA THAT MY MISSION WOULD TAKE ME SO FAR AWAY!
"'THE LARIFARS THEN SOUGHT TO DESTROY HIM BY CONCENTRATING THEIR ENERGIES IN A RAY OF FANTASTIC POWER...'"
WE HAVE NO I-FACTORS OF OUR OWN--THE ONLY WAY WE CAN GAIN THE KNOWLEDGE TO BECOME MASTERS OF THE UNIVERSE IS TO ABSORB HUMAN I-FACTORS INTO OURSELVES!

"*GREEN LANTERN* HANDLED THE THREAT BY FORMING A MIGHTY MIRROR THAT REFLECTED BACK THAT AWESOME RAY UNTIL THE ROCKS AROUND THE ENERGY— BEING BOILED AND BUBBLED!'"

"'BEFORE THE *LARIFARS* COULD RECOVER, I WAS WILLED TO FORM A GREAT GLOBE AROUND THEM WHICH ENCASED THEM SECURELY...'"

I'LL TAKE YOU OUT INTO SPACE-- PUT YOU IN ORBIT AROUND THE STAR-SUN OF THIS SYSTEM, TO REMAIN PRISONERS THE REST OF YOUR LIVES!

"'UNKNOWN TO *ABIN SUR* AT THAT MOMENT, ONE *LARIFAR* WAS STILL AT LARGE--ON THE DISTANT PLANET OF *ORLANA*...'"

WHAT IS DELAYING MY FELLOW-CREATURES? I WENT ON AHEAD TO FIND ANOTHER HUMAN-TYPE WORLD. THEY SHOULD BE HERE BY NOW!

"'THIS *LARIFAR--BALZONA--* LATER MENTIONED IN MY PRESENCE THAT IT WENT BACK SEARCHING FOR ITS FELLOWS AND FOUND THEM IMPRISONED IN THE ORBITING GLOBE ...'"

ONLY *GREEN LANTERN'S POWER RING* CAN FREE US!

THEN I SHALL SEEK HIM OUT-- AND TAKE IT AWAY FROM HIM!

WAIT--TO MAKE THE *POWER RING* WORK--I HAVE TO *HOLD IT*-- AND I HAVE NO WAY OF DOING THAT! IN THAT CASE, I MUST CAPTURE *GREEN LANTERN*-- COMPEL HIM TO FREE MY FELLOW-BEINGS WITH HIS RING!!

5

"AFTER RESTORING THE *I-FACTORS* TO THE HUMANOIDS WHO HAD BEEN ROBBED OF THEM, *ABIN SUR* RE-TURNED TO HIS HOME PLANET, UNAWARE THAT *BALZONA* ARRIVED THERE SOON AFTER...'"

MY FELLOW-BEINGS SAID *GREEN LANTERN* MENTIONED *UNGARA* AS HIS HOME WORLD! BUT SO FAR I'VE BEEN UNABLE TO FIND THIS UNIFORMED HERO! MAYBE I CAN GET HIM TO SHOW HIMSELF BY CREATING A *MENACE* HERE!

"BY SENDING OUT A BEAM OF RADIATION--AS THE ENERGY-BEAM LATER INFORMED US--*BALZONA* CAUSED A PLANETARY CRUST FAULT..'"

THIS GIGANTIC VOLCANO I CAUSED WILL DESTROY ALL LIFE ON THIS CONTINENT--UNLESS *GREEN LANTERN* COMES TO STOP IT!

"AS THAT AWESOME CATASTROPHE EXPLODED INTO A FIERY RAIN OF LAVA, PEOPLE FLED IN JET-BOATS AND GRAVITY-FLIERS...'"

"'IN HIS OTHER ROLE, *ABIN SUR* WAS A PROFESSOR OF HISTORY AT AN *UNGARAN* UNIVERSITY, WHERE WORD WAS FLASHED OF THE CATASTROPHE...'"

"ARRIVING OVER THE CRACK IN THE PLANET'S CRUST, HE USED ME TO FORM SCOOPS WITH WHICH TO CATCH THE ERUPT-ING LAVA...'"

I'LL STOP THE LAVA FROM HARMING ANYONE, FIRST OF ALL!

6

"'POURING THAT MOLTEN MAGMA BACK INTO THE GROUND, THE RING-WIELDER HARDENED IT AND WITH A MIGHTY SLEDGE, HAMMERED IT BACK INTO PLACE...'"

NEXT, I'LL RESTORE ALL VEGETATION AND DWELLINGS THAT WERE DAMAGED!

"'ABIN SUR DID NOT KNOW IT AT THAT TIME, BUT BALZONA WAS A MOST INTERESTED SPECTATOR OF WHAT HE WAS DOING...'"

I'LL KNOW HIS FACE ANYWHERE! I DARE NOT ATTACK WHILE HE HAS THE POWER RING! I'LL WAIT AND PICK A MORE OPPORTUNE MOMENT...CATCH HIM UNAWARES...

"'A FEW NIGHTS LATER, HAVING TRACKED DOWN ABIN SUR BY MEANS OF HIS CIVILIAN IDENTITY, BALZONA APPEARED...'"

WHILE HE SLEEPS, I SHALL ENTER HIS BODY-- AS WE ENTER HUMAN BODIES TO ROB OF THEIR I-FACTOR, AND SO GAIN CONTROL OVER HIM!

"'ABIN SUR WOKE DURING THAT STRANGE INVASION--AND FOUGHT HARD FOR HIS WILL AND BODILY CONTROLS--BUT SINCE AT THAT MOMENT, I WAS NOT CHARGED, HE SUCCUMBED...'"

IN A MOMENT I'LL HAVE GAINED MENTAL CONTROL OF HIM --AND WILL COMMAND HIM TO FREE MY FELLOW LARIFARS!

"'AFTER BALZONA EXPLAINED TO ABIN SUR WHAT HE HAD DONE, THE GREEN GLADIATOR REALIZED THAT THE ENERGY-BEING WAS NOT COMPLETELY FAMILIAR WITH ME, HIS POWER RING, AND KNEW NOTHING AT ALL OF THE POWER BATTERY...'"

I'LL FREE THEM-- IF I CAN!

IF YOU CAN? WHY CAN'T YOU? WHAT YOUR POWER RING DID, IT CAN UNDO!

BUT BY USING MY RING TO TAKE ME ACROSS SPACE TO THE STAR-SUN OF PENDARA, I'LL USE UP A GOOD DEAL OF ENERGY IN IT!

YOU MEAN-- THERE MAY NOT BE ENOUGH POWER LEFT IN IT TO RELEASE MY FELLOWS?

THAT'S NOT TRUE-- MY RING REMAINS FULLY CHARGED FOR 24 HOURS!

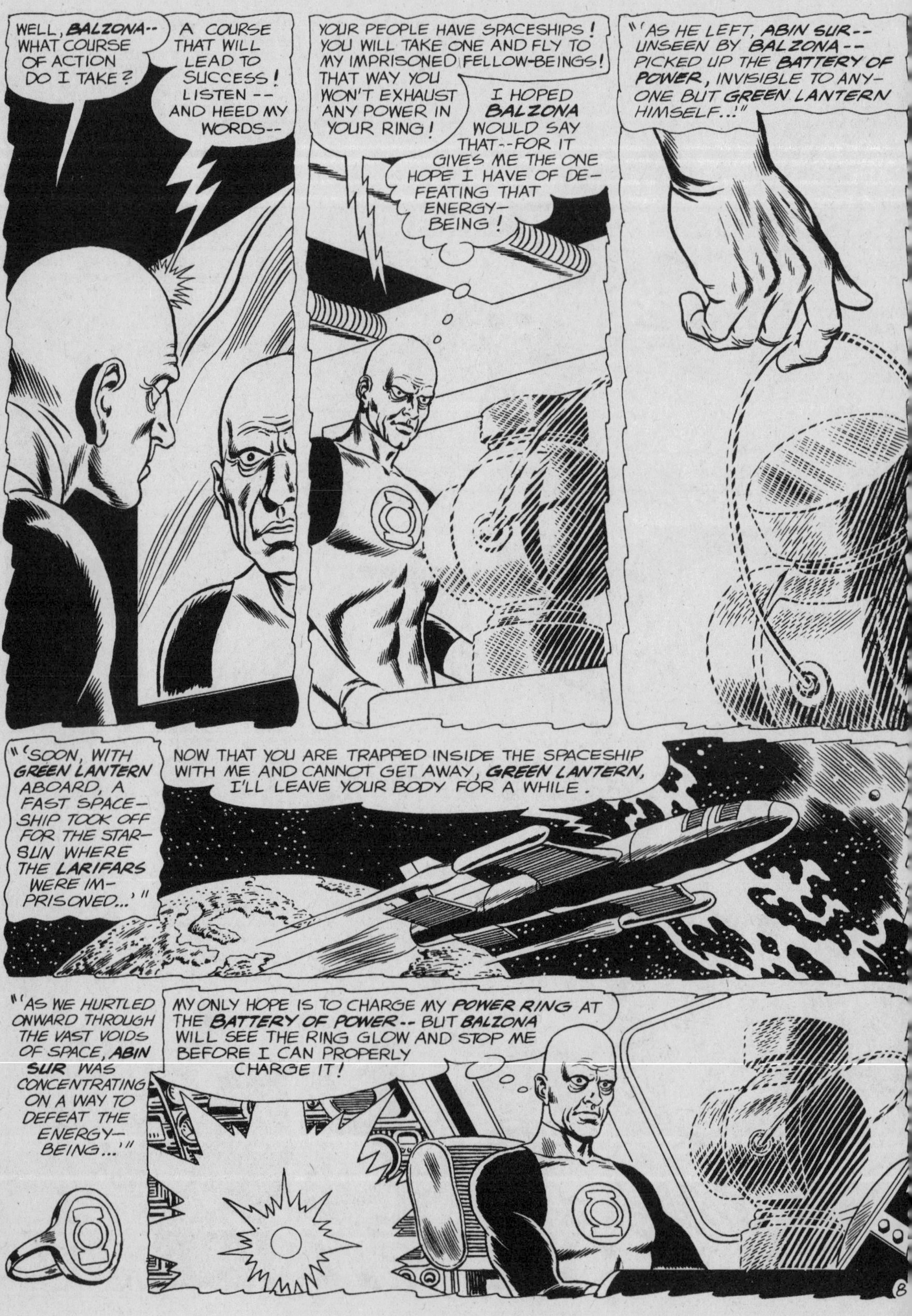
WELL, BALZONA-- WHAT COURSE OF ACTION DO I TAKE?
A COURSE THAT WILL LEAD TO SUCCESS! LISTEN -- AND HEED MY WORDS--
YOUR PEOPLE HAVE SPACESHIPS! YOU WILL TAKE ONE AND FLY TO MY IMPRISONED FELLOW-BEINGS! THAT WAY YOU WON'T EXHAUST ANY POWER IN YOUR RING!
I HOPED BALZONA WOULD SAY THAT--FOR IT GIVES ME THE ONE HOPE I HAVE OF DE-FEATING THAT ENERGY-BEING!
"'AS HE LEFT, ABIN SUR-- UNSEEN BY BALZONA-- PICKED UP THE BATTERY OF POWER, INVISIBLE TO ANY-ONE BUT GREEN LANTERN HIMSELF...'"
"'SOON, WITH GREEN LANTERN ABOARD, A FAST SPACE-SHIP TOOK OFF FOR THE STAR-SUN WHERE THE LARIFARS WERE IM-PRISONED...'"
NOW THAT YOU ARE TRAPPED INSIDE THE SPACESHIP WITH ME AND CANNOT GET AWAY, GREEN LANTERN, I'LL LEAVE YOUR BODY FOR A WHILE.
"'AS WE HURTLED ONWARD THROUGH THE VAST VOIDS OF SPACE, ABIN SUR WAS CONCENTRATING ON A WAY TO DEFEAT THE ENERGY-BEING...'"
MY ONLY HOPE IS TO CHARGE MY POWER RING AT THE BATTERY OF POWER-- BUT BALZONA WILL SEE THE RING GLOW AND STOP ME BEFORE I CAN PROPERLY CHARGE IT!
8

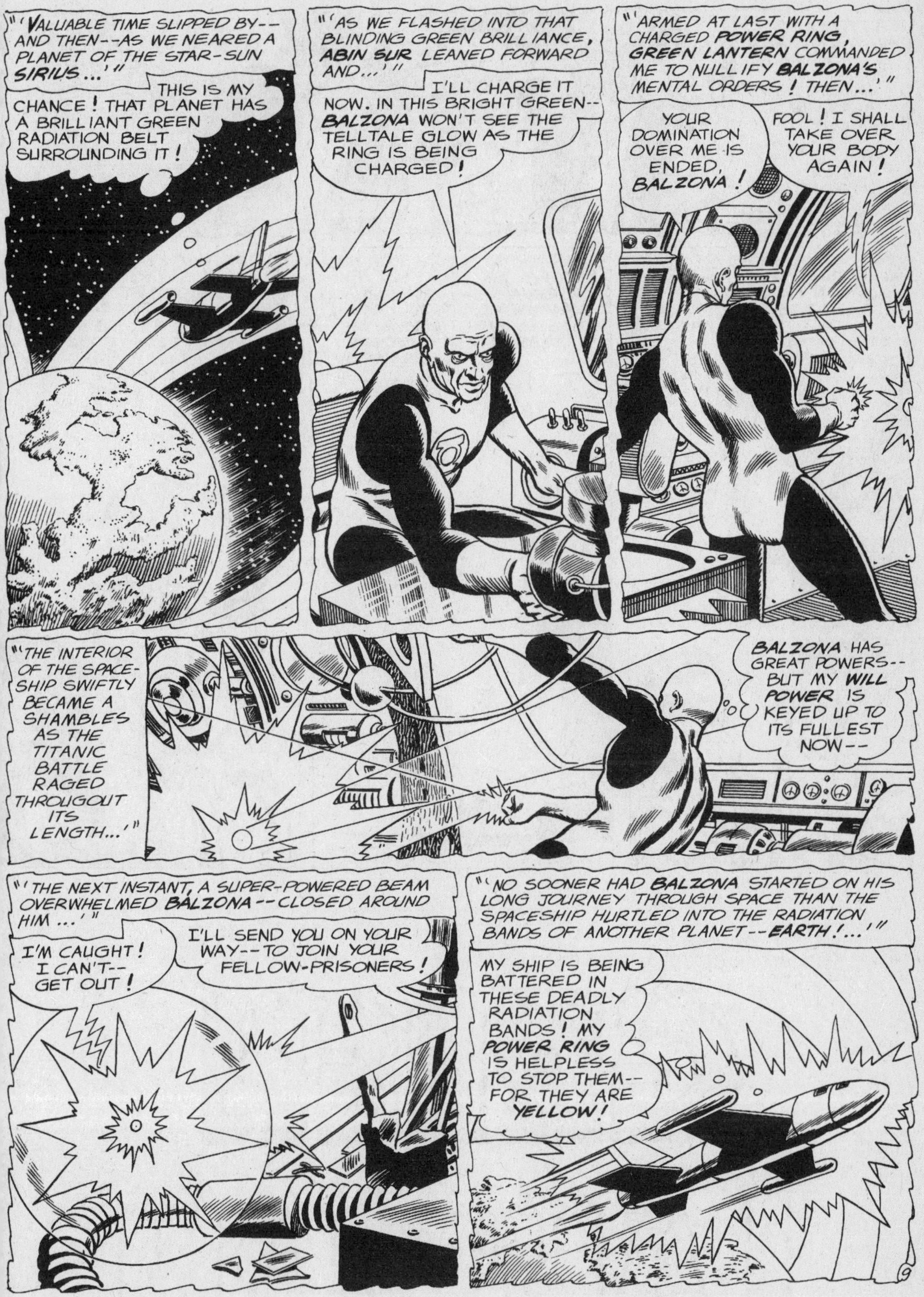
"'VALUABLE TIME SLIPPED BY--AND THEN--AS WE NEARED A PLANET OF THE STAR-SUN SIRIUS...'"
THIS IS MY CHANCE! THAT PLANET HAS A BRILLIANT GREEN RADIATION BELT SURROUNDING IT!
"'AS WE FLASHED INTO THAT BLINDING GREEN BRILLIANCE, ABIN SUR LEANED FORWARD AND...'"
I'LL CHARGE IT NOW. IN THIS BRIGHT GREEN--BALZONA WON'T SEE THE TELLTALE GLOW AS THE RING IS BEING CHARGED!
"'ARMED AT LAST WITH A CHARGED POWER RING, GREEN LANTERN COMMANDED ME TO NULLIFY BALZONA'S MENTAL ORDERS! THEN...'"
YOUR DOMINATION OVER ME IS ENDED, BALZONA!
FOOL! I SHALL TAKE OVER YOUR BODY AGAIN!
"'THE INTERIOR OF THE SPACESHIP SWIFTLY BECAME A SHAMBLES AS THE TITANIC BATTLE RAGED THROUGOUT ITS LENGTH...'"
BALZONA HAS GREAT POWERS--BUT MY WILL POWER IS KEYED UP TO ITS FULLEST NOW--
"'THE NEXT INSTANT, A SUPER-POWERED BEAM OVERWHELMED BALZONA--CLOSED AROUND HIM...'"
I'M CAUGHT! I CAN'T--GET OUT!
I'LL SEND YOU ON YOUR WAY--TO JOIN YOUR FELLOW-PRISONERS!
"'NO SOONER HAD BALZONA STARTED ON HIS LONG JOURNEY THROUGH SPACE THAN THE SPACESHIP HURTLED INTO THE RADIATION BANDS OF ANOTHER PLANET--EARTH!...'"
MY SHIP IS BEING BATTERED IN THESE DEADLY RADIATION BANDS! MY POWER RING IS HELPLESS TO STOP THEM--FOR THEY ARE YELLOW!

"*A* TERRIBLE YELLOW BRILLIANCE BLASTED *ABIN SUR* AT THE CONTROLS EVEN WHILE HE SOUGHT TO LIFT HIS SHIP FREE OF THAT DEADLY PERIL...*'*"

YELLOW LIGHT-- BLINDING ME!--

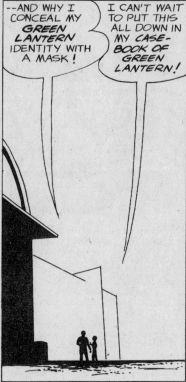

THE REST YOU KNOW, *PIEFACE*-- WHY I ALWAYS USE A NARROW, RADIATION-FREE CORRIDOR WHEN I LEAVE EARTH TO GO INTO SPACE, HOW I WAS MADE *GREEN LANTERN*--

--WHY *ABIN SUR* WAS IN A SPACESHIP WHEN HE CRASH-LANDED ON EARTH--

--AND WHY I CONCEAL MY *GREEN LANTERN* IDENTITY WITH A MASK!

I CAN'T WAIT TO PUT THIS ALL DOWN IN MY *CASE-BOOK OF GREEN LANTERN!*

FOR ONCE, *PIE*, LET *ME* GIVE YOU A TITLE FOR THIS ADVENTURE! I'VE ALWAYS LIKED TO THINK OF BRAVE *ABIN SUR*--WHO LOST HIS LIFE TO KEEP THE *LARIFARS* FROM SOMEDAY INVADING OUR PLANET-- AS *"EARTH'S FIRST GREEN LANTERN"!*

The End

GREEN LANTERN

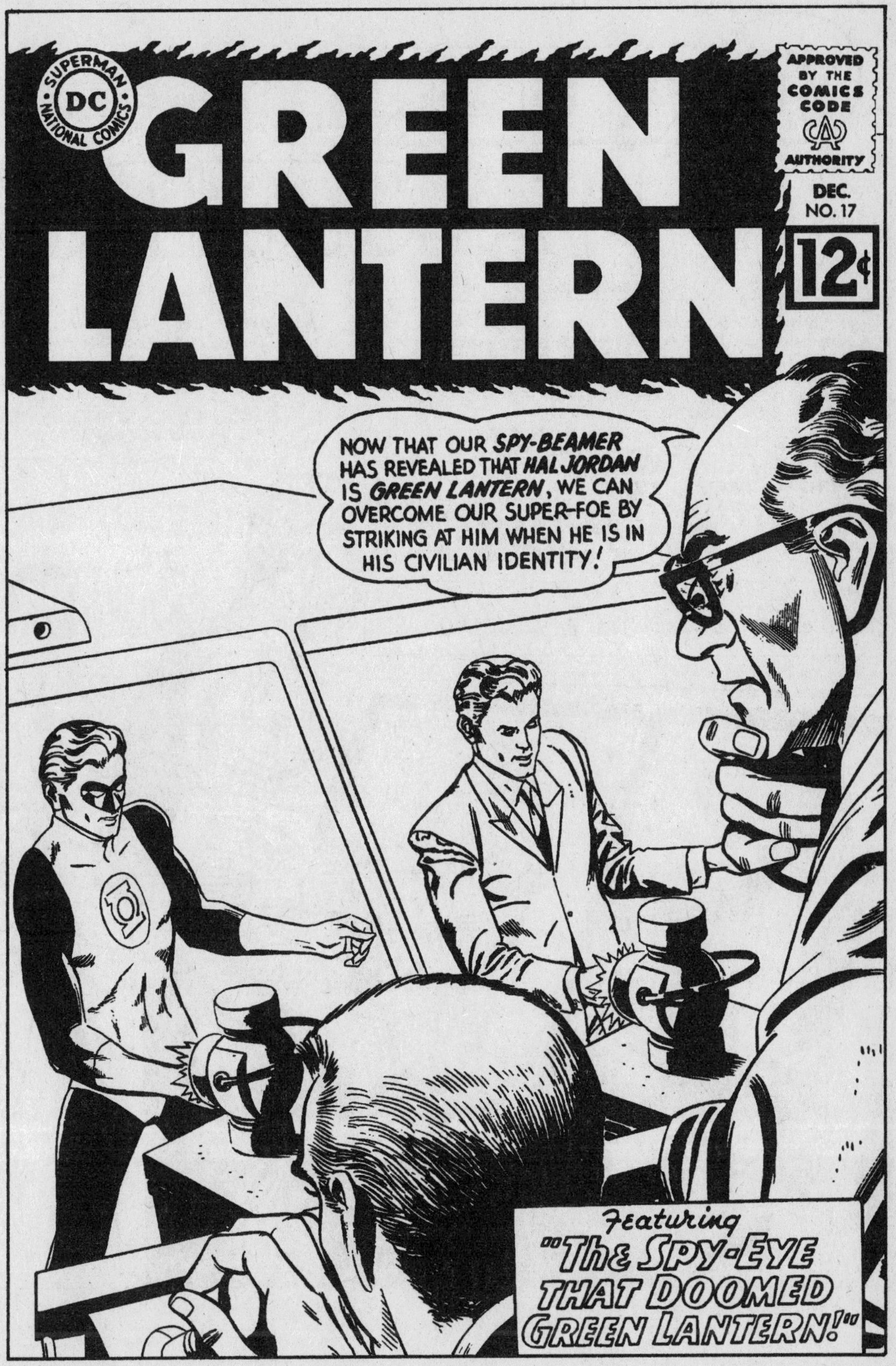
SUPERMAN DC NATIONAL COMICS
GREEN LANTERN
APPROVED BY THE COMICS CODE AUTHORITY
DEC. NO. 17
12¢
NOW THAT OUR SPY-BEAMER HAS REVEALED THAT HAL JORDAN IS GREEN LANTERN, WE CAN OVERCOME OUR SUPER-FOE BY STRIKING AT HIM WHEN HE IS IN HIS CIVILIAN IDENTITY!
Featuring "The Spy-Eye That Doomed Green Lantern!"

GREEN LANTERN

When a band of international spies put a **SPY-BEAM** on test pilot Hal Jordan in order to secure the plans of the **X-50** rocket plane, they are stunned to discover that Hal is also the famed crime-fighter **GREEN LANTERN!**
As a result, they abandon their idea of stealing the X-50 plans for a far greater prize--GREEN LANTERN'S POWER RING!--THE

SPY-EYE THAT DOOMED GREEN LANTERN!

There is our proof, Hal Jordan! You are--**GREEN LANTERN!** Now if you want to stay alive--hand over your **POWER RING!** We know it's over 24 hours since you charged it--so it's **POWERLESS** against us!

AS HAL JORDAN LEAVES HIS BOARDING HOUSE EARLY ONE MORNING FOR THE *FERRIS* AIRCRAFT FACTORY...

THERE'S JORDAN NOW! *GET* HIM!

A STRANGE INSTRUMENT IS LIFTED, POINTED DOWN AT THE YOUNG TEST PILOT...

IN THE NEXT INSTANT, AN INVISIBLE BEAM OF LIGHT HITS HAL JORDAN AND BATHES HIM IN AN UNSEEN AURA...

BETTER GET A MOVE ON. I HAVE A BUSY DAY COMING UP!

JORDAN DOESN'T KNOW IT-- BUT HE'S GOING TO HELP US SECURE THE PLANS FOR THE NEW *X-50* ORBITAL PLANE HE'S TESTING TOMORROW!

ALL WE HAVE TO DO IS TUNE IN ON HIM WITH OUR EYE *SPY-BEAM!*

MINUTES LATER, IN A PENTHOUSE APARTMENT NEAR THE JORDAN BOARDING HOUSE...

EXCELLENT! THIS SPY-APPARATUS WE BROUGHT FROM THE MOTHER COUNTRY IS FUNCTIONING PERFECTLY.

WE CAN'T PENETRATE WALLS OR PEOPLE WITH OUR *EYE-SPY* BEAM-- BUT WE *CAN* COAT PEOPLE WITH IT, TURNING THEM INTO WALKING TELEVISION CAMERAS-- AND SO FOLLOW THEM WITH THIS PRO-JECTOR WHEREVER THEY GO!

LEAVING HIS CAR AT THE *FERRIS* PARKING LOT, HAL WALKS TOWARD HIS HANGAR DRESSING ROOM, GREETING HIS YOUNG ESKIMO MECHANIC ON THE WAY...

BE RIGHT WITH YOU, *PIE* -- SOON'S I PUT ON SOME COVERALLS.

WE WANT TO CHECK OUT YOUR CONTROLS BE-FORE YOU TAKE THIS BABY UP TOMORROW, HAL !

IN THE HANGAR DRESSING ROOM, WHERE--AS *GREEN LANTERN*--HE KEEPS HIS *BATTERY OF POWER* *...

Hmm--AS LONG AS I'M HERE I MIGHT AS WELL RE-CHARGE MY *POWER RING*. IT'S BEEN OVER 20 HOURS SINCE I LAST CHARGED IT !

*Editor's Note: TO SAFEGUARD ITS PRESENCE THERE, GREEN LANTERN HAS WILL-POWERED AN INVISIBILITY SHIELD AROUND THE BATTERY.

STRETCHING OUT HIS ARM, THE TEST PILOT REPEATS HIS SOLEMN OATH...

IN BRIGHTEST DAY, IN BLACKEST NIGHT,
NO EVIL SHALL ESCAPE MY SIGHT!
LET THOSE WHO WORSHIP EVIL'S MIGHT
BEWARE MY POWER--
GREEN LANTERN'S LIGHT !

PUZZLED EYES WATCH AS HIS GLOWING BUT INVISIBLE *POWER RING* IS REFLECTED ON THE SPY-BEAMER SCREEN...

WHAT'S HE DOING ?

AND WHAT'S THAT GREEN GLOW ON HIS FINGER ?

HIS RING NOW FILLED WITH POWER FOR THE NEXT 24 HOURS, HAL JORDAN DONS A COVERALL ...

YOU NEARLY READY, HAL ?

BE RIGHT WITH YOU, *PIE*.

FOR THE NEXT SEVERAL HOURS, HAL AND *PIEFACE* CHECK OUT THE RADICAL NEW ROCKET-PLANE WITH WHICH IT IS HOPED MAN CAN *FLY INTO ORBIT--AND FLY OUT...*

3

 LATER THAT DAY, HAL KEEPS AN APPOINTMENT IN THE BRIEFING ROOM WITH SEVERAL SCIENTISTS AND AIR FORCE GENERALS...

RIGHT ON TIME, JORDAN. COME ALONG, TAKE A LAST LOOK AT THE *X-50* PLANS!

I HAVE THEM HERE. I'LL SPREAD THEM OUT!

IN THE PENTHOUSE WHERE THE *SPY-BEAMER* IS LOCATED...

HURRY, THIS IS WHAT WE'VE BEEN WAITING FOR! GET THAT CAMERA INTO POSITION! THEY ARE ABOUT TO EXAMINE *X-50* PLANS!

WITH OUR *SPY-BEAMER*, WE DON'T HAVE TO *STEAL* THOSE PLANS! SINCE HAL JORDAN IS OUR WALKING SPY-BEAM, WE CAN PHOTOGRAPH THEM IN PERFECT SAFETY! WHAT HE SEES, WE'LL SEE!

BUT AT THAT MOMENT...

I KNOW THOSE PLANS INSIDE-OUT, GENTLEMEN! I ASSURE YOU, NO FURTHER BRIEFING IS NECESSARY...

GOOD! THEN WE'LL PUT THEM AWAY!

BEFORE THE PLANS ARE PUT BACK IN THE SAFE, IT MIGHT BE A GOOD IDEA TO SAFE-GUARD THEM FROM THEFT BY COATING THEM WITH MY *POWER RING*! THAT WAY, IF THEY SHOULD BE STOLEN, MY RING WILL EMIT A TELLTALE GLOW!*

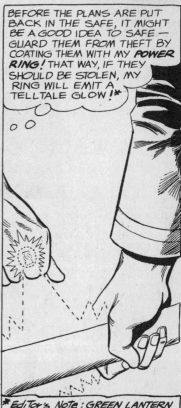

*Editor's Note: GREEN LANTERN FIRST USED THIS BURGLAR-ALARM SYSTEM IN "*The WHEEL OF MISFORTUNE!*" WHICH APPEARED IN *JUSTICE LEAGUE OF AMERICA*, #6.

④

CONSTERNATION OVERCOMES THE SPIES AS THEY SEE THEIR CAREFULLY LAID PLANS GO UP IN SMOKE...

JORDAN'S *"DOUBLE-CROSSED"* US! BY NOT LOOKING AT THE PLANS NEITHER CAN WE!

THIS *"SPOILS"* EVERYTHING! WHEN WE GO HOME AND REPORT FAILURE-- YOU KNOW WHAT WILL HAPPEN TO US!

WAIT! THERE'S STILL A WAY OUT! PHOTOGRAPH THE GENERAL AS HE OPENS THE SAFE! WE'LL BLOW UP THE PICTURES AND GET A CLOSE-UP OF THE COMBINATION--

--AND THEN WE'LL *STEAL* THE PLANS FROM THE SAFE!

WHEN THE BRIEFING PERIOD IS AT AN END, HAL FINDS HIS LADY BOSS, CAROL FERRIS, WAITING FOR HIM...

CAROL! IT'S GOOD TO SEE YOU!

TOMORROW'S A BIG DAY FOR *FERRIS*, HAL. I KNOW YOU HAVE TO GET TO BED EARLY AND HAVE A GOOD NIGHT'S SLEEP FOR ORBITING THE *X-50* TOMORROW, BUT--

HOW ABOUT PUTTING YOU IN A GOOD FRAME OF MIND BY HAVING AN EARLY DINNER WITH ME!

SOLD! WHERE WOULD YOU CARE TO DINE?

WE'RE GOING TO EAT AT *MY* PLACE, HAL! I'M GOING TO WHIP UP A MEAL WITH MY OWN HANDS!

SCORE A POINT FOR *HAL JORDAN* IN HIS BATTLE WITH *"GREEN LANTERN"* TO WIN CAROL'S AFFECTIONS! SHE'S NEVER INVITED MY ALTER EGO FOR A HOME-COOKED MEAL!

HAL JORDAN IS A HAPPY MAN AS HE WATCHES THE GIRL HE LOVES BRING TWO PLATES TO THE LITTLE TABLE WHERE THEY ARE TO DINE--WHEN...

MY RING-- STARTING TO GLOW!

IT'S SIGNALING ME SOMEBODY'S STEALING THE *X-50* PLANS! THERE'LL BE NO STEAK-FED HAL JORDAN TONIGHT!

IS SOMETHING WRONG, HAL? DIDN'T I PREPARE THE STEAK THE RIGHT WAY?

er--NOTHING LIKE THAT, CAROL... IT'S JUST THAT--er--I'M TOO EXCITED TO EAT! I'D BETTER BE RUNNING ALONG... GET THAT GOOD NIGHT'S SLEEP I'LL NEED...

WITH A WAN SMILE, HE BACKS FROM THE ROOM...

I'LL TAKE A RAIN-CHECK ON THAT DINNER, CAROL...

IT'LL BE A *REAL* RAINY DAY BEFORE YOU GET ANOTHER INVITE, MR. JORDAN--

HAL JORDAN FEELS BADLY ENOUGH ABOUT THE SUDDEN DEPARTURE-- BUT WHAT ABOUT CAROL?

I CAN'T FIGURE OUT THAT HAL JORDAN! I KNOW HE'S IN LOVE WITH ME--ALWAYS WANTS TO BE WITH ME-- AND YET WHEN HE GOT THE CHANCE, HE CHICKENED OUT! DOES HIS LOVE OF DUTY COME BEFORE HIS LOVE OF CAROL FERRIS? OH, I'M ALL MIXED UP!

OUTSIDE THE FERRIS HOME, HAL SWITCHES TO *GREEN LANTERN*...

WHEN I COATED THE PLANS WITH MY *POWER RING*, ORDERING IT TO GLOW IF ANYONE WERE REMOVING THEM--I DIDN'T THINK I'D GET SUCH A QUICK RESPONSE!

6

HIGH ABOVE *COAST CITY* STREAKS THE *EMERALD GLADIATOR*...

WHOEVER STOLE THOSE PLANS COULDN'T HAVE GONE VERY FAR IN THIS SHORT TIME. SINCE I ALREADY COATED THE PLANS BY MY RING, I CAN ORDER IT TO POINT TOWARD THEM!

HIS *POWER RING* POINTS AN ACCUSING FINGER DOWN AT A HIGH-POWERED CAR THAT HURTLES ALONG A LONELY ROAD...

THERE THEY ARE!

LOOK-- *GREEN LANTERN!*

TWIN SUBMACHINE-GUNS POINT SKYWARD AND ERUPT WITH A DEAFENING CLATTER...

RA-TA-TA-TAT!

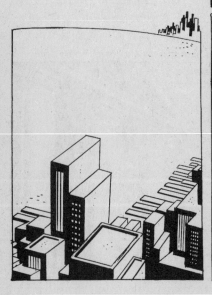

FROM THE *POWER RING,* VERDANT BEAMS OF POWER STAB DOWNWARD TO INTERCEPT THOSE SPEEDING LEAD PELLETS...

THE BULLETS THAT WERE MEANT TO STOP ME-- WILL STOP THEM!

7

INSTANTLY THE LEADEN BULLETS LENGTHEN...

WHAT'S HE DOING WITH OUR BULLETS?

THE TRANSFORMED BULLETS STAB INTO THE ROAD DIRECTLY AHEAD OF THE SPEEDING CAR...

WE'RE GOING TO CRASH INTO THE "BULLET-FENCE"!

AT EIGHTY MILES AN HOUR THE AUTOMOBILE SLAMS INTO THOSE UPRIGHT STAKES--BENDING THEM FAR OVER...

THEY AREN'T BREAKING-- JUST BENDING-- LIKE RUBBER!

WHEN THEY STRAIGHTEN OUT--WHAT'LL HAPPEN TO US?

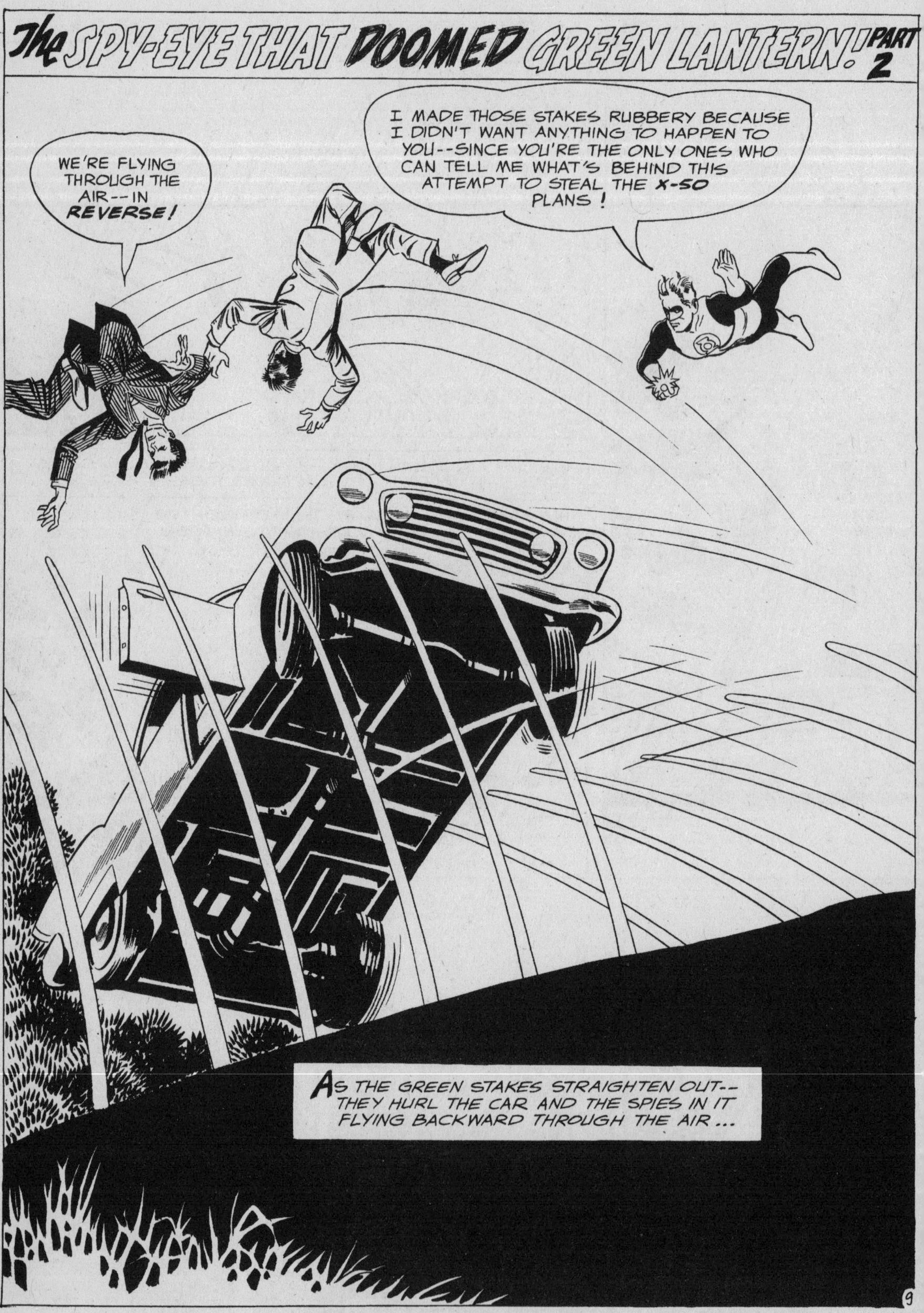
The SPY-EYE THAT DOOMED GREEN LANTERN! PART 2
WE'RE FLYING THROUGH THE AIR--IN REVERSE!
I MADE THOSE STAKES RUBBERY BECAUSE I DIDN'T WANT ANYTHING TO HAPPEN TO YOU--SINCE YOU'RE THE ONLY ONES WHO CAN TELL ME WHAT'S BEHIND THIS ATTEMPT TO STEAL THE X-50 PLANS!
AS THE GREEN STAKES STRAIGHTEN OUT--THEY HURL THE CAR AND THE SPIES IN IT FLYING BACKWARD THROUGH THE AIR...
9

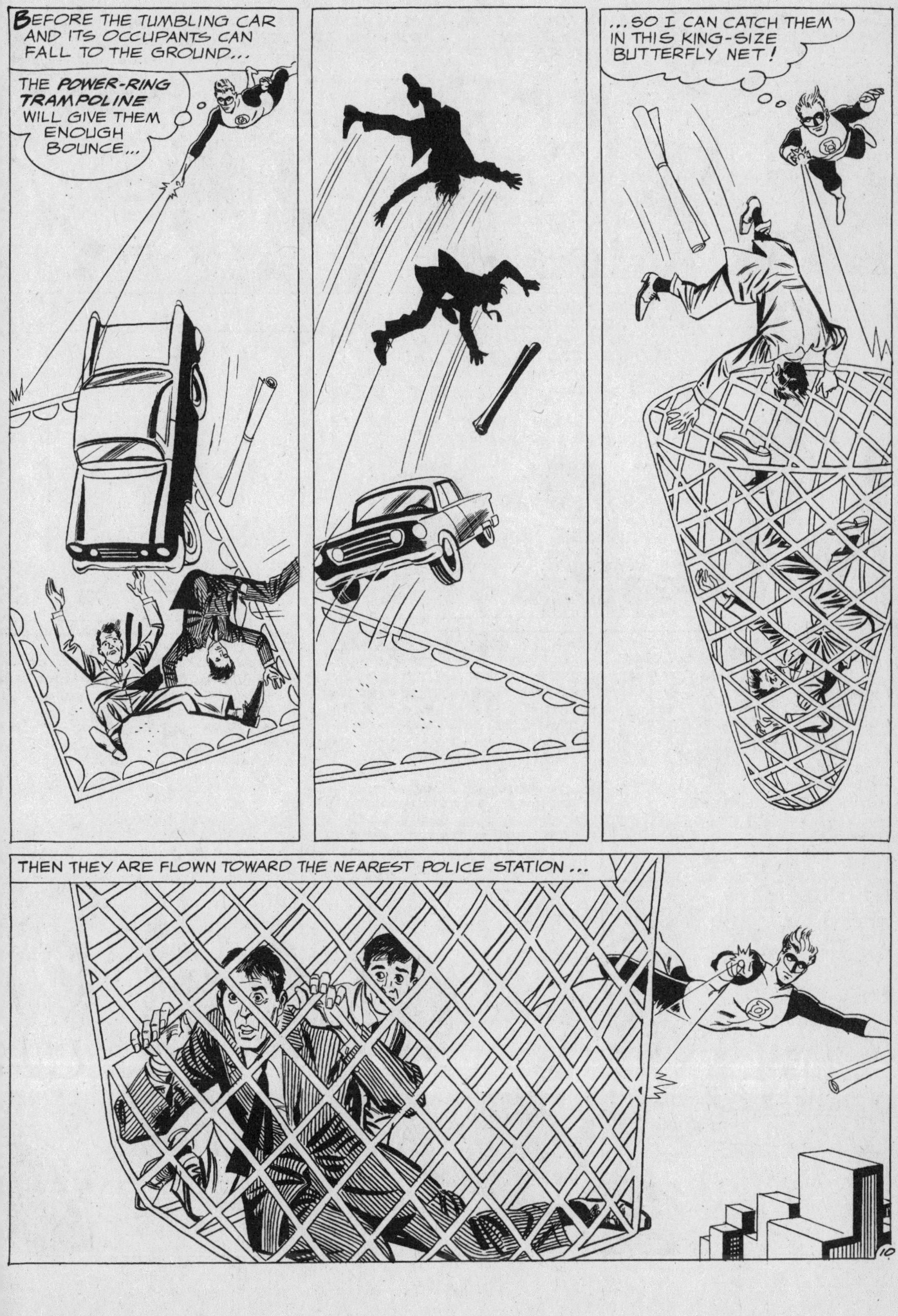
BEFORE THE TUMBLING CAR AND ITS OCCUPANTS CAN FALL TO THE GROUND...
THE POWER-RING TRAMPOLINE WILL GIVE THEM ENOUGH BOUNCE...
...SO I CAN CATCH THEM IN THIS KING-SIZE BUTTERFLY NET!
THEN THEY ARE FLOWN TOWARD THE NEAREST POLICE STATION...
10

IN THE PRECINCT HOUSE A LITTLE LATER...

THEY WON'T SAY A WORD, *GREEN LANTERN!* WE'RE STUCK!

I CAN HELP HERE, OFFICERS! ONE WAY OR ANOTHER, WE MUST LEARN WHAT SORT OF SPY SET-UP THEY HAVE!

WITH MY *POWER RING* I CAN PROBE THEIR MINDS--AND FLASH THEIR THOUGHTS ONTO A SCREEN ON THE WALL!

THE "MENTAL MOVIE" REVEALS HOW A *SPY-EYE* BEAM WAS PLAYED ON TEST PILOT *HAL JORDAN*...

WHEN THEY COATED HAL JORDAN WITH THAT SPY-BEAM--THEY ALSO COATED ME--*GREEN LANTERN*--AT THE SAME TIME! THEY CAN WATCH WHATEVER I DO!

AS THE *EMERALD GLADIATOR* AND THE POLICE OF *COAST CITY* WATCH IN UTTER FASCINATION, THE STORY OF THE THEFT OF THE *X-50* PLANS UNFOLDS...

THEY DON'T KNOW WHAT HAL JORDAN WAS DOING-- BUT *I* DO! I WAS CHARGING MY *POWER RING!* THE *POWER BATTERY* IS INVISIBLE, HOWEVER -- JUST AS IS THE *POWER RING* WHEN I WEAR IT AS HAL JORDAN!

THEY USED MY BODY AS A "CAMERA" TO LEARN THE SAFE COMBINATION--AND NOW ONE OF THESE SPIES IS OPENING THE SAFE WHERE THE *X-50* PLANS ARE KEPT!

11

WHEN THE "MENTAL MOVIE" IS OVER...

WHAT ABOUT THESE *X-50* PLANS YOU SAVED, *GREEN LANTERN*?

I'D BETTER TAKE THEM WITH ME UNTIL I CAN RETURN THEM TOMORROW!

AFTER LEAVING THE POLICE STATION, THE *GREEN GLADIATOR* HEADS TOWARD THE HEART OF *COAST CITY*...

I LEARNED SOME MORE THINGS FROM THOSE THREE SPIES--THE LOCATION OF THEIR HIDEOUT, WHERE THEIR MASTER SPY AND THE *EYE-SPY* BEAMER GADGET IS HIDDEN!...

HIGH ABOVE AN APARTMENT NOT FAR FROM HIS OWN BOARD-ING HOUSE (AS *HAL JORDAN*), *GREEN LANTERN* SENDS A MIGHTY BUZZ-SAW FLYING THROUGH THE AIR...

SINCE THE *SPY-RING* OCCUPIES THE ENTIRE TOP FLOOR I'LL REMOVE IT TO PREVENT ANY OF THEM FROM ESCAPING! I'LL REPAIR THE "DAMAGE" TO THE BUILDING AFTER I NAB THE SPIES!

THE GREEN TEETH OF THE FLYING SAW BITE DEEP INTO THE STEEL AND CONCRETE OF THE APARTMENT PENTHOUSE...

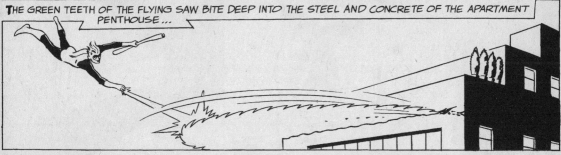

AS THE PENT-HOUSE COMES FREE OF THE BUILDING IT IS GRIPPED BY A MIGHTY BIRD AND...

NOW I HAVE THEM WHERE THEY CAN'T GET AWAY--OR USE ANY OF THEIR SPY-TRICKS!

BUT TO THE STUNNED AMAZEMENT OF THE *EMERALD GLADIATOR...*

THE PLACE IS EMPTY! THE REMAINING SPIES MUST HAVE FOLLOWED THE COURSE OF THE THEFT WITH THE SPY-BEAM--AND SAW ME CAPTURE THEIR FELLOW SPIES! THAT ALERTED THEM TO THEIR DANGER AND THEY FLED!

HE RETURNS THE PENTHOUSE TO THE APARTMENT BUILDING AS IF IT HAD NEVER BEEN REMOVED...

I'M CONCERNED ABOUT ANOTHER THING! *IF* THE SPIES HAVE BEEN CONTINUALLY FOLLOWING ME WITH THEIR *EYE-SPY* BEAM, THEY MAY HAVE GUESSED AT MY HAL JORDAN IDENTITY! BEFORE THIS CASE IS OVER, I'LL HAVE TO "PROVE" THEM *WRONG!*

THEY COULD STRIKE AT ME ANYWHERE, ANY-TIME, FOR THEY'LL ALWAYS KNOW WHERE I AM! THEY MAY NOT HAVE HAD TIME TO SET UP THE *SPY-BEAMER* IN THEIR NEW HIDEOUT YET--BUT I WON'T TAKE ANY CHANCES. I'LL SPEND THE NIGHT WHERE THEY CAN'T GET AT ME OR THE *X-50* PLANS!

WITH HIS *POWER RING* HE FORMS A BED MIDWAY BETWEEN THE EARTH AND MOON...

WITH THE SILENCE OF SPACE AROUND ME, I'LL SLEEP LIKE A BABY!

NOW I CAN GET THE SLEEP I NEED TO BE AT MY BEST FOR MY ORBITAL FLIGHT TOMORROW!

13

NEXT MORNING, A FULLY RE-FRESHED *GREEN LANTERN* TURNS OVER THE *X-50* PLANS TO AN AIR-FORCE GENERAL...

WE CAN'T THANK YOU ENOUGH FOR WHAT YOU DID LAST NIGHT. THESE PLANS COULD MEAN THE SAFETY OF OUR COUNTRY AND EVERYONE IN IT!

SOME MILES AWAY, MASTER SPY IVAR DOMANN HAS ONCE AGAIN SET UP HIS *SPY-EYE* MACHINE...

THAT *GREEN LANTERN!* IF IT WEREN'T FOR HIM -- WE'D BE ON OUR WAY TO THE MOTHER COUNTRY RIGHT NOW WITH THOSE PLANS!

SAY! I JUST NOTICED SOMETHING ODD! *WHERE IS HAL JORDAN?* WE COATED *HIM* WITH THE *SPY-EYE* -- AND HE OUGHT TO BE AROUND SOMEWHERE OR WE WOULDN'T GET ANY PICTURE!

JUST AS A CAMERA HAS TO BE THERE TO TAKE A PICTURE -- SO DOES SOMEONE COATED WITH THE *SPY-BEAM!* WE COATED ONLY *HAL JORDAN* -- SO WHERE IS HE?

CHIEF, DO YOU THINK--?

I THINK *HAL JORDAN* AND *GREEN LANTERN* ARE ONE AND THE SAME MAN...

WE MIGHT HAVE KNOWN FOR SURE IF WE HAD KEPT THE *SPY-BEAM* MACHINE TURNED ON AT ALL TIMES!

FROM NOW ON WE WILL FOLLOW THIS *GREEN LANTERN* VERY CLOSELY! IF WE SEE HIM CHANGE INTO THE FLYING TOGS OF HAL JORDAN AND TAKE THE *X-50* PLANE INTO ORBIT -- WE'LL HAVE OUR MAN!

14

BEFORE THE **EMERALD GLADIATOR** CHANGES INTO HIS PILOT'S GARB, HE ENTERS HIS HANGAR DRESSING ROOM, WHERE HE TOUCHES HIS RING TO THE **BATTERY OF POWER**, MADE TEMPORARILY VISIBLE...

IN BRIGHTEST DAY, IN BLACKEST NIGHT, NO EVIL SHALL ESCAPE MY SIGHT! LET THOSE WHO WORSHIP EVIL'S MIGHT BEWARE MY POWER-- GREEN LANTERN'S LIGHT!

SURPRISE AND DELIGHT CHANGE THE HARD FACE OF IVAR DOMANN...

SO? THAT IS THE VERY SAME POSE **HAL JORDAN** ASSUMED WHEN HE CAME INTO THE DRESSING ROOM! **NOW** I KNOW WHAT HE WAS DOING! GET THE TAPE WE MADE ON THAT!

AT THE MASTER SPY'S SUGGESTION, A "**POWER BATTERY**" IS QUICKLY PAINTED IN ON THE TAPE...

AHA! IT IS THE SAME! BUT TO MAKE DOUBLY SURE-- WE MUST COMPARE THEIR POSES SIDE BY SIDE!

FOR THE FIRST TIME IN HISTORY, HUMAN EYES SEE **HAL JORDAN** AND **GREEN LANTERN** CHARGING THE **POWER RING** AT THE SAME TIME...

THERE IS NO DOUBT OF IT! HAL JORDAN, TEST PILOT--IS ALSO **GREEN LANTERN**!

THIS CHANGES EVERYTHING! WE NO LONGER NEED THE PLANS FOR THE **X-50**! INSTEAD-- WE WILL STEAL THE **POWER RING** OF THE FAMOUS **GREEN LANTERN**! IT SHALL BE OUR SECRET WEAPON!

"AND WHAT A WEAPON IT SHALL BE! NO FLYING MISSILE WILL BE ABLE TO CROSS OUR BORDERS! WE SHALL DESTROY THEM FROM FAR AWAY!..."

"*NO ENEMY SUBMARINE WILL PENETRATE CLOSE ENOUGH TO FIRE A NUCLEAR BOMB AT US. WE SHALL SCOOP THEM ALL OUT OF THE SEA...*"

"*THEIR ARMIES WILL BE HELPLESS WHEN WE ENCLOSE THEM IN A GREEN DOME OUT OF WHICH THEY WILL BE UNABLE TO ESCAPE...*"

AND THEN EVEN AS THE MASTER SPY GLOATS IN TRIUMPH...

IVAR--LOOK! THE SCREEN WENT *BLANK!*

NO--NO! NOT WHEN WE ARE SO CLOSE TO THE GREATEST EXPLOIT EVER RECORDED BY ANY SPY! QUICKLY-- SEE WHAT IS WRONG WITH THE *SPY-EYE* MACHINE AND FIX IT!

WHILE AT THIS MOMENT, TEST PILOT HAL JORDAN IS WALKING TOWARD THE *X-50*--ABOUT TO GO INTO ORBIT FOR 36 HOURS...

SHE'S ALL YOURS NOW, HAL! GOOD LUCK!

I'LL BE SEEING YOU, *PIEFACE*--

SOONER THAN YOU THINK!

GREEN LANTERN

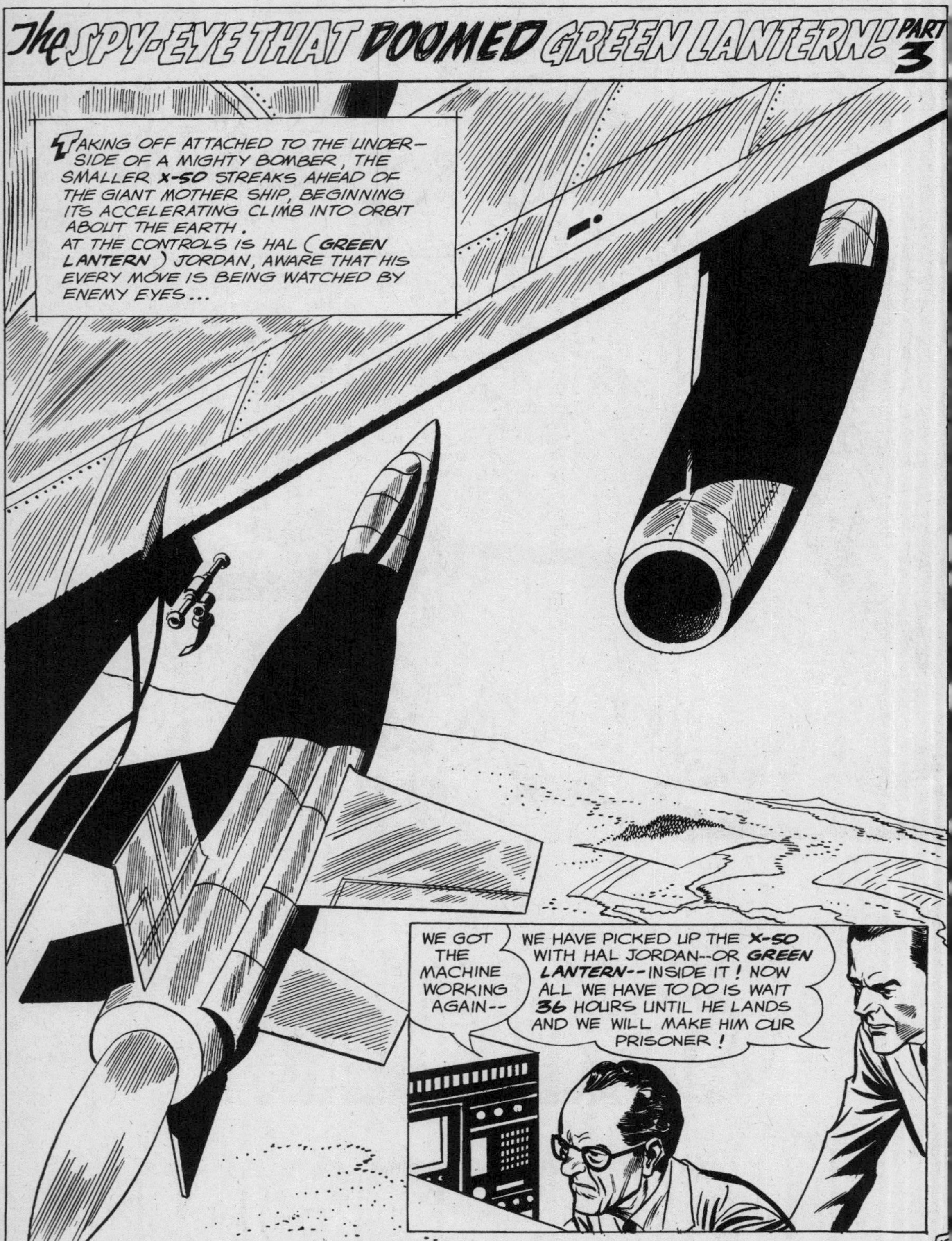
The SPY-EYE THAT DOOMED GREEN LANTERN! PART 3
TAKING OFF ATTACHED TO THE UNDER-SIDE OF A MIGHTY BOMBER, THE SMALLER X-50 STREAKS AHEAD OF THE GIANT MOTHER SHIP, BEGINNING ITS ACCELERATING CLIMB INTO ORBIT ABOUT THE EARTH. AT THE CONTROLS IS HAL (GREEN LANTERN) JORDAN, AWARE THAT HIS EVERY MOVE IS BEING WATCHED BY ENEMY EYES...
WE GOT THE MACHINE WORKING AGAIN--
WE HAVE PICKED UP THE X-50 WITH HAL JORDAN--OR GREEN LANTERN--INSIDE IT! NOW ALL WE HAVE TO DO IS WAIT 36 HOURS UNTIL HE LANDS AND WE WILL MAKE HIM OUR PRISONER!

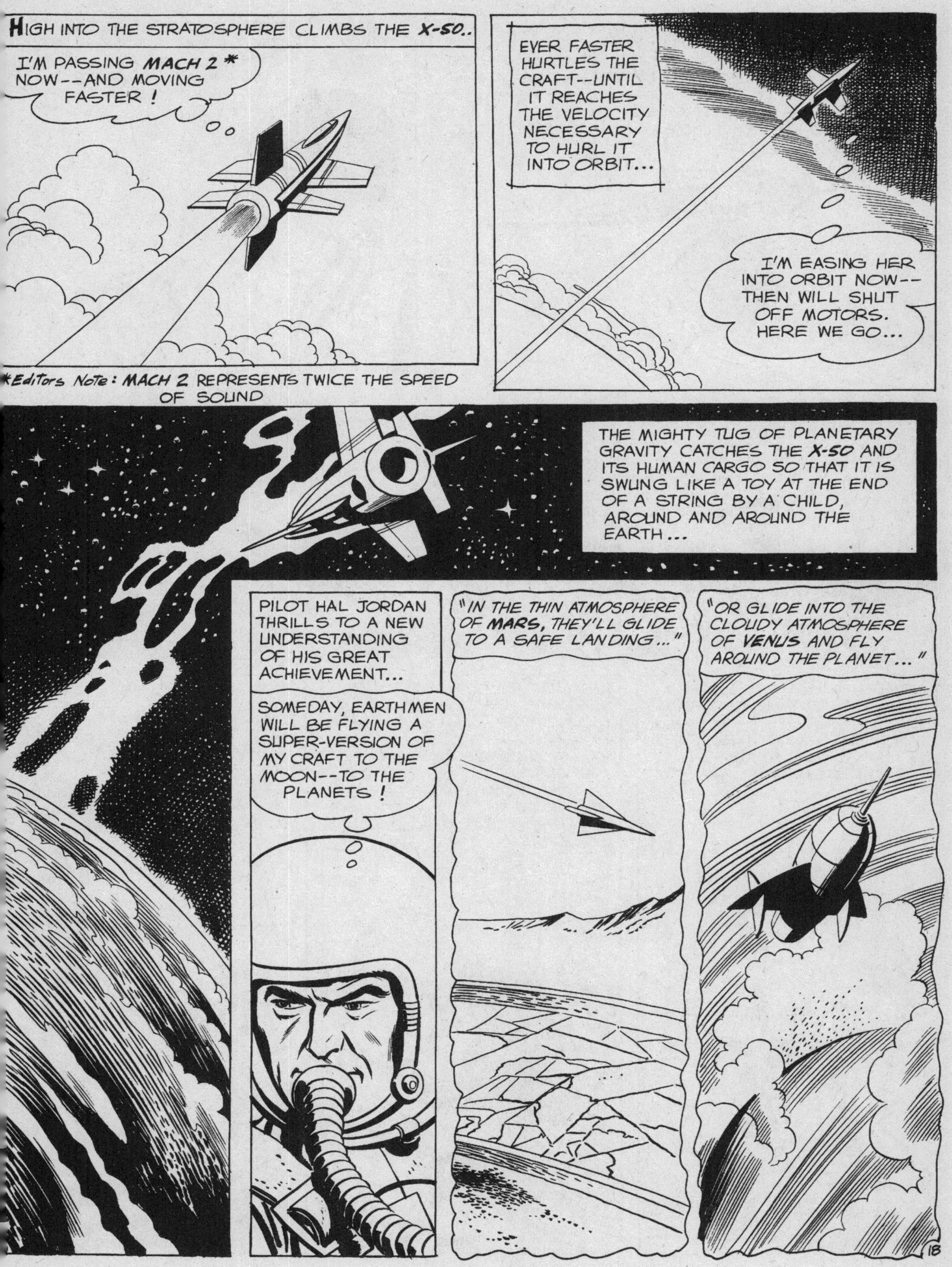
HIGH INTO THE STRATOSPHERE CLIMBS THE X-50..
I'M PASSING MACH 2* NOW--AND MOVING FASTER!
*Editors Note: MACH 2 REPRESENTS TWICE THE SPEED OF SOUND
EVER FASTER HURTLES THE CRAFT--UNTIL IT REACHES THE VELOCITY NECESSARY TO HURL IT INTO ORBIT...
I'M EASING HER INTO ORBIT NOW--THEN WILL SHUT OFF MOTORS. HERE WE GO...
THE MIGHTY TUG OF PLANETARY GRAVITY CATCHES THE X-50 AND ITS HUMAN CARGO SO THAT IT IS SWUNG LIKE A TOY AT THE END OF A STRING BY A CHILD, AROUND AND AROUND THE EARTH...
PILOT HAL JORDAN THRILLS TO A NEW UNDERSTANDING OF HIS GREAT ACHIEVEMENT...
SOMEDAY, EARTHMEN WILL BE FLYING A SUPER-VERSION OF MY CRAFT TO THE MOON--TO THE PLANETS!
"IN THE THIN ATMOSPHERE OF MARS, THEY'LL GLIDE TO A SAFE LANDING..."
"OR GLIDE INTO THE CLOUDY ATMOSPHERE OF VENUS AND FLY AROUND THE PLANET..."
18

FOR 36 HOURS, THE *X-50* CONTINUES TO CIRCUM—NAVIGATE THE PLANET, THEN JETS FREE OF ITS ORBITAL PATH AND MAKES A *"ROLLER-COASTER GLIDE"* TOWARD THE LANDING STRIPS OF THE *FERRIS* AIRCRAFT FACTORY...

HE HAS BEEN IN THE PLANE LONG ENOUGH FOR HIS RING TO BE EXHAUSTED OF POWER!

HE WILL BE POWERLESS TO RESIST US!

IS EVERYTHING READY?

TWO OF OUR MEN ARE TAKING CARE OF THE DETAILS RIGHT NOW! WHEN HE LANDS, IT WILL BE A SIMPLE MATTER TO CAPTURE HIM!

MOMENTS LATER, EAGER HANDS ASSIST HAL JORDAN FROM THE ORBITAL PLANE...

CONGRATULATIONS, JORDAN! WITH YOU AT THE CONTROLS, THE *X-50* PERFORMED PERFECTLY!

AIR FORCE MEDICOS RUSH FORWARD TO TAKE COMMAND...

WE'LL GET YOU TO A BASE HOSPITAL FOR A MEDICAL CHECK-UP!

AN IMPETUOUS CAROL FERRIS FORGETS HERSELF LONG ENOUGH TO...

HAL—YOU WERE MARVELOUS! AND THE MOMENT YOU'RE FREE, I WANT YOU TO COME OVER FOR DINNER--

MMM-- YOU'VE ALREADY GIVEN ME AN APPETIZER WITH THAT KISS, CAROL!

THEN HAL IS PUSHED INTO AN AMBULANCE...

WE'LL HAVE YOU IN AND OUT OF THE HOSPITAL IN JIG TIME, SIR!

ONCE INSIDE THE AMBULANCE, HOWEVER...

HEY, WHAT **IS** THIS?

DON'T MAKE A MOVE, JORDAN--IF YOU WANT TO LIVE! WE SUBSTITUTED OUR MEN FOR THE HOSPITAL ORDERLIES SO WE COULD CAPTURE YOU!

WHAT DO YOU WANT FROM ME? I DON'T KNOW ENOUGH ABOUT THE X-50 TO TELL YOU ANYTHING!

WE WANT YOU-- BECAUSE YOU ARE **GREEN LANTERN!**

THE AMBULANCE BRAKES TO A STOP AT A LONELY COUNTRY HOUSE, WHERE...

ME--GREEN LANTERN? WHERE DID YOU EVER GET A WILD IDEA LIKE THAT?

WE'LL SHOW YOU, INSIDE THE HOUSE!

MOMENTS LATER...

THOSE ARE TAPE RECORDINGS OF TWO SHOTS OF YOU WE TOOK. ONE SHOWS YOU CHARGING YOUR **POWER RING** AS **HAL JORDAN**--THE OTHER AS **GREEN LANTERN!**

HUH? WHAT'S THAT ABOUT **ME** CHARGING A RING?

I WAS--er--ONLY STRETCHING OUT MY ARM TO REMOVE A KINK IN IT! AS FOR THE "GREEN GLOW"--IT MUST HAVE BEEN CAUSED BY SOME DE-FECT IN YOUR APPARATUS!

SAY WHAT YOU WANT--WE KNOW YOU'RE **GREEN LANTERN!** AND WE'RE GOING TO TAKE AWAY YOUR RING!

I SUPPOSE THE ONLY THING THAT WOULD CONVINCE YOU THAT I'M NOT **GREEN LANTERN** IS FOR THE REAL **GREEN LANTERN** TO APPEAR!

THERE'S ONE TRICK YOU CAN'T DO! YOU'VE BEEN IN THE X-50 FOR **36** HOURS-- SO YOUR **POWER RING** HAS LOST ITS POWER! AND WE'VE HAD OUR EYES GLUED ON YOU TO MAKE SURE YOU DIDN'T LEAVE THE SHIP TO RECHARGE THE RING!

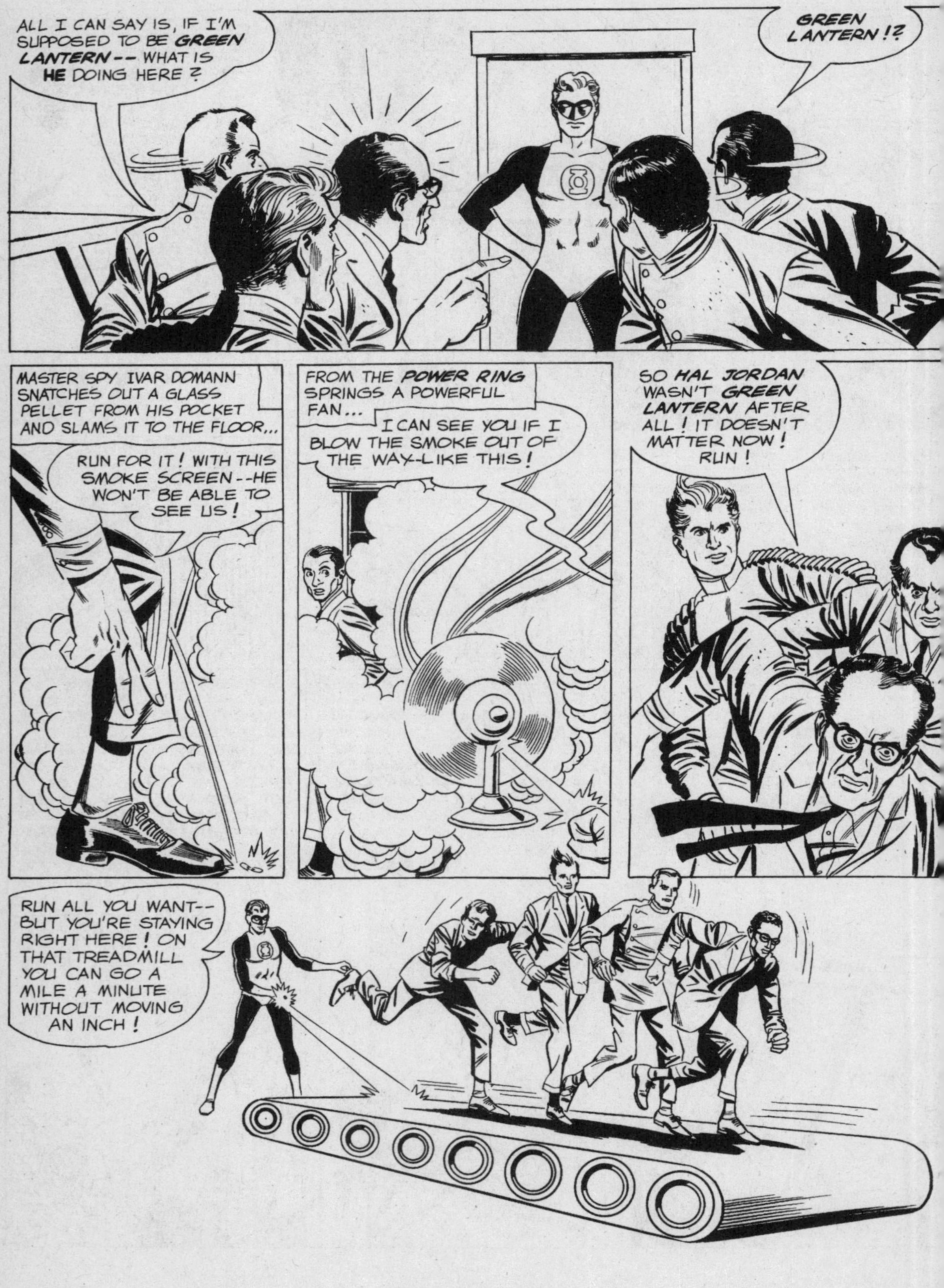
ALL I CAN SAY IS, IF I'M SUPPOSED TO BE GREEN LANTERN-- WHAT IS HE DOING HERE?
GREEN LANTERN!?
MASTER SPY IVAR DOMANN SNATCHES OUT A GLASS PELLET FROM HIS POCKET AND SLAMS IT TO THE FLOOR...
RUN FOR IT! WITH THIS SMOKE SCREEN--HE WON'T BE ABLE TO SEE US!
FROM THE POWER RING SPRINGS A POWERFUL FAN...
I CAN SEE YOU IF I BLOW THE SMOKE OUT OF THE WAY-LIKE THIS!
SO HAL JORDAN WASN'T GREEN LANTERN AFTER ALL! IT DOESN'T MATTER NOW! RUN!
RUN ALL YOU WANT-- BUT YOU'RE STAYING RIGHT HERE! ON THAT TREADMILL YOU CAN GO A MILE A MINUTE WITHOUT MOVING AN INCH!

POWER-RING HANDS REACH DOWN AND SEIZE THE "FLEEING" SPIES...

LET GO! LET GO!

GRIPPED BY THOSE MIGHTY FINGERS, THE SPIES ARE LIFTED AND CARRIED THROUGH THE AIR...

THANKS FOR EVERYTHING, GREEN LANTERN! I'LL CALL CENTRAL INTELLIGENCE AND GET THEM HERE TO IMPOUND THAT SPY-BEAMER MACHINE!

SAY NO MORE, HAL JORDAN! IT WAS A PLEASURE!

THE SPIES ARE HERDED TOWARD POLICE HEADQUARTERS...

WHAT A DISASTER THIS HAS TURNED OUT TO BE FOR US --

--AND OUR MOTHER COUNTRY!

LATER, AFTER HAL JORDAN HAS BEEN EXAMINED AND RELEASED BY THE REAL AIR FORCE MEDICAL TEAM, HE PAYS A BRIEF VISIT TO THE HOME OF HIS GOOD FRIEND PIEFACE...

HAL! JUST THE MAN I WANT TO SEE! I'VE BEEN READING THE PAPERS!

I FIGURED AS MUCH! NOW YOU WANT TO ASK SOME QUESTIONS!

THESE HEADLINES DON'T MAKE MUCH SENSE! HOW COULD GREEN LANTERN SAVE HAL JORDAN-- WHEN YOU ARE ONE AND THE SAME!

I DID IT BY MAKING ANOTHER GREEN LANTERN!

NEWS

GREEN LANTERN RESCUES X-50 PILOT! CRACKS SPY RING!

22

BUT THAT'S IMPOSSIBLE! YOU TOLD ME THAT ON THE WORLD OF *AKU* YOU MADE *DUPLICATE GREEN LANTERNS* OUT OF THIN AIR -- BUT ONLY BECAUSE THAT PLANET HAD UNIQUE SUPER-MAGNETIC FIELDS!* YOU COULD NEVER DO THIS ON *EARTH!*

THAT IS TRUE!

* Editor's Note: SEE *GREEN LANTERN #6: "The WORLD OF LIVING PHANTOMS!"*

THEN WHO WAS THIS OTHER *GREEN LANTERN* THAT SAVED YOU?

YOU WERE, *PIEFACE!*

ME? YOU'RE KIDDING! I WOULD HAVE KNOWN ABOUT IT!

NOT NECESSARILY! LISTEN...

I REALIZED THAT THE SPIES WERE CONTINUALLY WATCHING ME WITH THEIR *SPY-BEAMER!* THEY FIGURED THAT I COULDN'T CHARGE MY RING WHILE I WAS IN ORBIT AROUND THE EARTH WITHOUT THEIR SEEING ME DO IT!

"SO I HAD TO DEVISE SOME WAY OF GETTING TO THE *BATTERY OF POWER* WITHOUT THEIR KNOWING IT..."

I HAVE A PLAN THAT I THINK WILL WORK. BUT IT'S GOT TO BE DONE AT SUPER-FAST TIME... IN A MOMENT OR TWO!

"BEFORE THE 24-HOUR LIMIT ON MY *POWER RING* EXPIRED, I LEFT THE *X-SO* -- IN INVISIBLE FORM..."

THE PLANE WILL KEEP ON ORBITING IN PERFECT SAFETY WHILE I'M GONE!

"A SPLIT-SECOND LATER, WHILE STILL INVISIBLE, I WAS IN THE HANGAR DRESSING ROOM, CHARGING MY RING TO THE *BATTERY OF POWER* ..."

"THE NEXT INSTANT I WAS IN YOUR ROOM WHILE YOU WERE LISTENING TO THE RADIO REPORTS ON THE ORBITING *X-50* ..."

PIEFACE, I ORDER YOU TO BECOME *GREEN LANTERN* AS YOU DID ONCE BEFORE * --AND COME TO ME WHEN I SUMMON YOU--FOLLOW MY TELEPATHIC COMMANDS ...

*Editor's Note: SEE GREEN LANTERN #5: "The POWER RING THAT VANISHED!"

"THEN I RETURNED TO THE *X-50* TO RESUME MY OTHER IDENTITY AS HAL JORDAN, TEST PILOT, AND WAIT FOR FURTHER DEVELOPMENTS ..."

IN THE COUPLE OF SECONDS I WAS GONE, THE *SPY-SCREEN* WENT BLANK! I'M COUNTING ON THE SPIES THINKING THERE WAS A MOMENTARY DISTURBANCE ON THEIR SCREEN...

YOU DON'T REMEMBER COMING TO MY RESCUE BECAUSE YOU WERE SO EXHAUSTED FROM YOUR LONG VIGIL AT THE RADIO, FOLLOWING THE PROGRESS OF THE *X-50* TO ITS SAFE LANDING-- YOU HAD FALLEN INTO A DEEP SLUMBER.

HOW ABOUT THAT! ME--A SLEEP-- WALKING *GREEN LANTERN*! I MISSED ALL THE EXCITEMENT! IT WAS YOU SECRETLY MAKING ME CAPTURE THOSE SPIES!

ONE MORE THING! HOW COULD YOU BE SO SURE THE SPIES WOULDN'T BE ABLE TO SEE YOU ON THEIR *SPY-BEAM* IN YOUR *INVISIBLE* FORM?

FROM WHAT YOU KNOW OF THE STORY-- YOU OUGHT TO BE ABLE TO FIGURE THAT ONE OUT FOR *YOURSELF*!

24

THE YOUNG ESKIMO GREASE—MONKEY SINKS INTO A CHAIR AND THINKS——AND THINKS...

I GIVE UP! IT'S BEYOND ME!

TRY IT ONCE MORE! THE ANSWER IS RIGHT BEFORE YOUR EYES——

——BUT YOU CAN'T SEE IT...!

OHHH—— OF COURSE! WHEN THEY SAW YOU—— AS HAL JORDAN——CHARGE YOUR POWER RING—— THEY COULDN'T SEE THE BATTERY! THEY HAD TO SKETCH IT IN LATER!

SINCE YOU WILLED THE POWER BATTERY TO BE INVISIBLE—— YOU KNEW THAT ANYTHING ELSE YOU WILLED TO BE INVISIBLE WOULD BE UNSEEN BY THE SPY-BEAMER!

SO I KNEW I COULD NOT BE SEEN AS AN INVISIBLE GREEN LANTERN!

RIGHT!

NOW I CAN WRITE IN MY CASE BOOK THE TRUE EXPLANATION OF HOW GREEN LANTERN RESCUED HAL JORDAN!

WHILE I COLLECT A LITTLE PERSONAL BONUS ON THIS CASE—— THAT POSTPONED DINNER DATE WITH MY SWEETHEART, CAROL FERRIS!

The End

(2)

GREEN LANTERN

SHOWCASE

PRESENTS

LOOK FOR THESE OTHER TITLES FEATURING CLASSIC TALES OF THE MEMBERS OF THE JUSTICE LEAGUE OF AMERICA!

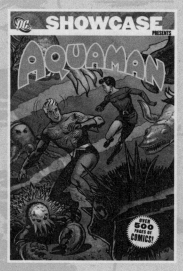

SHOWCASE
PRESENTS

LOOK FOR THESE OTHER TITLES FEATURING
CLASSIC TALES OF DC SUPER HEROES!